GO!

Premium Media Site

D0154649

Improve your grade with hands-on tools and resources!

- Master *Key Terms* to expand your vocabulary.
- Assess your knowledge with fun *Crossword Puzzles* and *Flipboards*, which let you flip through the definitions of the key terms and match them with the correct term.
- Prepare for exams by taking practice quizzes in the *Online Chapter Review*.
- Download *Student Data Files* for the application projects in each chapter.
- Answer matching and multiple choice questions to test what you learned in each chapter.

And for even more tools, you can access the following Premium Resources using your Access Code. Register now to get the most out of *GO!*.

- *Student Training Videos* for each Objective have been created by the author - a real instructor teaching the same types of courses that you take.*
- *GO! to Work* videos are short interviews with workers showing how they use Office in their job.*
- *GO! for Job Success* videos related to the projects in the chapter cover such important topics as Dressing for Success, Time Management, and Making Ethical Choices.*

*Access code required for these premium resources

Your Access Code is:

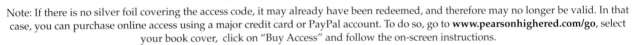

Note: If there is no silver foil covering the access code, it may already have been redeemed, and therefore may no longer be valid. In that case, you can purchase online access using a major credit card or PayPal account. To do so, go to **www.pearsonhighered.com/go**, select your book cover, click on "Buy Access" and follow the on-screen instructions.

To Register:

- To start you will need a valid email address and this access code.
- Go to **www.pearsonhighered.com/go** and scroll to find your text book.
- Once you've selected your text, on the Home Page for the book, click the link to access the Student Premium Content.
- Click the Register button and follow the on-screen instructions.
- After you register, you can sign in any time via the log-in area on the same screen.

System Requirements

Windows 7 Ultimate Edition; IE 8
Windows Vista Ultimate Edition SP1; IE 8
Windows XP Professional SP3; IE 7
Windows XP Professional SP3; Firefox 3.6.4
Mac OS 10.5.7; Firefox 3.6.4
Mac OS 10.6; Safari 5

Technical Support

http://247pearsoned.custhelp.com

Photo credits: Goodluz/wrangler/Elena Elisseeva/Shutterstock

GO!

with Microsoft®

Access 2013

Comprehensive

GO!
with Microsoft®

Access 2013
Comprehensive

Shelley Gaskin, Carolyn McLellan, and Nancy Graviett

PEARSON

Boston   Columbus   Indianapolis   New York   San Francisco   Upper Saddle River
Amsterdam   Cape Town   Dubai   London   Madrid   Milan   Munich   Paris   Montréal   Toronto
Delhi   Mexico City   São Paulo   Sydney   Hong Kong   Seoul   Singapore   Taipei   Tokyo

Editor in Chief: Michael Payne
Executive Acquisitions Editor: Jenifer Niles
Editorial Project Manager: Carly Prakapas
Product Development Manager: Laura Burgess
Development Editor: Toni Ackley
Editorial Assistant: Andra Skaalrud
Director of Marketing: Maggie Leen
Marketing Manager: Brad Forrester
Marketing Coordinator: Susan Osterlitz
Marketing Assistant: Darshika Vyas
Managing Editor: Camille Trentacoste
Senior Production Project Manager: Rhonda Aversa

Operations Specialist: Maura Zaldivar-Garcia
Senior Art Director: Jonathan Boylan
Cover Photo: © photobar/Fotolia
Associate Director of Design: Blair Brown
Director of Media Development: Taylor Ragan
Media Project Manager, Production: Renata Butera
Full-Service Project Management: PreMediaGlobal
Composition: PreMediaGlobal
Printer/Binder: Webcrafters, Inc.
Cover Printer: Lehigh-Phoenix Color/Hagerstown
Text Font: MinionPro

ISBN 10: 0-13-341505-8
ISBN 13: 978-0-13-341505-6

Brief Contents

Table of Contents

Access Introduction to Microsoft Access 2013 49

Chapter 1 Getting Started with Microsoft Access 2013 51

About the Authors

Shelley Gaskin, Series Editor, is a professor in the Business and Computer Technology Division at Pasadena City College in Pasadena, California. She holds a bachelor's degree in Business Administration from Robert Morris College (Pennsylvania), a master's degree in Business from Northern Illinois University, and a doctorate in Adult and Community Education from Ball State University (Indiana). Before joining Pasadena City College, she spent 12 years in the computer industry, where she was a systems analyst, sales representative, and director of Customer Education with Unisys Corporation. She also worked for Ernst & Young on the development of large systems applications for their clients. She has written and developed training materials for custom systems applications in both the public and private sector, and has also written and edited numerous computer application textbooks.

This book is dedicated to my students, who inspire me every day.

Carolyn McLellan is the dean of the Division of Information Technology and Business at Tidewater Community College in Virginia Beach, Virginia. She has a master's degree in Secondary Education from Regent University and a bachelor's degree in Business Education from Old Dominion University. She taught for Norfolk Public Schools for 17 years in Business Education and served as a faculty member at Tidewater Community College for eight years teaching networking, where she developed over 23 new courses and earned the Microsoft Certified Trainer and Microsoft Certified System Engineer industry certifications. In addition to teaching, Carolyn loves to play volleyball, boogie board at the beach, bicycle, crochet, cook, and read.

This book is dedicated to my daughters, Megan and Mandy, who have my eternal love;
to my mother, Jean, who always believes in me and encouraged me to become a teacher;
to my sister Debbie, who was my first student and who inspires me with her strength in
overcoming hardships; to my niece Jenna, for her bravery, composure, and beauty; to my
grandsons, Damon and Jordan, who bring me happiness and a renewed joie de vivre; and
to the students and IT faculty at Tidewater Community College.

Nancy Graviett is a professor in the Business and Computer Science department at St. Charles Community College in Cottleville, Missouri, where she is the program coordinator for the Business Administrative Systems program and teaches within the program. Nancy is also very active with distance learning and teaches in face-to-face, hybrid, and online formats. She holds a master's degree from University of Missouri. Nancy holds Microsoft® Certified Application Specialist certification in multiple applications and provides training both on and off campus. In her free time, Nancy enjoys quilting and spending time with family and friends.

I dedicate this book to my husband, David, my children (Matthew and Andrea), and my
parents, whose love and support I cherish more than they could ever know.

GO! with Access 2013

GO! with Access 2013 is the right solution for you and your students in today's fast-moving, mobile environment. The GO! Series content focuses on the real-world job skills students need to succeed in the workforce. They learn Office by working step-by-step through practical job-related projects that put the core functionality of Office in context. And as has always been true of the GO! Series, students learn the important concepts when they need them, and they never get lost in instruction, because the GO! Series uses Microsoft procedural syntax. Students learn how and learn why—at the teachable moment.

After completing the instructional projects, students are ready to apply the skills in a wide variety of progressively challenging projects that require them to solve problems, think critically, and create projects on their own. And, for those who want to go beyond the classroom and become certified, GO! provides clear MOS preparation guidelines so students know what is needed to ace the Core exam!

What's New

New Design reflects the look of Windows 8 and Office 2013 and enhances readability.

Enhanced Chapter Opener now includes a deeper introduction to the A and B instructional projects and more highly defined chapter Objectives and Learning Outcomes.

New Application Introductions provide a brief overview of the application and put the chapters in context for students.

Coverage of New Features of Office 2013 ensures that students are learning the skills they need to work in today's job market.

New Application Capstone Projects ensure that students are ready to move on to the next set of chapters. Each Application Capstone Project can be found on the Instructor Resource Center and is also a Grader project in MyITLab.

More Grader Projects based on the E, F, and G mastering-level projects, both homework and assessment versions! These projects are written by our GO! authors, who are all instructors in colleges like yours!

New Training and Assessment Simulations are now written by the authors to match the book one-to-one!

New MOS Map on the Instructor Resource Site and in the Annotated Instructor's Edition indicates clearly where each required MOS Objective is covered.

Three Types of Videos help students understand and succeed in the real world:

- *Student Training Videos* are broken down by Objective and created by the author—a real instructor teaching the same types of courses that you do. Real personal instruction.
- *GO! to Work* videos are short interviews with workers showing how they use Office in their jobs.
- *GO! for Job Success* videos relate to the projects in the chapter and cover important career topics such as *Dressing for Success*, *Time Management*, and *Making Ethical Choices*. **Available for Chapters 1–3 only**.

New GO! Learn It Online Section at the end of the chapter indicates where various student learning activities can be found, including multiple choice and matching activities.

New Styles for In-Text Boxed Content: Another Way, Notes, More Knowledge, Alerts, and **new *By Touch* instructions** are included in line with the instruction and not in the margins so that the student is more likely to read this information.

Clearly Indicated Build from Scratch Projects: GO! has always had many projects that begin "from scratch," and now we have an icon to really call them out!

New Visual Summary focuses on the four key concepts to remember from each chapter.

New Review and Assessment Guide summarizes the end-of-chapter assessments for a quick overview of the different types and levels of assignments and assessments for each chapter.

New Skills and Procedures Summary Chart (online at the Instructor Resource Center) summarizes all of the shortcuts and commands covered in the chapter.

New End-of-Chapter Key Term Glossary with Definitions for each chapter, plus a comprehensive end-of-book glossary.

New Flipboards and Crossword Puzzles enable students to review the concepts and key terms learned in each chapter by completing online challenges.

Teach the Course You Want in Less Time

A Microsoft® Office textbook designed for student success!

- **Project-Based –** Students learn by creating projects that they will use in the real world.

- **Microsoft Procedural Syntax –** Steps are written to put students in the right place at the right time.

- **Teachable Moment –** Expository text is woven into the steps—at the moment students need to know it—not chunked together in a block of text that will go unread.

- **Sequential Pagination –** Students have actual page numbers instead of confusing letters and abbreviations.

New Feature

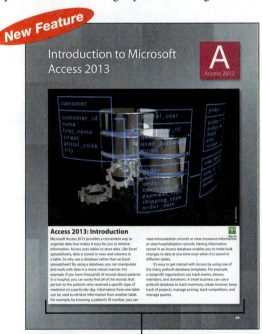

New Application Introductions – Provide an overview of the application to prepare students for the upcoming chapters.

Student Outcomes and Learning Objectives – Objectives are clustered around projects that result in student outcomes.

New Design – Provides a more visually appealing and concise display of important content.

Simulation Training and Assessment – Give your students the most realistic Office 2013 experience with open, realistic, high-fidelity simulations.

Scenario – Each chapter opens with a job-related scenario that sets the stage for the projects the student will create.

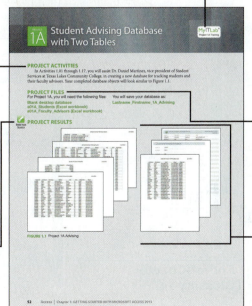

Project Activities – A project summary stated clearly and quickly.

New Build from Scratch Icons – Enable you to easily see all the projects that the student builds from scratch.

Project Files – Clearly shows students which files are needed for the project and the names they will use to save their documents.

Project Results – Shows students what successful completion looks like.

In-Text Features
Another Way, Notes, More Knowledge, Alerts, and By Touch Instructions

Microsoft Procedural Syntax – Steps are written to put the student at the right place at the right time.

Color Coding – Each chapter has two instructional projects, which is less overwhelming for students than one large chapter project. The two projects are differentiated by different colored numbering and headings.

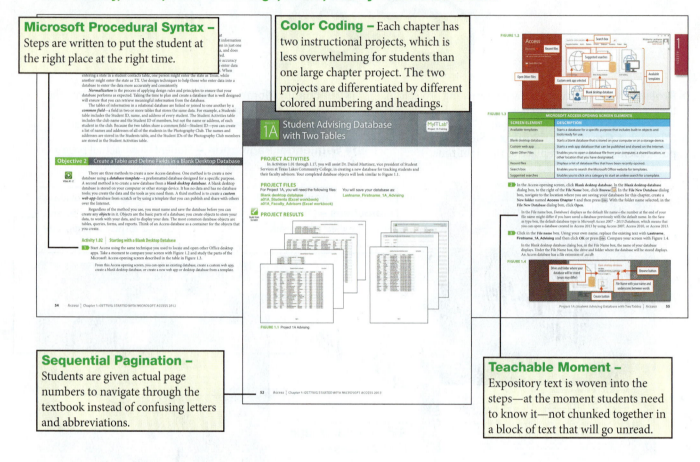

Sequential Pagination – Students are given actual page numbers to navigate through the textbook instead of confusing letters and abbreviations.

Teachable Moment – Expository text is woven into the steps—at the moment students need to know it—not chunked together in a block of text that will go unread.

End-of-Chapter
Content-Based Assessments – Assessments with defined solutions.

Objective List – Every end-of-chapter project includes a listing of covered objectives from Projects A and B.

Review and Assessment Chart – Displays a comprehensive list of each chapter assessment with a description and location to make planning easier.

End-of-Chapter Glossary – Gives students an easy way to review key terms.

End-of-Chapter

Content-Based Assessments – Assessments with defined solutions. (continued)

Grader Projects – Each chapter has six MyITLab Grader projects—three homework and three assessment—clearly indicated by the MyITLab logo.

Task-Specific Rubric – A matrix specific to the GO! Solve It projects that states the criteria and standards for grading these defined-solution projects.

End-of-Chapter

Outcomes-Based Assessments – Assessments with open-ended solutions.

GO! with MyITLab
Gives you a completely integrated solution
Instruction ■ **Training** ■ **Assessment**

All of the content in the book and MyITLab is written by the authors, who are instructors, so the instruction works seamlessly with the simulation trainings and grader projects — true 1:1. eText, Training and Assessment Simulations, and Grader Projects

Student Materials

Student Data Files – All student data files are available to all on the companion website: www.pearsonhighered.com/go.

Three Types of Videos help students understand and succeed in the real world:

- *Student Training Videos* are by Objective and created by the author—a real instructor teaching the same types of courses that you teach.
- *GO! to Work* videos are short interviews with workers showing how they use Office in their job.
- *GO! for Job Success* videos related to the projects in the chapter cover important career topics such as *Dressing for Success*, *Time Management*, and *Making Ethical Choices*. **Available for Chapters 1–3 only**.

Flipboards and Crossword Puzzles provide a variety of review options for content in each chapter.
Available on the companion website using the access code included with your book.
pearsonhighered.com/go

Instructor Materials

Annotated Instructor Edition – An instructor tool includes a full copy of the student textbook and a guide to implementing your course in three different ways, depending on the emphasis you want to place on digital engagement. Also included are teaching tips, discussion topics, and other useful pieces for teaching each chapter.

Student Assignment Tracker (previously called Assignment Sheets) **–** Lists all the assignments for the chapter. Just add the course information, due dates, and points. Providing these to students ensures they will know what is due and when.

Scripted Lectures – A script to guide your classroom lecture of each instructional project.

Annotated Solution Files – Coupled with the scorecards, these create a grading and scoring system that makes grading easy and efficient.

PowerPoint Lectures – PowerPoint presentations for each chapter.

Audio PowerPoints – Audio versions of the PowerPoint presentations for each chapter.

Scoring Rubrics – Can be used either by students to check their work or by you as a quick check-off for the items that need to be corrected.

Syllabus Templates – For 8-week, 12-week, and 16-week courses.

MOS Map – Provided at the Instructor Resource Center site and in the Annotated Instructor's Edition, showing where each required MOS Objective is covered either in the book or via additional instructional material provided.

Test Bank – Includes a variety of test questions for each chapter.

Companion Website – Online content such as the Online Chapter Review, Glossary, and Student Data Files are all at www.pearsonhighered.com/go.

Reviewers

GO! Focus Group Participants

Kenneth Mayer	Heald College
Carolyn Borne	Louisiana State University
Toribio Matamoros	Miami Dade College
Lynn Keane	University of South Carolina
Terri Hayes	Broward College
Michelle Carter	Paradise Valley Community College

GO! Reviewers

Abul Sheikh	Abraham Baldwin Agricultural College
John Percy	Atlantic Cape Community College
Janette Hicks	Binghamton University
Shannon Ogden	Black River Technical College
Karen May	Blinn College
Susan Fry	Boise State University
Chigurupati Rani	Borough of Manhattan Community College / CUNY
Ellen Glazer	Broward College
Kate LeGrand	Broward College
Mike Puopolo	Bunker Hill Community College
Nicole Lytle-Kosola	California State University, San Bernardino
Nisheeth Agrawal	Calhoun Community College
Pedro Diaz-Gomez	Cameron
Linda Friedel	Central Arizona College
Gregg Smith	Central Community College
Norm Cregger	Central Michigan University
Lisa LaCaria	Central Piedmont Community College
Steve Siedschlag	Chaffey College
Terri Helfand	Chaffey College
Susan Mills	Chambersburg
Mandy Reininger	Chemeketa Community College
Connie Crossley	Cincinnati State Technical and Community College
Marjorie Deutsch	City University of New York - Queensborough Community College
Mary Ann Zlotow	College of DuPage
Christine Bohnsak	College of Lake County
Gertrude Brier	College of Staten Island
Sharon Brown	College of The Albemarle
Terry Rigsby	Columbia College
Vicki Brooks	Columbia College
Donald Hames	Delgado Community College
Kristen King	Eastern Kentucky University
Kathie Richer	Edmonds Community College
Gary Smith	Elmhurst College
Wendi Kappersw	Embry-Riddle Aeronautical University
Nancy Woolridge	Fullerton College
Abigail Miller	Gateway Community & Technical College
Deep Ramanayake	Gateway Community & Technical College
Gwen White	Gateway Community & Technical College
Debbie Glinert	Gloria K School
Dana Smith	Golf Academy of America
Mary Locke	Greenville Technical College
Diane Marie Roselli	Harrisburg Area Community College
Linda Arnold	Harrisburg Area Community College - Lebanon
Daniel Schoedel	Harrisburg Area Community College - York Campus
Ken Mayer	Heald College
Xiaodong Qiao	Heald College
Donna Lamprecht	Hopkinsville Community College
Kristen Lancaster	Hopkinsville Community College
Johnny Hurley	Iowa Lakes Community College
Linda Halverson	Iowa Lakes Community College
Sarah Kilgo	Isothermal Community College
Chris DeGeare	Jefferson College
David McNair	Jefferson College
Diane Santurri	Johnson & Wales University
Roland Sparks	Johnson & Wales University
Ram Raghuraman	Joliet Junior College
Eduardo Suniga	Lansing Community College
Kenneth A. Hyatt	Lone Star College - Kingwood
Glenn Gray	Lone Star College - North Harris
Gene Carbonaro	Long Beach City College
Betty Pearman	Los Medanos College
Diane Kosharek	Madison College
Peter Meggison	Massasoit Community College
George Gabb	Miami Dade College
Lennie Alice Cooper	Miami Dade College
Richard Mabjish	Miami Dade College
Victor Giol	Miami Dade College
John Meir	Midlands Technical College
Greg Pauley	Moberly Area Community College
Catherine Glod	Mohawk Valley Community College
Robert Huyck	Mohawk Valley Community College
Kevin Engellant	Montana Western
Philip Lee	Nashville State Community College
Ruth Neal	Navarro College
Sharron Jordan	Navarro College
Richard Dale	New Mexico State University
Lori Townsend	Niagara County Community College
Judson Curry	North Park University
Mary Zegarski	Northampton Community College
Neal Stenlund	Northern Virginia Community College
Michael Goeken	Northwest Vista College
Mary Beth Tarver	Northwestern State University
Amy Rutledge	Oakland University
Marcia Braddock	Okefenokee Technical College
Richard Stocke	Oklahoma State University - OKC
Jane Stam	Onondaga Community College
Mike Michaelson	Palomar College
Kungwen (Dave) Chu	Purdue University Calumet
Wendy Ford	City University of New York - Queensborough Community College
Lewis Hall	Riverside City College
Karen Acree	San Juan College
Tim Ellis	Schoolcraft College
Dan Combellick	Scottsdale Community College
Pat Serrano	Scottsdale Community College
Rose Hendrickson	Sheridan College
Kit Carson	South Georgia College
Rebecca Futch	South Georgia State College
Brad Hagy	Southern Illinois University Carbondale
Mimi Spain	Southern Maine Community College
David Parker	Southern Oregon University
Madeline Baugher	Southwestern Oklahoma State University
Brian Holbert	St. Johns River State College
Bunny Howard	St. Johns River State College
Stephanie Cook	State College of Florida
Sharon Wavle	Tompkins Cortland Community College
George Fiori	Tri-County Technical College
Steve St. John	Tulsa Community College
Karen Thessing	University of Central Arkansas
Richard McMahon	University of Houston-Downtown
Shohreh Hashemi	University of Houston-Downtown
Donna Petty	Wallace Community College
Julia Bell	Walters State Community College
Ruby Kowaney	West Los Angeles College
Casey Thompson	Wiregrass Georgia Technical College
DeAnnia Clements	Wiregrass Georgia Technical College

Introduction to Microsoft Office 2013 Features

1

PROJECT 1A

OUTCOMES
Create, save, and print a Microsoft Office 2013 document.

OBJECTIVES

1. Use File Explorer to Download, Extract, and Locate Files and Folders
2. Use Start Search to Locate and Start a Microsoft Office 2013 Desktop App
3. Enter, Edit, and Check the Spelling of Text in an Office 2013 Program
4. Perform Commands from a Dialog Box
5. Create a Folder and Name and Save a File
6. Insert a Footer, Add Document Properties, Print a File, and Close a Desktop App

PROJECT 1B

OUTCOMES
Use the ribbon and dialog boxes to perform commands in Microsoft Office 2013.

OBJECTIVES

7. Open an Existing File and Save It with a New Name
8. Sign In to Office and Explore Options for a Microsoft Office Desktop App
9. Perform Commands from the Ribbon and Quick Access Toolbar
10. Apply Formatting in Office Programs
11. Compress Files and Use the Microsoft Office 2013 Help System
12. Install Apps for Office and Create a Microsoft Account

etse1112/Fotolia

In This Chapter

In this chapter, you will use File Explorer to navigate the Windows folder structure, create a folder, and save files in Microsoft Office 2013 programs. You will also practice using features in Microsoft Office 2013 that work similarly across Word, Excel, Access, and PowerPoint. These features include managing files, performing commands, adding document properties, signing in to Office, applying formatting, and using Help. You will also practice compressing files and installing Apps for Office from the Office Store. In this chapter, you will also learn how to set up a free Microsoft account so that you can use SkyDrive.

The projects in this chapter relate to **Skyline Metro Grill**, which is a chain of 25 casual, full-service restaurants based in Boston. The Skyline Metro Grill owners are planning an aggressive expansion program. To expand by 15 additional restaurants in Chicago, San Francisco, and Los Angeles by 2018, the company must attract new investors, develop new menus, develop new marketing strategies, and recruit new employees, all while adhering to the company's quality guidelines and maintaining its reputation for excellent service. To succeed, the company plans to build on its past success and maintain its quality elements.

PROJECT ACTIVITIES

In Activities 1.01 through 1.09, you will create a note form using Microsoft Word, save it in a folder that you create by using File Explorer, and then print the note form or submit it electronically as directed by your instructor. Your completed note form will look similar to Figure 1.1.

PROJECT FILES

For Project 1A, you will need the following file:

New blank Word document

You will save your file as:

Lastname_Firstname_1A_Note_Form

PROJECT RESULTS

Build from
Scratch

Skyline Metro Grill, Chef's Notes
Executive Chef, Sarah Jackson

Lastname_Firstname_1A_Note_Form

FIGURE 1.1 Project 1A Note Form

Objective 1   Use File Explorer to Download, Extract, and Locate Files and Folders

Video OF1-1

A *file* is a collection of information stored on a computer under a single name, for example, a Word document or a PowerPoint presentation. A file is stored in a *folder*—a container in which you store files—or a *subfolder*, which is a folder within a folder. The Windows operating system stores and organizes your files and folders, which is a primary task of an operating system.

You *navigate*—explore within the organizing structure of Windows—to create, save, and find your files and folders by using the *File Explorer* program. File Explorer displays the files and folders on your computer and is at work anytime you are viewing the contents of files and folders in a *window*. A window is a rectangular area on a computer screen in which programs and content appear; a window can be moved, resized, minimized, or closed.

Activity 1.01   Using File Explorer to Download, Extract, and Locate Files and Folders

1 ▶ Sign in to Windows 8 with your Microsoft account—or the account provided by your instructor—to display the Windows 8 **Start screen**, and then click the **Desktop** tile. Insert a **USB flash drive** in your computer; **Close** ☒ any messages or windows that display.

The *desktop* is the screen in Windows that simulates your work area. A *USB flash drive* is a small data storage device that plugs into a computer USB port.

2 ▶ On the taskbar, click **Internet Explorer** 🅔. Click in the **address bar** to select the existing text, type **www.pearsonhighered.com/go** and press Enter. Locate and click the name of this textbook, and then click the **STUDENT DATA FILES tab**.

The *taskbar* is the area along the lower edge of the desktop that displays buttons representing programs—also referred to as desktop apps. In the desktop version of Internet Explorer 10, the *address bar* is the area at the top of the Internet Explorer window that displays, and where you can type, a *URL—Uniform Resource Locator*—which is an address that uniquely identifies a location on the Internet.

3 On the list of files, move your mouse pointer over—*point* to—**Office Features Chapter 1** and then *click*—press the left button on your mouse pointing device one time.

4 In the **Windows Internet Explorer** dialog box, click **Save As**.

A *dialog box* is a small window that contains options for completing a task.

5 In the **Save As** dialog box, on the left, locate the **navigation pane**, and point to the vertical **scroll bar**.

The Save As dialog box is an example of a *common dialog box*; that is, this dialog box looks the same in Excel and in PowerPoint and in most other Windows-based desktop applications—also referred to as programs.

Use the *navigation pane* on the left side of the Save As dialog box to navigate to, open, and display favorites, libraries, folders, saved searches, and an expandable list of drives. A *pane* is a separate area of a window.

A *scroll bar* displays when a window, or a pane within a window, has information that is not in view. You can click the up or down scroll arrows—or the left and right scroll arrows in a horizontal scroll bar—to scroll the contents up and down or left and right in small increments.

You can also drag the *scroll box*—the box within the scroll bar—to scroll the window or pane in either direction.

This is a *compressed folder*—also called a *zipped folder*—which is a folder containing one or more files that have been reduced in size. A compressed folder takes up less storage space and can be transferred to other computers faster.

NOTE | **Comparing Your Screen with the Figures in This Textbook**

Your screen will match the figures shown in this textbook if you set your screen resolution to 1280 × 768. At other resolutions, your screen will closely resemble, but not match, the figures shown. To view your screen's resolution, on the desktop, right-click in a blank area, and then click Screen resolution.

---

6 In the **navigation pane**, if necessary, on the scroll bar click ⌄ to scroll down. If necessary, to the left of **Computer**, click ▷ to expand the list. Then click the name of your **USB flash drive**.

7 With *Office_Features* displayed in the **File name** box, in the lower right corner click **Save**.

At the bottom of your screen, the *Notification bar* displays information about pending downloads, security issues, add-ons, and other issues related to the operation of your computer.

8 In the **Notification bar**, when the download is complete, click **Open folder** to display the folder window for your **USB flash drive**.

A *folder window* displays the contents of the current location—folder, library, or drive—and contains helpful parts so that you can navigate within the file organizing structure of Windows.

9 With the compressed **Office_Features** folder selected, on the ribbon, click the **Extract tab** to display the **Compressed Folder Tools**, and then click **Extract all**.

The *ribbon* is a user interface in both Office 2013 and Windows 8 that groups the commands for performing related tasks on tabs across the upper portion of a window.

In the dialog box, you can *extract*—decompress or pull out—files from a compressed folder.

You can navigate to some other location by clicking the Browse button and navigating within your storage locations.

10 In the **Extract Compressed (Zipped) Folders** dialog box, click to the right of the selected text, and then press Backspace until only the drive letter of your USB and the colon following it display—for example G:—and then click **Extract**. Notice that a progress bar indicates the progress of the extract process, and that when the extract is complete, the **Office_Features** folder displays on the file list of your **USB flash drive**.

In a dialog box or taskbar button, a *progress bar* indicates visually the progress of a task such as a download or file transfer.

The *address bar* in File Explorer displays your current location in the folder structure as a series of links separated by arrows, which is referred to as the *path*—a sequence of folders that leads to a specific file or folder.

By pressing Backspace in the Extract dialog box, you avoid creating an unneeded folder level.

11 Because you no longer need the compressed (zipped) version of the folder, be sure it is selected, click the **Home tab**, and then click **Delete**. In the upper right corner of the **USB drive** folder window, click **Close** ☒. **Close** ☒ the **Internet Explorer** window and in the Internet Explorer message, click **Close all tabs**.

Your desktop redisplays.

Objective 2 Use Start Search to Locate and Start a Microsoft Office 2013 Desktop App

Video OF1-2

The term *desktop app* commonly refers to a computer program that is installed on your computer and requires a computer operating system such as Microsoft Windows or Apple OS to run. The programs in Microsoft Office 2013 are considered to be desktop apps. Apps that run from the *device software* on a smartphone or a tablet computer—for example, iOS, Android, or Windows Phone—or apps that run from *browser software* such as Internet Explorer, Safari, Firefox, or Chrome on a desktop PC or laptop PC are referred to simply as *apps*.

Activity 1.02 | Using Start Search to Locate and Start a Microsoft Office 2013 Desktop App

The easiest and fastest way to search for an app is to use the *Start search* feature—simply display the Windows 8 Start screen and start typing. By default, Windows 8 searches for apps; you can change it to search for files or settings.

1 With your desktop displayed, press [⊞] to display the Windows 8 **Start screen**, and then type **word 2013** With *word 2013* bordered in white in the search results, press Enter to return to the desktop and open Word. If you want to do so, in the upper right corner, sign in with your Microsoft account, and then compare your screen with Figure 1.2.

Documents that you have recently opened, if any, display on the left. On the right, you can select either a blank document or a *template*—a preformatted document that you can use as a starting point and then change to suit your needs.

BY TOUCH Swipe from the right edge of the screen to display the charms, and then tap Search. Tap in the Apps box, and then use the onscreen keyboard that displays to type *word 2013*. Tap the selected Word 2013 app name to open Word.

FIGURE 1.2

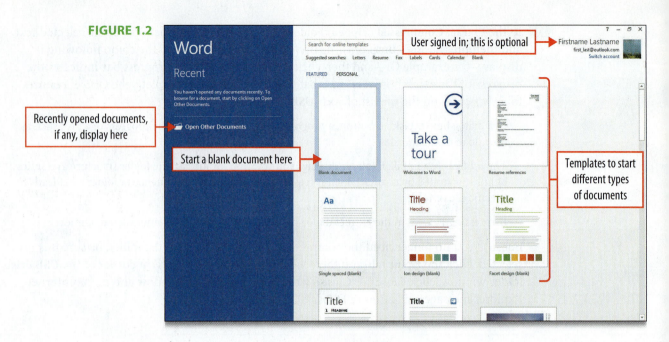

Recently opened documents, if any, display here

Start a blank document here

User signed in; this is optional

Templates to start different types of documents

2 Click **Blank document**. Compare your screen with Figure 1.3, and then take a moment to study the description of these screen elements in the table in Figure 1.4.

NOTE | **Displaying the Full Ribbon**

If your full ribbon does not display, click any tab, and then at the right end of the ribbon, click 📌 to pin the ribbon to keep it open while you work.

FIGURE 1.3

Quick Access Toolbar

Ribbon tabs

Help and window control buttons

Application icon

Title bar

Ribbon

FILE tab

Group names

Signed-in user

Status bar

FIGURE 1.4

MICROSOFT OFFICE SCREEN ELEMENTS	
SCREEN ELEMENT	**DESCRIPTION**
FILE tab	Displays Microsoft Office Backstage view, which is a centralized space for all of your file management tasks such as opening, saving, printing, publishing, or sharing a file—all the things you can do *with* a file.
Group names	Indicate the names of the groups of related commands on the displayed tab.
Help and window control buttons	Display Word Help and Full Screen Mode and enable you to Minimize, Restore Down, or Close the window.
Application icon	When clicked, displays a menu of window control commands including Restore, Minimize, and Close.
Quick Access Toolbar	Displays buttons to perform frequently used commands and use resources with a single click. The default commands include Save, Undo, and Redo. You can add and delete buttons to customize the Quick Access Toolbar for your convenience.
Ribbon	Displays a group of task-oriented tabs that contain the commands, styles, and resources you need to work in an Office 2013 desktop app. The look of your ribbon depends on your screen resolution. A high resolution will display more individual items and button names on the ribbon.
Ribbon tabs	Display the names of the task-oriented tabs relevant to the open program.
Status bar	Displays file information on the left; on the right displays buttons for Read Mode, Print Layout, and Web Layout views; on the far right displays Zoom controls.
Title bar	Displays the name of the file and the name of the program. The Help and window control buttons are grouped on the right side of the title bar.
Signed-in user	Name of the Windows 8 signed-in user.

Objective 3 | Enter, Edit, and Check the Spelling of Text in an Office 2013 Program

Video OF1-3

All of the programs in Office 2013 require some typed text. Your keyboard is still the primary method of entering information into your computer. Techniques to enter text and to *edit*—make changes to—text are similar among all of the Office 2013 programs.

Activity 1.03 | Entering and Editing Text in an Office 2013 Program

1 On the ribbon, on the HOME tab, in the Paragraph group, if necessary, click Show/Hide ¶ so that it is active—shaded. If necessary, on the VIEW tab, in the Show group, select the Ruler check box so that rulers display below the ribbon and on the left side of your window.

The *insertion point*—a blinking vertical line that indicates where text or graphics will be inserted—displays. In Office 2013 programs, the mouse *pointer*—any symbol that displays on your screen in response to moving your mouse device—displays in different shapes depending on the task you are performing and the area of the screen to which you are pointing.

When you press Enter, Spacebar, or Tab on your keyboard, characters display to represent these keystrokes. These screen characters do not print and are referred to as *formatting marks* or *nonprinting characters*.

2 ▸ Type **Skyline Grille Info** and notice how the insertion point moves to the right as you type. Point slightly to the right of the letter *e* in *Grille* and click to place the insertion point there. Compare your screen with Figure 1.5.

> A *paragraph symbol* (¶) indicates the end of a paragraph and displays each time you press Enter. This is a type of formatting mark and does not print.

FIGURE 1.5

3 ▸ On your keyboard, locate and then press the Backspace key to delete the letter *e*.

> Pressing Backspace removes a character to the left of the insertion point.

4 ▸ Press → one time to place the insertion point to the left of the *I* in *Info*. Type **Chef's** and then press Spacebar one time.

> By *default*, when you type text in an Office program, existing text moves to the right to make space for new typing. Default refers to the current selection or setting that is automatically used by a program unless you specify otherwise.

5 ▸ Press Del four times to delete *Info* and then type **Notes**

> Pressing Del removes a character to the right of the insertion point.

6 ▸ With your insertion point blinking after the word *Notes*, on your keyboard, hold down the Ctrl key. While holding down Ctrl, press ← three times to move the insertion point to the beginning of the word *Grill*.

> This is a *keyboard shortcut*—a key or combination of keys that performs a task that would otherwise require a mouse. This keyboard shortcut moves the insertion point to the beginning of the previous word.

> A keyboard shortcut is commonly indicated as Ctrl + ← (or some other combination of keys) to indicate that you hold down the first key while pressing the second key. A keyboard shortcut can also include three keys, in which case you hold down the first two and then press the third. For example, Ctrl + Shift + ← selects one word to the left.

7 ▸ With the insertion point blinking at the beginning of the word *Grill*, type **Metro** and press Spacebar.

8 ▸ Press Ctrl + End to place the insertion point after the letter *s* in *Notes*, and then press Enter one time. With the insertion point blinking, type the following and include the spelling error:
Exective Chef, Madison Dunham

9 With your mouse, point slightly to the left of the *M* in *Madison*, hold down the left mouse button, and then **drag**—hold down the left mouse button while moving your mouse—to the right to select the text *Madison Dunham* but not the paragraph mark following it, and then release the mouse button. Compare your screen with Figure 1.6.

> The **mini toolbar** displays commands that are commonly used with the selected object, which places common commands close to your pointer. When you move the pointer away from the mini toolbar, it fades from view.
>
> **Selecting** refers to highlighting, by dragging or clicking with your mouse, areas of text or data or graphics so that the selection can be edited, formatted, copied, or moved. The action of dragging includes releasing the left mouse button at the end of the area you want to select.
>
> The Office programs recognize a selected area as one unit to which you can make changes. Selecting text may require some practice. If you are not satisfied with your result, click anywhere outside of the selection, and then begin again.

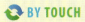 **BY TOUCH**   Tap once on *Madison* to display the gripper—small circle that acts as a handle—directly below the word. This establishes the start gripper. If necessary, with your finger, drag the gripper to the beginning of the word. Then drag the gripper to the end of Dunham to select the text and display the end gripper.

FIGURE 1.6

10 With the text *Madison Dunham* selected, type **Sarah Jackson**

> In any Windows-based program, such as the Microsoft Office 2013 programs, selected text is deleted and then replaced when you begin to type new text. You will save time by developing good techniques for selecting and then editing or replacing selected text, which is easier than pressing the ⌜Del⌟ key numerous times to delete text.

Activity 1.04 | Checking Spelling

Office 2013 has a dictionary of words against which all entered text is checked. In Word and PowerPoint, words that are not in the dictionary display a wavy red line, indicating a possible misspelled word or a proper name or an unusual word—none of which are in the Office 2013 dictionary.

In Excel and Access, you can initiate a check of the spelling, but red underlines do not display.

1 Notice that the misspelled word *Exective* displays with a wavy red underline.

2 Point to *Exective* and then **right-click**—click your right mouse button one time.

> A **shortcut menu** displays, which displays commands and options relevant to the selected text or object. These are **context-sensitive commands** because they relate to the item you right-clicked. These types of menus are also referred to as **context menus**. Here, the shortcut menu displays commands related to the misspelled word.

 BY TOUCH   Tap and hold a moment to select the misspelled word, then release your finger to display the shortcut menu.

3 Press Esc to cancel the shortcut menu, and then in the lower left corner of your screen, on the **status bar**, click the **Proofing icon** , which displays an *X* because some errors are detected. Compare your screen with Figure 1.7.

> The Spelling pane displays on the right. Here you have many more options for checking spelling than you have on the shortcut menu. The suggested correct word, *Executive*, is highlighted.
>
> You can click the speaker icon to hear the pronunciation of the selected word. You can also see some synonyms for *Executive*. Finally, if you have not already installed a dictionary, you can click *Get a Dictionary*—if you are signed in to Office with a Microsoft account—to find and install one from the online Office store; or if you have a dictionary app installed, it will display here and you can search it for more information.
>
> In the Spelling pane, you can ignore the word one time or in all occurrences, change the word to the suggested word, select a different suggestion, or add a word to the dictionary against which Word checks.

FIGURE 1.7

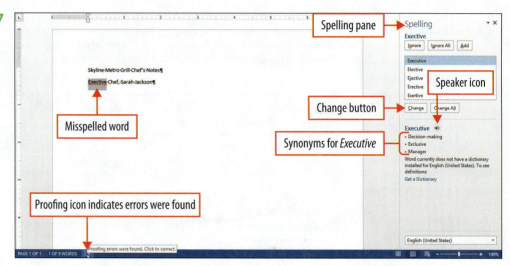

🔄 **ANOTHER WAY**   Press F7 to display the Spelling pane; or, on the Review tab, in the Proofing group, click Spelling & Grammar.

4 In the **Spelling** pane, click **Change** to change the spelling to *Executive*. In the message box that displays, click **OK**.

Objective 4 | Perform Commands from a Dialog Box

Video OF1-4

In a dialog box, you make decisions about an individual object or topic. In some dialog boxes, you can make multiple decisions in one place.

Activity 1.05 | Performing Commands from a Dialog Box

1 On the ribbon, click the **DESIGN tab**, and then in the **Page Background group**, click **Page Color**.

2 At the bottom of the menu, notice the command **Fill Effects** followed by an **ellipsis** (…). Compare your screen with Figure 1.8.

> An *ellipsis* is a set of three dots indicating incompleteness. An ellipsis following a command name indicates that a dialog box will display when you click the command.

FIGURE 1.8

DESIGN tab active

Page Color button

Fill Effects followed by ellipsis

3 ▶ Click **Fill Effects** to display the **Fill Effects** dialog box. Compare your screen with Figure 1.9.

Fill is the inside color of a page or object. The Gradient tab is active. In a *gradient fill*, one color fades into another. Here, the dialog box displays a set of tabs across the top from which you can display different sets of options. Some dialog boxes display the option group names on the left.

FIGURE 1.9

Fill Effects dialog box

Tabs within a dialog box

4 ▶ Under **Colors**, click the **One color** option button.

The dialog box displays settings related to the One color option. An *option button* is a round button that enables you to make one choice among two or more options.

5 ▶ Click the **Color 1 arrow**—the arrow under the text *Color 1*—and then in the third column, point to the second color to display the ScreenTip *Gray-25%, Background 2, Darker 10%*.

A *ScreenTip* displays useful information about mouse actions, such as pointing to screen elements or dragging.

6 ▶ Click **Gray-25%, Background 2, Darker 10%**, and then notice that the fill color displays in the **Color 1** box. In the **Dark Light** bar, click the **Light arrow** as many times as necessary until the scroll box is all the way to right. Under **Shading styles**, click the **Diagonal down** option button. Under **Variants**, click the upper right variant. Compare your screen with Figure 1.10.

FIGURE 1.10

One color option button

Gray-25%, Background 2, Darker 10%

Scroll box at Light end

Upper right variant selected

Diagonal down option button

Sample box shows effects

7 > At the bottom of the dialog box, click **OK**, and notice the subtle page color.

In Word, the gray shading page color will not print—even on a color printer—unless you set specific options to do so. However a subtle background page color is effective if people will be reading the document on a screen. Microsoft's research indicates that two-thirds of people who open Word documents never edit them; they only read them.

Activity 1.06 | Using Undo

1 > Point to the *S* in *Skyline*, and then drag down and to the right to select both paragraphs of text and include the paragraph marks. On the mini toolbar, click **Styles,** and then *point to* but do not click **Title**. Compare your screen with Figure 1.11.

A *style* is a group of *formatting* commands, such as font, font size, font color, paragraph alignment, and line spacing that can be applied to a paragraph with one command. Formatting is the process of establishing the overall appearance of text, graphics, and pages in an Office file—for example, in a Word document.

Live Preview is a technology that shows the result of applying an editing or formatting change as you point to possible results—before you actually apply it.

FIGURE 1.11

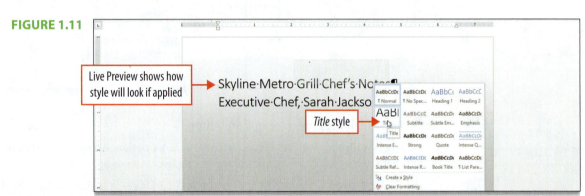

2 > In the **Styles** gallery, click **Title**.

A *gallery* is an Office feature that displays a list of potential results.

3 > On the ribbon, on the **HOME tab**, in the **Paragraph group**, click **Center** ☰ to center the two paragraphs.

Alignment refers to the placement of paragraph text relative to the left and right margins. *Center alignment* refers to text that is centered horizontally between the left and right margins. You can also align text at the left margin, which is the default alignment for text in Word, or at the right.

4 > With the two paragraphs still selected, on the **HOME tab**, in the **Font Group**, click **Text Effects and Typography** Ａ ▾ to display a gallery.

5 > In the second row, click the first effect—**Gradient Fill – Gray**. Click anywhere to *deselect*—cancel the selection—the text and notice the text effect.

6 ▶ Because this effect might be difficult to read, in the upper left corner of your screen, on the **Quick Access Toolbar**, click **Undo** ↺.

The **Undo** command reverses your last action.

🔄 **ANOTHER WAY**   Press Ctrl + Z as the keyboard shortcut for the Undo command.

7 ▶ Display the **Text Effects and Typography** gallery again, and then in the second row, click the second effect—**Gradient Fill – Blue, Accent 1, Reflection**. Click anywhere to deselect the text and notice the text effect. Compare your screen with Figure 1.12.

As you progress in your study of Microsoft Office, you will practice using many dialog boxes and applying interesting effects such as this to your Word documents, Excel worksheets, Access database objects, and PowerPoint slides.

FIGURE 1.12

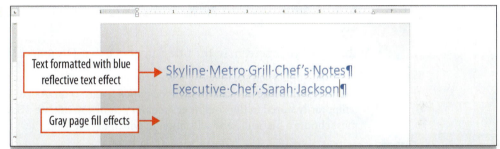

Text formatted with blue reflective text effect ➡ Skyline·Metro·Grill·Chef's·Notes¶
Executive·Chef,·Sarah·Jackson¶

Gray page fill effects ➡

Objective 5   Create a Folder and Name and Save a File

Video OF1-5

A *location* is any disk drive, folder, or other place in which you can store files and folders. Where you store your files depends on how and where you use your data. For example, for your college classes, you might decide to store on a removable USB flash drive so that you can carry your files to different locations and access your files on different computers.

If you do most of your work on a single computer, for example your home desktop system or your laptop computer that you take with you to school or work, then you can store your files in one of the Libraries—Documents, Music, Pictures, or Videos—that the Windows 8 operating system creates on your hard drive.

The best place to store files if you want them to be available anytime, anywhere, from almost any device is on your *SkyDrive*, which is Microsoft's free *cloud storage* for anyone with a free Microsoft account. Cloud storage refers to online storage of data so that you can access your data from different places and devices. *Cloud computing* refers to applications and services that are accessed over the Internet, rather than to applications that are installed on your local computer.

Because many people now have multiple computing devices—desktop, laptop, tablet, smartphone—it is common to store data *in the cloud* so that it is always available. *Synchronization*, also called *syncing*—pronounced SINK-ing—is the process of updating computer files that are in two or more locations according to specific rules. So if you create and save a Word document on your SkyDrive using your laptop, you can open and edit that document on your tablet. And then when you close the document again, the file is properly updated to reflect your changes.

You need not be connected to the Internet to access documents stored on SkyDrive because an up-to-date version of your content is synched to your local system and available on SkyDrive. You must, however, be connected to the Internet for the syncing to occur. Saving to SkyDrive will keep the local copy on your computer and the copy in the cloud synchronized for as long as you need it. If you open and edit on a different computer, log into the SkyDrive website, and then edit using Office 2013, Office 2010, or the **Office Web Apps**, you can save any changes back to SkyDrive. Office Web Apps are the free online companions to Microsoft Word, Excel, PowerPoint, Access, and OneNote. These changes will be synchronized back to any of your computers that run the SkyDrive for Windows application, which you get for free simply by logging in with your Microsoft account at skydrive.com.

The Windows operating system helps you to create and maintain a logical folder structure, so always take the time to name your files and folders consistently.

Activity 1.07 | Creating a Folder and Naming and Saving a File

A Word document is an example of a file. In this activity, you will create a folder on your USB flash drive in which to store your files. If you prefer to store on your SkyDrive or in the Documents library on your hard drive, you can use similar steps.

1 If necessary, insert your **USB flash drive** into your computer.

> As the first step in saving a file, determine where you want to save the file, and if necessary, insert a storage device.

2 At the top of your screen, in the title bar, notice that *Document1 – Word* displays.

> The Blank option on the opening screen of an Office 2013 program displays a new unsaved file with a default name—*Document1, Presentation1*, and so on. As you create your file, your work is temporarily stored in the computer's memory until you initiate a Save command, at which time you must choose a file name and a location in which to save your file.

3 In the upper left corner of your screen, click the **FILE tab** to display **Backstage** view. Compare your screen with Figure 1.13.

> **Backstage view** is a centralized space that groups commands related to *file* management; that is why the tab is labeled *FILE*. File management commands include opening, saving, printing, publishing, or sharing a file. The **Backstage tabs**—*Info, New, Open, Save, Save As, Print, Share, Export*, and *Close*—display along the left side. The tabs group file-related tasks together.
>
> Here, the **Info tab** displays information—*info*—about the current file, and file management commands display under Info. For example, if you click the Protect Document button, a list of options that you can set for this file that relate to who can open or edit the document displays.
>
> On the right, you can also examine the **document properties**. Document properties, also known as **metadata**, are details about a file that describe or identify it, such as the title, author name, subject, and keywords that identify the document's topic or contents. To close Backstage view and return to the document, you can click ⊛ in the upper left corner or press Esc.

FIGURE 1.13

4 On the left, click **Save As**, and notice that the default location for storing Office files is your **SkyDrive**—if you are signed in. Compare your screen with Figure 1.14.

When you are saving something for the first time, for example a new Word document, the Save and Save As commands are identical. That is, the Save As commands will display if you click Save or if you click Save As.

FIGURE 1.14

> **N O T E**   Saving after Your File Is Named
>
> After you name and save a file, the Save command on the Quick Access Toolbar saves any changes you make to the file without displaying Backstage view. The Save As command enables you to name and save a *new* file based on the current one—in a location that you choose. After you name and save the new document, the original document closes, and the new document—based on the original one—displays.

5 To store your Word file on your **USB flash drive**—instead of your SkyDrive—click the **Browse** button to display the **Save As** dialog box. On the left, in the navigation pane, scroll down, and then under **Computer**, click the name of your **USB flash drive**. Compare your screen with Figure 1.15.

In the Save As dialog box, you must indicate the name you want for the file and the location where you want to save the file. When working with your own data, it is good practice to pause at this point and determine the logical name and location for your file.

In the Save As dialog box, a *toolbar* displays. This is a row, column, or block of buttons or icons, that usually displays across the top of a window and that contains commands for tasks you perform with a single click.

FIGURE 1.15

6 On the toolbar, click **New folder**.

In the file list, Word creates a new folder, and the text *New folder* is selected.

7 Type **Office Features Chapter 1** and press Enter. Compare your screen with Figure 1.16.

In Windows-based programs, the Enter key confirms an action.

FIGURE 1.16

8 In the **file list**, double-click the name of your new folder to open it and display its name in the **address bar**.

9 In the lower portion of the dialog box, click in the **File name** box to select the existing text. Notice that Office inserts the text at the beginning of the document as a suggested file name.

10 On your keyboard, locate the hyphen ⊡ key. Notice that the Shift of this key produces the underscore character. With the text still selected and using your own name, type **Lastname_Firstname_1A_Note_Form** and then compare your screen with Figure 1.17.

You can use spaces in file names, however, some people prefer not to use spaces. Some programs, especially when transferring files over the Internet, may insert the extra characters *%20* in place of a space. This can happen in *SharePoint*, so using underscores instead of spaces can be a good habit to adopt. SharePoint is Microsoft's collaboration software with which people in an organization can set up team sites to share information, manage documents, and publish reports for others to see. In general, however, unless you encounter a problem, it is OK to use spaces. In this textbook, underscores are used instead of spaces in file names.

FIGURE 1.17

11 In the lower right corner, click **Save** or press Enter. Compare your screen with Figure 1.18.

The Word window redisplays and your new file name displays in the title bar, indicating that the file has been saved to a location that you have specified.

FIGURE 1.18

12 In the first paragraph, click to place the insertion point after the word *Grill* and type , (a comma). In the upper left corner of your screen, on the **Quick Access Toolbar**, click **Save** 🖫.

After a document is named and saved in a location, you can save any changes you have made since the last Save operation by using the Save command on the Quick Access Toolbar. When working on a document, it is good practice to save your changes from time to time.

Objective 6 | Insert a Footer, Add Document Properties, Print a File, and Close a Desktop App

Video OF1-6

For most of your files, especially in a workplace setting, it is useful to add identifying information to help in finding files later. You might also want to print your file on paper or create an electronic printout. The process of printing a file is similar in all of the Office applications.

Activity 1.08 | Inserting a Footer, Inserting Document Info, and Adding Document Properties

> **NOTE** | **Are You Printing or Submitting Your Files Electronically?**
>
> In this activity, you can either produce a paper printout or create an electronic file to submit to your instructor if required.

1 On the ribbon, click the **INSERT tab**, and then in the **Header & Footer group**, click **Footer**.

2 At the bottom of the list, click **Edit Footer**. On the ribbon, notice that the **HEADER & FOOTER TOOLS** display.

The *Header & Footer Tools Design* tab displays on the ribbon. The ribbon adapts to your work and will display additional tabs like this one—referred to as *contextual tabs*—when you need them.

A *footer* is a reserved area for text or graphics that displays at the bottom of each page in a document. Likewise, a *header* is a reserved area for text or graphics that displays at the top of each page in a document. When the footer (or header) area is active, the document area is dimmed, indicating it is unavailable.

3 On the ribbon, under **HEADER & FOOTER TOOLS**, on the **DESIGN tab**, in the **Insert group**, click **Document Info**, and then click **File Name** to insert the name of your file in the footer, which is a common business practice. Compare your screen with Figure 1.19.

Ribbon commands that display ▼ will, when clicked, display a list of options for the command.

FIGURE 1.19

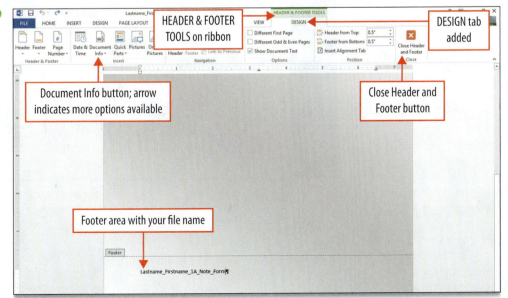

4 ▶ At the right end of the ribbon, click **Close Header and Footer**.

🔄 **ANOTHER WAY**   Double-click anywhere in the dimmed document to close the footer.

5 ▶ Click the **FILE tab** to display **Backstage** view. On the right, at the bottom of the **Properties** list, click **Show All Properties**.

🔄 **ANOTHER WAY**   Click the arrow to the right of Properties, and then click Show Document Panel to show and edit properties at the top of your document window.

6 ▶ On the list of **Properties**, click to the right of **Tags** to display an empty box, and then type **chef, notes, form**

> *Tags*, also referred to as *keywords*, are custom file properties in the form of words that you associate with a document to give an indication of the document's content. Adding tags to your documents makes it easier to search for and locate files in File Explorer and in systems such as Microsoft SharePoint document libraries.

🔄 **BY TOUCH**   Tap to the right of Tags to display the Tags box and the onscreen keyboard.

7 ▶ Click to the right of **Subject** to display an empty box, and then type your course name and section #; for example *CIS 10, #5543*.

8 ▶ Under **Related People**, be sure that your name displays as the author. If necessary, right-click the author name, click Edit Property, type your name, click outside of the Edit person dialog box, and then click OK. Compare your screen with Figure 1.20.

FIGURE 1.20

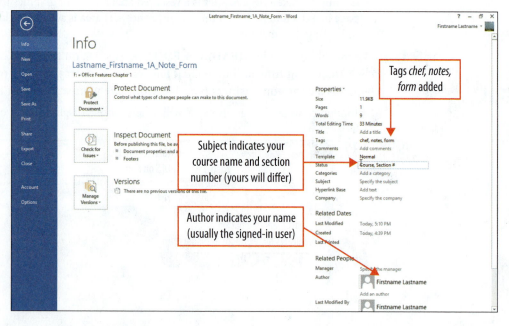

Activity 1.09 | Printing a File and Closing a Desktop App

1 On the left, click **Print**, and then compare your screen with Figure 1.21.

> Here you can select any printer connected to your system and adjust the settings related to how you want to print. On the right, the ***Print Preview*** displays, which is a view of a document as it will appear on paper when you print it.

> At the bottom of the Print Preview area, in the center, the number of pages and page navigation arrows with which you can move among the pages in Print Preview display. On the right, the Zoom slider enables you to shrink or enlarge the Print Preview. ***Zoom*** is the action of increasing or decreasing the viewing area of the screen.

🔄 **ANOTHER WAY**   From the document screen, press ⎡Ctrl⎤ + ⎡P⎤ or ⎡Ctrl⎤ + ⎡F2⎤ to display Print in Backstage view.

FIGURE 1.21

2 To submit your file electronically, skip this step and continue to Step 3. To print your document on paper using the default printer on your system, in the upper left portion of the screen, click the **Print** button.

> The document will print on your default printer; if you do not have a color printer, the blue text will print in shades of gray. The gray page color you applied to the document does not display in Print Preview nor does it print unless you specifically adjust some of Word's options. Backstage view closes and your file redisplays in the Word window.

3 To create an electronic file, on the left click **Export**. On the right, click the **Create PDF/XPS** button to display the **Publish as PDF or XPS** dialog box.

> ***PDF*** stands for ***Portable Document Format***, which is a technology that creates an image that preserves the look of your file. This is a popular format for sending documents electronically, because the document will display on most computers.

> ***XPS*** stands for ***XML Paper Specification***—a Microsoft file format that also creates an image of your document and that opens in the XPS viewer.

4 On the left in the **navigation pane**, if necessary expand ▷ Computer, and then navigate to your **Office Features Chapter 1** folder on your **USB flash drive**. Compare your screen with Figure 1.22.

FIGURE 1.22

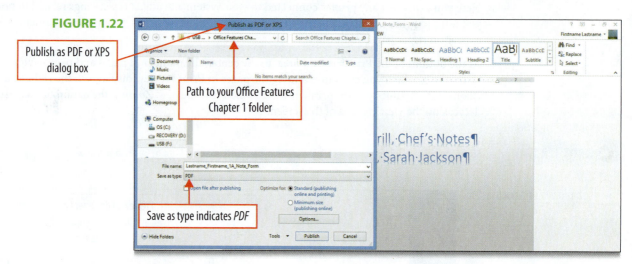

Publish as PDF or XPS dialog box

Path to your Office Features Chapter 1 folder

Save as type indicates *PDF*

5 In the lower right corner of the dialog box, click **Publish**; if your Adobe Acrobat or Adobe Reader program displays your PDF, in the upper right corner, click Close . Notice that your document redisplays in Word.

🔄 **ANOTHER WAY**   In Backstage view, click Save As, navigate to the location of your Chapter folder, click the Save as type arrow, on the list click PDF, and then click Save.

6 Click the **FILE tab** to redisplay **Backstage** view. On the left, click **Close**, if necessary click Save, and then compare your screen with Figure 1.23.

FIGURE 1.23

Close button

Word window with all documents closed

7 In the upper right corner of the Word window, click **Close** . If directed by your instructor to do so, submit your paper or electronic file.

END | You have completed Project 1A

PROJECT ACTIVITIES

In Activities 1.10 through 1.21, you will open, edit, and then compress a Word file. You will also use the Office Help system and install an app for Office. Your completed document will look similar to Figure 1.24.

PROJECT FILES

For Project 1B, you will need the following file:

of01B_Rehearsal_Dinner

You will save your file as:

Lastname_Firstname_1B_Rehearsal_Dinner

PROJECT RESULTS

Skyline Metro Grill

TO: Sarah Jackson, Executive Chef

FROM: Laura Mabry Hernandez, General Manager

DATE: February 17, 2016

SUBJECT: Wedding Rehearsal Dinners

In the spring and summer months, wedding rehearsal dinners provide a new marketing opportunity for Skyline Metro Grill at all of our locations. A rehearsal dinner is an informal meal following a wedding rehearsal at which the bride and groom typically thank those who have helped them make their wedding a special event.

Our smaller private dining rooms with sweeping city views are an ideal location for a rehearsal dinner. At each of our locations, I have directed the Sales and Marketing Coordinator to partner with local wedding planners to promote Skyline Metro Grill as a relaxed yet sophisticated venue for rehearsal dinners. The typical rehearsal dinner includes the wedding party, the immediate family of the bride and groom, and out-of-town guests.

Please develop six menus—in varying price ranges—to present to local wedding planners so that they can easily promote Skyline Metro Grill to couples who are planning a rehearsal dinner. In addition to a traditional dinner, we should also include options for a buffet-style dinner and a family-style dinner.

This marketing effort will require extensive communication with our Sales and Marketing Coordinators and with local wedding planners. Let's meet to discuss the details and the marketing challenges, and to create a promotional piece that begins something like this:

Skyline Metro Grill for Your Rehearsal Dinner

Lastname_Firstname_1B_Rehearsal_Dinner

FIGURE 1.24 Project 1B Memo

Video OF1-7

In any Office program, you can display the ***Open dialog box***, from which you can navigate to and then open an existing file that was created in that same program.

The Open dialog box, along with the Save and Save As dialog boxes, is a *common dialog box*. These dialog boxes, which are provided by the Windows programming interface, display in all Office programs in the same manner. So the Open, Save, and Save As dialog boxes will all look and perform the same regardless of the Office program in which you are working.

Activity 1.10 | Opening an Existing File and Saving It with a New Name

In this activity, you will display the Open dialog box, open an existing Word document, and then save it in your storage location with a new name.

1 Sign in to your computer, and then on the Windows 8 Start screen, type **word 2013** Press Enter to open Word on your desktop. If you want to do so, on the taskbar, right-click the **Word icon**, and then click **Pin this program to taskbar** to keep the Word program available from your desktop.

2 On Word's opening screen, on the left, click **Open Other Documents**. Under **Open**, click **Computer**, and then on the right click **Browse**.

3 In the **Open** dialog box, on the left in the **navigation pane**, scroll down, if necessary expand ▷ Computer, and then click the name of your **USB flash drive**. In the **file list**, double-click the **Office_Features** folder that you downloaded.

4 Double-click **of01B_Rehearsal_Dinner**. If **PROTECTED VIEW** displays at the top of your screen, in the center click **Enable Editing**.

In Office 2013, a file will open in ***Protected View*** if the file appears to be from a potentially risky location, such as the Internet. Protected View is a security feature in Office 2013 that protects your computer from malicious files by opening them in a restricted environment until you enable them. ***Trusted Documents*** is another security feature that remembers which files you have already enabled.

You might encounter these security features if you open a file from an email or download files from the Internet; for example, from your college's learning management system or from the Pearson website. So long as you trust the source of the file, click Enable Editing or Enable Content— depending on the type of file you receive—and then go ahead and work with the file.

5 With the document displayed in the Word window, be sure that **Show/Hide** is active; if necessary, on the HOME tab, in the Paragraph group, click Show/Hide to activate it. Compare your screen with Figure 1.25.

FIGURE 1.25

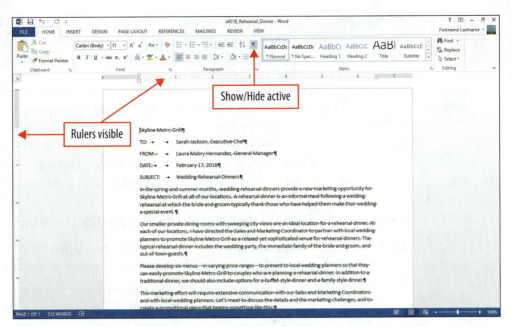

6 Click the **FILE tab** to display **Backstage** view, and then on the left, click **Save As**. On the right, click the folder under **Current Folder** to open the **Save As** dialog box. Notice that the current folder is the **Office_Features** folder you downloaded.

ANOTHER WAY   Press F12 to display the Save As dialog box.

7 In the upper left corner of the **Save As** dialog box, click the **Up** button ↑ to move up one level in the File Explorer hierarchy. In the **file list**, double-click your **Office Features Chapter 1** folder to open it.

8 Click in the **File name** box to select the existing text, and then, using your own name, type **Lastname_Firstname_1B_Rehearsal_Dinner** Compare your screen with Figure 1.26.

FIGURE 1.26

9 Click **Save** or press Enter; notice that your new file name displays in the title bar.

The original document closes, and your new document, based on the original, displays with the name in the title bar.

More Knowledge   **Read-Only**

Some files might display **Read-Only** in the title bar, which is a property assigned to a file that prevents the file from being modified or deleted; it indicates that you cannot save any changes to the displayed document unless you first save it with a new name.

Video OF1-8

If you sign in to Windows 8 with a Microsoft account, you may notice that you are also signed in to Office. This enables you to save files to and retrieve files from your SkyDrive and to **collaborate** with others on Office files when you want to do so. To collaborate means to work with others as a team in an intellectual endeavor to complete a shared task or to achieve a shared goal.

Within each Office application, an **Options dialog box** enables you to select program settings and other options and preferences. For example, you can set preferences for viewing and editing files.

Activity 1.11 | Signing In to Office and Viewing Application Options

1 In the upper right corner of your screen, if you are signed in with a Microsoft account, click the arrow to the right of your name, and then compare your screen with Figure 1.27.

Here you can change your photo, go to About me to edit your profile, examine your Account settings, or switch accounts to sign in with a different Microsoft account.

FIGURE 1.27

2 Click the **FILE tab** to display **Backstage** view. On the left, click the last tab—**Options**.

3 In the **Word Options** dialog box, on the left, click **Display**, and then on the right, locate the information under **Always show these formatting marks on the screen**.

4 Under **Always show these formatting marks on the screen**, be sure the last check box, **Show all formatting marks**, is selected—select it if necessary. Compare your screen with Figure 1.28.

FIGURE 1.28

Display tab selected

Word Options dialog box

Object anchors selected by default

Show all formatting marks selected

5 In the lower right corner of the dialog box, click **OK**.

Objective 9 Perform Commands from the Ribbon and Quick Access Toolbar

Video OF1-9

The ribbon that displays across the top of the program window groups commands in a manner that you would most logically use them. The ribbon in each Office program is slightly different, but all contain the same three elements: **tabs**, **groups**, and **commands**.

Tabs display across the top of the ribbon, and each tab relates to a type of activity; for example, laying out a page. Groups are sets of related commands for specific tasks. Commands—instructions to computer programs—are arranged in groups and might display as a button, a menu, or a box in which you type information.

You can also minimize the ribbon so only the tab names display, which is useful when working on a smaller screen such as a tablet computer where you want to maximize your screen viewing area.

Activity 1.12 | Performing Commands from and Customizing the Ribbon and the Quick Access Toolbar

1 Take a moment to examine the document on your screen. If necessary, on the ribbon, click the VIEW tab, and then in the Show group, click to place a check mark in the Ruler check box. Compare your screen with Figure 1.29.

This document is a memo from the General Manager to the Executive Chef regarding a new restaurant promotion for wedding rehearsal dinners.

When working in Word, display the rulers so that you can see how margin settings affect your document and how text and objects align. Additionally, if you set a tab stop or an indent, its location is visible on the ruler.

FIGURE 1.29

Ruler checkbox selected

VIEW tab active

Show group

Rulers display

2 In the upper left corner of your screen, above the ribbon, locate the **Quick Access Toolbar**.

Recall that the Quick Access Toolbar contains commands that you use frequently. By default, only the commands Save, Undo, and Redo display, but you can add and delete commands to suit your needs. Possibly the computer at which you are working already has additional commands added to the Quick Access Toolbar.

3 At the end of the **Quick Access Toolbar**, click the **Customize Quick Access Toolbar** button ⊤, and then compare your screen with Figure 1.30.

A list of commands that Office users commonly add to their Quick Access Toolbar displays, including New, Open, Email, Quick Print, and Print Preview and Print. Commands already on the Quick Access Toolbar display a check mark. Commands that you add to the Quick Access Toolbar are always just one click away.

Here you can also display the More Commands dialog box, from which you can select any command from any tab on the ribbon to add to the Quick Access Toolbar.

 BY TOUCH   Tap once on Quick Access Toolbar commands.

FIGURE 1.30

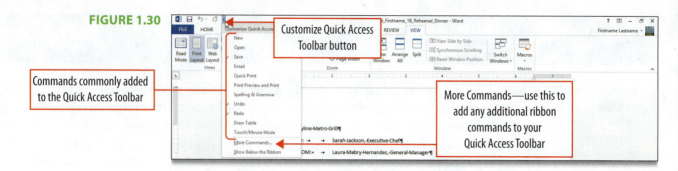

On the list, click **Print Preview and Print**, and then notice that the icon is added to the **Quick Access Toolbar**. Compare your screen with Figure 1.31.

> The icon that represents the Print Preview command displays on the Quick Access Toolbar. Because this is a command that you will use frequently while building Office documents, you might decide to have this command remain on your Quick Access Toolbar.

ANOTHER WAY   Right-click any command on the ribbon, and then on the shortcut menu, click Add to Quick Access Toolbar.

FIGURE 1.31

In the first line of the document, if necessary, click to the left of the *S* in *Skyline* to position the insertion point there, and then press `Enter` one time to insert a blank paragraph. Press `↑` one time to position the insertion point in the new blank paragraph. Compare your screen with Figure 1.32.

FIGURE 1.32

On the ribbon, click the **INSERT tab**. In the **Illustrations group**, *point* to the **Online Pictures** button to display its ScreenTip.

> Many buttons on the ribbon have this type of *enhanced ScreenTip*, which displays useful descriptive information about the command.

Click **Online Pictures**, and then compare your screen with Figure 1.33.

> In the Insert Pictures dialog box you can search for online pictures using Microsoft's Clip Art collection. *Clip art* refers to royalty-free photos and illustrations you can download from Microsoft's Office.com site.

> Here you can also search for images using the Bing search engine, and if you are signed in with your Microsoft account, you can also find images on your SkyDrive or on your computer by clicking Browse. At the bottom, you can click the Flickr logo and download pictures from your Flickr account if you have one.

FIGURE 1.33

8 Click **Office.com Clip Art** and in the box that displays to the right, type **salad in a bowl** and press [Enter]. As shown in Figure 1.34, point to the illustration of the salad bowl to display its keywords.

You can use various keywords to find clip art that is appropriate for your documents.

FIGURE 1.34

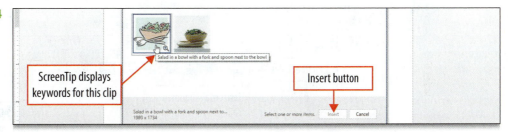

9 Click the illustration of the salad to select it, and then in the lower right corner, click **Insert**. In the upper right corner of the picture, point to the **Layout Options** button [icon] to display its ScreenTip, and then compare your screen with Figure 1.35. If you cannot find the image, select a similar image, and then drag one of the corner sizing handles to match the approximate size shown in the figure.

Inserted pictures anchor—attach to—the paragraph at the insertion point location—as indicated by the anchor symbol. *Layout Options* enable you to choose how the *object*—in this instance an inserted picture—interacts with the surrounding text. An object is a picture or other graphic such as a chart or table that you can select and then move and resize.

When a picture is selected, the PICTURE TOOLS become available on the ribbon. Additionally, *sizing handles*—small squares that indicate an object is selected—surround the selected picture.

FIGURE 1.35

10 With the image selected, click **Layout Options** 🖼, and then under **With Text Wrapping**, in the second row, click the first layout—**Top and Bottom**.

11 Point to the image to display the 🔀 pointer, hold down the left mouse button to display a green line at the left margin, and then drag the image to the right and slightly upward until a green line displays in the center of the image and at the top of the image, as shown in Figure 1.36, and then release the left mouse button. If you are not satisfied with your result, on the Quick Access Toolbar, click Undo 🔙 and begin again.

Alignment Guides are green lines that display to help you align objects with margins or at the center of a page.

FIGURE 1.36

12 On the ribbon, in the **Picture Styles group**, point to the first style to display the ScreenTip *Simple Frame, White*, and notice that the image displays with a white frame.

NOTE   The Size of Groups on the Ribbon Varies with Screen Resolution

Your monitor's screen resolution might be set higher than the resolution used to capture the figures in this book. At a higher resolution, the ribbon expands some groups to show more commands than are available with a single click, such as those in the Picture Styles group. Or, the group expands to add descriptive text to some buttons, such as those in the Adjust group. Regardless of your screen resolution, all Office commands are available to you. In higher resolutions, you will have a more robust view of the ribbon commands.

13 Watch the image as you point to the second picture style, and then to the third, and then to the fourth.

Recall that Live Preview shows the result of applying an editing or formatting change as you point to possible results—*before* you actually apply it.

14 In the **Picture Styles group**, click the second style—**Beveled Matte, White**—and then click anywhere outside of the image to deselect it. Notice that the *PICTURE TOOLS* no longer display on the ribbon. Compare your screen with Figure 1.37.

Contextual tabs on the ribbon display only when you need them.

FIGURE 1.37

15 On the **Quick Access Toolbar**, click **Save** 💾 to save the changes you have made.

Activity 1.13 | Minimizing and Using the Keyboard to Control the Ribbon

Instead of a mouse, some individuals prefer to navigate the ribbon by using keys on the keyboard.

1 On your keyboard, press Alt, and then on the ribbon, notice that small labels display. Press N to activate the commands on the **INSERT tab**, and then compare your screen with Figure 1.38.

Each label represents a *KeyTip*—an indication of the key that you can press to activate the command. For example, on the INSERT tab, you can press F to open the Online Pictures dialog box.

FIGURE 1.38

2 Press Esc to redisplay the KeyTips for the tabs. Then, press Alt or Esc again to turn off keyboard control of the ribbon.

3 Point to any tab on the ribbon and right-click to display a shortcut menu.

Here you can choose to display the Quick Access Toolbar below the ribbon or collapse the ribbon to maximize screen space. You can also customize the ribbon by adding, removing, renaming, or reordering tabs, groups, and commands, although this is not recommended until you become an expert Office user.

4 Click **Collapse the Ribbon**. Notice that only the ribbon tabs display. Click the **HOME tab** to display the commands. Click anywhere in the document, and notice that the ribbon goes back to the collapsed display.

5 Right-click any ribbon tab, and then click **Collapse the Ribbon** again to remove the check mark from this command.

Many expert Office users prefer the full ribbon display.

6 Point to any tab on the ribbon, and then on your mouse device, roll the mouse wheel. Notice that different tabs become active as you roll the mouse wheel.

You can make a tab active by using this technique instead of clicking the tab.

Objective 10   Apply Formatting in Office Programs

Video OF1-10

Activity 1.14 | Changing Page Orientation and Zoom Level

In this activity, you will practice common formatting techniques used in Office applications.

1 On the ribbon, click the **PAGE LAYOUT tab**. In the **Page Setup group**, click **Orientation**, and notice that two orientations display—*Portrait* and *Landscape*. Click **Landscape**.

In **portrait orientation**, the paper is taller than it is wide. In **landscape orientation**, the paper is wider than it is tall.

2 In the lower right corner of the screen, locate the **Zoom slider**.

Recall that to zoom means to increase or decrease the viewing area. You can zoom in to look closely at a section of a document, and then zoom out to see an entire page on the screen. You can also zoom to view multiple pages on the screen.

3 Drag the **Zoom slider** to the left until you have zoomed to approximately *60%*. Compare your screen with Figure 1.39.

FIGURE 1.39

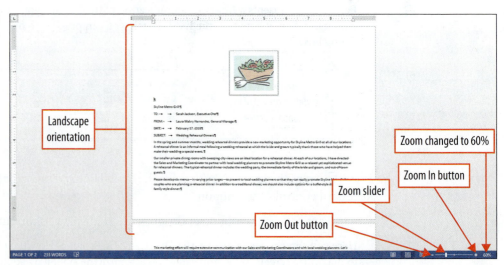

🔄 **BY TOUCH**   Drag the Zoom slider with your finger.

4 Use the technique you just practiced to change the **Orientation** back to **Portrait**.

The default orientation in Word is Portrait, which is commonly used for business documents such as letters and memos.

5 In the lower right corner, click the **Zoom In** button ➕ as many times as necessary to return to the **100%** zoom setting.

> Use the zoom feature to adjust the view of your document for editing and for your viewing comfort.

🔄 **ANOTHER WAY** You can also control Zoom from the ribbon. On the VIEW tab, in the Zoom group, you can control the Zoom level and also zoom to view multiple pages.

6 On the **Quick Access Toolbar**, click **Save** 🖫.

More Knowledge **Zooming to Page Width**

Some Office users prefer Page Width, which zooms the document so that the width of the page matches the width of the window. Find this command on the VIEW tab, in the Zoom group.

Activity 1.15 | Formatting Text by Using Fonts, Alignment, Font Colors, and Font Styles

1 If necessary, on the right side of your screen, drag the vertical scroll box to the top of the scroll bar. To the left of *Skyline Metro Grill*, point in the margin area to display the ⬚ pointer and click one time to select the entire paragraph. Compare your screen with Figure 1.40.

> Use this technique to select complete paragraphs from the margin area—drag downward to select multiple-line paragraphs—which is faster and more efficient than dragging through text.

FIGURE 1.40

2 On the ribbon, click the **HOME tab**, and then in the **Paragraph group**, click **Center** ≣ to center the paragraph.

3 On the **HOME tab**, in the **Font group**, click the **Font button arrow** [Calibri (Body) ▾]. On the alphabetical list of font names, scroll down and then locate and *point to* **Cambria**.

> A *font* is a set of characters with the same design and shape. The default font in a Word document is Calibri, which is a *sans serif* font—a font design with no lines or extensions on the ends of characters.

> The Cambria font is a *serif font*—a font design that includes small line extensions on the ends of the letters to guide the eye in reading from left to right.

> The list of fonts displays as a gallery showing potential results. For example, in the Font gallery, you can point to see the actual design and format of each font as it would look if applied to text.

4 Point to several other fonts and observe the effect on the selected text. Then, scroll back to the top of the **Font** gallery. Under **Theme Fonts**, click **Calibri Light**.

> A *theme* is a predesigned combination of colors, fonts, line, and fill effects that look good together and is applied to an entire document by a single selection. A theme combines two sets of fonts—one for text and one for headings. In the default Office theme, Calibri Light is the suggested font for headings.

5 With the paragraph *Skyline Metro Grill* still selected, on the **HOME tab**, in the **Font group**, click the **Font Size button arrow** 11 ▾ , point to **36**, and then notice how Live Preview displays the text in the font size to which you are pointing. Compare your screen with Figure 1.41.

FIGURE 1.41

Font Size button arrow

Font size list

Live Preview displays font as 36 pt., Calibri Light font

Skyline·Metro·Grill¶

6 On the list of font sizes, click **20**.

Fonts are measured in *points*, with one point equal to 1/72 of an inch. A higher point size indicates a larger font size. Headings and titles are often formatted by using a larger font size. The word *point* is abbreviated as *pt*.

7 With *Skyline Metro Grill* still selected, on the **HOME tab**, in the **Font group**, click the **Font Color button arrow** A ▾ . Under **Theme Colors**, in the last column, click the last color—**Green, Accent 6, Darker 50%**. Click anywhere to deselect the text.

8 To the left of *TO:*, point in the left margin area to display the pointer, hold down the left mouse button, and then drag down to select the four memo headings. Compare your screen with Figure 1.42.

Use this technique to select complete paragraphs from the margin area—drag downward to select multiple paragraphs—which is faster and more efficient than dragging through text.

BY TOUCH Tap once on TO: to display the gripper, then with your finger, drag to the right and down to select the four paragraphs.

FIGURE 1.42

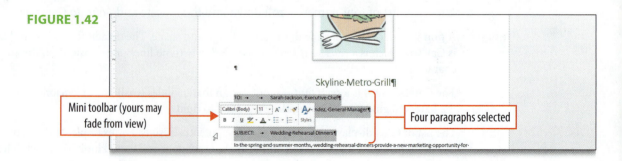

Mini toolbar (yours may fade from view)

Four paragraphs selected

9 With the four paragraphs selected, on the mini toolbar, click the **Font Color** button ![A], and notice that the text color of the four paragraphs changes.

> The font color button retains its most recently used color—Green, Accent 6, Darker 50%. As you progress in your study of Microsoft Office, you will use other buttons that behave in this manner; that is, they retain their most recently used format. This is commonly referred to as *MRU*—most recently used.

> Recall that the mini toolbar places commands that are commonly used for the selected text or object close by so that you reduce the distance that you must move your mouse to access a command. If you are using a touchscreen device, most commands that you need are close and easy to touch.

10 On the right, drag the vertical scroll box down slightly to position more of the text on the screen. Click anywhere in the paragraph that begins *In the spring*, and then **triple-click**—click the left mouse button three times—to select the entire paragraph. If the entire paragraph is not selected, click in the paragraph and begin again.

11 With the entire paragraph selected, on the mini toolbar, click the **Font Color button arrow** ![A], and then under **Theme Colors**, in the sixth column, click the last color— **Orange, Accent 2, Darker 50%**.

12 In the memo headings, select the guide word *TO:* and then on the mini toolbar, click **Bold** ![B] and **Italic** ![I].

> *Font styles* include bold, italic, and underline. Font styles emphasize text and are a visual cue to draw the reader's eye to important text.

13 On the mini toolbar, click **Italic** ![I] again to turn off the Italic formatting.

> A *toggle button* is a button that can be turned on by clicking it once, and then turned off by clicking it again.

Activity 1.16 | Using Format Painter

Use the Format Painter to copy the formatting of specific text or of a paragraph and then apply it in other locations in your document.

1 With *TO:* still selected, on the mini toolbar, click **Format Painter** ![icon]. Then, move your mouse under the word *Sarah*, and notice the ![icon] mouse pointer. Compare your screen with Figure 1.43.

> The pointer takes the shape of a paintbrush, and contains the formatting information from the paragraph where the insertion point is positioned. Information about the Format Painter and how to turn it off displays in the status bar.

FIGURE 1.43

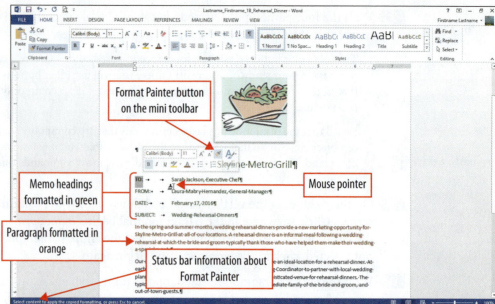

Format Painter button on the mini toolbar

Memo headings formatted in green

Mouse pointer

Paragraph formatted in orange

Status bar information about Format Painter

2 With the pointer, drag to select the guide word *FROM:* and notice that Bold formatting is applied. Then, point to the selected text *FROM:* and on the mini toolbar, *double-click* **Format Painter**.

3 Select the guide word *DATE:* to copy the Bold formatting, and notice that the pointer retains the shape.

When you *double-click* the Format Painter button, the Format Painter feature remains active until you either click the Format Painter button again, or press Esc to cancel it—as indicated on the status bar.

4 With Format Painter still active, select the guide word *SUBJECT:*, and then on the ribbon, on the **HOME tab**, in the **Clipboard group**, notice that **Format Painter** is selected, indicating that it is active. Compare your screen with Figure 1.44.

FIGURE 1.44

Format Painter button on ribbon active

Memo headings formatted with Bold; *SUBJECT:* still selected

Skyline·Metro·Grill¶

5 On the ribbon, click **Format Painter** to turn the command off.

 ANOTHER WAY   Press Esc to turn off Format Painter.

6 In the paragraph that begins *In the spring*, triple-click again to select the entire paragraph. On the mini toolbar, click **Bold** B and **Italic** I . Click anywhere to deselect.

7 On the **Quick Access Toolbar**, click **Save** to save the changes you have made to your document.

Activity 1.17 | Using Keyboard Shortcuts and Using the Clipboard to Copy, Cut, and Paste

The *Clipboard* is a temporary storage area that holds text or graphics that you select and then cut or copy. When you *copy* text or graphics, a copy is placed on the Clipboard and the original text or graphic remains in place. When you *cut* text or graphics, a copy is placed on the Clipboard, and the original text or graphic is removed—cut—from the document.

After copying or cutting, the contents of the Clipboard are available for you to *paste*—insert— in a new location in the current document, or into another Office file.

1 Hold down Ctrl and press Home to move to the beginning of your document, and then take a moment to study the table in Figure 1.45, which describes similar keyboard shortcuts with which you can navigate quickly in a document.

FIGURE 1.45

KEYBOARD SHORTCUTS TO NAVIGATE IN A DOCUMENT	
TO MOVE	**PRESS**
To the beginning of a document	Ctrl + Home
To the end of a document	Ctrl + End
To the beginning of a line	Home
To the end of a line	End
To the beginning of the previous word	Ctrl + ←
To the beginning of the next word	Ctrl + →
To the beginning of the current word (if insertion point is in the middle of a word)	Ctrl + ←
To the beginning of the previous paragraph	Ctrl + ↑
To the beginning of the next paragraph	Ctrl + ↓
To the beginning of the current paragraph (if insertion point is in the middle of a paragraph)	Ctrl + ↑
Up one screen	PgUp
Down one screen	PgDn

2 To the left of *Skyline Metro Grill*, point in the left margin area to display the pointer, and then click one time to select the entire paragraph. On the **HOME tab**, in the **Clipboard group**, click **Copy** .

Because anything that you select and then copy—or cut—is placed on the Clipboard, the Copy command and the Cut command display in the Clipboard group of commands on the ribbon. There is no visible indication that your copied selection has been placed on the Clipboard.

ANOTHER WAY   Right-click the selection, and then click Copy on the shortcut menu; or, use the keyboard shortcut Ctrl + C.

3 On the **HOME tab**, in the **Clipboard group**, to the right of the group name *Clipboard*, click the **Dialog Box Launcher** button ![icon], and then compare your screen with Figure 1.46.

The Clipboard pane displays with your copied text. In any ribbon group, the ***Dialog Box Launcher*** displays either a dialog box or a pane related to the group of commands. It is not necessary to display the Clipboard in this manner, although sometimes it is useful to do so.

FIGURE 1.46

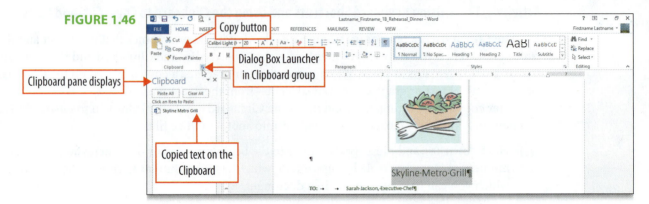

4 In the upper right corner of the **Clipboard** pane, click **Close** ![X].

5 Press [Ctrl] + [End] to move to the end of your document. Press [Enter] one time to create a new blank paragraph. On the **HOME tab**, in the **Clipboard group**, point to **Paste**, and then click the *upper* portion of this split button.

The Paste command pastes the most recently copied item on the Clipboard at the insertion point location. If you click the lower portion of the Paste button, a gallery of Paste Options displays. A ***split button*** is divided into two parts; clicking the main part of the button performs a command, and clicking the arrow displays a list or gallery with choices.

🔄 **ANOTHER WAY**　　Right-click, on the shortcut menu under Paste Options, click the desired option button; or, press [Ctrl] + [V].

6 Below the pasted text, click **Paste Options** ![icon] as shown in Figure 1.47.

Here you can view and apply various formatting options for pasting your copied or cut text. Typically you will click Paste on the ribbon and paste the item in its original format. If you want some other format for the pasted item, you can choose another format from the ***Paste Options gallery***.

The Paste Options gallery provides a Live Preview of the various options for changing the format of the pasted item with a single click. The Paste Options gallery is available in three places: on the ribbon by clicking the lower portion of the Paste button—the Paste button arrow; from the Paste Options button that displays below the pasted item following the paste operation; or on the shortcut menu if you right-click the pasted item.

FIGURE 1.47

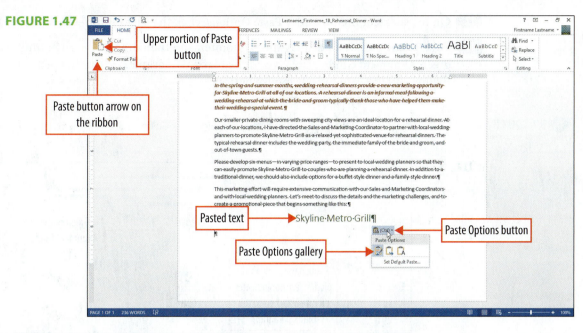

Upper portion of Paste button

Paste button arrow on the ribbon

Pasted text → Skyline·Metro·Grill¶

Paste Options button

Paste Options gallery

7 In the **Paste Options** gallery, *point* to each option to see the Live Preview of the format that would be applied if you clicked the button.

The contents of the Paste Options gallery are contextual; that is, they change based on what you copied and where you are pasting.

8 Press Esc to close the gallery; the button will remain displayed until you take some other screen action.

9 Press Ctrl + Home to move to the top of the document, and then click the **salad image** one time to select it. While pointing to the selected image, right-click, and then on the shortcut menu, click **Cut**.

Recall that the Cut command cuts—removes—the selection from the document and places it on the Clipboard.

 ANOTHER WAY   On the HOME tab, in the Clipboard group, click the Cut button; or, use the keyboard shortcut Ctrl + X.

10 Press Del one time to remove the blank paragraph from the top of the document, and then press Ctrl + End to move to the end of the document.

11 With the insertion point blinking in the blank paragraph at the end of the document, right-click, and notice that the **Paste Options** gallery displays on the shortcut menu. Compare your screen with Figure 1.48.

FIGURE 1.48

Paste Options on the shortcut menu

12 On the shortcut menu, under **Paste Options**, click the first button—**Keep Source Formatting**.

13 Point to the picture to display the pointer, and then drag to the right until the center green **Alignment Guide** displays and the blank paragraph is above the picture, as shown in Figure 1.49. Release the left mouse button.

FIGURE 1.49

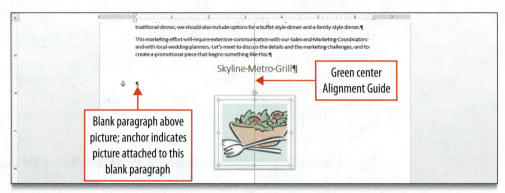

14 Above the picture, click to position the insertion point at the end of the word *Grill*, press Spacebar one time, type **for Your Rehearsal Dinner** and then **Save** 🖫 your document. Compare your screen with Figure 1.50.

FIGURE 1.50

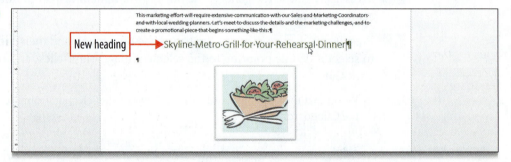

15 On the **INSERT tab**, in the **Header & Footer group**, click **Footer**. At the bottom of the list, click **Edit Footer**, and then with the **HEADER & FOOTER Design tab** active, in the **Insert group**, click **Document Info**. Click **File Name** to add the file name to the footer.

16 On the right end of the ribbon, click **Close Header and Footer**.

17 On the **Quick Access Toolbar**, point to the **Print Preview and Print icon** 🔍 you placed there, right-click, and then click **Remove from Quick Access Toolbar**.

   If you are working on your own computer and you want to do so, you can leave the icon on the toolbar; in a lab setting, you should return the software to its original settings.

18 Click **Save** 🖫 and then click the **FILE tab** to display **Backstage** view. With the **Info tab** active, in the lower right corner click **Show All Properties**. As **Tags**, type **weddings, rehearsal dinners, marketing**

19 As the **Subject**, type your course name and number—for example *CIS 10, #5543*. Under **Related People**, be sure your name displays as the author (edit it if necessary), and then on the left, click **Print** to display the Print Preview. Compare your screen with Figure 1.51.

FIGURE 1.51

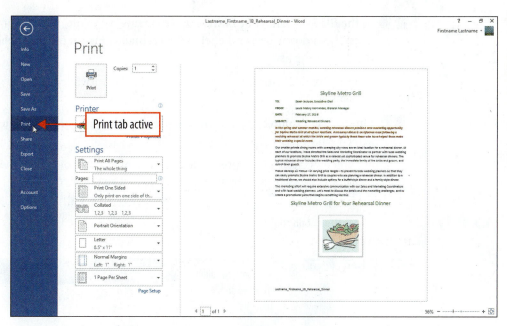

20 ▶ On the left side of **Backstage** view, click **Save**. As directed by your instructor, print or submit your file electronically as described in Project 1A, and then in the upper right corner of the Word window, click **Close** ☒ .

21 ▶ If a message indicates *Would you like to keep the last item you copied?* click **No**.

This message displays if you have copied some type of image to the Clipboard. If you click Yes, the items on the Clipboard will remain for you to use in another program or document.

Objective 11 | Compress Files and Use the Microsoft Office 2013 Help System

Video OF1-11

A *compressed file* is a file that has been reduced in size. Compressed files take up less storage space and can be transferred to other computers faster than uncompressed files. You can also combine a group of files into one compressed folder, which makes it easier to share a group of files.

Within each Office program, the Help feature provides information about all of the program's features and displays step-by-step instructions for performing many tasks.

Activity 1.18 | Compressing Files

In this activity, you will combine the two files you created in this chapter into one compressed file.

1 ▶ On the Windows taskbar, click **File Explorer** . On the left, in the **navigation pane**, navigate to your **USB flash drive**, and then open your **Office Features Chapter 1** folder. Compare your screen with Figure 1.52.

FIGURE 1.52

2 In the **file list**, click your **Lastname_Firstname_1A_Note_Form** Word file one time to select it. Then, hold down Ctrl, and click your **Lastname_Firstname_1B_Rehearsal_Dinner** file to select the files in the list.

> In any Windows-based program, holding down Ctrl while selecting enables you to select multiple items.

3 On the **File Explorer** ribbon, click **Share**, and then in the **Send group**, click **Zip**. Compare your screen with Figure 1.53.

> Windows creates a compressed folder containing a *copy* of each of the selected files. The folder name is selected—highlighted in blue—so that you can rename it.

 BY TOUCH   Tap the ribbon commands.

FIGURE 1.53

ANOTHER WAY   Point to the selected files in the File List, right-click, point to Send to, and then click Compressed (zipped) folder.

4 Using your own name, type **Lastname_Firstname_Office_Features_Chapter_1** and press Enter.

> The compressed folder is ready to attach to an email or share in some other format.

5 In the upper right corner of the folder window, click **Close** ⊠.

Activity 1.19 | Using the Microsoft Office 2013 Help System in Excel

In this activity, you will use the Microsoft Help feature to find information about formatting numbers in Excel.

1 Press ⊞ to display the Windows 8 **Start screen**, and then type **excel 2013** Press Enter to open the Excel desktop app.

2 On Excel's opening screen, click **Blank workbook**, and then in the upper right corner, click **Microsoft Excel Help** ❓.

ANOTHER WAY   Press F1 to display Help in any Office program.

3 In the **Excel Help** window, click in the **Search online help** box, type **formatting numbers** and then press Enter.

4 On the list of results, click **Format numbers as currency**. Compare your screen with Figure 1.54.

5 ▶ If you want to do so, at the top of the **Excel Help** window, click Print [printer icon] to print a copy of this information for your reference.

6 ▶ In the upper right corner of the Help window, click **Close** [×].

7 ▶ Leave Excel open for the next activity.

Objective 12 | Install Apps for Office and Create a Microsoft Account

A L E R T !   **Working with Web-Based Applications and Services**

Computer programs and services on the web receive continuous updates and improvements. Thus, the steps to complete the following web-based activities may differ from the ones shown. You can often look at the screens and the information presented to determine how to complete the activity.

Video OF1-12

Apps for Office 2013 and SharePoint 2013 are a collection of downloadable apps that enable you to create and view information within your familiar Office programs. Some of these apps are developed by Microsoft, but many more are developed by specialists in different fields. As new apps are developed, they will be available from the online Office Store.

An *app for Office* is a webpage that works within one of the Office applications, such as Excel, that you download from the Office Store. Office apps combine cloud services and web technologies within the user interface of Office and SharePoint. For example, in Excel, you can use an app to look up and gather search results for a new apartment by placing the information in an Excel worksheet, and then use maps to determine the distance of each apartment to work and to family members.

Activity 1.20 | Installing Apps for Office

A L E R T !   **You Must Be Signed In to Office with a Microsoft Account to Complete This Activity**

To download an Office app, you must be signed in to Office with a free Microsoft account. If you do not have a Microsoft account, refer to the next activity to create one by using Microsoft's outlook.com email service, which includes free SkyDrive cloud storage.

1 ▶ On the Excel ribbon, click the **INSERT tab**. In the **Apps group**, click the **Apps for Office** arrow, and then click **See All**.

2 ▶ Click **FEATURED APPS**, and then on the right, click in the **Search for apps on the Office Store** box, type **Bing Maps** and press Enter.

3 ▶ Click the **Bing logo**, and then click the **Add** button, and then if necessary, click Continue.

4 ▶ **Close** [×] Internet Explorer, and then **Close** [×] the **Apps for Office** box.

Project 1B: Memo | **Office** **41**

5 On the **INSERT tab**, in the **Apps group**, click **Apps for Office**, click **See All**, click **MY APPS**, click the **Bing Maps** app, and then in the lower right corner, click **Insert**.

6 On the Welcome message, click **Insert Sample Data**.

Here, the Bing map displays information related to the sample data. Each state in the sample data displays a small pie chart that represents the two sets of data. Compare your screen with Figure 1.55.

This is just one example of many apps downloadable from the Office store.

FIGURE 1.55

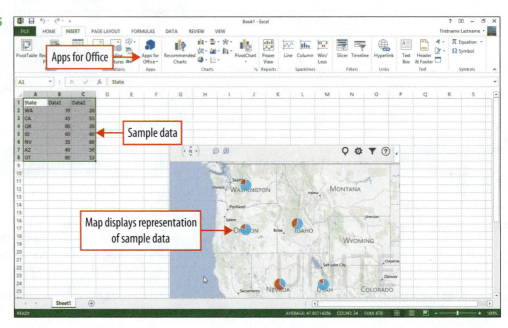

7 **Close** ✕ Excel without saving.

Activity 1.21 | Creating a Microsoft Account

In Windows 8, you can create a Microsoft account, and then use that account to sign in to *any* Windows 8 PC. Signing in with a Microsoft account is recommended because you can:

- Download Windows 8 apps from the Windows Store.
- Get your online content—email, social network updates, updated news—automatically displayed in an app on the Windows 8 Start screen when you sign in.
- Synch settings online to make every Windows 8 computer you use look and feel the same.
- Sign in to Office so that you can store documents on your SkyDrive and download Office apps.

1 Open Internet Explorer 🌐, and then go to **www.outlook.com**

2 Locate and click **Sign up now** to display a screen similar to Figure 1.56. Complete the form to create your account.

FIGURE 1.56

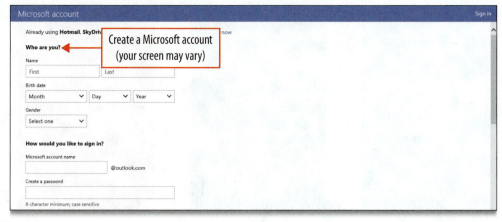

3 **Close** ⊠ Internet Explorer.

END | You have completed Project 1B

END OF CHAPTER

SUMMARY

Many Office features and commands, such as the Open and Save As dialog boxes, performing commands from the ribbon and from dialog boxes, and using the Clipboard are the same in all Office desktop apps.

A desktop app is installed on your computer and requires a computer operating system such as Microsoft Windows or Apple OS to run. The programs in Microsoft Office 2013 are considered to be desktop apps.

Apps that run on a smartphone or tablet computer—for example, iOS, Android, or Windows Phone—or apps that run from browser software such as Internet Explorer or Chrome on a PC, are referred to as apps.

Within each Office app, you can install additional Apps for Office from the Office Store. You must have a Microsoft account, which includes free SkyDrive storage, to download Windows 8 or Office apps.

GO! LEARN IT ONLINE

Review the concepts and key terms in this chapter by completing these online challenges, which you can find at **www.pearsonhighered.com/go**.

Matching and Multiple Choice: Answer matching and multiple choice questions to test what you learned in this chapter. MyITLab®

Crossword Puzzle: Spell out the words that match the numbered clues, and put them in the puzzle squares.

Flipboard: Flip through the definitions of the key terms in this chapter and match them with the correct term.

GLOSSARY

GLOSSARY OF CHAPTER KEY TERMS

Address bar (Internet Explorer) The area at the top of the Internet Explorer window that displays, and where you can type, a URL—Uniform Resource Locator—which is an address that uniquely identifies a location on the Internet.

Address bar (Windows) The bar at the top of a folder window with which you can navigate to a different folder or library, or go back to a previous one.

Alignment The placement of text or objects relative to the left and right margins.

Alignment guides Green lines that display when you move an object to assist in alignment.

App The term that commonly refers to computer programs that run from the device software on a smartphone or a tablet computer—for example, iOS, Android, or Windows Phone—or computer programs that run from the browser software on a desktop PC or laptop PC—for example Internet Explorer, Safari, Firefox, or Chrome.

App for Office A webpage that works within one of the Office applications, such as Excel, and that you download from the Office Store.

Apps for Office 2013 and SharePoint 2013 A collection of downloadable apps that enable you to create and view information within your familiar Office programs.

Backstage tabs The area along the left side of Backstage view with tabs to display screens with related groups of commands.

Backstage view A centralized space for file management tasks; for example, opening, saving, printing, publishing, or sharing a file. A navigation pane displays along the left side with tabs that group file-related tasks together.

Center alignment The alignment of text or objects that is centered horizontally between the left and right margins.

Click The action of pressing and releasing the left button on a mouse pointing device one time.

Clip art Downloadable predefined graphics available online from Office.com and other sites.

Clipboard A temporary storage area that holds text or graphics that you select and then cut or copy.

Cloud computing Refers to applications and services that are accessed over the Internet, rather than to applications that are installed on your local computer.

Cloud storage Online storage of data so that you can access your data from different places and devices.

Collaborate To work with others as a team in an intellectual endeavor to complete a shared task or to achieve a shared goal.

Commands An instruction to a computer program that causes an action to be carried out.

Common dialog boxes The set of dialog boxes that includes Open, Save, and Save As, which are provided by the Windows programming interface, and which display and operate in all of the Office programs in the same manner.

Compressed file A file that has been reduced in size and thus takes up less storage space and can be transferred to other computers quickly.

Compressed folder A folder that has been reduced in size and thus takes up less storage space and can be transferred to other computers quickly; also called a *zipped* folder.

Context menus Menus that display commands and options relevant to the selected text or object; also called *shortcut menus*.

Context-sensitive commands Commands that display on a shortcut menu that relate to the object or text that you right-clicked.

Contextual tabs Tabs that are added to the ribbon automatically when a specific object, such as a picture, is selected, and that contain commands relevant to the selected object.

Copy A command that duplicates a selection and places it on the Clipboard.

Cut A command that removes a selection and places it on the Clipboard.

Default The term that refers to the current selection or setting that is automatically used by a computer program unless you specify otherwise.

Deselect The action of canceling the selection of an object or block of text by clicking outside of the selection.

Desktop In Windows, the screen that simulates your work area.

Desktop app The term that commonly refers to a computer program that is installed on your computer and requires a computer operating system like Microsoft Windows or Apple OS to run.

Dialog box A small window that contains options for completing a task.

Dialog Box Launcher A small icon that displays to the right of some group names on the ribbon, and which opens a related dialog box or pane providing additional options and commands related to that group.

Document properties Details about a file that describe or identify it, including the title, author name, subject, and keywords that identify the document's topic or contents; also known as *metadata*.

Drag The action of holding down the left mouse button while moving your mouse.

Edit The process of making changes to text or graphics in an Office file.

Ellipsis A set of three dots indicating incompleteness; an ellipsis following a command name indicates that a dialog box will display if you click the command.

Enhanced ScreenTip A ScreenTip that displays more descriptive text than a normal ScreenTip.

Extract To decompress, or pull out, files from a compressed form.

File A collection of information stored on a computer under a single name, for example, a Word document or a PowerPoint presentation.

File Explorer The program that displays the files and folders on your computer, and which is at work anytime you are viewing the contents of files and folders in a window.

Fill The inside color of an object.

Folder A container in which you store files.

Folder window In Windows, a window that displays the contents of the current folder, library, or device, and contains helpful parts so that you can navigate the Windows file structure.

Font A set of characters with the same design and shape.

Font styles Formatting emphasis such as bold, italic, and underline.

Footer A reserved area for text or graphics that displays at the bottom of each page in a document.

Formatting The process of establishing the overall appearance of text, graphics, and pages in an Office file—for example, in a Word document.

Formatting marks Characters that display on the screen, but do not print, indicating where the Enter key, the Spacebar, and the Tab key were pressed; also called *nonprinting characters*.

Gallery An Office feature that displays a list of potential results instead of just the command name.

Gradient fill A fill effect in which one color fades into another.

Groups On the Office ribbon, the sets of related commands that you might need for a specific type of task.

Header A reserved area for text or graphics that displays at the top of each page in a document.

Info tab The tab in Backstage view that displays information about the current file.

Insertion point A blinking vertical line that indicates where text or graphics will be inserted.

Keyboard shortcut A combination of two or more keyboard keys, used to perform a task that would otherwise require a mouse.

KeyTip The letter that displays on a command in the ribbon and that indicates the key you can press to activate the command when keyboard control of the ribbon is activated.

Keywords Custom file properties in the form of words that you associate with a document to give an indication of the document's content; used to help find and organize files. Also called *tags*.

Landscape orientation A page orientation in which the paper is wider than it is tall.

Layout Options A button that displays when an object is selected and that has commands to choose how the object interacts with surrounding text.

Live Preview A technology that shows the result of applying an editing or formatting change as you point to possible results—*before* you actually apply it.

Location Any disk drive, folder, or other place in which you can store files and folders.

Metadata Details about a file that describe or identify it, including the title, author name, subject, and keywords that identify the document's topic or contents; also known as *document properties*.

Mini toolbar A small toolbar containing frequently used formatting commands that displays as a result of selecting text or objects.

MRU Acronym for *most recently used*, which refers to the state of some commands that retain the characteristic most recently applied; for example, the Font Color button retains the most recently used color until a new color is chosen.

Navigate The process of exploring within the organizing structure of Windows.

Navigation pane In a folder window, the area on the left in which you can navigate to, open, and display favorites, libraries, folders, saved searches, and an expandable list of drives.

Nonprinting characters Characters that display on the screen, but do not print, indicating where the Enter key, the Spacebar, and the Tab key were pressed; also called *formatting marks*.

Notification bar An area at the bottom of an Internet Explorer window that displays information about pending downloads, security issues, add-ons, and other issues related to the operation of your computer.

Object A text box, picture, table, or shape that you can select and then move and resize.

Office Web Apps The free online companions to Microsoft Word, Excel, PowerPoint, Access, and OneNote.

Open dialog box A dialog box from which you can navigate to, and then open on your screen, an existing file that was created in that same program.

Option button In a dialog box, a round button that enables you to make one choice among two or more options.

Options dialog box A dialog box within each Office application where you can select program settings and other options and preferences.

Pane A separate area of a window.

Paragraph symbol The symbol ¶ that represents the end of a paragraph.

Paste The action of placing text or objects that have been copied or cut from one location to another location.

Paste Options gallery A gallery of buttons that provides a Live Preview of all the Paste options available in the current context.

Path A sequence of folders that leads to a specific file or folder.

PDF The acronym for Portable Document Format, which is a file format that creates an image that preserves the look of your file; this is a popular format for sending documents electronically because the document will display on most computers.

Point The action of moving your mouse pointer over something on your screen.

Pointer Any symbol that displays on your screen in response to moving your mouse.

Points A measurement of the size of a font; there are 72 points in an inch.

Portable Document Format A file format that creates an image that preserves the look of your file, but that cannot be easily changed; a popular format for sending documents electronically, because the document will display on most computers.

Portrait orientation A page orientation in which the paper is taller than it is wide.

Print Preview A view of a document as it will appear when you print it.

Progress bar In a dialog box or taskbar button, a bar that indicates visually the progress of a task such as a download or file transfer.

Protected View A security feature in Office 2013 that protects your computer from malicious files by opening them in a restricted environment until you enable them; you might encounter this feature if you open a file from an email or download files from the Internet.

pt The abbreviation for *point*; for example, when referring to a font size.

Quick Access Toolbar In an Office program window, the small row of buttons in the upper left corner of the screen from which you can perform frequently used commands.

Read-Only A property assigned to a file that prevents the file from being modified or deleted; it indicates that you cannot save any changes to the displayed document unless you first save it with a new name.

Ribbon A user interface in both Office 2013 and File Explorer that groups the commands for performing related tasks on tabs across the upper portion of the program window.

Right-click The action of clicking the right mouse button one time.

Sans serif font A font design with no lines or extensions on the ends of characters.

ScreenTip A small box that that displays useful information when you perform various mouse actions such as pointing to screen elements or dragging.

Scroll bar A vertical or horizontal bar in a window or a pane to assist in bringing an area into view, and which contains a scroll box and scroll arrows.

Scroll box The box in the vertical and horizontal scroll bars that can be dragged to reposition the contents of a window or pane on the screen.

Selecting Highlighting, by dragging with your mouse, areas of text or data or graphics, so that the selection can be edited, formatted, copied, or moved.

Serif font A font design that includes small line extensions on the ends of the letters to guide the eye in reading from left to right.

SharePoint Collaboration software with which people in an organization can set up team sites to share information, manage documents, and publish reports for others to see.

Shortcut menu A menu that displays commands and options relevant to the selected text or object; also called a *context menu*.

Sizing handles Small squares that indicate a picture or object is selected.

SkyDrive Microsoft's free cloud storage for anyone with a free Microsoft account.

Split button A button divided into two parts and in which clicking the main part of the button performs a command and clicking the arrow opens a menu with choices.

Start search The search feature in Windows 8 in which, from the Start screen, you can begin to type and by default, Windows 8 searches for apps; you can adjust the search to search for files or settings.

Status bar The area along the lower edge of an Office program window that displays file information on the left and buttons to control how the window looks on the right.

Style A group of formatting commands, such as font, font size, font color, paragraph alignment, and line spacing that can be applied to a paragraph with one command.

Subfolder A folder within a folder.

Synchronization The process of updating computer files that are in two or more locations according to specific rules—also called *syncing*.

Syncing The process of updating computer files that are in two or more locations according to specific rules—also called *synchronization*.

Tabs (ribbon) On the Office ribbon, the name of each activity area.

Tags Custom file properties in the form of words that you associate with a document to give an indication of the document's content; used to help find and organize files. Also called *keywords*.

Taskbar The area along the lower edge of the desktop that displays buttons representing programs.

Template A preformatted document that you can use as a starting point and then change to suit your needs.

Theme A predesigned combination of colors, fonts, and effects that look good together and is applied to an entire document by a single selection.

Title bar The bar at the top edge of the program window that indicates the name of the current file and the program name.

Toggle button A button that can be turned on by clicking it once, and then turned off by clicking it again.

Toolbar In a folder window, a row of buttons with which you can perform common tasks, such as changing the view of your files and folders or burning files to a CD.

Triple-click The action of clicking the left mouse button three times in rapid succession.

Trusted Documents A security feature in Office that remembers which files you have already enabled; you might encounter this feature if you open a file from an email or download files from the Internet.

Uniform Resource Locator An address that uniquely identifies a location on the Internet.

URL The acronym for Uniform Resource Locator, which is an address that uniquely identifies a location on the Internet.

USB flash drive A small data storage device that plugs into a computer USB port.

Window A rectangular area on a computer screen in which programs and content appear, and which can be moved, resized, minimized, or closed.

XML Paper Specification A Microsoft file format that creates an image of your document and that opens in the XPS viewer.

XPS The acronym for XML Paper Specification—a Microsoft file format that creates an image of your document and that opens in the XPS viewer.

Zipped folder A folder that has been reduced in size and thus takes up less storage space and can be transferred to other computers quickly; also called a *compressed* folder.

Zoom The action of increasing or decreasing the size of the viewing area on the screen.

Introduction to Microsoft Access 2013

Access 2013

S. John/Fotolia

Access 2013: Introduction

Video AA

Microsoft Access 2013 provides a convenient way to organize data that makes it easy for you to retrieve information. Access uses tables to store data. Like Excel spreadsheets, data is stored in rows and columns in a table. So why use a database rather than an Excel spreadsheet? By using a database, you can manipulate and work with data in a more robust manner. For example, if you have thousands of records about patients in a hospital, you can easily find all of the records that pertain to the patients who received a specific type of medicine on a particular day. Information from one table can be used to retrieve information from another table. For example, by knowing a patient's ID number, you can

view immunization records or view insurance information or view hospitalization records. Having information stored in an Access database enables you to make bulk changes to data at one time even when it is stored in different tables.

It's easy to get started with Access by using one of the many prebuilt database templates. For example, a nonprofit organization can track events, donors, members, and donations. A small business can use a prebuilt database to track inventory, create invoices, keep track of projects, manage pricing, track competitors, and manage quotes.

Getting Started with Microsoft Access 2013

GO! to Work
Video A1

1

ACCESS 2013

PROJECT 1A

OUTCOMES
Create a new database.

PROJECT 1B

OUTCOMES
Create a database from a template.

OBJECTIVES

1. Identify Good Database Design
2. Create a Table and Define Fields in a Blank Desktop Database
3. Change the Structure of Tables and Add a Second Table
4. Create a Query, Form, and Report
5. Close a Database and Exit Access

OBJECTIVES

6. Use a Template to Create a Database
7. Organize Objects in the Navigation Pane
8. Create a New Table in a Database Created with a Template
9. Print a Report and a Table

Riccardo Piccinini/Fotolia

In This Chapter

In this chapter, you use Microsoft Access 2013 to organize a collection of related information. You will create new databases, create tables, and enter data into the tables. You will create a query, a form, and a report—all of which are Access objects that make a database useful for finding and analyzing information. You will also create a complete database from a template that you can use as provided, or that you can modify to suit your needs. In this chapter, you will also learn how to apply good database design principles to your Access database and to define the structure of a database.

The projects in this chapter relate to **Texas Lakes Community College**, which is located in the Austin, Texas, area. Its four campuses serve over 30,000 students and offer more than 140 certificate programs and degrees. The college has a highly acclaimed Distance Education program and an extensive Workforce Development program. The college makes positive contributions to the community through cultural and athletic programs and has significant partnerships with businesses and nonprofit organizations. Popular fields of study include nursing and health care, solar technology, computer technology, and graphic design.

PROJECT
1A

Student Advising Database
with Two Tables

MyITLab®
Project 1A Training

PROJECT ACTIVITIES

In Activities 1.01 through 1.17, you will assist Dr. Daniel Martinez, vice president of Student Services at Texas Lakes Community College, in creating a new database for tracking students and their faculty advisors. Your completed database objects will look similar to Figure 1.1.

PROJECT FILES

For Project 1A, you will need the following files:

Blank desktop database
a01A_Students (Excel workbook)
a01A_Faculty_Advisors (Excel workbook)

You will save your database as:

Lastname_Firstname_1A_Advising

Build from
Scratch

PROJECT RESULTS

FIGURE 1.1 Project 1A Advising

Objective 1   Identify Good Database Design

Video A1-1

A *database* is an organized collection of *data*—facts about people, events, things, or ideas—related to a specific topic or purpose. *Information* is data that is organized in a useful manner. Your contact list is a type of database because it is a collection of data about one topic—the people with whom you communicate. A simple database of this type is called a *flat database* because it is not related or linked to any other collection of data. Another example of a simple database is a list of your music collection. You do not keep information about your music collection in your contact list because the data is not related to the people in your contact list.

A more sophisticated type of database is a *relational database*, so-called because multiple collections of data in the database are related to one another; for example, data about the students, the courses, and the faculty members at a college. Microsoft Access 2013 is a relational *database management system*—also referred to as a *DBMS*—which is software that controls how related collections of data are stored, organized, retrieved, and secured.

Activity 1.01   Using Good Design Techniques to Plan a Database

Before creating a new database, the first step is to determine the information you want to keep track of by asking yourself, *What questions should this database be able to answer?* The purpose of a database is to store the data in a manner that makes it easy to get the information you need by asking questions. For example, in a student database for Texas Lakes Community College, the questions to be answered might include:

- How many students are enrolled at the college?
- How many students have not yet been assigned a faculty advisor?
- Which students live in Austin, Texas?
- Which students owe money for tuition?
- Which students are majoring in Information Systems Technology?

Tables are the foundation of an Access database because all of the data is stored in one or more tables. A table is similar in structure to an Excel worksheet because data is organized into rows and columns. Each table row is a *record*—all of the categories of data pertaining to one person, place, event, thing, or idea. Each table column is a *field*—a single piece of information for every record. For example, in a table storing student contact information, each row forms a record for only one student. Each column forms a field for every record; for example, the student ID number or the student last name.

When organizing the fields of information in your table, break each piece of information into its smallest, most useful part. For example, create three fields for the name of a student—one field for the last name, one field for the first name, and one field for the middle name or initial.

The **first principle of good database design** is to organize data in the tables so that *redundant*—duplicate—data does not occur. For example, record the student contact information in only *one* table, so that if a student's address changes, you can change the information in just one place. This conserves space, reduces the likelihood of errors when recording new data, and does not require remembering all of the different places where the student's address is stored.

The **second principle of good database design** is to use techniques that ensure the accuracy and consistency of data as it is entered into the table. Typically, many different people enter data into a database—think of all the people who enter data about students at your college. When entering a state in a student contacts table, one person might enter the state as *Texas*, while another might enter the state as *TX*. Use design techniques to help those who enter data into a database to enter the data more accurately and consistently.

Normalization is the process of applying design rules and principles to ensure that your database performs as expected. Taking the time to plan and create a database that is well designed will ensure that you can retrieve meaningful information from the database.

The tables of information in a relational database are linked or joined to one another by a **common field**—a field in two or more tables that stores the same data. For example, a Students table includes the Student ID, name, and address of every student. The Student Activities table includes the club name and the Student ID of members, but not the name or address, of each student in the club. Because the two tables share a common field—Student ID—you can create a list of names and addresses of all of the students in the Photography Club. The names and addresses are stored in the Students table, and the Student IDs of the Photography Club members are stored in the Student Activities table.

Objective 2   Create a Table and Define Fields in a Blank Desktop Database

Video A1-2

There are three methods to create a new Access database. One method is to create a new database using a **database template**—a preformatted database designed for a specific purpose. A second method is to create a new database from a **blank desktop database**. A blank desktop database is stored on your computer or other storage device. It has no data and has no database tools; you create the data and the tools as you need them. A third method is to create a **custom web app** database from scratch or by using a template that you can publish and share with others over the Internet.

Regardless of the method you use, you must name and save the database before you can create any **objects** in it. Objects are the basic parts of a database; you create objects to store your data, to work with your data, and to display your data. The most common database objects are tables, queries, forms, and reports. Think of an Access database as a container for the objects that you create.

Activity 1.02 | Starting with a Blank Desktop Database

1 Start Access using the same technique you used to locate and open other Office desktop apps. Take a moment to compare your screen with Figure 1.2 and study the parts of the Microsoft Access opening screen described in the table in Figure 1.3.

> From this Access opening screen, you can open an existing database, create a custom web app, create a blank desktop database, or create a new web app or desktop database from a template.

FIGURE 1.2

FIGURE 1.3

MICROSOFT ACCESS OPENING SCREEN ELEMENTS	
SCREEN ELEMENT	**DESCRIPTION**
Available templates	Starts a database for a specific purpose that includes built-in objects and tools ready for use.
Blank desktop database	Starts a blank database that is stored on your computer or on a storage device.
Custom web app	Starts a web app database that can be published and shared on the Internet.
Open Other Files	Enables you to open a database file from your computer, a shared location, or other location that you have designated.
Recent files	Displays a list of database files that have been recently opened.
Search box	Enables you to search the Microsoft Office website for templates.
Suggested searches	Enables you to click on a category to start an online search for a template.

2 In the Access opening screen, click **Blank desktop database**. In the **Blank desktop database** dialog box, to the right of the **File Name** box, click **Browse** 📁. In the **File New Database** dialog box, navigate to the location where you are saving your databases for this chapter, create a **New folder** named **Access Chapter 1** and then press Enter. With the folder name selected, in the **File New Database** dialog box, click **Open**.

In the File name box, *Database1* displays as the default file name—the number at the end of your file name might differ if you have saved a database previously with the default name. In the Save as type box, the default database type is *Microsoft Access 2007 – 2013 Databases*, which means that you can open a database created in Access 2013 by using Access 2007, Access 2010, or Access 2013.

3 Click in the **File name** box. Using your own name, replace the existing text with **Lastname_Firstname_1A_Advising** and then click **OK** or press Enter. Compare your screen with Figure 1.4.

In the Blank desktop database dialog box, in the File Name box, the name of your database displays. Under the File Name box, the drive and folder where the database will be stored displays. An Access database has a file extension of *.accdb*.

FIGURE 1.4

4 In the **Blank desktop database** dialog box, click **Create**. Compare your screen with Figure 1.5, and then take a moment to study the screen elements described in the table in Figure 1.6.

Access creates the new database and opens *Table1*. Recall that a table is an Access object that stores data in columns and rows, similar to the format of an Excel worksheet. Table objects are the foundation of a database because tables store the data that is used by other database objects.

FIGURE 1.5

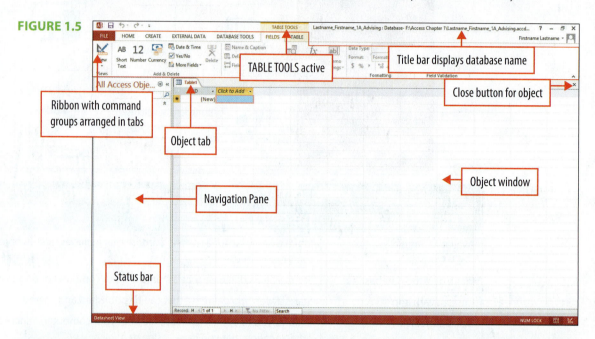

FIGURE 1.6

MICROSOFT ACCESS DATABASE WINDOW ELEMENTS	
ACCESS WINDOW ELEMENT	**DESCRIPTION**
Navigation Pane	Displays the database objects that you can open in the object window.
Object tab	Identifies and enables you to work with the open object.
Object window	Displays the active or open object (table, query, or other object).
Close button for object	Closes the active object (table, query, or other object).
Ribbon with command groups arranged in tabs	Groups the commands for performing related database tasks on tabs.
Status bar	Indicates the active view and the status of action occurring within the database on the left; provides buttons on the right to switch between Datasheet view and Design view.
Table Tools	Provides tools for working with a table object—only available when a table object is active.
Title bar	Displays the database name.

Activity 1.03 | Assigning the Data Type and Name to Fields

After you have named and saved your database, the next step is to consult your database design plan and then create the tables for your data. Limit the data in each table to *one* subject. For example, in this project, your database will have two tables—one for student information and one for faculty advisor information.

Recall that each column in a table is a field; field names display at the top of each column of the table. Recall also that each row in a table is a record—all of the data pertaining to one person, place, thing, event, or idea. Each record is broken up into its smallest usable parts—the fields. Use meaningful names for fields; for example, *Last Name*.

1 Notice the new blank table that displays in **Datasheet** view, and then take a moment to study the elements of the table's object window. Compare your screen with Figure 1.7.

The table displays in *Datasheet view*, which displays the data in columns and rows similar to the format of an Excel worksheet. Another way to view a table is in *Design view*, which displays the underlying design—the *structure*—of the table's fields. The *object window* displays the open object—in this instance, the table object.

In a new blank database, there is only one object—a new blank table. Because you have not yet named this table, the object tab displays a default name of *Table1*. Access creates the first field and names it *ID*. In the ID field, Access assigns a unique sequential number—each number incremented by one—to each record as it is entered into the table.

FIGURE 1.7

2 In the **Navigation Pane**, click **Shutter Bar Open/Close Button** [«] to collapse the **Navigation Pane** to a narrow bar on the left.

The *Navigation Pane* displays and organizes the names of the objects in a database. From the Navigation Pane, you can open objects. Collapse or close the Navigation Pane to display more of the object—in this case, the table.

🔄 **ANOTHER WAY**   Press [F11] to close or open the Navigation Pane.

3 In the field names row, click anywhere in the text *Click to Add* to display a list of data types. Compare your screen with Figure 1.8.

A *data type* defines the kind of data that you can store in a field, such as numbers, text, or dates. A field in a table can have only one data type. The data type of each field should be included in your database design. After selecting the data type, you can name the field.

🔄 **ANOTHER WAY**   To the right of *Click to Add*, click the arrow.

FIGURE 1.8

When clicked, displays list of data types

Navigation Pane closed

List of data types

4 ▶ On the list of data types, click **Short Text**, and notice that in the second column, *Click to Add* changes to *Field1*, which is selected. Type **Last Name** and then press Enter.

The second column displays *Last Name* as the field name, and, in the third column, the data type list displays. The ***Short Text data type*** describes text, a combination of text and numbers, or numbers that are not used in calculations, such as the Postal Code. This data type enables you to enter up to 255 characters in the field.

🔄 **ANOTHER WAY** With the list of data types displayed, type the character that is underscored to select the data type. For example, type *t* to select Short Text or type *u* to select Currency.

5 ▶ In the third field name box, type **t** to select *Short Text*, type **First Name** and then press Enter.

6 ▶ In the fourth field name box, click **Short Text**, type **Middle Initial** and then press Enter.

7 ▶ Create the remaining fields from the table given by first selecting the data type, typing the field name, and then pressing Enter. The field names in the table will display on one line—do not be concerned if the field names do not completely display in the column; you will adjust the column widths later.

Data Type		Short Text	Short Text	Short Text	Short Text	Short Text	Short Text	Short Text	Short Text	Short Text	Short Text	Currency
Field Name	ID	Last Name	First Name	Middle Initial	Address	City	State	Postal Code	Phone	Email	Faculty Advisor ID	Amount Owed

The Postal Code and Phone fields are assigned a data type of Short Text because the numbers are never used in calculations. The Amount Owed field is assigned the ***Currency data type***, which describes monetary values and numeric data that can be used in calculations and that have one to four decimal places. A U.S. dollar sign ($) and two decimal places are automatically included for all of the numbers in a field with the Currency data type.

8 ▶ If necessary, scroll to bring the first column—**ID**—into view, and then compare your screen with Figure 1.9.

Access automatically created the ID field, and you created 11 additional fields in the table.

FIGURE 1.9

Twelve fields created (you might have to scroll to display all of the fields)

More Knowledge | **Create Fields by Entering Data**

You can create a new field in Datasheet view by typing the data in a new column. Access automatically assigns a data type based on the data you enter. For example, if you enter a date, Access assigns the Date/Time data type. If you enter a monetary amount, Access assigns the Currency data type. If Access cannot determine the data type based on the data entered, the Short Text data type is assigned. You can always change the data type if an incorrect data type is assigned. If you use this method to create fields, you must check the assigned data types to be sure they are correct. You must also rename the fields because Access assigns the names as *Field1*, *Field2*, and so on.

Activity 1.04 | Renaming Fields and Changing Data Types in a Table

1 ▶ In the first column, click anywhere in the text *ID*. On the ribbon, under **TABLE TOOLS**, on the **FIELDS tab**, in the **Properties group**, click **Name & Caption**. In the **Enter Field Properties** dialog box, in the **Name** box, change *ID* to **Student ID**

The field name *Student ID* is a clearer and more precise description of this field's data. In the Enter Field Properties dialog box, you have the option to change the **Caption** to display a name for a field other than the name that displays in the Name box. Many database designers do not use spaces in field names; instead, they might name a field *LastName* or *LName* and then create a caption for the field so it displays as *Last Name* in tables, forms, or reports. In the Enter Field Properties dialog box, you can also provide a description for the field.

🔄 **ANOTHER WAY** | Right-click the field name to display the shortcut menu, and then click Rename Field; or, double-click the field name to select the existing text, and then type the new field name.

2 ▶ Click **OK** to close the **Enter Field Properties** dialog box. On the ribbon, in the **Formatting group**, notice that the **Data Type** for the **Student ID** field is *AutoNumber*. Click the **Data Type arrow**, click **Short Text**, and then compare your screen with Figure 1.10.

In the new record row, the Student ID field is selected. By default, Access creates an ID field for all new tables and sets the data type for the field to AutoNumber. The **AutoNumber data type** describes a unique sequential or random number assigned by Access as each record is entered. Changing the data type of this field to Short Text enables you to enter a custom student ID number.

When records in a database have *no* unique value, such as a book ISBN or a license plate number, the AutoNumber data type is a useful way to automatically create a unique number. In this manner, you are sure that every record is different from the others.

FIGURE 1.10

Activity 1.05 | Adding a Record to a Table

A new contact list is not useful until you fill it with names and phone numbers. Likewise, a new database is not useful until you ***populate*** it by filling one or more tables with data. You can populate a table with records by typing data directly into the table.

1 In the new record row, click in the **Student ID** field to display the insertion point, type **1023045** and then press Enter. Compare your screen with Figure 1.11.

> The pencil icon ✏ in the *record selector box* indicates that a record is being entered or edited. The record selector box is the small box at the left of a record in Datasheet view. When clicked, the entire record is selected.

↻ **ANOTHER WAY**   Press Tab to move the insertion point to the next field.

FIGURE 1.11

First Student ID is **1023045**

Pencil icon in record selector box indicates record being entered or edited

Insertion point in Last Name field

2 With the insertion point positioned in the **Last Name** field, type **Fresch** and then press Enter.

> **NOTE**   **Correcting Typing Errors**
>
> Correct any typing errors you make by using the techniques you have practiced in other Office applications. For example, use Backspace to remove characters to the left of the insertion point. Use Del to remove characters to the right of the insertion point. Or select the text you want to replace and type the correct information. Press Esc to exit out of a record that has not been completely entered.

---

3 In the **First Name** field, type **Jenna** and then press Enter.

4 In the **Middle Initial** field, type **A** and then press Enter.

5 In the **Address** field, type **7550 Douglas Ln** and then press Enter.

> Do not be concerned if the data does not completely display in the column. As you progress in your study of Access, you will adjust column widths so that you can view all of the data.

6 Continue entering data in the fields as indicated in the table given, pressing Enter to move to the next field.

City	State	Postal Code	Phone	Email	Faculty Advisor ID
Austin	**TX**	**78749**	**(512) 555-0857**	**jfresch@tlcc.edu**	**FAC-2289**

> **NOTE**   **Format for Typing Telephone Numbers in Access**
>
> Access does not require a specific format for typing telephone numbers in a record. The examples in this textbook use the format of Microsoft Outlook. Using such a format facilitates easy transfer of Outlook information to and from Access.

---

7 In the **Amount Owed** field, type **250** and then press Enter. Compare your screen with Figure 1.12.

> Pressing Enter or Tab in the last field moves the insertion point to the next row to begin a new record. Access automatically saves the record as soon as you move to the next row; you do not have to take any specific action to save a record.

FIGURE 1.12

First record entered and saved

Insertion point blinking in first field of new record row

8 To give your table a meaningful name, on the **Quick Access Toolbar**, click **Save** 💾. In the **Save As** dialog box, in the **Table Name** box, using your own name, replace the selected text by typing **Lastname Firstname 1A Students**

> Save each database object with a name that identifies the data that it contains. When you save objects within a database, it is not necessary to use underscores in place of the spaces between words. Your name is included as part of the object name so that you and your instructor can identify your printouts or electronic files easily.

9 In the **Save As** dialog box, click **OK**. Notice that the object tab—located directly above the **Student ID** field name—displays the new table name that you just entered.

More Knowledge | **Renaming or Deleting a Table**

To change the name of a table, close the table, display the Navigation Pane, right-click the table name, and then click Rename. Type the new name or edit as you would any selected text. To delete a table, close the table, display the Navigation Pane, right-click the table name, and then click Delete.

Activity 1.06 | Adding Additional Records to a Table

1 In the new record row, click in the **Student ID** field, and then enter the data for two additional students as shown in the table given. Press Enter or Tab to move from field to field. The data in each field will display on one line in the table.

udent	Last Name	First Name	Middle Initial	Address	City	State	Postal Code	Phone	Email	Faculty Advisor ID	Amount Owed
345677	Ingram	Joey	S	621 Hilltop Dr	Leander	TX	78646	(512) 555-0717	jingram@tlcc.edu	FAC-2377	378.5
456689	Snyder	Amanda	J	4786 Bluff St	Buda	TX	78610	(512) 555-9120	asnyder@tlcc.edu	FAC-9005	0

2 Compare your screen with Figure 1.13.

FIGURE 1.13

Some fields may be out of view on your screen

Records for three students entered

Activity 1.07 | Importing Data from an Excel Workbook into an Existing Access Table

You can type records directly into a table. You can also ***import*** data from a variety of sources. Importing is the process of copying data from one source or application to another application. For example, you can import data from a Word table or an Excel spreadsheet into an Access database because the data is arranged in columns and rows, similar to a table in Datasheet view.

In this activity, you will *append*—add on—data from an Excel spreadsheet to your *1A Students* table. To append data, the table must already be created, and it must be closed.

1 ▶ In the upper right corner of the table, below the ribbon, click **Object Close** ☒ to close your **1A Students** table. Notice that no objects are open.

2 ▶ On the ribbon, click the **EXTERNAL DATA tab**. In the **Import & Link group**, click **Excel**. In the **Get External Data – Excel Spreadsheet** dialog box, click **Browse**.

3 ▶ In the **File Open** dialog box, navigate to your student files, double-click the Excel file **a01A_Students**, and then compare your screen with Figure 1.14.

The path to the *source file*—the file being imported—displays in the File name box. There are three options for importing data from an Excel spreadsheet: import the data into a *new* table in the current database, append a copy of the records to an existing table, or link the data from the spreadsheet to a linked table in the database. A *link* is a connection to data in another file. When linking, Access creates a table that maintains a link to the source data, so that changes to the data in one file are automatically made in the other—linked—file.

 ANOTHER WAY   Click the file name, and then in the File Open dialog box, click Open.

FIGURE 1.14

4 ▶ Click the **Append a copy of the records to the table** option button, and then, in the box to the right, click the **arrow**.

Currently, your database has only one table, so no other tables display on the list. However, when a database has multiple tables, click the arrow to select the table to which you want to append records. The table into which you import or append data is referred to as the *destination table*.

5 ▶ Press Esc to cancel the list, and in the dialog box, click **OK**. Compare your screen with Figure 1.15.

The first screen of the Import Spreadsheet Wizard displays, and the presence of scroll bars indicates that records and fields are out of view in this window. To append records from an Excel workbook to an existing database table, the column headings in the Excel worksheet or spreadsheet must be identical to the field names in the table. The *wizard* identifies the first row of the spreadsheet as column headings, which are equivalent to field names. A wizard is a feature in a Microsoft Office program that walks you step by step through a process.

FIGURE 1.15

First row identified as column headings, which are equivalent to field names

Field names in Excel Spreadsheet exactly match the field names in the Access table

Scroll bars indicate more data

6 ▶ In the lower right corner of the wizard, click **Next**. Notice that the name of your table displays under **Import to Table**. In the lower right corner of the wizard, click **Finish**.

7 ▶ In the **Get External Data – Excel Spreadsheet** dialog box, click **Close**. Open » the **Navigation Pane**.

8 ▶ Point to the right edge of the **Navigation Pane** to display the ↔ pointer. Drag to the right to increase the width of the **Navigation Pane** so that the entire table name displays, and then compare your screen with Figure 1.16.

FIGURE 1.16

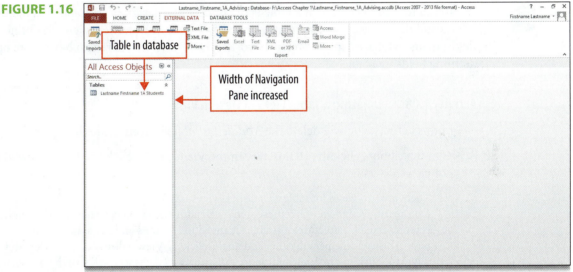

Table in database

Width of Navigation Pane increased

9 ▶ In the **Navigation Pane**, double-click your **1A Students** table to open the table in **Datasheet** view, and then **Close** « the **Navigation Pane**.

ANOTHER WAY   To open an object from the Navigation Pane, right-click the object name, and then click Open.

10 ▶ In the lower left corner of your screen, locate the navigation area, and notice that there are a total of **25** records in the table—you entered three records and imported 22 additional records. Compare your screen with Figure 1.17.

The records that you entered and the records you imported from the Excel spreadsheet display in your table; the first record in the table is selected. The **navigation area** indicates the number of records in the table and has controls in the form of arrows that you click in order to navigate among the records.

FIGURE 1.17

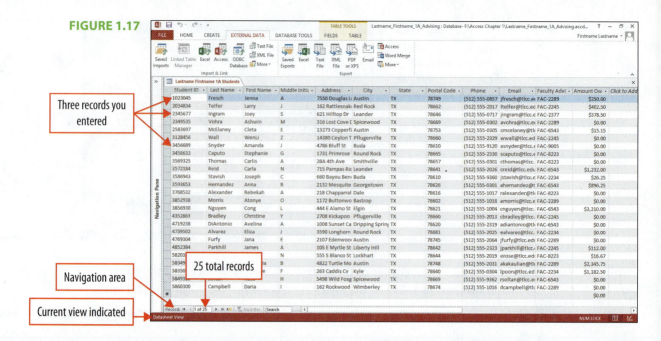

Three records you entered

Navigation area

Current view indicated

25 total records

Video A1-3

Recall that the structure of a table is the underlying design of the table and includes field names and data types. You can create or modify a table in Datasheet view. To define and modify fields, many database experts prefer to work in Design view, where you have more options for defining fields in a table.

Activity 1.08 | Deleting a Table Field in Design View

In this activity, you will delete the *Middle Initial* field from the table.

1 On the ribbon, click the **HOME tab**. In the **Views group**, click the **View arrow** to display a list of views.

There are two views for tables: Datasheet view and Design view. Other objects have different views. On the list, Design view is represented by a picture of a pencil, a ruler, and an angle. Datasheet view is represented by a picture of a table arranged in columns and rows. In the Views group, if the View button displays the pencil, ruler, and angle, clicking View will switch your view to Design view. Likewise, clicking the View button that displays as a datasheet will switch your view to Datasheet view.

2 On the list, click **Design View**, and then compare your screen with Figure 1.18.

Design view displays the underlying design—the structure—of the table and its fields. In Design view, the records with the data in the table do not display. You can only view the information about each field's characteristics. Each field name is listed, along with its data type. You can add more descriptive information about a field in the Description column.

You can decide how each field should look and behave in the Field Properties area. For example, you can set a specific field size in the Field Properties area. In the lower right corner, information displays about the active selection—in this case, the Field Name.

FIGURE 1.18

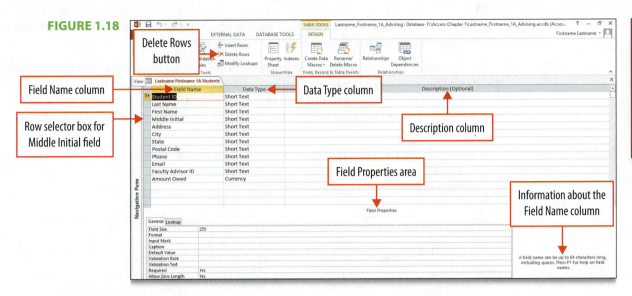

Delete Rows button

Field Name column

Row selector box for Middle Initial field

Data Type column

Description column

Field Properties area

Information about the Field Name column

3 In the **Field Name** column, to the left of **Middle Initial**, point to the row selector box to display the ➡ pointer, and then click one time to select the entire row.

4 Under **TABLE TOOLS**, on the **DESIGN tab**, in the **Tools group**, click **Delete Rows**. Read the message in the message box, and then click **Yes**.

Deleting a field deletes both the field and its data. After you save the changes, you cannot undo this action, so Access prompts you to be sure you want to proceed. If you change your mind after deleting a field and saving the changes, you must add the field back into the table and then reenter the data for that field for every record.

 ANOTHER WAY In Design view, right-click the selected row, and then click Delete Rows; or, in Datasheet view, select the field—column—and on the HOME tab, in the Records group, click Delete.

Activity 1.09 | Changing a Field Size and Adding a Description

Typically, many different individuals in an organization have the ability to enter data into a table. For example, at your college, many registration assistants enter and modify student and course information daily. Two ways to help reduce errors are to restrict what can be typed in a field and to add descriptive information to help the individuals when entering the data.

1 With your table still displayed in **Design** view, in the **Field Name** column, click anywhere in the **Student ID** field name.

2 In the lower area of the screen, under **Field Properties**, click **Field Size** to select *255*, type **7** and then press Enter.

This action limits the size of the Student ID field to no more than seven characters. **Field properties** control how the field displays and how data can be entered into the field. You can define properties for each field in the Field Properties area by first clicking on the field name.

The default field size for a Short Text field is 255. Limiting the Field Size property to seven ensures that no more than seven characters can be entered for each Student ID. However, this does not prevent someone from entering seven characters that are incorrect or entering fewer than seven characters. Setting the proper data type for the field and limiting the field size are two ways to *help* reduce errors during data entry.

 ANOTHER WAY In Datasheet view, click in the field. On the FIELDS tab, in the Properties group, click in the Field Size box, and then type the number that represents the maximum number of characters for that field.

3 In the **Student ID** row, click in the **Description** box, type **Seven-digit Student ID number** and then press Enter. Compare your screen with Figure 1.19.

Descriptions for fields in a table are optional. Include a description if the field name does not provide an obvious explanation of the type of data to be entered. If a description is provided for a field, when data is entered in that field in Datasheet view, the text in the Description displays on the left side of the status bar to provide additional information for the individuals who are entering the data.

When you enter a description for a field, a Property Update Options button displays below the text you typed, which enables you to copy the description for the field to all other database objects that use this table as an underlying source.

FIGURE 1.19

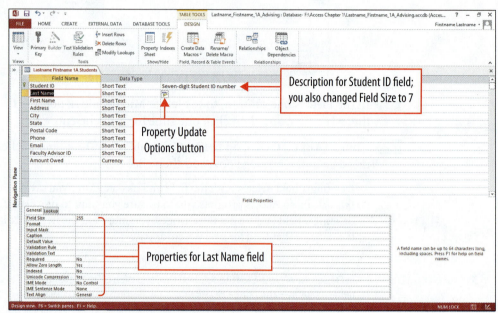

4 Click in the **State** field name box. In the **Field Properties** area, change the **Field Size** to **2** and in the **Description** box for this field, type **Two-character state abbreviation** and then press Enter.

5 Click in the **Faculty Advisor ID** field name box. In the **Field Properties** area, change the **Field Size** to **8** and in the **Description** box for this field, type **Eight-character ID of instructor assigned as advisor** and then press Enter.

6 On the **Quick Access Toolbar**, click **Save** 🖫 to save the design changes to your table, and then notice the message.

The message indicates that the field size property of one or more fields has changed to a shorter size. If more characters are currently present in the Student ID, State, or Faculty Advisor ID fields than you have set as the field size, the data will be *truncated*—cut off or shortened—because the fields were not previously restricted to these specific number of characters.

7 In the message box, click **Yes**.

Activity 1.10 | Viewing the Primary Key in Design View

Primary key refers to the field in the table that uniquely identifies a record. For example, in a college registration database, your Student ID number uniquely identifies you—no other student at the college has your exact student number. In the 1A Students table, the Student ID uniquely identifies each student.

When you create a table using the blank desktop database template, Access designates the first field as the primary key field and names the field ID. It is good database design practice to establish a primary key for every table, because doing so ensures that you do not enter the same record more than once. You can imagine the confusion if another student at your college had the same Student ID number as your own.

1 With your table still displayed in **Design** view, in the **Field Name** column, click in the **Student ID** field name box. To the left of the box, notice the small icon of a key, as shown in Figure 1.20.

Access automatically designates the first field as the primary key field, but you can set any field as the primary key by clicking the field name, and then in the Tools group, clicking Primary Key.

FIGURE 1.20

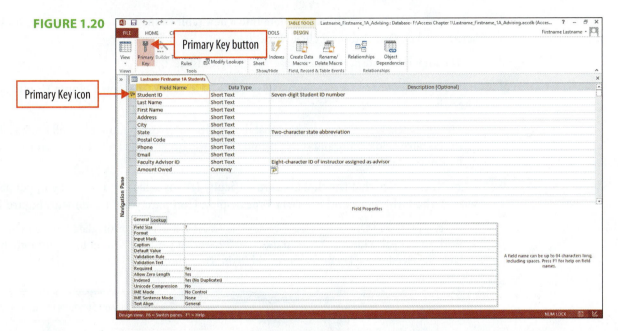

2 On the **DESIGN tab**, in the **Views group**, notice that the **View** button displays a picture of a datasheet, indicating that clicking **View** will switch the view to **Datasheet** view. Click the top of the **View** button.

If you make design changes to a table and switch views without first saving the table, Access prompts you to save the table before changing views.

Activity 1.11 | Adding a Second Table to a Database by Importing an Excel Spreadsheet

Many Microsoft Office users track data in an Excel spreadsheet. The sorting and filtering capabilities of Excel are useful for a simple database where all of the information resides in one large Excel spreadsheet. However, Excel is limited as a database management tool because it cannot *relate* the information in multiple spreadsheets in a way that you can ask a question and get a meaningful result. Because data in an Excel spreadsheet is arranged in columns and rows, the spreadsheet can easily become an Access table by importing the spreadsheet.

1 On the ribbon, click the **EXTERNAL DATA tab**, and then in the **Import & Link group**, click **Excel**. In the **Get External Data – Excel Spreadsheet** dialog box, click **Browse**.

2 In the **File Open** dialog box, navigate to the location where your student data files are stored, and then double-click **a01A_Faculty_Advisors**. Compare your screen with Figure 1.21.

FIGURE 1.21

3 ▶ Be sure that the **Import the source data into a new table in the current database** option button is selected, click **OK**, and then click **Next**.

The Import Spreadsheet Wizard displays the spreadsheet data.

4 ▶ In the upper left corner of the wizard, select the **First Row Contains Column Headings** check box.

The Excel data is framed, indicating that the first row of Excel column titles will become the Access table field names, and the remaining rows will become the individual records in the new Access table.

5 ▶ Click **Next**. Notice that the first column—**Faculty ID**—is selected, and in the upper area of the wizard, the **Field Name** and the **Data Type** display. Compare your screen with Figure 1.22.

Here, under Field Options, you can review and change the name or the data type of each selected field. You can also identify fields in the spreadsheet that you do not want to import into the Access table by selecting the Do not import field (Skip) check box.

FIGURE 1.22

6 ▶ Click **Next**. In the upper area of the wizard, click the **Choose my own primary key** option button, and then be sure that **Faculty ID** displays in the box to the right.

In the new table, Faculty ID will be the primary key. No two faculty members have the same Faculty ID. By default, Access selects the first field as the primary key, but you can click the arrow to select a different field.

7 ▶ Click **Next**. In the **Import to Table** box, using your own name, type **Lastname Firstname 1A Faculty Advisors** and then click **Finish**.

8 ▶ In the **Get External Data – Excel Spreadsheet** dialog box, click **Close**. Open ⏩ the **Navigation Pane**.

9 In the **Navigation Pane**, double-click your **1A Faculty Advisors** table to open it in **Datasheet** view, and then **Close** `«` the **Navigation Pane**.

Two tables that are identified by their object tabs are open in the object window. Your 1A Faculty Advisors table is the active table and displays the 29 records that you imported from the Excel spreadsheet.

10 In your **1A Faculty Advisors** table, click in the **Postal Code** field in the first record. On the ribbon, under **TABLE TOOLS**, click the **FIELDS tab**. In the **Formatting group**, click the **Data Type arrow**, and then click **Short Text**. Compare your screen with Figure 1.23.

When you import data from an Excel spreadsheet, check the data types of all fields to ensure they are correct. Recall that if a field, such as the Postal Code, contains numbers that are not used in calculations, the data type should be set to Short Text. To change the data type of a field, click in the field in any record.

FIGURE 1.23

Activity 1.12 | **Adjusting Column Widths**

You can adjust the column widths in a table displayed in Datasheet view by using techniques similar to those you use for Excel spreadsheets.

1 In the object window, click the **object tab** for your **1A Students** table to make it the active object and to display it in the object window.

Clicking the object tabs along the top of the object window enables you to display open objects and make them active so that you can work with them. All of the columns in the datasheet are the same width, regardless of the length of the data in the field, the length of the field name, or the field size that was set. If you print the table as currently displayed, some of the data or field names will not print fully, so you will want to adjust the column widths.

2 In the field names row, point to the right edge of the **Address** field to display the ⊞ pointer, and then compare your screen with Figure 1.24.

FIGURE 1.24

3 With the ⊞ pointer positioned as shown in Figure 1.24, double-click the right edge of the **Address** field.

The column width of the Address field widens to display fully the longest entry in the field. In this manner, the width of a column can be increased or decreased to fit its contents in the same manner as a column in an Excel spreadsheet. In Access, adjusting the column width to fit the contents is referred to as *Best Fit*.

4 ▶ Point to the **City** field name to display the ⬇ pointer, right-click to select the entire column, and then click **Field Width**. In the **Column Width** dialog box, click **Best Fit**.

This is a second way to adjust column widths.

5 ▶ If necessary, scroll to the right to view the last three fields. Point to the **Email** field name to display the ⬇ pointer, hold down the left mouse button, and then drag to the right to select this column, the **Faculty Advisor ID** column, and the **Amount Owed** column. Point to the right edge of any of the selected columns to display the ✛ pointer, and then double-click to apply **Best Fit** to all three columns.

You can select multiple columns and adjust the widths of all of them at one time by using this technique or by right-clicking any of the selected columns, clicking Field Width, and clicking Best Fit in the Column Width dialog box.

6 ▶ If necessary, scroll to the left to view the **Student ID** field. To the left of the **Student ID** field name, click **Select All** ▢. Notice that all of the fields are selected.

7 ▶ On the ribbon, click the **HOME tab**. In the **Records group**, click **More**, and then click **Field Width**. In the **Column Width** dialog box, click **Best Fit**. Click anywhere in the **Student ID** field, and then compare your screen with Figure 1.25.

Using the More command is a third way to adjust column widths. By using Select All, you can adjust the widths of all of the columns at one time. Adjusting the width of columns does not change the data in the table's records; it only changes the *display* of the data.

FIGURE 1.25

NOTE   **Adjusting Column Widths**

After adjusting column widths, scroll horizontally and vertically to be sure that all of the data displays in all of the fields. Access adjusts column widths to fit the screen size based on the displayed data. If data is not displayed on the screen when you adjust column widths—even if you use Select All—the column width might not be adjusted adequately to display all of the data in the field. After adjusting column widths, save the table before performing other tasks. The column width adjustments might not save with the table. When you reopen a table, be sure to readjust the column widths if you plan to print the table or work with the data in the table.

---

8 ▶ On the **Quick Access Toolbar**, click **Save** 🖫 to save the table design changes—changing the column widths.

If you do not save the table after making design changes, Access prompts you to save when you close the table.

Activity 1.13 | Printing a Table

There are times when you will want to print a table, even though a report may look more professional. For example, you may need a quick reference, or you may want to proofread the data that has been entered. Before printing a table, be sure to apply Best Fit to all of the columns in the table.

1 On the ribbon, click the **FILE tab**, click **Print**, and then click **Print Preview**. Compare your screen with Figure 1.26.

The table displays in Print Preview with the default zoom setting of Fit to Window, a view that enables you to see how your table will print on the page. It is a good idea to view any object in Print Preview before printing so that you can make changes to the object if needed before actually printing it. In the navigation area, the Next Page button is darker (available), an indication that more than one page will print.

FIGURE 1.26

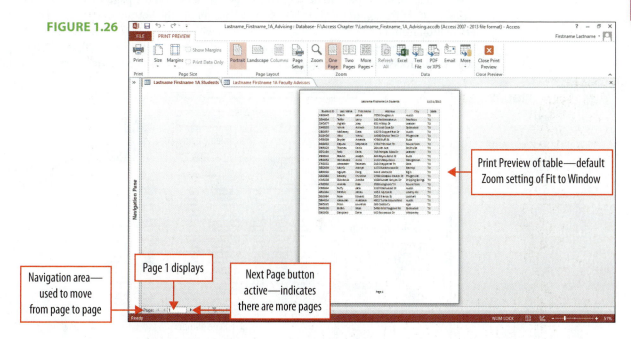

Print Preview of table—default Zoom setting of Fit to Window

Page 1 displays

Navigation area—used to move from page to page

Next Page button active—indicates there are more pages

2 In the navigation area, click **Next Page** ▶ to display Page 2. Point to the top of the page to display the 🔍 pointer, click one time to zoom in, and then compare your screen with Figure 1.27.

The Print Preview display enlarges, and the Zoom Out pointer displays. The second page of the table displays the last five fields. The Next Page button is dimmed, indicating that the button is unavailable because there are no more pages after Page 2. The Previous Page button is available, indicating that a page exists before this page.

FIGURE 1.27

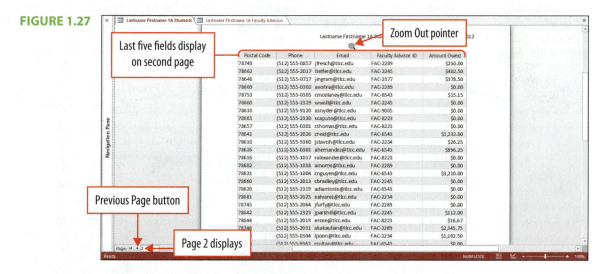

Zoom Out pointer

Last five fields display on second page

Previous Page button

Page 2 displays

3 On the ribbon, on the **PRINT PREVIEW tab**, in the **Zoom group**, click the top portion of the **Zoom** button to change the zoom setting back to the default setting of Fit to Window.

4 In the **Page Layout group**, click **Landscape**, and notice that there are only three fields on Page 2. In the navigation area, click **Previous Page** ◀ to display Page 1, and then compare your screen with Figure 1.28.

The orientation of the page to be printed changes. Included on the page are the table name and current date at the top of the page and the page number at the bottom of the page. The change in orientation from portrait to landscape is not saved with the table. Each time you print, you must check the page orientation, the margins, and any other print parameters so that the object prints as you intend. You should also be sure that Best Fit is applied to each column or to the entire table.

FIGURE 1.28

> **N O T E**   **Headers and Footers in Access Objects**
>
> The headers and footers in Access tables and queries are controlled by default settings; you cannot enter additional information or edit the information. The object name displays in the center of the header area, and the current date displays on the right. Adding your name to the object name is helpful in identifying your paper or electronic results. The page number displays in the center of the footer area. The headers and footers in Access forms and reports are more flexible; you can add to and edit the information.

5 On the **PRINT PREVIEW tab**, in the **Print group**, click **Print**. In the **Print** dialog box, under **Print Range**, verify that **All** is selected. Under **Copies**, verify that the **Number of Copies** is **1**. Compare your screen with Figure 1.29.

FIGURE 1.29

6 Determine whether your instructor wants you to submit your work for this project on paper or electronically. If submitting electronically, determine whether, in addition to submitting your Access database, your instructor wants you to create and submit electronic printouts of individual database objects.

7 To print on paper, in the **Print** dialog box, click **OK**; and then on the ribbon, in the **Close Preview group**, click **Close Print Preview**. If you are required to create and submit electronic printouts, in the **Print** dialog box, click **Cancel**, and then follow the steps in the following Note—or follow the specific directions provided by your instructor.

N O T E   **Creating a PDF Electronic Printout of an Access Object**

Display the object (table, query, form, report, and so on) in Print Preview and adjust margins and orientation as needed. On the PRINT PREVIEW tab, in the Data group, click PDF or XPS. In the Publish as PDF or XPS dialog box, navigate to your chapter folder. Use the default file name, or follow your instructor's directions to name the object. If wish to view the PDF file, in the dialog box, select the Open file after publishing check box. In the Publish as PDF or XPS dialog box, click Publish. If necessary, close the Windows 8 Reader, Adobe Reader, or Adobe Acrobat window and the Export – PDF dialog box. On the ribbon, click Close Print Preview; your electronic printout is saved.

---

8 In the upper right corner of the object window, click **Close Object** [×] to close your **1A Students** table. Notice that the **1A Faculty Advisors** table is the active object in the object window.

⟳ **ANOTHER WAY**   In the object window, right-click your 1A Students object tab, and then click Close.

---

9 In your **1A Faculty Advisors** table, to the left of the **Faculty ID** field name, click **Select All** [ ] to select all of the columns. On the **HOME tab**, in the **Records group**, click **More**, and then click **Field Width**. In the **Column Width** dialog box, click **Best Fit** to adjust the widths of all of the columns so that all of the data display. Scroll horizontally and vertically to be sure that all of the data display in each field; if necessary, use the techniques you practiced to apply **Best Fit** to individual columns. **Save** [ ] the changes you made to the table's column widths, and then click in any record to cancel the selection.

10 On the ribbon, click the **FILE tab**, click **Print**, and then click **Print Preview**. On the **PRINT PREVIEW tab**, in the **Page Layout group**, click **Landscape**. Notice that the table will print on more than one page. In the **Page Size group**, click **Margins**, click **Normal**, and then notice that one more column moved to the first page—your results may differ depending upon your printer's capabilities.

> In addition to changing the page orientation to Landscape, you can change the margins to Normal to see if all of the fields will print on one page. In this instance, there are still too many fields to print on one page, although the Postal Code field moved from Page 2 to Page 1.

11 If directed to do so by your instructor, create a paper or electronic printout of your **1A Faculty Advisors** table, and then click **Close Print Preview**.

12 In the object window, **Close** [×] your **1A Faculty Advisors** table.

> All of your database objects—your *1A Students* table and your *1A Faculty Advisors* table—are closed; the object window is empty.

Video A1-4

Recall that tables are the foundation of an Access database because all of the data is stored in one or more tables. You can display the data stored in tables in other database objects such as queries, forms, and reports.

Activity 1.14 | Creating a Query by Using the Simple Query Wizard

A *query* is a database object that retrieves specific data from one or more database objects—either tables or other queries—and then, in a single datasheet, displays only the data that you specify when you design the query. Because the word *query* means *to ask a question*, think of a query as a question formed in a manner that Access can answer.

A *select query* is one type of Access query. A select query, also called a *simple select query*, retrieves (selects) data from one or more tables or queries and then displays the selected data in a datasheet. A select query creates a subset of the data to answer specific questions; for example, *Which students live in Austin, TX?*

The objects from which a query selects the data are referred to as the query's *data source*. In this activity, you will create a simple select query using a wizard that walks you step by step through the process. The process involves selecting the data source and indicating the fields that you want to include in the query results. The query—the question you want to ask—is *What is the last name, first name, email address, phone number, and Student ID of every student?*

1 On the ribbon, click the **CREATE tab**, and then in the **Queries group**, click **Query Wizard**. In the **New Query** dialog box, be sure **Simple Query Wizard** is selected, and then click **OK**. Compare your screen with Figure 1.30.

FIGURE 1.30

2 In the wizard, click the **Tables/Queries arrow**, and then click **Table: Lastname Firstname 1A Students**.

> In the wizard, the displayed table or query name is the object that was last selected on the Navigation Pane. The last object you worked with was your 1A Faculty Advisors table, so that object name displayed in the wizard.

> To create a query, first select the data source—the object from which the query is to select the data. The information you need to answer the question is stored in your 1A Students table, so this table is your data source.

3 Under **Available Fields**, click **Last Name**, and then click **Add Field** `>` to move the field to the **Selected Fields** list on the right. Double-click the **First Name** field to add the field to the **Selected Fields** list.

> Use either method to add fields to the Selected Fields list—you can add fields in any order.

4 By using **Add Field** `>` or by double-clicking the field name, add the following fields to the **Selected Fields** list in the order specified: **Email, Phone,** and **Student ID**. Compare your screen with Figure 1.31.

> Selecting these five fields will answer the question, *What is the last name, first name, email address, phone number, and Student ID of every student?*

FIGURE 1.31

5 In the wizard, click **Next**. Click in the **What title do you want for your query?** box. Using your own name, edit as necessary so that the query name is **Lastname Firstname 1A All Students Query** and then compare your screen with Figure 1.32.

FIGURE 1.32

6 In the wizard, click **Finish**. Select all of the columns, apply **Best Fit**, and then **Save** 🖫 the query. In the first record, click in the **Last Name** field to cancel the selection. Compare your screen with Figure 1.33.

> Access *runs* the query—performs the actions indicated in your query design—by searching the records in the specified data source, and then finds the records that match specified criteria. The records that match the criteria display in a datasheet. A select query *selects*—finds and displays—*only* the information from the data source that you request, including the specified fields.

> In the object window, Access displays every student from your 1A Students table—the data source—but displays *only* the five fields that you moved to the Selected Fields list in the Simple Query Wizard.

FIGURE 1.33

Five fields selected in Simple Query Wizard

Query results display in the object window

All students from the data source display—25 records

7 > On the ribbon, click the **FILE tab**, click **Print**, and then click **Print Preview**. Notice that the query results will print on one page. As directed by your instructor, create a paper or electronic printout. Click **Close Print Preview**.

8 > In the object window, **Close** ⊠ the query.

Activity 1.15 | Creating and Printing a Form

A *form* is an Access object with which you can enter data, edit data, or display data from a table or query. In a form, the fields are laid out in an attractive format on the screen, which makes working with the database easier for those who must enter and look up data.

One type of form displays only one record at a time. Such a form is useful not only to the individual who performs the data entry—typing in the records—but also to anyone who has the job of viewing information in the database. For example, when you visit the Records office at your college to obtain a transcript, someone displays your record on the screen. For the viewer, it is much easier to look at one record at a time, using a form, than to look at all of the student records in the database table.

1 > **Open** » the **Navigation Pane**. Drag the right edge of the **Navigation Pane** to the right to increase the width of the pane so that all object names display fully. Notice that a table name displays with a datasheet icon, and a query name displays an icon of two overlapping datasheets. Right-click your **1A Students** table, and then compare your screen with Figure 1.34.

FIGURE 1.34

Navigation Pane Close button

Table icon

Query icon

Shortcut menu for your 1A Students table

2 > On the shortcut menu, click **Open** to display the table in the object window, and then **Close** « the **Navigation Pane** to maximize your object window space.

🔄 **ANOTHER WAY**   On the Navigation Pane, double-click the object name to open it.

3 ▶ Notice that there are 11 fields in the table. On the **CREATE tab**, in the **Forms group**, click **Form**, and then compare your screen with Figure 1.35.

The Form tool creates a form based on the active object—your 1A Students table. The form displays all of the fields from the underlying data source—one record at a time—in a simple top-to-bottom format with all 11 fields lined up in a single column. You can use this new form immediately, or you can modify it. Records that you create or edit in a form are automatically added to or updated in the underlying table or data source.

The new form displays in *Layout view*—the Access view in which you can make changes to an object while the object is open and displaying the data from the data source. Each field in the form displayed in Figure 1.35 displays the data for the first student record—*Jenna Fresch*—from your 1A Students table.

FIGURE 1.35

4 ▶ At the right side of the status bar, notice the three buttons. Point to each button to display its ScreenTip, and notice that **Layout View** 🗎 is active, indicating that the form is displayed in Layout view.

5 ▶ In the status bar, click **Form View** 🗎.

In *Form view*, you can view the records, create a new record, edit a record, and delete a record. You cannot change the layout or design of the form. Form view is useful for individuals who *access records* in your database. Layout view is useful for individuals who *design* the form.

🔄 **ANOTHER WAY**   On the DESIGN tab, or on the HOME tab, in the Views group, click the top portion of the View button when it displays an icon of a form.

6 ▶ In the navigation area, click **Next record** ▶ two times to display the third record—the record for *Joey Ingram*.

Use the navigation buttons to scroll among the records and to display any single record.

7 ▶ Using your own name, **Save** 🖫 the form as **Lastname Firstname 1A Student Form**

8 Be sure that Record 3 displays. On the ribbon, click the **FILE tab**, click **Print**, and then on the right, click **Print**—do *not* click **Print Preview** because you are going to print a *single* record—not all of the records.

9 In the **Print** dialog box, under **Print Range**, click the **Selected Record(s)** option button, and then click **Setup**.

10 In the **Page Setup** dialog box, click the **Columns tab**. Under **Column Size**, double-click in the **Width** box to select the existing value, type **7.5** and then click **OK**.

> Forms are usually not printed, so the default width for a form created with the Form command is larger than most printers can handle to print on one page. If you do not change the width, the form will print on two pages because the last column flows over the margins allowed by the printer. If, after changing the Width to 7.5, your form still prints on two pages, try entering a different Width; for example, 7 or 6.5.

11 If instructed to print your objects, in the **Print** dialog box, click **OK** to print the record for *Joey Ingram* on one page; otherwise, click **Cancel**. If instructed to print an electronic copy, follow the steps in the following Note or the directions provided by your instructor.

> After printing, along the left edge of the record, the narrow bar—the ***record selector bar***—displays in black, indicating that the record is selected.

| **N O T E** | **Printing a Single Form in PDF** |

On the FILE tab, click Print, and then on the right, click Print. In the Print dialog box, click Setup. In the Page Setup dialog box, click the Columns tab. Under Column Size, double-click in the Width box, type 7.5 and then click OK. In the Print dialog box, click Cancel. On the left edge of the form, click the record selector bar so that it is black—selected.

On the ribbon, click the EXTERNAL DATA tab. In the Export group, click PDF or XPS. In the Publish as PDF or XPS dialog box, navigate to your chapter folder, and at the lower right corner of the dialog box, click Options. In the Options dialog box, under Range, click the Selected records option button, and then click OK. In the Publish as PDF or XPS dialog box, click Publish. If necessary, close the Window 8 Reader, Adobe Reader, or Adobe Acrobat window.

---

12 Close ⊠ your **1A Student Form** object; leave your **1A Students** table open.

Activity 1.16 | Creating, Modifying, and Printing a Report

A ***report*** is a database object that displays the fields and records from a table or query in an easy-to-read format suitable for printing. Create professional-looking reports to summarize database information.

1 Open » the **Navigation Pane**, and then open your **1A Faculty Advisors** table by double-clicking the table name or by right-clicking the table name and clicking **Open**. Close « the **Navigation Pane**.

2 On the ribbon, click the **CREATE tab**. In the **Reports group**, click **Report**.

> The Report tool creates a report in Layout view and includes all of the fields and all of the records in the data source—your 1A Faculty Advisors table. Dotted lines indicate how the report will break across pages if you print it now. In Layout view, you can make quick changes to the report layout while viewing the data from the table.

3 In the report, click the **Faculty ID** field name, and then on the ribbon, under **REPORT LAYOUT TOOLS**, click the **ARRANGE tab**. In the **Rows & Columns group**, click **Select Column**, and then press Del. Using the same technique, delete the **Rank** field.

> The Faculty ID and Rank fields, along with the data, are deleted from the report. The fields readjust by moving to the left. Deleting the fields from the report does *not* delete the fields and data from the data source—your 1A Faculty Advisors table.

4 ▸ Click the **Address** field name, and then by using the scroll bar at the bottom of the screen, scroll to the right to display the **Cell Phone** field; be careful not to click in the report.

5 ▸ Hold down Shift, and then click the **Cell Phone** field name to select all of the fields from *Address* through *Cell Phone*. With the six field names selected—surrounded by a colored border—in the **Rows & Columns group**, click **Select Column**, and then press Del.

Use this method to select and delete multiple columns in Layout view.

6 ▸ Scroll to the left, and notice that the four remaining fields display within the dotted lines—they are within the margins of the report. Click the **Campus** field name. Hold down Shift, and then click the **First Name** field name to select the first three fields.

7 ▸ On the ribbon, under **REPORT LAYOUT TOOLS**, click the **DESIGN tab**. In the **Tools group**, click **Property Sheet**.

The *Property Sheet* for the selected columns displays on the right side of the screen. Every object and every item in an object has an associated Property Sheet where you can make precise changes to the properties—characteristics—of selected items.

8 ▸ In the **Property Sheet**, if necessary, click the **Format tab**. Click **Width**, type **1.5** and then press Enter. Compare your screen with Figure 1.36.

The width of the three selected field names and the columns changes to 1.5", and the fields readjust by moving to the left. When you change the Width property, you do not need to select the entire column. Change the Width property if you need to move columns within the margins of a report. In this report, the fields already displayed within the margins, but some reports may need this minor adjustment to print on one page.

FIGURE 1.36

9 ▸ **Close** ✕ the **Property Sheet**. Click the **Last Name** field name. On the ribbon, click the **HOME tab**, and then in the **Sort & Filter group**, click **Ascending**.

Access sorts the report in ascending alphabetical order by the Last Name field. By default, tables are sorted in ascending order by the primary key field—in this instance, the Faculty ID field. Changing the sort order in the report does *not* change the sort order in the underlying table.

10 ▸ At the top of the report, to the right of the green report icon, click anywhere in the title of the report to select the title. On the **HOME tab**, in the **Text Formatting group**, click the **Font Size arrow**, and then click **14**. Save 🖫 the report. In the **Save As** dialog box, in the **Report Name** box, add **Report** to the end of *Lastname Firstname 1A Faculty Advisors*, and then click **OK**.

11 On the **FILE tab**, click **Print**, and then click **Print Preview**. On the **PRINT PREVIEW tab**, in the **Zoom group**, click **Two Pages**, and then compare your screen with Figure 1.37.

As currently formatted, the report will print on two pages because the page number at the bottom of the report is positioned beyond the right margin of the report.

FIGURE 1.37

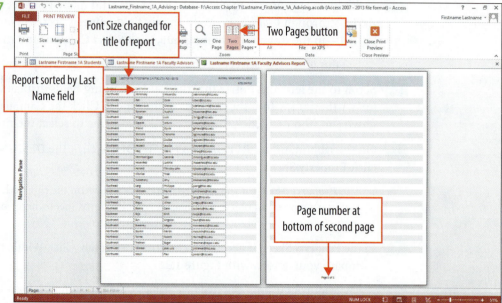

12 In the **Close Preview group**, click **Close Print Preview**. Scroll down to display the bottom of the report, and then, if necessary, scroll to the right to display the page number. Click the page number—**Page 1 of 1**—and then press ⌈Del⌋.

Because all of the data will print on one page, the page number is not necessary for this report. If you want the page number to display, you can drag it within the margins of the report.

13 Display the report in **Print Preview**, and notice that the report will now print on one page. In the **Zoom group**, click **One Page**. Click **Save** 🖫 to save the changes to the design of the report, and then create a paper or electronic printout as directed. Click **Close Print Preview**.

When you create a report by using the Report tool, the default margins are 0.25 inch. Some printers require a greater margin, so your printed report may result in two pages. As you progress in your study of Access, you will practice making these adjustments. Also, if a printer is not installed on your system, the electronic PDF printout may result in a two-page report.

14 In the object window, right-click any **object tab**, and then click **Close All** to close all of the open objects. Notice that the object window is empty.

Objective 5 | Close a Database and Exit Access

Video A1-5

When you close a table, any changes made to the records are saved automatically. If you make changes to the structure or adjust column widths, you are prompted to save the table when you close the table or when you switch views. Likewise, you are prompted to save queries, forms, and reports if you make changes to the layout or design. If the Navigation Pane is open when you exit Access, it will display when you reopen the database. When you are finished using your database, close the database, and then exit Access.

Activity 1.17 | Closing a Database and Exiting Access

1 **Open** » the **Navigation Pane**. If necessary, increase the width of the **Navigation Pane** so that all object names display fully. Notice that your report object displays with a green report icon. Compare your screen with Figure 1.38.

FIGURE 1.38

2 On the ribbon, click the **FILE tab**. Click **Close** to close the database but leave Access open. This action enables you to continue working in Access with another database if you want to do so. In the Access opening screen, in the upper right corner, click **Close** [×] to exit Access. As directed by your instructor, submit your database and the paper or electronic printouts of the five objects—two tables, one query, one form, and one report—that are the results of this project. Specifically, in this project, using your own name, you created the following database and printouts or electronic printouts:

1. Lastname_Firstname_1A_Advising	Database file
2. Lastname Firstname 1A Students	Table (printout or electronic printout – two pages)
3. Lastname Firstname 1A Faculty Advisors	Table (printout or electronic printout – two pages)
4. Lastname Firstname 1A All Students Query	Query (printout or electronic printout)
5. Lastname Firstname 1A Student Form	Form (printout or electronic printout – Record 3)
6. Lastname Firstname 1A Faculty Advisors Report	Report (printout or electronic printout)

 ANOTHER WAY   On the left side of the title bar, click [AB] and then click Close, or on the right side of the title bar, click [×] to close the database and to exit Access.

END | You have completed Project 1A

GO! with Office Web Apps

| Objective | Export an Access Table to an Excel Spreadsheet, Save to SkyDrive, Edit a Record, and Save to Your Computer |

Access web apps are designed to work with Microsoft's **SharePoint**, an application for setting up websites to share and manage documents. Your college may not have SharePoint installed, so you will use other tools to share objects from your database so that you can work collaboratively with others. Recall that Window's SkyDrive is a free file storage and file sharing service. For Access, you can export a database object to an Excel worksheet, a PDF file, or a text file, and then save the file to SkyDrive.

> **ALERT!** Working with Web-Based Applications and Services
>
> Computer programs and services on the web receive continuous updates and improvements. Therefore, the steps to complete this web-based activity may differ from the ones shown. You can often look at the screens and the information presented to determine how to complete the activity.

Activity | **Exporting an Access Table to an Excel Spreadsheet, Saving the Spreadsheet to SkyDrive, Editing a Record in SkyDrive, and Saving to Your Computer**

In this activity, you will *export*—copy data from one file into another file—your 1A Students table to an Excel spreadsheet, upload your Excel file to SkyDrive, edit a record in SkyDrive, and then download a copy of the edited spreadsheet to your computer.

1 Start Access, navigate to your **Access Chapter 1** folder, and then open your **1A_Advising** database file. If necessary, on the Message Bar, click Enable Content. In the **Navigation Pane**, click your **1A Students** table to select it—do not open it.

2 On the ribbon, click the **EXTERNAL DATA tab**, and then in the **Export group**, click **Excel**. In the **Export – Excel Spreadsheet** dialog box, click **Browse**, and then navigate to your **Access Chapter 1** folder. In the **File Save** dialog box, click in the **File name** box, type **Lastname_Firstname_AC_1A_Web** and then click **Save**.

3 In the **Export – Excel Spreadsheet** dialog box, under **Specify export options**, select the first two check boxes—**Export data with formatting and layout** and **Open the destination file after the export operation is complete**—and then click **OK**. In the **Microsoft Excel**

window, in the column headings row, to the left of column **A**, click **Select All**. On the **HOME tab**, in the **Cells group**, click **Format**, and then click **AutoFit Column Width**. Click in cell **A1** to cancel the selection, and then compare your screen with Figure A.

4 **Save** the spreadsheet, and then **Close** Excel. In the **Export – Excel Spreadsheet** dialog box, click **Close**, and then **Close** Access.

5 From the desktop, start Internet Explorer. Navigate to **http://skydrive.com**, and then sign in to your Microsoft account. Open your **GO! Web Projects** folder—or create and then open this folder if necessary.

6 On the menu bar, click **Upload**. In the **Choose File to Upload** dialog box, navigate to your **Access Chapter 1** folder, and then double-click your **AC_1A_Web** Excel file to upload it to SkyDrive.

FIGURE A

1A Students table exported to Excel spreadsheet

(GO! with Office Web Apps continues on the next page)

7 When the upload is completed, in your **GO! Web Projects** folder, click your **AC_1A_Web** file to open it in Microsoft Excel Web App.

On the ribbon, notice that you can open this worksheet in Excel instead of using the web app. If you are working on a computer that does not have Microsoft Excel installed, you can still create and modify workbooks in your web browser by using the Microsoft Excel Web app.

8 In the first record, click in the **Last Name** field. Using your own last name, type **Lastname** and then press Tab to replace *Fresch* with your last name. In the **First Name** field, using your own first name, type **Firstname** to replace *Jenna* with your own first name, and then press ↓ to save the record. Compare your screen with Figure B.

9 On the ribbon, click the **FILE tab**, click **Save As**, and then click **Download**. In the message box—usually displays at the bottom of your screen—click the **Save arrow**, and then click **Save as**. In the **Save As** dialog box, navigate to your **Access Chapter 1** folder, and then click in the **File name** box. Type **Lastname_Firstname_AC_1A_Web_Download** and then click **Save**. **Close** the message box.

10 In SkyDrive, on the title bar, click **SkyDrive** to return to your home page. At the top right corner of your screen, click your SkyDrive name, and then click **Sign out**. **Close** your browser window.

11 Start Excel. In the Excel opening screen, click **Open Other Workbooks**. Under **Open**, click **Computer**. Under **Computer**, click **Browse**. Navigate to your **Access Chapter 1** folder, and then double-click your **AC_1A_Web** Excel file. Notice that this file is the original file—the first record is not changed. If you are required to print your documents, use one of the methods in the Note box given. **Close** your Excel file, saving the changes to your worksheet, and then **Open** and print your **AC_1A_Web_Download** file by using one of the methods in the following Note. **Close** Excel, saving the changes to your worksheet. As directed by your instructor, submit your two workbooks and the two paper or electronic printouts that are the results of this project.

NOTE Adding the File Name to the Footer and Printing or Creating an Electronic Printout of an Excel Spreadsheet on One Page

Click the FILE tab, click Print, and then click Page Setup. In the Page Setup dialog box, on the Page tab, under Orientation, click Landscape. Under Scaling, click the Fit to option button. In the Page Setup dialog box, click the Header/Footer tab, and then click Custom Footer. With the insertion point blinking in the Left section box, click the Insert File Name button, and then click OK. In the Page Setup dialog box, click OK.

To print on paper, click Print. To create an electronic file of your printout, on the left side of your screen, click Export. Under Export, be sure Create PDF/XPS Document is selected, and then, on the right, click Create PDF/XPS. Navigate to your Access Chapter 1 folder, and then click Publish to save the file with the default name and an extension of pdf.

FIGURE B

PROJECT
1B

Student Workshops Database

PROJECT ACTIVITIES

In Activities 1.18 through 1.25, you will assist Dr. Miriam Yong, director of student activities, in creating a database to store information about student workshops held at Texas Lakes Community College campuses. You will use a database template that tracks event information, add workshop information to the database, and then print the results. Your completed report and table will look similar to Figure 1.39.

PROJECT FILES

For Project 1B, you will need the following files:

Desktop Event Management template
a01B_Workshops (Excel workbook)

You will save your database as:

Lastname_Firstname_1B_Student_Workshops

Build from
Scratch

PROJECT RESULTS

Lastname Firstname 1B All Events   Sunday, November 11, 2012   11:13:13 PM

Title	Start Time	End Time	Location
Your Online Reputation	3/9/2018 7:00:00 PM	3/9/2018 9:00:00 PM	Northeast Campus
Internet Safety			
Writing a Research Paper	3/10/2018 4:00:00 PM	3/10/2018 6:00:00 PM	Southwest Campus
Computer Skills			
Resume Writing	3/18/2018 2:00:00 PM	3/18/2018 4:00:00 PM	Northwest Campus
Job Skills			
Careers in the Legal Profession	3/19/2018 2:00:00 PM	3/19/2018 4:00:00 PM	Southeast Campus
Careers			
Transferring to a 4-Year University	4/8/2018 11:00:00 AM	4/8/2018 12:30:00 PM	Northeast Campus
Transfer			
Financial Aid	4/14/2018 7:00:00 PM	4/14/2018 8:30:00 PM	Southeast Campus
CC info			
Sensitivity Training	4/15/2018 8:00:00 AM	4/15/2018 9:00:00 AM	Northwest Campus
Human Behavior			
Preparing for the Job Interview	4/15/2018 12:30:00 PM	4/15/2018 2:00:00 PM	Northwest Campus
Job Skills			
Class Note Taking	4/18/2018 12:30:00 PM	4/18/2018 1:30:00 PM	Southeast Campus
Study Skills			
Managing Time and Stress	4/18/2018 6:00:00 PM	4/18/2018 7:30:00 PM	Southwest Campus
Study Skills			
Work Smart at Your Computer	4/20/2018 10:00:00 AM	4/20/2018 11:00:00 AM	Northeast Campus
Computer Skills			
Preparing for Tests	4/20/2018 4:00:00 PM	4/20/2018 5:00:00 PM	Southeast Campus
Study Skills			

Page 1 of 1

Lastname Firstname 1B Workshop Locations   11/11/2012

Room ID	Campus/Location	Room	Seats	Room Arrangement	Equipment
NE-01	Northeast Campus	H265	150	Theater	Computer Projector, Surround Sound, Microphone
NE-02	Northeast Campus	B105	25	U-shaped	25 Computers, Projectors
NW-01	Northwest Campus	C202	50	Lecture Classroom	Smart Board
SE-01	Southeast Campus	D148	20	U-shaped	White Board
SW-01	Southwest Campus	A15	35	Lecture Classroom	Computer Projector

Page 1

FIGURE 1.39 Project 1B Student Workshops

Video A1-6

A ***database template*** contains prebuilt tables, queries, forms, and reports that perform a specific task, such as tracking a large number of events. For example, your college may hold events such as athletic contests, plays, lectures, concerts, and club meetings. Using a predefined template, your college's activities director can quickly create a database to manage these events. The advantage of using a template to start a new database is that you do not have to create the objects—all you need to do is enter the data and modify the prebuilt objects to suit your needs.

The purpose of the database in this project is to track the student workshops that are held by Texas Lakes Community College. The questions to be answered might include:

- What workshops will be offered, and when will they be offered?
- In what rooms and on what campuses will the workshops be held?
- Which workshop locations have a computer projector for PowerPoint presentations?

Activity 1.18 | Using a Template to Create a Database

There are two types of database templates—those that will be stored on your desktop and those that are designed to share with others over the Internet. In this activity, you will use a desktop template to create your database.

1 Start Access. In the Access opening screen, scroll down until the last templates display. Notice that there is a **Task management** template and a **Desktop task management** template. Compare your screen with Figure 1.40.

> These templates are included with the Access program. To store a database to manage tasks on your desktop, select the *Desktop task management* template. To publish a database to manage tasks and share it with others, select the *Task management* template—the one that displays a globe image. The names of templates designed to create databases stored on your computer start with the word *Desktop*.

> You can search the Microsoft Office website for more templates. You can also click on a category under the search box, where templates will be suggested.

FIGURE 1.40

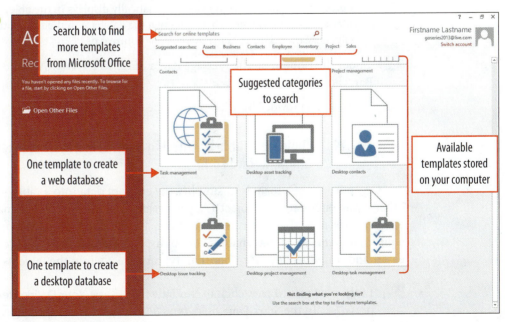

2 At the top of the window, click in the **Search for online templates** box, type **event** and then press Enter. Compare your screen with Figure 1.41.

You must have an Internet connection to search for online templates. Access displays several templates, including the Desktop Event Management template.

FIGURE 1.41

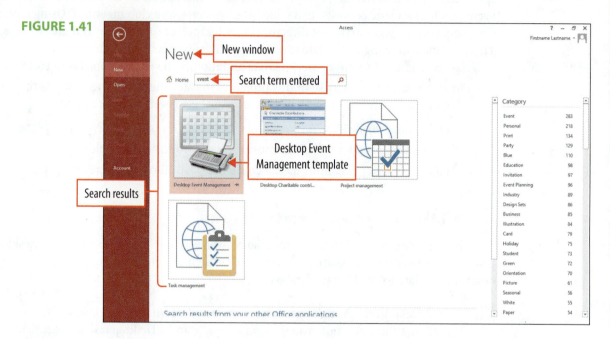

3 Click the **Desktop Event Management** template. In the dialog box, to the right of the **File Name** box, click **Browse** 📁, and then navigate to your **Access Chapter 1** folder.

4 In the **File New Database** dialog box, click in the **File name** box to select the existing text. Using your own name, type **Lastname_Firstname_1B_Student_Workshops** and then press Enter.

5 In the **Desktop Event Management** dialog box, click **Create** to download the template and to save the database.

Access creates the *1B_Student_Workshops* database, and the database name displays in the title bar. A predesigned *form*—Event List—automatically displays in the object window. Although you can enter events for any date, when you open the database in the future, the Event List form will display only those events for the current date and future dates.

6 Under the ribbon, on the **Message Bar**, a *SECURITY WARNING* displays. On the **Message Bar**, click **Enable Content**.

Databases provided by Microsoft are safe to use on your computer.

Activity 1.19 | Building a Table by Entering Records in a Multiple-Items Form and a Single-Record Form

One purpose of a form is to simplify the entry of data into a table—either for you or for others who enter data. In Project 1A, you created a simple form that enabled you to display or enter records in a table, one record at a time. The Desktop Event Management template contains a ***multiple-items form*** that enables you to display or enter *multiple* records in a table, but with an easier and simplified layout rather than typing directly into the table itself.

1 In the new record row, click in the **Title** field. Type **Your Online Reputation** and then press Tab. In the **Start Time** field, type **3/9/18 7p** and then press Tab.

Access formats the date and time. As you enter dates and times, a small calendar displays to the right of the field. You can use the calendar to select a date instead of typing it.

2 ▶ In the **End Time** field, type **3/9/18 9p** and then press Tab. In the **Description** field, type **Internet Safety** and then press Tab. In the **Location** field, type **Northeast Campus** and then press Tab three times to move to the **Title** field in the new record row. Compare your screen with Figure 1.42.

Because the workshops have no unique value, Access uses the AutoNumber data type in the ID field to assign a unique, sequential number to each record.

FIGURE 1.42

3 ▶ In the form, directly above the field names row, click **New Event**.

A ***single-record form*** with the name *Event Details* displays, similar to the simple form you created in Project 1A. A single-record form enables you to display or enter one record at a time into a table.

4 ▶ Using Tab to move from field to field, enter the following record in the **Event Details** form—press Tab three times to move from the **End Time** field to the **Description** field. Then compare your screen with Figure 1.43.

Title	Location	Start Time	End Time	Description
Writing a Research Paper	**Southwest Campus**	**3/10/18 4p**	**3/10/18 6p**	**Computer Skills**

FIGURE 1.43

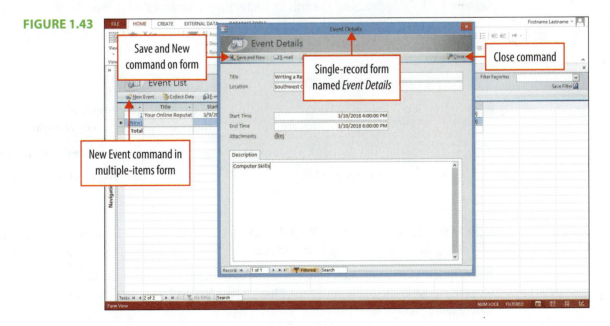

5 ▶ In the **Event Details** single-record form, in the upper right corner, click **Close**, and notice that the new record displays in the multiple-items form—*Event List*.

6 Enter the following records by using either the **Event List** form—the multiple-items form—or the **Event Details** form—the single-record form that is accessed by clicking the *New Event* command on the **Event List** form. The data in the table given is arranged in the same order as the **Event List** form. Be sure the multiple-items form displays, and then compare your screen with Figure 1.44.

ID	Title	Start Time	End Time	Description	Location
3	**Resume Writing**	3/18/18 2p	3/18/18 4p	**Job Skills**	**Northwest Campus**
4	**Careers in the Legal Profession**	3/19/18 2p	3/19/18 4p	**Careers**	**Southeast Campus**

ALERT!   Does a Single-Record Form—*Event Details*–Open?

In the multiple-items form, pressing Enter three times at the end of the row to begin a new record will display the single-record form—*Event Details*. If you prefer to use the multiple-items form—Event List—close the single-record form and continue entering records, using the Tab key to move from field to field.

FIGURE 1.44

Four records entered

7 In the object window, click **Close** ☒ to close the **Event List** form.

Activity 1.20 | Appending Records by Importing from an Excel Spreadsheet

In this activity, you will append records to the table that stores the data that displays in the Events List form. You will import the records from an Excel spreadsheet.

1 On the ribbon, click the **EXTERNAL DATA tab**. In the **Import & Link group**, click **Excel**.

2 In the **Get External Data – Excel Spreadsheet** dialog box, click **Browse**. Navigate to the location where your student data files are stored, and then double-click **a01B_Workshops**.

3 Click the second option button—**Append a copy of the records to the table**—and then click **OK**.

The table that stores the data is named *Events*. Recall that other objects, such as forms, queries, and reports, display data from tables; so the Event Details form displays data that is stored in the Events table.

4 In the **Import Spreadsheet Wizard**, click **Next**, and then click **Finish**. In the **Get External Data – Excel Spreadsheet** dialog box, click **Close**.

5 **Open** » the **Navigation Pane**. Double-click **Event List** to open the form that displays data from the **Events** table, and then **Close** « the **Navigation Pane**. Compare your screen with Figure 1.45.

A total of 12 records display; you entered four records, and you appended eight records from the a01B_Workshops Excel workbook. The data is truncated in several fields because the columns are not wide enough to display all of the data.

FIGURE 1.45

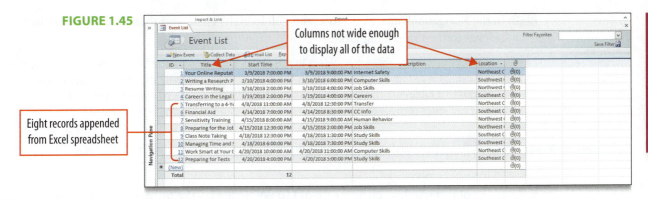

Eight records appended from Excel spreadsheet

6 To the left of the **ID** field name, click **Select All** to select all of the columns and rows.

7 In the field names row, point to the right edge of any of the selected columns to display the pointer, and then double-click to apply **Best Fit** to all of the columns. **Save** the form, and then click in any field to cancel the selection.

Objective 7 | Organize Objects in the Navigation Pane

Video A1-7

Use the Navigation Pane to open objects, organize database objects, and perform common tasks, such as renaming an object or deleting an object.

Activity 1.21 | Grouping Database Objects in the Navigation Pane

The Navigation Pane groups and displays your database objects and can do so in predefined arrangements. In this activity, you will group your database objects using the *Tables and Related Views* category, which groups objects by the table to which the objects are related. This grouping is useful because you can determine easily the table that is the data source of queries, forms, and reports.

1 **Open** ⟩ the **Navigation Pane**. At the top right side of the **Navigation Pane**, click ⊙. On the list, under **Navigate To Category**, click **Tables and Related Views**. Compare your screen with Figure 1.46.

In the Navigation Pane, you can see the number of objects that are included in the Desktop Event Management template, including the table named *Events*. Other objects in the database that display data from the Events table include one query, two forms, and five reports. In the Navigation Pane, the Event List form is selected because it is open in the object window and is the active object. Other objects might display on the Navigation Pane; for example, Filters and Unrelated Objects. These filters are objects created for use by the Desktop Event Management template.

FIGURE 1.46

One table—data source for all other objects

Two forms

Five reports

Filters included with the template

One query

Object not directly related to any table

2 In the **Navigation Pane**, point to **Events: Table**, right-click, and then click **Open** to display the records in the underlying table.

> The Events table is the active object in the object window. Use the Navigation Pane to open objects for use. The 12 records that display in the Event List multiple-items form are stored in this table. Recall that tables are the foundation of your database because your data must be stored in a table. You can enter records directly into a table or you can use a form to enter records.

ANOTHER WAY   Double-click the table name to open it in the object window.

3 In the object window, click the **Event List tab** to display the form as the active object in the object window.

> Recall that a form presents a more user-friendly screen for entering records into a table.

4 In the **Navigation Pane**, double-click the **Current Events** *report* (green icon) to open the report. Compare your screen with Figure 1.47.

> An advantage of using a template to create a database is that many objects, such as reports, are already designed for you.

FIGURE 1.47

5 In the object window, **Close** ☒ the **Current Events** report.

6 By double-clicking or right-clicking, from the **Navigation Pane**, open the **Events by Week** report.

> In this predesigned report, the events are displayed by week. After entering records in the form or table, the preformatted reports are updated with the records from the table.

7 In the object window, right-click any one of the **object tabs**, and then click **Close All** to close all of the objects. **Close** ☒ the **Navigation Pane**.

Objective 8   Create a New Table in a Database Created with a Template

Video A1-8

The Desktop Event Management template included only one table—the *Events* table. It is easy to start a database with a template, and then you can add additional objects as needed.

Activity 1.22 | Using the Table Tool to Create a New Table

Dr. Yong has information about the various locations where workshops are held. For example, on the Northeast Campus, she has information about the room, seating arrangements, number of seats, and multimedia equipment. In the Events table, workshops are scheduled in rooms at each of the four campuses. It would not make sense to store information about the campus rooms multiple times in the same table. It is *not* considered good database design to have duplicate information in a table.

When data becomes redundant, it is usually an indication that you need a new table to store that information. In this activity, you will create a table to track the workshop locations, the equipment, and the seating arrangements in each location.

1 On the ribbon, click the **CREATE tab**, and then in the **Tables group**, click **Table**.

2 In the field names row, click **Click to Add**, click **Short Text**, type **Campus/Location** and then press ⏎.

3 In the third column, click **Short Text**, type **Room** and then press ⏎. In the fourth column, click **Number**, type **Seats** and then press ⏎.

> The *Number data type* describes numbers that may be used in calculations. For the Seats field, you may need to determine the number of seats remaining after reservations are booked for a room. In the new record row, a *0* displays in the field.

4 In the fifth column, type **t** to select *Short Text*, type **Room Arrangement** and then press ⏎. In the sixth column, type **t** and then type **Equipment** On your keyboard, press ⬇.

> With the data type list displayed, you can select the data type by either clicking it or typing the letter that is underscored for the data type.

> This table has six fields. Access automatically creates the first field in the table—the ID field—to ensure that every record has a unique value. Before naming each field, you must define the data type for the field.

5 Right-click the **ID** field name, and then click **Rename Field**. Type **Room ID** and then press ⏎. On the ribbon, under **TABLE TOOLS**, on the **FIELDS tab**, in the **Formatting group**, click the **Data Type arrow**, and then click **Short Text**. On the ribbon, in the **Field Validation group**, notice that **Unique** is selected.

> Recall that, by default, Access creates the ID field with the AutoNumber data type so that the field can be used as the primary key. Here, this field will store a unique room ID that is a combination of letters, symbols, and numbers; therefore, it is appropriate to change the data type to Short Text. In Datasheet view, the primary key field is identified by the selection of the Unique check box.

Activity 1.23 | Entering Records into a New Table

1 If necessary, in the new record row, click in the **Room ID** field. Enter the following record, pressing ⏎ or ⇥ to move from one field to the next. Do not be concerned that all of your text does not display; you will adjust the column widths later. After entering the record, compare your screen with Figure 1.48.

> Recall that Access saves a record when you move to another row within the table. You can press either ⏎ or ⇥ to move between fields in a table.

Room ID	Campus/ Location	Room	Seats	Room Arrangement	Equipment
NE-01	Northeast Campus	H265	150	Theater	Computer Projector, Surround Sound, Microphone

FIGURE 1.48

2 In the **Views group**, click the top of the **View** button to switch to **Design** view. In the **Save As** dialog box, in the **Table Name** box, using your own name, type **Lastname Firstname 1B Workshop Locations** and then click **OK**.

> Recall that when you switch views or when you close a table, Access prompts you to save the table if you have not previously saved it.

ANOTHER WAY   On the right side of the status bar, click Design View to switch to Design view.

3 In the **Field Name** column, to the left of **Room ID**, notice the key icon.

> In Design view, the key icon indicates that the field—Room ID—is the primary key field.

4 In the **Views group**, click the top of the **View** button to switch back to **Datasheet** view.

ANOTHER WAY   On the right side of the status bar, click Datasheet View to switch to Datasheet view.

5 In the new record row, click in the **Room ID** field. Enter the following records, pressing Enter or Tab to move from one field to the next.

Room ID	Campus/Location	Room	Seats	Room Arrangement	Equipment
SW-01	Southwest Campus	A15	35	Lecture Classroom	Computer Projector
NW-01	Northwest Campus	C202	50	Lecture Classroom	Smart Board
SE-01	Southeast Campus	D148	20	U-shaped	White Board
NE-02	Northeast Campus	B105	25	U-shaped	25 Computers, Projector

6 To the left of the **Room ID** field name, click **Select All** to select all of the columns and rows in the table. On the **HOME tab**, in the **Records group**, click **More**, and then click **Field Width**. In the **Column Width** dialog box, click **Best Fit** to display all of the data in each column. **Save** the changes to the table, and then click in any field to cancel the selection. In the object window, **Close** your **1B Workshop Locations** table.

7 Open the **Navigation Pane**, and notice that your new table name displays in its own group. Point to the right edge of the **Navigation Pane** to display the pointer. Drag to the right to increase the width of the **Navigation Pane** so that your entire table name displays. Compare your screen with Figure 1.49.

> Recall that by organizing the Navigation Pane by Tables and Related Views, the Navigation Pane groups the objects by each table and displays the related objects under each table name.

FIGURE 1.49

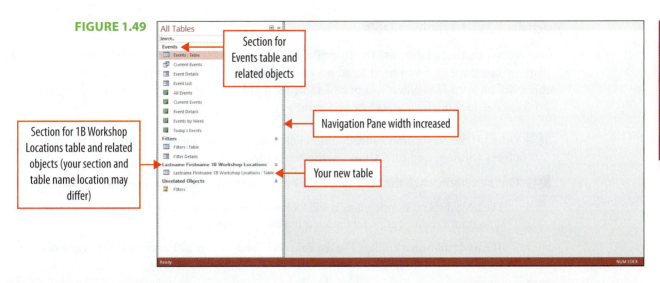

Section for 1B Workshop Locations table and related objects (your section and table name location may differ)

Section for Events table and related objects

Navigation Pane width increased

Your new table

Objective 9 Print a Report and a Table

Video A1-9

Recall that one advantage to starting a new database with a template, instead of from a blank database, is that many report objects are already created for you.

Activity 1.24 | Viewing Reports and Printing a Report

1 In the **Navigation Pane**, double-click the report (not the form) named **Event Details** to open it in the object window.

This prebuilt Event Details report displays in an attractively arranged format.

2 **Close** ✕ the **Event Details** report. Open the **All Events** report, and then **Close** « the **Navigation Pane**. On the **HOME** tab, in the **Views group**, click the top of the **View** button to switch to **Layout** view.

Recall that Layout view enables you to make changes to an object while viewing the data in the fields. Each prebuilt report displays the records in the table in different useful formats.

⟳ ANOTHER WAY On the right side of the status bar, click Layout View 📧 to switch to Layout view.

3 At the top of the report, click the title—*All Events*—to display a colored border around the title. Click to the left of the letter *A* to place the insertion point there. Using your own name, type **Lastname Firstname 1B** and then press Spacebar. Press Enter, and then **Save** 🖫 the report.

Including your name in the title will help you and your instructor identify any submitted work.

4 On the right side of the status bar, click **Print Preview** 🔍. In the navigation area, notice that the navigation arrows are unavailable, an indication that this report will print on one page.

⟳ ANOTHER WAY On the HOME tab, in the Views group, click the View arrow, and then click Print Preview. Or, on the FILE tab, click Print, and then click Print Preview. Or, right-click the object tab, and then click Print Preview.

5 Create a paper or electronic printout as instructed. Click **Close Print Preview**, and then **Close** ✕ the report.

Activity 1.25 | Printing a Table

When printing a table, use the Print Preview command to determine whether the table will print on one page or if you need to adjust column widths, margins, or page orientation. Recall that there will be occasions when you print a table for a quick reference or for proofreading. For a more professional-looking format, create and print a report.

1 Open » the **Navigation Pane**, double-click your **1B Workshop Locations** table to open it in the object window, and then **Close** « the **Navigation Pane**.

2 On the ribbon, click the **FILE tab**, click **Print**, and then click **Print Preview**.

The table displays showing how it will look when printed. Generally, tables are not printed, so there is no Print Preview option on the View button or on the status bar.

The navigation area displays *1* in the Pages box, and the navigation arrows to the right of the box are active, an indication that the table will print on more than one page.

3 In the navigation area, click **Next Page** ▶.

The second page of the table displays the last field. Whenever possible, try to print all of the fields horizontally on one page. Of course, if there are many records, more than one page may be needed to print all of the records and all of the fields.

4 On the **PRINT PREVIEW tab**, in the **Page Layout group**, click **Landscape**, and then compare your screen with Figure 1.50. In landscape orientation, notice that the entire table will print on one page—all of the navigation buttons are unavailable.

FIGURE 1.50

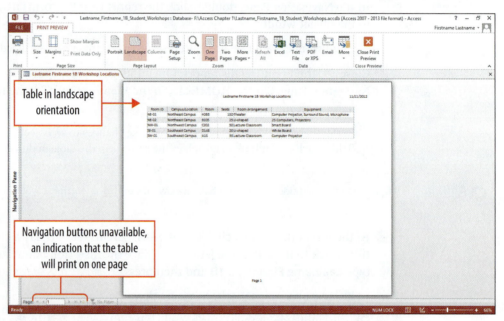

5 Create a paper or electronic printout as instructed, and then click **Close Print Preview**.

6 Close ✕ your **1B Workshop Locations** table. For the convenience of the next individual opening the database, **Open** » the **Navigation Pane**.

7 On the right side of the title bar, click **Close** ☒ to close the database and to exit Access. As directed by your instructor, submit your database and the paper or electronic printouts of the two objects—one report and one table—that are the results of this project. Specifically, in this project, using your own name, you created the following database and printouts or electronic printouts:

1. Lastname_Firstname_1B_Student_Workshops	Database file
2. All Events	Report (printout or electronic printout)
3. Lastname Firstname 1B Workshop Locations	Table (printout or electronic printout)

END | You have completed Project 1B

Objective   Export an Access Table to an Excel Spreadsheet, Save to Google Drive, Add a Record, and Save to Your Computer

Access web apps are designed to work with Microsoft's SharePoint, a service for setting up websites to share and manage documents. Your college may not have SharePoint installed, so you will use other tools to share objects from your database so that you can work collaboratively with others. Recall that Google Docs is Google's free, web-based word processor, spreadsheet, slide show, form, and data storage service. Google Drive is Google's free file storage and sharing service. For Access, you can export a database object to an Excel worksheet, a PDF file, or a text file, and then save the file to Google Drive.

ALERT!   **Working with Web-Based Applications and Services**

Computer programs and services on the web receive continuous updates and improvements. Therefore, the steps to complete this web-based activity may differ from the ones shown. You can often look at the screens and the information presented to determine how to complete the activity.

Activity | **Exporting an Access Table to an Excel Spreadsheet, Saving the Spreadsheet to Google Drive, Editing a Record in Google Drive, and Saving to Your Computer**

In this activity, you will export your 1B Workshop Locations table to an Excel spreadsheet, upload your Excel file to Google Drive as a Google Doc, add a record in Google Drive, and then download a copy of the edited spreadsheet to your computer.

1 Start Access, navigate to your **Access Chapter 1** folder, and then **Open** your **1B_Student_Workshops** database file. If necessary, on the Message Bar, click Enable Content, and then **Close** the **Event List** form. In the **Navigation Pane**, click your **1B Workshop Locations** table to select it—do not open it.

2 On the ribbon, click the **EXTERNAL DATA tab**, and then in the **Export group**, click **Excel**. In the **Export – Excel Spreadsheet** dialog box, click **Browse**, and then navigate to your **Access Chapter 1** folder. In the **File Save** dialog box, click in the **File name** box, type **Lastname_Firstname_AC_1B_Web** and then click **Save**.

3 In the **Export – Excel Spreadsheet** dialog box, under **Specify export options**, select the first two check boxes—**Export data with formatting and layout** and **Open the destination file after the export operation is complete**—and then click **OK**. Take a moment to examine the data in the file, and then **Close** Excel. In the **Export – Excel Spreadsheet** dialog box, click **Close**, and then **Close** Access.

4 From the desktop, start Internet Explorer, navigate to **http://drive.google.com**, and sign in to your Google account; if necessary, create a new Google account and then sign in. On the right side of the screen, click the **Settings arrow**, and then point to **Upload settings**. Be sure that **Convert uploaded files to Google Docs format** is selected.

If this setting is not selected, your document will upload as a pdf file and cannot be edited without further action.

5 Open your **GO! Web Projects** folder—or create and then open this folder by clicking **New folder**. Under **Drive**, to the right of **Create**, click **Upload**, and then click **Files**. In the **Choose File to Upload** dialog box, navigate to your **Access Chapter 1** folder, and then double-click your **AC_1B_Web** Excel file to upload it to Google Drive. When the title bar of the message box indicates *Upload complete*, **Close** the message box. Compare your screen with Figure A.

FIGURE A

(GO! with Office Web Apps continues on the next page)

6 Click your **AC_1B_Web** file to open the file in Google Drive. If necessary, maximize the window.

The worksheet displays column letters, row numbers, and data.

7 Click in cell **A7**, type **SW-02** and then press Tab. In cell **B7**, type **Southwest Campus** and then press Tab. In cell **C7**, type **B101** and then press Tab. In cell **D7**, type **25** and then press ↓ to save the record.

The new record might display with a different font than the other records.

8 Above row **1** and to the left of column **A**, click **Select All**. On the menu bar, click **Format**, and then click **Clear formatting** so that the font is the same for all data. Click in cell **A8**, and then compare your screen with Figure B.

9 On the menu, click **File**, point to **Download as**, and then click **Microsoft Excel (.xlsx)**. In the message box—usually displays at the bottom of your screen—click the **Save arrow**, and then click **Save as**. In the **Save As** dialog box, navigate to your **Access Chapter 1** folder, click in the **File name** box, type **Lastname_Firstname_AC_1B_Web_Download** and then click **Save**. **Close** the message box.

10 In Google Drive, at the top right corner of your screen, click your user name, and then click **Sign out**. **Close** your browser window.

11 Start Excel. In the Excel opening screen, click **Open Other Workbooks**. Under **Open**, click **Computer**. On the right, under **Computer**, click **Browse**. Navigate to your **Access Chapter 1** folder, and then double-click your **AC_1B_Web** Excel file. Notice that this file is the original file—the new record is not entered. If you are required to print your documents, use one of the methods in following Note. **Close** your Excel file; and, if prompted, save the changes to your worksheet. Then **Open** and print your **AC_1B_Web_Download** Excel file using one of the methods in the following Note. **Close** Excel; and, if prompted, save the changes to your worksheet. As directed by your instructor, submit your two workbooks and the two paper or electronic printouts that are the results of this project.

NOTE — Adding the File Name to the Footer and Printing or Creating an Electronic Printout of an Excel Spreadsheet on One Page

Click the FILE tab, click Print, and then click Page Setup. In the Page Setup dialog box, on the Page tab, under Orientation, click Landscape. Under Scaling, click the Fit to option button. In the Page Setup dialog box, click the Header/Footer tab, and then click Custom Footer. With the insertion point blinking in the Left section box, click the Insert File Name button, and then click OK. In the Page Setup dialog box, click OK.

To print on paper, click Print. To create an electronic file of your printout, on the left side of your screen, click Export. Under Export, be sure Create PDF/XPS Document is selected, and then, on the right, click Create PDF/XPS. Navigate to your Access Chapter 1 folder, and then click Publish to save the file with the default name and an extension of pdf.

FIGURE B

Office 365 includes business-class security and is backed by Microsoft. For an organization, what does that mean?

When you and a few classmates work together on a class project, you are not concerned about the security of your data. You probably use free personal email services such as Hotmail, Gmail, or Yahoo Mail to exchange documents, or perhaps you post your documents to free services such as Google Docs.

Organizations, on the other hand—even small ones with only two or three employees—must be concerned with the privacy and security of their data. Organizations cannot entrust their data and confidential communications to free services that may change frequently or that have no legal responsibility for the security of the data.

Organizations must provide each employee with a company email address rather than having each employee use his or her own personal free email address for business communications. Organizations must provide a central storage location for its data rather than having employees store data on flash drives or local hard drives with no control or oversight.

An organization must have a *secure environment*, which is a system that uses controlled *servers*—computers that provide services on a network such as an email server or a file server—to ensure the security and privacy of email, to control the storage and use of information, and to protect against the loss of confidential data.

Most small organizations cannot afford to hire the people with the skills necessary to install and maintain servers. So to establish and maintain a secure environment, many small organizations contract with and rely on small IT—the acronym for *Information Technology*—hosting companies to host their email communications and to provide secure storage.

Activity | Using the Exchange Online Outlook Meeting Tool to Collaborate

This group project relates to the **Bell Orchid Hotels**. If your instructor assigns this project to your class, you can expect to use the **Outlook Meeting tool** in **Office 365 Exchange Online** to collaborate on the following tasks for this chapter:

- If you are in the **Accounting Group**, you and your teammates will meet virtually to create a Stockholders Database to track individuals who have purchased stock in the hotel.

- If you are in the **Engineering Group**, you and your teammates will meet virtually to create a Subcontractors Database to track companies used by the Hotel for maintenance and renovation projects.

- If you are in the **Food and Beverage Group**, you and your teammates will meet virtually to create a Banquet Clients Database to track the types of functions taking place in the Hotel's banquet rooms.

- If you are in the **Human Resources Group**, you and your teammates will meet virtually to create an Employee Database for salaried employees.

- If you are in the **Operations Group**, you and your teammates will meet virtually to create a Guests Database to track guest information, as well as room rates and availability.

- If you are in the **Sales and Marketing Group**, you and your teammates will meet virtually to create an Associations Database to track industry and trade associations that book conventions for large groups.

FIGURE A

END OF CHAPTER

SUMMARY

Principles of good database design, also known as normalization, help ensure that the data in your database is accurate and organized in a way that you can retrieve information that is useful.

Databases can be created from scratch by using the blank desktop database template or a custom web app or by using a template that contains prebuilt tables, queries, forms, reports, and other objects.

Before entering records in a table, which is the foundation of a database, you must define data types and name the fields. Common data types are Short Text, Number, Currency, and Date/Time.

Forms are used to enter data into a table or view the data in a table. Queries are used to retrieve information from tables, and reports display information from tables in a professional-looking format.

GO! LEARN IT ONLINE

Review the concepts and key terms in this chapter by completing these online challenges, which you can find at **www.pearsonhighered.com/go.**

Matching and Multiple Choice: Answer matching and multiple choice questions to test what you learned in this chapter. MyITLab®

Crossword Puzzle: Spell out the words that match the numbered clues, and put them in the puzzle squares.

Flipboard: Flip through the definitions of the key terms in this chapter and match them with the correct term.

GO! FOR JOB SUCCESS

Video: Goal Setting

Your instructor may assign this video to your class, and then ask you to think about, or discuss with your classmates, these questions:

FotolEdhar / Fotolia

Is there anything you would change about Theo's behavior at his performance evaluation? Why or why not?

SMART goals are goals that are specific, measurable, achievable, realistic, and time-frame specific. Is Theo's first goal of beating his sales numbers by 10 percent next year a SMART goal?

How important do you think it is to set career development goals for yourself? Why?

END OF CHAPTER

REVIEW AND ASSESSMENT GUIDE FOR ACCESS CHAPTER 1

Your instructor may assign one or more of these projects to help you review the chapter and assess your mastery and understanding of the chapter.

		Review and Assessment Guide for Access Chapter 1	
Project	**Apply Skills from These Chapter Objectives**	**Project Type**	**Project Location**
1C	Objectives 1-5 from Project 1A	**1C Skills Review** A guided review of the skills from Project 1A.	On the following pages
1D	Objectives 6-9 from Project 1B	**1D Skills Review** A guided review of the skills from Project 1B.	On the following pages
1E	Objectives 1-5 from Project 1A	**1E Mastery (Grader Project)** A demonstration of your mastery of the skills in Project 1A with extensive decision making.	In MyITLab and on the following pages
1F	Objectives 6-9 from Project 1B	**1F Mastery (Grader Project)** A demonstration of your mastery of the skills in Project 1B with extensive decision making.	In MyITLab and on the following pages
1G	Objectives 1-9 from Projects 1A and 1B	**1G Mastery (Grader Project)** A demonstration of your mastery of the skills in Projects 1A and 1B with extensive decision making.	In MyITLab and on the following pages
1H	Combination of Objectives from Projects 1A and 1B	**1H GO! Fix It** A demonstration of your mastery of the skills in Projects 1A and 1B by creating a correct result from a document that contains errors you must find.	Online
1I	Combination of Objectives from Projects 1A and 1B	**1I GO! Make It** A demonstration of your mastery of the skills in Projects 1A and 1B by creating a result from a supplied picture.	Online
1J	Combination of Objectives from Projects 1A and 1B	**1J GO! Solve It** A demonstration of your mastery of the skills in Projects 1A and 1B, your decision-making skills, and your critical thinking skills. A task-specific rubric helps you self-assess your result.	Online
1K	Combination of Objectives from Projects 1A and 1B	**1K GO! Solve It** A demonstration of your mastery of the skills in Projects 1A and 1B, your decision-making skills, and your critical thinking skills. A task-specific rubric helps you self-assess your result.	On the following pages
1L	Combination of Objectives from Projects 1A and 1B	**1L GO! Think** A demonstration of your understanding of the chapter concepts applied in a manner that you would outside of college. An analytic rubric helps you and your instructor grade the quality of your work by comparing it to the work an expert in the discipline would create.	On the following pages
1M	Combination of Objectives from Projects 1A and 1B	**1M GO! Think** A demonstration of your understanding of the chapter concepts applied in a manner that you would outside of college. An analytic rubric helps you and your instructor grade the quality of your work by comparing it to the work an expert in the discipline would create.	Online
1N	Combination of Objectives from Projects 1A and 1B	**1N You and GO!** A demonstration of your understanding of the chapter concepts applied in a manner that you would in a personal situation. An analytic rubric helps you and your instructor grade the quality of your work.	Online
1O	Combination of Objectives from Projects 1A and 1B	**1O Cumulative Group Project for Access Chapter 1** A demonstration of your understanding of concepts and your ability to work collaboratively in a group role-playing assessment, requiring both collaboration and self-management.	Online

GLOSSARY

GLOSSARY OF CHAPTER KEY TERMS

Append To add on to the end of an object; for example, to add records to the end of an existing table.

AutoNumber data type A data type that describes a unique sequential or random number assigned by Access as each record is entered and that is useful for data that has no distinct field that can be considered unique.

Best Fit An Access command that adjusts the width of a column to accommodate the column's longest entry.

Blank desktop database A database that has no data and has no database tools—you must create the data and tools as you need them; the database is stored on your computer or other storage device.

Caption A property setting that displays a name for a field in a table, query, form, or report other than that listed as the field name.

Common field A field in two or more tables that stores the same data.

Currency data type An Access data type that describes monetary values and numeric data that can be used in mathematical calculations involving values with one to four decimal places.

Custom web app A database that you can publish and share with others over the Internet.

Data Facts about people, events, things, or ideas.

Data source The table or tables from which a query, form, or report retrieves its data.

Data type The characteristic that defines the kind of data that can be stored in a field, such as numbers, text, or dates.

Database An organized collection of facts about people, events, things, or ideas related to a specific topic or purpose.

Database management system (DBMS) Database software that controls how related collections of data are stored, organized, retrieved, and secured; also known as a DBMS.

Database template A preformatted database that contains prebuilt tables, queries, forms, and reports that perform a specific task, such as tracking events.

Datasheet view The Access view that displays data organized in columns and rows similar to an Excel worksheet.

DBMS An acronym for database management system.

Design view An Access view that displays the detailed structure of a table, query, form, or report. For forms and reports, may be the view in which some tasks must be performed, and only the controls, and not the data, display in this view.

Destination table The table to which you import or append data.

Export The process of copying data from one file into another file, such as an Access table into an Excel spreadsheet.

Field A single piece of information that is stored in every record; represented by a column in a database table.

Field properties Characteristics of a field that control how the field displays and how data can be entered in the field.

First principle of good database design A principle of good database design stating that data is organized in tables so that there is no redundant data.

Flat database A simple database file that is not related or linked to any other collection of data.

Form An Access object you can use to enter new records into a table, edit or delete existing records in a table, or display existing records.

Form view The Access view in which you can view records, but you cannot change the layout or design of the form.

Import The process of copying data from another file, such as a Word table or an Excel workbook, into a separate file, such as an Access database.

Information Data that is organized in a useful manner.

Layout view The Access view in which you can make changes to a form or report while the object is open—the data from the underlying data source displays.

Link A connection to data in another file.

Multiple-items form A form that enables you to display or enter multiple records in a table.

Navigation area An area at the bottom of the Access window that indicates the number of records in the table and contains controls in the form of arrows

that you click to navigate among the records.

Navigation Pane An area of the Access window that displays and organizes the names of the objects in a database; from here, you open objects for use.

Normalization The process of applying design rules and principles to ensure that your database performs as expected.

Number data type An Access data type that describes numbers that might be used in calculations.

Object tab In the object window, a tab that identifies the object and which enables you to make the open object active.

Object window An area of the Access window that displays open objects, such as tables, queries, forms, or reports; by default, each object displays on its own tab.

Objects The basic parts of a database that you create to store your data and to work with your data; for example, tables, queries, forms, and reports.

Populate The action of filling a database table with records.

Primary key The field in a table that uniquely identifies a record; for example, a Student ID number at a college.

Property Sheet A list of characteristics—properties—for fields or controls on a form or report in which you can make precise changes to each property associated with the field or control.

Query A database object that retrieves specific data from one or more database objects—either tables or other queries—and then, in a single datasheet, displays only the data you specify.

Record All of the categories of data pertaining to one person, place, event, thing, or idea; represented by a row in a database table.

Record selector bar The bar at the left edge of a record when it is displayed in a form, and which is used to select an entire record.

Record selector box The small box at the left of a record in Datasheet view that, when clicked, selects the entire record.

Redundant In a database, information that is duplicated in a manner that indicates poor database design.

Relational database A sophisticated type of database that has multiple collections of data within the file that are related to one another.

Report A database object that summarizes the fields and records from a table or query in an easy-to-read format suitable for printing.

Run The process in which Access searches the records in the table(s) included in the query design, finds the records that match the specified criteria, and then displays the records in a datasheet; only the fields that have been included in the query design display.

Second principle of good database design A principle stating that appropriate database techniques are used to ensure the accuracy and consistency of data as it is entered into the table.

Secure environment A system that uses controlled servers to ensure the security and privacy of email, to control the storage and use of information and to protect against the loss of confidential data.

Select query A type of Access query that retrieves (selects) data from one or more tables or queries, displaying the selected data in a datasheet; also known as a simple select query.

Server A computer that provides services on a network such as an email server or a file server.

SharePoint A Microsoft application used for setting up websites to share and manage documents.

Short Text data type An Access data type that describes text, a combination of text and numbers, or numbers that are not used in calculations, such as a Postal Code.

Simple select query Another name for a select query.

Single-record form A form that enables you to display or enter one record at a time in a table.

Source file When importing a file, refers to the file being imported.

Structure In Access, the underlying design of a table, including field names, data types, descriptions, and field properties.

Table A format for information that organizes and presents text and data in columns and rows; the foundation of a database.

Tables and Related Views An arrangement in the Navigation Pane that groups objects by the table to which they are related.

Truncated Refers to data that is cut off or shortened because the field or column is not wide enough to display all of the data or the field size is too small to contain all of the data.

Wizard A feature in Microsoft Office that walks you step by step through a process.

CHAPTER REVIEW

Apply 1A skills from these Objectives:

1. Identify Good Database Design
2. Create a Table and Define Fields in a Blank Desktop Database
3. Change the Structure of Tables and Add a Second Table
4. Create a Query, Form, and Report
5. Close a Database and Exit Access

In the following Skills Review, you will create a database to store information about the administrators of Texas Lakes Community College and their departments. Your completed database objects will look similar to Figure 1.51.

PROJECT FILES

For Project 1C, you will need the following files:

Blank desktop database
a01C_Administrators (Excel workbook)
a01C_Departments (Excel workbook)

You will save your database as:

Lastname_Firstname_1C_College_Administrators

Build from Scratch

PROJECT RESULTS

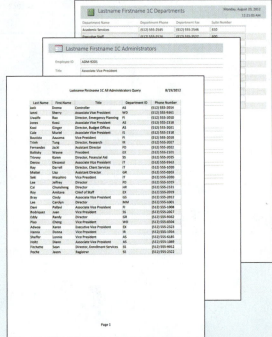

FIGURE 1.51

(Project 1C College Administrators continues on the next page)

CHAPTER REVIEW

1 Start Access. In the Access opening screen, click **Blank desktop database**. In the **Blank desktop database** dialog box, to the right of the **File Name** box, click **Browse**. In the **File New Database** dialog box, navigate to your **Access Chapter 1** folder. In the **File New Database** dialog box, click in the **File name** box, type **Lastname_Firstname_1C_College_Administrators** and then press Enter. In the **Blank desktop database** dialog box, click **Create**.

a. **Close** the **Navigation Pane**. In the field names row, click in the text *Click to Add*, and then click **Short Text**. Type **Title** and then press Enter.

b. In the third field name box, click **Short Text**, type **Last Name** and then press Enter. In the fourth field name box, click **Short Text**, type **First Name** and then press Enter. Create the remaining fields shown in **Table 1**, pressing Enter after the last field name. All of the data is typed on one line.

c. If necessary, scroll to bring the first column into view, and then click the **ID** field name. Under **TABLE TOOLS**, on the **FIELDS tab**, in the **Properties group**, click **Name & Caption**. In the **Name** box, change *ID* to **Employee ID** and then click **OK**. On the ribbon, in the **Formatting group**, click the **Data Type arrow**, and then click **Short Text**.

d. In the new record row, click in the **Employee ID** field, type, **ADM-9200** and press Enter. In the **Title** field, type **Vice President** and press Enter. Continue entering data in the fields shown in **Table 2**, pressing Enter or Tab to move to the next field and to the next row.

e. On the **Quick Access Toolbar**, click **Save**. In the **Save As** dialog box, in the **Table Name** box, using your own name, replace the selected text by typing **Lastname Firstname 1C Administrators** and then click **OK**.

f. In the new record row, enter the data for two college administrators shown in **Table 3**, pressing Enter or Tab to move from field to field and to the next row.

TABLE 1

Data Type		Short Text	Short Text	Short Text	Short Text	Short Text	Short Text	Short Text	Short Text	Short Text	Short Text	Currency
Field Name	ID	Title	Last Name	First Name	**Middle Initial**	**Address**	**City**	**State**	**Postal Code**	**Phone Number**	**Department ID**	**Salary**

Return to Step 1c

TABLE 2

Last Name	First Name	Middle Initial	Address	City	State	Postal Code	Phone Number	Department ID	Salary
Shaffer	**Lonnie**	**J**	**489 Ben Ave**	**Austin**	**TX**	**78734**	**(512) 555-6185**	**AS**	**123500**

Return to Step 1e

TABLE 3

Employee ID	Title	Last Name	First Name	Middle Initial	Address	City	State	Postal Code	Phone Number	Department ID	Salary
ADM-9201	Associate Vice President	Holtz	Diann	S	8416 Spencer Ln	Georgetown	TX	78627	(512) 555-1069	AS	101524
ADM-9202	Director, Enrollment Services	Fitchette	Sean	H	3245 Deer Trl	Spicewood	TX	78669	(512) 555-9012	SS	45070

Return to Step 1g

(Project 1C College Administrators continues on the next page)

g. **Close** your **1C Administrators** table. On the ribbon, click the **EXTERNAL DATA tab**, in the **Import & Link group**, click **Excel**. In the **Get External Data – Excel Spreadsheet** dialog box, click **Browse**. In the **File Open** dialog box, navigate to your student data files, and then double-click the **a01C_Administrators** Excel file.

h. Click the **Append a copy of the records to the table** option button, and then click **OK**. In the **Import Spreadsheet Wizard**, click **Next**, and then click **Finish**. In the **Get External Data – Excel Spreadsheet** dialog box, click **Close**.

i. **Open** the **Navigation Pane**. Point to the right edge of the **Navigation Pane** to display the ⟷ pointer, and then drag to the right so that the entire table name displays. In the **Navigation Pane**, double-click your **1C Administrators** table to open it, and then **Close** the **Navigation Pane**—there are 30 records in this table.

2 ▸ Click the **HOME tab**, and then in the **Views group**, click the top of the **View** button to switch to **Design** view. In the **Field Name** column, to the left of **Middle Initial**, click the row selector box to select the entire row. Under **TABLE TOOLS, o**n the **DESIGN tab**, in the **Tools group**, click **Delete Rows**. In the message box, click **Yes**.

a. Click in the **Employee ID** field name box. Under **Field Properties**, click **Field Size** to select the existing text. Type **8** and then in the **Employee ID** field row, click in the **Description** box. Type **Eight-character Employee ID** and then press `Enter`.

b. Click in the **State** field name box. In the **Field Properties** area, click **Field Size**, and then type **2** In the **State Description** box, type **Two-character state abbreviation** and then press `Enter`.

c. **Save** the design changes to your table, and in the message box, click **Yes**. On the **DESIGN tab**, in the **Views group**, click the top of the **View** button to switch to **Datasheet** view.

d. On the ribbon, click the **EXTERNAL DATA tab**, and then in the **Import & Link group**, click **Excel**. In the **Get External Data – Excel Spreadsheet** dialog box, to the right of the **File name** box, click **Browse**. In the

File Open dialog box, navigate to your student data files, and then double-click **a01C_Departments**. Be sure that the **Import the source data into a new table in the current database** option button is selected, and then click **OK**.

e. In the upper left corner of the wizard, select the **First Row Contains Column Headings** check box, and then click **Next**. Click **Next** again. Click the **Choose my own primary key** option button, be sure that **Department ID** displays, and then click **Next**. In the **Import to Table** box, type **Lastname Firstname 1C Departments** and then click **Finish**. In the **Get External Data – Excel Spreadsheet** dialog box, click **Close**.

f. **Open** the **Navigation Pane**, double-click your **1C Departments** table, and then **Close** the **Navigation Pane**. There are 12 records in your **1C Departments** table.

g. To the left of the **Department** field name, click **Select All**. On the ribbon, click the **HOME tab**. In the **Records group**, click **More**, and then click **Field Width**. In the **Column Width** dialog box, click **Best Fit**. **Save** the table, and then click in any field to cancel the selection. In the object window, click the **object tab** for your **1C Administrators** table. Using the techniques you just practiced, apply **Best Fit** to the columns, **Save** the table, and then cancel the selection.

h. With your **1C Administrators** table displayed, on the ribbon, click the **FILE tab**, click **Print**, and then click **Print Preview**. On the **PRINT PREVIEW tab**, in the **Page Layout group**, click **Landscape**. Create a paper or electronic printout as directed by your instructor—two pages result. On the ribbon, click **Close Print Preview**, and then **Close** your **1C Administrators** table.

i. With your **1C Departments** table displayed, view the table in **Print Preview**. Change the orientation to **Landscape**, and then create a paper or electronic printout as directed by your instructor—one page results. Click **Close Print Preview**, and then **Close** your **1C Departments** table.

(Project 1C College Administrators continues on the next page)

CHAPTER REVIEW

3 On the ribbon, click the **CREATE tab**, and then in the **Queries group**, click **Query Wizard**. In the **New Query** dialog box, be sure **Simple Query Wizard** is selected, and then click **OK**. In the wizard, click the **Tables/Queries arrow**, and then, if necessary, click **Table: Lastname Firstname 1C Administrators**.

a. Under **Available Fields**, click **Last Name**, and then click **Add Field** to move the field to the **Selected Fields** list on the right. Double-click the **First Name** field to move it to the **Selected Fields** list. By using **Add Field** or by double-clicking the field name, add the following fields to the **Selected Fields** list in the order specified: **Title**, **Department ID**, and **Phone Number**. This query will answer the question, *What is the last name, first name, title, Department ID, and phone number of every administrator?*

b. In the wizard, click **Next**. Click in the **What title do you want for your query?** box. Using your own name, edit as necessary so that the query name is **Lastname Firstname 1C All Administrators Query** and then click **Finish**. If necessary, apply **Best Fit** to the columns, and then **Save** the query. Display the query in **Print Preview**, and then create a paper or electronic printout as directed—one page results. Click **Close Print Preview**, and then **Close** the query.

c. **Open** the Navigation Pane, right-click your **1C Administrators** table, and then click **Open** to display the table in the object window. **Close** the **Navigation Pane**. Notice that the table has 11 fields. On the ribbon, click the **CREATE tab**, and in the **Forms group**, click **Form**. On the **Quick Access Toolbar**, click **Save**. In the **Save As** dialog box, click in the **Form Name** box, edit to name the form **Lastname Firstname 1C Administrator Form** and then click **OK**.

d. In the navigation area, click **Last record**, and then click **Previous record** two times to display the record for *Diann Holtz*. Using the instructions in Activity 1.15, print or create an electronic printout of only this record on one page. **Close** the form object, saving it if prompted. Your **1C Administrators** table object remains open.

e. **Open** the Navigation Pane, open your **1C Departments** table by double-clicking the table name or by right-clicking the table name and clicking **Open**. **Close** the **Navigation Pane**. On the **CREATE tab**, in the **Reports group**, click **Report**.

f. Click the **Department ID** field name, and then on the ribbon, click the **ARRANGE tab**. In the **Rows & Columns group**, click **Select Column**, and then press Del. Using the same technique, delete the **Department Email** field.

g. Click the **Department Phone** field name. Hold down Shift, and then click the **Suite Number** field name to select the last three field names. On the ribbon, click the **DESIGN tab**, and then in the **Tools group**, click **Property Sheet**. In the **Property Sheet**, on the **Format tab**, click **Width**, type **1.5** and then press Enter. **Close** the **Property Sheet**.

h. Click the **Department Name** field name. On the ribbon, click the **HOME tab**. In the **Sort & Filter group**, click **Ascending** to sort the report in alphabetic order by *Department Name*. At the bottom of the report, on the right side, click **Page 1 of 1**, and then press Del.

i. **Save** the report as **Lastname Firstname 1C Departments Report** and then click **OK**. Display the report in **Print Preview**, and then create a paper or electronic printout of the report as directed. Click **Close Print Preview**. In the object window, right-click any **object tab**, and then click **Close All** to close all open objects, leaving the object window empty.

(Project 1C College Administrators continues on the next page)

CHAPTER REVIEW

4 **Open** the **Navigation Pane**. If necessary, increase the width of the **Navigation Pane** so that all object names display fully. On the right side of the title bar, click **Close** to close the database and to exit Access. As directed by your instructor, submit your database and the paper or electronic printouts of the five objects—two tables, one query, one form, and one report—that are the results of this project. Specifically, in this project, using your own name, you created the following database and printouts or electronic printouts:

1. Lastname_Firstname_1C_College_Administrators	Database file
2. Lastname Firstname 1C Administrators	Table (printout or electronic printout – two pages)
3. Lastname Firstname 1C Departments	Table (printout or electronic printout)
4. Lastname Firstname 1C All Administrators Query	Query (printout or electronic printout)
5. Lastname Firstname 1C Administrator Form	Form (printout or electronic printout – Record 28)
6. Lastname Firstname 1C Departments Report	Report (printout or electronic printout)

END | You have completed Project 1C

CHAPTER REVIEW

Apply 1B skills from these Objectives:

6 Use a Template to Create a Database

7 Organize Objects in the Navigation Pane

8 Create a New Table in a Database Created with a Template

9 Print a Report and a Table

Skills Review | Project 1D Certification Events

In the following Skills Review, you will create a database to store information about certification test preparation events at Texas Lakes Community College. Your completed report and table will look similar to Figure 1.52.

PROJECT FILES

For Project 1D, you will need the following files:

Desktop Event Management template
a01D_Certification_Events (Excel workbook)

You will save your database as:

Lastname_Firstname_1D_Certification_Events

Build from Scratch

PROJECT RESULTS

FIGURE 1.52

(Project 1D Certification Events continues on the next page)

1 Start Access. In the Access opening screen, click in the **Search** box, type **event** and then press Enter to search for a template to manage events. Click the **Desktop Event Management** template. In the **Desktop Event Management** dialog box, to the right of the **File Name** box, click **Browse**, and then navigate to your **Access Chapter 1** folder. In the **File New Database** dialog box, click in the **File name** box to select the existing text. Using your own name, type **Lastname_Firstname_1D_Certification_Events** and then press Enter. In the **Desktop Event Management** dialog box, click **Create** to download the template and to save the database. Under the ribbon, on the **Message Bar**, click **Enable Content**.

a. In the first row, click in the **Title** field, type **Word 2013** and then press Tab. In the **Start Time** field, type **7/9/18 9a** and then press Tab. In the **End Time** field, type **7/9/18 3p** and then press Tab. In the **Description** field, type **Office 2013** and then press Tab. In the **Location** field, type **Southwest Campus** and then press Tab three times to move to the **Title** field in the new record row.

b. In the form, directly above the field names row, click **New Event** to open the **Event Details** single-record form. Using Tab to move from field to field, enter the record shown in **Table 1**. Press Tab three times to move from the **End Time** field to the **Description** field.

c. In the **Events Detail** form, click **Close**. Using either the **Event List** multiple-items form or the **Event Details** single-record form, enter the records shown in **Table 2**. If you use the **Events Detail** form, be sure to close it after entering records to display the records in the **Event List** form.

d. **Close** the **Event List** form. On the ribbon, click the **EXTERNAL DATA tab**, and in the **Import & Link group**, click **Excel**. In the **Get External Data – Excel Spreadsheet** dialog box, click **Browse**. Navigate to your student data files, and then double-click **a01D_Certification_Events**. Click the second option button—**Append a copy of the records to the table**—and then click **OK**.

e. In the **Import Spreadsheet Wizard**, click **Next**, and then click **Finish**. In the **Get External Data – Excel Spreadsheet** dialog box, click **Close**. Open the **Navigation Pane**, and then double-click **Event List** to open the form that displays data stored in the **Events** table—12 total records display. **Close** the **Navigation Pane**.

f. To the left of the **ID** field name, click **Select All**. In the field names row, point to the right edge of any of the selected columns to display the ✛ pointer, and then double-click to apply **Best Fit** to all of the columns. **Save** the form, and then click in any field to cancel the selection.

2 **Open** the **Navigation Pane**. At the top of the **Navigation Pane**, click the arrow. On the list, under **Navigate To Category**, click **Tables and Related Views**.

a. In the **Navigation Pane**, point to **Events: Table**, right-click, and then click **Open** to display the records in the underlying table. In the **Navigation Pane**, double-click the **Current Events** *report* (green icon) to view this predesigned report. From the **Navigation Pane**, open the **Events by Week** report to view this predesigned report.

TABLE 1

Title	Location	Start Time	End Time	Description	
Excel 2013	Northeast Campus	7/16/18 10a	7/16/18 4p	Office 2013	- - - ▸ (Return to Step 1c)

TABLE 2

ID	Title	Start Time	End Time	Description	Location	
3	Access 2013	7/23/18 12p	7/23/18 6p	Office 2013	Southeast Campus	
4	PowerPoint 2013	7/30/18 9a	7/30/18 3p	Office 2013	Northwest Campus	- - - ▸ (Return to Step 1d)

(Project 1D Certification Events continues on the next page)

CHAPTER REVIEW

b. In the object window, right-click any of the **object tabs**, and then click **Close All**. **Close** the **Navigation Pane**.

3 On the ribbon, click the **CREATE tab**, and in the **Tables group**, click **Table**.

a. In the field names row, click **Click to Add**, click **Short Text**, type **Campus Location** and then press **Enter**. In the third column, click **Short Text**, type **Lab** and then press **Enter**. In the fourth column, click **Number**, type **# Computers** and then press **Enter**. In the fifth column, click **Short Text**, type **Additional Equipment** and then press **↓**.

b. Right-click the **ID** field name, and then click **Rename Field**. Type **Lab ID** and then press **Enter**. On the **FIELDS tab**, in the **Formatting group**, click the **Data Type arrow**, and then click **Short Text**.

c. In the new record row, click in the **Lab ID** field, and then enter the records shown in **Table 3**, pressing **Enter** or **Tab** to move from one field to the next.

d. In the **Views group**, click the top of the **View** button to switch to **Design** view. In the **Save As** dialog box, in the **Table Name** box, using your own name, type **Lastname Firstname 1D Cert Prep Locations** and then click **OK**. Notice that the **Lab ID** field is the **Primary Key**. On the **DESIGN tab**, in the **Views group**, click the top of the **View** button to switch to **Datasheet** view.

e. To the left of the **Lab ID** field name, click **Select All** to select all of the columns and rows in the table. On the **HOME tab**, in the **Records group**, click **More**, and then click **Field Width**. In the **Column Width** dialog box, click **Best Fit**. **Save** the changes to the table, and then click in any field to cancel the selection. **Close** the table, and then **Open** the **Navigation Pane**. Increase the width of the **Navigation Pane** so that your entire table name displays.

4 In the **Navigation Pane**, double-click the **All Events** report to open it in the object window. **Close** the **Navigation Pane**. On the **HOME tab**, in the **Views group**, click the top of the **View** button to switch to **Layout** view. At the top of the report, click the title—*All Events*—to display a colored border around the title. Click to the left of the letter *A* to place the insertion point there. Using your own name, type **Lastname Firstname 1D** and then press **Spacebar**. Press **Enter**, and then **Save** the report.

a. On the right side of the status bar, click **Print Preview**, and notice that the report will print on one page. Create a paper or electronic printout as instructed. Click **Close Print Preview**, and then **Close** the report.

b. **Open** the **Navigation Pane**, double-click your **1D Cert Prep Locations** table, and then **Close** the **Navigation Pane**. On the ribbon, click the **FILE tab**, click **Print**, and then click **Print Preview**. On the **PRINT PREVIEW tab**, in the **Page Layout group**, click **Landscape**. Create a paper or electronic printout as directed, and then click **Close Print Preview**. Close your **1D Cert Prep Locations** table.

TABLE 3

Lab ID	Campus Location	Lab	# Computers	Additional Equipment
NW-L01	Northwest Campus	H202	35	3 printers, projector, DVD player
SE-L01	Southeast Campus	E145	25	Projector, document camera, smart board
NE-L01	Northeast Campus	F32	40	4 printers, smart board, instructor touch screen
SW-L01	Southwest Campus	G332	30	Projector, 4 digital displays
SE-L02	Southeast Campus	A225	25	Projector, white board, instructor touch screen

(Return to Step 3d)

(Project 1D Certification Events continues on the next page)

CHAPTER REVIEW

c. **Open** the **Navigation Pane**. On the right side of the title bar, click **Close** to close the database and to exit Access. As directed by your instructor, submit your database and the paper or electronic printouts of the two objects—one report and one table—that are the results of this project. Specifically, in this project, using your own name, you created the following database and printouts or electronic printouts:

1. Lastname_Firstname_1D_Certification_Events	Database file
2. Lastname Firstname 1D Cert Prep Locations	Table (printout or electronic printout)
3. All Events	Report (printout or electronic printout)

END | You have completed Project 1D

CONTENT-BASED ASSESSMENTS

In the following Mastering Access project, you will create a database to track information about the inventory of items for sale in the kiosk located in the snack bar at the Southeast Campus of Texas Lakes Community College. Your completed database objects will look similar to Figure 1.53.

Apply **1A** skills from these Objectives:

1 Identify Good Database Design

2 Create a Table and Define Fields in a Blank Desktop Database

3 Change the Structure of Tables and Add a Second Table

4 Create a Query, Form, and Report

5 Close a Database and Exit Access

PROJECT FILES

For Project 1E, you will need the following files:

Blank desktop database

a01E_Inventory (Excel workbook)

a01E_Inventory_Storage (Excel workbook)

You will save your database as:

Lastname_Firstname_1E_Kiosk_Inventory

PROJECT RESULTS

Build from Scratch

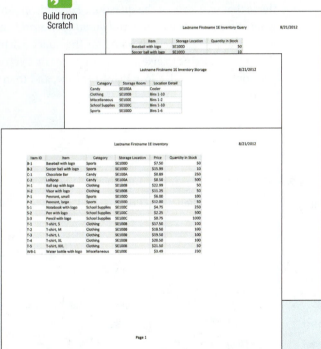

FIGURE 1.53

(Project 1E Kiosk Inventory continues on the next page)

CONTENT-BASED ASSESSMENTS

1 Start Access. Create a **Blank desktop database** in your **Access Chapter 1** folder. Name the database **Lastname_Firstname_1E_Kiosk_Inventory** and then **Close** the **Navigation Pane**. Create the fields shown in **Table 1**.

2 For the **ID** field, change the **Data Type** to **Short Text**, rename the field to **Item ID** and then enter the records shown in **Table 2**.

3 Save the table as **Lastname Firstname 1E Inventory** and then **Close** the table. From your student data files, import and then **Append** the data in the Excel file **a01E_Inventory** to your **1E Inventory** table. After importing, open your **1E Inventory** table—17 records display.

4 In **Design** view, delete the **Campus** field, which is redundant data. For the **Category** field, change the **Field Size** to **25** and enter a **Description** of **Enter the category of the item** For the **Item ID** field, change the **Field Size** to **10** and then **Save** the changes to your table. Switch to **Datasheet** view, apply **Best Fit** to all of the fields in the table, and then **Save** your changes. Display the table in **Print Preview**, change the orientation to **Landscape**, and then create a paper or electronic printout as directed by your instructor. **Close Print Preview**, and then **Close** the table.

5 From your student data files, import the **Excel** file **a01E_Inventory_Storage** into the database as a new table; designate the first row as column headings and the **Category** field as the primary key. In the wizard, name the table **Lastname Firstname 1E Inventory Storage** and then open your **1E Inventory Storage** table—five records display. In **Design** view, for the **Location Detail** field, change the **Field Size** to **30** and enter a **Description** of **Room and bin number or alternate location of inventory item Save** the design changes, switch to **Datasheet** view, apply **Best Fit** to all of the fields, and then **Save** your changes. Display the table in **Print Preview**, create a paper or electronic printout as directed, **Close Print Preview**, and then **Close** the table.

6 Use the **Query Wizard** to create a simple query based on your **1E Inventory** table. Include only the three fields that will answer the question, *For all item names, what is the storage location and quantity in stock?* In the wizard, accept the default name for the query. Display the query in **Print Preview**, create a paper or electronic printout as directed, **Close Print Preview**, and then **Close** the query.

TABLE 1

Data Type		Short Text	Short Text	Short Text	Short Text	Currency	Number
Field Name	ID	Item	Category	Campus	Storage Location	Price	Quantity in Stock

(Return to Step 2)

TABLE 2

Item ID	Item	Category	Campus	Storage Location	Price	Quantity in Stock
C-1	Chocolate Bar	Candy	Southeast	SE100A	.89	250
C-2	Lollipop	Candy	Southeast	SE100A	.5	500
T-1	T-shirt, S	Clothing	Southeast	SE100B	17.5	100

(Return to Step 3)

(Project 1E Kiosk Inventory continues on the next page)

CONTENT-BASED ASSESSMENTS

7 Open your **1E Inventory** table, and then create a **Form** for this table. **Save** the form as **Lastname Firstname 1E Inventory Form** and then display and select the fifth record. By using the instructions in Activity 1.15, create a paper or electronic printout of only this record on one page, as directed by your instructor. **Close** the form object, saving changes if prompted.

8 With your **1E Inventory** table open, create a **Report**. Delete the **Category** and **Price** fields, and then sort the **Item ID** field in **Ascending** order. Using the **Property Sheet**, for the **Item ID** field, change the **Width** to **0.75** and then for the **Storage Location** field, change the **Width** to **1.5** Scroll to display the bottom of the report, and then

delete the page number—**Page 1 of 1**. **Save** the report as **Lastname Firstname 1E Inventory Report** and then display the report in **Print Preview**. Create a paper or electronic printout as directed. Click **Close Print Preview**.

9 **Close All** open objects. **Open** the **Navigation Pane** and be sure that all object names display fully. **Close** the database, and then **Close** Access. As directed by your instructor, submit your database and the paper or electronic printouts of the five objects—two tables, one query, one form, and one report—that are the results of this project. Specifically, in this project, using your own name, you created the following database and printouts or electronic printouts:

1. Lastname_Firstname_1E_Kiosk_Inventory	Database file
2. Lastname Firstname 1E Inventory	Table (printout or electronic printout)
3. Lastname Firstname 1E Inventory Storage	Table (printout or electronic printout)
4. Lastname Firstname 1E Inventory Query	Query (printout or electronic printout)
5. Lastname Firstname 1E Inventory Form	Form (printout or electronic printout – Record 5)
6. Lastname Firstname 1E Inventory Report	Report (printout or electronic printout)

END | You have completed Project 1E

CONTENT-BASED ASSESSMENTS

In the following Mastering Access project, you will create a database to store information about the recruiting events that are scheduled to attract new students to Texas Lakes Community College. Your completed report and tables will look similar to Figure 1.54.

Apply 1B skills from these Objectives:

6 Use a Template to Create a Database

7 Organize Objects in the Navigation Pane

8 Create a New Table in a Database Created with a Template

9 Print a Report and a Table

Build from Scratch

PROJECT FILES

For Project 1F, you will need the following files:

Desktop Event Management template
a01F_Recruiting_Events (Excel workbook)

You will save your database as:

Lastname_Firstname_1F_Recruiting_Events

PROJECT RESULTS

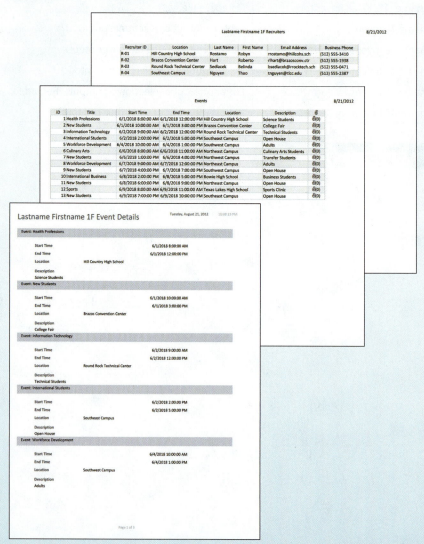

FIGURE 1.54

(Project 1F Recruiting Events continues on the next page)

CONTENT-BASED ASSESSMENTS

1 Start Access. In the Access opening screen, search for **event** and then click the **Desktop Event Management** template. Save the database in your **Access Chapter 1** folder as **Lastname_Firstname_1F_Recruiting_Events** and on the **Message Bar**, click **Enable Content**.

2 In the **Event List** multiple-items form or the **Event Details** single-record form—open by clicking **New Event** on the **Event List** form—enter the records shown in **Table 1**.

3 **Close** the **Event List** form. From your student data files, import and append the data from the **Excel** file **a01F_Recruiting_Events** to the **Events** table. **Open** the **Navigation Pane**, organize the objects by **Tables and Related Views**, and then open the **Events** table to display 13 records. **Close** the table, and then **Close** the **Navigation Pane**.

4 Create a new **Table** defining the new fields shown in **Table 2**.

5 For the **ID** field, change the **Data Type** to **Short Text**, rename the field to **Recruiter ID** and then enter the records shown in **Table 3**.

TABLE 1

ID	Title	Start Time	End Time	Description	Location
1	Health Professions	6/1/18 8a	6/1/18 12p	Science Students	Hill Country High School
2	New Students	6/1/18 10a	6/1/18 3p	College Fair	Brazos Convention Center
3	Information Technology	6/2/18 9a	6/2/18 12p	Technical Students	Round Rock Technical Center
4	International Students	6/2/18 2p	6/2/18 5p	Open House	Southeast Campus

Return to Step 3

TABLE 2

Data Type		Short Text	Short Text	Short Text	Short Text	Short Text
Field Name	ID	Location	Last Name	First Name	Email Address	Business Phone

Return to Step 5

TABLE 3

Recruiter ID	Location	Last Name	First Name	Email Address	Business Phone
R-01	Hill Country High School	Rostamo	Robyn	rrostamo@hillcohs.sch	(512) 555-3410
R-02	Brazos Convention Center	Hart	Roberto	rlhart@brazosconv.ctr	(512) 555-1938
R-03	Round Rock Technical Center	Sedlacek	Belinda	bsedlacek@rrocktech.sch	(512) 555-0471
R-04	Southeast Campus	Nguyen	Thao	tnguyen@tlcc.edu	(512) 555-2387

Return to Step 6

(Project 1F Recruiting Events continues on the next page)

CONTENT-BASED ASSESSMENTS

6 Apply **Best Fit** to all of the columns. **Save** the table as **Lastname Firstname 1F Recruiters** and then **Close** the table.

7 From the **Navigation Pane**, open the **Event Details** *report* (green icon). Switch to **Layout** view. In the report, click in the title—*Event Details*—and then click to position the insertion point to the left of the word *Event*. Using your own name, type **Lastname Firstname 1F** and then press Spacebar and Enter. If necessary, decrease the font size of the title so that the title does not overlap the date on the right side or does not extend to two lines.

     Save the report, and then display it in **Print Preview**. If directed to create a paper printout, in the **Print group**, click **Print**. In the **Print** dialog box, under **Print Range**, to the right of **Pages**, click in the **From** box, type **1** and then click in the **To** box and type **1** and then click **OK** to print only the first page. If directed to create an electronic printout, in the **Publish as PDF or XPS** dialog box, click **Options**, and then under **Range**, click the **Pages** option button, and then click **OK**. **Close Print Preview**, and then **Close** the report.

8 From the **Navigation Pane**, open the **Events** table, select all of the columns, and then apply **Best Fit** to all of the columns by double-clicking the right edge of any one of the selected columns. **Save** the table, and then cancel the selection. Display the table in **Print Preview**, change the orientation to **Landscape**, change the **Margins** to **Normal**, and then create a paper or electronic printout as directed. **Close Print Preview**, and then **Close** the table.

9 From the **Navigation Pane**, open your **1F Recruiters** table. Display the table in **Print Preview**, change the orientation to **Landscape**, and then create a paper or electronic printout as directed. **Close Print Preview**, and then **Close** the table.

10 Open the **Navigation Pane**, and be sure that all object names display fully. **Close** Access. As directed by your instructor, submit your database and the paper or electronic printouts of the three objects—one report and two tables—that are the results of this project. Specifically, in this project, using your own name, you created the following database and printouts or electronic printouts:

1. Lastname_Firstname_1F_Recruiting_Events	Database file
2. Event Details	Report (printout or electronic printout – Page 1)
3. Events	Table (printout or electronic printout)
4. Lastname Firstname 1F Recruiters	Table (printout or electronic printout)

END | You have completed Project 1F

CONTENT-BASED ASSESSMENTS

Mastering Access | Project 1G College Construction

Apply 1A and 1B skills from these Objectives:

1 Identify Good Database Design

2 Create a Table and Define Fields in a Blank Desktop Database

3 Change the Structure of Tables and Add a Second Table

4 Create a Query, Form, and Report

5 Close a Database and Exit Access

6 Use a Template to Create a Database

7 Organize Objects in the Navigation Pane

8 Create a New Table in a Database Created with a Template

9 Print a Report and a Table

In the following Mastering Access project, you will create one database to store information about construction projects for Texas Lakes Community College and a second database to store information about the public events related to the construction projects. Your completed database objects will look similar to Figure 1.55.

PROJECT FILES

For Project 1G, you will need the following files:

Blank desktop database
a01G_Projects (Excel workbook)
a01G_Contractors (Excel workbook)
Desktop Event Management template

You will save your databases as:

Lastname_Firstname_1G_College_Construction
Lastname_Firstname_1G_Public_Events

PROJECT RESULTS

Build from Scratch

FIGURE 1.55

(Project 1G College Construction continues on the next page)

CONTENT-BASED ASSESSMENTS

1 Start Access. Create a **Blank desktop database** in your **Access Chapter 1** folder. Name the database **Lastname_Firstname_1G_College_Construction** and then **Close** the **Navigation Pane**. Create the fields shown in **Table 1**.

2 For the **ID** field, change the **Data Type** to **Short Text**, rename the field to **Project ID** and then enter the three records shown in **Table 2**.

3 **Save** the table as **Lastname Firstname 1G Projects** and then **Close** the table. From your student data files, import and then append the data in the **Excel** file **a01G_Projects** to your **1G Projects** table. After importing, open your **1G Projects** table—eight records display.

4 In **Design** view, for the **Project ID** field, change the **Field Size** to **5** and then enter a **Description** of **Enter the Project ID using the format P-###** Save the changes to your table. Switch to **Datasheet** view, apply **Best Fit** to all of the fields in the table, and then **Save** your changes. Display the table in **Print Preview**, change the orientation to **Landscape**, and then create a paper or electronic printout as directed by your instructor. **Close Print Preview**, and then **Close** the table.

5 From your student data files, import the **Excel** file **a01G_Contractors** into the database as a new table; designate the first row as column headings and the **ID** field as the primary key. In the wizard, name the table **Lastname Firstname 1G Contractors** and then open your **1G Contractors** table—four records display. Apply **Best Fit** to all of the fields, and then **Save** your changes. Display the table in **Print Preview**, change the orientation to **Landscape**, and then create a paper or electronic printout as directed. **Close Print Preview**, and then **Close** the table.

6 Use the **Query Wizard** to create a simple query based on your **1G Projects** table. Include only the three fields that will answer the question, *For every site, what is the building project and the budget amount?* In the wizard, accept the default name for the query. Display the query in **Print Preview**, create a paper or electronic printout as directed, **Close Print Preview**, and then **Close** the query.

7 Open your **1G Projects** table, and then create a **Form** for this table. **Save** the form as **Lastname Firstname 1G Project Form** and then display and select the seventh record. By using the instructions in Activity 1.15, create a paper or electronic printout of only this record on one page as directed by your instructor. **Close** the form object, saving changes if prompted.

8 With your **1G Projects** table open, create a **Report**. Delete the **Budget Amount** field, and then sort the **Building Project** field in **Ascending** order. For the **Building Project**, **Site**, and **Contractor** fields, using the **Property Sheet**, change the **Width** of all three fields to **2** At the bottom of the report, delete the page number—**Page 1 of 1**. **Save** the report as **Lastname Firstname 1G Projects Report** and then display the report in **Print Preview**. Create a paper or electronic printout as directed. **Close Print Preview**.

9 **Close All** open objects. **Open** the **Navigation Pane**, arrange the objects by **Tables and Related Views**, and be sure that all object names display fully. **Close** the database, but do *not* close Access.

TABLE 1

Data Type		Short Text	Short Text	Short Text	Currency
Field Name	ID	Building Project	Site	Contractor	Budget Amount

Return to Step 2

TABLE 2

Project ID	Building Project	Site	Contractor	Budget Amount
P-356	Student Center, 3-story	Northeast Campus	RR Construction	61450000
P-823	Student Center, 2-story	Southeast Campus	RR Construction	41960000
P-157	Health Professions Center	Northwest Campus	Marshall Ellis Construction	42630000

Return to Step 3

(Project 1G College Construction continues on the next page)

CONTENT-BASED ASSESSMENTS

10 In the Access opening screen, search for **event** and then click the **Desktop Event Management** template. Save the database in your **Access Chapter 1** folder as **Lastname_Firstname_1G_Public_Events** and on the **Message Bar**, click **Enable Content**.

11 In the **Event List** multiple-items form or the **Event Details** single-record form—open by clicking **New Event** on the **Event List** form—enter the three records shown in **Table 3**.

12 **Close** the **Event List** form. **Open** the **Navigation Pane**, organize the objects by **Tables and Related Views**, and then open the **Current Events** *report* (green icon). Switch to **Layout** view. In the report, click in the title—*Current Events*—and then click to position the insertion point to the left of the letter *C*. Using your own name, type **Lastname Firstname 1G** and then press

Spacebar and Enter. If necessary, decrease the font size of the title so that the title does not overlap the date on the right side or does not extend to two lines. **Save** the report, display it in **Print Preview**, and then create a paper or electronic printout as directed. **Close Print Preview**, and then **Close** the report.

13 Open the **Navigation Pane**, and be sure that all object names display fully. **Close** Access. As directed by your instructor, submit your database and the paper or electronic printouts of the six objects—two tables, one query, one form, and two reports—that are the results of this project. Specifically, in this project, using your own name, you created the following database and printouts or electronic printouts:

1. Lastname_Firstname_1G_College_Construction	Database file
2. Lastname_Firstname_1G_Public_Events	Database file
3. Lastname Firstname 1G Projects	Table (printout or electronic printout)
4. Lastname Firstname 1G Contractors	Table (printout or electronic printout)
5. Lastname Firstname 1G Projects Query	Query (printout or electronic printout)
6. Lastname Firstname 1G Project Form	Form (printout or electronic printout - Record 7)
7. Lastname Firstname 1G Projects Report	Report (printout or electronic printout)
8. Current Events	Report (printout or electronic printout)

TABLE 3

ID	Title	Start Time	End Time	Description	Location
1	Groundbreaking	6/13/18 10a	6/13/18 11a	Student Center groundbreaking	Northeast Campus
2	Dedication	8/26/18 12:30 p	8/26/18 2p	Gymnasium building dedication	Southwest Campus
3	Community Arts Expo	10/5/18 6p	10/5/18 9p	Book and Art Expo at Library	Southeast Campus

(Return to Step 12)

END | You have completed Project 1G

CONTENT-BASED ASSESSMENTS

Apply a combination of the **1A** and **1B** skills.

Build from Scratch

| GO! Fix It | Project 1H Scholarships | Online |

Build from Scratch

| GO! Make It | Project 1I Theater Events | Online |

| GO! Solve It | Project 1J Athletic Scholarships | Online |

| GO! Solve It | Project 1K Student Activities | |

Build from Scratch

PROJECT FILES

For Project 1K, you will need the following files:

Desktop Event Management template
a01K_Student_Activities (Word document)

You will save your database as:

Lastname_Firstname_1K_Student_Activities

Use the Desktop Event Management template to create a database, and save it in your Access Chapter 1 folder as **Lastname_Firstname_1K_Student_Activities** From your student data files, use the information in the Word document a01K_Student_Activities to enter data into the Event List multiple-items form. Each event begins at 6 p.m. and ends at 10 p.m.

After entering the records, close the form, and arrange the Navigation Pane by Tables and Related Views. Open the Event Details *report*, and then add **Lastname Firstname 1K** to the beginning of the report title. If necessary, decrease the font size of the title so that it does not overlap the date and so that it displays on one line. Create a paper or electronic printout as directed—two pages result. As directed, submit your database and the paper or electronic printout of the report that are the results of this project. Specifically, in this project, using your own name, you created the following database and printout or electronic printout:

| 1. Lastname_Firstname_1K_Student_Activities | Database file |
| 2. Lastname Firstname 1K Event Details | Report (printout or electronic printout) |

Performance Level

Performance Criteria		Exemplary	Proficient	Developing
	Create database using Desktop Event Management template and enter data	Database created using the correct template, named correctly, and all data entered correctly.	Database created using the correct template, named correctly, but not all data entered correctly.	Database created using the correct template, but numerous errors in database name and data.
	Modify report	Event Details report title includes name and project on one line.	Event Details report title includes name and project, but not on one line.	Event Details report title does not include name and project.
	Create report printout	Event Details report printout is correct.	Event Details printout is incorrect.	Event Details report printout not created.

END | You have completed Project 1K

OUTCOMES-BASED ASSESSMENTS

RUBRIC

The following outcomes-based assessments are *open-ended assessments*. That is, there is no specific correct result; your result will depend on your approach to the information provided. Make *Professional Quality* your goal. Use the following scoring rubric to guide you in *how* to approach the problem and then to evaluate *how well* your approach solves the problem.

The *criteria*—Software Mastery, Content, Format & Layout, and Process—represent the knowledge and skills you have gained that you can apply to solving the problem. The *levels of performance*—Professional Quality, Approaching Professional Quality, or Needs Quality Improvements—help you and your instructor evaluate your result.

	Your completed project is of Professional Quality if you:	Your completed project is Approaching Professional Quality if you:	Your completed project Needs Quality Improvements if you:
1-Software Mastery	Choose and apply the most appropriate skills, tools, and features and identify efficient methods to solve the problem.	Choose and apply some appropriate skills, tools, and features, but not in the most efficient manner.	Choose inappropriate skills, tools, or features, or are inefficient in solving the problem.
2-Content	Construct a solution that is clear and well organized, contains content that is accurate, appropriate to the audience and purpose, and is complete. Provide a solution that contains no errors in spelling, grammar, or style.	Construct a solution in which some components are unclear, poorly organized, inconsistent, or incomplete. Misjudge the needs of the audience. Have some errors in spelling, grammar, or style, but the errors do not detract from comprehension.	Construct a solution that is unclear, incomplete, or poorly organized; contains some inaccurate or inappropriate content; and contains many errors in spelling, grammar, or style. Do not solve the problem.
3-Format & Layout	Format and arrange all elements to communicate information and ideas, clarify function, illustrate relationships, and indicate relative importance.	Apply appropriate format and layout features to some elements, but not others. Overuse features, causing minor distraction.	Apply format and layout that does not communicate information or ideas clearly. Do not use format and layout features to clarify function, illustrate relationships, or indicate relative importance. Use available features excessively, causing distraction.
4-Process	Use an organized approach that integrates planning, development, self-assessment, revision, and reflection.	Demonstrate an organized approach in some areas, but not others; or, use an insufficient process of organization throughout.	Do not use an organized approach to solve the problem.

OUTCOMES-BASED ASSESSMENTS

Build from
Scratch

GO! Think   Project 1L Student Clubs

PROJECT FILES

For Project 1L, you will need the following files:

Blank desktop database
a01L_Clubs (Word document)
a01L_Student_Clubs (Excel workbook)
a01L_Club_Presidents (Excel workbook)

You will save your database as

Lastname_Firstname_1L_Student_Clubs

Dr. Daniel Martinez, vice president of Student Services, needs a database that tracks information about student clubs. The database should contain two tables—one for club information and one for contact information for the club presidents.

Create a desktop database, and save the database in your Access Chapter 1 folder as **Lastname_Firstname_1L_Student_Clubs** From your student data files, use the information in the Word document a01L_Clubs to create the first table and to enter two records. Name the table appropriately to include your name and 1L, and then append the 23 records from the Excel workbook a01L_Student_Clubs to your table. For the Club ID and President ID fields, add a description and change the field size.

Create a second table in the database by importing 25 records from the Excel workbook a01L_Club_Presidents, and name the table appropriately to include your name and 1L. For the State and Postal Code fields, add a description and change the field size. Be sure that the field data types are correct—recall that numbers that are not used in calculations should have a data type of Short Text. Be sure all of the data and field names display in each table.

Create a simple query based on the Clubs table that answers the question, *What is the club name, meeting day, meeting time, campus, and Room ID for all of the clubs?* Create a form based on the Clubs table, saving it with an appropriate name that includes your name and 1L. Create a report based on the Presidents table, saving it with an appropriate name that includes your name and 1L, that displays the president's last name (in ascending order), the president's first name, and the phone number of every president. Change the width of the three fields so that there is less space between them, but being sure that each record prints on a single line. Delete the page number from the report.

Create paper or electronic printouts of the two tables, the query, only Record 21 of the form, and the report as directed and being sure that each object prints on one page. Organize the objects on the Navigation Pane by Tables and Related Views, and be sure that all object names display fully. As directed, submit your database and the paper or electronic printouts of the five objects—two tables, one query, one form, and one report—that are the results of this project.

Build from
Scratch

END | You have completed Project 1L

Build from
Scratch

GO! Think   Project 1M Faculty Training   Online

You and GO!   Project 1N Personal Contacts   Online

Build from
Scratch

GO! Cumulative Group Project   Project 1O Bell Orchid Hotels
                                                                  Online

Sort and Query a Database

GO! to Work
Video A2

ACCESS 2013

PROJECT 2A

OUTCOMES
Sort and query a database.

OBJECTIVES

1. Open and Save an Existing Database
2. Create Table Relationships
3. Sort Records in a Table
4. Create a Query in Design View
5. Create a New Query from an Existing Query
6. Sort Query Results
7. Specify Criteria in a Query

PROJECT 2B

OUTCOMES
Create complex queries.

OBJECTIVES

8. Specify Numeric Criteria in a Query
9. Use Compound Criteria in a Query
10. Create a Query Based on More Than One Table
11. Use Wildcards in a Query
12. Create Calculated Fields in a Query
13. Calculate Statistics and Group Data in a Query
14. Create a Crosstab Query
15. Create a Parameter Query

Robert Kneschke/Fotolia

In This Chapter

In this chapter, you will sort Access database tables and create and modify queries. To convert data into meaningful information, you must manipulate your data in a way that you can answer questions. One question might be: *Which students have a grade point average of 3.0 or higher?* By having this list of students, you could send information about scholarships or internships to those who meet the grade point average criteria. Queries are one of the most powerful tools in an Access database—a query not only answers questions, but it also provides data for meaningful reports.

The projects in this chapter relate to **Texas Lakes Community College**, which is located in the Austin, Texas, area. Its four campuses serve more than 30,000 students and offer more than 140 certificate programs and degrees. The college has a highly acclaimed Distance Education program and an extensive Workforce Development program. The college makes positive contributions to the community through cultural and athletic programs and has significant partnerships with businesses and nonprofit organizations. Popular fields of study include nursing and health care, solar technology, computer technology, and graphic design.

PROJECT 2A Instructors and Courses Database

MyITLab®
Project 2A Training

PROJECT ACTIVITIES

In Activities 2.01 through 2.17, you will assist Dr. Carolyn Judkins, dean of the Business Division at the Northeast Campus of Texas Lakes Community College, in locating information about instructors and courses in the division. Your completed database objects will look similar to Figure 2.1.

PROJECT FILES

For Project 2A, you will need the following file:

a02A_Instructors_Courses

You will save your database as:

Lastname_Firstname_2A_Instructors_Courses

PROJECT RESULTS

FIGURE 2.1 Project 2A Instructors and Courses

Objective 1   Open and Save an Existing Database

Video A2-1

There will be instances when you need to work with a database and still keep the original, unaltered version of the database. Like the other Microsoft Office 2013 applications, you can open a database file and save it with another name.

Activity 2.01 | Opening and Saving an Existing Database

1 ▶ **Start** Access. In the Access opening screen, click **Open Other Files**. Under **Open**, click **Computer**, and then on the right, click **Browse**. In the **Open** dialog box, navigate to the location where your student data files for this chapter are stored, and then double-click **a02A_Instructors_Courses** to open the database.

2 ▶ On the ribbon, click the **FILE tab**, and then click **Save As**. Under **File Types**, be sure **Save Database As** is selected. On the right, under **Database File Types**, be sure **Access Database** is selected, and then at the bottom of the screen, click **Save As**.

The Access Database file type saves your database in a format that enables the database to be opened with Access 2007, Access 2010, or Access 2013. If you are sharing your database with individuals who have an earlier version of Access, you can save the database in a version that is compatible with that application, although some functionality might be lost if an earlier version of Access does not have the same feature as the later version of Access.

3 ▶ In the **Save As** dialog box, navigate to the location where you are saving your databases. Create a **New folder** named **Access Chapter 2**, and then **Open** the folder. Click in the **File name** box, drag to select the existing text, and using your own name, type **Lastname_ Firstname_2A_Instructors_Courses** and then click **Save** or press Enter.

Use this technique when you need to keep a copy of the original database file.

4 ▶ On the **Message Bar**, notice the **SECURITY WARNING**. In the **Navigation Pane**, notice that this database contains two table objects. Compare your screen with Figure 2.2.

FIGURE 2.2

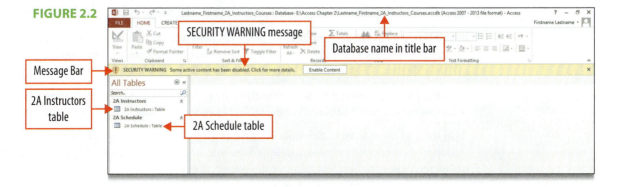

Activity 2.02 | Resolving Security Alerts and Renaming Tables

The *Message Bar* is the area directly below the ribbon that displays information such as security alerts when there is potentially unsafe, active content in an Office document that you open. Settings that determine the alerts that display on your Message Bar are set in the Access *Trust Center*, an area in Access where you can view the security and privacy settings for your Access installation.

You may not be able to change the settings in the Trust Center, depending upon decisions made by your organization. To display the Trust Center, click the FILE tab, click Options, and then click Trust Center.

1 On the **Message Bar**, click **Enable Content**.

> When working with the student data files that accompany this textbook, repeat this action each time you see the security warning. Databases for this textbook are safe to use on your computer.

2 In the **Navigation Pane**, right-click the **2A Instructors** table, and then click **Rename**. With the table name selected and using your own name, type **Lastname Firstname 2A Instructors** and then press Enter to rename the table. Use the same technique to **Rename** the **2A Schedule** table to **Lastname Firstname 2A Schedule**

> Including your name in the table enables you and your instructor to easily identify your work, because Access includes the table name in the header of your paper or electronic printouts.

3 Point to the right edge of the **Navigation Pane** to display the ⟷ pointer. Drag to the right to increase the width of the pane until both table names display fully.

Objective 2 | Create Table Relationships

Video A2-2

Access databases are relational databases because the tables in the database can relate—actually connect—to other tables through common fields. Recall that common fields are fields in two or more tables that store the same data; for example, a Student ID number may be stored in two tables in the same database.

After you have a table for each subject in your database, you must provide a way to connect the data in the tables when you need to obtain meaningful information from the stored data. To do this, create common fields in the related tables, and then define table *relationships*. A relationship is an association that you establish between two tables based on common fields. After the relationship is established, you can create a query, form, or report that displays information from more than one table.

Activity 2.03 | Selecting the Tables and Common Field to Establish the Table Relationship

In this activity, you will select the two tables in the database that you will use to establish the table relationship and identify the common field that will connect the tables.

1 In the **Navigation Pane**, double-click your **2A Instructors** table to open it in the object window. Examine the fields in the table. Double-click your **2A Schedule** table, and examine the fields in the table.

> In the 2A Instructors table, *Instructor ID* is the primary key field, which ensures that each instructor has only one record in the table. No two instructors have the same Instructor ID.

> In the 2A Schedule table, *Schedule ID* is the primary key field. Every scheduled course section during an academic term has a unique Schedule ID. Some colleges refer to this as the *Section Number*.

2 In the **2A Schedule** table, scroll to display the **Instructor ID** field—third from last column—and then compare your screen with Figure 2.3.

Both the 2A Instructors table and the 2A Schedule table include the *Instructor ID* field, which is the common field of the two tables. Because *one* instructor can teach *many* different courses, *one* Instructor ID can be present *many* times in the 2A Schedule table. When the relationship is established, it will be a ***one-to-many relationship***, which is the most common type of relationship in a relational database.

FIGURE 2.3

3 In the object window, right-click the **2A Schedule object tab**, and then click **Close All** to close both tables. On the ribbon, click the **DATABASE TOOLS tab**, and then in the **Relationships group**, click **Relationships**. Compare your screen with Figure 2.4.

You can close all of the open objects by right-clicking any object tab. The Show Table dialog box displays in the Relationships window. In the Show Table dialog box, the Tables tab displays the two tables that are in this database.

FIGURE 2.4

4 Point to the title bar of the **Show Table** dialog box, and then drag downward and to the right to move the dialog box away from the top of the **Relationships** window.

Moving the Show Table dialog box enables you to see the tables as they are added to the Relationships window.

5 In the **Show Table** dialog box, if necessary, click your **2A Instructors** table, and then click **Add**. In the **Show Table** dialog box, double-click your **2A Schedule** table to add it to the **Relationships** window. In the **Show Table** dialog box, click **Close**, and then compare your screen with Figure 2.5.

You can use either technique to add a table to the Relationships window. A ***field list***—a list of the field names in a table—for each of the two table objects displays, and each table's primary key is identified by the key icon. Although this database has only two tables, larger databases have many tables. Scroll bars in a field list indicate that there are fields that are not currently in view.

FIGURE 2.5

Field list for 2A Instructors table

Field list for 2A Schedule table

Primary key icon

Scroll bar indicates there are fields out of view

A L E R T ! **Are There More Than Two Field Lists in the Relationships Window?**

In the Show Table dialog box, if you double-click a table name more than one time, a duplicate field list displays in the Relationships window. To remove a field list from the Relationships window, right-click the title bar of the field list, and then click Hide Table. Alternatively, click anywhere in the field list, and then on the DESIGN tab, in the Relationships group, click Hide Table.

6 ▶ In the **2A Schedule** field list—the field list on the right—point to the title bar to display the ⬚ pointer. Drag the field list to the right until there are about two inches of space between the field lists.

7 ▶ In the **2A Instructors** field list—the field list on the left—point to the lower right corner of the field list to display the ⬚ pointer, and then drag downward and to the right to increase the height and width of the field list until the entire name of the table in the title bar displays and all of the field names display.

This action enables you to see all of the available fields and removes the vertical scroll bar.

8 ▶ Use the same technique to resize the **2A Schedule** field list so that the table name and all of the field names display as shown in Figure 2.6.

Recall that *one* instructor can teach *many* scheduled courses. The arrangement of field lists in the Relationships window displays the *one table* on the left side and the *many table* on the right side. Recall also that the primary key in each table is the field that contains the data that uniquely identifies each record in the table. In the 2A Instructors table, each instructor is uniquely identified by the Instructor ID. In the 2A Schedule table, each scheduled course section is uniquely identified by the Schedule ID.

FIGURE 2.6

Table on the *one* side of the relationship

Table on the *many* side of the relationship

Instructor ID is common field for the two tables

N O T E **The Field That Is Highlighted Does Not Matter**

After you rearrange the field lists in the Relationships window, the highlighted field name indicates the active field list, which is the list that you moved or resized last. This is of no consequence for this activity.

9 In the **2A Instructors** field list, point to **Instructor ID**, and then drag the field name downward and to the right into the **2A Schedule** field list until the ⬚ pointer's arrow is on top of **Instructor ID**. Release the mouse button to display the **Edit Relationships** dialog box.

> As you drag, a small graphic displays to indicate that you are dragging a field name from one field list to another. A table relationship works by matching data in two fields—the common field. In these two tables, the common field has the same name—*Instructor ID*. Common fields are not required to have the same name; however, they must have the same data type and field size.

 ANOTHER WAY On the DESIGN tab, in the Tools group, click Edit Relationships. In the Edit Relationships dialog box, click Create New. In the Create New dialog box, designate the tables and fields that will create the relationship and click OK.

10 Point to the title bar of the **Edit Relationships** dialog box, and then drag the dialog box downward and to the right below the two field lists as shown in Figure 2.7.

> By dragging the common field, you create the *one-to-many* relationship. In the 2A Instructors table, Instructor ID is the primary key. In the 2A Schedule table, Instructor ID is the *foreign key* field. The foreign key is the field in the related table used to connect to the primary key in another table. The field on the *one* side of the relationship is typically the primary key.

FIGURE 2.7

Activity 2.04 | Setting Relationship Options

In this activity, you will set relationship options that enable you to work with records in the two related tables.

1 In the **Edit Relationships** dialog box, click to select the **Enforce Referential Integrity** check box. Notice that the two options under **Enforce Referential Integrity** are now available.

> *Referential integrity* is a set of rules that Access uses to ensure that the data between related tables is valid. Enforcing referential integrity ensures that an Instructor ID cannot be added to a course in the 2A Schedule table if the Instructor ID is *not* included in the 2A Instructors table. Similarly, enforcing referential integrity without selecting a cascade option below ensures that you cannot delete an instructor from the 2A Instructors table if there is a course that has been assigned to that instructor in the 2A Schedule table.

> After selecting Enforce Referential Integrity, *cascade options*—relationship options that enable you to update records in related tables when referential integrity is enforced—become available for use.

2 ▶ In the **Edit Relationships** dialog box, click to select the **Cascade Update Related Fields** check box.

The *Cascade Update Related Fields* option enables you to change the data in the primary key field for the table on the *one* side of the relationship, and updates that change to any fields in the related table that store the same data. For example, in the 2A Instructors table, if you change the data in the Instructor ID field for one instructor, Access automatically finds every scheduled course assigned to that instructor in the 2A Schedule table and changes the data in the common field, in this case, the Instructor ID field. Without this option, if you try to change the Instructor ID number for an instructor, an error message displays if there is a related record in the related table on the *many* side of the relationship.

3 ▶ In the **Edit Relationships** dialog box, click to select the **Cascade Delete Related Records** check box, and then compare your screen with Figure 2.8.

The *Cascade Delete Related Records* option enables you to delete a record in the table on the *one* side of the relationship and also delete all of the related records in related tables. For example, if an instructor retires or leaves the college and the courses that the instructor teaches must be canceled because no other instructor can be found, you can delete the instructor's record from the 2A Instructors table, and then all of the courses that are assigned to that instructor in the 2A Schedule table are also deleted. Without this option, an error message displays if you try to delete the instructor's record from the 2A Instructors table.

FIGURE 2.8

4 ▶ In the **Edit Relationships** dialog box, click **Create**, and then compare your screen with Figure 2.9.

The Edit Relationships dialog box closes and a *join line*—the line connecting or joining the two tables—displays between the two field lists. The join line connects the primary key field—Instructor ID—in the 2A Instructors field list to the common field—Instructor ID—in the 2A Schedule field list. On the join line, *1* indicates the *one* side of the relationship, and the infinity symbol (∞) indicates the *many* side of the relationship. These symbols display when referential integrity is enforced.

FIGURE 2.9

Activity 2.05 | Printing and Saving a Relationship Report

The Relationships window provides a map of how your database tables are related, and you can print and save this information as a report.

1 Under **RELATIONSHIP TOOLS**, on the **DESIGN tab**, in the **Tools group**, click **Relationship Report**.

The report is created and displays in the object window in Print Preview.

2 On the **PRINT PREVIEW tab**, in the **Page Size group**, click **Margins**, and then click **Normal** to increase the margins slightly—some printers cannot print with narrow margins. Compare your screen with Figure 2.10. Create a paper or electronic printout of the relationship report as directed.

FIGURE 2.10

3 On the **Quick Access Toolbar**, click **Save** 🖫. In the **Save As** dialog box, click **OK** to accept the default report name.

The report name displays in the Navigation Pane under *Unrelated Objects*. Because the report is just a map of the relationship between the tables, and not a report containing records from a table, it is not associated with or related to any tables.

4 In the object window, click **Close** ☒ to close the report, and then **Close** ☒ the **Relationships** window.

> **NOTE** | **Close Print Preview and the Relationship Report**
>
> If you click Close Print Preview when the report is displayed in Print Preview, the Relationship Report displays in Design view in the object window. If this happens, you can Close the object while it is displayed in this view.

Activity 2.06 | Displaying Subdatasheet Records

When you open the table on the *one* side of the relationship, the related records from the table on the *many* side are available for you to view and to modify.

1 In the **Navigation Pane**, double-click your **2A Instructors** table to open it in the object window, and then **Close** ☒ the **Navigation Pane**.

> **2** On the left side of the first record—*Instructor ID* of *1224567*—click ⊞, and then compare your screen with Figure 2.11.

> The ⊞ symbol to the left of a record in a table indicates that *related* records may exist in another table. Click ⊞ to display the related records in a ***subdatasheet***. In the first record for *Craig Fresch*, you can see that related records exist in the 2A Schedule table—he is scheduled to teach five LGL (Legal) courses. The ⊞ symbol to the left of each record displays because you created a relationship between the two tables using the Instructor ID field—the common field.

> When you click ⊞ to display the subdatasheet, the symbol changes to ⊟, an indication that the subdatasheet is expanded. Click ⊟ to collapse the subdatasheet.

FIGURE 2.11

Course sections from your 2A Schedule table for *Associate Professor Craig Fresch*

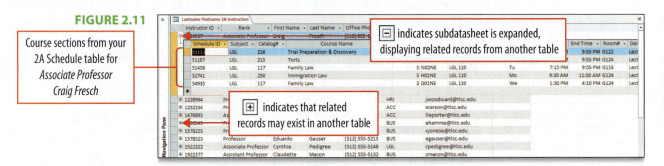

| *More* **Knowledge** | **Other Types of Relationships: One-to-One and Many-to-Many** |

The type of relationship is determined by the placement of the primary key field. A one-to-one relationship exists between two tables when a record in one table is related to only one record in a second table. In this case, both tables use the same field as the primary key. This is most often used when data is placed in a separate table because access to that information is restricted; for example, using an Employee ID field as the primary key field, there is one table for contact information and a second table with payroll information.

A many-to-many relationship between tables exists when many records in one table are related to many records in another table. For example, many students can enroll in many courses. To create a many-to-many relationship, you must create a third table that contains the primary key fields from both tables. In the Relationships window, you create a join line from this table to the other two tables. In effect, you create multiple one-to-many relationships.

Activity 2.07 | Testing Cascade Options

Recall that cascade options enable you to make changes to records on the *one* side table of the relationship and update or delete records in the table on the *many* side of the relationship. In this activity, you will change the data in the Instructor ID field—the primary key field—for one instructor, and then delete all of the records associated with another instructor from both tables.

> **1** In the subdatasheet for the first record—*Instructor ID* of *1224567*—notice that the first course that this instructor is scheduled to teach has a *Schedule ID* of *51113—LGL 216*. In the **2A Instructors** table, to the left of the first record, click ⊟ to collapse the subdatasheet.

> **2** If necessary, in the first record, in the **Instructor ID** field, select the data—**1224567**. Type **8224567** and then press ↓ to save the record.

> Because you enabled Cascade Update Related Fields in the Edit Relationships dialog box, you can change the data in the Instructor ID field—the primary key field—and all records in the 2A Schedule table that store that Instructor ID number are automatically updated. If this option is not enabled, an error message displays.

> **3** **Open** ≫ the **Navigation Pane**. In the **Navigation Pane**, double-click your **2A Schedule** table to open it, and then **Close** ≪ the **Navigation Pane**.

 ANOTHER WAY   Press F11 to open or close the Navigation Pane.

4 Scroll to locate the record with a **Schedule ID** of **51113**—*LGL 216*. If necessary, scroll to the right to display the **Instructor ID** field, and notice that for this record, the **Instructor ID** is **8224567**. Compare your screen with Figure 2.12.

The Cascade Update Related Fields option enables you to change the data in the primary key field in your 2A Instructors table, and the five related records for *Craig Fresch* in the 2A Schedule table were updated to store his new Instructor ID of *8224567*.

FIGURE 2.12

Course assigned to *Craig Fresch*

Instructor ID updated by changing Instructor ID in 2A Instructors table

5 **Close** ☒ your **2A Schedule** table. In your **2A Instructors** table, scroll to display the last few records. On the left side of the record for **Instructor ID** of **6145288**—*Professor Ivey Clarke*—click ⊞ to display the subdatasheet. Notice that this instructor is scheduled to teach two courses—*Schedule IDs* of *42837* and *42930*.

6 Click ⊟ to collapse the subdatasheet. For the same record—*Instructor ID* of *6145288*—point to the record selector box to display the ➡ pointer, and then click to select the record. On the **HOME tab**, in the **Records group**, click **Delete**.

A message displays warning you that this record and related records in related tables will be deleted. The record you selected does not display in the table, and the next record is selected. Because you enabled Cascade Delete Related Records, you are able to delete the record for Professor Ivey Clarke and delete the two courses she is scheduled to teach from the 2A Schedule table—with no error message.

🔄 **ANOTHER WAY**   With the record selected, press ⌨Del; or with the record selected, right-click within the record, and then click Delete Record.

7 In the message box, click **Yes**.

The record for *Instructor ID* of *6145288* is deleted, and the two courses she was scheduled to teach are deleted from the 2A Schedule table. On the Quick Access Toolbar, Undo is unavailable—if you mistakenly delete a record and its related records, you must enter them again in both tables.

8 **Open** ☒ the **Navigation Pane**, open your **2A Schedule** table, and then **Close** ☒ the **Navigation Pane**. Scroll through the records and notice that the records for a **Schedule ID** of **42837** and **42930** have been deleted from the table.

The Cascade Delete Related Records option in the Edit Relationships dialog box enables you to delete a record in the table on the *one* side of the relationship—2A Instructors—and simultaneously delete the records in the table on the *many* side of the relationship—2A Schedule—that are related to the deleted record.

9 In the object window, right-click either **object tab**, and then click **Close All** to close both tables.

Video A2-3

Sorting is the process of arranging data in a specific order based on the value in a field. For example, you can sort the names in your contact list alphabetically by each person's last name, or you can sort your music collection by the artist. Initially, records in an Access table display in the order they are entered into the table. After you close the table and reopen it, the records display in order by the primary key field.

Activity 2.08 | Sorting Records in a Table in Ascending or Descending Order

In this activity, you will determine the departments of the faculty in the Business Division by sorting the data. Data can be sorted in either *ascending order* or *descending order*. Ascending order sorts text alphabetically (A to Z) and sorts numbers from the lowest number to the highest number. Descending order sorts text in reverse alphabetical order (Z to A) and sorts numbers from the highest number to the lowest number.

1 **Open** [»] the **Navigation Pane**, open your **2A Instructors** table, and then **Close** [«] the **Navigation Pane**. Notice that the records in the table are sorted in ascending order by the **Instructor ID** field, which is the primary key field.

2 In the field names row, click the **Department arrow**, click **Sort A to Z**, and then compare your screen with Figure 2.13.

> To sort records in a table, click the arrow to the right of the field name in the column on which you want to sort, and then click the sort order. After a field is sorted, a small arrow in the field name box indicates the sort order. For the Department field, the small arrow points upward, indicating an ascending sort; on the ribbon, Ascending is selected.

> The records display in alphabetical order by the Department field. Because the department names are now grouped together, you can quickly scroll through the table to see the instructors for each department. The first record in the table has no data in the Department field because the *Instructor ID* of 9999999 is reserved for *Staff*, a designation that is used until a scheduled course has been assigned to a specific instructor.

🔁 **ANOTHER WAY**   Click in the field in any record, and then on the HOME tab, in the Sort & Filter group, click Ascending; or right-click in the field in any record, and then click Sort A to Z.

FIGURE 2.13

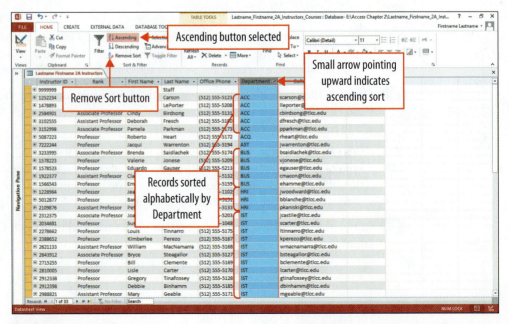

3 On the **HOME tab**, in the **Sort & Filter group**, click **Remove Sort** to clear the sort and to return the records to the default sort order, which is by the primary key field—**Instructor ID**.

4 Click the **Last Name arrow**, and then click **Sort Z to A**.

The records in the table are sorted by the Last Name field in reverse alphabetical order. The small arrow in the field name box points downward, indicating a descending sort. On the ribbon, Descending is selected.

5 In the **Sort & Filter group**, click **Remove Sort** to clear the sort.

Activity 2.09 | Sorting Records in a Table on Multiple Fields

To sort a table on two or more fields, first identify the fields that will act as the *outermost sort field* and the *innermost sort field*. The outermost sort field is the first level of sorting, and the innermost sort field is the second level of sorting. To alphabetize a table by Last Name and then First Name—also called First Name within Last Name—the Last Name field is identified as the outermost sort field. If there are duplicate last names, the records should be further sorted by the First Name field—the innermost sort field. For tables, you sort the *innermost* field *first* and then sort the outermost field.

In this activity, you will sort the records by Last Name—innermost sort field—within the Department—outermost sort field.

1 In the **Last Name** field, click in any record. On the ribbon, on the **HOME tab**, in the **Sort & Filter group**, click **Ascending**.

The records are sorted in ascending order by Last Name—the innermost sort field.

2 In any record, point in the **Department** field, right-click, and then click **Sort Z to A**. Compare your screen with Figure 2.14.

The records are sorted in descending order first by Department—the outermost sort field. Within each Department grouping, the records are sorted in ascending order by Last Name—the innermost sort field. Records can be sorted on multiple fields using both ascending and descending order.

FIGURE 2.14

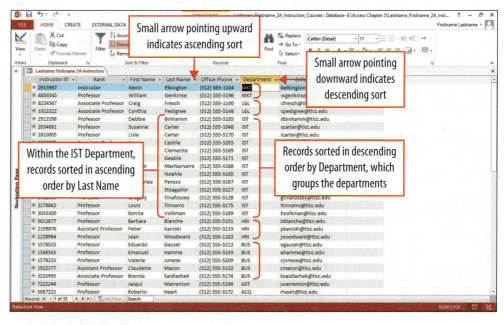

3 On the ribbon, click the **FILE tab**, click **Print**, and then click **Print Preview**. On the **PRINT PREVIEW tab**, in the **Page Layout group**, click **Landscape**. In the **Zoom group**, click **Two Pages**, and notice that the table will print on two pages.

4 In the **Print group**, click **Print**. In the **Print** dialog box, under **Print Range**, click in the **From** box, type **1** and then click in the **To** box. Type **1** to print only the first page. If directed to submit a paper printout, click **OK**. If directed to create an electronic printout, in the **Print** dialog box, click **Cancel**. On the **PRINT PREVIEW tab**, in the **Data group**, click **PDF or XPS**, click **Options**, and then under **Range**, click the **Pages** option button, click **OK**, and then click **Publish**.

5 In the object window, **Close** ☒ the table. In the message box, click **Yes** to save the changes to the sort order.

6 **Open** ☒ the **Navigation Pane**, double-click your **2A Instructors** table to open it, and then **Close** ☒ the **Navigation Pane**. Notice that the table displays the sort order you specified.

7 On the **HOME tab**, in the **Sort & Filter group**, click **Remove Sort**. **Close** ☒ the table, and in the message box, click **Yes** to save the table with the sort removed.

> Generally, tables are not stored with the data sorted. Instead, queries are created that sort the data, and then reports are created to display the sorted data.

Objective 4   Create a Query in Design View

Video A2-4

Recall that a select query is a database object that retrieves (selects) specific data from one or more tables and then displays the specified data in a table in Datasheet view. A query answers a question, such as *Which instructors teach courses in the IST department?* Unless a query has already been designed to ask this question, you must create a new query.

Database users rarely need to see all of the records in all of the tables. That is why a query is so useful; it creates a ***subset*** of records—a portion of the total records—according to your specifications and then displays only those records.

Activity 2.10 │ Creating a New Select Query in Design View

Previously, you created a query using the Query Wizard. To create more complex queries, use Query Design view. The table (or tables) from which a query selects its data is referred to as the ***data source***.

1 On the ribbon, click the **CREATE tab**, and then in the **Queries group**, click **Query Design**. Compare your screen with Figure 2.15.

> A new query opens in Design view, and the Show Table dialog box displays, which lists both tables in the database.

FIGURE 2.15

2 In the **Show Table** dialog box, double-click **2A Instructors**, and then, in the dialog box, click **Close**.

> A field list for your 2A Instructors table displays in the upper area of the query window. Instructor ID is the primary key field in this table.

> The query window has two parts: the upper area called the *table area* that displays the field lists for tables that are used in the query, and the lower area called the *design grid* that displays the design of the query.

ALERT!   **Is There More Than One Field List in the Table Area?**

If you double-click a table more than one time, a duplicate field list displays in the table area of the query window. To remove a field list from the query window, right-click the title bar of the field list, and then click Remove Table.

3 Point to the lower right corner of the field list to display the ⬦ pointer, and then drag downward and to the right to resize the field list, displaying all of the field names and the entire table name. In the **2A Instructors** field list, double-click **Rank**, and then look at the design grid.

> The Rank field name displays in the design grid in the Field row. You limit the fields that display in the query results by placing only the desired field names in the design grid.

4 In the **2A Instructors** field list, point to **First Name**, drag the field name down into the design grid until the ⬦ pointer displays in the **Field** row in the second column, and then release the mouse button. Compare your screen with Figure 2.16.

> This is a second way to add field names to the design grid. As you drag the field, a small rectangular shape attaches to the mouse pointer. When you release the mouse button, the field name displays in the Field row.

FIGURE 2.16

5 In the design grid, in the **Field** row, click in the third column, and then click the **arrow** that displays. From the list, click **Last Name** to add the field to the design grid.

> This is a third way to add field names to the design grid.

6 Using one of the three techniques you just practiced, add the **Office Phone** field to the fourth column and the **Department** field to the fifth column in the design grid.

ALERT!   **Is There a Duplicate Field Name or an Incorrect Field Name in the Design Grid?**

If you double-click a field name more than one time, a duplicate field name displays in the design grid. To remove a duplicate field name, in the design grid, in the Field row, right-click the duplicate field name, and then click Cut. Use this same method to delete a field name that you placed in the design grid by mistake. As you progress in your study of query design, you will learn alternate ways to delete field names from the design grid.

Activity 2.11 | Running, Saving, Printing, and Closing a Query

After you design a query, you *run* the query to display the results. When you run a query, Access looks at the records in the table (or tables) you have included in the query, finds the records that match the specified conditions (if any), and displays only those records in a datasheet. Only the fields that you have added to the design grid display in the query results. The query always runs using the current table or tables, presenting the most up-to-date information.

1 Under **QUERY TOOLS**, on the **DESIGN tab**, in the **Results group**, click **Run**, and then compare your screen with Figure 2.17.

> This query answers the question, *What is the rank, first name, last name, office phone number, and department of all of the instructors in the 2A Instructors table?* A query is a subset of the records in the table, arranged in Datasheet view, using the fields and conditions that you specify in the design grid. The five fields you specified in the design grid display in columns, and the records from the 2A Instructors table display in rows.

ANOTHER WAY   On the DESIGN tab, in the Results group, click the top portion of the View button, which runs the query by switching to Datasheet view.

FIGURE 2.17

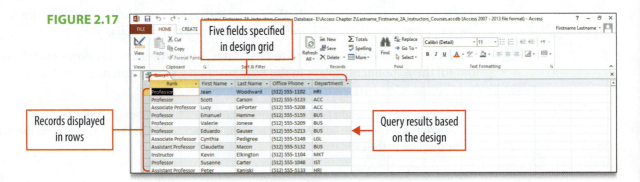

2 On the **Quick Access Toolbar**, click **Save**. In the **Save As** dialog box, type **Lastname Firstname 2A Instructors Query** and then click **OK**.

> The query name displays on the object tab in the object window. Save your queries if you are likely to ask the same question again; doing so will save you the effort of creating the query again to answer the same question.

ALERT!   **Does a Message Display After Entering a Query Name?**

Query names are limited to 64 characters. For all projects, if you have a long last name or first name that results in your query name exceeding the 64-character limit, use your first initial instead of your first name.

---

3 On the ribbon, click the **FILE tab**, click **Print**, and then click **Print Preview**. Create a paper or electronic printout as directed, and then click **Close Print Preview**.

> Queries answer questions and gather information from the data in tables. Typically, queries are created as a basis for a report, but query results can be printed just like any table of data.

4 **Close** the query. **Open** the **Navigation Pane**, and then notice that your **2A Instructors Query** object displays under your **2A Instructors** table object.

> The new query name displays in the Navigation Pane under the table with which it is related—the 2A Instructors table, which is the data source. Only the design of the query is saved; the records reside in the table object. Each time you open a query, Access runs it again and displays the results based on the data stored in the data source. Thus, the results of the query always reflect the most up-to-date information.

Video A2-5

You can create a new query from scratch, or you can copy an existing query and modify the design to answer another question. Using an existing query saves you time if your new query uses all or some of the same fields and conditions in an existing query.

Activity 2.12 | Copying an Existing Query

1 In the **Navigation Pane**, right-click your **2A Instructors Query**, and then click **Copy**.

> **ANOTHER WAY**
> To create a copy of the query, in the Navigation Pane, click the query name to select it. On the HOME tab, in the Clipboard group, click Copy.

2 In the **Navigation Pane**, point to a blank area, right-click, and then click **Paste**.

The Paste As dialog box displays, which enables you to name the copied query.

> **ANOTHER WAY**
> On the HOME tab, in the Clipboard group, click Paste.

3 In the **Paste As** dialog box, type **Lastname Firstname 2A Instructor IDs Query** and then click **OK**.

A new query, based on a copy of your 2A Instructors Query is created and displays in the Navigation Pane under its data source—your 2A Instructors table object.

4 In the **Navigation Pane**, double-click your **2A Instructor IDs Query** to run the query and open the query results in **Datasheet** view. **Close** `«` the **Navigation Pane**.

Activity 2.13 | Modifying the Design of a Query

1 On the **HOME tab**, in the **Views group**, click the top portion of the **View** button to switch to **Design** view.

> **ANOTHER WAY**
> On the HOME tab, in the Views group, click the View arrow, and then click Design View; or on the right side of the status bar, click Design View. If the query is not open, in the Navigation Pane, right-click the query name, and then click Design View.

2 In the design grid, point to the thin gray selection bar above the **Office Phone** field name to display the ↓ pointer, and then compare your screen with Figure 2.18.

FIGURE 2.18

3 With the ⊥ pointer displayed in the selection bar above the **Office Phone** field name, click to select the column, and then press Del.

This action deletes the field from the query design only—it has no effect on the field in the data source—2A Instructors table. The Department field moves to the left. Similarly, by using the selection bar, you can drag to select multiple fields and delete them at one time.

↻ ANOTHER WAY   In the design grid, click in the field name. On the DESIGN tab, in the Query Setup group, click Delete Columns; or right-click the field name, and then click Cut; or select the column, and on the HOME tab, in the Records group, click Delete.

4 Point to the selection bar above the **First Name** column, and then click to select the column. In the selected column, point to the selection bar, hold down the left mouse button to display the ▧ pointer, and then drag to the right until a dark vertical line displays on the right side of the **Last Name** column. Release the mouse button to position the **First Name** field in the third column.

To rearrange fields in a query, first select the field to move, and then drag it to a new position in the design grid.

5 Using the technique you just practiced, move the **Department** field to the left of the **Rank** field.

6 From the field list, drag the **Instructor ID** field down to the first column in the design grid until the ▧ pointer displays, and then release the mouse button. Compare your screen with Figure 2.19.

The Instructor ID field displays in the first column, and the remaining four fields move to the right. Use this method to insert a field to the left of a field already displayed in the design grid.

FIGURE 2.19

7 On the **DESIGN tab**, in the **Results group**, click **Run**.

This query answers the question, *What is the instructor ID, department, rank, last name, and first name of every instructor in the 2A Instructors table?* The results of the query are a subset of the records stored in the 2A Instructors table. The records are sorted by the table's primary key field—Instructor ID.

8 On the **FILE tab**, click **Print**, and then click **Print Preview**. Create a paper or electronic printout as directed, and then click **Close Print Preview**.

9 **Close** ✕ the query. In the message box, click **Yes** to save the changes to the query design—deleting a field, moving two fields, and adding a field. **Open** » the **Navigation Pane**.

The query is saved and closed, and the query name displays in the Navigation Pane under the related table. Recall that only the *design* of the query is saved; the records reside in the related table.

Video A2-6

You can sort the results of a query in ascending or descending order in either Datasheet view or Design view. Use Design view if your query results should always display in a specified sort order or if you intend to use the sorted results in a report.

Activity 2.14 | Sorting Query Results

In this activity, you will copy an existing query and then sort the query results by using the Sort row in Design view.

1 In the **Navigation Pane**, right-click your **2A Instructor IDs Query**, and then click **Copy**. In the **Navigation Pane**, point to a blank area, right-click, and then click **Paste**.

2 In the **Paste As** dialog box, type **Lastname Firstname 2A Department Sort Query** and then click **OK**. Increase the width of the **Navigation Pane** so that the names of all of the objects display fully.

> A new query is created based on a copy of your 2A Instructor IDs Query; that is, the new query includes the same fields in the same order as the query that you copied.

3 In the **Navigation Pane**, right-click your **2A Department Sort Query**, and then click **Design View**. **Close** « the **Navigation Pane**.

> Use this technique to display the query in Design view if you are redesigning the query. Recall that if you double-click a query name in the Navigation Pane, Access runs the query and displays the query results.

4 In the design grid, in the **Sort** row, under **Last Name**, click to display the insertion point and an arrow. Click the **arrow**, click **Ascending**, and then compare your screen with Figure 2.20.

FIGURE 2.20

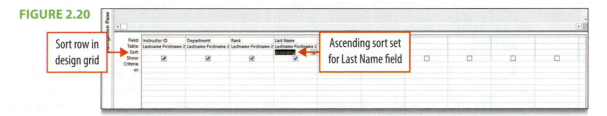

Sort row in design grid

Ascending sort set for Last Name field

5 On the **DESIGN tab**, in the **Results group**, click **Run**.

> In the query results, the records are sorted in ascending order by the Last Name field, and two instructors have the same last name of *Carter*—*Susanne* and *Lisle*.

6 On the **HOME tab**, in the **Views group**, click the top of the **View** button to switch to **Design** view.

7 In the design grid, click in the **Sort** row under **First Name**, click the **arrow**, and then click **Ascending**. **Run** the query.

> In the query results, the records are sorted first by the Last Name field. If two instructors have the same last name, then those records are sorted by the First Name field. The two instructors with the same last name of *Carter* are sorted by their first names, and the two records with the same last name of *Fresch* are sorted by their first names.

8 Switch to **Design** view. In the design grid, click in the **Sort** row under **Department**, click the **arrow**, and then click **Descending**. **Run** the query, and then compare your screen with Figure 2.21.

In Design view, fields with a Sort setting are sorted from left to right. That is, the sorted field on the left becomes the outermost sort field, and the sorted field on the right becomes the innermost sort field. Thus, the records in this query are sorted first in descending order by the Department field—the leftmost sort field. Then, within each department, the records are sorted in ascending order by the Last Name field. And, finally, within each duplicate last name, the records are sorted in ascending order by the First Name field.

If you run a query and the sorted results are not what you intended, be sure the fields are displayed from left to right according to the groupings that you desire.

FIGURE 2.21

9 Display the query results in **Print Preview**. Create a paper or electronic printout as directed, and then click **Close Print Preview**. **Close** ⊠ the query. In the message box, click **Yes** to save the changes to the query design.

> **More Knowledge**   **Sorting in Design View or Datasheet View**
>
> If you add a sort order to the *design* of a query, it remains as a permanent part of the query design. If you use the sort buttons in Datasheet view, the sort order will override the sort order of the query design and can be saved as part of the query. A sort order designated in Datasheet view does not display in the Sort row of the query design grid. As with sorting tables, in Datasheet view, a small arrow displays to the right of the field name to indicate the sort order of the field.

Objective 7   Specify Criteria in a Query

Video A2-7

Queries locate information in a table based on *criteria* that you specify as part of the query design. Criteria are conditions that identify the specific records that you are looking for. Criteria enable you to ask a more specific question; therefore, you will get a more specific result. For example, to find out how many instructors are in the IST department, limit the results to display only that specific department by entering criteria in the design grid.

Activity 2.15 | Specifying Text Criteria in a Query

In this activity, you will assist Dean Judkins by creating a query to answer the question, *How many instructors are in the IST Department?*

1 On the ribbon, click the **CREATE tab**, and then in the **Queries group**, click **Query Design**.

2 In the **Show Table** dialog box, double-click your **2A Instructors** table to add it to the table area, and then **Close** the **Show Table** dialog box.

3 By dragging the lower right corner downward and to the right, resize the field list to display all of the field names and the table name. Add the following fields to the design grid in the order given: **Department**, **Instructor ID**, **Rank**, **Last Name**, and **First Name**.

4 In the design grid, click in the **Criteria** row under **Department**, type **IST** and then press Enter. Compare your screen with Figure 2.22.

Access places quotation marks around the criteria to indicate that this is a ***text string***—a sequence of characters. Use the Criteria row to specify the criteria that will limit the results of the query to your exact specifications. The criteria is not case sensitive; you can type *ist* instead of *IST*.

FIGURE 2.22

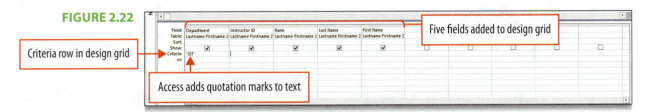

Criteria row in design grid

Five fields added to design grid

Access adds quotation marks to text

---

5 In the design grid, click in the **Sort** row under **Last Name**, click the **arrow**, and then click **Ascending**. Click in the **Sort** row under **First Name**, click the **arrow**, and then click **Ascending**.

6 **Run** the query, and then compare your screen with Figure 2.23.

Thirteen records display. There are 13 instructors in the IST Department; or, more specifically, there are 13 records that have *IST* in the Department field. The records are sorted in ascending order, first by the Last Name field and then by the First Name field.

FIGURE 2.23

Thirteen records match criteria—*IST* in the Department field

Within Last Name field, records sorted in ascending order by the First Name field

Records sorted in ascending order by the Last Name field

---

7 **Save** 💾 the query as **Lastname Firstname 2A IST Query** and then display the query results in **Print Preview**. Create a paper or electronic printout as directed, and then click **Close Print Preview**.

8 Close ⊠ the query, **Open** ⧉ the **Navigation Pane**, and then notice that your **2A IST Query** object name displays under your **2A Instructors** table—its data source.

> Recall that in the Navigation Pane, queries display an icon of two overlapping datasheets.

Activity 2.16 | Specifying Criteria and Hiding the Field in the Query Results

So far, all of the fields that you included in the query design have also been included in the query results. There are times when you need to use the field in the query design, but you do not need to display that field in the results, usually, when the data in the field is the same for all of the records. In this activity, you will create a query to answer the question, *Which instructors have a rank of professor?*

1 Close ⧉ the **Navigation Pane**. On the ribbon, click the **CREATE tab**, and then in the **Queries group**, click **Query Design**.

2 In the **Show Table** dialog box, double-click your **2A Instructors** table to add it to the table area, and then **Close** the **Show Table** dialog box.

3 Resize the field list, and then add the following fields to the design grid in the order given: **Instructor ID**, **Last Name**, **First Name**, and **Rank**.

4 Click in the **Sort** row under **Last Name**, click the **arrow**, and then click **Ascending**. Click in the **Sort** row under **First Name**, click the **arrow**, and then click **Ascending**.

5 Click in the **Criteria** row under **Rank**, type **professor** and then press Enter. Compare your screen with Figure 2.24.

> Recall that criteria is not case sensitive. As you start typing *professor*, a list of functions displays, from which you can select if a function is included in your criteria. After pressing Enter, the insertion point moves to the next criteria box, and quotation marks are added around the text string that you entered.

FIGURE 2.24

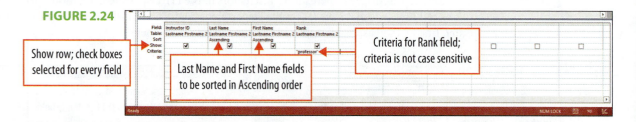

Show row; check boxes selected for every field

Last Name and First Name fields to be sorted in Ascending order

Criteria for Rank field; criteria is not case sensitive

6 In the design grid, in the **Show** row, notice that a check box is selected for every field. **Run** the query.

> Eighteen records meet the criteria—*professor* in the *Rank* field. In the Rank column, every record displays *Professor*, and the records are sorted in ascending order by the First Name field within the Last Name field.

7 Switch to **Design** view. In the design grid, in the **Show** row under **Rank**, click to clear the check box.

> Because it is repetitive and not particularly useful to display *Professor* for every record in the query results, clear the Show check box so that the field is hidden and does not display. It is good practice, however, to run the query first before clearing the Show check box to be sure that the correct records display.

8 **Run** the query, and then notice that the *Rank* field does not display even though it is used to specify criteria in the query.

The same 18 records display, but the *Rank* field is hidden from the query results. Although the Rank field is included in the query design so that you can specify the criteria of *professor*, it is not necessary to display the field in the results. When appropriate, clear the Show check box to avoid cluttering the query results with data that is not useful.

9 **Save** 💾 the query as **Lastname Firstname 2A Professor Query** and then display the query results in **Print Preview**. Create a paper or electronic printout as directed, and then click **Close Print Preview**. **Close** ⊠ the query.

Activity 2.17 | Using *Is Null* Criteria to Find Empty Fields

Sometimes you must locate records where data is missing. You can locate such records by using *Is Null* as the criteria in a field. *Is Null* is used to find empty fields. Additionally, you can display only the records where data has been entered in the field by using the criteria of *Is Not Null*, which excludes records where the specified field is empty. In this activity, you will design a query to answer the question, *Which scheduled courses have no credits listed?*

1 On the ribbon, click the **CREATE tab**, and then in the **Queries group**, click **Query Design**. In the **Show Table** dialog box, double-click your **2A Schedule** table to add it to the table area, and then **Close** the **Show Table** dialog box.

2 Resize the field list, and then add the following fields to the design grid in the order given: **Subject**, **Catalog#**, **Section**, **Course Name**, and **Credits**.

3 Click in the **Criteria** row under **Credits**, type **is null** and then press Enter.

Access capitalizes *is null*. The criteria *Is Null* examines the Credits field and locates records that do *not* have any data entered in the field.

4 Click in the **Sort** row under **Subject**, click the **arrow**, and then click **Ascending**. **Sort** the **Catalog#** field in **Ascending** order, and then **Sort** the **Section** field in **Ascending** order. Compare your screen with Figure 2.25.

FIGURE 2.25

Three fields sorted in Ascending order

Is Null criteria for Credits field

5 **Run** the query, and then compare your screen with Figure 2.26.

Four scheduled courses do not have credits listed—the Credits field is empty. The records are sorted in ascending order first by the Subject field. Within the Subject field, the records are sorted in ascending order by the Catalog# field. Within the Catalog# field, the records are sorted in ascending order by the Section field. Using the information displayed in the query results, a course scheduler can more easily locate the records in the table and enter the credits for these courses.

FIGURE 2.26

Sorted first by Subject

Within Subject, sorted by Catalog#

Within Catalog#, sorted by Section

Credits field empty (null) for four courses

6 Save 💾 the query as **Lastname Firstname 2A No Credits Query**, and then display the query results in **Print Preview**. Create a paper or electronic printout as instructed, click **Close Print Preview**, and then **Close** ✕ the query.

7 **Open** » the **Navigation Pane**, and then notice that your **2A No Credits Query** object displays under your **2A Schedule** table object, its data source.

8 On the right side of the title bar, click **Close** ✕ to close the database and to exit Access. As directed by your instructor, submit your database and the paper or electronic printouts of the eight objects—relationship report, sorted table, and six queries—that are the results of this project. Specifically, in this project, using your own name, you created the following database and printouts or electronic printouts:

1. Lastname_Firstname_2A_Instructors_Courses	Database file
2. Relationships for Lastname_Firstname_2A_Instructors_Courses	Relationships Report (printout or electronic printout)
3. Lastname Firstname 2A Instructors table sorted (not saved)	Table sorted (printout or electronic printout - Page 1)
4. Lastname Firstname 2A Instructors Query	Query (printout or electronic printout)
5. Lastname Firstname 2A Instructor IDs Query	Query (printout or electronic printout)
6. Lastname Firstname 2A Department Sort Query	Query (printout or electronic printout)
7. Lastname Firstname 2A IST Query	Query (printout or electronic printout)
8. Lastname Firstname 2A Professor Query	Query (printout or electronic printout)
9. Lastname Firstname 2A No Credits Query	Query (printout or electronic printout)

END | You have completed Project 2A

GO! with Office Web Apps

Objective	Export an Access Query to a PDF File, Save to SkyDrive, and Add a Description to the PDF File

Access web apps are designed to work with Microsoft's SharePoint, an application for setting up websites to share and manage documents. Your college may not have SharePoint installed, so you will use other tools to share objects from your database so that you can work collaboratively with others. When you have information that you want to share with others, you can upload files to SkyDrive. Some files can be opened in SkyDrive; some can only be downloaded. Because database files are typically large in size, and free storage space on SkyDrive is limited, you can export database objects to different formats and then upload those files to SkyDrive.

> **ALERT!** **Working with Web-Based Applications and Services**
>
> Computer programs and services on the web receive continuous updates and improvements. Thus, the steps to complete this web-based activity may differ from the ones shown. You can often look at the screens and the information presented to determine how to complete the activity.

Activity | Exporting an Access Query to a PDF File, Uploading a PDF File to SkyDrive, and Adding a Description to a PDF File

In this activity, you will export your 2A No Credits Query object to a PDF file, upload your PDF file to SkyDrive, and then add a description to the PDF File. Recall that PDF stands for Portable Document Format—a file format that creates an image that preserves the look of your file, but that cannot be easily changed. The results of the query will be available for individuals with whom you have shared your SkyDrive files or folders.

1 **Start** Access, navigate to your **Access Chapter 2** folder, and then **Open** your **2A_Instructors_Courses** database file. If necessary, on the Message Bar, click Enable Content. In the **Navigation Pane**, click your **2A No Credits Query** object to select it—do not open it.

2 On the ribbon, click the **EXTERNAL DATA tab**, and then in the **Export group**, click **PDF or XPS**. In the **Publish as PDF or XPS** dialog box, navigate to your **Access Chapter 2** folder. Click in the **File name** box, type **Lastname_Firstname_AC_2A_Web** and then be sure the **Open file after publishing** check box is selected, and the **Minimum size (publishing online)** option button is

selected. Click **Publish**, and then compare your screen with Figure A.

> The PDF file is created and opens in the Windows 8 Reader, Adobe Reader, or Adobe Acrobat, depending on the software that is installed on your computer.

3 **Close** your **AC_2A_Web** file. In the **Export – PDF** dialog box, click **Close**, and then **Close** Access.

4 From the desktop, start Internet Explorer, navigate to **http://skydrive.com**, and then sign in to your Microsoft account. Open your **GO! Web Projects** folder—or create and then open this folder if necessary.

FIGURE A

Your 2A No Credits Query exported as a PDF file and opened in Adobe Reader (yours may open in Windows 8 Reader or Adobe Acrobat)

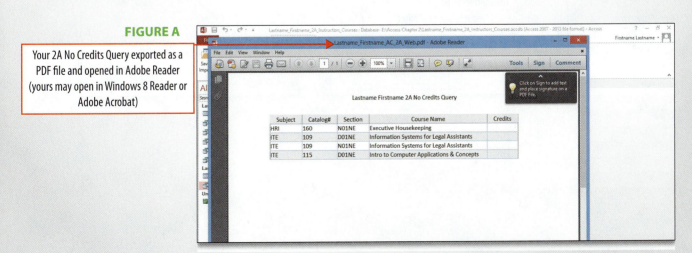

(GO! with Office Web Apps continues on the next page)

5 On the menu bar, click **Upload**. In the **Choose File to Upload** dialog box, navigate to your **Access Chapter 2** folder, and then double-click your **AC_2A_Web** file to upload it to SkyDrive.

6 In your **GO! Web Projects** folder, right-click your **AC_2A_Web** file, and then click **Properties**.

A properties panel displays on the right side of the window.

7 In the properties panel, click **Add a description**. In the box, type **This query displays courses in the schedule that do not have credits assigned to them.** and then press Enter. Compare your screen with Figure B.

8 On your keyboard, press the ⊞ key, type **snip**, and then click **Snipping Tool**. In the **Snipping Tool** dialog box, click the **New arrow**, and then click **Full-screen snip**.

9 On the **Snipping Tool** toolbar, click **Save Snip** 🔲. In the **Save As** dialog box, navigate to your **Access Chapter 2** folder. Click in the **File name** box, type **Lastname_Firstname_AC_2A_Web_Snip** and then click the **Save as type arrow**. Click **JPEG file**, and then click **Save. Close** ❎ the **Snipping Tool** window.

10 In SkyDrive, on the title bar, click **SkyDrive** to return to your home page. At the top right corner of your screen, click your SkyDrive name, and then click **Sign out**. **Close** your browser window.

11 If directed to submit a paper printout of your pdf and snip file, follow the directions given in the Note. As directed by your instructor, submit your pdf file and your snip file that are the results of this project.

N O T E **Printing Your PDF and Snip .jpeg File**

Using Windows Explorer, navigate to your Access Chapter 2 folder. Locate and double-click your AC_2A_Web file. On the toolbar, click the Print file button. Then Close the Windows 8 Reader, Adobe Reader, or Adobe Acrobat window. In your Access Chapter 2 folder, locate and double-click your AC_2A_Web_Snip file. If this is the first time you have tried to open a .jpeg file, you will be asked to identify a program. If you are not sure which program to use, select Windows Photo Viewer. From the ribbon, menu bar, or toolbar, click the Print command, and then Close the program window.

FIGURE B

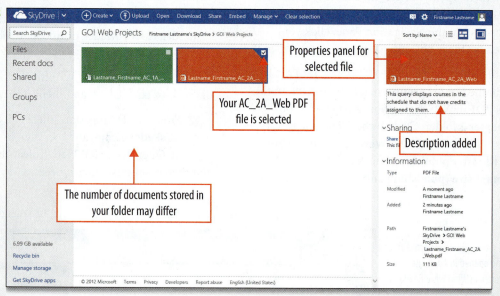

PROJECT ACTIVITIES

In Activities 2.18 through 2.33, you will assist Roberto Garza, athletic director for Texas Lakes Community College, in creating queries to locate information about athletic scholarships that are awarded to students. Your completed database objects will look similar to Figure 2.27.

PROJECT FILES

For Project 2B, you will need the following files:

a02B_Athletes_Scholarships
a02B_Athletes (Excel workbook)

You will save your database as:

Lastname_Firstname_2B_Athletes_Scholarships

PROJECT RESULTS

FIGURE 2.27 Project 2B Athletic Scholarships

Video A2-8

Criteria can be set for fields containing numeric data. When you design your table, set the appropriate data type for fields that will contain numbers, currency, or dates so that mathematical calculations can be performed.

Activity 2.18 | Opening, Renaming, and Saving an Existing Database and Importing a Spreadsheet as a New Table

In this activity, you will open, rename, and save an existing database, and then import an Excel spreadsheet as a new table in the database.

1 **Start** Access. In the Access opening screen, click **Open Other Files**. Under **Open**, click **Computer**. Under **Recent Folders**, if displayed, click the location where your student data files are stored; otherwise, click **Browse** and then navigate to the location where your student data files are stored. Double-click **a02B_Athletes_Scholarships** to open the database.

2 Click the **FILE tab**, click **Save As**, and then under **File Types**, be sure **Save Database As** is selected. On the right, under **Database File Types**, be sure **Access Database** is selected, and then click **Save As**. In the **Save As** dialog box, navigate to your **Access Chapter 2** folder, click in the **File name** box, type **Lastname_Firstname_2B_Athletes_Scholarships** and then press Enter.

3 On the **Message Bar**, click **Enable Content**. In the **Navigation Pane**, right-click **2B Scholarships Awarded**, and then click **Rename**. Using your own name, type **Lastname Firstname 2B Scholarships Awarded** and then press Enter. In the **Navigation Pane**, double-click the table name to open it in **Datasheet** view. **Close** « the **Navigation Pane**, and then examine the data in the table. Compare your screen with Figure 2.28.

In this table, Mr. Garza tracks the names and amounts of scholarships awarded to student athletes. Students are identified only by their Student ID numbers, and the primary key is the Scholarship ID field.

FIGURE 2.28

4 **Close** × the table. On the ribbon, click the **EXTERNAL DATA tab**, and then in the **Import & Link group**, click **Excel**. In the **Get External Data – Excel Spreadsheet** dialog box, to the right of the **File name** box, click **Browse**.

5 In the **File Open** dialog box, navigate to your student data files, and then double-click **a02B_Athletes**. Be sure that the **Import the source data into a new table in the current database** option button is selected, and then click **OK**.

The Import Spreadsheet Wizard opens and displays the spreadsheet data.

6 In the wizard, click **Next**. In the upper left area of the wizard, select the **First Row Contains Column Headings** check box, click **Next**, and then click **Next** again.

7 In the wizard, click the **Choose my own primary key** option button, and then be sure that **Student ID** displays in the box.

In the new table, Student ID will be designated as the primary key. No two students have the same Student ID.

8 Click **Next**. With the text selected in the **Import to Table** box, type **Lastname Firstname 2B Athletes** and then click **Finish**. In the **Get External Data – Excel Spreadsheet** dialog box, click **Close**.

9 Open ⟩⟩ the **Navigation Pane**, and increase the width of the pane so that the two table names display fully. In the **Navigation Pane**, right-click your **2B Athletes** table, and then click **Design View**. Close ⟨⟨ the **Navigation Pane**.

10 To the right of **Student ID**, click in the **Data Type** box, click the **arrow**, and then click **Short Text**. For the **Postal Code** field, change the **Data Type** to **Short Text**, and in the **Field Properties** area, click **Field Size**, type **5** and then press Enter. In the **Field Name** column, click **State**, set the **Field Size** to **2** and then press Enter. Compare your screen with Figure 2.29.

Recall that numeric data that is not used in a calculation, such as the Student ID and Postal Code, should be assigned a data type of Short Text.

FIGURE 2.29

11 On the **DESIGN tab**, in the **Views group**, click the top of the **View** button to switch to **Datasheet** view. In the message box, click **Yes** to save the table. In the second message box, click **Yes**—no data will be lost. Take a moment to examine the data in the imported table.

12 In the datasheet, to the left of the **Student ID** field name, click **Select All** ☐. On the **HOME tab**, in the **Records group**, click **More**, and then click **Field Width**. In the **Column Width** dialog box, click **Best Fit. Save** 🖫 the table, click in any record to cancel the selection, and then **Close** ☒ the table.

Activity 2.19 | Creating a One-to-Many Table Relationship

In this activity, you will create a one-to-many relationship between your 2B Athletes table and your 2B Scholarships Awarded table by using the common field—*Student ID*.

1 On the ribbon, click the **DATABASE TOOLS tab**, and then in the **Relationships group**, click **Relationships**.

2 In the **Show Table** dialog box, double-click your **2B Athletes** table, and then double-click your **2B Scholarships Awarded** table to add both tables to the **Relationships** window. **Close** the **Show Table** dialog box.

3 ▶ Point to the title bar of the field list on the right, and drag the field list to the right until there are approximately three inches of space between the field lists. By dragging the lower right corner of the field list downward and to the right, resize each field list to display all of the field names and the entire table name.

Repositioning and resizing the field lists are not required, but doing so makes it easier for you to view the field names and the join line when creating relationships.

4 ▶ In the **2B Athletes** field list, point to **Student ID**, and then drag the field name into the **2B Scholarships Awarded** field list on top of **Student ID**. Release the mouse button to display the **Edit Relationships** dialog box.

5 ▶ Point to the title bar of the **Edit Relationships** dialog box, and then drag it downward below the two field lists. In the **Edit Relationships** dialog box, be sure that **Student ID** displays as the common field for both tables.

Repositioning the Edit Relationships dialog is not required, but doing so enables you to see the field lists. The Relationship Type is *One-To-Many*—*one* athlete can have *many* scholarships. The common field in both tables is the *Student ID* field. In the 2B Athletes table, Student ID is the primary key. In the 2B Scholarships Awarded table, Student ID is the foreign key.

6 ▶ In the **Edit Relationships** dialog box, click to select the **Enforce Referential Integrity** check box, the **Cascade Update Related Fields** check box, and the **Cascade Delete Related Records** check box. Click **Create**, and then compare your screen with Figure 2.30.

The one-to-many relationship is established. The *1* and ∞ symbols indicate that referential integrity is enforced, which ensures that a scholarship cannot be awarded to a student whose Student ID is not included in the 2B Athletes table. Recall that the Cascade options enable you to update and delete records automatically on the *many* side of the relationship when changes are made in the table on the *one* side of the relationship.

FIGURE 2.30

7 ▶ Under **RELATIONSHIP TOOLS**, on the **DESIGN tab**, in the **Tools group**, click **Relationship Report**. On the **PRINT PREVIEW tab**, in the **Page Size group**, click **Margins**, and then click **Normal**. Save 💾 the report as **Lastname Firstname 2B Relationships** and then create a paper or electronic printout as directed.

8 ▶ In the object window, right-click either **object tab**, and then click **Close All** to close the **Relationship Report** and the **Relationships** window.

9 ▶ Open » the **Navigation Pane**, double-click your **2B Athletes** table to open it, and then Close « the **Navigation Pane**. On the left side of the first record, click ⊞ to display the subdatasheet for the record.

In the first record, for *Joel Barthmaier*, one related record exists in the 2B Scholarships Awarded table. Joel has been awarded the *Austin Jump Ball Award* in the amount of *$300*. The subdatasheet displays because you created a relationship between the two tables using Student ID as the common field.

10 Close ☒ the **2B Athletes** table.

When you close the table, the subdatasheet collapses—you do not need to click ⊟ before closing a table.

Activity 2.20 | Specifying Numeric Criteria in a Query

In this activity, you will create a query to answer the question, *Which scholarships are in the amount of $300, and for which sports?*

1 On the ribbon, click the **CREATE tab**. In the **Queries group**, click **Query Design**.

2 In the **Show Table** dialog box, double-click your **2B Scholarships Awarded** table to add it to the table area, and then **Close** the **Show Table** dialog box. Resize the field list to display all of the fields and the entire table name.

3 Add the following fields to the design grid in the order given: **Sport**, **Scholarship Name**, and **Amount**.

4 Click in the **Sort** row under **Sport**, click the **arrow**, and then click **Ascending**. Click in the **Sort** row under **Scholarship Name**, click the **arrow**, and then click **Ascending**.

The records will be sorted in ascending order by the Scholarship Name field within the Sport field.

5 Click in the **Criteria** row under **Amount**, type **300** and then press [Enter]. Compare your screen with Figure 2.31.

When you enter currency values as criteria, do not type the dollar sign. Include a decimal point only if you are looking for a specific amount that includes cents; for example, 300.49. Access does not insert quotation marks around the criteria because the data type of the field is Currency, which is a numeric format.

FIGURE 2.31

6 Under **QUERY TOOLS**, on the **DESIGN tab**, in the **Results group**, click **Run** to display the query results.

Five scholarships in the exact amount of $300 were awarded to student athletes. In the navigation area, *1 of 5* displays—1 represents the first record that is selected, and 5 represents the total number of records that meet the criteria.

7 On the **HOME tab**, in the **Views group**, click the top of the **View** button to switch to **Design** view.

Activity 2.21 | Using Comparison Operators in Criteria

Comparison operators are symbols you can use to evaluate data in the field to determine if it is the same (=), greater than (>), less than (<), or in between a range of values as specified by the criteria. If no comparison operator is specified, equal (=) is assumed. For example, in the previous activity, you created a query to display only those records where the *Amount* is *300*. The comparison operator of = was assumed, and the query results displayed only those records that had values in the Amount field equal to 300.

1 In the design grid, in the **Criteria** row under **Amount**, select the existing criteria of *300*. Type **>300** and then press Enter. **Run** the query.

> Fourteen records display, and each has a value *greater than* $300 in the Amount field; there are no records for which the Amount is *equal to* $300.

2 Switch to **Design** view. In the **Criteria** row under **Amount**, select the existing criteria of *>300*. Type **<300** and then press Enter. **Run** the query.

> Eleven records display, and each has a value *less than* $300 in the Amount field; there are no records for which the Amount is *equal to* $300.

3 Switch to **Design** view. In the **Criteria** row under **Amount**, select the existing criteria of *<300*. Type **>=300** and then press Enter. **Run** the query, and then compare your screen with Figure 2.32.

> Nineteen records display, including the records for scholarships in the exact amount of $300. The records include scholarships *greater than* or *equal to* $300. In this manner, comparison operators can be combined. This query answers the question, *Which scholarships have been awarded in the amount of $300 or more, and for which sports, arranged alphabetically by sport?*

FIGURE 2.32

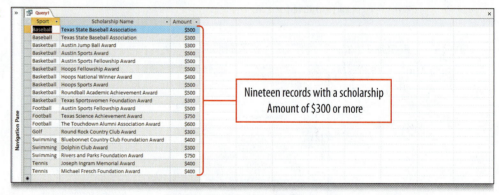

4 Save the query as **Lastname Firstname 2B $300 or More Query** and then display the query results in **Print Preview**. Create a paper or electronic printout as directed, and then click **Close Print Preview**.

5 **Close** the query. **Open** the **Navigation Pane**, and notice that this new query displays under *2B Scholarships Awarded*, its data source.

Activity 2.22 | Using the Between ... And Comparison Operator

The *Between ... And operator* is a comparison operator that looks for values within a range. It is useful when you need to locate records that are within a range of dates; for example, scholarships awarded between May 1 and June 30.

In this activity, you will create a new query from an existing query, and then add criteria to look for values within a range of dates. The query will answer the question, *Which scholarships were awarded between May 1 and June 30?*

1 In the **Navigation Pane**, right-click your **2B $300 or More Query** object, and then click **Copy**. In the **Navigation Pane**, point to a blank area, right-click, and then click **Paste**.

2 In the **Paste As** dialog box, type **Lastname Firstname 2B Awards May-June Query** and then click **OK**.

A new query, based on a copy of your 2B $300 or More Query is created and displays in the Navigation Pane under its data source—your 2B Scholarships Awarded table.

3 In the **Navigation Pane**, right-click your **2B Awards May-June Query** object, click **Design View**, and then **Close** «</> the **Navigation Pane**.

4 In the **2B Scholarships Awarded** field list, double-click **Award Date** to add it as the fourth column in the design grid.

5 In the **Criteria** row under **Amount**, select the existing criteria of >=*300*, and then press Del so that the query is not restricted by a monetary value.

6 Click in the **Criteria** row under **Award Date**, type **between 5/1/18 and 6/30/18** and then press Enter.

7 Click in the **Sort** row under **Sport**, click the **arrow**, and then click (**not sorted**) to remove the sort from this field. Click in the **Sort** row under **Scholarship Name**, click the **arrow**, and then click (**not sorted**) to remove the sort from this field. Click in the **Sort** row under **Award Date**, click the **arrow**, and then click **Ascending**.

8 In the selection bar of the design grid, point to the right edge of the **Award Date** column to display the ⊞ pointer, and then double-click to apply Best Fit to this column. Compare your screen with Figure 2.33.

The width of the Award Date column is increased to fit the longest entry in the column, which enables you to see all of the criteria. Access places pound signs (#) around the dates and capitalizes *between* and *and*. This criteria instructs Access to look for values in the Award Date field that begin with 5/1/18 and end with 6/30/18. Both the beginning and ending dates will be included in the query results.

FIGURE 2.33

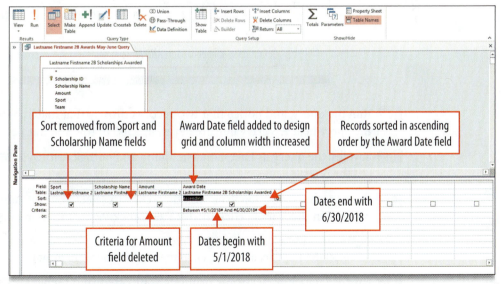

9 **Run** the query, and notice that eight scholarships were awarded between 5/1/2018 and 6/30/2018.

10 Display the query results in **Print Preview**, create a paper or electronic printout as directed, and then click **Close Print Preview**. **Close** ✕ the query, and in the message box, click **Yes** to save the changes to the query design.

Video A2-9

You can specify more than one condition—criteria—in a query; this is called *compound criteria*. Compound criteria use *logical operators* such as AND and OR. Logical operators evaluate data to determine if a condition is met (true) or not met (false). The AND and OR logical operators enable you to enter multiple criteria for the same field or for different fields.

Activity 2.23 | Using AND Criteria in a Query

The ***AND condition*** is an example of a compound criteria you can use to display records that match all parts of the specified criteria. In this activity, you will design a query to answer the question, *Which scholarships over $500 were awarded for football?*

1 On the ribbon, click the **CREATE tab**, and in the **Queries group**, click **Query Design**. In the **Show Table** dialog box, double-click your **2B Scholarships Awarded** table to add it to the table area, and then **Close** the **Show Table** dialog box. Resize the field list to display all of the fields and the entire table name.

2 Add the following fields to the design grid in the order given: **Scholarship Name**, **Sport**, and **Amount**.

3 Click in the **Criteria** row under **Sport**, type **football** and then press Enter.

4 In the **Criteria** row under **Amount**, type **>500** and then press Enter. Compare your screen with Figure 2.34.

> You create the AND condition by placing the criteria for both fields on the same line in the Criteria row. The criteria indicates that records should be located that contain *Football* in the Sport field AND a value greater than *500* in the Amount field. Both conditions must exist or be true for the records to display in the query results.

FIGURE 2.34

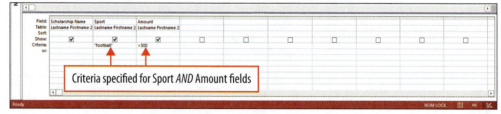

Criteria specified for Sport *AND* Amount fields

5 **Run** the query, and notice that two records display that match both conditions—*Football* in the **Sport** field AND a value greater than *$500* in the **Amount** field.

6 Save the query as **Lastname Firstname 2B Football AND Over $500 Query** and then **Close** the query.

7 Open the **Navigation Pane**, and then click to select your **2B Football AND Over $500 Query** object. On the ribbon, click the **FILE tab**, click **Print**, and then click **Print Preview**.

> You can view an object in Print Preview or print any selected object in the Navigation Pane—the object does not need to be open in the object window to print it.

8 Create a paper or electronic printout as directed, and then click **Close Print Preview**. **Close** the **Navigation Pane**.

Activity 2.24 | Using OR Criteria in a Query

The *OR condition* is an example of a compound criteria you can use to display records that meet one or more parts of the specified criteria. The OR condition can specify criteria in a single field or in different fields. In this activity, you will help Mr. Garza answer the question, *Which scholarships over $200 were awarded for volleyball or golf, and what is the award date of each?*

1 On the ribbon, click the **CREATE tab**. In the **Queries group**, click **Query Design**.

2 In the **Show Table** dialog box, double-click your **2B Scholarships Awarded** table to add it to the table area, and then **Close** the **Show Table** dialog box. Resize the field list, and then add the following fields to the design grid in the order given: **Scholarship Name**, **Sport**, **Amount**, and **Award Date**.

3 In the design grid, click in the **Criteria** row under **Sport**, type **volleyball** and then press ⬇.

The insertion point is blinking in the *or* row under Sport.

4 In the **or** row under **Sport**, type **golf** and then press Enter. **Run** the query.

Six records were located in the 2B Scholarships Awarded table that have either *volleyball* OR *golf* stored in the Sport field. This is an example of using the OR condition to locate records that meet one or more parts of the specified criteria in a single field—*Sport*.

5 Switch to **Design** view. In the **or** row under **Sport**, select *"golf"* and then press Del. In the **Criteria** row under **Sport**, select and delete *"volleyball"*. Type **volleyball or golf** and then press Enter.

6 In the **Criteria** row under **Amount**, type **>200** and then press Enter. Compare your screen with Figure 2.35.

This is an alternative way to enter the OR condition in the Sport field and is a good method to use when you add an AND condition to the criteria. Access will locate records where the Sport field contains *volleyball* OR *golf* AND where the Amount field contains a value greater than *200*.

If you enter *volleyball* in the Criteria row, and *golf* in the or row for the Sport field, then you must enter *>200* in both the Criteria row and the or row for the Amount field so that the correct records are located when you run the query.

FIGURE 2.35

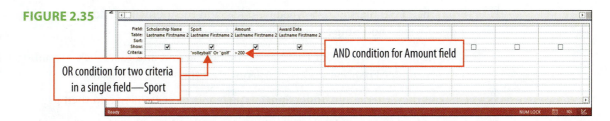

OR condition for two criteria in a single field—Sport

AND condition for Amount field

7 **Run** the query.

Two records were located in the 2B Scholarships Awarded table that have either *Volleyball* OR *Golf* stored in the Sport field AND a value greater than $200 stored in the Amount field. This is an example of using the OR condition in combination with an AND condition.

8 Save 🖫 the query as **Lastname Firstname 2B Volleyball OR Golf AND Over $200 Query** and then display the query results in **Print Preview**. Create a paper or electronic printout as directed, click **Close Print Preview**, and then **Close** ✕ the query.

Video A2-10

In a relational database, you can retrieve information from more than one table. Recall that a table in a relational database contains all of the records about a single topic. Tables are joined to one another by relating the primary key in one table to the foreign key in another table. This common field is used to create the relationship and is used to find records from multiple tables when the query is created and run.

For example, the Athletes table stores all of the data about the student athletes—name, address, and so on. The Scholarships Awarded table stores data about the scholarship name, the amount, and so on. When an athlete receives a scholarship, only the Student ID of the athlete is used to identify the athlete in the Scholarships Awarded table. It is not necessary to include any other data about the athlete in the Scholarships Awarded table; doing so would result in redundant data.

Activity 2.25 │ Creating a Query Based on More Than One Table

In this activity, you will create a query that selects records from two tables. This is possible because you created a relationship between the two tables in the database. The query will answer the questions, *What is the name, email address, and phone number of athletes who have received a scholarship for tennis or swimming, and what is the name and amount of the scholarship?*

1 On the ribbon, click the **CREATE tab**, and then in the **Queries group**, click **Query Design**. In the **Show Table** dialog box, double-click your **2B Athletes** table, and then double-click your **2B Scholarships Awarded** table to add both tables to the table area. In the **Show Table** dialog box, click **Close**. Drag the **2B Scholarships Awarded** field list—the field list on the right—to the right so that there are approximately three inches of space between the two field lists, and then resize each field list to display all of the field names and the table names.

> The join line displays because you created a one-to-many relationship between the two tables using the common field of Student ID; *one* athlete can receive *many* scholarships.

2 From the **2B Athletes** field list, add the following fields to the design grid in the order given: **Last Name**, **First Name**, **College Email**, and **Home Phone**.

3 From the **2B Scholarships Awarded** field list, add the following fields to the design grid in the order given: **Scholarship Name**, **Sport**, and **Amount**.

4 Click in the **Sort** row under **Last Name**, click the **arrow**, and then click **Ascending**. Click in the **Sort** row under **First Name**, click the **arrow**, and then click **Ascending**.

5 Click in the **Criteria** row under **Sport**, type **tennis or swimming** and then press Enter.

6 In the selection bar of the design grid, point to the right edge of the **Home Phone** column to display the ⊞ pointer, and then double-click to increase the width of the column and to display the entire table name on the **Table** row. Using the same technique, increase the width of the **Scholarship Name** column. If necessary, scroll to the right to display both of these columns in the design grid, and then compare your screen with Figure 2.36.

> When locating data from multiple tables, the information in the Table row is helpful, especially when different tables include the same field name, such as Address. Although the field name is the same, the data may be different; for example, you might have an athlete's address or a coach's address from two different related tables.

FIGURE 2.36

Table row indicates data source

Sorted in ascending order by Last Name and First Name fields

Criteria entered for Sport field

7 ▸ **Run** the query, and then compare your screen with Figure 2.37.

Eight records display for athletes who received either a Tennis *or* Swimming scholarship, and the records are sorted in ascending order by the Last Name field, and then the First Name field. Because the common field of Student ID is included in both tables, Access can locate the specified fields in both tables by using one query. Two students—*Carla Reid* and *Florence Zimmerman*—received two scholarships, one for tennis and one for swimming. Recall that *one* student athlete can receive *many* scholarships.

FIGURE 2.37

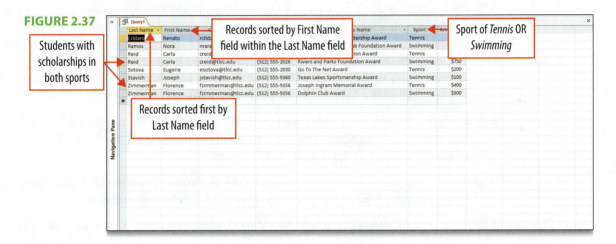

Students with scholarships in both sports

Records sorted by First Name field within the Last Name field

Sport of *Tennis* OR *Swimming*

Records sorted first by Last Name field

8 ▸ **Save** 🖫 the query as **Lastname Firstname 2B Tennis OR Swimming Query** and then display the query results in **Print Preview**. Change the orientation to **Landscape**, and the **Margins** to **Normal**. Create a paper or electronic printout as directed, and then click **Close Print Preview**.

9 ▸ **Close** ✕ the query, **Open** » the **Navigation Pane**, increase the width of the **Navigation Pane** to display all object names fully, and then compare your screen with Figure 2.38.

Your *2B Tennis OR Swimming Query* object name displays under both tables from which it selected records.

FIGURE 2.38

Query displays under both of its data sources

10 ▸ **Close** « the **Navigation Pane**.

Video A2-11

Wildcard characters serve as a placeholder for one or more unknown characters in criteria. When you are unsure of the specific character or set of characters to include in the criteria, use a wildcard character in place of the character.

Activity 2.26 | Using a Wildcard in a Query

Use the asterisk (*) wildcard character to represent one or more unknown characters. For example, entering Fo* as the criteria in a last name field will result in displaying records containing last names of Foster, Forrester, Fossil, or any other last name that begins with *Fo*. In this activity, you will use the asterisk (*) wildcard character in criteria to answer the question, *Which athletes received scholarships from local rotary clubs, country clubs, or foundations?*

1 On the ribbon, click the **CREATE tab**, and then in the **Queries group**, click **Query Design**. In the **Show Table** dialog box, double-click your **2B Athletes** table, and then double-click your **2B Scholarships Awarded** table to add both tables to the table area. In the **Show Table** dialog box, click **Close**. Drag the **2B Scholarships Awarded** field list to the right so that there are approximately three inches of space between the two field lists, and then resize each field list to display all of the field names and the table names.

2 From the **2B Athletes** field list, add the following fields to the design grid in the order given: **Last Name** and **First Name**. From the **2B Scholarships Awarded** field list, add the **Awarding Organization** field to the design grid.

3 Click in the **Sort** row under **Last Name**, click the **arrow**, and then click **Ascending**. Click in the **Sort** row under **First Name**, click the **arrow**, and then click **Ascending**.

4 Click in the **Criteria** row under **Awarding Organization**, type **rotary*** and then press Enter.

The * wildcard character is a placeholder you can use to match one or more unknown characters. After pressing Enter, Access adds *Like* to the beginning of the criteria and places quotation marks around *rotary**.

5 **Run** the query, and then compare your screen with Figure 2.39.

Three athletes received scholarships from a rotary club from different cities. The results are sorted alphabetically by the Last Name field. If there were two athletes with the same Last Name, the records would be sorted by the First Name field.

FIGURE 2.39

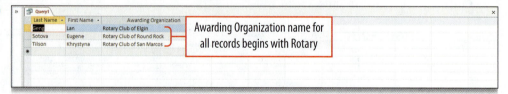

Awarding Organization name for all records begins with Rotary

6 Switch to **Design** view. Click in the **or** row under **Awarding Organization**, type ***country club** and then press Enter.

You can use the * wildcard character at the beginning, middle, or end of the criteria. The position of the * determines the location of the unknown characters. By entering *country club*, Access will locate records with an Awarding Organization name that ends in *Country Club*.

7 **Run** the query.

Six records display for students receiving scholarships; three from organizations with a name that begins with *Rotary*, and three from organizations with a name that ends with *Country Club*.

8 ▷ Switch to **Design** view. In the design grid under **Awarding Organization** and under **Like** "***country club**", type ***foundation*** and then press Enter. Compare your screen with Figure 2.40.

This query will also display records where the Awarding Organization has *Foundation* anywhere in its name—at the beginning, in the middle, or at the end of the organization name. Three *OR* criteria have been entered for the Awarding Organization field. When run, this query will locate records where the Awarding Organization has a name that begins with *Rotary*, OR ends with *Country Club*, OR has *Foundation* anywhere in its name.

FIGURE 2.40

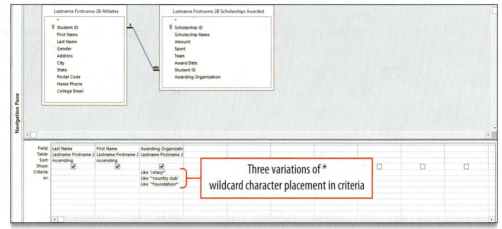

Three variations of *
wildcard character placement in criteria

9 ▷ **Run** the query.

Twenty-eight scholarships were awarded from organizations where the name of the organization begins with *Rotary*, ends with *Country Club*, or has *Foundation* anywhere in its name. The records are sorted alphabetically by the Last Name field and then by the First Name field.

10 ▷ **Save** 🖫 the query as **Lastname Firstname 2B Wildcard Query** and then display the query results in **Print Preview**. Create a paper or electronic printout as directed, and then click **Close Print Preview**.

11 ▷ **Close** ✕ the query, and then **Open** » the **Navigation Pane**. Notice that your **2B Wildcard Query** displays under both tables because the query selected data from both tables—the data sources.

| More Knowledge | Using the ? Wildcard Character to Search for a Single Unknown Character |

You can use the question mark (?) wildcard character to search for a single unknown character. For each question mark included in the criteria, the query results can display any character. For example, entering *b?d* as the criteria will result in the display of words such as *bed*, *bid*, or *bud*, or any three-character word that begins with *b* and ends with *d*. Entering *b??d* as the criteria will result in the display of words such as *bard*, *bend*, or *bind*, or any four-character word that begins with *b* and ends with *d*.

Objective 12 Create Calculated Fields in a Query

Video A2-12

Queries can create calculated values that are stored in a **_calculated field_**. A calculated field stores the value of a mathematical operation. For example, you can multiply the value stored in a field named Total Hours Worked by the value stored in a field named Hourly Pay to display the Gross Pay value for each work study student.

There are two steps to create a calculated field in a query. First, name the field that will store the results of the calculation. Second, enter the **_expression_**—the formula—that will perform the calculation. When entering the information for the calculated field in the query, the new field name must be followed by a colon (:), and each field name used in the expression must be enclosed within its own pair of brackets.

Activity 2.27 | Creating a Calculated Field in a Query

For each scholarship received by student athletes, the Texas Lakes Community College Alumni Association will donate an amount equal to 50 percent of each scholarship amount. In this activity, you will create a calculated field to determine the amount that the Alumni Association will donate for each scholarship. The query will answer the question, *How much money will the Alumni Association donate for each student athlete who is awarded a scholarship?*

1 ▶ Close « the **Navigation Pane**. On the ribbon, click the **CREATE tab**, and then in the **Queries group**, click **Query Design**. In the **Show Table** dialog box, double-click your **2B Scholarships Awarded** table to add the table to the table area, **Close** the **Show Table** dialog box, and then resize the field list.

2 ▶ Add the following fields to the design grid in the order given: **Student ID**, **Scholarship Name**, and **Amount**. Click in the **Sort** row under **Student ID**, click the **arrow**, and then click **Ascending**.

3 ▶ In the **Field** row, right-click in the first empty column to display a shortcut menu, and then click **Zoom**.

Although the calculation can be typed directly in the empty Field box, the Zoom dialog box gives you more working space and enables you to see the entire calculation as you enter it.

4 ▶ In the **Zoom** dialog box, type **Alumni Donation:[Amount]*0.5** and then compare your screen with Figure 2.41.

The first element, *Alumni Donation*, is the new field name that will display the result of the calculation when the query is run. The new field name is followed by a colon (:), which separates the new field name from the expression. *Amount* is enclosed in brackets because it is an existing field name in your 2B Scholarships Awarded table; it contains the numeric data on which the calculation is performed. Following the right square bracket is the asterisk (*), the mathematical operator for multiplication. Finally, the percentage expressed as a decimal—*0.5*—displays.

FIGURE 2.41

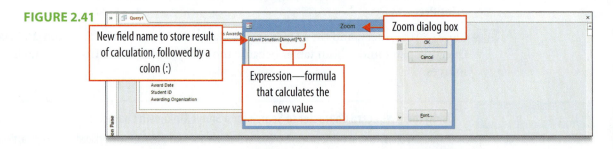

New field name to store result of calculation, followed by a colon (:)

Zoom dialog box

Expression—formula that calculates the new value

5 ▶ In the **Zoom** dialog box, click **OK**, **Run** the query, and then compare your screen with Figure 2.42.

The query results display three fields from your 2B Scholarships Awarded table and a fourth field—*Alumni Donation*—that displays a calculated value. Each calculated value equals the value in the Amount field multiplied by 0.5 or 50%.

FIGURE 2.42

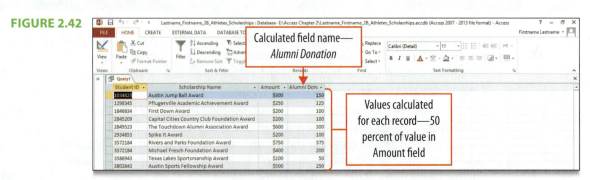

Calculated field name—*Alumni Donation*

Values calculated for each record—50 percent of value in Amount field

6 Notice the formatting of the values in the **Alumni Donation** field—there are no dollar signs to match the formatting in the **Amount** field; you will adjust the formatting of this field later.

> When using a number, such as 0.5, in an expression, the values that display in the calculated field might not be formatted the same as the existing field that was part of the calculation.

Activity 2.28 | Creating a Second Calculated Field in a Query

In this activity, you will create a calculated field to determine the total value of each scholarship after the Alumni Association donates an additional 50% based on the amount awarded by various organizations. The query will answer the question, *What is the total value of each scholarship after the Alumni Association donates an additional 50%?*

1 Switch to **Design** view. In the **Field** row, right-click in the first empty column to display a shortcut menu, and then click **Zoom**.

2 In the **Zoom** dialog box, type **Total Scholarship:[Amount]+[Alumni Donation]** and then compare your screen with Figure 2.43.

> Each existing field name—*Amount* and *Alumni Donation*—must be enclosed in separate pairs of brackets.

FIGURE 2.43

3 In the **Zoom** dialog box, click **OK**, and then **Run** the query.

> The value in the *Total Scholarship* field is calculated by adding together the values in the Amount field and the Alumni Donation field. The values in the Total Scholarship field are formatted with dollar signs, commas, and decimal points, which is carried over from the Currency format in the Amount field.

Activity 2.29 | Formatting Calculated Fields

In this activity, you will format the calculated fields so that the values display in a consistent manner.

1 Switch to **Design** view. In the **Field** row, click in the **Alumni Donation** field name box.

2 Under **QUERY TOOLS**, on the **DESIGN tab**, in the **Show/Hide group**, click **Property Sheet**.

> The Property Sheet displays on the right. Recall that a Property Sheet enables you to make precise changes to the properties—characteristics—of selected items, in this case, a field.

 ANOTHER WAY   In the design grid, on the Field row, right-click in the Alumni Donation field name box, and then click Properties.

3 In the **Property Sheet**, on the **General tab**, click **Format**. In the property setting box, click the **arrow**, and then compare your screen with Figure 2.44.

A list of available formats for the Alumni Donation field displays.

FIGURE 2.44

4 On the list, click **Currency**. In the **Property Sheet**, click **Decimal Places**. In the property setting box, click the **arrow**, and then click **0**.

5 In the design grid, in the **Field** row, click in the **Total Scholarship** field name. In the **Property Sheet**, set the **Decimal Places** property setting to **0**.

You do not need to set the Format setting to Currency as the field already displays with the currency symbol.

6 Close ☒ the **Property Sheet**, and then **Run** the query.

The Alumni Donation and Total Scholarship fields are formatted as Currency with 0 decimal places.

7 To the left of the **Student ID** field name, click **Select All** ☐. On the **HOME tab**, in the **Records group**, click **More**, and then click **Field Width**. In the **Column Width** dialog box, click **Best Fit**. Save ☐ the query as **Lastname Firstname 2B Alumni Donations Query** and then click in any field to cancel the selection.

The field widths adjust to display fully the calculated field names.

8 Display the query results in **Print Preview**. On the **PRINT PREVIEW tab**, in the **Page Layout group**, click **Landscape**. Create a paper or electronic printout as directed, and then click **Close Print Preview**. Close ☒ the query.

Objective 13   Calculate Statistics and Group Data in a Query

Video A2-13

You can use queries to perform statistical calculations known as ***aggregate functions*** on a group of records. For example, you can find the total or average amount for a group of records, or you can find the lowest or highest number in a group of records.

Activity 2.30 | Using the Min, Max, Avg, and Sum Functions in a Query

In this activity, you will use aggregate functions to find the lowest and highest scholarship amounts and the average and total scholarship amounts. The last query in this activity will answer the question, *What is the total dollar amount of all scholarships awarded?*

1 On the ribbon, click the **CREATE tab**, and then in the **Queries group**, click **Query Design**. In the **Show Table** dialog box, double-click your **2B Scholarships Awarded** table to add the table to the table area, **Close** the **Show Table** dialog box, and then resize the field list.

2 Add the **Amount** field to the design grid.

Include only the field to summarize in the design grid, so that the aggregate function is applied only to that field.

3 Under **QUERY TOOLS**, on the **DESIGN tab**, in the **Show/Hide group**, click **Totals** to add a **Total** row as the third row in the design grid. Notice that in the design grid, on the **Total** row under **Amount**, *Group By* displays.

Use the Total row to select an aggregate function for the selected field.

4 In the **Total** row under **Amount**, click in the box that displays *Group By*, and then click the **arrow** to display a list of aggregate functions. Compare your screen with Figure 2.45, and then take a moment to review the available aggregate functions and the purpose of each function as shown in Table 2.46.

FIGURE 2.45

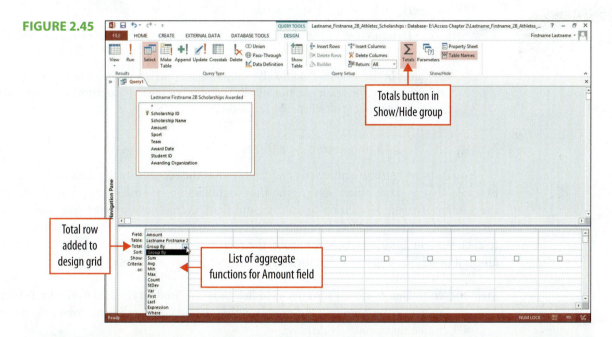

FIGURE 2.46

AGGREGATE FUNCTIONS	
FUNCTION NAME	**PURPOSE**
Group By	Groups the records alphabetically, for example, groups by Sport.
Sum	Totals the values in a field.
Avg	Averages the values in a field.
Min	Locates the smallest value in a field.
Max	Locates the largest value in a field.
Count	Displays the number of records based on a field.
StDev	Calculates the standard deviation for the values in a field.
Var	Calculates the variance for the values in a field.
First	Displays the first value in a field or column.
Last	Displays the last value in a field or column.
Expression	Creates a calculated field that includes an aggregate function.
Where	Limits the records to those that match a condition specified in the Criteria row of a field.

5 In the list of functions, click **Min**, and then **Run** the query. Point to the right edge of the first column to display the ⊞ pointer, and then double-click to apply Best Fit to the field.

> Access locates the minimum (smallest) value—*$100*—in the Amount field for all of the records in the 2B Scholarships Awarded table. The field name *MinOfAmount* is automatically created. This query answers the question, *What is the minimum (smallest) scholarship amount awarded to athletes?*

6 Switch to **Design** view. In the **Total** row under **Amount**, click the **arrow**, and then click **Max**. **Run** the query.

> The maximum (largest) value for a scholarship award amount is *$750.00*.

7 Switch to **Design** view. In the **Total** row, under **Amount**, click the **arrow**, and then click **Avg**. **Run** the query.

> The average scholarship award amount is *$358.33*.

8 Switch to **Design** view. In the **Total** row, under **Amount**, click the **arrow**, and then click **Sum**. **Run** the query.

> The values in the Amount field for all records are summed displaying a result of *$10,750.00*. The field name *SumOfAmount* is automatically created. The query answers the question, *What is the total dollar amount of all scholarships awarded?*

Activity 2.31 | Grouping Records in a Query

You can use aggregate functions and then group the records by the data in a field. For example, to group (summarize) the amount of scholarships awarded to each student, you include the Student ID field in addition to the Amount field. Using the Sum aggregate function, the records will be grouped by the Student ID so you can see the total amount of scholarships awarded to each student. Similarly, you can group the records by the Sport field so you can see the total amount of scholarships awarded for each sport.

1 Switch to **Design** view. From the field list, drag the **Student ID** field to the first column of the design grid—the **Amount** field moves to the second column. In the **Total** row, under **Student ID**, notice that *Group By* displays.

> This query will group—summarize—the records by Student ID and will calculate a total amount for each student.

2 **Run** the query, and then compare your screen with Figure 2.47.

> The query calculates the total amount of all scholarships for each student.

FIGURE 2.47

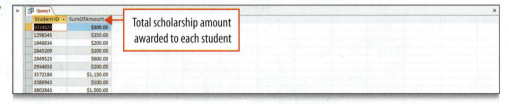

Total scholarship amount awarded to each student

3 Switch to **Design** view. In the design grid, above **Student ID**, point to the selection bar to display the ↓ pointer. Click to select the column, and then press Del to remove the **Student ID** field from the design grid.

4 From the field list, drag the **Sport** field to the first column in the design grid—the **Amount** field moves to the second column. Click in the **Sort** row under **Amount**, click the **arrow**, and then click **Descending**.

5 ▸ On the **DESIGN tab**, in the **Show/Hide group**, click **Property Sheet**. In the **Property Sheet**, set the **Decimal Places** property to **0**, and then **Close** ⊠ the **Property Sheet**.

6 ▸ **Run** the query, and then compare your screen with Figure 2.48.

> Access groups—summarizes—the records by each sport and displays the groupings in descending order by the total amount of scholarships awarded for each sport. Basketball scholarships were awarded the largest total amount—*$3,500*—and Volleyball scholarships were awarded the smallest total amount—*$650*.

FIGURE 2.48

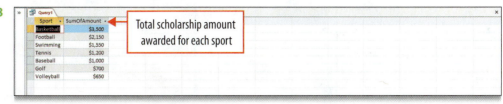

Total scholarship amount awarded for each sport

7 ▸ **Save** 🖫 the query as **Lastname Firstname 2B Total by Sport Query** and then display the query results in **Print Preview**. Create a paper or electronic printout as directed, click **Close Print Preview**, and then **Close** ⊠ the query.

Objective 14 | Create a Crosstab Query

Video A2-14

A **crosstab query** uses an aggregate function for data that can be grouped by two types of information, and then displays the data in a compact, spreadsheet-like format with column headings and row headings. A crosstab query always has at least one row heading, one column heading, and one summary field. Use a crosstab query to summarize a large amount of data in a compact space that is easy to read.

Activity 2.32 | Creating a Crosstab Query Using the Query Wizard

In this activity, you will create a crosstab query that displays the total amount of scholarships awarded for each sport and for each type of team—men's or women's.

1 ▸ On the ribbon, click the **CREATE tab**, and then in the **Queries group**, click **Query Wizard**.

2 ▸ In the **New Query** dialog box, click **Crosstab Query Wizard**, and then click **OK**.

3 ▸ In the **Crosstab Query Wizard**, click your **Table: 2B Scholarships Awarded**, and then click **Next**.

4 ▸ In the wizard under **Available Fields**, double-click **Sport** to move the field to the **Selected Fields** list and to group the scholarship amounts by the sports—the sports will display as row headings. Click **Next**, and then compare your screen with Figure 2.49.

> The sport names will be grouped and displayed as row headings, and you are prompted to select column headings.

FIGURE 2.49

Crosstab Query Wizard

Field designated as column headings

Sport names will be grouped and display as row headings

Scholarship ID will be grouped and display as column headings

5 In the wizard, in the field list, click **Team** to select the column headings. Click **Next**, and then compare your screen with Figure 2.50.

The Team types—*Men's* and *Women's*—will display as column headings, and you are prompted to select a field to summarize.

FIGURE 2.50

6 In the wizard under **Fields**, click **Amount**. Under **Functions**, click **Sum**.

The crosstab query will calculate the total scholarship amount for each sport and for each type of team.

7 Click **Next**. In the **What do you want to name your query?** box, select the existing text, type **Lastname Firstname 2B Sport and Team Crosstab Query** and then click **Finish**. Apply **Best Fit** to the datasheet, **Save** 🖫 the query, click in any field to cancel the selection, and then compare your screen with Figure 2.51.

The field widths adjust to display fully the calculated field names.

FIGURE 2.51

8 Display the query results in **Print Preview**. Create a paper or electronic printout as directed, click **Close Print Preview**, and then **Close** ☒ the query.

More **Knowledge**   **Creating a Crosstab Query Using Data from Two Related Tables**

To create a crosstab query using fields from more than one table, you must first create a select query with the fields from both tables, and then use the query as the data source for the crosstab query.

Video A2-15

A *parameter query* prompts you for criteria before running the query. For example, you might need to display the records for students who live in different cities serviced by Texas Lakes Community College. You can create a select query and enter the criteria for a city such as Austin, but when you open the query, only the records for those students who live in Austin will display. To find the students who live in Round Rock, you must open the query in Design view, change the criteria, and then run the query again.

A parameter query eliminates the need to change the design of a select query. You create a single query that prompts you to enter the city; the results are based upon the criteria you enter when prompted.

Activity 2.33 │ Creating a Parameter Query with One Criteria

In this activity, you will create a parameter query that displays student athletes from a specified city in the areas serviced by Texas Lakes Community College.

1▶ On the **CREATE tab**, in the **Queries group**, click **Query Design**.

2▶ In the **Show Table** dialog box, double-click your **2B Athletes** table to add it to the table area, **Close** the **Show Table** dialog box, and then resize the field list.

3▶ Add the following fields to the design grid in the order given: **Last Name**, **First Name**, **Address**, **City**, **State**, and **Postal Code**.

4▶ Click in the **Sort** row under **Last Name**, click the **arrow**, and then click **Ascending**. Click in the **Sort** row under **First Name**, click the **arrow**, and then click **Ascending**.

5▶ In the **Criteria** row under **City**, type **[Enter a City]** and then press Enter. Compare your screen with Figure 2.52.

The bracketed text indicates a *parameter*—a value that can be changed—rather than specific criteria.

FIGURE 2.52

Parameter for City field

Last Name and First Name fields sorted in ascending order

6▶ **Run** the query. In the **Enter Parameter Value** dialog box, type **austin** and then compare your screen with Figure 2.53.

The Enter Parameter Value dialog box prompts you to *Enter a City*, which is the text enclosed in brackets that you entered in the Criteria row under City. The city you enter will be set as the criteria for the query. Because you are prompted for the criteria, you can reuse this query without having to edit the Criteria row in Design view. The value you enter is not case sensitive—you can enter *austin*, *Austin*, or *AUSTIN*.

FIGURE 2.53

Enter Parameter Value dialog box

Value entered—*austin*—will be used as criteria for City field

Field:	Last Name	First Name	Address	City	State	Postal Code				
Table:	Lastname Firstname 2	Lastname Firstname 2	Lastname Firstname 2	Lastname Firstname 2	Lastname Firstname 2	Lastname Firstname 2				
Sort:	Ascending	Ascending								
Show:	☑	☑	☑	☑	☑	☑	☐	☐	☐	☐
Criteria:				[Enter a City]						
or:										

ALERT! **Did the Enter Parameter Value Dialog Box Not Display?**

If the Enter Parameter Value dialog box does not display, you may have typed the parameter incorrectly in the design grid. Common errors include using parentheses or curly braces instead of brackets around the parameter text, which Access interprets as specific criteria, resulting in no records matching the criteria. If you type curly braces instead of brackets, the query will not run. To correct, display the query in Design view and correct the parameter entered in the Criteria row.

---

7 In the **Enter Parameter Value** dialog box, click **OK**.

Twenty-three students live in the city of Austin, and the records are sorted in alphabetical order by the Last Name field. If students have the same last name, those records will be sorted by the First Name field.

8 Save 🖫 the query as **Lastname Firstname 2B City Parameter Query** and then **Close** ✕ the query.

Recall that only the query design is saved; each time you open a query, it is run using the most up-to-date information from the data source.

9 Open 》 the **Navigation Pane**. In the **Navigation Pane**, under your **2B Athletes** table, double-click your **2B City Parameter Query**. In the **Enter Parameter Value** dialog box, type **round rock** and then click **OK**. **Close** 《 the **Navigation Pane**. Compare your screen with Figure 2.54.

Nine students live in the city of Round Rock. Every time you open a parameter query, you are prompted to enter criteria. You may have to apply Best Fit to the columns if all of the data in the fields does not display and you wish to print the query results—the length of the data in the fields changes as new records display depending upon the criteria entered.

FIGURE 2.54

Nine students live in Round Rock

10 Display the query results in **Print Preview**, and change the orientation to **Landscape**. Create a paper or electronic printout as directed, click **Close Print Preview**, and then **Close** ✕ the query.

11 > **Open** » the **Navigation Pane**, and, if necessary increase the width of the pane so that all object names display fully. On the right side of the title bar, click **Close** ✖ to close the database and to exit Access. As directed by your instructor, submit your database and the paper or electronic printouts of the 11 objects—relationship report and 10 queries—that are the results of this project. Specifically, in this project, using your own name, you created the following database and printouts or electronic printouts:

1. Lastname_Firstname_2B_Athletes_Scholarships	Database file
2. Lastname Firstname 2B Relationships	Relationships Report (printout or electronic printout)
3. Lastname Firstname 2B $300 or More Query	Query (printout or electronic printout)
4. Lastname Firstname 2B Awards May-June Query	Query (printout or electronic printout)
5. Lastname Firstname 2B Football AND Over $500 Query	Query (printout or electronic printout)
6. Lastname Firstname 2B Volleyball OR Golf AND Over $200 Query	Query (printout or electronic printout)
7. Lastname Firstname 2B Tennis OR Swimming Query	Query (printout or electronic printout)
8. Lastname Firstname 2B Wildcard Query	Query (printout or electronic printout)
9. Lastname Firstname 2B Alumni Donations Query	Query (printout or electronic printout)
10. Lastname Firstname 2B Total by Sport Query	Query (printout or electronic printout)
11. Lastname Firstname 2B Sport and Team Crosstab Query	Query (printout or electronic printout)
12. Lastname Firstname 2B City Parameter Query	Query (printout or electronic printout - Round Rock)

More Knowledge   **Parameter Query Prompts**

Be sure that the parameter you enter in the Criteria row as a prompt is not the same as the field name. For example, do not use *[City]* as the parameter. Access interprets this as the field name of *City*. Recall that you entered a field name in brackets when creating a calculated field in a query. If you use a field name as the parameter, the Enter Parameter Value dialog box *will not* display, and all of the records *will* display.

The parameter should inform the individual running the query of the data required to display the correct results. If you want to use the field name by itself as the prompt, type a question mark at the end of the text; for example, *[City?]*. You cannot use a period, exclamation mark (!), curly braces ({ }), another set of brackets ([ ]), or the ampersand (&) as part of the parameter.

END | You have completed Project 2B

GO! with Office Web Apps

Objective Export an Access Query to a PDF File, Save the PDF File to Google Drive, and Share the File

Access web apps are designed to work with Microsoft's SharePoint, a service for setting up websites to share and manage documents. Your college may not have SharePoint installed, so you will use other tools to share objects from your database so that you can work collaboratively with others. Recall that Google Docs is Google's free, web-based word processor, spreadsheet, slide show, form, and data storage service. Google Drive is Google's free file storage and sharing service. For Access, you can export a database object to an Excel worksheet, a PDF file, or a text file, and then save the file to Google Drive.

> **ALERT!** **Working with Web-Based Applications and Services**
>
> Computer programs and services on the web receive continuous updates and improvements. Thus, the steps to complete this web-based activity may differ from the ones shown. You can often look at the screens and the information presented to determine how to complete the activity.

Activity | **Exporting an Access Query to a PDF File, Saving the PDF file to Google Drive, and Sharing the File**

In this activity, you will export your 2B Sport and Team Crosstab Query object to a PDF file, upload your PDF file to Google Drive, and then share the file.

1 **Start** Access, navigate to your **Access Chapter 2** folder, and then **Open** your **2B_Athletes_Scholarships** database file. If necessary, on the Message Bar, click **Enable Content**. In the **Navigation Pane**, click your **2B Sport and Team Crosstab Query** object to select it—do not open it.

2 On the ribbon, click the **EXTERNAL DATA tab**, and then in the **Export group**, click **PDF or XPS**. In the **Publish as PDF or XPS** dialog box, navigate to your

Access Chapter 2 folder. Click in the **File name** box. Using your own name, type **Lastname_Firstname_AC_2B_Web** and then be sure that the **Open file after publishing** check box is selected, and the **Minimum size (publishing online)** option button is selected. Click **Publish**, and then compare your screen with Figure A.

The PDF file is created and opens in Windows 8 Reader, Adobe Reader, or Adobe Acrobat, depending on the software that is installed on your computer.

FIGURE A

> Your 2B Sport and Team Crosstab Query exported as a PDF file and opened in Adobe Reader (yours may open in Windows Reader 8 or Adobe Acrobat)

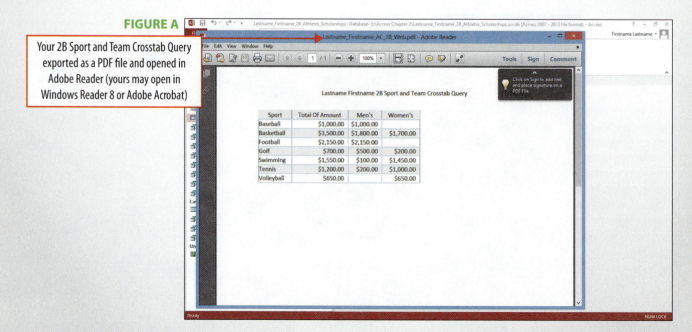

Sport	Total Of Amount	Men's	Women's
Baseball	$1,000.00	$1,000.00	
Basketball	$3,500.00	$1,800.00	$1,700.00
Football	$2,150.00	$2,150.00	
Golf	$700.00	$500.00	$200.00
Swimming	$1,550.00	$100.00	$1,450.00
Tennis	$1,200.00	$200.00	$1,000.00
Volleyball	$650.00		$650.00

Lastname Firstname 2B Sport and Team Crosstab Query

(GO! with Office Web Apps continues on the next page)

3 **Close** your **AC_2B_Web** file. In the **Export – PDF** dialog box, click **Close**, and then **Close** Access.

4 From the desktop, start Internet Explorer, navigate to **http://drive.google.com**, and sign in to your Google account, or create one.

5 Open your **GO! Web Projects** folder—or create and open this folder if necessary. Under **Drive**, to the right of **Create**, click **Upload** 📤, and then click **Files**. In the **Choose File to Upload** dialog box, navigate to your **Access Chapter 2** folder, and then double-click your **AC_2B_Web** file to upload it to Google Drive. When the title bar of the message box indicates *Upload complete*, **Close** the message box.

6 Click your **AC_2B_Web** file to open the file in Google Drive. Notice that it displays as a PDF file on a separate tab in the browser window.

7 In the browser window, locate the tab for the PDF file, and then **Close** the tab to display your folder in Google Drive.

8 Right-click your **AC_2B_Web** file, point to **Share**, and then click **Share**.

9 In the **Sharing settings** dialog box, click in the **Add people** box, and then type your own email address that you use at your college. Click the **Can edit arrow**, and click **Can comment**. Click **Add message**, type **Please share your comments about the results of this**

crosstab query. and then compare your screen with Figure B.

10 On your keyboard, press the ⊞ key, type **snip** and then click **Snipping Tool**. In the **Snipping Tool** dialog box, click the **New arrow**, and then click **Full-screen snip**.

11 On the **Snipping Tool** toolbar, click **Save Snip** 💾. In the **Save As** dialog box, navigate to your **Access Chapter 2** folder. Click in the **File name** box, type **Lastname_Firstname_AC_2B_Web_Snip** and then be sure that the **Save as type** box displays **JPEG file**. Click **Save**, and then **Close** ❎ the **Snipping Tool** window.

12 In the **Sharing settings** dialog box, click **Share & save**. In the **Sharing settings** dialog box, click **Done**.

> You can change who has access to the file in the Sharing settings dialog box. By default, the file is private and is shared only with specific people you have designated. You can grant access to anyone on the web or to anyone who has the link to this file.

13 In Google Drive, click your Google Drive name, and then click **Sign out**. **Close** your browser window.

14 If directed to submit a paper printout of your pdf and snip file, follow the directions given in the Note. As directed by your instructor, submit your pdf file and your snip file that are the results of this project. Your instructor may also request that you submit a copy of the email that was sent to you notifying you of the shared file.

N O T E Printing Your PDF and Snip .jpeg File

Use File Explorer to navigate to your Access Chapter 2 folder. Locate and double-click your AC_2B_Web file. On the toolbar, click the Print file button. Then Close the Windows 8 Reader, Adobe Reader, or Adobe Acrobat window. In your Access Chapter 2 folder, locate and double-click your AC_2B_Web_Snip file. If this is the first time you have tried to open a .jpeg file, you will be asked to identify a program. If you are not sure which program to use, select Windows Photo Viewer. From the ribbon, menu bar, or toolbar, click the Print command, and then Close the program window.

FIGURE B

Andrew Rodriguez / Fotolia; FotolEdhar/ Fotolia; apops/ Fotolia; Yuri Arcurs/ Fotolia

Sharing Your Calendar in Office 365: With Office 365, you set up your Calendar in Outlook—either in Outlook Web App or on the desktop app—and then you can share your calendar, add appointments and meetings, and see your calendar from anywhere that you have Internet access. Recall that Outlook Web App and the Outlook desktop app work seamlessly together. When you use the desktop app, you have some additional features that are not available in Outlook Web App, but any information you add is available in either app. You will be able to view your calendar—and use email—from your smartphone or from anywhere you have an Internet connection.

In an Office 365 environment, the most important thing to do with your calendar is to share it with others. Recall that Office 365 is specifically designed to help teams work together, and the first step to working together successfully is to share as much information as possible to facilitate good communication.

When you create an appointment in your calendar, Outlook displays one of four indicators associated with your availability for that date and time: Busy, Free, Tentative, or Out of Office. This is referred to as your *free/busy information*. Outlook's default setting for all appointments is Busy. The free/busy indicators also display when others view your calendar on the Office 365 shared Exchange server. Recall that Exchange Server is Microsoft's system for sharing Outlook information among members on a network. Your free/busy schedule is shared automatically with all other users.

In an Exchange Online environment, you can share your calendar with other Exchange Online users in your organization. Additionally, you can publish your calendar to the Internet and other people so they can access it. You could even share your calendar with a customer or client.

Activity | Sharing Calendars

This group project relates to the **Bell Orchid Hotels**. If your instructor assigns this project to your class, you can expect to use your **Outlook Calendar** in **Office 365 Exchange Online** to set meeting times for the following tasks for this chapter:

- If you are in the **Accounting Group**, you and your teammates will set meeting times to sort, filter, and create queries for the Stockholders database you created in Chapter 1.

- If you are in the **Engineering Group**, you and your teammates will set meeting times to sort, filter, and create queries for the Subcontractors database you created in Chapter 1.

- If you are in the **Food and Beverage Group**, you and your teammates will set meeting times to sort, filter, and create queries for the Banquet Clients database you created in Chapter 1.

- If you are in the **Human Resources Group**, you and your teammates will set meeting times to sort, filter, and create queries for the Employee database you created in Chapter 1.

- If you are in the **Operations Group**, you and your teammates will set meeting times to sort, filter, and create queries for the Guests database you created in Chapter 1.

- If you are in the **Sales and Marketing Group**, you and your teammates will set meeting times to sort, filter, and create queries for the Associations database you created in Chapter 1.

FIGURE A

END OF CHAPTER

SUMMARY

Table relationships are created by joining the common fields in tables and provide a means for you to extract information from multiple tables when you create queries, forms, and reports.

Queries are created to answer questions and to extract information from your database tables; saving a query with your database saves you time when you need to answer the question many times.

Queries range from simple queries where you ask a single question to complex queries where you use compound criteria, wildcard characters, logical operators, and create calculated fields.

A crosstab query displays information grouped by two fields that is an easy way to display complex data, and a parameter query prompts you to enter the criteria when you open or run the query.

GO! LEARN IT ONLINE

Review the concepts and key terms in this chapter by completing these online challenges, which you can find at **www.pearsonhighered.com/go**.

Matching and Multiple Choice:
Answer matching and multiple choice questions to test what you learned in this chapter. MyITLab®

Crossword Puzzle:
Spell out the words that match the numbered clues, and put them in the puzzle squares.

Flipboard:
Flip through the definitions of the key terms in this chapter and match them with the correct term.

GO! FOR JOB SUCCESS

Video: Making Ethical Choices

Your instructor may assign this video to your class, and then ask you to think about, or discuss with your classmates, these questions:

FotolEdhar / Fotolia

Which behaviors in this video do you think were unethical?

Is it unethical to "borrow" things from your employer? Why? What would you do if you saw this behavior going on?

What do you think an employer could do to prevent unethical behavior?

END OF CHAPTER

REVIEW AND ASSESSMENT GUIDE FOR ACCESS CHAPTER 2

Your instructor may assign one or more of these projects to help you review the chapter and assess your mastery and understanding of the chapter.

	Review and Assessment Guide for Access Chapter 2		
Project	**Apply Skills from These Chapter Objectives**	**Project Type**	**Project Location**
2C	Objectives 1–7 from Project 2A	**2C Skills Review** A guided review of the skills from Project 2A.	On the following pages
2D	Objectives 8–15 from Project 2B	**2D Skills Review** A guided review of the skills from Project 2B.	On the following pages
2E	Objectives 1–7 from Project 2A	**2E Mastery (Grader Project)** A demonstration of your mastery of the skills in Project 2A with extensive decision making.	In MyITLab and on the following pages
2F	Objectives 8–15 from Project 2B	**2F Mastery (Grader Project)** A demonstration of your mastery of the skills in Project 2B with extensive decision making.	In MyITLab and on the following pages
2G	Objectives 1–15 from Projects 2A and 2B	**2G Mastery (Grader Project)** A demonstration of your mastery of the skills in Projects 2A and 2B with extensive decision making.	In MyITLab and on the following pages
2H	Combination of Objectives from Projects 2A and 2B	**2H GO! Fix It** A demonstration of your mastery of the skills in Projects 2A and 2B by creating a correct result from a document that contains errors you must find.	Online
2I	Combination of Objectives from Projects 2A and 2B	**2I GO! Make It** A demonstration of your mastery of the skills in Projects 2A and 2B by creating a result from a supplied picture.	Online
2J	Combination of Objectives from Projects 2A and 2B	**2J GO! Solve It** A demonstration of your mastery of the skills in Projects 2A and 2B, your decision-making skills, and your critical thinking skills. A task-specific rubric helps you self-assess your result.	Online
2K	Combination of Objectives from Projects 2A and 2B	**2K GO! Solve It** A demonstration of your mastery of the skills in Projects 2A and 2B, your decision-making skills, and your critical thinking skills. A task-specific rubric helps you self-assess your result.	On the following pages
2L	Combination of Objectives from Projects 2A and 2B	**2L GO! Think** A demonstration of your understanding of the chapter concepts applied in a manner that you would outside of college. An analytic rubric helps you and your instructor grade the quality of your work by comparing it to the work an expert in the discipline would create.	On the following pages
2M	Combination of Objectives from Projects 2A and 2B	**2M GO! Think** A demonstration of your understanding of the chapter concepts applied in a manner that you would outside of college. An analytic rubric helps you and your instructor grade the quality of your work by comparing it to the work an expert in the discipline would create.	Online
2N	Combination of Objectives from Projects 2A and 2B	**2N You and GO!** A demonstration of your understanding of the chapter concepts applied in a manner that you would in a personal situation. An analytic rubric helps you and your instructor grade the quality of your work.	Online
2O	Combination of Objectives from Projects 2A and 2B	**2O Cumulative Group Project for Access Chapter 2** A demonstration of your understanding of concepts and your ability to work collaboratively in a group role-playing assessment, requiring both collaboration and self-management.	Online

GLOSSARY

GLOSSARY OF CHAPTER KEY TERMS

Aggregate functions Calculations such as Min, Max, Avg, and Sum that are performed on a group of records.

AND condition A compound criteria used to display records that match all parts of the specified criteria.

Ascending order A sorting order that arranges text alphabetically (A to Z) and numbers from the lowest number to the highest number.

Between ... And operator A comparison operator that looks for values within a range.

Calculated field A field that stores the value of a mathematical operation.

Cascade Delete Related Records A cascade option that enables you to delete a record in a table on the *one* side of the relationship and also delete all of the related records in related tables.

Cascade options Relationship options that enable you to update records in related tables when referential integrity is enforced.

Cascade Update Related Fields A cascade option that enables you to change the data in the primary key field in the table on the *one* side of the relationship and update that change to any fields storing that same data in related tables.

Comparison operators Symbols that are used to evaluate data in the field to determine if it is the same (=), greater than (>), less than (<), or in between a range of values as specified by the criteria.

Compound criteria Multiple conditions in a query or filter.

Criteria Conditions in a query that identify the specific records you are looking for.

Crosstab query A query that uses an aggregate function for data that can be grouped by two types of information and displays the data in a compact, spreadsheet-like format with column headings and row headings.

Data source The table or tables from which a form, query, or report retrieves its data.

Descending order A sorting order that arranges text in reverse alphabetical order (Z to A) and numbers from the highest number to the lowest number.

Design grid The lower area of the query window that displays the design of the query.

Expression A formula.

Field list A list of field names in a table.

Foreign key The field that is included in the related table so the field can be joined with the primary key in another table for the purpose of creating a relationship.

Free/Busy information In the Outlook calendar, one of four indicators—Busy, Free, Tentative, or Out of Office—associated with your availability for a specific date and time.

Innermost sort field When sorting on multiple fields in Datasheet view, the field that is used for the second level of sorting.

Is Not Null A criteria that searches for fields that are not empty.

Is Null A criteria that searches for fields that are empty.

Join line In the Relationships window, the line joining two tables that visually indicates the common fields and the type of relationship.

Logical operators Operators that are used to evaluate data to determine if a condition is met (true) or not met (false). With two criteria, AND requires that both conditions be met and OR requires that either condition be met for a record to display in the query results.

Message Bar The area directly below the ribbon that displays information such as security alerts when there is potentially unsafe, active content in an Office document that you open.

One-to-many relationship A relationship between two tables where one record in the first table corresponds to many records in the second table—the most common type of relationship in Access.

OR condition A compound criteria used to display records that match at least one of the specified criteria.

Outermost sort field When sorting on multiple fields in Datasheet view, the field that is used for the first level of sorting.

Parameter A value that can be changed.

Parameter query A query that prompts you for criteria before running the query.

Referential integrity A set of rules that Access uses to ensure that the data between related tables is valid.

Relationship An association that you establish between two tables based on common fields.

Run The process in which Access looks at the records in the table(s) included in the query design, finds the records that match the specified criteria, and then displays the records in a datasheet; only the fields included in the query design display.

Sorting The process of arranging data in a specific order based on the value in a field.

Subdatasheet A format for displaying related records when you click ⊞ next to a record in a table on the *one* side of the relationship.

Subset A portion of the total records available.

Table area The upper area of the query window that displays field lists for the tables that are used in a query.

Text string A sequence of characters.

Trust Center An area of Access where you can view the security and privacy settings for your Access installation.

Wildcard character In a query, a character that serves as a placeholder for one or more unknown characters in criteria; an asterisk (*) represents one or more unknown characters, and a question mark (?) represents a single unknown character.

CHAPTER REVIEW

Skills Review   Project 2C Freshman Orientation

In the following Skills Review, you will assist Dr. Wendy Bowie, the director of counseling at the Southwest Campus, in using her database to answer several questions about the freshman orientation sessions that will be held prior to class registration. Your completed database objects will look similar to Figure 2.55.

PROJECT FILES

For Project 2C, you will need the following file:

a02C_Freshman_Orientation

You will save your database as:

Lastname_Firstname_2C_Freshman_Orientation

PROJECT RESULTS

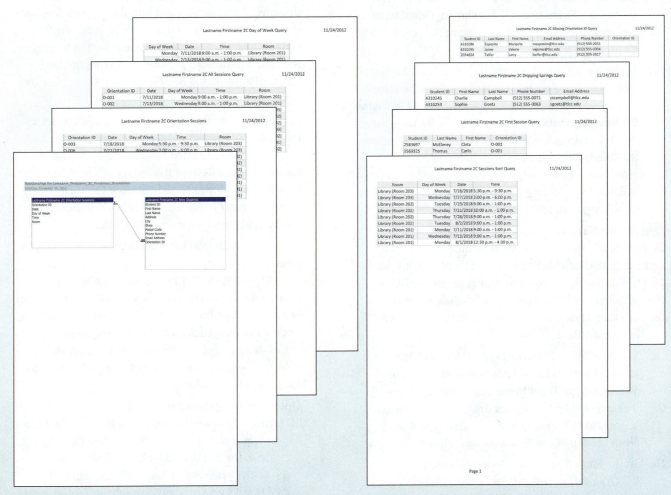

FIGURE 2.55

(Project 2C Freshman Orientation continues on the next page)

CHAPTER REVIEW

1 ▶ Start Access. In the Access opening screen, click **Open Other Files**. Under **Open**, click **Computer**. Under **Recent Folders**, if displayed, click the location where your student data files are stored; otherwise, click **Browse** and then navigate to the location where your student data files are stored. Double-click **a02C_Freshman_Orientation** to open the database.

a. On the ribbon, click the **FILE tab**, and then click **Save As**. Under **File Types**, be sure **Save Database As** is selected. On the right, under **Database File Types**, be sure **Access Database** is selected, and then click **Save As**.

b. In the **Save As** dialog box, navigate to your **Access Chapter 2** folder. Click in the **File name** box, type **Lastname_Firstname_2C_Freshman_Orientation** and then press Enter. On the **Message Bar**, click **Enable Content**.

c. In the **Navigation Pane**, right-click **2C New Students**, and then click **Rename**. With the table name selected and using your own name, type **Lastname Firstname 2C New Students** and then press Enter. **Rename** the 2C Orientation Sessions table to **Lastname Firstname 2C Orientation Sessions** and then point to the right edge of the **Navigation Pane** to display the ⟷ pointer. Drag to the right to increase the width of the pane until both tables names display fully.

2 ▶ In the **Navigation Pane**, double-click your 2C New Students table to open it in the object window, and examine the fields in the table. Double-click your 2C Orientation Sessions table, and examine the fields in the table. In the object window, right-click either **object tab**, and then click **Close All** to close both tables. **Close** the **Navigation Pane**.

a. On the ribbon, click the **DATABASE TOOLS tab**, and then in the **Relationships group**, click **Relationships**. Point to the title bar of the **Show Table** dialog box, and then drag downward and slightly to the right to move the dialog box away from the top of the **Relationships** window.

b. In the **Show Table** dialog box, click your 2C Orientation Sessions table, and then click **Add**. In the **Show Table** dialog box, double-click your **2C New Students** table to add it to the **Relationships** window. In the **Show Table** dialog box, click **Close**.

c. In the **2C New Students** field list—the field list on the right—point to the title bar to display the ↖ pointer, and then drag the field list to the right until there are approximately three inches of space between the field lists. In the **2C New Students** field list, point to the lower right corner of the field list to display the ⬊ pointer, and then drag downward and to the right to resize the field list and display all of the field names and the entire table name. Use the same technique to resize the **2C Orientation Sessions** field list—the field list on the left—so that the table name displays fully.

d. In the **2C Orientation Sessions** field list, point to **Orientation ID**, and then drag the field name downward and to the right into the **2C New Students** field list until the ⬊ pointer's arrow is on top of **Orientation ID**. Release the mouse button to display the **Edit Relationships** dialog box. Drag the **Edit Relationships** dialog box downward below the two field lists.

e. In the **Edit Relationships** dialog box, click to select the **Enforce Referential Integrity** check box, the **Cascade Update Related Fields** check box, and the **Cascade Delete Related Records** check box. In the **Edit Relationships** dialog box, click **Create** to create a one-to-many relationship—*one* orientation session can be scheduled for *many* new students.

f. Under **RELATIONSHIP TOOLS**, on the **DESIGN tab**, in the **Tools group**, click **Relationship Report**. On the **PRINT PREVIEW tab**, in the **Page Size group**, click **Margins**, and then click **Normal**. Create a paper or electronic printout as directed. On the **Quick Access Toolbar**, click **Save**. In the **Save As** dialog box, click **OK** to accept the default report name. In the object window, **Close** the report, and then **Close** the **Relationships** window.

g. **Open** the **Navigation Pane**, double-click your 2C Orientation Sessions table to open it in the object window, and then **Close** the **Navigation Pane**. On the left side of the last record—*Orientation ID* of *O-1*—click ⊞ to display the subdatasheet, and notice that 13 new students are scheduled to attend this orientation session. Click ⊟ to collapse the subdatasheet.

(Project 2C Freshman Orientation continues on the next page)

CHAPTER REVIEW

h. In the last record, in the **Orientation ID** field, select the existing data—*O-1*—and then type **O-001**—the first character is the letter *O* followed by a hyphen, two zeros, and the number *1*— to make the data consistent with the Orientation IDs of the other sessions. The 13 related records in your 2C New Students table are updated with the new Orientation ID because you selected **Cascade Update Related Fields** in the **Edit Relationships** dialog box.

i. Display the subdatasheet for the record with an **Orientation ID** of O-010, and notice that one student—*Student ID* of *8273485*—is scheduled for this orientation session. Collapse the subdatasheet. To the left of the record, point to the record selector box to display the ➔ pointer, and then click to select the record. On the **HOME tab**, in the **Records group**, click **Delete**. In the message box, click **Yes** to delete this record and the related student record in the **2C New Students** table.

3 ▶ In the **Date** field, click in any record. On the **HOME tab**, in the **Sort & Filter group**, click **Ascending** to sort the records by the date. In the field names row, click the **Room arrow**, and then click **Sort Z to A** to sort the rooms from Room 203 to Room 201. The records are sorted first by the **Room** field and then by the **Date** field. On the **FILE tab**, click **Print**, and then click **Print Preview**. Create a paper or electronic printout as directed, and then click **Close Print Preview**. On the **HOME tab**, in the **Sort & Filter group**, click **Remove Sort**. **Close** the table, and in the message box, click **No**; you do not need to save any design changes to the table.

4 ▶ On the ribbon, click the **CREATE tab**, and then in the **Queries group**, click **Query Design**. In the **Show Table** dialog box, double-click your **2C Orientation Sessions** table, and then **Close** the **Show Table** dialog box. Point to the lower right corner of the field list to display the ⬉ pointer, and then drag downward and to the right to resize the field list, displaying all of the field names and the entire table name.

a. In the field list, double-click **Orientation ID** to add the field to the first column in the design grid. In the field list, point to **Date**, and then drag the field name down into the design grid until the ⬉ pointer displays in the **Field** row in the second

column, and then release the mouse button. In the design grid, in the **Field** row, click in the third column, click the **arrow**, and then click **Day of Week** to add the field to the design grid. Using one of the three techniques you just practiced, add the **Time** field to the fourth column and the **Room** field to the fifth column in the design grid.

b. Under **QUERY TOOLS**, on the **DESIGN tab**, in the **Results group**, click **Run**. This query answers the question, *What is the Orientation ID, date, day of week, time, and room for all of the orientation sessions in the 2C Orientation Sessions table?*

c. On the **Quick Access Toolbar**, click **Save**. In the **Save As** dialog box, type **Lastname Firstname 2C All Sessions Query** and then click **OK**. On the ribbon, click the **FILE tab**, click **Print**, and then click **Print Preview**. Create a paper or electronic printout as directed, and then click **Close Print Preview**. **Close** your **2C All Sessions Query**, and then **Open** the **Navigation Pane**.

5 ▶ In the **Navigation Pane**, right-click your **2C All Sessions Query** object, and then click **Copy**. In the **Navigation Pane**, point to a blank area, right-click, and then click **Paste**. In the **Paste As** dialog box, type **Lastname Firstname 2C Day of Week Query** and then click **OK** to create a new query based on an existing query.

a. In the **Navigation Pane**, right click your **2C Day of Week Query** object, and then click **Design View**. **Close** the **Navigation Pane**. In the design grid, point to the thin gray selection bar above the **Orientation ID** field name to display the ⬇ pointer, click to select the column, and then press [Del].

b. Point to the selection bar above the **Day of Week** field name to display the ⬉ pointer, and then drag to the left until a dark vertical line displays on the left side of the **Date** column. Release the mouse button to position the **Day of Week** field in the first column.

c. **Run** the query. The query results display four fields. This query answers the question, *What is the day of week, date, time, and room for every orientation session in the 2C Orientation Sessions table?*

(Project 2C Freshman Orientation continues on the next page)

d. On the **FILE tab**, click **Print**, and then click **Print Preview**. Create a paper or electronic printout as directed, and then click **Close Print Preview**. **Close** the query, and in the message box, click **Yes** to save the changes to the design—you deleted one field and moved another field. **Open** the **Navigation Pane**.

6 In the **Navigation Pane**, right-click your **2C Day of Week Query** object, and then click **Copy**. In the **Navigation Pane**, point to a blank area, right-click, and then click **Paste**. In the **Paste As** dialog box, type **Lastname Firstname 2C Sessions Sort Query** and then click **OK** to create a new query based on an existing query. Increase the width of the **Navigation Pane** so that the names of all of the objects display fully.

a. In the **Navigation Pane**, right-click your **2C Sessions Sort Query** click **Design View**, and then **Close** the **Navigation Pane**. In the design grid, drag the **Room** field to the left of the **Day of Week** field to position it in the first column. In the design grid, click in the **Sort** row under **Room**, click the **arrow**, and then click **Descending**. Click in the **Sort** row under **Date**, click the **arrow**, and then click **Ascending**.

b. **Run** the query. This query answers the question, *For every session, within each room (with the Room field sorted in descending order), what is the day of week, date (with the Date field sorted in ascending order), and time?*

c. Display the query results in **Print Preview**, create a paper or electronic printout as directed, and then click **Close Print Preview**. **Close** the query, and in the message box, click **Yes** to save the changes to the query design.

7 On the ribbon, click the **CREATE tab**, and then in the **Queries group**, click **Query Design**. In the **Show Table** dialog box, double-click your **2C New Students** table to add it to the table area, and then **Close** the **Show Table** dialog box. Resize the field list to display all of the field names and the entire table name. Add the following fields to the design grid in the order given: **Student ID**, **Last Name**, **First Name**, and **Orientation ID**.

a. In the design grid, click in the **Criteria** row under **Orientation ID**, type **O-001**—the first character is the letter *O* followed by a hyphen, two zeros, and the number *1*—and then press [Enter].

b. **Run** the query to display 13 records that meet the specified criteria—records that have *O-001* in the *Orientation ID* field. **Save** the query as **Lastname Firstname 2C First Session Query** and then display the query results in **Print Preview**. Create a paper or electronic printout as directed, click **Close Print Preview**, and then **Close** the query.

c. On the ribbon, click the **CREATE tab**, and then in the **Queries group**, click **Query Design**. In the **Show Table** dialog box, double-click your **2C New Students** table to add it to the table area, and then **Close** the **Show Table** dialog box. Resize the field list, and then add the following fields to the design grid in the order given: **Student ID**, **First Name**, **Last Name**, **Phone Number**, **Email Address**, and **City**. Click in the **Criteria** row under **City**, type **dripping springs** and then press [Enter].

d. **Run** the query to display the five new students who live in *Dripping Springs*. Switch to **Design** view. In the design grid, in the **Show** row under **City**, click to clear the check box. Recall that if all of the results use the same criteria, such as *dripping springs*, it is not necessary to display that field in the query results. **Run** the query again. **Save** the query as **Lastname Firstname 2C Dripping Springs Query** and then display the query results in **Print Preview**. Create a paper or electronic printout as directed, click **Close Print Preview**, and then **Close** the query.

e. On the ribbon, click the **CREATE tab**, and then in the **Queries group**, click **Query Design**. In the **Show Table** dialog box, double-click your **2C New Students** table to add it to the table area, and then **Close** the **Show Table** dialog box. Resize the field list, and then add the following fields to the design grid in the order given: **Student ID**, **Last Name**, **First Name**, **Email Address**, **Phone Number**, and **Orientation ID**. Click in the **Sort** row under **Last Name**, click the **arrow**, and then click **Ascending**. Click in the **Sort** row under **First Name**, click the **arrow**, and then click **Ascending**. Click in the **Criteria** row under **Orientation ID**, type **is null** and then press [Enter].

(Project 2C Freshman Orientation continues on the next page)

CHAPTER REVIEW

f. Run the query to display the three new students who have not signed up for an orientation session. **Save** the query as **Lastname Firstname 2C Missing Orientation ID Query** and then display the query results in **Print Preview**. On the **PRINT PREVIEW** tab, in the **Page Size group**, click **Margins**, and then click **Normal**. Create a paper or electronic printout as directed, click **Close Print Preview**, and then **Close** the query.

g. Open the **Navigation Pane**. If necessary, increase the width of the pane so that all object names display fully. On the right side of the title bar, click **Close** to close the database and to exit Access. As directed by your instructor, submit your database and the paper or electronic printouts of the eight objects—relationship report, sorted table, and six queries—that are the results of this project. Specifically, in this project, using your own name, you created the following database and printouts or electronic printouts:

1. Lastname_Firstname_2C_Freshman_Orientation	Database file
2. Relationships for Lastname_Firstname_2C_Freshman_Orientation	Relationships Report (printout or electronic printout)
3. Lastname Firstname 2C Orientation Sessions table sorted (not saved)	Table sorted (printout or electronic printout)
4. Lastname Firstname 2C All Sessions Query	Query (printout or electronic printout)
5. Lastname Firstname 2C Day of Week Query	Query (printout or electronic printout)
6. Lastname Firstname 2C Sessions Sort Query	Query (printout or electronic printout)
7. Lastname Firstname 2C First Session Query	Query (printout or electronic printout)
8. Lastname Firstname 2C Dripping Springs Query	Query (printout or electronic printout)
9. Lastname Firstname 2C Missing Orientation ID Query	Query (printout or electronic printout)

END | You have completed Project 2C

CHAPTER REVIEW

Apply **2B** skills from these Objectives:

8 Specify Numeric Criteria in a Query

9 Use Compound Criteria in a Query

10 Create a Query Based on More Than One Table

11 Use Wildcards in a Query

12 Create Calculated Fields in a Query

13 Calculate Statistics and Group Data in a Query

14 Create a Crosstab Query

15 Create a Parameter Query

Skills Review   Project 2D Club Fundraisers

In the following Skills Review, you will assist Dr. Michael Bransford, the student activities director for Texas Lakes Community College, in answering his questions about fundraisers, clubs, donations, dates of fundraiser events, and fundraiser locations. Your completed database objects will look similar to Figure 2.56.

PROJECT FILES

For Project 2D, you will need the following files:

a02D_Club_Fundraisers
a02D_Clubs (Excel workbook)

You will save your database as:

Lastname_Firstname_2D_Club_Fundraisers

PROJECT RESULTS

FIGURE 2.56

(Project 2D Club Fundraisers continues on the next page)

CHAPTER REVIEW

1 ▶ Start Access. In the Access opening screen, click **Open Other Files**. Under **Open**, click **Computer**. Under **Recent Folders**, if displayed, click the location where your student data files are stored; otherwise, click **Browse** and then navigate to the location where your student data files are stored. Double-click **a02D_Club_Fundraisers** to open the database.

a. On the ribbon, click the **FILE tab**, and then click **Save As**. Under **File Types**, be sure **Save Database As** is selected. On the right, under **Database File Types**, be sure **Access Database** is selected, and then at the bottom of the screen, click **Save As**. In the **Save As** dialog box, navigate to your **Access Chapter 2** folder. Click in the **File name** box, type **Lastname_Firstname_2D_Club_Fundraisers** and then press Enter. On the **Message Bar**, click **Enable Content**.

b. In the **Navigation Pane**, right-click **2D Fundraisers**, click **Rename**, type **Lastname Firstname 2D Fundraisers** and then press Enter. Increase the width of the **Navigation Pane** to display the entire table name. Double-click the table name to open it, examine the fields in the table, and then **Close** the table.

c. On the ribbon, click the **EXTERNAL DATA tab**, and then in the **Import & Link group**, click **Excel**. In the **Get External Data – Excel Spreadsheet** dialog box, to the right of the **File name** box, click **Browse**. In the **File Open** dialog box, navigate to your student data files, and then double-click **a02D_Clubs**. Be sure that the **Import the source data into a new table in the current database** option button is selected, and then click **OK**.

d. In the upper left area of the wizard, select the **First Row Contains Column Headings** check box, click **Next**, and then click **Next** again. In the wizard, click the **Choose my own primary key** option button, be sure that **Club ID** displays, and then click **Next**. With the text selected in the **Import to Table** box and using your own name, type **Lastname Firstname 2D Clubs**, and then click **Finish**. In the **Get External Data – Excel Spreadsheet** dialog box, click **Close**.

e. In the **Navigation Pane**, right-click your **2D Clubs** table, and then click **Design View**. **Close** the **Navigation Pane**. In the **Field Name** column, click

Club ID. In the **Field Properties** area, click **Field Size**, type **8** and then press Enter. Under **TABLE TOOLS**, on the **DESIGN tab**, in the **Views group**, click the upper portion of the **View** button to switch to **Datasheet** view. In the message box, click **Yes** to save the design changes. In the second message box, click **Yes**—no data will be lost. Examine the fields and data in the table. To the left of the **Club ID** field name, click **Select All**. On the **HOME tab**, in the **Records group**, click **More**, and then click **Field Width**. In the **Column Width** dialog box, click **Best Fit**. **Save** the table, click in any record to cancel the selection, and then **Close** the table.

f. On the ribbon, click the **DATABASE TOOLS tab**, and then in the **Relationships group**, click **Relationships**. In the **Show Table** dialog box, double-click your **2D Clubs** table, and then double-click your **2D Fundraisers** table to add both tables to the **Relationships** window. **Close** the **Show Table** dialog box. Point to the title bar of the field list on the right, and drag the field list to the right until there are approximately two inches of space between the field lists. By dragging the lower right corner of the field list, resize each field list to display all of the field names and the entire table name.

g. In the **2D Clubs** field list, point to **Club ID**, drag the field name into the **2D Fundraisers** table on top of **Club ID**, and then release the mouse button. Point to the title bar of the **Edit Relationships** dialog box, and then drag it downward below the two field lists. In the **Edit Relationships** dialog box, select the **Enforce Referential Integrity** check box, the **Cascade Update Related Fields** check box, the **Cascade Delete Related Records** check box, and then click **Create**. A *one-to-many* relationship is established; *one* student club can raise money for *many* fundraising events.

h. Under **RELATIONSHIP TOOLS**, on the **DESIGN tab**, in the **Tools group**, click **Relationship Report**. On the **PRINT PREVIEW tab**, in the **Page Size group**, click **Margins**, and then click **Normal**. **Save** the report as **Lastname Firstname 2D Relationships** and then create a paper or electronic printout as directed. In the object window, right-click either **object tab**, and then click **Close All**.

(Project 2D Club Fundraisers continues on the next page)

CHAPTER REVIEW

2 ▶ On the ribbon, click the **CREATE tab**. In the **Queries group**, click **Query Design**. In the **Show Table** dialog box, double-click your **2D Fundraisers** table to add it to the table area, and then **Close** the **Show Table** dialog box. Resize the field list. Add the following fields to the design grid in the order given: **Fundraiser Name**, **Donation**, and **Fundraiser Location**.

a. Click in the **Sort** row under **Fundraiser Name**, click the **arrow**, and then click **Ascending**. Click in the **Criteria** row under **Donation**, type **>=1000** and then press Enter. **Run** the query, and notice that seven records match the criteria. This query answers the question, *Where was each fundraiser held (in alphabetical order by the Fundraiser Name field) for fundraisers with a donation greater than or equal to $1,000?*

b. **Save** the query as **Lastname Firstname 2D $1000 or More Donation Query** and then display the query results in **Print Preview**. Create a paper or electronic printout as directed, click **Close Print preview**, and then **Close** your query object. **Open** the **Navigation Pane**.

c. In the **Navigation Pane**, right-click your **2D $1000 or More Donation Query** object, and then click **Copy**. In the **Navigation Pane**, point to a blank area, right-click, and then click **Paste**. In the **Paste As** dialog box, type **Lastname Firstname 2D Fundraisers June-July Query** and then click **OK**. In the **Navigation Pane**, right-click your **2D Fundraisers June-July Query** object, and then click **Design View**. **Close** the **Navigation Pane**.

d. In the **2D Fundraisers** field list, double-click **Date** to add it to the fourth column in the design grid. Click in the **Sort** row under **Fundraiser Name**, click the **arrow**, and then click **(not sorted)**. Click in the **Sort** row under **Date**, click the **arrow**, and then click **Ascending**.

e. In the **Criteria** row under **Donation**, select the existing criteria of *>=1000*, and then press Del so that the query results are not restricted by a monetary value. Click in the **Criteria** row under **Date**, type **between 6/1/18 and 7/31/18** and then press Enter. **Run** the query, and notice that four records match the criteria. This query answers the question, *What is the fundraiser name, donation, fundraiser location, and date (in chronological order) for events held between June 1, 2018 and July 31, 2018?*

f. Display the query results in **Print Preview**, create a paper or electronic printout as directed, and then click **Close Print Preview**. **Close** the query, and in the message box, click **Yes** to save the changes to the query design.

3 ▶ On the ribbon, click the **CREATE tab**, and in the **Queries group**, click **Query Design**. In the **Show Table** dialog box, double-click your **2D Fundraisers** table to add it to the table area, and then **Close** the **Show Table** dialog box. Resize the field list. Add the following fields to the design grid in the order given: **Fundraiser Name**, **Fundraiser Location**, **Donation**, and **Club ID**.

a. Click in the **Sort** row under **Fundraiser Name**, click the **arrow**, and then click **Ascending**. Click in the **Criteria** row under **Club ID**, type **club-109** and then press Enter. Click in the **Criteria** row under **Donation**, type **<=1000** and then press Enter. **Run** the query, and notice that two records match the criteria. Switch back to **Design** view, and in the **Show** row under **Club ID**, clear the check box. **Run** the query again. This query answers the question, *Which fundraiser events with their locations listed had donations raised by CLUB-109 of $1,000 or less?*

b. **Save** the query as **Lastname Firstname 2D CLUB-109 Low Donations Query** and then display the query results in **Print Preview**. Create a paper or electronic printout as directed, click **Close Print Preview**, and then **Close** the query.

c. On the ribbon, click the **CREATE tab**, and then in the **Queries group**, click **Query Design**. In the **Show Table** dialog box, double-click your **2D Fundraisers** table to add it to the table area, and then **Close** the **Show Table** dialog box. Resize the field list. Add the following fields to the design grid in the order given: **Club ID**, **Fundraiser Name**, **Date**, and **Donation**.

d. Click in the **Sort** row under **Date**, click the **arrow**, and then click **Ascending**. Click in the **Criteria** row under **Club ID**, type **club-107 or club-115** and then press Enter. Click in the **Criteria** row under **Donation**, type **>1000** and then press Enter. **Run** the query, and notice that two records match the criteria. This query answers the questions, *Which fundraiser events received donations over $1,000 from either CLUB-107 or CLUB-115, and on what dates (in chronological order) were the fundraiser events held?*

(Project 2D Club Fundraisers continues on the next page)

CHAPTER REVIEW

e. **Save** the query as **Lastname Firstname 2D CLUB 107 OR 115 Over $1000 Query** and then display the query results in **Print Preview**. Create a paper or electronic printout as directed, click **Close Print Preview**, and then **Close** the query.

4 On the ribbon, click the **CREATE tab**, and then in the **Queries group**, click **Query Design**. In the **Show Table** dialog box, double-click your **2D Clubs** table, and then double-click your **2D Fundraisers** table to add both tables to the table area. **Close** the **Show Table** dialog box. Drag the field list on the right side to the right until there are approximately two inches of space between the field lists, and then resize each field list.

a. From the **2D Clubs** field list, add the following fields to the design grid in the order given: **Club Name**, **Campus**, and **Club Email**. From the **2D Fundraisers** field list, add the following fields to the design grid in the order given: **Fundraiser Name**, **Date**, and **Donation**. In the design grid, drag the **Donation** field to the left to position it as the first column.

b. Click in the **Sort** row under **Donation**, click the **arrow**, and then click **Descending**. Click in the **Criteria** row under **Campus**, type **southeast** and then press ⏎. Click in the **or** row under **Campus**, type **northeast** and then press ⏎. **Run** the query, and notice that 10 records match the criteria. This query answers the question, *For the Southeast and Northeast campuses, what is the donation (in descending order), club name, campus name, club email address, fundraiser name, and date of all fundraising events?*

c. **Save** the query as **Lastname Firstname 2D SE OR NE Donations Query** and then display the query results in **Print Preview**. On the **PRINT PREVIEW tab**, in the **Page Layout group**, click **Landscape**. In the **Page Size group**, click **Margins**, and then click **Normal**. Create a paper or electronic printout as directed, click **Close Print Preview**, and then **Close** the query.

5 On the ribbon, click the **CREATE tab**, and then in the **Queries group**, click **Query Design**. In the **Show Table** dialog box, double-click your **2D Clubs** table, and then double-click your **2D Fundraisers** table to add both tables to the table area. **Close** the **Show Table** dialog box. Drag the field list on the right side to the right until there are approximately two inches of space between the field lists, and then resize each field list. From the **2D Clubs** field

list, add the **Club Name** field to the design grid. From the **2D Fundraisers** field list, add the **Fundraiser Name** field to the design grid.

a. Click in the **Sort** row under **Club Name**, click the **arrow**, and then click **Ascending**. Click in the **Criteria** row under **Club Name**, type **phi*** and then press ⏎. In the **Criteria** row under **Fundraiser Name**, type ***walk*** and then press ⏎. **Run** the query, and notice that two records match the criteria—Club Name begins with *Phi* and Fundraiser Name has *Walk* anywhere in its name. This query answers the question, *Which clubs (in alphabetical order) that have names starting with Phi have raised money for fundraisers that involve walking?*

b. **Save** the query as **Lastname Firstname 2D Phi Walk Query** and then display the query results in **Print Preview**. Create a paper or electronic printout as directed, click **Close Print Preview**, and then **Close** the query.

6 On the ribbon, click the **CREATE tab**, and then in the **Queries group**, click **Query Design**. In the **Show Table** dialog box, double-click your **2D Clubs** table, and then double-click your **2D Fundraisers** table to add both tables to the table area. **Close** the **Show Table** dialog box. Drag the field list on the right side to the right until there are approximately two inches of space between the field lists, and then resize each field list. From the field lists, add the following fields to the design grid in the order given: **Fundraiser ID**, **Club Name**, and **Donation**.

a. Click in the **Sort** row under **Fundraiser ID**, click the **arrow**, and then click **Ascending**. Alumni will donate an additional 25 percent based on the value in the **Donation** field. In the **Field** row, right-click in the fourth column, and then click **Zoom**. In the **Zoom** dialog box, type **Alumni Donation:[Donation]*0.25** and then click **OK**. **Run** the query to be sure the new field—*Alumni Donation*—displays. In the first record, the *Alumni Donation* displays as *156.25*.

b. Switch to **Design** view. In the **Field** row, right-click in the first empty column, and then click **Zoom**. In the **Zoom** dialog box, type **Total Donation:[Donation]+[Alumni Donation]** and then click **OK**. **Run** the query to be sure that the new field—*Total Donation*—displays. In the first record, the *Total Donation* displays as *$781.25*.

(Project 2D Club Fundraisers continues on the next page)

c.   Switch to **Design** view. In the **Field** row, click in the **Alumni Donation** field name box. Under **QUERY TOOLS**, on the **DESIGN tab**, in the **Show/Hide group**, click **Property Sheet**. In the **Property Sheet**, click **Format**. In the property setting box, click the **arrow**, and then click **Currency**. In the **Property Sheet**, click **Decimal Places**. In the property setting box, click the **arrow**, and then click **2**. **Close** the **Property Sheet**, and then **Run** the query. This query answers the question, *In ascending order by Fundraiser ID, what is the club name, donation, alumni donation, and total donation for each fundraising event if the alumni donate an additional 25 percent based on the value in the Donation field?*

d.   To the left of the **Fundraiser ID** field name, click **Select All**. On the **HOME tab**, in the **Records group**, click **More**, and then click **Field Width**. In the **Column Width** dialog box, click **Best Fit**. Save the query as **Lastname Firstname 2D Alumni Donation Query** and then click in any field to cancel the selection. Display the query results in **Print Preview**. On the **PRINT PREVIEW tab**, in the **Page Layout group**, click **Landscape**. Create a paper or electronic printout as directed, click **Close Print Preview**, and then **Close** the query.

7   On the ribbon, click the **CREATE tab**, and then in the **Queries group**, click **Query Design**. In the **Show Table** dialog box, double-click your **2D Fundraisers** table to add the table to the table area. **Close** the **Show Table** dialog box. Resize the field list, and then add the **Donation** field to the design grid.

a.   Under **QUERY TOOLS**, on the **DESIGN tab**, in the **Show/Hide group**, click **Totals** to add a **Total** row as the third row in the design grid. In the **Total** row under **Donation**, click in the box that displays *Group By*, click the **arrow**, and then click **Sum**. In the **Show/Hide group**, click **Property Sheet**. In the **Property Sheet**, set **Decimal Places** to **0**, and then **Close** the **Property Sheet**. **Run** the query. Point to the right edge of the first column to display the ⬌ pointer, and then double-click to apply Best Fit to the field. The sum of the Donation fields is *$20,259.*

b.   Switch to **Design** view. From the field list, drag the **Club ID** field to the first column in the design grid—the **Donation** field moves to the second column. **Run** the query. This query answers the question, *For each club ID, what are the total donations?*

c.   **Save** the query as **Lastname Firstname 2D Total Donations by Club Query** and then display the query results in **Print Preview**. Create a paper or electronic printout as directed, click **Close Print Preview**, and then **Close** the query.

8   On the ribbon, click the **CREATE tab**, and then in the **Queries group**, click **Query Wizard**. In the **New Query** dialog box, click **Crosstab Query Wizard**, and then click **OK**. In the **Crosstab Query Wizard**, click your **Table: 2D Fundraisers**, and then click **Next**. In the wizard under **Available Fields**, double-click **Fundraiser ID** to group the records by this field and display the Fundraiser IDs as row headings. Click **Next**.

a.   In the wizard, in the field list, click **Club ID** to select the column headings, and then click **Next**. Under **Fields**, click **Donation**. Under **Functions**, click **Sum**, and then click **Next**. In the **What do you want to name your query?** box, select the existing text, type **Lastname Firstname 2D Fundraisers and Clubs Crosstab Query** and then click **Finish**.

b.   On the ribbon, click the **HOME** tab, and then switch to **Design** view. In the design grid, click in the **[Donation]** column. Under **QUERY TOOLS**, on the **DESIGN tab**, in the **Show/Hide group**, click **Property Sheet**. In the **Property Sheet**, click **Decimal Places**. In the property settings box, click the **arrow**, and then click **0**. In the design grid, click in the **Total Of Donation** column, set the **Decimal Places** to **0**, and then **Close** the **Property Sheet**. **Run** the query. Select all of the columns, apply **Best Fit**, and then **Save** the query. This query answers the question, *Grouped by Fundraiser ID and Club ID, what are the total donations?*

c.   Display the query results in **Print Preview**. On the **PRINT PREVIEW tab**, in the **Page Layout group**, click **Landscape**. Create a paper or electronic printout as directed—two pages result. Click **Close Print Preview**, and then **Close** the query.

9   On the ribbon, click the **CREATE tab**, and then in the **Queries group**, click **Query Design**. In the **Show Table** dialog box, double-click your **2D Fundraisers** table to add the table to the table area. **Close** the **Show Table** dialog box, and then resize the field list. Add the following fields to the design grid in the order given: **Club ID**, **Fundraiser Location**, and **Date**.

(Project 2D Club Fundraisers continues on the next page)

CHAPTER REVIEW

a. Click in the **Sort** row under **Date**, click the **arrow**, and then click **Ascending**. In the **Criteria** row under **Club ID**, right-click, and then click **Zoom**. In the **Zoom** dialog box, type **[Enter a Club ID in the format club-###]** and then click **OK**. **Run** the query. In the **Enter Parameter Value** dialog box, type **club-109** and then click **OK**. Three records match the criteria.

b. **Save** the query as **Lastname Firstname 2D Club ID Parameter Query** and then display the query results in **Print Preview**. Create a paper or electronic printout as directed, click **Close Print Preview**, and then **Close** the query.

c. **Open** the **Navigation Pane**, and increase the width of the pane so that all object names display fully. On the right side of the title bar, click **Close** to close the database and to exit Access. As directed by your instructor, submit your database and the paper or electronic printouts of the 11 objects—relationship report and 10 queries, one of which printed on two pages—that are the results of this project. Specifically, in this project, using your own name, you created the following database and printouts or electronic printouts:

1. Lastname_Firstname_2D_Clubs_Fundraisers	Database file
2. Lastname Firstname 2D Relationships	Relationships Report (printout or electronic printout)
3. Lastname Firstname 2D $1000 or More Donation Query	Query (printout or electronic printout)
4. Lastname Firstname 2D Fundraisers June-July Query	Query (printout or electronic printout)
5. Lastname Firstname 2D CLUB-109 Low Donations Query	Query (printout or electronic printout)
6. Lastname Firstname 2D CLUB-107 OR 115 Over $1000 Query	Query (printout or electronic printout)
7. Lastname Firstname 2D SE OR NE Donations Query	Query (printout or electronic printout)
8. Lastname Firstname 2D Phi Walk Query	Query (printout or electronic printout)
9. Lastname Firstname 2D Alumni Donation Query	Query (printout or electronic printout)
10. Lastname Firstname 2D Total Donations by Club Query	Query (printout or electronic printout)
11. Lastname Firstname 2D Fundraisers and Clubs Crosstab Query	Query (printout or electronic printout - two pages)
12. Lastname Firstname 2D Club ID Parameter Query	Query (printout or electronic printout - CLUB-109)

END | You have completed Project 2D

CONTENT-BASED ASSESSMENTS

| Mastering Access | Project 2E Biology Supplies |

In the following Mastering Access project, you will assist Greg Franklin, chair of the Biology Department at the Southwest Campus, in using his database to answer questions about biology laboratory supplies. Your completed database objects will look similar to Figure 2.57.

PROJECT FILES

For Project 2E, you will need the following file:

a02E_Biology_Supplies

You will save your database as:

Lastname_Firstname_2E_Biology_Supplies

PROJECT RESULTS

Apply 2A skills from these Objectives:

1 Open and Save an Existing Database

2 Create Table Relationships

3 Sort Records in a Table

4 Create a Query in Design View

5 Create a New Query from an Existing Query

6 Sort Query Results

7 Specify Criteria in a Query

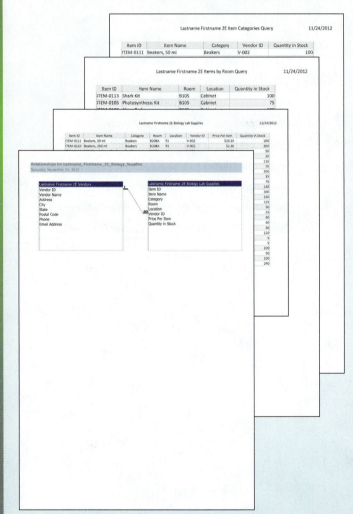

FIGURE 2.57

(Project 2E Biology Supplies continues on the next page)

CONTENT-BASED ASSESSMENTS

Mastering Access   Project 2E Biology Supplies (continued)

1 **Start** Access. From your student data files, open **a02E_Biology_Supplies**. Save the database in your **Access Chapter 2** folder as **Lastname_Firstname_2E_Biology_Supplies** and then enable the content. In the **Navigation Pane**, **Rename** each table by adding **Lastname Firstname** to the beginning of the table name. Increase the width of the **Navigation Pane** so that all object names display fully.

2 Open both tables to examine the fields and data, and then **Close** both tables. Create a *one-to-many* relationship between your **2E Vendors** table and your **2E Biology Lab Supplies** table using the common field **Vendor ID**. **Enforce Referential Integrity**, and enable both cascade options. *One* vendor can be the provider of *many* supplies. Create a **Relationship Report** with **Normal Margins**, saving it with the default name. Create a paper or electronic printout as directed, and then **Close All** open objects. Open your **2E Vendors** table. In the last record, in the **Vendor ID** field, select **V-100**, type **V-001** and then press ↓ to save the record. **Close** the table.

3 Open your **2E Biology Lab Supplies** table. Sort the records first in **Descending** order by **Price Per Item** and then in **Ascending** order by **Category**. Using **Landscape** orientation, create a paper or electronic printout as directed. **Close** the table, and do *not* save changes to the table.

4 Create a query in **Query Design** view using your **2E Biology Lab Supplies** table to answer the question, *What is the item ID, item name, room, location, and quantity in stock for all of the items, sorted in ascending order by the Room field and the Location field?* Display the fields in the order listed in the question. **Save** the query as **Lastname Firstname 2E Items by Room Query** and then create a paper or electronic printout as directed. **Close** the query.

5 From the **Navigation Pane**, copy your **2E Items by Room Query** object to create a new query object named **Lastname Firstname 2E Item Categories Query** and then redesign the query to answer the question, *What is the item ID, item name, category, vendor ID, and quantity*

in stock for all items, sorted in ascending order by the Category field and in ascending order by the Vendor ID field?* Display only the fields necessary to answer the question and in the order listed in the question. Create a paper or electronic printout as directed. **Close** the query, saving the design changes.

6 From the **Navigation Pane**, copy your **2E Items by Room Query** object to create a new query object named **Lastname Firstname 2E Supplies Sort Query** and then redesign the query to answer the question, *What is the item name, category, price per item, and quantity in stock for all supplies, sorted in ascending order by the Category field and then in descending order by the Price Per Item field?* Display only the fields necessary to answer the question and in the order listed in the question. Create a paper or electronic printout as directed. **Close** the query, saving the design changes.

7 From the **Navigation Pane**, copy your **2E Supplies Sort Query** object to create a new query object named **Lastname Firstname 2E Kits Query** and then redesign the query to answer the question, *What is the item name, category, price per item, quantity in stock, and vendor ID for all items that have a category of kits, sorted in ascending order only by the Item Name field?* Do not display the **Category** field in the query results, and display the rest of the fields in the order listed in the question. Six records match the criteria. Create a paper or electronic printout as directed. **Close** the query, saving the design changes.

8 Create a query in **Query Design** view using your **2E Vendors** table to answer the question, *What is the vendor ID and vendor name where the phone number is missing from the table, sorted in ascending order by the Vendor Name field?* Display the fields in the order listed in the question. Two records match the criteria. **Save** the query as **Lastname Firstname 2E Missing Phone Query** and then create a paper or electronic printout as directed. **Close** the query.

(Project 2E Biology Supplies continues on the next page)

CONTENT-BASED ASSESSMENTS

9 Be sure all objects are closed. **Open** the **Navigation Pane**, be sure that all object names display fully, and then **Close** Access. As directed by your instructor, submit your database and the paper or electronic printouts of the seven objects—relationship report, sorted table, and five queries—that are the results of this project. Specifically, in this project, using your own name, you created the following database and printouts or electronic printouts:

1. Lastname_Firstname_2E_Biology_Supplies	Database file
2. Relationships for Lastname_Firstname_2E_Biology_Supplies	Relationships Report (printout or electronic printout)
3. Lastname Firstname 2E Biology Lab Supplies table sorted (not saved)	Table sorted (printout or electronic printout - one page)
4. Lastname Firstname 2E Items by Room Query	Query (printout or electronic printout)
5. Lastname Firstname 2E Item Categories Query	Query (printout or electronic printout)
6. Lastname Firstname 2E Supplies Sort Query	Query (printout or electronic printout)
7. Lastname Firstname 2E Kits Query	Query (printout or electronic printout)
8. Lastname Firstname 2E Missing Phone Query	Query (printout or electronic printout)

END | You have completed Project 2E

CONTENT-BASED ASSESSMENTS

Mastering Access | Project 2F Student Publications

In the following Mastering Access project, you will assist Siobhan Reiss, the English Writing Lab coordinator, in using her database to answer questions about student publications. Your completed database objects will look similar to Figure 2.58.

Apply 2B skills from these Objectives:

8 Specify Numeric Criteria in a Query
9 Use Compound Criteria in a Query
10 Create a Query Based on More Than One Table
11 Use Wildcards in a Query
12 Create Calculated Fields in a Query
13 Calculate Statistics and Group Data in a Query
14 Create a Crosstab Query
15 Create a Parameter Query

PROJECT FILES

For Project 2F, you will need the following files:

a02F_Student_Publications
a02F_Student_Papers (Excel workbook)

You will save your database as:

Lastname_Firstname_2F_Student_Publications

PROJECT RESULTS

FIGURE 2.58

(Project 2F Student Publications continues on the next page)

CONTENT-BASED ASSESSMENTS

1 **Start** Access. From your student data files, open **a02F_Student_Publications**. Save the database in your **Access Chapter 2** folder as **Lastname_Firstname_2F_Student_Publications** and then enable the content. In the **Navigation Pane**, **Rename** the **2F Publishers** table by adding **Lastname Firstname** to the beginning of the table name. From your student data files, import the **a02F_Student_Papers** Excel file as a new table in the database. Designate the first row of the spreadsheet as column headings, and designate **Paper ID** as the primary key. Name the new table **Lastname Firstname 2F Student Papers** and then increase the width of the **Navigation Pane** so that all object names display fully.

Open your **2F Student Papers** table in **Design** view. For the **Student ID** field, change the **Data Type** to **Short Text**. Switch to **Datasheet** view, saving the change, apply **Best Fit** to all of the columns, and then **Save** the table. Examine the fields and data in this table. Open your **2F Publishers** table, examine the fields and data, and then **Close All** open objects.

Create a *one-to-many* relationship between your **2F Publishers** table and your **2F Student Papers** table using the common field **Publisher ID**. **Enforce Referential Integrity**, and enable both cascade options. *One* publisher can publish *many* student papers. Create a **Relationship Report** with **Normal Margins**, saving it as **Lastname Firstname 2F Relationships** and then create a paper or electronic printout as directed. **Close All** open objects.

2 Create a query in **Query Design** view using your **2F Student Papers** table to answer the question, *What is the student ID, home campus, award paid, and publisher ID for awards greater than or equal to $50, sorted in ascending order by the Student ID field?* Display the fields in the order listed in the question. Five records match the criteria. **Save** the query as **Lastname Firstname 2F Awards $50 or More Query** and then create a paper or electronic printout as directed. **Close** the query.

3 From the **Navigation Pane**, copy your **2F Awards $50 or More Query** object to create a new query object named **Lastname Firstname 2F 2nd Qtr NW Students Query** and then redesign the query to answer the questions, *Which students (Student ID) from the Northwest campus had papers published between 4/1/18 and 6/30/18, and what was the paper name, the award paid, and the category, sorted in ascending order only by the Publication Date field?* Do not restrict the results by **Award Paid**. Do not display the **Home Campus** field in

the query results, and display the rest of the fields in the order listed in the question. Three records match the criteria. Using **Landscape** orientation, create a paper or electronic printout as directed. **Close** the query, saving the design changes.

4 Create a query in **Query Design** view using your **2F Student Papers** table to answer the question, *Which paper IDs, paper names, and category for students from the Southeast or Northeast campuses were published that had an award paid greater than $25, sorted in descending order by the Award Paid field?* Display the fields in the order listed in the question. Six records match the criteria. **Save** the query as **Lastname Firstname 2F SE OR NE Over $25 Query** and then using **Normal Margins**, create a paper or electronic printout as directed. **Close** the query.

5 Create a query in **Query Design** view using both tables to answer the questions, *Which paper names were published with a publisher name that has Texas as part of its name, what is the contact name and contact phone number, and what was the award paid, sorted in descending order by the Award Paid field?* (Hint: Use a wildcard character in the **Criteria** row.) Display the fields in the order listed in the question. Eight records match the criteria. **Save** the query as **Lastname Firstname 2F Texas Publishers Query** and then using **Landscape** orientation, create a paper or electronic printout as directed. **Close** the query.

6 The college's Federation of English Faculty will donate money to the English Writing Lab based on 50 percent of the awards paid to the students. Create a query in **Query Design** view using your **2F Student Papers** table to answer the question, *In ascending order by the Paper ID field, what will be the total of each donation to the Writing Lab if the Federation donates an additional 50 percent of each award paid to students?* (Hint: First calculate the amount of the donation, naming the new field **Federation Donation**, and then run the query to be sure the correct results display. Then calculate the total donation, naming the new field **Total Donation**.) Change the property settings of the **Federation Donation** field to display with a **Format** of **Currency** and with **Decimal Places** set to **2**. For the **Publisher ID** of **P-20**, the *Federation Donation* is *$22.50*, and the *Total Donation* is *$67.50*. Apply **Best Fit** to all of the columns, **Save** the query as **Lastname Firstname 2F Federation Donation Query** and then create a paper or electronic printout as directed. **Close** the query.

(Project 2F Student Publications continues on the next page)

CONTENT-BASED ASSESSMENTS

7 Create a query in **Query Design** view using your **2F Student Papers** table and the **Sum** aggregate function to answer the question, *What are the total awards paid for each category, sorted in descending order by the Award Paid field?* Display the fields in the order listed in the question. Change the property settings of the **Award Paid** field to display with **Decimal Places** set to **0**. For the **Category** of **Student Life**, total awards paid are *$265*. Apply **Best Fit** to the **SumOfAward Paid** column. **Save** the query as **Lastname Firstname 2F Awards by Category Query** and then create a paper or electronic printout as directed. **Close** the query.

8 Use the **Query Wizard** to create a crosstab query based on your **2F Student Papers** table. Select **Home Campus** as the row headings and **Category** as the column headings. **Sum** the **Award Paid** field. Name the query **Lastname Firstname 2F Campus and Category Crosstab Query** In **Design** view, change the property settings of the last two fields to display with **Decimal Places** set to **0**. This query answers the question, *What are the total awards paid for student publications by each home campus and by each category?* Apply **Best Fit** to all of the columns, and then **Save** the query. Using **Landscape** orientation and **Normal Margins**, create a paper or electronic printout as directed. **Close** the query.

9 Create a query in **Query Design** view using your **2F Student Papers** table that prompts you to enter the **Home Campus**, and then answers the question, *What is the home campus, student ID, paper name, category, and publication date for student publications, sorted in ascending order by the Publication Date field?* Display the fields in the order listed in the question. **Run** the query, entering **southwest** when prompted for criteria. Seven records match the criteria. **Save** the query as **Lastname Firstname 2F Campus Parameter Query** and then using **Normal Margins**, create a paper or electronic printout as directed. **Close** the query.

10 Open the **Navigation Pane**, and be sure that all object names display fully. **Close** Access. As directed by your instructor, submit your database and the paper or electronic printouts of the nine objects—relationship report and eight queries—that are the results of this project. Specifically, in this project, using your own name, you created the following database and printouts or electronic printouts:

1. Lastname_Firstname_2F_Student_Publications	Database file
2. Lastname Firstname 2F Relationships	Relationships Report (printout or electronic printout)
3. Lastname Firstname 2F Awards $50 or More Query	Query (printout or electronic printout)
4. Lastname Firstname 2F 2nd Qtr NW Students Query	Query (printout or electronic printout)
5. Lastname Firstname 2F SE OR NE Over $25 Query	Query (printout or electronic printout)
6. Lastname Firstname 2F Texas Publishers Query	Query (printout or electronic printout)
7. Lastname Firstname 2F Federation Donation Query	Query (printout or electronic printout)
8. Lastname Firstname 2F Awards by Category Query	Query (printout or electronic printout)
9. Lastname Firstname 2F Campus and Category Crosstab Query	Query (printout or electronic printout)
10. Lastname Firstname 2F Campus Parameter Query	Query (printout or electronic printout - Southwest)

END | You have completed Project 2F

CONTENT-BASED ASSESSMENTS

Apply 2A and 2B skills from these Objectives:

1 Open and Save an Existing Database

2 Create Table Relationships

3 Sort Records in a Table

4 Create a Query in Design View

5 Create a New Query from an Existing Query

6 Sort Query Results

7 Specify Criteria in a Query

8 Specify Numeric Criteria in a Query

9 Use Compound Criteria in a Query

10 Create a Query Based on More Than One Table

11 Use Wildcards in a Query

12 Create Calculated Fields in a Query

13 Calculate Statistics and Group Data in a Query

14 Create a Crosstab Query

15 Create a Parameter Query

In the following Mastering Access project, you will assist Kim Ngo, director of Academic Scholarships, in using her database to answer questions about scholarships awarded to students. Your completed database objects will look similar to Figure 2.59.

PROJECT FILES

For Project 2G, you will need the following file:

a02G_Student_Scholarships

You will save your database as:

Lastname_Firstname_2G_Student_Scholarships

PROJECT RESULTS

FIGURE 2.59

(Project 2G Student Scholarships continues on the next page)

1 ▶ **Start** Access. From your student data files, open **a02G_Student_Scholarships**. Save the database in your **Access Chapter 2** folder as **Lastname_Firstname_2G_ Student_Scholarships** and then enable the content. In the **Navigation Pane**, **Rename** each table by adding **Lastname Firstname** to the beginning of the table name. Increase the width of the **Navigation Pane** so that all object names display fully.

2 ▶ Open both tables to examine the fields and data, and then **Close** both tables. Create a *one-to-many* relationship between your **2G Students** table and your **2G Scholarships Awarded** table using the common field **Student ID**. **Enforce Referential Integrity**, and enable both cascade options. *One* student can have *many* scholarships. Create a **Relationship Report** with **Normal Margins**, saving it with the default name. Create a paper or electronic printout as directed, and then **Close All** open objects. Open your **2G Students** table. In the last record, in the **Student ID** field, select **9999999**, type **2839403** and then press ↓ to save the record. **Close** the table.

3 ▶ Create a query in **Query Design** view using your **2G Scholarships Awarded** table to answer the question, *What is the scholarship name, amount, and major for scholarships greater than or equal to $500, sorted in ascending order by the Scholarship Name field?* Display the fields in the order listed in the question. Eight records match the criteria. **Save** the query as **Lastname Firstname 2G Amount $500 or More Query** and then create a paper or electronic printout as directed. **Close** the query.

4 ▶ From the **Navigation Pane**, copy your **2G Amount $500 or More Query** object to create a new query object named **Lastname Firstname 2G Awards 4th Qtr Query** and then redesign the query to answer the question, *Which scholarships (Scholarship Name) were awarded between 10/1/18 and 12/31/18, for what amount, and for which student (Student ID), sorted in ascending order only by the Award Date field?* Display only the fields necessary to answer the question and in the order listed in the question. Do not restrict the results by amount. Five records match the criteria. Create a paper or electronic printout as directed. **Close** the query, saving the design changes.

5 ▶ Create a query in **Query Design** view using your **2G Scholarships Awarded** table to answer the question, *Which scholarships (Scholarship Name) were awarded for either Math or Business majors for amounts of more than $200, sorted in descending order by the Amount field?*

Display the fields in the order listed in the question. Four records match the criteria. (Hint: If six records display, switch to **Design** view and combine the majors on one criteria line using OR.) **Save** the query as **Lastname Firstname 2G Math OR Business Over $200 Query** and then create a paper or electronic printout as directed. **Close** the query.

6 ▶ Create a query in **Query Design** view using your **2G Students** table and a wildcard character to answer the question, *What is the city, student ID, last name, and first name of students from cities that begin with the letter L, sorted in ascending order by the City field, in ascending order by the Last Name field, and ascending order by the First Name field?* Display the fields in the order listed in the question. Five records match the criteria. **Save** the query as **Lastname Firstname 2G L Cities Query** and then create a paper or electronic printout as directed. **Close** the query.

7 ▶ Create a query in **Query Design** view using your **2G Students** table and all of the fields in the same order that they display in the field list to answer the question, *For which students is the Postal Code missing?* Three records match the criteria. **Save** the query as **Lastname Firstname 2G Missing Postal Code Query** and then using **Normal Margins**, create a paper or electronic printout as directed. **Close** the query.

8 ▶ The Board of Trustees for the college will donate an amount equal to 50 percent of each scholarship amount. Create a query in **Query Design** view using both tables to answer the question, *In ascending order by the Scholarship Name field, and including the first name and last name of the scholarship recipient, what will be the total value of each scholarship if the Board of Trustees donates an additional 50 percent of each award paid to students?* (Hint: First calculate the amount of the donation, naming the new field **Board Donation**, and then run the query to be sure the correct results display. Then calculate the total donation, naming the new field **Total Donation**.) Change the property settings of the appropriate fields to display with a **Format** of **Currency** and with **Decimal Places** set to **0**. For the **Scholarship Name** of **Amanda Snyder Foundation Scholarship**, the *Board Donation* is *$125*, and the *Total Donation* is *$375*. Apply **Best Fit** to all of the columns, **Save** the query as **Lastname Firstname 2G Board Donation Query** and then using **Landscape** orientation, create a paper or electronic printout as directed. **Close** the query.

(Project 2G Student Scholarships continues on the next page)

CONTENT-BASED ASSESSMENTS

9 Create a query in **Query Design** view using your **2G Scholarships Awarded** table and the **Sum** aggregate function to answer the question, *For each major, what is the total scholarship amount, sorted in descending order by the Amount field?* Display the fields in the order listed in the question. Change the property settings of the **Amount** field to display with **Decimal Places** set to **0**. For the **Major** of **History**, the total scholarship amount is *$1,850*. Apply **Best Fit** to all of the columns. **Save** the query as **Lastname Firstname 2G Amount by Major Query** and then create a paper or electronic printout as directed. **Close** the query.

10 Use the **Query Wizard** to create a crosstab query based on your **2G Scholarships Awarded** table. Select **Student ID** as the row headings and **Major** as the column headings. **Sum** the **Amount** field. Name the query **Lastname Firstname 2G Student ID and Major Crosstab Query** In **Design** view, change the property settings of the last two fields to display with **Decimal Places** set to **0**. This query answers the question, *What are the total scholarship amounts paid by each student ID and by each major?* Apply **Best Fit** to all of the columns, and then **Save** the query. Using **Landscape** orientation, create a paper or electronic printout as directed—two pages result. **Close** the query.

11 Create a query in **Query Design** view using your **2G Scholarships Awarded** table that prompts you to enter the **Major**, and then answers the question, *What is the scholarship name and amount for a major, sorted in ascending order by the Scholarship Name field?* Display the fields in the order listed in the question. **Run** the query, entering **history** when prompted for criteria. Four records match the criteria. **Save** the query as **Lastname Firstname 2G Major Parameter Query** and then create a paper or electronic printout as directed. **Close** the query.

12 Open the **Navigation Pane**, and be sure that all object names display fully. **Close** Access. As directed by your instructor, submit your database and the paper or electronic printouts of the 10 objects—relationship report and nine queries, one of which prints on two pages—that are the results of this project. Specifically, in this project, using your own name, you created the following database and printouts or electronic printouts:

1. Lastname_Firstname_2G_Student_Scholarships	Database file
2. Relationships for Lastname_Firstname_2G_Student_Scholarships	Relationships Report (printout or electronic printout)
3. Lastname Firstname 2G Amount $500 or More Query	Query (printout or electronic printout)
4. Lastname Firstname 2G Awards 4th Qtr Query	Query (printout or electronic printout)
5. Lastname Firstname 2G Math OR Business Over $200 Query	Query (printout or electronic printout)
6. Lastname Firstname 2G L Cities Query	Query (printout or electronic printout)
7. Lastname Firstname 2G Missing Postal Code Query	Query (printout or electronic printout)
8. Lastname Firstname 2G Board Donation Query	Query (printout or electronic printout)
9. Lastname Firstname 2G Amount by Major Query	Query (printout or electronic printout)
10. Lastname Firstname 2G Student ID and Major Crosstab Query	Query (printout or electronic printout - two pages)
11. Lastname Firstname 2G Major Parameter Query (using History)	Query (printout or electronic printout)

END | You have completed Project 2G

CONTENT-BASED ASSESSMENTS

Apply a combination of the **2A** and **2B** skills.

GO! Fix It	Project 2H Social Sciences	Online
GO! Make It	Project 2I Faculty Awards	Online
GO! Solve It	Project 2J Student Refunds	Online
GO! Solve It	Project 2K Leave	

PROJECT FILES

For Project 2K, you will need the following file:

a02K_Leave

You will save your database as:

Lastname_Firstname_2K_Leave

Start Access, navigate to your student data files, open a02K_Leave, and then save the database in your Access Chapter 2 folder as **Lastname_Firstname_2K_Leave** Add **Lastname Firstname** to the beginning of both table names, create a one-to-many relationship with cascade options between the two tables—*one* employee can have *many* leave transactions—and then create a relationship report saving it as **Lastname Firstname 2K Relationships**

Create and save four queries to answer the following questions:

- What is the last name and first name of employees who have used personal leave, sorted in ascending order by the Last Name and First Name fields? Do not display the Leave field in the query results.

- What is the last name, first name, and email address of employees who have no phone number listed, sorted in ascending order by the Last Name and First Name fields?

- Grouped by the Leave Classification field, what is the total of each type of leave used? (Hint: Use the aggregate function Count.)

- What is the total number of leave transactions grouped in rows by the Employee# field and grouped in columns by the Leave Classification field?

As directed, create paper or electronic printouts of the relationship report and the four queries. Be sure that each object prints on one page, and that the object names display fully in the Navigation Pane. As directed, submit your database and the paper or electronic printouts of the five objects that are the results of this project.

(Project 2K Leave continues on the next page)

CONTENT-BASED ASSESSMENTS

Performance Level

Performance Criteria	Exemplary	Proficient	Developing
Create relationship and relationship report	Relationship and relationship report created correctly.	Relationship and relationship report created with one error.	Relationship and relationship report created with two or more errors, or missing entirely.
Create Personal Leave query	Query created with correct name, fields, sorting, and criteria.	Query created with one element incorrect.	Query created with two or more elements incorrect, or missing entirely.
Create Missing Phone query	Query created with correct name, fields, sorting, and criteria.	Query created with one element incorrect.	Query created with two or more elements incorrect, or missing entirely.
Create Type of Leave query	Query created with correct name, fields, and aggregate function.	Query created with one element incorrect.	Query created with two or more elements incorrect, or missing entirely.
Create Crosstab query	Query created with correct name, row headings, column headings, and aggregate function.	Query created with one element incorrect.	Query created with two or more elements incorrect, or missing entirely.

END | You have completed Project 2K

OUTCOMES-BASED ASSESSMENTS

RUBRIC

The following outcomes-based assessments are *open-ended assessments*. That is, there is no specific correct result; your result will depend on your approach to the information provided. Make *Professional Quality* your goal. Use the following scoring rubric to guide you in *how* to approach the problem and then to evaluate *how well* your approach solves the problem.

The *criteria*—Software Mastery, Content, Format & Layout, and Process—represent the knowledge and skills you have gained that you can apply to solving the problem. The *levels of performance*—Professional Quality, Approaching Professional Quality, or Needs Quality Improvements—help you and your instructor evaluate your result.

	Your completed project is of Professional Quality if you:	Your completed project is Approaching Professional Quality if you:	Your completed project Needs Quality Improvements if you:
1-Software Mastery	Choose and apply the most appropriate skills, tools, and features and identify efficient methods to solve the problem.	Choose and apply some appropriate skills, tools, and features, but not in the most efficient manner.	Choose inappropriate skills, tools, or features, or are inefficient in solving the problem.
2-Content	Construct a solution that is clear and well organized, contains content that is accurate, appropriate to the audience and purpose, and is complete. Provide a solution that contains no errors in spelling, grammar, or style.	Construct a solution in which some components are unclear, poorly organized, inconsistent, or incomplete. Misjudge the needs of the audience. Have some errors in spelling, grammar, or style, but the errors do not detract from comprehension.	Construct a solution that is unclear, incomplete, or poorly organized; contains some inaccurate or inappropriate content; and contains many errors in spelling, grammar, or style. Do not solve the problem.
3-Format & Layout	Format and arrange all elements to communicate information and ideas, clarify function, illustrate relationships, and indicate relative importance.	Apply appropriate format and layout features to some elements, but not others. Overuse features, causing minor distraction.	Apply format and layout that does not communicate information or ideas clearly. Do not use format and layout features to clarify function, illustrate relationships, or indicate relative importance. Use available features excessively, causing distraction.
4-Process	Use an organized approach that integrates planning, development, self-assessment, revision, and reflection.	Demonstrate an organized approach in some areas, but not others; or, use an insufficient process of organization throughout.	Do not use an organized approach to solve the problem.

OUTCOMES-BASED ASSESSMENTS

Apply a combination of the **2A** and **2B** skills.

GO! Think   Project 2L Coaches

PROJECT FILES

For Project 2L, you will need the following file:

a02L_Coaches

You will save your database as

Lastname_Firstname_2L_Coaches

Start Access, navigate to your student data files, open a02L_Coaches, and then save the database in your Access Chapter 2 folder as **Lastname_Firstname_2L_Coaches** Add **Lastname Firstname** to the beginning of both table names, create a one-to-many relationship with cascade options between the two tables—*one* coach can participate in *many* activities—and then create a relationship report saving it as **Lastname Firstname 2L Relationships**

Create queries to assist Randy Garza, the athletic director, in answering the following questions about the coaches at Texas Lakes Community College:

- What is the last name and first name of every coach involved in *Dive* activities, sorted in ascending order by the Last Name field and First Name fields?
- What is the last name and first name of every coach involved in basketball or football activities, sorted in ascending order first by the Activity Name field and then by the Last Name and First Name fields?
- Grouped by division, what is the total number of activity names, sorted in descending order by the total number? (Hint: Use the Count aggregate function.)
- What is the skill specialty, last name, first name, and phone number for coaches in a specified position that is entered when prompted for the Position, sorted in ascending order first by the Skill Specialty field and then by the Last Name and First Name fields? (When prompted, enter the position of *director* for your paper or electronic printout.)

As directed, create paper or electronic printouts of the relationship report and the four queries. Be sure that each object prints on one page, and that the object names display fully in the Navigation Pane. As directed, submit your database and the paper or electronic printouts of the five objects that are the results of this project.

END | You have completed Project 2L

GO! Think   Project 2M Club Donations   **Online**

Build from Scratch

You and GO!   Project 2N Personal Inventory   **Online**

Build from Scratch

GO! Cumulative Group Project   Project 2O Bell Orchid Hotels
Online

Forms, Filters, and Reports

GO! to Work
Video A3

PROJECT 3A	OUTCOMES
	Create forms to enter and delete records and to display data in a database.

OBJECTIVES

1. Create and Use a Form to Add and Delete Records
2. Filter Records
3. Create a Form by Using the Form Wizard
4. Modify a Form in Layout View and in Design View

PROJECT 3B	OUTCOMES
	Create reports to display database information.

OBJECTIVES

5. Create a Report by Using the Report Tool and Modify the Report in Layout View
6. Create a Report by Using the Report Wizard
7. Modify the Design of a Report
8. Keep Grouped Data Together in a Printed Report

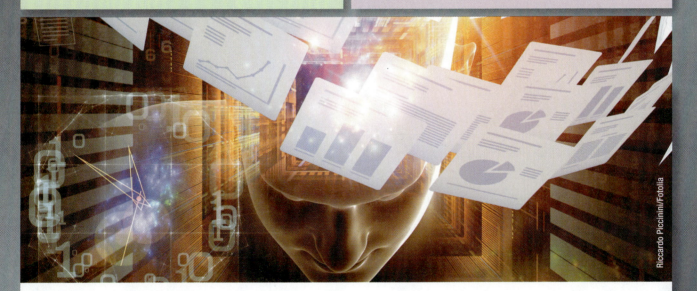

Riccardo Piccinini/Fotolia

In This Chapter

In this chapter, you will create forms to enter and delete data and to view data in database tables. Forms can display one record at a time with fields placed in the same order to match a paper source document. Records in a form or table can be filtered to display a subset of the records based on matching specific values. You will modify forms by adding fields, changing field widths, and adding labels to the forms. You will create professional-looking reports that summarize the data stored in a query or table. You will modify the reports by changing the fields in the report, by changing the layout of the report, by grouping data, and by making sure that groupings of data stay together on the printed page.

The projects in this chapter relate to **Texas Lakes Community College**, which is located in the Austin, Texas, area. Its four campuses serve over 30,000 students and offer more than 140 certificate programs and degrees. The college has a highly acclaimed Distance Education program and an extensive Workforce Development program. The college makes positive contributions to the community through cultural and athletic programs and has significant partnerships with businesses and nonprofit organizations. Popular fields of study include nursing and health care, solar technology, computer technology, and graphic design.

Students and Majors Database

PROJECT ACTIVITIES

In Activities 3.01 through 3.15, you will assist Sean Fitchette, director of Enrollment Services at Texas Lakes Community College, in using his Access database to track new students and their major fields of study. Your completed forms will look similar to Figure 3.1.

PROJECT FILES

For Project 3A, you will need the following file:

a03A_Students_Majors

You will save your database as:

Lastname_Firstname_3A_Students_Majors

PROJECT RESULTS

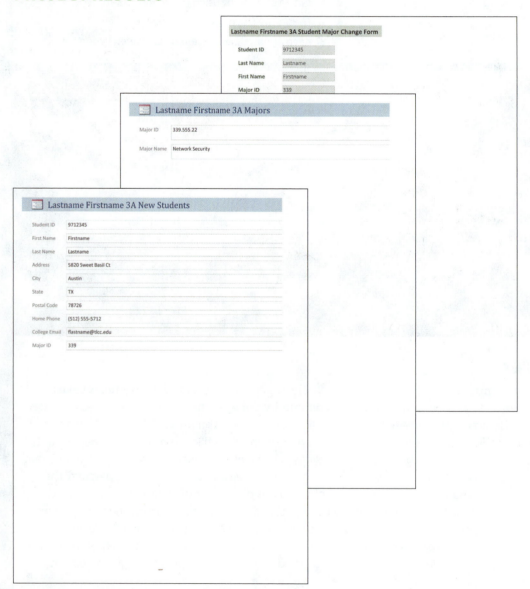

FIGURE 3.1 Project 3A Students and Majors

Objective 1   Create and Use a Form to Add and Delete Records

Video A3-1

A *form* is a database object that you can use to enter new records into a table, or to edit, delete, or display existing records in a table. A form is useful to control access to the data. For example, you can design a form for college registration assistants so that they can see and enter the courses scheduled and fees paid by an individual student. However, they cannot see or enter grades for a student.

Some forms display only one record at a time; other forms display multiple records at the same time. A form that displays only one record at a time is useful not only to the individual who performs the *data entry*—entering the actual records—but also to anyone who has the job of viewing information in a database. For example, when you request a transcript from your college, someone displays your record on the screen. For the individual viewing your transcript, it is much easier to look at one record at a time, using a form, than to look at all of the student transcripts in the database.

Activity 3.01 | Opening and Saving an Existing Database, Renaming Tables, and Viewing a Table Relationship

1 Start Access. In the Access opening screen, click **Open Other Files**. Under **Open**, click **Computer**, and then on the right, click **Browse**. In the **Open** dialog box, navigate to the location where your student data files for this chapter are stored, and then double-click **a03A_Students_Majors** to open the database.

2 On the ribbon, click the **FILE tab**, and then click **Save As**. Under **File Types**, be sure **Save Database As** is selected. On the right, under **Database File Types**, be sure **Access Database** is selected, and then at the bottom of the screen, click **Save As**.

3 In the **Save As** dialog box, navigate to the location where you are saving your databases. Create a **New folder** named **Access Chapter 3**, and then **Open** the folder. In the **File name** box and using your own name, replace the existing text with **Lastname_Firstname_3A_Students_Majors** and then click **Save** or press [Enter].

4 On the **Message Bar**, click **Enable Content**. In the **Navigation Pane**, right-click the **3A Majors** table, and then click **Rename**. With the table name selected and using your own name, type **Lastname Firstname 3A Majors** and then press [Enter] to rename the table. Use the same technique to **Rename** the **3A New Students** table to **Lastname Firstname 3A New Students**

5 Point to the right edge of the **Navigation Pane** to display the ↔ pointer. Drag to the right to increase the width of the pane until both table names display fully.

6 On the ribbon, click the **DATABASE TOOLS tab**. In the **Relationships group**, click **Relationships**. On the **DESIGN tab**, in the **Relationships group**, click **All Relationships**. If necessary, resize and move the field lists so that the entire table name and fields display for each field list.

> Because you renamed the tables, the field lists do not automatically display in the Relationships window.

7 In the **Relationships** window, click the **join line** between the two field lists. In the **Tools group**, click **Edit Relationships**. Point to the title bar of the **Edit Relationships** dialog box, and drag the dialog box downward below the two field lists. Compare your screen with Figure 3.2.

> *One* major is associated with *many* students. A one-to-many relationship is established between your 3A Majors table and your 3A New Students table using the Major ID field as the common field. Recall that Cascade Update Related Fields enables you to change the primary key in the 3A Majors table, and then the data in the foreign key field in the 3A New Students field is automatically updated. Recall that Cascade Delete Related Records enables you to delete a record in the 3A Majors table, and then all related records in the 3A New Students table are automatically deleted.

🔄 **ANOTHER WAY**   In the Relationships window, double-click the join line to display the Edit Relationships dialog box.

FIGURE 3.2

ALERT!   **Is Your Edit Relationships Dialog Box Empty?**

The Edit Relationships dialog box does not display any information if you do not first click the join line. If this happens, close the Edit Relationships dialog box, and then be sure that you click the join line—when selected, the join line is darker.

---

8 Close ⊠ the **Edit Relationships** dialog box, and then **Close** ☒ the **Relationships** window. In the message box, click **Yes** to save changes to the layout of the relationships.

Activity 3.02 | Creating a Form and Viewing Records

There are several ways to create a form in Access, but the fastest and easiest way is to use the ***Form tool***. With a single mouse click, all fields from the data source are placed on the form. You can use the new form immediately, or you can modify the form in Layout view or in Design view.

The Form tool uses all of the field names and all of the records from an existing table or query. Records that you create or edit using a form are automatically updated in the underlying table or tables. In this activity, you will create a form and then view records from the underlying table—the data source.

1 In the **Navigation Pane**, double-click your **3A New Students** table to open it. Scroll as needed to view all 10 fields—*Student ID, First Name, Last Name, Address, City, State, Postal Code, Home Phone, College Email,* and *Major ID*. **Close** ☒ the table.

2 In the **Navigation Pane**, be sure your **3A New Students** table is selected. On the ribbon, click the **CREATE tab**, and then in the **Forms group**, click **Form**. **Close** ◄◄ the **Navigation Pane**, and then compare your screen with Figure 3.3.

The form is created based on the currently selected object—your 3A New Students table—and displays in *Layout view*. In Layout view, you can modify the form with the data displayed in the fields. For example, you can adjust the size of the text boxes to fit the data.

The form is created in a simple top-to-bottom layout, with all 10 fields from your 3A New Students table lined up in a single column. The data for the first record in the data source displays.

FIGURE 3.3

Data for Record 1 of 101 displays in form

Dotted lines indicate form is displayed in Layout view

Form displays all 10 fields from your 3A New Students table

Current record box

New (blank) record button

Layout View button active

Navigation area

3 In the navigation area, click **Next record** ▶ four times to display the fifth record—*Student ID 1298345*. In the navigation area, select the text in the Current record box, type **62** and then press [Enter] to display the record for *Student ID 5720358*. In the navigation area, click **Last record** ▶❙ to display the record for *Student ID 9583924*, and then click **First record** ❙◀ to display the record for *Student ID 1034823*.

Use the navigation buttons to scroll among the records or the Current record box to display any single record.

4 Save 🖫 the form as **Lastname Firstname 3A New Student Form** and then **Close** ☒ the form object.

5 Open ◄◄ the **Navigation Pane**. Notice that your new form displays under the table with which it is related—your **3A New Students** table.

Activity 3.03 | Creating a Second Form

In this activity, you will use the Form tool to create a form for your 3A Majors table.

1 ▶ In the **Navigation Pane**, click your **3A Majors** table to select it. On the ribbon, click the **CREATE tab**, and then in the **Forms group**, click **Form**. **Close** « the **Navigation Pane**, and then compare your screen with Figure 3.4.

Because a one-to-many relationship is established, the form displays related records in the 3A New Students table for each record in the 3A Majors table. Five new students have selected a major of *Diagnostic Medical Sonography—Major ID 105.*

FIGURE 3.4

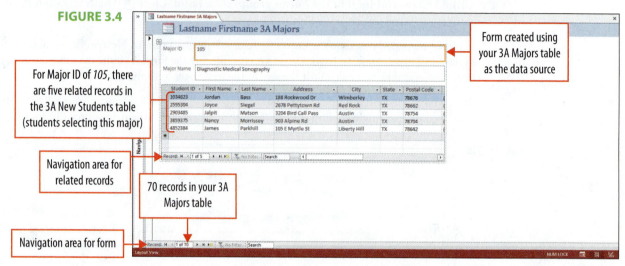

Form created using your 3A Majors table as the data source

For Major ID of *105*, there are five related records in the 3A New Students table (students selecting this major)

Navigation area for related records

70 records in your 3A Majors table

Navigation area for form

2 ▶ **Close** × your **3A Majors** form. In the message box, click **Yes**. In the **Save As** dialog box, in the **Form Name** box, type **Lastname Firstname 3A Major Form** and then click **OK**.

Recall that if you do not save an object, you are prompted to do so when you close the object.

3 ▶ **Open** » the **Navigation Pane**. Notice that your new form displays under the table with which it is related—your **3A Majors** table.

Activity 3.04 | Adding Records to a Table by Using a Form

By using a single-record form to add, modify, and delete records, you can reduce the number of data entry errors, because the individual performing the data entry is looking at only one record at a time. Recall that your database is useful only if the information is accurate—just like your contact list is useful only if it contains accurate phone numbers and email addresses.

Forms are based on—also referred to as *bound* to—the table where the records are stored. When a record is entered in a form, the new record is added to the underlying table. The reverse is also true—when a record is added to the table, the new record can be viewed in the related form.

In this activity, you will add a new record to both tables by using the forms that you just created.

1 ▶ In the **Navigation Pane**, double-click your **3A New Student Form** object to open it, and then **Close** « the **Navigation Pane**. In the navigation area, click **New (blank) record** ▶⊞ to display a new blank form.

When you open a form, the first record in the underlying table displays in *Form view*, which is used to view, add, modify, and delete records stored in the table.

2 ▶ In the **Student ID** field, type **9712345** and then press ⟨Tab⟩.

Use the ⟨Tab⟩ key to move from field to field in a form. *Tab order* is the order in which the insertion point moves from one field to the next when you press the ⟨Tab⟩ key. As you start typing, the pencil icon displays in the *record selector bar* at the left—the bar used to select an entire record. The pencil icon displays when a record is being created or edited.

ANOTHER WAY Press the Enter key, provided there are no special links on the form, such as a link to create a new form or a link to print the form.

3 Using your own first name and last name and using the first initial of your first name and your last name for the *College Email* field, continue entering the data shown in the following table, and then compare your screen with Figure 3.5.

Student ID	First Name	Last Name	Address	City	State	Postal Code	Home Phone	College Email	Major ID
9712345	First Name	Last Name	5820 Sweet Basil Ct	Austin	TX	78726	(512) 555-5712	flastname@ tlcc.edu	339

FIGURE 3.5

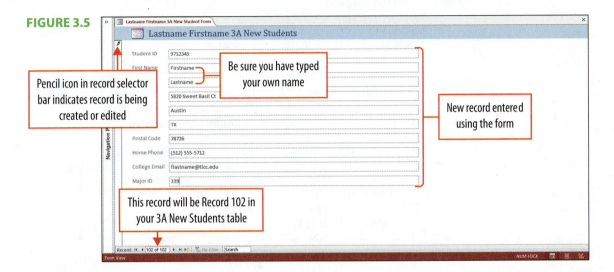

4 With the insertion point positioned in the last field, press Tab to save the record and display a new blank record. **Close** ☒ your **3A New Student Form** object.

5 **Open** ☒ the **Navigation Pane**, and then double-click your **3A New Students** table to open it. In the navigation area, click **Last record** ⏮ to verify that the record you entered in the form is stored in the underlying table. **Close** ☒ your **3A New Students** table.

6 In the **Navigation Pane**, double-click your **3A Major Form** object to open it. At the bottom of the screen, in the navigation area for the form—*not* the navigation area for the subdatasheet—click **New (blank) record** ⏭. In the blank form enter the data shown in the following table:

Major ID	Major Name
339.555.22	Network Security

7 **Close** ☒ your **3A Major Form** object. In the **Navigation Pane**, double-click your **3A Majors** table, and then scroll to verify that the record for *Major ID 339.555.22 Network Security* displays in the table—records are sorted by the *Major ID* field. **Close** ☒ the table.

Activity 3.05 | Deleting Records from a Table by Using a Form

You can delete records from a database table by using a form. In this activity, you will delete the record for *Major ID 800.03* because the program has been discontinued.

1 In the **Navigation Pane**, double-click your **3A Major Form** object to open it, and then **Close** `«` the **Navigation Pane**. On the **HOME tab**, in the **Find group**, click **Find** to open the **Find and Replace** dialog box.

🔄 **ANOTHER WAY**   Press `Ctrl` + `F` to open the Find and Replace dialog box.

2 In the **Look In** box, notice that *Current field* displays. In the **Find What** box, type **800.03** and then click **Find Next**. Compare your screen with Figure 3.6, and verify that the record for *Major ID 800.03* displays.

> Because the insertion point was positioned in the *Major ID* field before opening the dialog box, Access will search for data in this field—the *Current field*.

FIGURE 3.6

Record for *Major ID 800.03* displays

Find and Replace dialog box

Look In box indicates that Access will search the Current field—*Major ID*

Find What box

3 **Close** ❌ the **Find and Replace** dialog box. On the **HOME tab**, in the **Records group**, click the **Delete arrow**, and then click **Delete Record**.

> The record is removed from the screen, and a message displays alerting you that you are about to delete *1 record(s)*. Once you click *Yes*, you cannot click Undo to reverse this action. If you delete a record by mistake, you must re-create the record by reentering the data. Because no students are associated with this major and the program is being discontinued, you can delete it from the table.

4 In the message box, click **Yes** to delete the record. In the navigation area for the form, notice that the total number of records in the table is *70*. **Close** ❌ your **3A Major Form** object.

5 **Open** `»` the **Navigation Pane**, and then double-click your **3A Majors** table to open it. Examine the table to verify that the *Major ID 800.03* record has been deleted from the table, and then **Close** ❌ the table.

> Adding and deleting records in a form updates the records stored in the underlying table.

Activity 3.06 | Printing a Form

When a form is displayed, clicking Print causes *all* of the records to print in the form layout. In this activity, you will print only *one* record.

1 In the **Navigation Pane**, double-click your **3A New Student Form** object to open it, and then **Close** `«` the **Navigation Pane**. Press `Ctrl` + `F` to open the **Find and Replace** dialog box. In the **Find What** box, type **9712345** and then click **Find Next** to display the record with your name. **Close** ❌ the **Find and Replace** dialog box.

2 ▶ On the ribbon, click the **FILE tab**, click **Print**, and then on the right, click **Print**. In the **Print** dialog box, under **Print Range**, click the **Selected Record(s)** option button. In the lower left corner of the dialog box, click **Setup**.

3 ▶ In the **Page Setup** dialog box, click the **Columns tab**. Under **Column Size**, double-click in the **Width** box to select the existing value, type **7.5** and then compare your screen with Figure 3.7.

Change the width of the column in this manner so that the form prints on one page. Forms are not typically printed, so the width of the column in a form might be greater than the width of the paper on which you are printing. The maximum column width that you can enter is dependent upon the printer that is installed on your system. This setting is saved when you save or close the form.

FIGURE 3.7

Page Setup dialog box

Record with your name

Column Size Width set to 7.5 so that form will print on one page

4 ▶ In the **Page Setup** dialog box, click **OK**. To create a paper printout, in the **Print** dialog box click **OK**. To create an electronic printout of this single form, click **Cancel** and then follow the instructions in the Note below.

N O T E Printing a Single Form in PDF

To create an electronic printout of a single form in PDF, change the column width to 7.5 as described in Step 3 above, and then in the Print dialog box, click Cancel. On the left side of the form, click the Record Selector bar so that it is black—selected. On the ribbon, click the EXTERNAL DATA tab. In the Export group, click PDF or XPS.

In the Publish as PDF or XPS dialog box, navigate to your chapter folder. In the File name box, the form has the same name as the form. Be sure that the Open file after publishing check box is selected, and that the Minimum size (publishing online) option button is selected. In the Publish as PDF or XPS dialog box, Click Options. In the Options dialog box, under Range, click the Selected records option button, click OK, and then click Publish. Close the Windows 8 Reader, Adobe Reader or Adobe Acrobat window, and then submit the file as directed by your instructor.

---

5 ▶ **Close** ✕ your **3A New Student Form** object, **Open** » the **Navigation Pane**, and then double-click your **3A Major Form** object to open it. **Close** « the **Navigation Pane**.

6 ▶ Use the techniques you just practiced to **Find** the record for the **Major ID** of **339.555.22**, and then create a paper or electronic printout as directed by your instructor of that record only on one page. After printing, **Close** ✕ your **3A Major Form** object.

If there are no related records in the subdatasheet, the empty subdatasheet does not display in the printed form.

Objective 2 | Filter Records

Video A3-2

Filtering records in a form displays only a portion of the total records—a *subset*—based on matching specific values. Filters are commonly used to provide a quick answer, and the result is not generally saved for future use. For example, by filtering records in a form, you can quickly display a subset of records for students majoring in Information Systems Technology, which is identified by the Major ID of 339.

A form provides an interface for the database. For example, because of security reasons, the registration assistants at your college may not have access to the entire student database. Rather, by using a form, they can access and edit only some information—the information necessary for them to do their jobs. Filtering records within a form provides individuals who do not have access to the entire database a way to ask questions of the database without constructing a query. You can save the filter with the form if you are going to use the filter frequently.

Activity 3.07 | Filtering Data by Selection of One Field

In this activity, you will assist a counselor at the college who wants to see records for students majoring in Information Systems Technology. In a form, you can use the *Filter By Selection* command to display only the records that contain the value in the selected field and to hide the records that do *not* contain the value in the selected field.

> **1** Open ⟩⟩ the **Navigation Pane**, double-click your **3A New Student Form** object to open it in **Form** view, and then **Close** ⟨⟨ the **Navigation Pane**.

> **2** In the first record, click the **Major ID** field name—or you can click in the field box. Press ⟨Ctrl⟩ + ⟨F⟩ to display the **Find and Replace** dialog box. In the **Find What** box, type **339** If necessary, in the Match box, click the arrow, and then click Whole Field. Click **Find Next**, and then compare your screen with Figure 3.8.

This action finds and displays a record with a *Major ID* of 339—the major of *Information Systems Technology*. You will use this action to filter the records using the value of *339*.

FIGURE 3.8

> **3** Close ⟨X⟩ the **Find and Replace** dialog box. On the **HOME tab**, in the **Sort & Filter group**, click **Selection**, and then click **Equals "339"**. Compare your screen with Figure 3.9.

Seven records match the contents of the selected Major ID field—*339*—the Major ID for the Information Systems Technology major. In the navigation area, *Filtered* with a funnel icon displays next to the number of records. *Filtered* also displays on the right side of the status bar to indicate that a filter is applied. On the HOME tab, in the Sort & Filter group, Toggle Filter is active.

 ANOTHER WAY   With the data selected in the field, right-click the selection, and then click Equals "339".

FIGURE 3.9

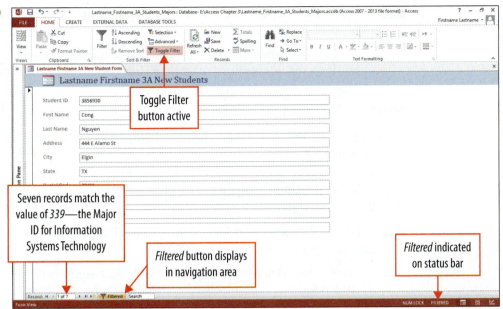

4 ▶ On the **HOME tab**, in the **Sort & Filter group**, click **Toggle Filter** to remove the filter and display all 102 records. Notice *Unfiltered* in the navigation area, which indicates a filter is created but is not active.

ANOTHER WAY Click Filtered in the navigation area to remove the filter.

NOTE **The Toggle Filter Button**

On the HOME tab, in the Sort & Filter group, the Toggle Filter button is used to apply or remove a filter. If no filter is created, the button is not available. After a filter is created, the button becomes available. Because it is a toggle button used to apply or remove a filter, the ScreenTip that displays for this button alternates between Apply Filter—when a filter is created but is not currently applied—and Remove Filter—when a filter is applied.

5 ▶ Be sure that the first record—for *Jordan Bass*—displays. On the **HOME tab**, in the **Sort & Filter group**, click **Toggle Filter** to reapply the filter. In the navigation area, click **Last record** ▶❙ to display the last of the seven records that match a Major ID of *339*.

The record for *Student ID 9712345* displays—the record with your name. Use Toggle Filter to apply or remove filters as needed.

6 ▶ In the navigation area, click **Filtered** to remove the filter and display all of the records.

In the navigation area, *Filtered* changes to *Unfiltered*.

7 ▶ In the first record for *Jordan Bass*, in the **Last Name** field, select the first letter—**B**—in *Bass*. In the **Sort & Filter group**, click **Selection**, and then click **Begins with "B"**.

A new filter is applied that displays eight records in which the *Last Name* begins with the letter *B*.

ANOTHER WAY With the letter *B* selected, right-click the selection, and then click Begins with "B".

8 ▶ Use either **Toggle Filter** in the **Sort & Filter group** or **Filtered** in the navigation area to remove the filter and display all of the records.

9 In the **Sort & Filter group**, click **Advanced**, and then click **Clear All Filters**. Notice, that in the navigation area, *Unfiltered* changed to *No Filter*.

The filter is removed from the form and must be recreated to apply it. If you toggle the filter off and save the form, the filter is saved with the form even though the filter is not currently applied.

Activity 3.08 | Using Filter By Form

Use the *Filter By Form* command to filter the records based on one or more fields, or based on more than one value in the same field. The Filter By Form command offers greater flexibility than the Filter By Selection command and can be used to answer a question that requires matching multiple values. In this activity, you will filter records to help Mr. Fitchette determine how many students live in Dripping Springs or Austin.

1 On the **HOME tab**, in the **Sort & Filter group**, click **Advanced**, and then click **Filter By Form**. Compare your screen with Figure 3.10.

The Filter by Form window displays all of the field names, but without any data. In the empty text box for each field, you can type a value or select a value from a list. The *Look for* and *Or* tabs display at the bottom.

FIGURE 3.10

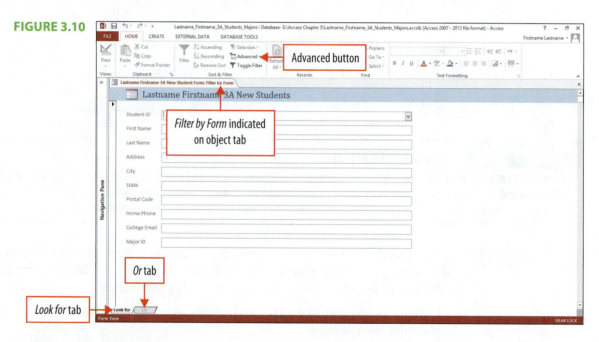

2 In the form, click the **City** field name to position the insertion point in the **City** field box. At the right edge of the **City** field box, click the **arrow**, and then click **Dripping Springs**. In the **Sort & Filter group**, click **Toggle Filter**.

As displayed in the navigation area, four student records have *Dripping Springs* stored in the City field.

3 In the **Sort & Filter group**, click **Advanced**, and then click **Filter By Form**. In the lower left corner of the form, click the **Or tab**. Click the **City** field box **arrow**, and then click **Austin**. In the **Sort & Filter group**, click **Toggle Filter**, and then compare your screen with Figure 3.11.

As displayed in the navigation area, 28 student records have either *Dripping Springs* OR *Austin* stored in the City field. You have created an **OR condition**; that is, records display where, in this instance, either of two values—Dripping Springs *or* Austin—is present in the selected field.

 ANOTHER WAY   Click in the field box, and type the criteria separated by the word *or*. For example, in the City field box, type *Dripping Springs or Austin*.

FIGURE 3.11

28 students live in either *Dripping Springs* or *Austin*

Indicates filter is applied

> 4 In the **Sort & Filter group**, click **Advanced**, and then click **Clear All Filters** to display all 102 records.

Activity 3.09 | Using Advanced Filter/Sort

In this activity, you will use the Advanced Filter/Sort command to filter records to locate students who live in Austin with a Major ID of *339*—Information Systems Technology.

> 1 In the **Sort & Filter group**, click **Advanced**, and then click **Advanced Filter/Sort**.

The Advanced Filter design grid displays, which is similar to the query design grid. A field list for the underlying table of the form displays.

> 2 In the table area, resize the field list so that the entire table name and all of the field names display.

> 3 In the **3A New Students** field list, double-click **City**, and then double-click **Major ID** to add both fields to the design grid. In the **Criteria** row under **City**, type **Austin** and then press Enter. In the **Criteria** row under **Major ID**, type **339** and then press Enter. Compare your screen with Figure 3.12.

FIGURE 3.12

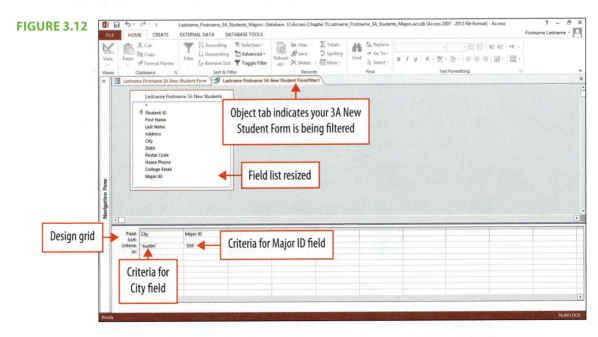

Object tab indicates your 3A New Student Form is being filtered

Field list resized

Design grid

Criteria for Major ID field

Criteria for City field

> **4** ▶ In the **Sort & Filter group**, click **Toggle Filter** to display the filtered records.

Three records match the criteria. You have created an **AND condition**; that is, only records where both values—Austin *and* 339—are present in the selected fields display. There are three students who live in Austin who have declared a major of Information Systems Technology.

> **5** ▶ In the **Sort & Filter group**, click **Toggle Filter** to remove the filter and to display all of the records.

In the navigation area, *Unfiltered* displays, which indicates that a filter has been created for this form. Unless you click Clear All Filters, the filter is saved with the form when the form is closed. When you reopen the form, you can click Toggle Filter or Unfiltered to reapply the filter.

> **6** ▶ **Close** ⌧ your **3A New Student Form** object, and notice that the Advanced Filter grid also closes.

> **More Knowledge**   **Using the Filter Button**
>
> You can filter a form in a manner similar to the way you filter records in a table. Click in the field you wish to use for the filter. On the HOME tab, in the Sort & Filter group, click Filter to display a shortcut menu. Select the (Select All) check box to clear the option, and then select the data by which you want to filter your records by clicking the check boxes preceding the data. To remove the filter, redisplay the menu, and then select the (Select All) check box.

Objective 3   Create a Form by Using the Form Wizard

Video A3-3

The **Form Wizard** walks you step by step through the creation of a form and gives you more flexibility in the design, layout, and number of fields in a form than the Form tool. Design a form for the individuals who use the form—either for entering new records or viewing records. For example, when your college counselor displays student information, it may be easier for the counselor to view the information if the fields are arranged in a layout that more closely matches a paper form.

Activity 3.10 | Creating a Form by Using the Form Wizard

In this activity, you will create a form to match the layout of a paper form that a student at Texas Lakes Community College completes when that student changes his or her major. This will make it easier for the individual who changes the data in the database.

> **1** ▶ On the ribbon, click the **CREATE tab**, and then in the **Forms group**, click **Form Wizard**.

The Form Wizard walks you step by step through the process of creating a form by asking questions. In the first wizard screen, you select the fields to include on the form. The fields can come from more than one table or query.

> **2** ▶ In the **Tables/Queries** box, click the **arrow** to display a list of available tables and queries from which you can create the form.

There are two tables in the database from which you can create a new form. The selected table is the one that you last worked with.

> **3** ▶ Click **Table: Lastname Firstname 3A New Students**, and then compare your screen with Figure 3.13.

In the Available Fields list, the field names from your 3A New Students table display.

FIGURE 3.13

Form Wizard button

Your 3A New Students table selected

Available Fields list displays field names in your 3A New Students table

Selected Fields list box

> **4** In the **Available Fields** list, double-click the following field names in the order given to move them to the **Selected Fields** list: **First Name**, **Last Name**, and **Major ID**. Compare your screen with Figure 3.14.

Three field names from your 3A New Students table display in the Selected Fields list.

ANOTHER WAY Click the field name, and then click One Field ▸ to move a field from the Available Fields list to the Selected Fields list.

FIGURE 3.14

Three fields that will display in the form

> **5** Click **Next**. In the wizard, be sure **Columnar** is selected as the layout, and then click **Next**. In the **What title do you want for your form?** box, select the existing text, type **Lastname Firstname 3A Student Major Change Form** and then click **Finish** to close the wizard and create the form.

The three fields and the data from the first record in your 3A New Students table display in Form view.

> **6** Open » the **Navigation Pane**. If necessary, increase the width of the Navigation Pane so that all object names display fully. Compare your screen with Figure 3.15.

In the Navigation Pane, the form displays under its data source—your 3A New Students table.

FIGURE 3.15

Form created using the Form Wizard

Data from first record in your 3A New Students table displays in form

New form displays under its data source

Video A3-4

After you create a form, you can make changes to it. For example, you can group the fields, resize the fields, add more fields to the form, and change the style of the form. Layout view enables you to see the data in the form as you modify the form. Most changes to a form can be made in Layout view.

Activity 3.11 | Grouping Controls in Layout View

In this activity, you will group *controls* in the form so that you can work with them as one unit. Controls are objects on a form that display data or text, perform actions, and let you view and work with information.

1 **Close** `«` the **Navigation Pane**, and be sure that your **3A Student Major Change Form** object displays in the object window. On the **HOME tab**, in the **Views group**, click the top portion of the **View** button to switch to **Layout** view. If the Field List pane displays on the right side of your screen, click Close `✕` to close the pane. Compare your screen with Figure 3.16.

The field names and data for the first record in your 3A New Students record display in controls. The data for the first record displays in **text box controls**. The most commonly used control is the text box control, which typically displays data from a field in the underlying table. A text box control is a **bound control**—its data comes from a field in a table or query.

The field names—*First Name*, *Last Name*, and *Major ID*—display in **label controls**. A label control displays to the left of a text box control and contains descriptive information that displays on the form, usually the field name. A control that does not have a data source is an **unbound control**. Another example of an unbound control is a label control that displays the title of a form.

ANOTHER WAY   On the right side of the status bar, click Layout View 🗐 to switch from Form view to Layout view.

FIGURE 3.16

Label control, an unbound control

Label controls that display the field names

Text box controls that display the data—bound controls

2 Click the **First Name label control**. Hold down `Shift`, and then click the **Last Name label control**, the **Major ID label control**, and the three **text box controls** to select all of the label and text box controls on the form.

ALERT!   **Do Your Controls Change Order When Selecting?**

If, when selecting multiple controls, the controls change order, click Undo, and then select the controls again. Be careful not to drag the mouse when you are selecting multiple controls.

---

3 With all six controls selected—surrounded by a colored border—on the ribbon, under **FORM LAYOUT TOOLS**, click the **ARRANGE tab**. In the **Table group**, click **Stacked**. Click the **First Name label control** to cancel the selection of all of the controls and to surround the **First Name label control** with a colored border. Compare your screen with Figure 3.17.

This action groups the controls together in the *Stacked layout* format—a layout similar to a paper form, with labels to the left of each field. Because the controls are grouped, you can move and edit the controls more easily as you redesign your form.

A dotted line forms a border around the controls, which indicates that the controls are grouped together. Above and to the left of the first label control that displays *First Name*, the *layout selector* displays. The layout selector is used to select and move or format the entire group of controls.

FIGURE 3.17

Activity 3.12 | Applying a Theme and Formatting a Form in Layout View

In this activity, you will apply a *theme* to the form in Layout view. A theme is a predesigned set of colors, fonts, lines, and fill effects that look good together and that can be applied to all of the objects in the database or to individual objects in the database.

1 On the ribbon, under **FORM LAYOUT TOOLS**, click the **DESIGN tab**. In the **Themes group**, click **Themes**. In the **Themes** gallery, using the ScreenTips, point to the **Retrospect** theme, right-click, and then click **Apply Theme to This Object Only**.

Right-click a theme so that you can apply the theme to an individual object within the database. Apply a theme before formatting any other controls in your form.

NOTE | **Applying a Theme to an Object and Determining the Applied Theme**

If you click a theme rather than right-clicking it and selecting an option, the theme is applied to all objects in the database. You cannot click Undo to cancel the application of the theme to all objects. To determine the applied theme, in the Themes group, point to Themes. The ScreenTip displays the name of the current theme.

---

2 Click anywhere in the title of the form—*Lastname Firstname 3A Student Major Change Form*—to select the title. On the ribbon, under **FORM LAYOUT TOOLS**, click the **FORMAT tab**. In the **Font group**, click the **Font Size arrow**, and then click **14**. In the **Font group**, click **Bold** **B**. Click the **Font Color arrow**, and then under **Theme Colors**, in the fourth column, click the last color—**Olive Green, Text 2, Darker 50%**.

Activity 3.13 | Adding, Resizing, and Moving Controls in Layout View

In Layout view, you can change the form's *control layout*—the grouped arrangement of controls.

1 Be sure that your **3A Student Major Change Form** object displays in **Layout** view. On the ribbon, click the **DESIGN tab**, and in the **Tools group**, click **Add Existing Fields**. Compare your screen with Figure 3.18.

> The Field List pane displays, which lists the fields in the underlying table—your 3A New Students table.

FIGURE 3.18

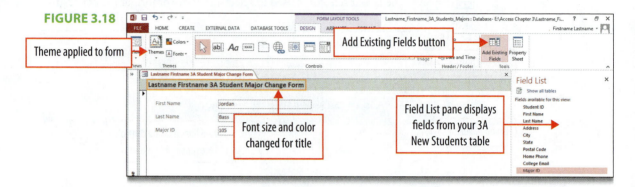

Theme applied to form

Add Existing Fields button

Font size and color changed for title

Field List pane displays fields from your 3A New Students table

2 In the **Field List** pane, click **Student ID**, and then drag the field name to the left until the ▓ pointer displays above the **First Name label control** and a colored line displays above the control. Release the mouse button, and then compare your screen with Figure 3.19. If you are not satisfied with the result, click Undo, and begin again.

> This action adds the Student ID label control and text box control to the form above the First Name controls.

FIGURE 3.19

Student ID label control

Student ID text box control

Student ID field added to the form

3 **Close** ☒ the **Field List** pane. Click the **Student ID text box control**, which displays *1034823*, to surround it with a border and to remove the border from the label control.

4 On the **DESIGN tab**, in the **Tools group**, click **Property Sheet**.

> The Property Sheet for the Student ID text box control displays. Recall that each control has an associated Property Sheet where precise changes to the properties—characteristics—of selected controls can be made. At the top of the Property Sheet, to the right of *Selection type:*, *Text Box* displays because you selected the Student ID text box control.

5 In the **Property Sheet**, click the **Format tab**. Click **Width** to select the property setting, type **1.5** and then press Enter to decrease the width of the text box controls. Compare your screen with Figure 3.20.

All four text box controls are resized simultaneously. Because the controls are grouped together in a stacked layout, you can adjust the width of all of the text box controls at one time without having to select all of the controls. By decreasing the width of the text box controls, you have more space in which to rearrange the form controls. Because you can see the data in Layout view, you can determine visually that the space you have allotted is adequate to display all of the data in every field for every record.

🔁 **ANOTHER WAY**   With the text box control selected, point to the right edge of the text box control until the ↔ pointer displays, and then drag left to the desired location.

FIGURE 3.20

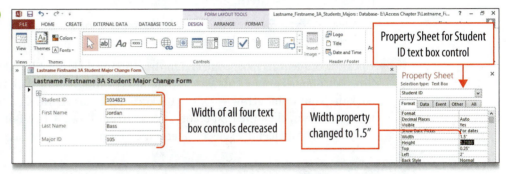

6 Close ☒ the **Property Sheet**. Click the **Last Name text box control**, which displays *Bass*. On the ribbon, under **FORM LAYOUT TOOLS**, click the **ARRANGE tab**. In the **Rows & Columns group**, click **Select Row** to select the text box control and its associated label control.

7 In the **Move group**, click **Move Up** to move both controls above the **First Name** controls, and then compare your screen with Figure 3.21.

🔁 **ANOTHER WAY**   Drag the selected controls to the desired location and then release the mouse button.

FIGURE 3.21

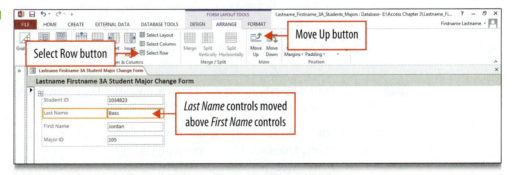

ALERT!   **Did the Last Name Label Control Not Move with the Last Name Text Box Control?**

Be sure to select both the text box control and the label control before moving the controls; otherwise, only one of the controls will move. If this happens, click Undo, select both controls, and try again. Controls are stacked from top to bottom, not right to left.

8 Save 🖫 the changes you have made to the design of your form.

Activity 3.14 | Formatting Controls in Layout View

In this activity, you will format and change the property settings for multiple controls.

1 With the form displayed in **Layout** view, click the **Student ID text box control**, which displays *1034823*. On the **ARRANGE tab**, in the **Rows & Columns group**, click **Select Column** to select all four text box controls.

ANOTHER WAY   Click the first text box control, hold down Shift, and then click the last text box control to select all four text box controls.

2 With all four text box controls selected, on the ribbon, click the **FORMAT tab**. In the **Font group**, click the **Background Color arrow**. Under **Theme Colors**, in the last column, click the second color—**Green, Accent 6, Lighter 80%**.

All of the text box controls display a background color of light green. This formatting is not applied to the label controls on the left.

3 Click the **Student ID label control**. On the ribbon, click the **ARRANGE tab**, and then in the **Rows & Columns group**, click **Select Column**. On the ribbon, click the **FORMAT tab**, and then click the **Font Color arrow**—*not* the **Background Color arrow**. Under **Theme Colors**, in the fourth column, click the first color—**Olive Green, Text 2**. Click **Bold B**. Click in a blank area of the form to cancel the selection, and then compare your screen with Figure 3.22.

FIGURE 3.22

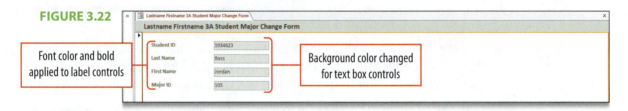

Font color and bold applied to label controls

Background color changed for text box controls

4 Click any **label control** to display the **layout selector**, and then click the **layout selector** to select all of the grouped controls.

Recall that the layout selector, which displays to the left and above the Student ID label control, enables you to select and move the entire group of controls in Layout view.

ANOTHER WAY   Click any control, and then on the ARRANGE tab, in the Rows & Columns group, click Select Layout.

5 On the **FORMAT tab**, in the **Font group**, click the **Font Size arrow**, and then click **12** to change the font size of all of the text in all of the controls.

6 With all of the controls still selected, on the ribbon, click the **DESIGN tab**. In the **Tools group**, click **Property Sheet**, and then compare your screen with Figure 3.23.

The Property Sheet for the selected controls displays. At the top of the Property Sheet, to the right of *Selection type:*, *Multiple selection* displays because you have more than one control selected.

FIGURE 3.23

Property Sheet for selected controls

Selected label and text box controls

7 In the **Property Sheet**, click **Height**, type **0.25** and then press Enter to change the height of each selected control.

8 Click the **Student ID label control** to cancel the selection of all of the controls and to select only this label control. In the **Property Sheet**, click **Width**, type **1.25** and then press Enter.

The width of every label control changed to 1.25 inches. Recall that because the label controls are arranged in a stacked layout, you can change the width of all controls by selecting only one control. This is one of the few properties that can be changed without first selecting the column.

9 Close ☒ the **Property Sheet**, and then **Save** 🖫 the design changes to your form.

Activity 3.15 | Modifying a Form in Design View

Design view presents a detailed view of the structure of your form. Because the form is not actually running when displayed in Design view, the data does not display in the text box controls. However, some tasks, such as resizing sections, must be completed in Design view.

1 On the status bar, click **Design View** 📐, and then compare your screen with Figure 3.24.

The form in Design view displays three sections, each designated by a *section bar* at the top of each section. The *Form Header* contains information, such as the form title, that displays at the top of the screen in Form view or Layout view and is printed at the top of the first page when records are printed as forms. The *Detail section* displays the records from the underlying table, and the *Form Footer* displays at the bottom of the screen in Form view or Layout view and is printed after the last detail section on the last page of a printout.

> **🔄 ANOTHER WAY**   On the HOME tab, in the Views group, click the View arrow, and then click Design view; or right-click the object tab, and then click Design View.

FIGURE 3.24

2 At the bottom of the form, click the **Form Footer section bar** to select it. On the ribbon, click the **DESIGN tab**, and in the **Tools group**, click **Property Sheet**. In the **Property Sheet**, on the **Format tab**, click **Height**, type **0.5** and then press Enter. Compare your screen with Figure 3.25.

In addition to properties for controls, you can make precise changes to sections of the form. Because you selected the Form Footer section bar, the Property Sheet displays a *Selection type* of *Section*, and the section is identified as *Form Footer*.

> **🔄 ANOTHER WAY**   At the bottom of the form, point to the lower edge of the Form Footer section bar to display the ➕ pointer, and then drag downward approximately 0.5 inch to increase the height of the section.

FIGURE 3.25

3 ▶ On the **DESIGN tab**, in the **Controls group**, click **Label** [Aa]. Move the [+A] pointer into the **Form Footer** section and then position the plus sign of the [+A] pointer at approximately **0.25 inch on the horizontal ruler** and even with the lower edge of the **Form Footer section bar**—the position does not need to be precise. Compare your screen with Figure 3.26.

FIGURE 3.26

4 ▶ Click one time. Type **Texas Lakes Community College** and then press Enter. With the **label control** selected, on the ribbon, click the **FORMAT tab**. In the **Font group**, click **Bold** [B]. Click the **Font Color arrow**, and then under **Theme Colors**, in the fourth column, click the first color—**Olive Green, Text 2**.

5 ▶ With the **label control** still selected, in the **Property Sheet**, click **Top**, type **0.1** and then press Enter. In the **Property Sheet**, in the **Left** property setting, type **0.6** and then press Enter. **Close** [X] the **Property Sheet**, and then **Save** [💾] the design changes to your form.

The top edge of the label control in the Form Footer section displays 0.1 inch from the lower edge of the Form Footer Section bar. The left edge of the label control aligns at 0.6 inch from the left margin of the form. In this manner, you can place a control in a specific location on the form.

6 ▶ On the right side of the status bar, click **Form View** [🗔], and then compare your screen with Figure 3.27.

Form Footer text displays on the screen at the bottom of the form and prints only on the last page if all of the forms are printed. Recall, that in Form view, you can add, modify, or delete records stored in the underlying table.

 ANOTHER WAY   On the HOME tab, in the Views group, click the View arrow, and then click Form View; or right-click the object tab, and then click Form View.

FIGURE 3.27

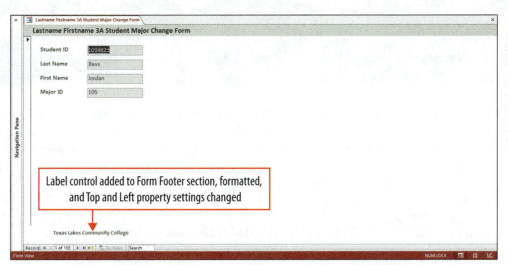

Label control added to Form Footer section, formatted, and Top and Left property settings changed

7 In the navigation area, click **Last record** ▶| to display the record containing your name.

8 On the ribbon, click the **FILE tab**, click **Print**, and then on the right, click **Print**. In the **Print** dialog box, under **Print Range**, click the **Selected Records(s)** option button. Create a paper or electronic printout as directed by your instructor. To create an electronic printout, follow the directions given in the Note in Activity 3.06.

> Because you decreased the width of the text box controls, you do *not* have to adjust the Column size Width in the Page Setup dialog box as you did with the form you created by using the Form tool.

9 **Close** ⨉ all open objects, and then **Open** » the **Navigation Pane**. On the right side of the title bar, click **Close** ⨉ to close the database and to exit Access. As directed by your instructor, submit your database and the paper or electronic printouts of the three forms that are the results of this project. Specifically, in this project, using your own name, you created the following database and printouts or electronic printouts:

1. Lastname_Firstname_3A_Students_Majors	Database file
2. Lastname Firstname 3A New Student Form	Form (printout or electronic printout - Record 102)
3. Lastname Firstname 3A Major Form	Form (printout or electronic printout - Record 33)
4. Lastname Firstname 3A Student Major Change Form	Form (printout or electronic printout - Record 102)

END | You have completed Project 3A

GO! with Office Web Apps

Objective	**Export** an Access Form to an Excel Spreadsheet, Save to SkyDrive, Edit a Record, and Save to Your Computer

Access web apps are designed to work with Microsoft's SharePoint, an application for setting up websites to share and manage documents. Your college may not have SharePoint installed, so you will use other tools to share objects from your database so that you can work collaboratively with others. Recall that Window's SkyDrive is a free file storage and file sharing service. For Access, you can export a database object to an Excel worksheet, a PDF file, or a text file, and then save the file to SkyDrive.

> **ALERT!** **Working with Web-Based Applications and Services**
>
> Computer programs and services on the web receive continuous updates and improvements. Thus, the steps to complete this web-based activity may differ from the ones shown. You can often look at the screens and the information presented to determine how to complete the activity.

Activity | Exporting an Access Form to an Excel Spreadsheet, Saving the Spreadsheet to SkyDrive, Editing a Record in SkyDrive, and Saving to Your Computer

In this activity, you will export your 3A Student Major Change Form object to an Excel spreadsheet, upload your Excel file to SkyDrive, edit a record in SkyDrive, and then download a copy of the edited spreadsheet to your computer.

1 Start Access, navigate to your **Access Chapter 3** folder, and then **Open** your **3A_Students_Majors** database file. If necessary, on the Message Bar, click Enable Content. In the **Navigation Pane**, click your **3A Student Major Change Form** object to select it.

2 On the ribbon, click the **EXTERNAL DATA tab**, and in the **Export group**, click **Excel**. In the **Export – Excel Spreadsheet** dialog box, click **Browse**, and then navigate to your **Access Chapter 3** folder. In the **File Save** dialog box, click in the **File name** box, type **Lastname_Firstname_AC_3A_Web** and then click **Save**.

3 In the **Export – Excel Spreadsheet** dialog box, under **Specify export options**, select the second check box—**Open the destination file after the export operation is complete**—and then click **OK**.

The records from the underlying table of the form display in Excel. When you export a form to Excel, the formatting and layout are automatically saved. For example, notice the olive green background color of the cells, which was the color that was applied to the text box controls in the form.

4 In the **Microsoft Excel** window, in the column headings row, to the left of column **A**, click **Select All**. On the **HOME tab**, in the **Cells group**, click **Format**, and then click **AutoFit Column Width**. Click in cell **A1** to cancel the selection, and then compare your screen with Figure A.

FIGURE A

Your 3A Student Major form exported to Excel spreadsheet and opened in Excel

Four fields and 102 records from underlying table

(GO! with Office Web Apps continues on the next page)

5 **Save** the spreadsheet, and then **Close** Excel. In the **Export – Excel Spreadsheet** dialog box, click **Close**, and then **Close** Access.

6 From the desktop, start Internet Explorer, navigate to **http://skydrive.com**, and then sign in to your Microsoft account. Open your **GO! Web Projects** folder—or create and then open this folder if necessary.

7 On the menu bar, click **Upload**. In the **Choose File to Upload** dialog box, navigate to your **Access Chapter 3** folder, and then double-click your **AC_3A_Web** file to upload it to SkyDrive.

8 In your **GO! Web Projects** folder, click your **AC_3A_Web** file to open it in Microsoft Excel Web App.

On the ribbon, notice that you can open this worksheet in Excel instead of using the web app. If you are working on a computer that does not have Microsoft Excel installed, you can still create and modify workbooks in your web browser by using the Microsoft Excel Web App.

9 In the second record, click in the **Last Name** field, using your own last name, type **Lastname** and then press Tab. In the **First Name** field, using your own first name, type **Firstname** and then press ↓ to save the record. Compare your screen with Figure B.

10 On the ribbon, click the **FILE tab**, click **Save As**, and then click **Download**. In the message box—which usually displays at the bottom of your screen—click the **Save arrow**, and then click **Save as**. In the **Save As** dialog box, navigate to your **Access Chapter 3** folder, click in the **File name** box, and then type **Lastname_Firstname_A3A_Web_Download** and then click **Save**. **Close** the message box.

11 In SkyDrive, on the title bar, click **SkyDrive** to return to your home page. At the top right corner of your screen, click your SkyDrive name, and then click **Sign out**. **Close** your browser window.

12 Start Excel. In the Excel opening screen, click **Open Other Workbooks**. Under **Open**, click **Computer**, and then on the right, click **Browse**. Navigate to your **Access Chapter 3** folder, and then double-click your **A3A_Web** file. Notice that this file is the original file—the second record is not changed. If you are required to print your documents, use one of the methods in the Note box below. **Close** your Excel file, saving the changes to your worksheet, and then **Open** and print your **A3A_Web_Download** file following one of the methods in the Note box below. **Close** Excel, saving the changes to your worksheet. As directed by your instructor, submit your two workbooks and the two paper or electronic printouts that are the results of this project.

> **N O T E** **Adding the File Name to the Footer and Printing or Creating an Electronic Printout of an Excel Spreadsheet of Only One Page**
>
> Click the FILE tab, click Print, and then click Page Setup. In the Page Setup dialog box, click the Header/Footer tab, and then click Custom Footer. With the insertion point blinking in the Left section box, click the Insert File Name button, and then click OK. In the Page Setup dialog box, click OK. Under Settings, click the *Pages* spin box up arrow to display *1* in the box. Click the *to* spin box up arrow to display *1* in the box.
>
> To print on paper, click Print. To create an electronic file of your printout, on the left side of your screen, click Export. Under Export, be sure Create PDF/XPS Document is selected, and then click Create PDF/XPS. In the Publish as PDF or XPS dialog box, click Options. In the Options dialog box, under Page range, click Pages, and be sure the From box displays *1* and the To box displays *1*; then click OK. Navigate to your Access Chapter 3 folder, and then click Publish to save the file with the default name and an extension of pdf.

FIGURE B

Job Openings Database

PROJECT ACTIVITIES

In Activities 3.16 through 3.24, you will assist Jack Woods, director of the Career Center for Texas Lakes Community College, in using his Access database to track the employees and job openings advertised for the annual job fair. Your completed reports will look similar to Figure 3.28.

PROJECT FILES

For Project 3B, you will need the following file:

a03B_Job_Openings

You will save your database as:

Lastname_Firstname_3B_Job_Openings

PROJECT RESULTS

FIGURE 3.28 Project 3B Job Openings

Video A3-5

A *report* is a database object that summarizes the fields and records from a query or from a table in an easy-to-read format suitable for printing. A report consists of information extracted from queries or tables and report design controls, such as labels, headings, and graphics. The queries or tables that provide the underlying data for a report are referred to as the report's *record source*.

Activity 3.16 | Opening and Saving an Existing Database, Renaming Objects, and Viewing a Table Relationship

1 Start Access. In the Access opening screen, click **Open Other Files**. Under **Open**, click **Computer**. Under **Recent Folders**, if displayed, click the location where your student data files are stored; otherwise, click **Browse** and then navigate to the location where your student data files are stored. Double-click **a03B_Job_Openings** to open the database.

2 On the **FILE tab**, click **Save As**. Under **File Types**, be sure **Save Database As** is selected. On the right, under **Database File Types**, be sure **Access Database** is selected, and then click **Save As**. In the **Save As** dialog box, navigate to your **Access Chapter 3** folder. In the **File name** box, replace the existing text with **Lastname_Firstname_3B_Job_Openings** and then press ⏎.

3 On the **Message Bar**, click **Enable Content**. In the **Navigation Pane**, right-click the **3B Employers** table, and then click **Rename**. With the table name selected and using your own name, type **Lastname Firstname 3B Employers** and then press ⏎ to rename the table. Use the same technique to **Rename** the **3B Job Openings** table to **Lastname Firstname 3B Job Openings** and then **Rename** the first **3B Salary $40,000 or More Query** object to **Lastname Firstname 3B Salary $40,000 or More Query**

> Recall that a query that selects data from more than one table displays under both table names in the Navigation Pane. When you rename one of the query objects, the name of the second occurrence automatically changes.

4 Point to the right edge of the **Navigation Pane** to display the ⟷ pointer. Drag to the right to increase the width of the pane until all object names display fully.

5 On the ribbon, click the **DATABASE TOOLS tab**. In the **Relationships group**, click **Relationships**. Under **RELATIONSHIP TOOLS**, on the **DESIGN tab**, in the **Relationships group**, click **All Relationships**. Resize and move the field lists so that the entire table name and fields display for each field list.

> Because you renamed the tables, the field lists do not automatically display in the Relationships window.

6 In the **Relationships** window, click the **join line** between the two field lists. In the **Tools group**, click **Edit Relationships**. Point to the title bar of the **Edit Relationships** dialog box, and drag the dialog box downward below the **3B Job Openings** field list. Compare your screen with Figure 3.29.

> *One* employer is associated with *many* job openings. Thus, a one-to-many relationship is established between the 3B Employers table and the 3B Job Openings table by using Employee ID as the common field. Referential integrity is enforced, and cascade options are selected.

FIGURE 3.29

All objects renamed

Width of Navigation Pane increased

Join line with symbols indicating one-to-many relationships with referential integrity enforced

Edit Relationships dialog box

Employer ID is the common field

Cascade options selected

---

7 ▸ **Close** ✕ the **Edit Relationships** dialog box, and then **Close** ✕ the **Relationships** window. In the message box, click **Yes** to save changes to the layout of the relationships.

8 ▸ In the **Navigation Pane**, double-click each table, and then examine the fields and data in each table. Double-click the query object to run the query and examine the query results, apply **Best Fit** to the query results, and then **Save** the query. Switch to **Design** view to examine the design grid.

> Because you renamed the tables that are the underlying source of data for the query, you have to reapply Best Fit to the query results. The query answers the question, *What is the Job ID, position, employer name, number of job openings, and annual salary for job openings that have an annual salary of $40,000 or more, in ascending order by the Employer Name field within the Position field?*

9 ▸ In the object window, right-click any **object tab**, and then click **Close All**.

Activity 3.17 | Creating a Report by Using the Report Tool and Applying a Theme to the Report

The *Report tool* is the fastest way to create a report. This tool displays all of the fields and records from the record source that you select. You can use the Report tool to look at the underlying data quickly in an easy-to-read format, after which you can save the report and modify it in Layout view or in Design view.

In this activity, you will use the Report tool to create a report from a query that lists all of the job openings with an annual salary of at least $40,000 and apply a theme to the report.

1 ▸ In the **Navigation Pane**, if necessary, click to select your **3B Salary $40,000 or More Query** object. On the ribbon, click the **CREATE tab**, and in the **Reports group**, click **Report. Close** « the **Navigation Pane**, and then compare your screen with Figure 3.30.

> The report is created using the query as the record source and displays in Layout view. The report includes all of the fields and all of the records from the query and the title of the query. In Layout view, the broken lines indicate the page margins in the report.

FIGURE 3.30

Title of the report is the query name

Broken lines indicate margins

All fields and records from the query display in the report

2 Under **REPORT LAYOUT TOOLS**, on the **DESIGN tab**, in the **Themes group**, click **Themes**. In the **Themes** gallery, use the ScreenTips to locate the **Integral** theme, right-click the **Integral** theme, and then click **Apply Theme to This Object Only**.

> Recall that right-clicking a theme enables you to apply a predefined format to the active object only, which is a quick way to apply a professional look to a report. Apply a theme before formatting any other controls on the report.

Activity 3.18 | Modifying a Report in Layout View

After you create a report, you can make changes to it. For example, you can add or delete fields, resize the fields, and change the style of the report. Layout view enables you to see the data in the report as you modify the report. Most changes to a report can be made in Layout view.

1 Click the **Job ID** field name. On the ribbon, under **REPORT LAYOUT TOOLS**, click the **ARRANGE tab**. In the **Rows & Columns group**, click **Select Column** to select the field name and all of the data for each record in the field. Press Del to remove the field from the report.

> The Job ID field is deleted, and the remaining fields move to the left. No fields extend beyond the right margin of the report.

 ANOTHER WAY   With the column selected, on the HOME tab, in the Records group, click Delete; or right-click the selected column, and then click Delete or Delete Column.

2 Scroll down, and notice that for the position of *Estimating Manager*, there is an extra blank line in the fields for this record. In the **Employer Name** field, click in the **text box control** that displays *Monroe Heating & Air Conditioning* to select all of the text box controls in this field.

3 On the ribbon, under **REPORT LAYOUT TOOLS**, click the **DESIGN tab**. In the **Tools group**, click **Property Sheet**. In the **Property Sheet**, on the **Format tab**, click **Width**, type **2.5** and then press Enter. Compare your screen with Figure 3.31.

> Recall that you can use the Property Sheet to make precise changes to control properties.

 ANOTHER WAY   Point to the right edge of the text box control to display the ↔ pointer. Drag to the right slightly until the data in the text box control displays on one line.

FIGURE 3.31

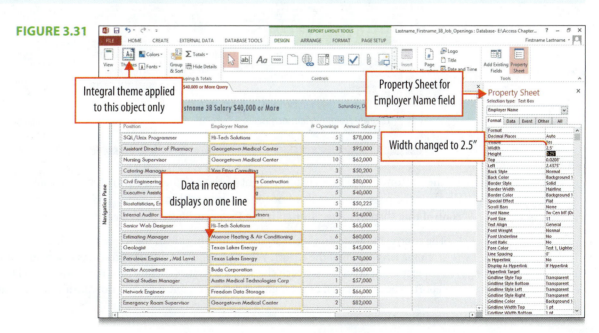

4 **Close** [X] the **Property Sheet**. Click the **Position** field name, and then on the ribbon, click the **HOME tab**. In the **Sort & Filter group**, click **Ascending** to sort the records in ascending order by the Position field.

🔄 **ANOTHER WAY**   Right-click the selected field name and then click Sort A to Z.

5 Scroll to the bottom of the report, and then click the **calculated control** that displays *$2,157,625*, which is truncated at the bottom. Press [Del] to remove this control.

In a report created by using the Report tool, a ***calculated control*** is automatically created to sum any field that is formatted as currency. A calculated control contains an expression, often a formula or a function. Here, the total is not a useful number and thus can be deleted.

6 Scroll to the bottom of the report again, and then under the last column, click the horizontal line that is the border between the last record and the calculated control that you deleted. Press [Del] to remove this line, and then scroll to the bottom of the report to verify that the line has been deleted.

7 Scroll to the top of the report, and then click the **# Openings** field name. On the ribbon, click the **DESIGN tab**. In the **Grouping & Totals group**, click **Totals**, and then click **Sum**.

8 Scroll to the bottom of the report, and then click the **calculated control** that displays *100*. On the **DESIGN tab**, in the **Tools group**, click **Property Sheet**. In the **Property Sheet**, on the **Format tab**, click **Height**, type **0.25** and then press [Enter]. Compare your screen with Figure 3.32.

The total number of job openings for positions with a salary of $40,000 or more is 100.

🔄 **ANOTHER WAY**   Point to the lower edge of the text box control to display the [↕] pointer, and then double-click to resize the control, or drag downward to increase the height of the control.

FIGURE 3.32

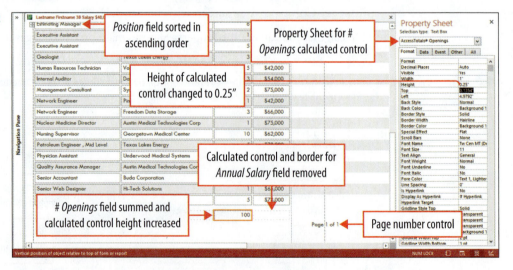

9 At the bottom of the report to the right of the calculated control, notice that the control that displays the page number does not fit entirely within the margins of the report. Click the **control** that displays *Page 1 of 1*. In the **Property Sheet**, click **Left**, type **2.5** and then press [Enter].

The control moves within the margins of the report with the left edge of the control 2.5 inches in from the left margin of the report. When you click on different controls in a report or form, the Property Sheet changes to match the selected control. Before printing, always scroll through the report to be sure that all of the controls display on one page and not outside of the margins.

🔄 **ANOTHER WAY**   Click the control, point to the selected control to display the 🔲 pointer, and then drag the control to the left within the margins of the report.

10 ▶ Scroll to the top of the report, and then click the **label control** that displays the title of the report—*Lastname Firstname 3B Salary $40,000 or More Query*. On the ribbon, under **REPORT LAYOUT TOOLS**, click the **FORMAT tab**. In the **Font group**, click the **Font Size arrow**, and then click **14**.

11 ▶ With the **label control** for the title still selected, double-click **Query** to select the word, type **Report** and then press ⏎ to change the name of the report to *Lastname Firstname 3B Salary $40,000 or More Report*.

12 ▶ Click the **Position** field name. In the **Property Sheet**, click **Left**, type **0.5** and then press ⏎ to move this field 0.5 inch in from the left margin of the report. Compare your screen with Figure 3.33.

> The other fields adjust by moving to the right. The fields are centered approximately within the margins of the report.

🔄 **ANOTHER WAY**   Click the layout selector ⊞ to select all of the controls, and then drag it slightly downward and to the right until the columns are visually centered between the margins of the report. If your columns rearrange, click Undo and begin again.

FIGURE 3.33

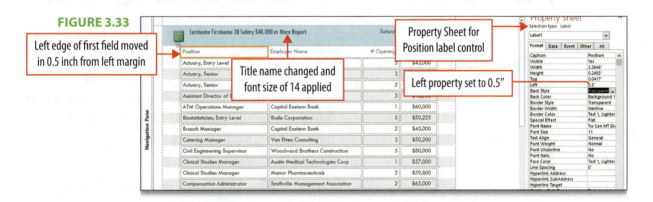

Left edge of first field moved in 0.5 inch from left margin

Title name changed and font size of 14 applied

Property Sheet for Position label control

Left property set to 0.5"

13 ▶ **Close** ☒ the **Property Sheet**, and then **Save** 💾 the report as **Lastname Firstname 3B Salary $40,000 or More Report**

Activity 3.19 | Printing a Report

In this activity, you will view your report in Print Preview and display the two pages of the report.

1 ▶ On the right side of the status bar, click **Print Preview** 🔍.

🔄 **ANOTHER WAY**   On the DESIGN tab or the HOME tab, in the Views group, click the View arrow, and then click Print Preview; or, in the object window, right-click the object tab, and then click Print Preview.

2 ▶ On the **PRINT PREVIEW tab**, in the **Zoom group**, click **Two Pages** to view the two pages of your report. Notice that the page number displays at the bottom of each page.

3 Create a paper or electronic printout as directed—two pages result, and then click **Close Print Preview**. **Close** ☒ the report, and then **Open** ⨠ the **Navigation Pane**.

The report displays under both tables from which the query was created. The report object name displays with a small green notebook icon.

4 **Close** � the **Navigation Pane**.

Video A3-6

Objective 6 Create a Report by Using the Report Wizard

Use the *Report Wizard* when you need more flexibility in the design of your report. You can group and sort data by using the wizard and use fields from more than one table or query if you have created the relationships between tables. The Report Wizard is similar to the Form Wizard; the wizard walks you step by step through the process of creating the report by asking you questions and then designs the report based on your answers.

Activity 3.20 | Creating a Report by Using the Report Wizard

In this activity, you will prepare a report for Mr. Woods that displays the employers, grouped by industry, and the total fees paid by employers for renting a booth at the Job Fair.

1 On the ribbon, click the **CREATE tab**, and then in the **Reports group**, click **Report Wizard**.

In the first wizard screen, you select the fields to include on the report. The fields can come from more than one table or query.

2 In the **Tables/Queries** box, click the **arrow**, and then click **Table: Lastname Firstname 3B Employers**. In the **Available Fields** list, double-click the following field names in the order given to move them to the **Selected Fields** list: **Industry**, **Employer Name**, and **Fee Paid** (scroll as necessary to locate the *Fee Paid* field). Compare your screen with Figure 3.34.

Three field names from your 3B Employers table display in the Selected Fields list.

 ANOTHER WAY Click the field name, and then click One Field ⯈ to move a field from the Available Fields list to the Selected Fields list.

FIGURE 3.34

Fields selected from your 3B Employers table

First screen of Report Wizard

Three fields that will display in the report

3 Click **Next**. In the wizard, notice that you can add grouping levels and that a preview of the grouping level displays on the right.

Grouping data helps to organize and summarize the data in your report.

4 On the left, double-click **Industry**, and then compare your screen with Figure 3.35.

The preview displays how the data will be grouped in the report. Grouping data in a report places all of the records that have the same data in a field together as a group—in this instance, the records will be grouped by *Industry*. Within each Industry name, the Employer Name and Fee Paid will display.

FIGURE 3.35

Records will be grouped by *Industry* names

Fields that will display within each *Industry* grouping

Preview of grouping

5 Click **Next**. Click the **1** box **arrow**, click **Employer Name**, and then compare your screen with Figure 3.36.

In this step of the wizard, you indicate how you want to sort the records and summarize the information. You can sort up to four fields. The Summary Options button displays because the data is grouped, and at least one of the fields—*Fee Paid*—contains numerical or currency data. Within each Industry grouping, the records will be sorted alphabetically by the Employer Name. Sorting records in a report presents a more organized view of the records.

FIGURE 3.36

Field that will be sorted

Type of sort

Summary Options button displays because *Fee Paid* contains currency data

6 In the wizard, click **Summary Options**, and then compare your screen with Figure 3.37.

The Summary Options dialog box displays. The *Fee Paid* field can be summarized by selecting one of the four check boxes for Sum, Avg, Min, or Max. You can also display only summary information or display both the details—each record—and the summary information. The default setting is to display *Detail and Summary*.

FIGURE 3.37

Summary Options dialog box

Show options

Aggregate functions for *Fee Paid* field

7 In the **Summary Options** dialog box, click to select the **Sum** check box. Under **Show**, be sure that **Detail and Summary** is selected, and then click **OK**. In the wizard, click **Next**.

> In this step of the wizard, you select the layout and page orientation. A preview of the layout displays on the left.

8 Click each **Layout** option button, noticing the changes in the preview, and then click **Stepped** to select it as the layout for your report. Under **Orientation**, be sure that **Portrait** is selected. At the bottom of the wizard, be sure that the **Adjust the field width so all fields fit on a page** check box is selected, and then click **Next**.

9 In the **What title do you want for your report?** box, select the existing text, type **Lastname Firstname 3B Booth Fees by Industry Report** and then click **Finish**. Compare your screen with Figure 3.38.

> The report is saved and displays in Print Preview using the specifications you defined in the Report Wizard. The records are grouped by Industry. Within each Industry, the records display in ascending order by the Employer Name. Within each Industry grouping, the Fee paid is summed or totaled—the word *Sum* displays at the end of each grouping.

FIGURE 3.38

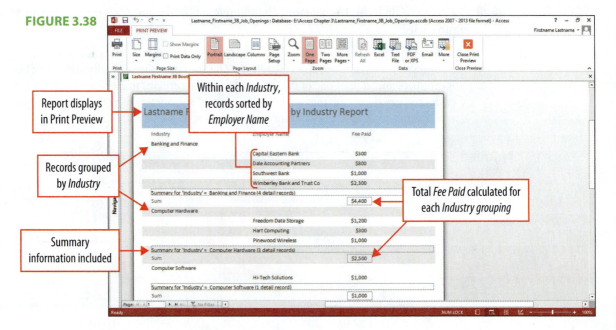

10 In the object window, right-click the **object tab** for the report, and then click **Layout View**.

 ANOTHER WAY   On the status bar, click Layout View 🗐 ; or click Close Print Preview, and then on the HOME tab or the DESIGN tab, click the View arrow, and then click Layout View.

Objective 7 | Modify the Design of a Report

Video A3-7

You can modify the design of a report that is created using the Report Wizard by using the same techniques and tools that you use to modify a report created with the Report tool. Recall that most report modifications can be made in Layout view.

Activity 3.21 | Formatting and Deleting Controls in Layout View

In this activity, you will apply a theme to the report, format the title of the report, and delete the summary information controls.

1 Be sure that your **3B Booth Fees by Industry Report** object is displayed in **Layout** view. Under **REPORT LAYOUT TOOLS**, on the **DESIGN tab**, in the **Themes group**, click **Themes**. In the **Themes** gallery, use the ScreenTips to locate the **Ion Boardroom** theme, right-click the **Ion Boardroom** theme, and then click **Apply Theme to This Object Only**.

Recall that you should apply a theme before applying any other formatting changes. Also, recall that if you click a theme—instead of right-clicking—the theme is applied to all of the objects in the database.

2 At the top of the report, click the title—*Lastname Firstname 3B Booth Fees by Industry*—to display a border around the label control. On the ribbon, under **REPORT LAYOUT TOOLS**, click the **FORMAT tab**. In the **Font group**, click the **Font Size arrow**, and then click **14**. In the **Font group**, click **Bold** B.

By changing the font size, the report name is no longer truncated and includes the word *Report*.

3 Within each *Industry* grouping, notice the **Summary for 'Industry'** information.

Because you selected Summary Options, a summary line is included at the end of each grouping that details what is being summarized—in this case, summed—and the number of records that are included in the summary total. Now that Mr. Woods has viewed the report, he has decided that this information is not necessary and can be removed.

4 Click any one of the controls that begins with **Summary for 'Industry'**.

The control that you clicked is surrounded by a border, and all of the other summary information controls are surrounded by paler borders to indicate that all controls are selected.

5 Press [Del] to remove the controls from the report, and then compare your screen with Figure 3.39.

ANOTHER WAY Right-click any of the selected controls, and then click Delete to remove the controls from the report.

FIGURE 3.39

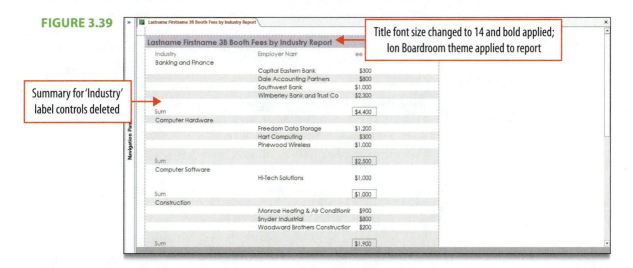

Title font size changed to 14 and bold applied; Ion Boardroom theme applied to report

Summary for 'Industry' label controls deleted

6 **Save** 💾 the changes you have made to the design of the report.

Activity 3.22 | Modifying Controls in Layout View

In this activity, you will modify the text in controls, move controls, resize controls, and add a control to the report in Layout view.

1 On the left side of the report, click a **Sum label control**, which selects all of the related controls. Double-click the control to select the text—*Sum*. Type **Total Booth Fees by Industry** and then press Enter. Compare your screen with Figure 3.40.

This text states more clearly what is being summed.

FIGURE 3.40

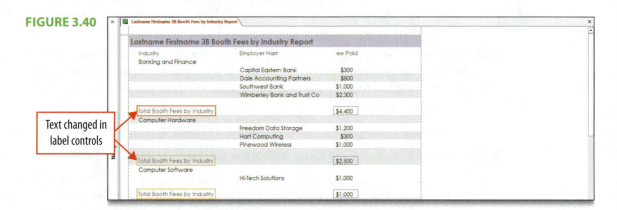

Text changed in label controls

2 At the top of the report, click the **Industry label control** to select it. Hold down Shift, click the **Employer Name label control**, and then click the **Fee Paid label control** to select all three field names. On the **FORMAT tab**, in the **Font group**, click **Bold** **B**.

Clicking Bold also increases the size of the controls so that the text is no longer truncated.

3 At the top of the report, under the **Fee Paid label control**, click the **text box control** that displays *$300* to select the text box controls for all of the records for this field. On the ribbon, click the **DESIGN tab**. In the **Tools group**, click **Property Sheet**. In the **Property Sheet**, on the **Format tab**, click **Left**, type **7** and then press Enter. Compare your screen with Figure 3.41.

All of the Fee Paid text box controls move to the right—7" in from the left margin. Do not be concerned that the summary total and the field name are not aligned with the data; you will correct this in the next activity. The field is moved to the right so that you can increase the width of the Employer Name text box controls so that all of the data for every record displays.

FIGURE 3.41

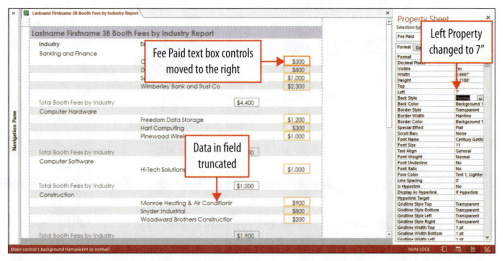

Fee Paid text box controls moved to the right

Left Property changed to 7"

Data in field truncated

4 ▶ Scroll to view the bottom of the report. Click to select the **calculated control** for the **Grand Total,** which displays *20,400* and part of the dollar symbol. In the **Property Sheet**, click **Width**, type **0.8** and then press Enter.

> The width of the calculated control increases to display the dollar symbol. Do not be concerned that the right edge of the control no longer aligns with the control above it; you will correct this in the next activity. Recall that a calculated control contains an expression—a formula or function—that displays the result of the expression when the report is displayed in Report view, Print Preview, or Layout view.

ANOTHER WAY Point to the left edge of the control to display the ↔ pointer. Drag to the left slightly to increase the width of the calculated control.

5 ▶ At the bottom of the report, on the left side, click the **Grand Total label control**. In the **Property Sheet**, click **Width**, type **1** and then press Enter. Compare your screen with Figure 3.42.

> The width of the label control is increased so that all of the text displays.

ANOTHER WAY Point to the right edge of the control to display the ↔ pointer, and then double-click to resize the control.

FIGURE 3.42

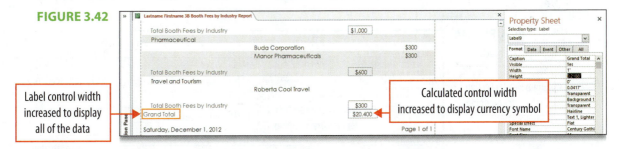

Label control width increased to display all of the data

Calculated control width increased to display currency symbol

6 ▶ Scroll to the top to display the Industry grouping of **Construction**, and notice that the first and third records have truncated data in the **Employer Name** field. In the **Construction** grouping, click, the **Employer Name text box control** that starts with *Monroe Heating* to select all of the text box controls for this field.

7 ▶ In the **Property Sheet**, click **Width**, type **3** and then press Enter. **Save** the design changes to your report, and then compare your screen with Figure 3.43.

> The width of the Employer Name text box controls is increased so that all of the data in this field for every record displays. Recall that you moved the Fee Paid text box controls to the right to make room for the increased width of these controls.

FIGURE 3.43

Width of Employer Name text box control increased to 3"

Text is no longer truncated

Activity 3.23 | Aligning Controls in Design View

Design view gives you a more detailed view of the structure of your report. You can see the header and footer sections for the report, for the page, and for groups. In Design view, your report is not running, so you cannot see the data from the table in the controls. In the same manner as forms, you can add labels to the Page Footer section or increase the height of sections. Some tasks, such as aligning controls, must be completed in Design view.

1 Close ☒ the **Property Sheet**. On the status bar, click **Design View** ☑, and then compare your screen with Figure 3.44.

Design view for a report is similar to Design view for a form. You can modify the layout of the report in this view, and use the dotted grid pattern to align controls. This report has several sections. The **Report Header** displays information at the top of the *first page* of a report. The **Page Header** displays information at the top of *every page* of a report. The **Group Header** displays the name of data in the field by which the records are grouped; in this case, the *Industry* name. The **Detail** section displays the data for each record. The **Group Footer** displays the summary information for each grouping; in this case, the Industry name. The **Page Footer** displays information at the bottom of *every page* of the report. The **Report Footer** displays information at the bottom of the *last page* of the report.

If you do not group data in a report, the Group Header section and Group Footer section will not display. If you do not summarize the data, the Group Footer section will not display.

FIGURE 3.44

2 In the **Page Footer** section of the report, examine the two controls in this section. Recall that information in the Page Footer section displays at the bottom of every page in the report.

On the left side, the **date control** displays *=Now( )*, which inserts the current date each time the report is opened. On the right side, the **page number control** displays *="Page " & [Page] & " of " & [Pages]*, which inserts the page number, for example *Page 1 of 2*, when the report is displayed in Print Preview or when printed. Both of these controls contain examples of functions that are used by Access to create controls in a report.

3 In the **Industry Footer** section, click the **Total Booth Fees by Industry label control**. Hold down Shift, and in the **Report Footer** section, click the **Grand Total label control** to select both label controls.

4 On the ribbon, under **REPORT DESIGN TOOLS**, click the **ARRANGE tab**. In the **Sizing & Ordering group**, click **Align**, and then click **Left**.

The left edge of the *Grand Total label control* is aligned with the left edge of the *Total Booth Fees by Industry label control*. When using the Align Left command, the left edges of the selected controls are aligned with the control that is the farthest to the left in the report.

5 In the **Page Header** section, click the **Fee Paid label control**. Hold down Shift while you click the following: in the **Detail** section, click the **Fee Paid text box control**; in the **Industry Footer** section, click the **calculated control** that begins with =*Sum*; and in the **Report Footer** section, click the **calculated control** that begins with =*Sum*.

Four controls are selected.

6 On the **ARRANGE tab**, in the **Sizing & Ordering group**, click **Align**, and then click **Right**. Save 💾 the design changes to your report, and then compare your screen with Figure 3.45.

The right edges of the four selected controls are aligned with the right edge of the *Fee Paid text box control*. When using the Align Right command, the right edges of the selected controls are aligned with the control that is the farthest to the right in the report.

FIGURE 3.45

7 On the status bar, click **Layout View** ▤ to display the underlying data in the controls. Scroll to view the bottom of the report. On the left side, notice that the **Total Booth Fees by Industry label control** and the **Grand Total label control** are left aligned. Also, notice the right alignment of the controls in the **Fee Paid** column.

Objective 8 — Keep Grouped Data Together in a Printed Report

Video A3-8

Before you print a report, examine the report in Print Preview to be sure that all of the labels and data display fully and to be sure that all of the data is properly grouped. Sometimes a page break occurs in the middle of a group of data, leaving the labels on one page and the data or summary information on another page.

Activity 3.24 | Keeping Grouped Data Together in a Printed Report

In this activity, you will preview the document and then will keep the data in each group together so a grouping is not split between two pages of the report. This is possible if the data in a grouping does not exceed the length of a page.

1 On the status bar, click **Print Preview** 🔍. On the **PRINT PREVIEW tab**, in the **Zoom group**, click **Two Pages**, and then compare your screen with Figure 3.46.

The report will print on two pages. For the Industry grouping of *Hotel and Food Service*, one record and the summary data display at the top of Page 2 and is separated from the rest of the grouping that displays at the bottom of page 1. Your display may differ depending upon your printer configuration.

In Print Preview, the One Page or Two Pages Zoom view causes the records to be compressed slightly and might display with the bottoms of records truncated. The records, however, will print correctly.

FIGURE 3.46

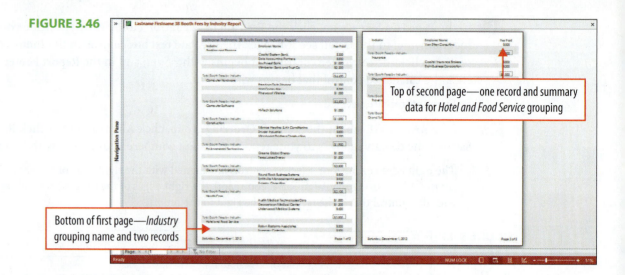

Top of second page—one record and summary data for *Hotel and Food Service* grouping

Bottom of first page—*Industry* grouping name and two records

2 On the ribbon, click **Close Print Preview** to return to **Layout** view. On the **DESIGN tab**, in the **Grouping & Totals group**, click **Group & Sort**.

At the bottom of the screen, the *Group, Sort, and Total pane* displays. This pane is used to control how information is grouped, sorted, or totaled. Layout view is the preferred view in which to accomplish these tasks because you can see how the changes affect the display of the data in the report.

3 In the **Group, Sort, and Total** pane, on the **Group on Industry** bar, click **More**. To the right of **do not keep group together on one page**, click the **arrow**, and then compare your screen with Figure 3.47.

The *keep whole group together on one page* command keeps each industry group together, from the name in the Group Header section through the summary information in the Group Footer section. The default setting is *do not keep group together on one page*. Next to *Group on Industry*, with A on top indicates that the industry names are sorted in ascending order.

FIGURE 3.47

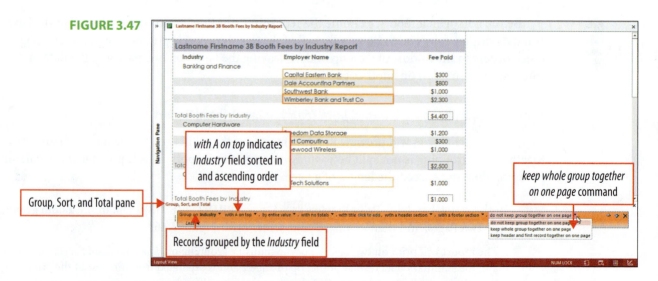

with A on top indicates *Industry* field sorted in and ascending order

keep whole group together on one page command

Group, Sort, and Total pane

Records grouped by the *Industry* field

4 Click **keep whole group together on one page**. On the **DESIGN tab**, in the **Grouping & Totals group**, click **Group & Sort** to close the **Group, Sort, and Total** pane.

5 On the status bar, click **Print Preview** 🔍. If necessary, in the Zoom group, click Two Pages. Compare your screen with Figure 3.48.

The entire grouping for the Industry of *Hotel and Food Service* displays at the top of page 2. The grouping no longer breaks between page 1 and page 2. Recall that even though the bottoms of records display truncated because of the compressed Print Preview setting of Two Pages, the records will print correctly.

FIGURE 3.48

Entire *Hotel and Food Service* grouping kept together at top of second page

6 **Save** 💾 the design changes to your report, and then create a paper or electronic printout of the report as directed—two pages result.

7 **Close** ✕ the report, and then **Open** ❯❯ the **Navigation Pane**. If necessary, increase the width of the Navigation Pane so that all object names display fully.

8 On the right side of the title bar, click **Close** ✕ to close the database and to exit Access. As directed by your instructor, submit your database and the paper or electronic printouts of the two reports—each report is two pages—that are the results of this project. Specifically, in this project, using your own name you created the following database and printouts or electronic printouts:

1. Lastname_Firstname_3B_Job_Openings	Database file
2. Lastname Firstname 3B Salary $40,000 or More Report	Report (printout or electronic printout - two pages)
3. Lastname Firstname 3B Booth Fees by Industry Report	Report (printout or electronic printout - two pages)

END | You have completed Project 3B

GO! with Office Web Apps

Objective | **Export** an Access Report to a Word File, Save to SkyDrive, and Add a Description to the Word File

Access web apps are designed to work with Microsoft's SharePoint, an application for setting up websites to share and manage documents. Your college may not have SharePoint installed, so you will use other tools to share objects from your database so that you can work collaboratively with others. When you have information that you want to share with others, you can upload files to SkyDrive. Some files can be opened in SkyDrive; some can only be downloaded. Because database files are typically large in size, and free storage space on SkyDrive is limited, you can export database objects to different formats and then upload those files to SkyDrive.

> **ALERT!** **Working with Web-Based Applications and Services**
>
> Computer programs and services on the web receive continuous updates and improvements. Thus, the steps to complete this web-based activity may differ from the ones shown. You can often look at the screens and the information presented to determine how to complete the activity.

Activity | **Exporting an Access Report to a Word File, Uploading the Word File to SkyDrive, and Adding a Description to the Word File**

In this activity, you will export your 3B Salary $40,000 or More Report object to a Word file, upload your Word file to SkyDrive, and then add a description to the Word file. The report will be available for individuals with whom you have shared your SkyDrive files or folders.

1 Start Access, navigate to your **Access Chapter 3** folder, and then **Open** your **3B_Job_Openings** database file. If necessary, on the Message Bar, click Enable Content. In the **Navigation Pane**, click your **3B Salary $40,000 or More Report** object to select it.

2 On the ribbon, click the **EXTERNAL DATA tab**, and in the **Export group**, click **More**, and then click **Word**.

The report will be exported as a *Rich Text Format (RTF)*—a standard file format that contains text and some formatting such as underline, bold, italic, font sizes, and colors. RTF documents can be opened in many word processing programs and text editors.

3 In the **Export – RTF File** dialog box, navigate to your **Access Chapter 3** folder. In the **File Save** dialog box, click in the **File name** box to select the existing text. Type **Lastname_Firstname_AC_3B_Web** and then click **Save**. In the **Export – RTF File** dialog box, select the **Open the destination file after the export operation is complete** check box, and then click **OK**. Compare your screen with Figure A.

The RTF file is created and opens in Word.

4 **Close** ☒ Word. In the **Export – RTF File** dialog box, click **Close**, and then **Close** ☒ Access.

FIGURE A

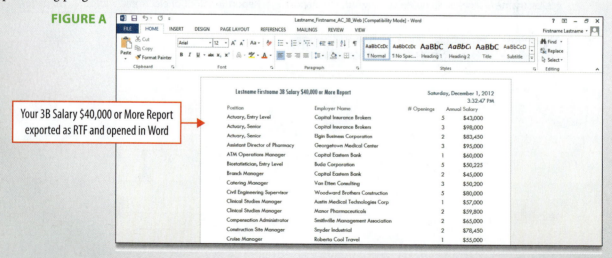

Your 3B Salary $40,000 or More Report exported as RTF and opened in Word

(GO! with Office Web Apps continues on the next page)

5 From the desktop, start Internet Explorer, navigate to **http://skydrive.com**, and then sign in to your Microsoft account. Open your **GO! Web Projects** folder—or create and then open this folder if necessary.

6 On the menu bar, click **Upload**. In the **Choose File to Upload** dialog box, navigate to your **Access Chapter 3** folder, and then double-click your **AC_3B_Web** file to upload it to SkyDrive.

7 After the file is uploaded, in your **GO! Web Projects** folder, right-click your **AC_3B_Web** file, and then click **Properties**.

A Properties panel displays on the right side of your screen.

8 In the **Properties** panel, click **Add a description**. In the box, type **This report displays job openings in our area that have a salary of $40,000 or more for which our students can apply.** Press Enter, and then compare your screen with Figure B.

9 On your keyboard, press the ⊞ key, type **snip**, and then click **Snipping Tool**. In the **Snipping Tool** dialog box, click the **New arrow**, and then click **Full-screen Snip**.

10 On the **Snipping Tool** toolbar, click **Save Snip** 🖫. In the **Save As** dialog box, navigate to your **Access Chapter 3** folder. Click in the **File name** box to select the existing text. Type **Lastname_Firstname_AC_3B_Web_Snip** and then, if necessary, click the **Save as type arrow**, and click **JPEG file**. In the **Save As** dialog box, click **Save**, and then **Close** ⊠ the **Snipping Tool** window.

11 In SkyDrive, on the title bar, click **SkyDrive** to return to your home page. At the top right corner of your screen, click your SkyDrive name, and then click **Sign out**. **Close** your browser window.

12 If directed to submit a paper printout of your RTF document and snip file, follow the directions given in the Note below. As directed by your instructor, submit your RTF document, which is two pages, and your snip file that are the results of this project.

N O T E   **Printing your RTF Document and Your Snip .JPEG File**

Using Windows Explorer, navigate to your Access Chapter 3 folder. Locate and double-click your AC_3B_Web file—it will open in Word. On the ribbon, click the FILE tab, and then click Print. To print on paper, on the right, click Print. To create an electronic file of your printout, on the left side of your screen, click Export. Under Export, be sure Create PDF/XPS Document is selected, and then click Create PDF/XPS. Navigate to your Access Chapter 3 folder, and then click Publish to save the file with the default name and an extension of pdf.

In your Access Chapter 3 folder, locate and double-click your AC_3B_Web_Snip file. If this is the first time you have tried to open a .jpeg file, you will be asked to identify a program. If you are not sure which program to use, select Windows Photo Viewer. From the ribbon, menu bar, or toolbar, click the Print command, and then Close the program window.

FIGURE B

The advantage of using Office 365 is that your organization does not have to purchase and install server hardware and software for sophisticated business applications and does not need a full-time IT person or staff just to manage the technology your teams need.

By using Office 365, you are able to have business-class services for your employees without investing in expensive hardware, software, and personnel. However, at least one person in an organization must be designated as the *Office 365 Administrator*—the person who creates and manages the account, adds new users, sets up the services your organization wants to use, sets permission levels, and manages the SharePoint team sites. You can have more than one administrator if you want to share these tasks with others.

Microsoft provides easy-to-use instructions and videos to get you started, and you might also have contact with a Microsoft representative. You will probably find, however, that subscribing to and setting up the account, adding users, and activating services is a straightforward process that requires little or no assistance.

After purchasing the required number of licenses, you will add each team member as a user that includes his or her email address. The Admin Overview page, as shown in Figure A, assists the Office 365 Administrator. On the left, there are links to manage the users and domains in your Office 365 account. This is where you can add new users, delete users, set permission levels, enter and change passwords, and update the user properties and the licenses.

On this page, you can see the various services available to you in Office 365. In the site shown in Figure A, Outlook, Lync, SharePoint (team sites), and a public-facing website are all part of the services.

Activity | Using a Team Site to Collaborate

This group project relates to the **Bell Orchid Hotels**. If your instructor assigns this project to your class, you will use a SharePoint team site in **Office 365** to collaborate on the following tasks for this chapter:

- If you are in the **Accounting Group**, you and your teammates will finalize the Stockholders database and post it on the SharePoint team site.

- If you are in the **Engineering Group**, you and your teammates will finalize the Subcontractors database and post it on the SharePoint team site.

- If you are in the **Food and Beverage Group**, you and your teammates will finalize Banquet Clients database and post it on the SharePoint team site.

- If you are in the **Human Resources Group**, you and your teammates will finalize the Employees database and post it on the SharePoint team site.

- If you are in the **Operations Group**, you and your teammates will finalize the Guests Database and post it on the SharePoint team site.

- If you are in the **Sales and Marketing Group**, you and your teammates will finalize the Associations database and post it on the SharePoint team site.

FIGURE A

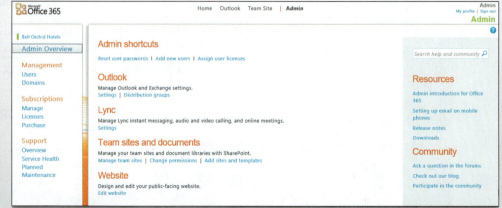

END OF CHAPTER

SUMMARY

A form is a database object that you can use to enter new records into a table, or to edit, delete, or display existing records in a table and can be used to control access to the data in a database.

Filter records in a form to display only a subset of the total records based on matching specific values to provide a quick answer to a question. Filters are generally not saved with a form.

A report is a database object that summarizes the fields and records from a query or from a table, in an easy-to-read format suitable for printing. You can group records and summarize the data in a report.

Most changes to forms and reports can be done in Layout view where the underlying data displays in the controls; however, some modifications, such as aligning controls, must be done in Design view.

GO! LEARN IT ONLINE

Review the concepts and key terms in this chapter by completing these online challenges, which you can find at **www.pearsonhighered.com/go**.

Matching and Multiple Choice: Answer matching and multiple choice questions to test what you learned in this chapter. MyITLab®

Crossword Puzzle: Spell out the words that match the numbered clues, and put them in the puzzle squares.

Flipboard: Flip through the definitions of the key terms in this chapter and match them with the correct term.

GO! FOR JOB SUCCESS

Video: Performance Evaluations

Your instructor may assign this video to your class, and then ask you to think about, or discuss with your classmates, these questions:

FotolEdhar / Fotolia

What kind of message is Sara sending by forgetting to do the self-assessment review she was assigned for her evaluation? Why is it important to do a self-assessment for a review?

How should Sara react to her supervisor's criticisms in her review?

How important is it to follow a company's dress code policy? Do you think Sara's response to not following the dress code is appropriate? Why or why not?

END OF CHAPTER

REVIEW AND ASSESSMENT GUIDE FOR ACCESS CHAPTER 3

Your instructor may assign one or more of these projects to help you review the chapter and assess your mastery and understanding of the chapter.

Project	Apply Skills from These Chapter Objectives	Project Type	Project Location
3C	Objectives 1-4 from Project 3A	**3C Skills Review** A guided review of the skills from Project 3A.	On the following pages
3D	Objectives 5-8 from Project 3B	**3D Skills Review** A guided review of the skills from Project 3B.	On the following pages
3E	Objectives 1-4 from Project 3A	**3E Mastery (Grader Project)** A demonstration of your mastery of the skills in Project 3A with extensive decision making.	In MyITLab and on the following pages
3F	Objectives 5-8 from Project 3B	**3F Mastery (Grader Project)** A demonstration of your mastery of the skills in Project 3B with extensive decision making.	In MyITLab and on the following pages
3G	Objectives 1-8 from Projects 3A and 3B	**3G Mastery (Grader Project)** A demonstration of your mastery of the skills in Projects 3A and 3B with extensive decision making.	In MyITLab and on the following pages
3H	Combination of Objectives from Projects 3A and 3B	**3H GO! Fix It** A demonstration of your mastery of the skills in Projects 3A and 3B by creating a correct result from a document that contains errors you must find.	Online
3I	Combination of Objectives from Projects 3A and 3B	**3I GO! Make It** A demonstration of your mastery of the skills in Projects 3A and 3B by creating a result from a supplied picture.	Online
3J	Combination of Objectives from Projects 3A and 3B	**3J GO! Solve It** A demonstration of your mastery of the skills in Projects 3A and 3B, your decision-making skills, and your critical thinking skills. A task-specific rubric helps you self-assess your result.	Online
3K	Combination of Objectives from Projects 3A and 3B	**3K GO! Solve It** A demonstration of your mastery of the skills in Projects 3A and 3B, your decision-making skills, and your critical thinking skills. A task-specific rubric helps you self-assess your result.	On the following pages
3L	Combination of Objectives from Projects 3A and 3B	**3L GO! Think** A demonstration of your understanding of the chapter concepts applied in a manner that you would outside of college. An analytic rubric helps you and your instructor grade the quality of your work by comparing it to the work an expert in the discipline would create.	On the following pages
3M	Combination of Objectives from Projects 3A and 3B	**3M GO! Think** A demonstration of your understanding of the chapter concepts applied in a manner that you would outside of college. An analytic rubric helps you and your instructor grade the quality of your work by comparing it to the work an expert in the discipline would create.	Online
3N	Combination of Objectives from Projects 3A and 3B	**3N You and GO!** A demonstration of your understanding of the chapter concepts applied in a manner that you would in a personal situation. An analytic rubric helps you and your instructor grade the quality of your work.	Online
3O	Combination of Objectives from Projects 3A and 3B	**3O Cumulative Group Project for Access Chapter 3** A demonstration of your understanding of concepts and your ability to work collaboratively in a group role-playing assessment, requiring both collaboration and self-management.	Online
Capstone Project for Access Chapters 1-3	Combination of Objectives from Projects 1A, 1B, 2A, 2B, 3A, and 3B	A demonstration of your mastery of the skills in Chapters 1-3 with extensive decision making. **(Grader Project)**	In MyITLab and online

GLOSSARY

GLOSSARY OF CHAPTER KEY TERMS

AND condition A condition in which records display only when all of the values are present in the selected fields.

Bound A term used to describe objects and controls that are based on data that is stored in tables.

Bound control A control that retrieves its data from an underlying table or query; a text box control is an example of a bound control.

Calculated control A control that contains an expression, often a formula or function, that most often summarizes a field that contains numerical data.

Control An object on a form or report that displays data or text, performs actions, and lets you view and work with information.

Control layout The grouped arrangement of controls on a form or report; for example, the Stacked layout.

Data entry The action of entering the data into a record in a database table or form.

Date control A control on a form or report that inserts the current date each time the form or report is opened.

Design view The Access view that displays the detailed structure of a query, form, or report; for forms and reports, may be the view in which some tasks must be performed, and only the controls, and not the data, display.

Detail section The section of a form or report that displays the records from the underlying table or query.

Filter by Form An Access command that filters the records in a form based on one or more fields, or based on more than one value in the field.

Filter by Selection An Access command that displays only the records that contain the value in the selected field and hides the records that do not contain the value.

Filtering The process of displaying only a portion of the total records (a subset) based on matching specific values to provide a quick answer to a question.

Form A database object that you can use to enter new records into a table, or to edit, delete, and display existing records in a table.

Form Footer Information at the bottom of the screen in Form view or Layout view that is printed after the last detail section on the last page of a printout.

Form Header Information such as a form's title that displays at the top of the screen in Form view or Layout view and is printed at the top of the first page when records are printed as forms.

Form tool An Access tool that creates a form with a single mouse click, which includes all of the fields from the underlying data source (table or query).

Form view The Access view in which you can view, modify, delete, or add records in a table; but you cannot change the layout or design of the form.

Form Wizard An Access tool that walks you step by step through the creation of a form and that gives you more flexibility in the design, layout, and number of fields in a form.

Group Footer Information printed at the end of each group of records; used to display summary information for the group.

Group Header Information printed at the beginning of each new group of records; for example, the group name.

Group, Sort, and Total pane A pane that displays at the bottom of the screen in which you can control how information is sorted and grouped in a report; provides the most flexibility for adding or modifying groups, sort orders, or totals options on a report.

Label control A control on a form or report that contains descriptive information, usually a field name or title.

Layout selector A small symbol that displays in the upper left corner of a selected control layout in a form or report that is displayed in Layout view or Design view; used to move or format an entire group of controls.

Layout view The Access view in which you can make changes to a form or report while the object is running—the data from the underlying data source displays.

Office 365 Administrator In Office 365, the person who creates and manages the account, adds new users, sets up the services your organization wants to use, sets permission levels, and manages the SharePoint team sites.

OR condition A condition in which records display that match at least one of the specified values.

Page Footer Information printed at the bottom of every page in a report; most often includes the page number.

Page Header Information printed at the top of every page in a report.

Page number control A control on a form or report that inserts the page numbers when displayed in Print Preview or when printed.

Record selector bar The vertical bar at the left edge of a record when it is displayed in a form that is used to select an entire record.

Record source The tables or queries that provide the underlying data for a form or report.

Report A database object that summarizes the fields and records from a query or table in an easy-to-read format suitable for printing.

Report Footer Information printed at the bottom of the last page of a report.

Report Header Information printed on the first page of a report; used for logos, titles, and dates.

Report tool An Access tool that creates a report with one mouse click and displays all of the fields and records from the record source that you select.

Report Wizard An Access tool that walks you step by step through the creation of a report and that gives you more flexibility in the design, layout, and number of fields in a report.

Rich Text Format (RTF) A standard file format that contains text and some formatting such as underline, bold, italic, font sizes, and colors; RTF documents can be opened in many word processing programs and text editors.

Section bar In Design view, a gray bar in a form or report that identifies and separates one section from another; used to select the section and to change the size of the section.

Stacked layout A control layout format that is similar to a paper form, with label controls placed to the left of each text box control; the controls are grouped together for easy editing.

Subset A portion of the total records available.

Tab order The order in which the insertion point moves from one field to another in a form when you press the Tab key.

Text box control A bound control on a form or report that displays the data from the underlying table or query.

Theme A predesigned set of colors, fonts, lines, and fill effects that look good together and that can be applied to all of the objects in the database or to individual objects in the database.

Unbound control A control that does not have a source of data, such as the title in a form or report.

3

ACCESS

CHAPTER REVIEW

Skills Review   Project 3C Student Internships

    In the following Skills Review, you will assist Erinique Jerlin, the dean of Business at the Northwest Campus, in using her database to track business students and their internship placements for the current semester. Your completed forms will look similar to Figure 3.49.

PROJECT FILES

For Project 3C, you will need the following file:

a03C_Student_Internships

You will save your database as:

Lastname_Firstname_3C_Student_Internships

PROJECT RESULTS

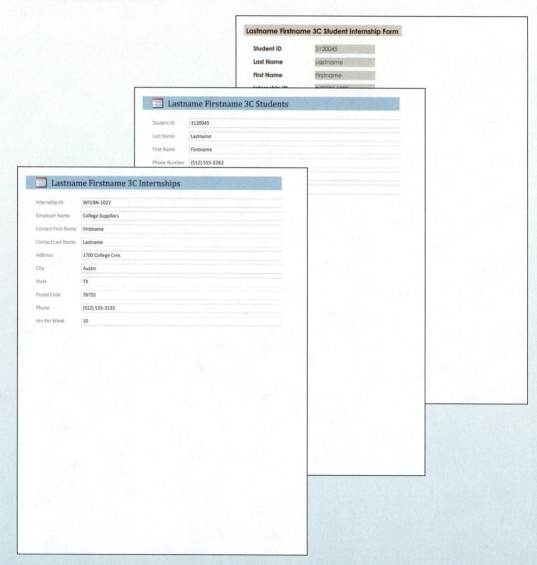

FIGURE 3.49

(Project 3C Student Internships continues on the next page)

CHAPTER REVIEW

1 ▶ Start Access. In the Access opening screen, click **Open Other Files**. Under **Open**, click **Computer**. Under **Recent Folders**, if displayed, click the location where your student data files are stored; otherwise, click **Browse** and then navigate to the location where your student data files are stored. Double-click **a03C_Student_Internships** to open the database.

a. On the ribbon, click the **FILE tab**, and then click **Save As**. Under **File Types**, be sure **Save Database As** is selected. On the right, under **Database File Types**, be sure **Access Database** is selected, and then click **Save As**.

b. In the **Save As** dialog box, navigate to your **Access Chapter 3** folder. In the **File name** box, replace the existing text with **Lastname_Firstname_3C_Student_Internships** and then press [Enter]. On the **Message Bar**, click **Enable Content**.

c. In the **Navigation Pane**, right-click **3C Students**, and then click **Rename**. With the table name selected and using your own name, type **Lastname Firstname 3C Students** and then press [Enter]. **Rename** the **3C Internships** table to **Lastname Firstname 3C Internships** and then point to the right edge of the **Navigation Pane** to display the ↔ pointer. Drag to the right to increase the width of the pane until both tables names display fully.

d. On the ribbon, click the **DATABASE TOOLS tab**, and then in the **Relationships group**, click **Relationships**. Under **RELATIONSHIP TOOLS**, on the **DESIGN tab**, in the **Relationships group**, click **All Relationships**. Resize and move the field lists so that the entire table name and fields display for each field list. In the **Relationships** window, click the **join line** between the two field lists. In the **Tools group**, click **Edit Relationships**. Point to the title bar of the **Edit Relationships** dialog box, and drag the dialog box downward below the two field lists. Notice that a *one-to-many* relationship is established between

the two tables by using *Internship ID* as the common field. **Close** the **Edit Relationships** dialog box, and then **Close** the **Relationships** window. In the message box, click **Yes** to save changes to the layout of the relationships.

e. In the **Navigation Pane**, click your **3C Students** table to select it. On the ribbon, click the **CREATE tab**, and then in the **Forms group**, click **Form**. **Save** the form as **Lastname Firstname 3C Student Form** and then **Close** the form object.

f. In the **Navigation Pane**, click your **3C Internships** table to select it. On the ribbon, click the **CREATE tab**, and then in the **Forms group**, click **Form**. Notice that for the first record—*Internship ID INTERN-1000* for *Lakes Realty Inc*—there are two student records in the subdatasheet—two students have been assigned internships for this employer. **Close** the form, and in the message box, click **Yes** to save the form. In the **Save As** dialog box, type **Lastname Firstname 3C Internship Company Form** and then press [Enter]. If necessary, increase the width of the Navigation Pane so that all object names display fully.

g. In the **Navigation Pane**, double-click your **3C Student Form** object to open it, and then **Close** the **Navigation Pane**. In the navigation area, click **New (blank) record** to display a new blank form. In the **Student ID** field, type **3120045** and then press [Tab]. Using your own last name and first name, continue entering the data as shown in **Table 1**.

h. With the insertion point positioned in the last field, press [Tab] to save the record and display a new blank record. **Close** your **3C Student Form** object, and then **Open** the **Navigation Pane**. Double-click your **3C Internship Company Form** object to open it, and then **Close** the **Navigation Pane**. Notice that for the first record, in the subdatasheet, the record you just entered displays. Scroll to view the bottom of

TABLE 1

Student ID	Last Name	First Name	Phone Number	Email	Internship ID
3120045	**Lastname**	**Firstname**	**(512) 555-3263**	**ns3120@tlcc.edu**	**INTERN-1000**

┈┈➤(Return to Step 1-h)

(Project 3C Student Internships continues on the next page)

the form. In the navigation area for the form—*not* the navigation area for the subdatasheet—click **New (blank) record**. In the blank form, using your own first name and last name, enter the data as shown in **Table 2**.

i. In the navigation area for the form, click **First record**. Click in the **Employer Name** field, and then on the **HOME tab**, in the **Find group**, click **Find**. In the **Find and Replace** dialog box, in the **Find What** box, type **Jones Consulting** and then click **Find Next**. **Close** the **Find and Replace** dialog box. On the **HOME tab**, in the **Records group**, click the **Delete arrow**, and then click **Delete Record**. In the message box, click **Yes** to delete the record. In the navigation area for the form, notice that the total number of records is *27*.

j. Use the technique you just practiced to **Find** the form for the **Internship ID** of INTERN-1027, and then **Close** the **Find and Replace** dialog box. On the ribbon, click the **FILE tab**, click **Print**, and then on the right, click **Print**. In the **Print** dialog box, under **Print Range**, click the **Selected Record(s)** option button. In the lower left corner of the dialog box, click **Setup**. In the **Page Setup** dialog box, click the **Columns tab**. Under **Column Size**, double-click in the **Width** box to select the existing value, type **7.5** and then click **OK**. If directed to print the form, in the **Print** dialog box, click **OK**. If directed to submit an electronic printout of the form, click **Cancel**, and then follow the directions given in the Note in Activity 3.06.

k. **Close** your **3C Internship Company Form** object, and then **Open** the **Navigation Pane**. In the **Navigation Pane**, double-click your **3C Student Form** object to open it, and then **Close** the **Navigation Pane**. Use the **Find** command to display the record where the **Last Name** field contains your last name, and then create a paper or electronic printout of only

that record, being sure to change the **Column Size Width** to **7.5**

2 With your **3C Student Form** object displayed in **Form** view, in the navigation area, click **First record**, and then click the **Internship ID** field name to select the text in the field box. Press Ctrl + F to display the **Find and Replace** dialog box. In the **Find What** box, type **INTERN-1009** and then click **Find Next** to find and display the record for *Michael Fresch*. **Close** the **Find and Replace** dialog box. On the **HOME tab**, in the **Sort & Filter group**, click **Selection**, and then click **Equals "INTERN-1009"**. In the navigation area, notice that two students are assigned internships with the company identified as INTERN-1009.

a. In the **Sort & Filter group**, click **Toggle Filter** to remove the filter and display all 52 records. **Close** the form. If prompted, click **Yes** to save the form.

b. **Open** the **Navigation Pane**, double-click your **3C Internship Company Form** object to open it, and then **Close** the **Navigation Pane**. On the **HOME tab**, in the **Sort & Filter group**, click **Advanced**, and then click **Filter By Form**. In the form, click the **City** field name to position the insertion point in the **City** field box, click the **arrow**, and then click **Georgetown**. In the **Sort & Filter group**, click **Toggle Filter** to display the filtered records. In the navigation area for the form, notice that three internships are located in the *City* of *Georgetown*.

c. In the **Sort & Filter group**, click **Advanced**, and then click **Filter By Form**. In the lower left corner of the form, click the **Or tab**. Click the **City** field box **arrow**, and then click **Elgin**. In the **Sort & Filter group**, click **Toggle Filter**. In the navigation area for the form, notice that five internships are located in either *Georgetown* or *Elgin*. In the **Sort & Filter group**, click **Advanced**, and then click **Clear All Filters** to display all 27 records.

TABLE 2

Internship ID	Employer Name	Contact First Name	Contact Last Name	Address	City	State	Postal Code	Phone	Hrs Per Week
INTERN-1027	**College Suppliers**	**Firstname**	**Lastname**	1700 College Cres	**Austin**	**TX**	78755	(512) 555-3133	10

Return to Step 1-i

(Project 3C Student Internships continues on the next page)

CHAPTER REVIEW

d. In the **Sort & Filter group**, click **Advanced**, and then click **Advanced Filter/Sort**. Resize the field list. In the **3C Internships** field list, double-click **City**, and then double-click **Hrs Per Week** to add both fields to the design grid. Click in the **Criteria** row under **City**, type **Austin** and then press Enter. In the **Criteria** row under **Hrs Per Week**, type **>10** and then press Enter. In the **Sort & Filter group**, click **Toggle Filter** to display the filtered records, and notice that that there are five internships in the *City* of *Austin* offering *more than 10* hours per week of work. In the **Sort & Filter group**, click **Toggle Filter** to remove the filter and display all 27 records. **Save** and then **Close** your **3C Internship Company Form** object, which also closes the Advanced Filter grid.

3 On the ribbon, click the **CREATE tab**, and then in the **Forms group**, click **Form Wizard**. In the **Tables/Queries** box, click the **arrow**, and then click **Table: Lastname Firstname 3C Students**. In the **Available Fields** list, double-click the following field names in the order given to move them to the **Selected Fields** list: **First Name**, **Last Name**, and **Internship ID**. Click **Next**. In the wizard, be sure **Columnar** is selected as the layout, and then click **Next**. In the **What title do you want for your form?** box, select the existing text, type **Lastname Firstname 3C Student Internship Form** and then click **Finish** to close the wizard and create the form.

4 On the **HOME tab**, in the **Views group**, click the top portion of the **View** button to switch to **Layout** view. If the **Field List** pane displays on the right side of your screen, close the pane. Click the **First Name label control**. Hold down Shift, and then click the **Last Name label control**, the **Internship ID label control**, and the three **text box controls** to select all of the controls. On the ribbon, under **FORM LAYOUT TOOLS**, click the **ARRANGE tab**. In the **Table group**, click **Stacked** to group all of the controls. Click the **First Name label control** to cancel the selection of all of the controls.

a. On the ribbon, under **FORM LAYOUT TOOLS**, click the **DESIGN tab**. In the **Themes group** click **Themes**. In the **Themes** gallery, using the ScreenTips, point to the **Wisp** theme, right-click, and then click **Apply Theme to This Object Only**. Click anywhere in the title—*Lastname Firstname 3C Student Internship*

Form—to select the title. On the ribbon, under **FORM LAYOUT TOOLS**, click the **FORMAT tab**. In the **Font group**, click the **Font Size arrow**, and then click **14**. In the **Font group**, click **Bold**. Click the **Font Color arrow**, and then under **Theme Colors**, in the sixth column, click the last color—**Orange, Accent 2, Darker 50%**.

b. On the ribbon, click the **DESIGN tab**. In the **Tools group**, click **Add Existing Fields**. In the **Field List** pane, click **Student ID**, and then drag the field name to the left until the pointer displays above the **First Name label control** and a colored line displays above the control. Release the mouse button to add the *Student ID* controls to the form, and then **Close** the **Field List** pane.

c. Click the **First Name text box control**, which displays *Jordan*, to select it. On the **DESIGN tab**, in the **Tools group**, click **Property Sheet**. In the **Property Sheet**, on the **Format tab**, click **Width**, type **1.75** and then press Enter to decrease the width of the text box controls. **Close** the **Property Sheet**. Be sure that the **First Name text box control** is still selected. On the ribbon, click the **ARRANGE tab**, and in the **Rows & Columns group**, click **Select Row**. In the **Move group**, click **Move Down** to move both controls below the **Last Name** controls. **Save** the changes you have made to the design of your form.

d. Click the **Student ID text box control**, which displays *1010101*. On the **ARRANGE tab**, in the **Rows & Columns group**, click **Select Column** to select all four text box controls. On the ribbon, click the **FORMAT tab**, and in the **Font group**, click the **Background Color arrow**. Under **Theme Colors**, in the fourth column, click the second color—**Brown, Text 2, Lighter 80%**.

e. Click the **Student ID label control**, and then on the ribbon, click the **ARRANGE tab**. In the **Rows & Columns group**, click **Select Column** to select all four label controls. On the ribbon, click the **FORMAT tab**, and then click the **Font Color arrow**—*not* the **Background Color arrow**. Under **Theme Colors**, in the fourth column, click the first color—**Brown, Text 2**. In the **Font group**, click **Bold**.

(Project 3C Student Internships continues on the next page)

CHAPTER REVIEW

f. Click the **layout selector** [⊞] to select all of the controls. In the **Font group**, click the **Font Size arrow**, and then click **12**. With all of the controls still selected, on the ribbon, click the **DESIGN tab**, and in the **Tools group**, click **Property Sheet**. In the **Property Sheet**, on the **Format tab**, click **Height**, type **0.25** and then press [Enter] to change the height of each selected control.

g. Click the **Student ID label control** to select only that control. In the **Property Sheet**, click **Width**, type **1.75** and then press [Enter] to change the width of all of the label controls. **Save** the design changes to your form.

h. On the status bar, click **Design View**. At the bottom of the form, click the **Form Footer section bar** to select it. In the **Property Sheet**, click **Height**, type **0.5** and then press [Enter] to increase the height of the **Form Footer** section.

i. On the ribbon, under **FORM DESIGN TOOLS**, click the **DESIGN tab**. In the **Controls group**, click **Label**. Move the pointer into the **Form Footer** section and then position the plus sign of the pointer at approximately **0.25 inch on the horizontal ruler** and even with the lower edge of the **Form Footer section bar**—the placement does not need to be precise. Click one time, type **Texas Lakes Community College** and then press [Enter].

j. With the **label control** selected, on the ribbon, click the **FORMAT tab**. In the **Font group**, click **Bold**. Click the **Font Color arrow**, and then under **Theme Colors**, in the fourth column, click the first

color—**Brown, Text 2**. If necessary, double-click the right edge of the label control to resize the control so that all of the data displays.

k. With the **label control** still selected, in the **Property Sheet**, click **Top**, type **0.1** and then press [Enter]. In the **Property Sheet**, in the **Left** property setting box, type **0.9** and then press [Enter]. **Close** the **Property Sheet**, and then **Save** the design changes to your form.

l. On the right side of the status bar, click **Form View**. In the navigation area, click **Last record** to display the record containing your name. On the ribbon, click the **FILE tab**, and then click **Print**. In the **Print** dialog box, under **Print Range**, click the **Selected Records(s)** option button. Because you changed the field widths, you do not need to change the Column Size Width in the **Print** dialog box. Create a paper or electronic printout as directed by your instructor. To create an electronic printout, follow the directions given in the Note in Activity 3.06.

m. **Close** all open objects, and then **Open** the **Navigation Pane**. If necessary, increase the width of the pane so that all object names display fully. On the right side of the title bar, click **Close** to close the database and to exit Access. As directed by your instructor, submit your database and the paper or electronic printouts of the three forms that are the results of this project. Specifically, in this project, using your own name, you created the following database and printouts or electronic printouts:

1. Lastname_Firstname_3C_Student_Internships	Database file
2. Lastname Firstname 3C Student Form	Form (printout or electronic printout - Record 52)
3. Lastname Firstname 3C Internship Company Form	Form (printout or electronic printout - Record 27)
4. Lastname Firstname 3C Student Internship Form	Form (printout or electronic printout - Record 52)

END | You have completed Project 3C

CHAPTER REVIEW

Skills Review   Project 3D Student Parking

In the following Skills Review, you will assist Carlos Medina, the chief of security, in using his Access database to track the details about students who have paid for parking in designated lots at the Southeast Campus of Texas Lakes Community College. Your completed reports will look similar to Figure 3.50.

PROJECT FILES

For Project 3D, you will need the following file:

a03D_Student_Parking

You will save your database as:

Lastname_Firstname_3D_Student_Parking

PROJECT RESULTS

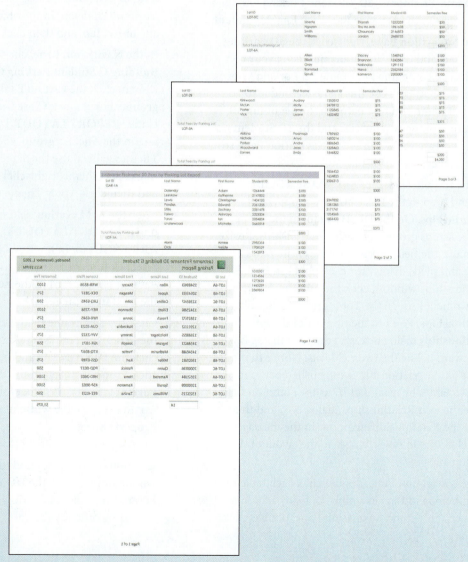

FIGURE 3.50

(Project 3D Student Parking continues on the next page)

CHAPTER REVIEW

1 Start Access. In the Access opening screen, click **Open Other Files**. Under **Open**, click **Computer**. Under **Recent Folders**, if displayed, click the location where your student data files are stored; otherwise, click **Browse** and then navigate to the location where your student data files are stored. Double-click **a03D_Student_Parking** to open the database.

a. On the ribbon, click the **FILE tab**, and then click **Save As**. Under **File Types**, be sure **Save Database As** is selected. On the right, under **Database File Types**, be sure **Access Database** is selected, and then at the bottom of the screen, click **Save As**. In the **Save As** dialog box, navigate to your **Access Chapter 3** folder. In the **File name** box, replace the existing text with **Lastname_Firstname_3D_Student_Parking** and then press Enter. On the **Message Bar**, click **Enable Content**.

b. In the **Navigation Pane**, right-click the **3D Parking Lots** table, and then click **Rename**. Using your own name, type **Lastname Firstname 3D Parking Lots** and then press Enter. Use this same technique to add your last name and first name to the beginning of the names of the two queries and the **3D Students** table. Increase the width of the **Navigation Pane** so that all object names display fully.

c. On the ribbon, click the **DATABASE TOOLS tab**, and then in the **Relationships group**, click **Relationships**. On the **DESIGN tab**, in the **Relationships group**, click **All Relationships**. Resize and move the field lists so that the entire table name and fields display for each field list. In the **Relationships** window, click the **join line** between the two field lists. In the **Tools group**, click **Edit Relationships**. Point to the title bar of the **Edit Relationships** dialog box, and drag the dialog box downward below the two field lists. Notice that a *one-to-many* relationship is established between the two tables by using *Lot ID* as the common field. **Close** the **Edit Relationships** dialog box, and then **Close** the **Relationships** window. In the message box, click **Yes** to save changes to the layout of the relationships.

d. In the **Navigation Pane**, double-click each table to open them, and then examine the fields and data in each table. In the **Navigation Pane**, double-click

your **3D Building G Student Parking Query** object to run the query and view the results. Apply **Best Fit** to the query results, and then **Save** the query. Switch to **Design** view to examine the design grid. This query answers the question, *What is the lot ID, lot location, student ID, student last name, student first name, license plate, and semester fee for students who have paid for parking in front of Building G, in ascending order by the Last Name field?* In the **Navigation Pane**, double-click your **3D Student Parking by Lots Query** object, apply **Best Fit** to the query results, **Save** the query, and then switch to **Design** view to examine the design grid. This query answers the question, *What is the lot ID, student ID, student last name, student first name, license plate, state, and semester fee for all students?* In the object window, right-click any **object tab**, and then click **Close All**.

e. In the **Navigation Pane**, click to select your **3D Building G Student Parking Query** object. On the ribbon, click the **CREATE tab**, and in the **Reports group**, click **Report**. **Close** the **Navigation Pane**. Under **REPORT LAYOUT TOOLS**, on the **DESIGN tab**, in the **Themes group**, click **Themes**. In the **Themes** gallery, use the ScreenTips to locate the **Retrospect** theme, right-click the **Retrospect** theme, and then click **Apply Theme to This Object Only**.

f. Click the **Lot Location** field name. On the ribbon, under **REPORT LAYOUT TOOLS**, click the **ARRANGE tab**. In the **Rows & Columns group**, click **Select Column** to select the field name and all of the data for each record in the field. Press Del to remove the field from the report.

g. Click the **Last Name** field name, hold down Shift, and then click the **First Name** field name. On the ribbon, click the **DESIGN tab**, and in the **Tools group**, click **Property Sheet**. In the **Property Sheet**, on the **Format tab**, click **Width**, type **1.25** and then press Enter to decrease the width of the two fields. **Close** the **Property Sheet**.

h. Click the **Last Name** field name to cancel the selection of both fields and to select only this field. On the ribbon, click the **HOME tab**, and in the **Sort & Filter group**, click **Ascending** to sort the records in ascending order by the Last Name field.

(Project 3D Student Parking continues on the next page)

i. If necessary, scroll to the bottom of the report, and notice that the *Semester Fee* column is automatically totaled. At the top of the report, click the **Student ID** field name. On the ribbon, click the **DESIGN tab**. In the **Grouping & Totals group**, click **Totals**, and then click **Count Records**. If necessary, scroll to the bottom of the report, and notice that *14* students have paid for parking in front of Building G.

j. At the bottom of the report, under **Student ID**, click the **calculated control** that displays *14*. Hold down Ctrl, and then under **Semester Fee**, click the **calculated control** that displays *$1,075*—the two calculated controls are selected. On the **DESIGN tab**, in the **Tools group**, click **Property Sheet**. In the **Property Sheet**, click **Height**, type **0.25** and then press Enter to increase the height of both controls. At the bottom of the report, to the right of the **calculated control** that displays *$1,075*, click the **control** that displays *Page 1 of 1*. In the **Property Sheet**, click **Left**, type **2.5** and then press Enter to move the page number within the margins of the report.

k. At the top of the report, click the **label control** that displays the title of the report—*Lastname Firstname 3D Building G Student Parking Query*. On the ribbon, under **REPORT LAYOUT TOOLS**, click the **FORMAT tab**. In the **Font group**, click the **Font Size arrow**, and then click **14**. With the **label control** still selected, double-click **Query** to select the word, type **Report** and then press Enter to change the title of the report to *Lastname Firstname 3D Building G Student Parking Report*.

l. Click the **Lot ID** field name. In the **Property Sheet**, click **Left**, type **0.25** and then press Enter to move all of the fields slightly to the right from the left margin. **Close** the **Property Sheet**, and then **Save** the report as **Lastname Firstname 3D Building G Student Parking Report**

m. On the right side of the status bar, click **Print Preview**. On the **PRINT PREVIEW tab**, in the **Zoom group**, click **Two Pages**, and notice that the report will print on one page. Create a paper or electronic printout as directed, click **Close Print Preview**, and then **Close** the report.

2 ▶ On the ribbon, click the **CREATE tab**, and then in the **Reports group**, click **Report Wizard**. In the **Tables/Queries** box, click the **arrow**, and then click

Query: Lastname Firstname 3D Student Parking by Lots Query. In the **Available Fields** list, double-click the following field names in the order given to move them to the **Selected Fields** list: **Lot ID**, **Last Name**, **First Name**, **Student ID**, and **Semester Fee**.

a. Click **Next**. In the **How do you want to view your data?** box, click **by Lastname Firstname 3D Students**, and then click **Next**. In the list on the left, double-click **Lot ID** to group the records by this field, and then click **Next**. Click the **1 box arrow**, and then click **Last Name** to sort the records by the student's last name within each Lot ID.

b. In the wizard, click **Summary Options**. In the **Summary Options** dialog box, to the right of **Semester Fee**, click to select the **Sum** check box. Under **Show**, be sure that **Detail and Summary** is selected, and then click **OK**. In the wizard, click **Next**.

c. In the wizard, under **Layout**, be sure that **Stepped** is selected. Under **Orientation**, click **Landscape**. At the bottom of the wizard, be sure that the **Adjust the field width so all fields fit on a page** check box is selected, and then click **Next**. In the **What title do you want for your report?** box, select the existing text, type **Lastname Firstname 3D Fees by Parking Lot Report** and then click **Finish**. In the object window, right-click the **object tab** for the report, and then click **Layout View**.

3 ▶ Under **REPORT LAYOUT TOOLS**, on the **DESIGN tab**, in the **Themes group**, click **Themes**. In the **Themes** gallery, use the ScreenTips to locate the **Ion Boardroom** theme, right-click the **Ion Boardroom** theme, and then click **Apply Theme to This Object Only**. In the report, click the title—*Lastname Firstname 3D Fees by Parking Lot*—to display a border around the label control. On the ribbon, under **REPORT LAYOUT TOOLS**, click the **FORMAT tab**. In the **Font group**, click the **Font Size arrow**, and then click **14**. In the **Font group**, click **Bold**. In the body of the report, click any one of the controls that begins with **Summary for 'Lot ID'**, and then press Del. **Save** the design changes to your report.

a. On the left side of the report, click a **Sum label control**, which will select all of the related controls. Double-click the control to select the text—*Sum*. Type **Total Fees by Parking Lot** and then press Enter.

(Project 3D Student Parking continues on the next page)

CHAPTER REVIEW

b. At the top of the report, click the **Lot ID label control** to select it. Hold down Shift, and then click each one of the four other label controls that display the field names to select all five label controls. On the **FORMAT tab**, in the **Font group**, click **Bold**.

c. In the report, under **Last Name**, click the **text box control** that displays *Dolensky*. Hold down Shift, and then under **First Name**, click the **text box control** that displays *Adam*. On the ribbon, click the **DESIGN tab**. In the **Tools group**, click **Property Sheet**. In the **Property Sheet**, click **Width**, type **1.5** and then press Enter.

d. In the report, click the **Student ID label control**. In the **Property Sheet**, click **Left**, type **7.25** and then press Enter. Do not be concerned that the data in the field is not aligned with the field name; you will adjust this later in this project. Scroll to the bottom of the report, and then click the **Grand Total label control**. In the **Property Sheet**, click **Width**, type **1** and then press Enter. **Close** the **Property Sheet**, and then **Save** the design changes to your report.

e. On the status bar, click **Design View**. In the **Lot ID Footer** section, click the **Total Fees by Parking Lot label control**. Hold down Shift, and in the **Report Footer** section, click the **Grand Total label control** to select both controls. On the ribbon, under **REPORT DESIGN TOOLS**, click the **ARRANGE tab**. In the **Sizing & Ordering group**, click **Align**, and then click **Left**.

f. In the report, in the **Page Header** section, click the **Student ID label control**. Hold down Shift, and in the **Detail** section, click the **Student ID text box control**. On the **ARRANGE tab**, in the **Sizing & Ordering group**, click **Align**, and then click **Left**. On the status bar, click **Layout View** and notice the left alignment of the two sets of controls.

4 On the status bar, click **Print Preview**. On the **PRINT PREVIEW tab**, in the **Zoom group**, click **More Pages**, and then click **Four Pages** to view how your report is currently laid out. In the **Zoom group**, click the **Zoom arrow**, and then click **50%**. Notice at the bottom of Page 1 and the top of Page 2, that the grouping for **LOT-2B** breaks across these two pages. Notice at the bottom of Page 2 and the top of Page 3, that the grouping for **LOT-6A** breaks across these two pages. Your pages may display differently depending upon the printer that is installed on your system.

a. On the ribbon, click **Close Print Preview** to return to Layout view. On the **DESIGN tab**, in the **Grouping & Totals group**, click **Group & Sort**. In the **Group, Sort, and Total** pane, on the **Group on Lot ID** bar, click **More**. Click the **do not keep group together on one page arrow**, and then click **keep whole group together on one page**. On the **DESIGN tab**, in the **Grouping & Totals group**, click **Group & Sort** to close the **Group, Sort, and Total** pane. **Save** the design changes to your report.

b. On the status bar, click **Print Preview**. Notice that the entire grouping for **LOT-2B** displays at the top of Page 2. Keeping this group together forced the groupings for **LOT-5C** and **LOT-6A** to move to the top of Page 3—your groupings may display differently depending upon the printer that is installed on your system. Create a paper or electronic printout as directed—three pages result.

c. **Close** the report, and then **Open** the **Navigation Pane**. If necessary, increase the width of the pane so that all object names display fully. On the right side of the title bar, click **Close** to close the database and to exit Access. As directed by your instructor, submit your database and the paper or electronic printouts of the two reports—one report is three pages—that are the results of this project. Specifically, in this project, using your own name, you created the following database and printouts or electronic printouts:

1. Lastname_Firstname_3D_Student_Parking	Database file
2. Lastname Firstname 3D Building G Student Parking Report	Report (printout or electronic printout)
3. Lastname Firstname 3D Fees by Parking Lot Report	Report (printout or electronic printout - three pages)

END | You have completed Project 3D

CONTENT-BASED ASSESSMENTS

Mastering Access   Project 3E Textbook Publishers

In the following Mastering Access project, you will assist Donna Rider, manager of the bookstore, in using her database to track textbooks and publishers for courses being offered by the Science Department at the Northeast Campus of Texas Lakes Community College. Your completed forms will look similar to Figure 3.51.

Apply 3A skills from these Objectives:

1 Create and Use a Form to Add and Delete Records

2 Filter Records

3 Create a Form by Using the Form Wizard

4 Modify a Form in Layout View and in Design View

PROJECT FILES

For Project 3E, you will need the following file:

a03E_Textbook_Publishers

You will save your database as:

Lastname_Firstname_3E_Textbook_Publishers

PROJECT RESULTS

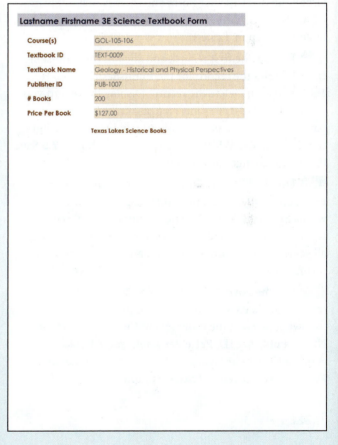

FIGURE 3.51

(Project 3E Textbook Publishers continues on the next page)

CONTENT-BASED ASSESSMENTS

1 Start Access. From your student data files, open **a03E_Textbook_Publishers**. Save the database in your **Access Chapter 3** folder as **Lastname_Firstname_3E_Textbook_Publishers** and then enable the content. In the **Navigation Pane**, **Rename** each table by adding **Lastname Firstname** to the beginning of the table name. Increase the width of the **Navigation Pane** so that all object names display fully. View the relationship between the *3E Publishers* table and the *3E Science Textbooks* table; *one* publisher can provide *many* textbooks for the science courses. Save the changes to the layout of the relationships.

2 Based on your **3E Publishers** table, use the **Form** tool to create a form. **Save** the form as **Lastname Firstname 3E Publisher Form** and then switch to **Form** view. Using the form, add a new record to the underlying table as shown in **Table 1**.

3 Display the first record, and click in the **Publisher ID** field. **Find** the record for the **Publisher ID** of **PUB-1006**, and then **Delete** the record. Display the record you entered for **PUB-1008**, and then, as directed, create a paper or electronic printout of only that record, changing the **Column Size Width** in the **Print** dialog box to **7.5 Save** the design changes to your form.

4 Use the **Filter By Form** tool in your **3E Publisher Form** object to create a filter that displays records with a **State** of **CA** or **TX**. After verifying that three records match this criteria, click **Toggle Filter** to display all seven records. **Save** your form, and then **Close** your form.

5 Use the **Form Wizard** to create a form based on your **3E Science Textbooks** table that includes the following fields in the order given: **Course(s)**, **Textbook Name**, **Publisher ID**, **Price Per Book**, and **# Books**. Apply a **Columnar** layout, and name the form **Lastname Firstname 3E Science Textbook Form.**

6 In **Layout** view, apply the **Stacked** layout to all of the controls, and then apply the **Ion Boardroom** theme to this form only. For the title of the form, change the **Font Size** to **16**, apply **Bold**, and then change the **Font Color** to **Dark Purple, Text 2**—under **Theme Colors**, in the fourth column, the first color. **Save** the design changes to the form.

7 From the **Field List** pane, add the **Textbook ID** field to the form directly above the **Textbook Name** field. Move the **# Books** controls directly above the **Price Per Book** controls. **Close** the **Field List** pane. Display Record 9—this record's textbook name is the longest entry of all records. Click the **Textbook Name text box control**, set the **Width** property to **4** and then **Save** the design changes to your form.

8 Select all six **text box controls**, and change the **Background Color** to **Orange, Accent 4, Lighter 80%**—under **Theme Colors**, in the eighth column, the second color. Select all six **label controls**, and change the **Font Color** to **Orange, Accent 4, Darker 50%**—under **Theme Colors**, in the eighth column, the last color. Apply **Bold** to the **label controls**. With the **label controls** still selected, set the **Width** property to **1.75** and then select all of the **label controls** and all of the **text box controls**. Change the **Font Size** to **12**, set the **Height** property to **0.25** and then **Save** the design changes to your form.

9 In **Design** view, set the **Form Footer** section **Height** property to **0.5** Add a **Label control** to the **Form Footer** section that displays **Texas Lakes Science Books** For this **label control**, change the **Font Color** to **Orange, Accent 4, Darker 50%**—under **Theme Colors**, in the eighth column, the last color—and then apply **Bold**. For this **label control**, set the **Width** property to **2.2** Set the **Top** property to **0.1** and then set the **Left** property to **1.95**

TABLE 1

Publisher ID	Publisher Name	Address	City	State	Postal Code	Phone Number	Publisher Web Site
PUB-1008	Hidden Hills Publishing Co	5100 Live Oak St	Dallas	TX	75201	(214) 555-0857	http://www.hhpubco.pub

(Return to Step 3)

(Project 3E Textbook Publishers continues on the next page)

CONTENT-BASED ASSESSMENTS

10 ▶ **Close** the **Property Sheet**, **Save** your form, and then switch to **Form** view. **Find** the record for the **Textbook ID** of **TEXT-0009**, and then, as directed, create a paper or electronic printout of only this record. Because you changed the field widths, you do not need to change the Column Size Width in the **Print** dialog box.

11 ▶ **Close** all open objects, and then **Open** the **Navigation Pane**. If necessary, increase the width of the pane so that all object names display fully. **Close** Access. As directed by your instructor, submit your database and the paper or electronic printouts of the two forms that are the results of this project. Specifically, in this project, using your own name, you created the following database and printouts or electronic printouts:

1. Lastname_Firstname_3E_Textbook_Publishers	Database file
2. Lastname Firstname 3E Publisher Form	Form (printout or electronic printout - Record 7)
3. Lastname Firstname 3E Science Textbook Form	Form (printout or electronic printout - Record 9)

END | You have completed Project 3E

CONTENT-BASED ASSESSMENTS

Mastering Access   Project 3F Degrees and Students

In the following Mastering Access project, you will assist Tom Catogrides, the registrar, in using his database to track degrees and grade point averages for honor students in the health professions program in preparation for graduation. Your completed database objects will look similar to Figure 3.52.

Apply 3B skills from these Objectives:

5 Create a Report by Using the Report Tool and Modify the Report in Layout View

6 Create a Report by Using the Report Wizard

7 Modify the Design of a Report

8 Keep Grouped Data Together in a Printed Report

PROJECT FILES

For Project 3F, you will need the following file:

a03F_Degrees_Students

You will save your database as:

Lastname_Firstname_3F_Degrees_Students

PROJECT RESULTS

FIGURE 3.52

(Project 3F Degrees and Students continues on the next page)

CONTENT-BASED ASSESSMENTS

1 Start Access. From your student data files, open **a03F_Degrees_Students**. **Save** the database in your **Access Chapter 3** folder as **Lastname_Firstname_3F_Degrees_ Students** and then enable the content. In the **Navigation Pane**, **Rename** the two tables and two queries by adding **Lastname Firstname** to the beginning of each object name, and then increase the width of the **Navigation Pane** so that all object names display fully. View the relationship that is established between the *3F Degrees* tables and the *3F Students* table—*one* type of degree can be awarded to *many* students. Save the changes to the layout of the relationships. **Run** each query to display the query results, apply **Best Fit**, and then **Save** each query.

Open each query in **Design** view to examine the design grid. The *3F Summa Cum Laude Graduates Query* answers the question, *What is the GPA, student ID, last name, first name, degree, and program for students graduating with a grade point average of 3.8 or higher, in descending order by GPA?* The *3F GPAs by Degree Program Query* answers the question, *What is the program, last name, first name, and GPA for all students, in ascending order by the Last Name field within the Program field?* **Close All** objects.

Based on your **3F Summa Cum Laude Graduates Query** object, use the **Report** tool to create a report. Apply the **Facet** theme to only this report. Delete the **Student ID** field from the report. For the **Last Name**, **First Name**, and **Degree text box controls**, set the **Width** property to **1.25** and then **Sort** the **Last Name** field in **Ascending** order. For the **Program text box controls**, set the **Width** property to **2.5**

At the bottom of the report, for the **calculated control**, which displays *8*, set the **Height** to **0.25** and then for the **page number control**, set the **Left** property to **5** For the title of the report, set the **Font Size** to **14** and change the word *Query* to **Report** For the **GPA** field, set the **Left** property to **0.25** to approximately center the fields within the margins of the report. **Save** the report as **Lastname Firstname 3F Summa Cum Laude Graduates Report** and then create a paper or electronic printout as directed. **Close Print Preview**, **Close** the **Property Sheet**, and then **Close** the report.

2 Use the **Report Wizard** to create a report based on your **3F GPAs by Degree Program Query** object that includes the following fields in the order given: **Program**, **GPA**, **Last Name**, and **First Name**. View your data **by 3F Degrees** and do not add any other grouping to the report. Sort first in **Descending** order by **GPA**, and second in **Ascending** order by **Last Name**. Summarize the report by averaging the **GPA** field. Be sure the layout is **Stepped** and the orientation is **Portrait**. For the report title, type **Lastname Firstname 3F GPAs by Program Report** and then switch to **Layout** view.

3 Apply the **Wisp** theme to only this report. For the report title, change the **Font Size** to **16**, and then apply **Bold**. Delete the controls that begin with **Summary for 'Program'**. Under **Program**, for the **text box controls**, set the **Width** property to **2.75** Change the text in the **Avg label control** to **Average GPA by Program** At the top of the report, select the four **label controls** that display the field names, and then apply **Bold**. Select the **GPA label control**, the **GPA text box controls**, and the **calculated controls** for the average GPA, and then set the **Width** property to **1** and the **Left** property to **3 Close** the **Property Sheet**. Display the report in **Design** view. Under **Program Header**, click the **Program text box control**, hold down Shift, and under **Program Footer**, click the **Average GPA by Program label control**. **Align** the controls on the **Right**, and then **Save** the design changes to your report.

4 Switch to **Print Preview**, **Zoom** to display **Two Pages** of the report, and examine how the groupings break across the pages. Switch to **Layout** view, display the **Group, Sort, and Total** pane, select **keep whole group together on one page**, and then close the **Group, Sort, and Total** pane. Switch to **Print Preview**, and notice that the groupings are not split between pages. **Save** the report, and then create a paper or electronic printout as directed—two pages result.

(Project 3F Degrees and Students continues on the next page)

Mastering Access   Project 3F Degrees and Students (continued)

5 **Close Print Preview**, and then **Close** the report. **Open** the **Navigation Pane**, and, if necessary, increase the width of the pane so that all object names display fully. On the right side of the title bar, click **Close** to close the database and to exit Access. As directed by your instructor, submit your database and the paper or electronic printouts of the two reports—one report is two pages—that are the results of this project. Specifically, in this project, using your own name, you created the following database and printouts or electronic printouts:

1. Lastname_Firstname_3F_Degrees_Students	Database file
2. Lastname Firstname 3F Summa Cum Laude Graduates Report	Report (printout or electronic printout)
3. Lastname Firstname 3F GPAs by Program Report	Report (printout or electronic printout - two pages)

END | You have completed Project 3F

CONTENT-BASED ASSESSMENTS

Mastering Access   Project 3G Career Books

In the following Mastering Access project, you will assist Rebecca Hennelly, head librarian at the Southwest Campus of Texas Lakes Community College, in using her database to track publishers and book titles that assist students in finding employment. Your completed forms and report will look similar to Figure 3.53.

Apply 3A and 3B skills from these Objectives:

1 Create and Use a Form to Add and Delete Records

2 Filter Records

3 Create a Form by Using the Form Wizard

4 Modify a Form in Layout View and in Design View

5 Create a Report by Using the Report Tool and Modify the Report in Layout View

6 Create a Report by Using the Report Wizard

7 Modify the Design of a Report

8 Keep Grouped Data Together in a Printed Report

PROJECT FILES

For Project 3G, you will need the following file:

a03G_Career_Books

You will save your database as:

Lastname_Firstname_3G_Career_Books

PROJECT RESULTS

FIGURE 3.53

(Project 3G Career Books continues on the next page)

CONTENT-BASED ASSESSMENTS

1 Start Access. From your student data files, open **a03G_Career_Books**. Save the database in your **Access Chapter 3** folder as **Lastname_Firstname_3G_Career_ Books** and then enable the content. In the **Navigation Pane**, **Rename** the two tables and one query by adding **Lastname Firstname** to the beginning of each object name. Increase the width of the **Navigation Pane** so that all object names display fully. View the relationship that is established between the *3G Publishers* tables and the *3G Career Books* table—*one* publisher can publish *many* career books. Save the changes to the layout of the relationships.

Open the **3G Resume or Interview Books Query**, apply **Best Fit**, and then **Save** the query. Switch the query to **Design** view, examine the design of the query, and then **Close** the query object.

2 Based on your **3G Career Books** table, use the **Form** tool to create a form. **Save** the form as **Lastname Firstname 3G Career Book Form** and then switch to **Form** view. Using the form, add a new record to the underlying table as shown in **Table 1**.

3 Display the first record, and click in the **Title ID** field. **Find** the record for the **Title ID** of **T-19**, and then **Delete** the record. Display the record you entered for T-25, and then, as directed, create a paper or electronic printout of only that record, changing the **Column Size Width** in the **Print** dialog box to **7.5 Save** the design changes to your form.

4 Use the **Filter By Form** tool in your **3G Career Book Form** object to create a filter that displays records with a **Category** of **Interviewing Strategies** or **Resumes**. After verifying that 10 records match this criteria, click **Toggle Filter** to display all 24 records. **Save** the form, and then **Close** the form.

5 Use the **Form Wizard** to create a form based on your **3G Publishers** table that includes the following fields in the order given: **Company Name**, **Rep Last Name**, **Rep First Name**, **Job Title**, and **Phone Number**. Apply a **Columnar** layout, and name the form **Lastname Firstname 3G Publisher Form**

6 In **Layout** view, apply the **Stacked** layout to all of the controls, and then apply the **Integral** theme to this form only. For the title of the form, change the **Font Size** to **16**, apply **Bold**, and then change the **Font Color** to **Dark Teal, Text 2, Darker 50%**—under **Theme Colors**, in the fourth column, the last color. **Save** the design changes to the form.

7 From the **Field List** pane, add the **Publisher ID** field to the form directly above the **Company Name** field. **Close** the **Field List** pane. Move the **Rep First Name** controls directly above the **Rep Last Name** controls. Click the **Job Title text box control**, set the **Width** property to **2.5** and then **Save** the design changes to your form.

8 Select all six **text box controls**, and change the **Background Color** to **Turquoise, Accent 1, Lighter 80%**—under **Theme Colors**, in the fifth column, the second color. Select all six **label controls**, and change the **Font Color** to **Dark Teal, Text 2, Darker 50%**—under **Theme Colors**, in the fourth column, the last color. Apply **Bold** to the **label controls**. With the **label controls** still selected, set the **Width** property to **1.75** and then select all of the **label controls** and all of the **text box controls**. Change the **Font Size** to **12**, set the **Height** property to **0.25** and then **Save** the design changes to your form.

TABLE 1

Title ID	Title	Author Last Name	Author First Name	Publisher ID	Category	Copies On Hand	Value of Books
T-25	Effective Networking	Nunez	Charlene	PUB-109	Job Search	6	180

Return to Step 3

(Project 3G Career Books continues on the next page)

9 In **Design** view, set the **Form Footer** section **Height** property to **0.5** Add a **Label** control to the **Form Footer** section that displays **Texas Lakes Southwest Campus** For this **label control**, change the **Font Color** to **Dark Teal, Text 2, Darker 50%**—under **Theme Colors**, in the fourth column, the last color —and then apply **Bold**. For this **label control**, set the **Width** property to **2.2** Set the **Top** property to **0.1** and then set the **Left** property to **1 Close** the **Property Sheet**, **Save** your form, and then switch to **Form** view. Using the form, add a new record to the underlying table as shown in **Table 2**.

10 Display the record that you just created, and then, as directed, create a paper or electronic printout of only this record. Because you changed the field widths, you do not need to change the Column Size Width in the **Print** dialog box. **Close** the form.

11 Based on your **3G Resume or Interview Books Query** object, use the **Report** tool to create a report. Apply the **Retrospect** theme to only this report. Delete the following fields from the report: **Publisher ID**, **Category**, and **Company Name**. For the **Title text box controls**, set the **Width** property to **3** and then **Sort** the **Title** field in **Ascending** order. For the **Author Last Name text box controls** and the **Author First Name text box controls**, set the **Width** property to **1.5**

12 Click the **Title** field name, and then add a calculated control that counts the number of records. At the bottom of the report, for the **calculated control**, which displays *10*, set the **Height** to **0.25** and then for the **page number control**, set the **Left** property to **5** For the title of the report, set the **Font Size** to **14** and change the word *Query* to **Report** Click the **Title** field name, and then set the **Left** property to **0.75** to move all of the controls to the right. **Save** the report as **Lastname Firstname 3G Resume or Interview Books Report** and then create a paper or electronic printout as directed. **Close Print Preview**, **Close** the **Property Sheet**, and then **Close** the report.

13 Use the **Report Wizard** to create a report based on your **3G Career Books** table that includes the following fields in the order given: **Category**, **Title**, and **Value of Books**. Group your data by **Category**, sort in **Ascending** order by **Title**, and then summarize the report by summing the **Value of Books** field. Be sure the layout is **Stepped** and the orientation is **Portrait**. For the report title, type **Lastname Firstname 3G Book Values by Category Report** and then switch to **Layout** view.

14 Apply the **Ion Boardroom** theme to only this report. For the report title, change the **Font Size** to **14**, and then apply **Bold**. Delete the controls that begin with **Summary for 'Category'**. Select the **Category**, **Title**, and **Value of Books label controls**, and then apply **Bold**. Under **Title**, for the **text box controls**, set the **Width** property to **3.5** For the **Value of Books label control**, set the **Left** property to **6** and then **Save** the design changes to your report.

15 At the bottom of the report in the last column, select the following three controls: **text box control** that displays *$420*, **calculated control** that displays *$945*, and the **calculated control** that displays *7,730*. Set the **Width** property to **1.25** and the **Left** property to **6** For the **Grand Total label control**, set the **Width** property to **1** and then change the text in the **Sum label control** to **Total Value of Books by Category** Click any **Title text box control**, set the **Height** property to **0.35** and then **Save** your report.

16 **Close** the **Property Sheet**, and then display your report in **Design** view. Under **Category Footer**, click the **label control** that displays *Total Value of Books by Category*, hold down Shift, and then under **Report Footer**, click the **Grand Total label control**. **Align** the controls on the **Left**, and then **Save** the design changes to your report.

TABLE 2

Publisher ID	Company Name	Rep First Name	Rep Last Name	Job Title	Phone Number
PUB-111	**Associated Publishers**	**Marquis**	**Sullivan**	**Sales Associate**	**(512) 555-7373**

(Return to Step 10)

(Project 3G Career Books continues on the next page)

CONTENT-BASED ASSESSMENTS

17 Switch to **Print Preview**, **Zoom** to display **Two Pages** of the report, and examine how the groupings break across the pages. Switch to **Layout** view, display the **Group, Sort, and Total** pane, select **keep whole group together on one page**, and then close the **Group, Sort, and Total** pane. Switch to **Print Preview**, and notice that the groupings are no longer split between pages. **Save** the report, and then create a paper or electronic printout as directed—two pages result.

18 **Close Print Preview**, and then **Close** the report. **Open** the **Navigation Pane**, and, if necessary, increase the width of the pane so that all object names display fully. On the right side of the title bar, click **Close** to close the database and to exit Access. As directed by your instructor, submit your database and the paper or electronic printouts of the two forms and two reports—one report is two pages—that are the results of this project. Specifically, in this project, using your own name, you created the following database and printouts or electronic printouts:

1. Lastname_Firstname_3G_Career_Books	Database file
2. Lastname Firstname 3G Career Book Form	Form (printout or electronic printout - Record 24)
3. Lastname Firstname 3G Publisher Form	Form (printout or electronic printout - Record 12)
4. Lastname Firstname 3G Resume or Interview Books Report	Report (printout or electronic printout)
5. Lastname Firstname 3G Book Values by Category Report	Report (printout or electronic printout - two pages)

END | You have completed Project 3G

CONTENT-BASED ASSESSMENTS

GO! Fix It   Project 3H Resume Workshops   Online

GO! Make It   Project 3I Study Abroad   Online

GO! Solve It   Project 3J Job Offers   Online

GO! Solve It   Project 3K Financial Aid

PROJECT FILES

For Project 3K, you will need the following file:

a03K_Financial_Aid

You will save your database as:

Lastname_Firstname_3K_Financial_Aid

Start Access, navigate to your student data files, open a03K_Financial_Aid, and then save the database in your **Access Chapter 3** folder as **Lastname_Firstname_3K_Financial_Aid** Using your own name, add **Lastname Firstname** to the beginning of both table names and the query name. Sivia Long, the financial aid director, would like you to create an attractive form and a report for this database, using the following guidelines:

- The form will be used to update student records in the 3K FA Students table. Be sure that the Last Name field displays above the First Name field. After the form is created, enter a new record using your own information with a Student ID of **9091246** and Financial Aid ID of **FA-07** and a Home Phone of **(512) 555-9876** and a College Email of **ns246@tlcc.edu** Create a filter that when toggled on displays the records for those students whose last names begin with the letter *S*. Add a footer to the form that displays **Texas Lakes Community College Financial Aid** Save the form as **Lastname Firstname 3K FA Student Update Form** and then create a paper or electronic printout of your record only.

- The report should use the query and list the Award Name, the Student ID, and the Award Amount for financial aid offered to students, grouped by the Award Name field, and sorted in ascending order by the Student ID field. Include a total for the Award Amount field, save the report as **Lastname Firstname 3K FA Amount by Award Report** and be sure the groupings do not break across pages when the report is printed. Create a paper or electronic printout as directed—multiple pages result.

Open the Navigation Pane, be sure that all object names display fully, and then close Access. As directed, submit your database and the paper or electronic printout of the form and report—the report is multiple pages—that are the results of this project. Specifically, in this project, using your own name, you created the following database and printouts or electronic printouts:

1. Lastname_Firstname_3K_Financial_Aid	Database file
2. Lastname Firstname 3K FA Student Update Form	Form (printout or electronic printout - Record 35)
3. Lastname Firstname 3K FA Amount by Award Report	Report (printout or electronic printout - multiple pages)

(Project 3K Financial Aid continues on the next page)

CONTENT-BASED ASSESSMENTS

Performance Level

	Exemplary	Proficient	Developing
Create 3K FA Student Update Form	Form created with correct fields, new record, footer, and filter in an attractive format.	Form created with no more than two missing elements.	Form created with more than two missing elements.
Create 3K FA Amount by Award Report	Report created with correct fields, grouped, sorted, and summarized correctly, with groupings kept together in an attractive format.	Report created with no more than two missing elements.	Report created with more than two missing elements.

Performance Criteria

END | You have completed Project 3K

OUTCOMES-BASED ASSESSMENTS

RUBRIC

The following outcomes-based assessments are *open-ended assessments*. That is, there is no specific correct result; your result will depend on your approach to the information provided. Make *Professional Quality* your goal. Use the following scoring rubric to guide you in *how* to approach the problem and then to evaluate *how well* your approach solves the problem.

The *criteria*—Software Mastery, Content, Format & Layout, and Process—represent the knowledge and skills you have gained that you can apply to solving the problem. The *levels of performance*—Professional Quality, Approaching Professional Quality, or Needs Quality Improvements—help you and your instructor evaluate your result.

	Your completed project is of Professional Quality if you:	Your completed project is Approaching Professional Quality if you:	Your completed project Needs Quality Improvements if you:
1-Software Mastery	Choose and apply the most appropriate skills, tools, and features and identify efficient methods to solve the problem.	Choose and apply some appropriate skills, tools, and features, but not in the most efficient manner.	Choose inappropriate skills, tools, or features, or are inefficient in solving the problem.
2-Content	Construct a solution that is clear and well organized, contains content that is accurate, appropriate to the audience and purpose, and is complete. Provide a solution that contains no errors in spelling, grammar, or style.	Construct a solution in which some components are unclear, poorly organized, inconsistent, or incomplete. Misjudge the needs of the audience. Have some errors in spelling, grammar, or style, but the errors do not detract from comprehension.	Construct a solution that is unclear, incomplete, or poorly organized; contains some inaccurate or inappropriate content; and contains many errors in spelling, grammar, or style. Do not solve the problem.
3-Format & Layout	Format and arrange all elements to communicate information and ideas, clarify function, illustrate relationships, and indicate relative importance.	Apply appropriate format and layout features to some elements, but not others. Overuse features, causing minor distraction.	Apply format and layout that does not communicate information or ideas clearly. Do not use format and layout features to clarify function, illustrate relationships, or indicate relative importance. Use available features excessively, causing distraction.
4-Process	Use an organized approach that integrates planning, development, self-assessment, revision, and reflection.	Demonstrate an organized approach in some areas, but not others; or, use an insufficient process of organization throughout.	Do not use an organized approach to solve the problem.

OUTCOMES-BASED ASSESSMENTS

Apply a combination of the 3A and 3B skills.

GO! Think   Project 3L Food Services

PROJECT FILES

For Project 3L, you will need the following file:

a03L_Food_Services

You will save your database as:

Lastname_Firstname_3L_Food_Services

Start Access, navigate to your student data files, open a03L_Food_Services, save the database in your **Access Chapter 3** folder as **Lastname_Firstname_3L_Food_Services** and then enable the content. Using your own name, add **Lastname Firstname** to the beginning of both table names. Luciano Gonzalez, the hospitality director, would like you to create to create an attractive form and a report to assist him with the staff scheduling of food services for a two-day student orientation workshop using the following guidelines:

- The form will be used to update records in the 3L Staff table. Be sure that the Last Name field displays above the First Name field. After the form is created, enter a new record using your own last name and first name with a Staff ID of **STAFF-1119** and a Phone Number of **(512) 555-0845** and a Title of **Server** Create a filter that when toggled on displays the records for staff with a Title of *Server*. Add a footer to the form that displays **Texas Lakes Community College Hospitality Services** Save the form as **Lastname Firstname 3L Staff Update Form** and then create a paper or electronic printout of your record only.

- The report will be used by Mr. Gonzalez to call staff members when the schedule changes. Add a report footer that displays **Texas Lakes Community College Hospitality Services** and then save the report as **Lastname Firstname 3L Staff Phone List** Create a paper or electronic printout as directed.

Open the Navigation Pane, be sure that all object names display fully, and then close Access. As directed, submit your database and the paper or electronic printout of the form and report that are the results of this project. Specifically, in this project, using your own name, you created the following database and printouts or electronic printouts:

1. Lastname_Firstname_3L_Food_Services	Database file
2. Lastname Firstname 3L Staff Update Form	Form (printout or electronic printout - Record 19)
3. Lastname Firstname 3L Staff Phone List	Report (printout or electronic printout)

END | You have completed Project 3L

GO! Think   Project 3M Donor Gifts   **Online**

Build from Scratch

You and GO!   Project 3N Personal Inventory   **Online**

Build from Scratch

GO! Cumulative Group Project   Project 3O Bell Orchid Hotels

Online

Enhancing Tables

ACCESS 2013

GO! to Work
Video A4

PROJECT 4A	OUTCOMES Maneuver and manage data.

OBJECTIVES
1. Manage Existing Tables
2. Modify Existing Tables
3. Change Data Types
4. Attach Files to Records

PROJECT 4B	OUTCOMES Format tables and validate data entry.

OBJECTIVES
5. Create a Table in Design View
6. Create a Lookup Field
7. Set Field Properties
8. Create Data Validation Rules and Validation Text

In This Chapter

In this chapter, you will enhance tables and improve data accuracy and data entry. You will begin by identifying secure locations where databases will be stored and by backing up existing databases to protect the data. You will edit existing tables for more effective design and copy data and table design across tables. You will create a new table in Design view and determine the best data type for each field based on its characteristics. You will use the field properties to enhance the table and to improve data accuracy and data entry, including looking up data in another table and attaching an existing document to a record.

Golden Grove, California, is a growing city located between Los Angeles and San Diego. Just 10 years ago the population was under 100,000; today it has grown to almost 300,000. Its growth in population is based on its growth as a community. Community leaders have always focused on quality of life and economic development in decisions on housing, open space, education, and infrastructure, making the city a model for other communities its size around the United States. The city provides many recreational and cultural opportunities with a large park system and library system, thriving arts, and a friendly business atmosphere.

PROJECT

4A

City Directory

PROJECT ACTIVITIES

Dario Soto, the new city manager of Golden Grove, has a database of city directory information. This database has three tables that have duplicate information in them. In Activities 4.01 through 4.12, you will redesign the tables, edit and proofread data, change data types, and attach files to records. Your completed tables will look similar to those in Figure 4.1.

PROJECT FILES

For Project 4A, you will need the following files:

a04A_GG_Directory
a04A_GG_Employees
a04A_PZ_Schedule
a04A_Bldg_Permit_App

You will save your databases as:

Lastname_Firstname_4A_GG_Directory
Lastname_Firstname_a04A_GG_
    Directory_2015-08-22 (date will vary)
Lastname_Firstname_4A_GG_Employees

PROJECT RESULTS

FIGURE 4.1 Project 4A City Directory

Video A4-1

A database is most effective when the data is maintained accurately and efficiently. It is important to back up your database often to be sure you can always obtain a clean copy if the data is corrupted or lost. Maintaining the accuracy of the field design and data is also critical to have a useful database; regular reviews and updates of design and data are necessary. It is also helpful to avoid rekeying data that already exists in a database; using copy/paste or appending records reduces the chances for additional errors as long as the source data is accurate.

Activity 4.01 | Backing Up a Database

Before modifying the structure of an existing database, it is important to **back up** the database so that a copy of the original database will be available if you need it. It is also important to back up databases regularly to avoid losing data.

1 **Start** Access. Navigate to the location where the student data files for this textbook are saved. Locate and open the **a04A_GG_Directory** file and enable the content.

2 Display **Backstage** view, click **Save As**, and then, under **Save Database As**, double-click **Back Up Database**. In the **Save As** dialog box, navigate to the drive on which you will be saving your folders and projects for this chapter. Create a new folder named **Access Chapter 4** and then compare your screen with Figure 4.2.

Access appends the date to the file name as a suggested name for the backed-up database. Having the date as part of the file name assists you in determining the copy that is the most current.

FIGURE 4.2

3 In the **File name** box, before the file name, type **Lastname_Firstname_** In the **Save As** dialog box, click **Save**. In the title bar, notice that the original database file—not the backed-up file—is open.

4 On the taskbar, click **File Explorer** , and then navigate to the location of your **Access Chapter 4** folder. Open the folder to verify that the backed-up database exists, but do not open the file. **Close** the Access Chapter 4 window.

5 **Save As** an **Access Database** in your **Access Chapter 4** folder, and then name the database **Lastname_Firstname_4A_GG_Directory**

This is another method of making a copy of a database. The original file exists with the original name—the date is not appended to the database name, and the newly saved file is open.

More Knowledge | **Recover Data from a Backup**

If your database file is damaged, restore a backup to replace the damaged file.

• Open File Explorer, and Browse to the location where the good copy (backup) is stored.
• Copy the backup file to the location where the damaged file is located, replacing the existing file if necessary.

Activity 4.02 | Adding File Locations to Trusted Locations

In this activity, you will add the location of your database files for this chapter and the location of the student data files to the ***Trust Center***—a security feature that checks documents for macros and digital signatures. When you open any database from a location displayed in the Trust Center, no security warning will display. You should not designate the My Documents folder as a trusted location because others may try to gain access to this known folder.

1 Display **Backstage** view, and click the **Enable Content** button. Click **Advanced Options** to display the **Microsoft Office Security Options** dialog box. In the lower left corner, click **Open the Trust Center**.

2 In the **Trust Center** window, in the left pane, click **Trusted Locations**. Compare your screen with Figure 4.3.

The right pane displays the locations that are trusted sources. A ***trusted source*** is a person or organization that you know will not send you databases with malicious code. Under Path and User Locations, there is already an entry. A ***path*** is the location of a folder or file on your computer or storage device.

FIGURE 4.3

3 In the **Trusted Locations** pane, at the lower right, click **Add new location**. In the **Microsoft Office Trusted Location** dialog box, click **Browse**. In the **Browse** dialog box, navigate to where you saved your *Access Chapter 4* folder, double-click **Access Chapter 4**, and then click **OK**. Compare your screen with Figure 4.4.

The Microsoft Office Trusted Location dialog box displays the path to a trusted source of databases. Notice that you can trust any subfolders in the *Access Chapter 4* folder by checking the *Subfolders of this location are also trusted* option.

FIGURE 4.4

4 In the **Microsoft Office Trusted Location** dialog box, under **Description**, using your own first and last name, type **Databases created by Firstname Lastname** and then click **OK**.

The Trusted Locations pane displays the path of the *Access Chapter 4* folder. You will no longer receive a security warning when you open databases from this location.

5 Using the technique you just practiced, add the location of your student data files to the Trust Center. For the description, type **Student data files created for GO! Series**

Only locations that you know are secure should be added to the Trust Center. If other people have access to the databases and can change the information in the database, the location is not secure.

6 At the lower right corner of the **Trust Center** dialog box, click **OK**. In the displayed **Microsoft Office Security Options** dialog box, click **OK**.

The message bar no longer displays—you opened the database from a trusted location.

7 Display **Backstage** view, and then click **Close**. Open **Lastname_Firstname_4A_GG_Directory**.

The database opens, and the message bar with the Security Alert does not display. Using the Trust Center button is an efficient way to open databases that are saved in a safe location.

> **More Knowledge** | **Remove a Trusted Location**
>
> Display Backstage view, and then click the Options button. In the Access Options dialog box, in the left pane, click Trust Center. In the right pane, click the Trust Center Settings button, and then click Trusted Locations. Under Path, click the trusted location that you want to remove, and then click the Remove button. Click OK to close the dialog box.

Activity 4.03 | Duplicating a Table and Modifying the Structure

In this activity, you will duplicate the *4A Departments* table, modify the structure by deleting fields and data that are duplicated in other tables, and then designate a primary key field.

1 In the **Navigation Pane**, double-click **4A Departments** to open the table. **Close** « the **Navigation Pane**. Click the **FILE tab**, and then, from **Backstage** view, click **Save As**. Under **Database File Types**, double-click **Save Object As**. Compare your screen to Figure 4.5.

The Save As command displays the Save As dialog box where you can name and save a new object based on the currently displayed object. After you name and save the new table, the original table closes, and the new table—based on the original one—displays.

FIGURE 4.5

2 In the displayed **Save As** dialog box, under **Save '4A Departments' to:**, type **Lastname Firstname 4A Departments Revised** and then click **OK**.

The *4A Departments Revised* table is open; it is an exact duplicate of the *4A Departments* table. Working with a duplicate table ensures that the original table will be available if needed.

3 Point to the **Dept Head** field name until the ⬇ pointer displays. Drag to the right to the **Admin Asst** field name to select both fields. On the **HOME tab**, in the **Records group**, click the **Delete** button. In the displayed message box, click **Yes** to permanently delete the fields and the data.

> The names of the employees are deleted from this table to avoid having employee data in more than one table. Recall that a table should store data about one subject—this table now stores only departmental data. In addition to removing duplicate data, the fields that you deleted were also poorly designed. They combined both the first and last names in the same field, limiting the use of the data to entire names only.

4 Switch to **Design** view. To the left of **Department**, click the row selector box. On the **TABLE TOOLS DESIGN tab**, in the **Tools group**, click the **Insert Rows** button to insert a blank row (field) above the *Department* field.

5 Under **Field Name**, click in the blank field name box, type **Dept ID** and then press `Tab`. In the **Data Type** box, type **a** and then press `Tab`. Alternatively, click the Data Type arrow, and then select the AutoNumber data type. On the **TABLE TOOLS DESIGN tab**, in the **Tools group**, click the **Primary Key** button, and then compare your screen with Figure 4.6.

> Recall that a primary key field is used to ensure that each record is unique. Because each department has a unique name, you might question why the *Department* field is not designated as the primary key field. Primary key fields should be data that does not change often. When organizations or companies are reorganized, department names are often changed.

FIGURE 4.6

6 Switch to **Datasheet** view, and in the displayed message box, click **Yes** to save the table.

> Because the *Dept ID* field has a data type of AutoNumber, each record is sequentially numbered. The data in this field cannot be changed because it is generated by Access.

7 In the datasheet, next to **Department**, click the **Sort and Filter arrow** ⌄ , and then click **Sort A to Z**.

> Sorting the records by the department name makes it easier to locate a department.

8 Save 💾 the table. **Close** ✕ the table. **Open** » the **Navigation Pane**.

Activity 4.04 | Copying and Appending Records to a Table

In this activity, you will copy the *4A City Council Members* table to use as the basis for a single employees table. You will then copy the data in the *4A Police Dept Employees* table and ***append***—add on—the data to the new employees table.

1 In the **Navigation Pane**, click **4A City Council Members**. On the **HOME tab**, in the **Clipboard group**, click the **Copy** button. In the **Clipboard group**, click the **Paste** button.

> ***Copy*** sends a duplicate version of the selected table to the Clipboard, leaving the original table intact. The ***Clipboard*** is a temporary storage area in Office that can store up to 24 items. ***Paste*** moves the copy of the selected table from the Clipboard into a new location. Because two tables cannot have the same name in a database, you must rename the pasted version.

2 In the displayed **Paste Table As** dialog box, under **Table Name**, type **Lastname Firstname 4A Employees** and then compare your screen with Figure 4.7.

Under Paste Options, you can copy the structure only, including all the items that are displayed in Design view—field names, data types, descriptions, and field properties. To make an exact duplicate of the table, click Structure and Data. To copy the data from the table into another existing table, click Append Data to Existing Table.

FIGURE 4.7

Copies fields, data types, field descriptions, and field properties only

Table name

Copies structure from above and the data

Adds the data in the table to an existing table

🔄 **ANOTHER WAY**   There are two other methods to copy and paste selected tables:

- In the Navigation Pane, right-click the table, and from the displayed list, click Copy. To paste the table, right-click the Navigation Pane, and click Paste from the options listed.
- In the Navigation Pane, click the table, hold down `Ctrl`, and then press `C`. To paste the table, point to the Navigation Pane, hold down `Ctrl`, and then press `V`.

3 Under **Paste Options**, be sure that the **Structure and Data** option button is selected, and then click **OK**. Notice that the copied table displays in the **Navigation Pane**. Resize the **Navigation Pane** so that all table names display entirely.

An exact duplicate of the *4A City Council Members* table is created. The *4A Employees* table will be used to build a table of all employees.

More Knowledge   **Table Description**

To provide more information about a table, you can add a Table Description:

- In the Navigation Pane, right-click the table name, and then click Table Properties.
- In the Properties dialog box, click in the Description box, and then type information about the table. For example, in the 4A Employees table, you could type *Table copied from the 4A City Council Members table*.

---

4 Open the **4A Employees** table, and notice the duplicate records that were copied from the *4A City Council Members* table.

5 Copy the **4A Police Dept Employees** table, and then click the **Paste** button. In the **Paste Table As** dialog box, under **Table Name**, type **Lastname Firstname 4A Employees** Under **Paste Options**, click the **Append Data to Existing Table** option button, and then click **OK**. With the **4A Employees table** active, in the **Records group**, click the **Refresh All** button, and then compare your screen with Figure 4.8.

The table to which you are appending the records must exist before using the Append option. Clicking the Refresh All button causes Access to refresh or update the view of the table, displaying the newly appended records. The *4A Employees* table then displays the two records for the Police department employees—last names of *Farmer* and *Forbes*—and the records are arranged in ascending order by the first field. The records still exist in the *4A Police Dept Employees* table. If separate tables existed for the employees for each department, you would repeat these steps until every employee's record is appended to the *4A Employees* table.

FIGURE 4.8

Farmer and Forbes records appended to the table

ALERT! **Does a Message Box Display?**

If a message box displays stating that the Microsoft Office Access database engine could not find the object, you probably mistyped the name of the table in the Paste Table As dialog box. In the Navigation Pane, note the spelling of the table name to which you are copying the records. In the message box, click OK, and then in the Paste Table As dialog box, under Table Name, correctly type the table name.

6 ▶ **Close** the table.

More Knowledge **Appending Records**

Access appends all records from the *source table*—the table from which you are copying records—into the *destination table*—the table to which the records are appended—as long as the field names and data types are the same in both tables. Exceptions include:

• If the source table does not have all of the fields that the destination table has, Access will still append the records, leaving the data in the missing fields blank in the destination table.

• If the source table has a field name that does not exist in the destination table or the data type is incompatible, the append procedure will fail.

Before performing an append procedure, carefully analyze the structure of both the source table and the destination table.

Activity 4.05 | Splitting a Table into Two Tables

The *4A Employees* table stores personal data and office data about the employees. Although the table contains data about one subject—employees—you will split the table into two separate tables to keep the personal information separate from the office information.

1 ▶ Double-click the **4A Employees** table to open it in **Datasheet** view. **Close** « the **Navigation Pane**. Click the **FILE tab**, and then from **Backstage** view, click **Save As**. Under **Database File Types**, double-click **Save Object As**.

2 ▶ In the **Save As** dialog box, in the **Save to** box, type **Lastname Firstname 4A Employees Office** Notice the *As* box displays Table, and then click **OK**. Using the techniques you just practiced, create a copy of the open table named **Lastname Firstname 4A Employees Personal**

These two new tables will be used to split the *4A Employees* table into two separate tables, one storing personal data and the other storing office data.

3 ▶ In the **4A Employees Personal** table, scroll to the right, if needed, to display the **Date Hired**, **Office Phone**, **Position**, **Office Email**, and **Notes** fields. Select all five fields. On the **HOME tab**, in the **Records group**, click the **Delete** button. In the displayed message box, click **Yes** to permanently delete the fields and data.

Because these fields contain office data, they are deleted from the *4A Employees Personal* table. These fields will be stored in the *4A Employees Office* table.

4 ▶ Select the **Title, First Name, MI,** and **Last Name** fields, and then delete the fields. **Save** 🖫 and **Close** ☒ the table.

The fields you deleted are stored in the *4A Employees Office* table. You have deleted redundant data from the *4A Employees Personal* table.

5 ▸ **Open** » the **Navigation Pane**. Open the **4A Employees Office** table. **Close** « the **Navigation Pane**. Point to the **Street** field name until the pointer displays. Drag to the right to the **Home Phone** field name, and then compare your screen with Figure 4.9.

> Five fields are selected and will be deleted from this table. This is duplicate data that exists in the *4A Employees Personal* table. The *Empl ID* field will be the common field between the two tables.

FIGURE 4.9

Common field—4A Employees Office table and 4A Employees Personal table

Duplicate data—also stored in 4A Employees Personal table

6 ▸ Delete the selected fields and data from the table.

> The *4A Employees Office* table now stores only office data about the employees and can be linked to the *4A Employees Personal* table through the common field, *Empl ID*.

7 ▸ Click the **Position** field name. On the **TABLE TOOLS FIELDS tab**, in the **Add & Delete group**, click the **Number** button.

> A blank field is inserted between the *Position* field and the *Office Email* field, and it holds numeric data. Because this field will be used to link to the *4A Departments Revised* Dept ID field, which has a data type of AutoNumber, this field must use a data type of Number, even though it will not be used in a calculation.

8 ▸ The default name *Field1* is currently selected; type **Dept** to replace it and name the new field. Press Enter.

9 ▸ **Open** » the **Navigation Pane**. Open the **4A Departments Revised** table.

> The *4A Departments Revised* table opens in Datasheet view, and the records are sorted in ascending order by the *Department* field.

10 ▸ Locate the **Dept ID** for the City Police department. On the **tab row**, click the **4A Employees Office tab** to make the table active. In the record for Andrew Farmer, enter the City Police Dept ID, **14** in the **Dept** field. Press ↓ two times. In the third record, for Colette Forbes, type **14**

11 ▸ Using the techniques you just practiced, find the **Dept ID** for the City Council department, and then enter that number in the **Dept** field for the second and fourth records in the **4A Employees Office** table. Compare your screen with Figure 4.10.

> The *Dept* field is a common field with the *Dept ID* field in the *4A Departments Revised* table and will be used to link or join the two tables.

FIGURE 4.10

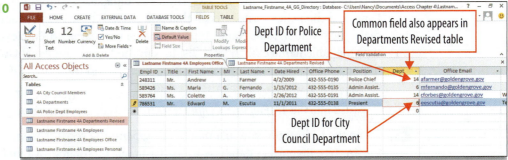

12 ▸ On the **tab row**, right-click any table tab, and then click **Close All**.

Activity 4.06 | Appending Records from Another Database

Additional employee records are stored in another database. In this activity, you will open a second database to copy and paste records from tables in the second database to tables in the *4A_GG_Directory* database.

🔄 **BY TOUCH**   Tap the Start screen icon.

1 ▶ Point to the lower left corner of your screen to display the **Start** screen icon ▦, and then click one time to display the Start screen. Right-click **Access 2013**, and then, from the taskbar, click **Open new window** to open a second instance of Access.

2 ▶ On the left side of the Access startup window, at the bottom, click **Open Other Files**. Under **Places**, click **Computer**, and then on the right, click **Browse**. In the **Open** dialog box, navigate to the location where the student data files for this textbook are saved. Locate and open the **a04A_GG_Employees** file. Display **Backstage** view, click **Save As**, and save the database as **Lastname_Firstname_4A_GG_Employees** in your **Access Chapter 4** folder.

🔄 **BY TOUCH**   On the taskbar, use the Swipe to Select technique—swipe upward with a short quick movement—to display the Jump List. On the list, tap Open new window.

3 ▶ In the **4A_GG_Employees** database window, in the **Navigation Pane**, right-click **4A Office**, and then click **Copy**. Click the **Access icon** in the taskbar to see two instances of Access open. Compare your screen with Figure 4.11.

Each time you start Access, you open an *instance* of it. Two instances of Access are open, and each instance displays in the taskbar.

FIGURE 4.11

You cannot open multiple databases in one instance of Access. If you open a second database in the same instance, Access closes the first database. You can, however, open multiple instances of Access that display different databases. The number of times you can start Access at the same time is limited by the amount of your computer's available RAM.

4 ▶ Point to each thumbnail to display the ScreenTip, and then click the button for the **4A_GG_Directory** database. In the **4A_GG_Directory** database window, right-click the **Navigation Pane**, and then click **Paste**—recall that you copied the *4A Office* table. In the **Paste Table As** dialog box, under **Table Name**, type **Lastname Firstname 4A Employees Office** being careful to type the table name exactly as it displays in the **Navigation Pane**. Under **Paste Options**, click the **Append Data to Existing Table** option button, and then click **OK**.

The records from the *4A Office* table in the source database—*4A_GG_Employees*—are copied and pasted into the *4A Employees Office* table in the destination database—*4A_GG_Directory*.

5 ▶ Using the techniques you just practiced, append the records from the **4A Personal** table in the **4A_GG_Employees** database to the **Lastname Firstname 4A Employees Personal** table in the **4A_GG_Directory** database.

6 ▶ Make the **4A_GG_Employees** database active, and then on the title bar for the **4A_GG_Employees** database window, click the **Close** button. If a message displays, click **Yes**.

7 ▸ If the **4A_GG_Directory** database is not current, on the taskbar, click the **Microsoft Access** button. Open the **4A Employees Personal** table, and then open the **4A Employees Office** table. **Close** « the **Navigation Pane**.

8 ▸ If necessary, on the tab row, click the 4A Employees Office tab to make the table active, and then compare your screen with Figure 4.12.

In addition to appending records, you can copy a single record or data in a field from a table in the source database file to a table in the destination database file. Now that you have finished restructuring the database, you can see that it is wise to plan your database before creating the tables and entering data.

FIGURE 4.12

Three appended records

Empl ID	Title	First Name	MI	Last Name	Date Hired	Office Phone	Position	Dept	Office Email	Notes	Click to Add
248311	Mr.	Andrew	J.	Farmer	4/2/2009	432-555-0190	Police Chief	14	afarmer@goldengrove.gov		
456789	Ms.	Sheila	J.	Kehoe	11/1/2012	714-555-0100	Mayor	35	skehoe@goldengrove.gov	Term expires 2019	
532268	Miss	Katherine	C.	Bothski	3/17/2015	714-555-0135	Director	1	kbothski@goldengrove.gov		
589426	Ms.	Marla	G.	Fernando	1/15/2012	432-555-0135	Admin Assist.	6	mfernando@goldengrove.gov		
589764	Ms.	Colette	A.	Forbes	2/26/2012	432-555-0191	Admin Assist.	14	cforbes@goldengrove.gov	Word and Access certifie	
689444	Mr.	Dario	T.	Soto	11/10/2014	714-555-0101	City Manager	7	dsoto@goldengrove.gov		
786531	Mr.	Edward	M.	Escutia	11/1/2011	432-555-0138	Presient	6	eescutia@goldengrove.gov	Term expires May 2018	
*								0			

9 ▸ On the **tab row**, right-click any table tab, and then click **Close All**.

Objective 2 Modify Existing Tables

Video A4-2

Data in a database is usually **dynamic**—changing. Records can be created, deleted, and edited in a table. It is important that the data is always up-to-date and accurate in order for the database to provide useful information.

Activity 4.07 ▌ Finding and Deleting Records

1 ▸ **Open** » the **Navigation Pane**. Open the **4A Departments Revised** table. **Close** « the **Navigation Pane**. In the datasheet, next to Dept ID, click the **Sort and Filter arrow** ▼, and then click **Sort Smallest to Largest**.

Sorting the records by the department ID returns the data to its primary key order.

2 ▸ In the table, in the **Department** field, click in the record containing the City Treasurer— Record 8. On the **HOME tab**, in the **Find group**, click the **Find** button. Alternatively, hold down Ctrl, and then press F.

The Find and Replace dialog box displays with the Find tab active.

3 ▸ In the **Find and Replace** dialog box, in the **Find What** box, type **Assessor**

The Look In box displays *Current field*, which refers to the Department field because you clicked in that field before you clicked the Find button.

4 ▸ In the **Find and Replace** dialog box, click the **Look in box arrow**. Notice that Access can search for the data in the entire Contacts table instead of only the Department field. Leaving the entry as **Current field**, click the **Look in box arrow** one time to close the list, and then click the **Find Next** button. Compare your screen with Figure 4.13.

If Access did not locate Record 5, ensure that you typed *Assessor* correctly in the Find What box. If you misspelled *Assessor* in the table, type the misspelled version in the Find What box. This is an example of how important accuracy is when entering data in your tables.

FIGURE 4.13

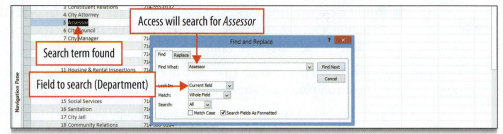

5 In the **Find and Replace** dialog box, click **Cancel** to close the dialog box.

The table displays with *Assessor* selected in Record 5. Even though you can locate this record easily in the table because there are a limited number of records, keep in mind that most database tables contain many more records. Using the Find button is an efficient way to locate a record in the table.

6 Point to the **Record Selector** box for the *Assessor* record until the ➔ pointer displays. Click one time to ensure that the entire record is selected, and then compare your screen with Figure 4.14.

FIGURE 4.14

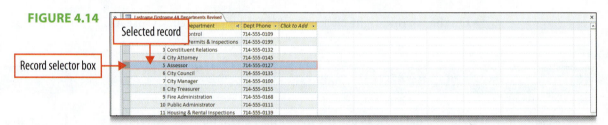

7 On the **HOME tab**, in the **Records group,** click the **Delete** button to delete the active record, and then compare your screen with Figure 4.15.

Notice that Access displays a message stating that you are about to delete one record and will be unable to undo the Delete operation.

> **ANOTHER WAY**
>
> There are two other methods to delete selected records in a table:
> - On the selected record, right-click and then click Delete Record.
> - From the keyboard, press Delete.

FIGURE 4.15

8 In the message box, click **Yes** to confirm the deletion.

The record holding information for *Assessor* no longer displays in the table; it has been permanently deleted from the table, and will no longer display in any other objects that were created using the Contacts table. The record number of Dept ID 6—City Council—is now record 5 and is the current record.

Activity 4.08 | Finding and Modifying Records

When data needs to be changed or updated, you must locate and modify the record with the data. Recall that you can move among records in a table using the navigation buttons at the bottom of the window and that you can use Find to locate specific data. Other navigation methods include using keys on the keyboard and using the Search box in the navigation area.

1 ▶ Take a moment to review the table in Figure 4.16, which lists the key combinations you can use to navigate within an Access table.

FIGURE 4.16

KEY COMBINATIONS FOR NAVIGATING A TABLE	
KEYSTROKE	**MOVEMENT**
↑	Moves the selection up one record at a time.
↓	Moves the selection down one record at a time.
PageUp	Moves the selection up one screen at a time.
PageDown	Moves the selection down one screen at a time.
Ctrl + Home	Moves the selection to the first field in the table or the beginning of the selected field.
Ctrl + End	Moves the selection to the last field in the table or the end of the selected field.
Tab	Moves the selection to the next field in the table.
Shift + Tab	Moves the selection to the previous field in the table.
Enter	Moves the selection to the next field in the table.

2 ▶ On the keyboard, press ↓ to move the selection down one record. Record 6—*City Manager*—is now the current record.

3 ▶ On the keyboard, hold down Ctrl, and then press Home to move to the first field of the first record in the table—Dept ID *1*.

4 ▶ In the navigation area, click the **Next record** button six times to navigate to Record 7— Dept ID 8.

5 ▶ On the keyboard, hold down Ctrl, and then press End to move to the last field in the last record in the table—Dept Phone *714-555-0151*.

6 ▶ On the keyboard, hold down Shift, and then press Tab to move to the previous field in the same record in the table—*City Planner* in the Department field.

7 ▶ In the navigation area, click in the **Search** box. In the **Search** box, type **b**

Record 2 is selected, and the letter *B* in *Building Permits & Inspections* is highlighted. Search found the first occurrence of the letter *b*. It is not necessary to type capital letters in the Search box; Access will locate the words regardless of capitalization.

8 In the **Search** box, type **sani**

Record 15 is selected, and the letters *Sani* in *Sanitation* are highlighted. Search found the first occurrence of the letters *sani*. This is the record that needs to be modified. It is not necessary to type an entire word in the Search box to locate a record containing that word.

9 In the field box, double-click the word *Sanitation* to select it. Type **Trash Pickup** to replace the current entry. The **Small Pencil** icon in the **Record Selector** box means that the record is being edited and has not yet been saved. Press ⬇ to move to the next record and save the change.

If you must edit part of a name, drag through letters or words to select them. You can then type the new letters or words over the selection to replace the text without having to press Delete or Backspace.

10 Save 🖫 and Close ⨉ the table. Open ⟩⟩ the Navigation Pane.

Activity 4.09   Adding and Moving Fields in Design View and Datasheet View

In this activity, you will add and move fields in Design view and in Datasheet view.

1 Right-click the **4A Employees Personal** table to display a shortcut menu, and click **Design View** to open the table in **Design** view. Alternatively, double-click the table name in the Navigation Pane to open the table in Datasheet view, and then click the View button to switch to Design view. **Close** ⟨⟨ the **Navigation Pane**.

2 In the **Field Name** column, click the **Field Name** box below the **Home Phone** field name.

A new row is inserted below the *Home Phone* field. Recall that a row in Design view is a field.

3 In the empty **Field Name** box, type **Birthdate** and then press Tab to move to the **Data Type** column. Click the **Data Type arrow** to display the list of data types, and then click **Date/Time** to set the data type for this field. Compare your screen with Figure 4.17.

A new field to display the employee's date of birth has been created in the *Lastname Firstname 4A Employees Personal* table. An advantage of adding a field in Design view is that you name the field and set the data type when you insert the field.

FIGURE 4.17

New field added →

Date/Time data type assigned to Birthdate

4 In the **Field Name** column, locate **Home Phone**, and then click the **Row Selector** box to select the field. Point to the **Row Selector** box to display the ➡ pointer. Drag the field up until you see a dark horizontal line following *Empl ID*, and then release the mouse button.

5 Switch the **Lastname Firstname 4A Employees Personal** table to **Datasheet** view. In the displayed message box, click **Yes** to save the design changes.

The *Home Phone* field displays to the left of the *Street* field.

6 In the first record—248311—click in the **Birthdate** field. Using the techniques you have practiced, enter the birthdate for each record shown in the following list, pressing ⬇ after each entry to move to the next record. Compare your screen with Figure 4.18.

Empl ID	Birthdate
248311	4/21/1955
456789	6/1/1964
532268	12/14/1984
589426	7/27/1990
589764	12/30/1972
689444	8/13/1980
786531	10/6/1966

FIGURE 4.18

Birthdates entered

7 Adjust all column widths, ensuring that all of the field names and all of the field data display. View the table in **Print Preview**. On the **PRINT PREVIEW tab**, in the **Page Layout group**, click the **Landscape** button. If you are instructed to submit this result, create a paper or electronic printout. On the **PRINT PREVIEW tab**, in the **Close Preview group**, click the **Close Print Preview** button.

8 Close the **4A Employees Personal** table. Open [»] the **Navigation Pane**. Open the **4A Employees Office** table in **Datasheet** view. Close [«] the **Navigation Pane**.

9 Select the **Office Phone** column. On the **TABLE TOOLS FIELDS tab**, in the **Add & Delete group**, click **Short Text**. Alternatively, right-click the selected field and, from the shortcut menu, click Insert Column. A new column is inserted to the right of *Office Phone*.

10 If necessary, double-click Field1—the name of your field may differ if you have been experimenting with adding fields—to select the field name. Type **Work Site** and press Enter to save the field name.

11 In the first record—248311—click in the **Work Site** field. Using the techniques you have practiced, enter the work site for each record shown in the following list, pressing ⬇ after each entry to move to the next record.

Empl ID	Work Site
248311	Justice Center
456789	City Hall
532268	B-121
589426	A-214
589764	Justice Center
689444	City Hall
786531	A-214

12 ▷ Point to **Position** until the pointer displays, and then click one time to select the column. Drag the field left until you see a dark vertical line between *Date Hired* and *Office Phone*, and then release the mouse button. Compare your screen with Figure 4.19.

The *Position* field is moved after the *Date Hired* field and before the *Office Phone* field. If you move a field to the wrong position, select the field again, and then drag it to the correct position. Alternatively, on the Quick Access Toolbar, click the Undo button to place the field back in its previous position.

FIGURE 4.19

Position field moved between Date Hired and Office Phone fields

---

More Knowledge   **Hide/Unhide Fields in a Table**

If you do not want a field to display in Datasheet view or on a printed copy of the table, you can hide the field.

- Right-click the field name at the top of the column.
- From the shortcut menu, click **Hide Fields**.
- To display the field again, right-click any column heading. From the shortcut menu, click Unhide Fields. In the dialog box, click the fields to unhide, and then click OK.

Activity 4.10 | Checking Spelling

In this exercise, you will use the Spell Check feature to find spelling errors in your data. It is important to realize that this will not find all data entry mistakes, so you will need to use additional proofreading methods to ensure the accuracy of the data.

1 ▷ In the first record—248311—click in the **Empl ID** field. On the **HOME tab**, in the **Records group**, click the **Spelling** button. Alternatively, press F7. Compare your screen with Figure 4.20.

The Spelling dialog box displays, and *Bothski* is highlighted because it is not in the Office dictionary. Many proper names will be *flagged*—highlighted—by the spelling checker. Take a moment to review the options in the Spelling dialog box; these are described in the table in Figure 4.21.

FIGURE 4.20

Word not in dictionary

Suggested alternatives

FIGURE 4.21

SPELLING DIALOG BOX BUTTONS	
BUTTON	**ACTION**
Ignore 'Last Name' Field	Ignores any words in the selected field.
Ignore	Ignores this one occurrence of the word but continues to flag other instances of the word.
Ignore All	Discontinues flagging any instance of the word anywhere in the table.
Change	Changes the identified word to the word highlighted under Suggestions.
Change All	Changes every instance of the word in the table to the word highlighted under Suggestions.
Add	Adds the highlighted word to a custom dictionary, which can be edited. This option does not change the built-in Office dictionary.
AutoCorrect	Adds the flagged word to the AutoCorrect list, which will subsequently correct the word automatically if misspelled in the future.
Options	Displays the Access Options dialog box.
Undo Last	Undoes the last change.

2 In the **Spelling** dialog box, click the **Ignore 'Last Name' Field** button.

Presient, which displays in the Position field, is flagged by the spelling checker. In the Spelling dialog box under Suggestions, *President* is highlighted.

3 In the **Spelling** dialog box, click the **Change** button to change the word from *Presient* to *President*.

When the spelling checker has completed checking the table and has found no other words missing from its dictionary, a message displays stating *The spelling check is complete*.

4 In the message box, click **OK**.

Objective 3 | Change Data Types

Video A4-3

Before creating a table, it is important to decide on the data types for the fields in the table. Setting a specific data type helps to ensure that the proper data will be entered into a field; for example, it is not possible to enter text into a field with a Currency data type. It is also important to choose a number data type when it is appropriate to avoid problems with calculations and sorting.

Activity 4.11 | Changing Data Types

Once data is entered into a field, caution must be exercised when changing the data type—existing data may not be completely visible or may be deleted. You can change the data type in either Datasheet view or Design view.

1 With the **4A Employees Office** table open, switch to **Design** view. Change the **Data Type** for the **Date Hired** field to **Date/Time**. Press F6 to move to the **Field Properties** pane at the bottom of the screen. Click in the **Format** property and select **Short Date**.

The data type of Date/Time is more appropriate for this field because it will display dates and restrict other entries. This will also allow the field to be accurately used in calculations, comparisons, and sorts.

2 Change the data type for the **Notes** field to **Long Text**, and then compare your screen with Figure 4.22.

The data type of Long Text is more appropriate for this field because it may require more than 255 characters and spaces to effectively describe notes associated with an employee.

FIGURE 4.22

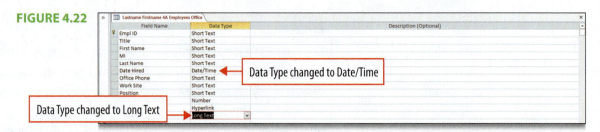

3 Switch to **Datasheet** view, saving changes to the table. Adjust all column widths, ensuring that all of the field names and all of the field data display. View the table in **Print Preview**, and then change the orientation to **Landscape**. If you are instructed to submit this result, create a paper or electronic printout. **Close Print Preview.**

4 Close ⊠ the **4A Employees Office** table, saving changes.

Objective 4 | Attach Files to Records

Video A4-4

The attachment data type can be used to add one or more files to the records in a database. For example, if you have a database for an antique collection, you can attach a picture of each antique and a Word document that contains a description of the item. Access stores the attached files in their native formats—if you attach a Word document, it is saved as a Word document. By default, fields contain only one piece of data; however, you can attach more than one file by using the attachment data type. As you attach files to a record, Access creates one or more *system tables* to keep track of the multiple entries in the field. You cannot view or work with these system tables.

Activity 4.12 | Attaching a Word Document to a Record

In this activity, you will attach documents to records in the *4A Departments Revised* table.

1 Open » the **Navigation Pane**. Open the **4A Departments Revised** table, and then switch to **Design** view. **Close** « the **Navigation Pane**. Click in the empty **Field Name** box under **Dept Phone**, type **Information** and then press Tab to move to the **Data Type** box. Click the **Data Type arrow**, click **Attachment**, and then press Enter. Under **Field Properties**, on the **General tab**, notice that only two field properties—**Caption** and **Required**—are displayed for an **Attachment** field.

2 Switch to **Datasheet** view, saving changes to the table. In the **Attachment** field, notice that the field name of *Information* does not display; instead, a paper clip symbol displays. In the first record, *(0)* displays after the paper clip symbol, indicating that there are no attachments for this record.

Because multiple files can be attached to a record, the name of the field displays the paper clip symbol.

3 In record 12, double-click in the **Attachment** field. In the displayed **Attachments** dialog box, click **Add**. Navigate to the location where the student data files for this textbook are saved. In the **Choose File** dialog box, double-click **a04A_PZ_Schedule**, and then compare your screen with Figure 4.23.

The Word document will be added to the Attachments dialog box. You can attach multiple files to the same record.

FIGURE 4.23

4 In the **Attachments** dialog box, click **OK**. Notice that the **Attachment** field now indicates there is **1** attachment for record 12. Double-click in the **Attachment** field. In the **Attachments** dialog box, click **a04A_PZ_Schedule.docx**, and then click **Open**.

Word opens, and the document displays. You can make changes to the document, and then save it in the database.

5 **Close** Word. In the **Attachments** dialog box, click **OK**. Press ⬇ to save the record.

6 In the second record, double-click in the **Attachment** field. In the displayed **Attachments** dialog box, click **Add**. Navigate to the location where the student data files for this textbook are saved. In the **Choose File** dialog box, double-click **a04A_Bldg_Permit_App**. In the **Attachments** dialog box, click **OK**.

The PDF document is added to the Attachments dialog box.

NOTE   **Saving Changes to an Attached File**

When you open an attached file in the program that was used to create it, Access places a temporary copy of the file in a temporary folder on the hard drive of your computer. If you change the file and save changes, Access saves the changes in the temporary copy. Closing the program used to view the attachment returns you to Access. When you click OK to close the Attachments dialog box, Access prompts you to save the attached file again. Click Yes to save the changes to the attached file in the database, or click No to keep the original, unedited version in the database.

To find the location of your temporary folder, start Internet Explorer. On the Tools menu, click Internet options. On the General tab, in the Browsing History section, click Settings. In the Website Data Settings dialog box, the temporary folder path displays in the Current location section.

---

7 Adjust all column widths, ensuring that all of the field names and all of the field data display. View the table in **Print Preview**. If you are instructed to submit this result, create a paper or electronic printout.

8 **Close** the table, saving changes. **Open** ⟩⟩ the **Navigation Pane**. **Close** the database, and **Exit** Access.

9 As directed by your instructor, submit your database and the paper or electronic printout of the three tables that are the result of this project. Specifically, in this project, using your own name you created the following database and printouts or electronic printouts:

1. Lastname_Firstname_4A_GG_Directory	Database file
2. Lastname Firstname 4A Employees Personal	Table (printed or electronic printout)
3. Lastname Firstname 4A Employees Office	Table (printed or electronic printout)
4. Lastname Firstname 4A Departments Revised	Table (printed or electronic printout)

END | You have completed Project 4A

PROJECT 4B | IT Tasks

PROJECT ACTIVITIES

Matthew Shoaf, director of the information technology department, has created a table to keep track of tasks that he has assigned to the employees in his department. In Activities 4.13 through 4.23, you will create a table in Design view that stores records about assigned tasks, modify its properties, and customize its fields. You will add features to the database table that will help to reduce data entry errors and that will make data entry easier. Your completed tables will look similar to the tables shown in Figure 4.24.

PROJECT FILES

For Project 4B, you will need the following file:
a04B_IT_Workload

You will save your database as:
Lastname_Firstname_4B_IT_Workload

PROJECT RESULTS

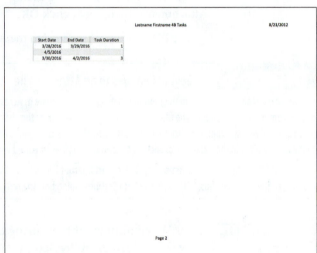

FIGURE 4.24 Project 4B IT Tasks

Video A4-5

In this activity, you will create a second table in a database using Design view.

Activity 4.13 | Creating a Table in Design View

In this activity, you will create a table to keep track of the tasks that the IT department will be completing. Creating a table in Design view gives you the most control over the characteristics of the table and the fields. Most database designers use Design view to create tables, setting the data types and formats before entering any records. Design view is a good way to create a table when you know exactly how you want to set up your fields.

1 ▶ **Start** Access. On the left side of the Access startup window, click **Open Other Files**. Under **Open Places**, click **Computer**, and then on the right, click **Browse**. In the **Open** dialog box, navigate to the student data files for this textbook. Locate and open **a04B_IT_Workload** file. **Save** the database in the **Microsoft Access Database** format in your **Access Chapter 4** folder as **Lastname_Firstname_4B_IT_Workload**

2 ▶ If you did not add the **Access Chapter 4** folder to the Trust Center, enable the content. In the **Navigation Pane**, under **Tables**, rename **4B Employees** by adding **Lastname Firstname** to the beginning of the table name. **Close** « the **Navigation Pane**.

3 ▶ On the Ribbon, click the **CREATE tab**. In the **Tables group**, click the **Table Design** button to open an empty table in Design view, and then compare your screen with Figure 4.25.

FIGURE 4.25

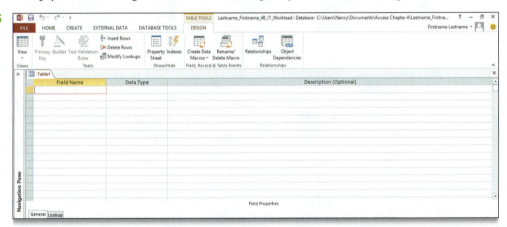

4 ▶ In the first **Field Name box**, type **WO#** press Tab, and then on the **DESIGN tab**, in the **Tools group**, click the **Primary Key** button.

5 ▶ Click the **Data Type arrow** to display a list of data types, as shown in Figure 4.26. Take a moment to study the table in Figure 4.27 that describes all 12 possible data types.

In Design view, all the data types are displayed. In Datasheet view, the list depends on the data entered in the field and does not display Lookup Wizard.

FIGURE 4.26

List of data types

FIGURE 4.27

DATA TYPES		
DATA TYPE	**DESCRIPTION**	**EXAMPLE**
Short Text	Text or combinations of text and numbers; also, numbers that are not used in calculations. Limited to 255 characters or length set on field, whichever is less. Access does not reserve space for unused portions of the text field. This is the default data type.	An inventory item, such as towels, or a phone number or postal code that is not used in calculations and that may contain characters other than numbers
Long Text	Lengthy text or combinations of text and numbers that can hold up to 65,535 characters depending on the size of the database.	A description of a product
Number	Numeric data used in mathematical calculations with varying field sizes.	A quantity, such as 500
Date/Time	Date and time values for the years 100 through 9999.	An order date, such as 11/10/2012 3:30 p.m.
Currency	Monetary values and numeric data that can be used in mathematical calculations involving data with one to four decimal places. Accurate to 15 digits on the left side of the decimal separator and to 4 digits on the right side. Use this data type to store financial data and when you do not want Access to round values.	An item price, such as $8.50
AutoNumber	Available in Design view. A unique sequential or random number assigned by Access as each record is entered that cannot be updated.	An inventory item number, such as 1, 2, 3, or a randomly assigned employee number, such as 3852788
Yes/No	Contains only one of two values—Yes/No, True/False, or On/Off. Access assigns 1 for all Yes values and 0 for all No values.	Whether an item was ordered— Yes or No
OLE Object	An object created by programs other than Access that is linked to or embedded in the table. *OLE* is an abbreviation for *object linking and embedding*, a technology for transferring and sharing information among programs. Stores up to two gigabytes of data (the size limit for all Access databases). Must have an OLE server registered on the server that runs the database. Should usually use Attachment data type instead.	A graphics file, such as a picture of a product, a sound file, a Word document, or an Excel spreadsheet stored as a bitmap image
Hyperlink	Web or email addresses.	An email address, such as dwalker@ityourway.com, or a Web page, such as http://www .ityourway.com
Attachment	Any supported type of file—images, spreadsheet files, documents, or charts. Similar to email attachments.	Same as OLE Object
Calculated	Available in Design view. Opens the Expression Builder to create an expression based on existing fields or numbers. Field must be designated as a Calculated field when it is inserted into the table; the expression can be edited in the Field Properties.	Adding two existing fields such as [field1]+[field2], or performing a calculation with a field and a number such as [field3]*.5
Lookup Wizard	Available in Design view. Not really a data type, but will display in the list of data types. Links to fields in other tables to display a list of data instead of having to manually type the data.	Link to another field in the same or another table

6 From the displayed list, click **Short Text**, and then press ⌨Tab to move to the **Description** box. In the **Description** box, type **Identification number assigned to task reported on work order form**

> Field names should be short; use the description box to display more information about the contents of the field.

7 Press ⌨F6 to move to the **Field Properties** pane at the bottom of the screen. In the **Field Size** box, type **8** to replace the 255. Compare your screen with Figure 4.28.

> Pressing ⌨F6 while in the Data Type column moves the insertion point to the first field property box in the Field Properties pane. Alternatively, click in the Field Size property box.

> Recall that a field with a data type of Short Text can store up to 255 characters. You can change the field size to limit the number of characters that can be entered into the field to ensure accuracy. For example, if you use the two-letter state abbreviations for a state field, limit the size of the field to two characters. When entering a state in the field, you will be unable to type more than two characters.

FIGURE 4.28

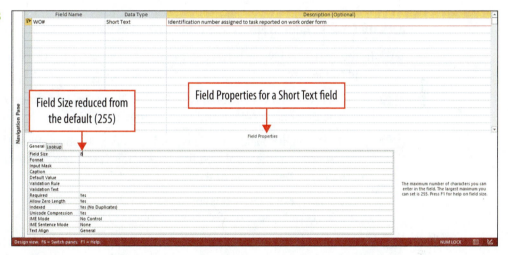

8 Click in the second **Field Name** box, type **Priority** and then press ⌨Tab two times to move to the **Description** box. Type **Indicate the priority level of this task** Press ⌨F6 to move to the **Field Properties** pane at the bottom of the screen. Click in the **Format** box and type **>**

> Because Short Text is the default data type, you do not have to select it if it is the correct data type for the field. Additionally, if the field name is descriptive enough, the Description box is optional.

> A greater than symbol (>) in the Format property box in a Text field converts all entries in the field to uppercase. Using a less than symbol (<) would force all entries to be lowercase.

More Knowledge | **About the Caption Property**

The Caption property is used to give a name to fields used on forms and reports. Many database administrators create field names in tables that are short and abbreviated. In a form or report based on the table, a more descriptive name is desired. The value in the Caption property is used in label controls on forms and reports instead of the field name. If the Caption property is blank, the field name is used in the label control. A caption can contain up to 2,048 characters.

---

9 In the third **Field Name** box, type **Status** and then press ⌨Tab three times to move to the next **Field Name** box.

10 In the fourth **Field Name** box, type **%Complete** Press [Tab] and then click the **Data Type arrow**. From the displayed list, click **Number**. Press [Tab] to move to the **Description** box, and then type **Percentage of the task that has been completed** Press [F6] to move to the **Field Properties** pane. Click the **Field Size** property arrow and select **Single**. Click the **Format** property arrow and select **Percent**. Set the **Decimal Places** property to 0.

> The data type of Number is appropriate for this field because it will display only the amount of a task that has been completed. Defining the number as a percent with zero decimal places further restricts the entries. This allows the field to be used accurately in calculations, comparisons, and sorts.

11 In the fifth **Field Name** box, type **Parts** Press [Tab] and then click the **Data Type arrow**. From the displayed list, click **Yes/No**. Press [Tab] to move to the **Description** box. Type **Click the field to indicate parts have been ordered to complete the task**

> The data type of Yes/No is appropriate for this field because there are only two choices, parts are on order (yes) or parts are not on order (no). In Datasheet view, click the check box to indicate yes with a checkmark.

Activity 4.14 | Adding Fields to a Table in Design View

1 In the sixth **Field Name** box, type **Tech** and then press [Tab] three times to move to the next **Field Name** box.

2 In the seventh **Field Name** box, type **Phone#** Press [Tab] two times to move to the **Description** box, type **Enter as ###-####** and then change the **Field Size** property to **8**

3 Click in the eighth **Field Name** box, and then type **Problem** Press [Tab] and then click the **Data Type arrow**. From the displayed list, click **Long Text**. Press [Tab] to move to the **Description** box, and then type **Description of the IT problem**

> The data type of Long Text is appropriate for this field because it may require more than 255 characters and spaces to effectively describe the IT problem that needs attention.

4 Click in the ninth **Field Name** box, and then type **Start Date** Press [Tab] and then click the **Data Type arrow**. From the displayed list, click **Date/Time**.

> The data type of Date/Time is appropriate for this field because it will only display date information. Because Date/Time is a type of number, this field can be used in calculations.

5 Click in the tenth **Field Name** box and then type **End Date** Press [Tab] and then click the **Data Type arrow**. From the displayed list, click **Date/Time**.

6 Click in the eleventh **Field Name** box and then type **Task Duration** Press [Tab] and then click the **Data Type arrow**. From the displayed list, click **Calculated**. Press [Tab], and the **Expression Builder** dialog box appears. In the **Expression Builder** dialog box, type **[End Date]-[Start Date]** and then compare your screen to Figure 4.29.

> The data type of Calculated is appropriate for this field because the entry is calculated with an expression—subtracting *Start Date* from *End Date*. The *Task Duration* field will remain blank if the task has not yet been completed; nothing can be entered in the field.

> The *Expression Builder* is a feature used to create formulas (expressions) in calculated fields, query criteria, form and report properties, and table validation rules. An expression can be entered using field names or numbers where the only spaces included are those that separate words in field names. Any time a field name is used in the expression, it should be enclosed in square brackets. An existing field cannot be changed to a Calculated data type; it must be assigned when the field is added to the table. The expression can be edited in the Field Properties.

FIGURE 4.29

7 ▶ Click **OK**. In the **Description** box, type **Number of days necessary to complete the task** Press
F6 to move to the **Field Properties** pane at the bottom of the screen. Click in the **Result Type**
property arrow, and then select **Single**.

8 ▶ On the **Quick Access** toolbar, click **Save** 🔲. In the **Save As** dialog box, type **Lastname
Firstname 4B Tasks** and then click **OK**. Switch to **Datasheet** view to view the table you have
just created; there are no records in the table yet.

Objective 6 ▏ Create a Lookup Field

Video A4-6

Creating a *lookup field* can restrict the data entered in a field because the person entering
data selects that data from a list retrieved from another table, query, or list of entered values. The
choices can be displayed in a *list box*—a box containing a list of choices—or a *combo box*—a
box that is a combination of a list box and a text box. You can create a lookup field by using the
Lookup Wizard or manually by setting the field's lookup field properties. Whenever possible, use
the Lookup Wizard because it simplifies the process, ensures consistent data entry, automatically
populates the associated field properties, and creates the needed table relationships.

Activity 4.15 ▏ Creating a Lookup Field Based on a List of Values

In this activity, you will create a lookup field for the Status field.

1 ▶ With the **4B Tasks** table open, switch to **Design** view. In the **Status** field, click in the **Data Type**
box, and then click the **arrow**. From the displayed list of data types, click **Lookup Wizard**.

2 ▶ In the first **Lookup Wizard** dialog box, click the **I will type in the values that I want** option
button, and then click **Next**. Compare your screen with Figure 4.30.

The first step of the Lookup Wizard enables you to choose whether you want Access to locate the
information from another table or query or whether you would like to type the information to
create a list.

The second step enables you to select the number of columns you want to include in the lookup
field. The values are typed in the grid, and you can adjust the column width of the displayed list.

FIGURE 4.30

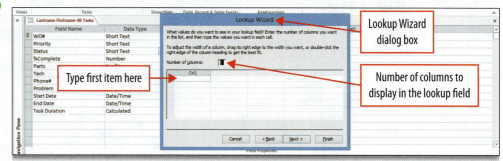

3 Be sure the number of columns is **1**. Under **Col1**, click in the first row, type **Not Started** and then press [Tab] or [↓] to save the first item.

> If you mistakenly press [Enter], the next dialog box of the wizard displays. If that happens, click the Back button.

4 Type the following data, and then compare your screen with Figure 4.31.

FIGURE 4.31

5 Double-click the right edge of Col1 to adjust the column width so all entries display, if necessary, and then click **Next**. In the final dialog box, click **Finish**. With the **Status** field selected, under **Field Properties**, click the **Lookup tab**.

> The Lookup Wizard populates the Lookup property boxes. The *Row Source Type* property indicates that the data is retrieved from a Value List, a list that you created. The *Row Source* property displays the data you entered in the list. The *Limit to List* property displays No, so you can type alternative data in the field if necessary.

6 **Save** the changes, and switch to **Datasheet** view. Click the **Status** field in the first record, and then click the **arrow** to view the lookup list. Press [Esc] to return to a blank field.

Activity 4.16 | Creating a Lookup Field Based on Data in Another Table

In this activity, you will create a lookup field for the Tech field.

1 In the **4B Tasks** table, switch to **Design** view. In the **Tech** field, click in the **Data Type** box, and then click the **Data Type arrow**. From the displayed list of data types, click **Lookup Wizard**.

2 In the first **Lookup Wizard** dialog box, be sure that the **I want the lookup field to get the values from another table or query** option button is selected.

3 Click **Next**. The **4B Employees** table is selected.

4 Click **Next** to display the third **Lookup Wizard** dialog box. Under **Available Fields**, click **Last Name**, and then click the **Add Field** (>) button to move the field to the **Selected Fields** box. Move the **First Name** and **Job Title** fields from the **Available Fields** box to the **Selected Fields** box. Compare your screen with Figure 4.32.

> Because there might be several people with the same last name, the First Name field and the Job Title field are included.

FIGURE 4.32

5 Click **Next** to display the fourth **Lookup Wizard** dialog box. In the **1** box, click the **arrow**, and then click **Last Name**. In the **2** box, click the **arrow**, and then click **First Name**. In the **3** box, click the **arrow**, and then click **Job Title**. Leave all three sort orders as **Ascending**.

> The list will first display last names in ascending order. If there are duplicate last names, then the duplicate last names will then be sorted by the first name in ascending order. If there are duplicate last names and first names, then those names will be sorted in ascending order by the job title.

6 Click **Next** to display the fifth **Lookup Wizard** dialog box. This screen enables you to change the width of the lookup field and to display the primary key field. Be sure the **Hide key column (recommended)** check box is selected, and then click **Next** to display the sixth and final **Lookup Wizard** dialog box.

> The actual data that is stored in the lookup field is the data in the primary key field.

7 Under **What label would you like for your lookup field?**, leave the default of **Tech** and be sure that **Allow Multiple Values** is *not* selected.

> Because you have already named the field, the default name is appropriate. If you were creating a new field that had not yet been named, a label should be entered on this screen. If you want to allow the selection of more than one last name when the lookup field displays and then store the multiple values, select the Allow Multiple Values check box, which changes the lookup field to a multivalued field. A *multivalued field* holds multiple values, such as a list of people to whom you have assigned the same task.

8 Click **Finish**. A message displays stating that the table must be saved before Access can create the needed relationship between the *4B Tasks* table and the *4B Employees* table. Click **Yes**.

9 With the **Tech** field selected, under **Field Properties**, click the Lookup tab, if necessary.

> The Lookup Wizard populates the Lookup properties boxes. The *Row Source Type* property indicates that the data is retrieved from a table or query. The *Row Source* property displays the SQL statement that is used to retrieve the data from the fields in the *4B Employees* table. The *Limit to List* property displays Yes, which means you must select the data from the list and cannot type data in the field.

10 Click the **General tab** to display the list of general field properties.

Video A4-7

A *field property* is an attribute or characteristic of a field that controls the display and input of data. You previously used field properties to change the size of a field and to specify a specific format for data types. When you click in any of the property boxes, a description of the property displays to the right. Available field properties depend upon the data type of each field.

Activity 4.17 | Creating an Input Mask Using the Input Mask Wizard

An *input mask* is a field property that determines the data that can be entered, how the data displays, and how the data is stored. For example, an input mask can require individuals to enter telephone numbers in a specific format like (636) 555-1212. If you enter the telephone number without supplying an area code, you will be unable to save the record until the area code is entered. Input masks provide *data validation*—rules that help prevent individuals from entering invalid data—and help ensure that individuals enter data in a consistent manner. By default, you can apply input masks to fields with a data type of Short Text, Number, Currency, and Date/Time. The Input Mask Wizard can be used to apply input masks to fields with a data type of Short Text or Date/Time only.

1 ▶ Under **Field Name**, click **Phone#**. Under **Field Properties**, click in the **Input Mask** box. At the right side of the Field Properties, notice the description given for this property. In the **Input Mask** box, click the **Build** ⋯ button. Compare your screen with Figure 4.33.

> The Build button displays after you click in a field property box so you can further define the property. The Input Mask Wizard starts, which enables you to create an input mask using one of several standard masks that Access has designed, such as Phone Number, Social Security Number, Zip Code, and so on. Clicking in the Try It box enables you to enter data to test the input mask.

FIGURE 4.33

2 ▶ In the displayed **Input Mask Wizard** dialog box, with **Phone Number** selected, click **Next**, and then compare your screen with Figure 4.34. In the **Input Mask Wizard** dialog box, notice the entry in the **Input Mask** box.

> A *0* indicates a required digit; a *9* indicates an optional digit or space. The area code is enclosed in parentheses, and a hyphen (-) separates the three-digit prefix from the four-digit number. The exclamation point (!) causes the input mask to fill in from left to right. The Placeholder character indicates that the field will display an underscore character (_) for each digit before data is entered in Datasheet view.

FIGURE 4.34

3 In the **Input Mask Wizard** dialog box, click **Back**, and then click **Edit List**.

The Customize Input Mask Wizard dialog box displays, which enables you to edit the default input mask or add an input mask.

4 In the **Customize Input Mask Wizard** dialog box, in the navigation area, click the **New (blank) record** button . In the **Description** box, type **Local Phone Number** Click in the **Input Mask** box, and type **!000-0000** Click in the **Placeholder** box, and type **#** Click in the **Sample Data** box, and type **555-2090** Compare your screen with Figure 4.35.

Because tasks are assigned to local personnel, the area code is unnecessary. Instead of displaying an underscore as the placeholder in the field, the number sign (#) displays.

FIGURE 4.35

5 In the **Customize Input Mask Wizard** dialog box, click **Close**.

The newly created input mask for Local Phone Number displays below the input mask for Password.

6 Under **Input Mask**, click **Local Phone Number**, and then click **Next**. Click the **Placeholder character arrow** to display other symbols that can be used as placeholders. Be sure that # is displayed as the placeholder character, and then click **Next**.

After creating an input mask to be used with the Input Mask Wizard, you can change the placeholder character for individual fields.

7 The next wizard screen enables you to decide how you want to store the data. Be sure that the **Without the symbols in the mask, like this** option button is selected, as shown in Figure 4.36.

Saving the data without the symbols makes the database size smaller.

FIGURE 4.36

8 ▶ Click **Next**. In the final wizard screen, click **Finish**. Notice that the entry in the **Input Mask** box displays as **!000\-0000;;#**. **Save** 🖫 the table.

Recall that the exclamation point (!) fills the input mask from left to right, and the 0s indicate required digits. The two semicolons (;) are used by Access to separate the input mask into three sections. This input mask has data in the first section—the 0s—and in the third section—the placeholder of #.

The second and third sections of an input mask are optional. The second section, which is not used in this input mask, determines whether the literal characters—in this case, the hyphen (-)—are stored with the data. A *0* in the second section will store the literal characters; a *1* or leaving it blank stores only the characters entered in the field. The third section of the input mask indicates the placeholder character—in this case, the # sign. If you want to leave the fill-in spaces blank instead of using a placeholder, type " "—there is a space between the quotation marks—in the third section.

9 ▶ Take a moment to study the table shown in Figure 4.37, which describes the characters that can be used to create a custom input mask.

FIGURE 4.37

MOST COMMON INPUT MASK CHARACTERS	
CHARACTER	**DESCRIPTION**
0	Required digit (0 through 9).
9	Optional digit or space.
#	Optional digit, space, plus sign, or minus sign; blank positions are converted to spaces.
L	Required letter (A through Z).
?	Optional letter.
A	Required digit or letter.
a	Optional digit or letter.
&	Any character or space; required.
C	Any character or space; optional.
<	All characters that follow are converted to lowercase.
>	All characters that follow are converted to uppercase.
!	Characters typed into the mask are filled from left to right. The exclamation point can be included anywhere in the input mask.
\	Character that follows is displayed as text. This is the same as enclosing a character in quotation marks.
Password	Creates a password entry box that displays asterisks (*) as you type. Access stores the characters.
" "	Used to enclose displayed text.
.	Decimal separator.
,	Thousands separator.
: ; - /	Date and time separators; character used depends on your regional settings.

Activity 4.18 | **Creating an Input Mask Using the Input Mask Properties Box**

In addition to using the wizard, input masks can be created directly in the Input Mask Properties box. In this activity, you will use the Input Mask Properties box to create a mask that will ensure the Work Order # is entered according to departmental policy. An example of a work order number used by the Information Technology department is WO CM-46341. WO is an abbreviation for Work Order. CM represents the initials of the person entering the work order data. A hyphen separates the initials from a number assigned to the work order.

1 With the **4B Tasks** table displayed in **Design** view, click in the **WO#** field. Under **Field Properties**, click in the **Input Mask** box, type **WO** press the [Spacebar], type **>LL-99** and then compare your screen with Figure 4.38.

The letters *WO* and a space will display at the beginning of every Work Order # (WO#). The greater than (>) sign converts any text following it to uppercase. Each *L* indicates that a letter (not a number) is required. A hyphen (-) follows the two letters, and the two 9s indicate optional numbers.

Take a moment to study the examples of input masks shown in Figure 4.39.

FIGURE 4.38

FIGURE 4.39

EXAMPLES OF INPUT MASKS		
INPUT MASK	**SAMPLE DATA**	**DESCRIPTION**
(000) 000-0000	(712) 555-5011	Must enter an area code because of the 0s enclosed in parentheses.
(999) 000-0000!	(702) 555-6331 ( ) 555-6331	Area code is optional because of the 9s enclosed in parentheses. Exclamation point causes mask to fill in from left to right.
(000) AAA-AAAA	(712) 555-TELE	Enables you to substitute the last seven digits of a U.S.–style phone number with letters. Area code is required.
#999	-20 2009	Can accept any positive or negative number of no more than four characters and no thousands separator or decimal places.
>L????L?000L0	GREENGR339M3 MAY R 452B7	Allows a combination of required (L) and optional (?) letters and required numbers (0). The greater than (>) sign changes letters to uppercase.
00000-9999	23703-5100	Requires the five-digit postal code (0) and optional plus-four section (9).
>L<???????????????	Elizabeth Rose	Enables up to 15 letters in which the first letter is required and is capitalized; all other letters are lowercase.
ISBN 0-&&&&&&&&&-0	ISBN 0-13-232762-7	Allows a book number with text of ISBN, required first and last digits, and any combination of characters between those digits.
>LL00000-0000	AG23703-0323	Accepts a combination of two required letters, both uppercase, followed by five required numbers, a hyphen, and then four required numbers. Could be used with part or inventory numbers.

2 Click in the **Start Date** field to make the field active. Under **Field Properties**, click in the **Format** box, and then click the **arrow**. From the displayed list, click **Short Date**. Also set the format of **End Date** to **Short Date**.

More Knowledge | **The Differences Between Input Masks and Display Formats**

You can define input masks to control how data is entered into a field and then apply a separate display format to the same data. For example, you can require individuals to enter dates in a format such as 30 Dec. 2015 by using an input mask of DD MMM. YYYY. By using the Format property, you can specify a format of Short Date, which will display the data as 12/30/2015, regardless of how the data was entered.

---

3 Switch to **Datasheet** view, click **Yes** to save the table. In the **WO#** field in the first record, type **da3** and then press Tab or Enter to go to the next field.

> The input mask adds the WO and a space. The da is automatically capitalized, and the hyphen is inserted before the 3.

4 In the **Priority** field, type **High** and then press Tab or Enter to go to the next field.

5 In the **Status** field, type **C** to display the **Completed** item in the lookup list, and then press Tab or Enter to move to the next field.

6 In the **%Complete** field, type **100** and then press Tab or Enter three times to bypass the **Parts** and **Tech** fields.

> Leaving the Yes/No field blank assigns a No value in the Parts field, so parts are not on order for this task.

7 In the **Phone#** field, type **5558735** and then press Tab or Enter to move to the next field.

8 In the **Problem** field, type **Computer 14 has a computer virus** and then press Tab or Enter to move to the next field.

9 In the **Start Date** field, type **3/28/2016** and then press Tab or Enter to move to the next field.

10 In the **End Date** field, type **3/29/16** and then press Tab or Enter to move to the **Task Duration** field. Notice the calculated field now displays a 1. Compare your screen with Figure 4.40.

FIGURE 4.40

Task Duration is calculated

11 Switch to **Design** view. The data entry is automatically saved when the record is complete.

Activity 4.19 | Specifying a Required Field

Recall that if a table has a field designated as the primary key field, an entry for the field is *required*; it cannot be left empty. You can set this requirement on other fields in either Design view or Datasheet view. In this activity, you will require an entry in the Status field. Use the Required field property to ensure that a field contains data and is not left blank.

1 Click in the **Status** field, and then under **Field Properties**, click in the **Required** box. Click the **Required arrow**, and then compare your screen with Figure 4.41.

> Only Yes and No options display in the list.

FIGURE 4.41

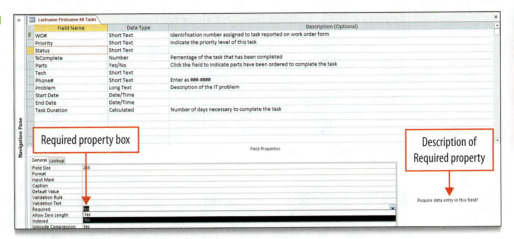

2 Click **Yes** to require an individual to enter the status for each record. **Save** 🖫 the changes to the table.

> A message displays stating that data integrity rules have been changed and that existing data may not be valid for the new rules. This message displays when you change field properties where data exists in the field. Clicking Yes requires Access to examine the field in every record to see if the existing data meets the new data validation rule. For each record Access finds where data does not meet the new validation rule, a new message displays that prompts you to keep testing with the new setting. You also can revert to the prior validation setting and continue testing or cancel testing of the data.

3 If the message is displayed, click **No**. Switch to **Datasheet** view. Click in the **Status** field. On the **TABLE TOOLS FIELDS tab**, in the **Field Validation group**, notice that the **Required** check box is selected.

4 In the table, click in the **Tech** field. On the **TABLE TOOLS FIELDS tab**, in the **Field Validation group**, click the **Required** check box. Compare your screen with Figure 4.42.

> A message displays stating that the existing data violates the Required property for the Tech field because the field is currently blank.

FIGURE 4.42

5 In the message box, click **Cancel**. Click the **arrow** at the right of the **Tech** field, and then select **Ron Lee**.

More Knowledge **Allowing Blank Data in a Required Text or Memo Field**

By default, all fields except the primary key field can be empty—null. If the Required property for a field is set to Yes, a value must be entered into the field. If data is required, Access will not save the record until a value is entered; however, you may not have the data to enter into a text or memo field where the Required property is set to Yes. To allow for this situation, you can set the Allow Zero Length property for the field to Yes. A *zero-length string* is created by typing two quotation marks with no space between them (""), which indicates that no value exists for a required text or memo field.

Activity 4.20 | Setting Default Values for Fields

You can use the Default Value field property to display a value in a field for new records. As you enter data, you can change the *default value* in the field to another value within the parameters of any validation rules. Setting a default value for fields that contain the same data for multiple records increases the efficiency of data entry. For example, if all of the employees in the organization live in California, set the default value of the state field to CA. If most of the employees in your organization live in the city of Golden Grove, set the default value of the city field to Golden Grove. If an employee lives in another city, type the new value over the displayed default value.

1 Switch to **Design** view. Under **Field Name**, click the **Priority** field. Under **Field Properties**, click in the **Default Value** box, and then type **Low** Switch to **Datasheet** view, and then **Save** 🔲 changes to the table. Notice that the **Priority** field displays *LOW* in the **New Record** row.

> Setting a default value does not change the data in saved records; the default value will display in new records and will be saved only if nothing else is typed in the field.

2 Switch back to **Design** view. Using the technique you just practiced, for the **Status** field, set the **Default Value** property to **Not Started** If necessary, for the %Complete field, set the Default Value property to **0**

3 For the **Start Date** field, set the **Default Value** to **3/30/16** Switch to **Datasheet** view, saving changes to the table. Compare your screen with Figure 4.43.

> The Status field shows a default value of *Not "Started"*. *Not* is an Access logical operator; therefore, Access excluded the word *Not* from the text expression.

FIGURE 4.43

4 Switch to **Design** view. Click in the **Status** field. Under **Field Properties**, in the **Default Value** box, select the text, and then type **"Not Started"** Click in the **Start Date** field, and notice that in the **Default Value** box, Access displays the date as **#3/30/2016#**. Switch to **Datasheet** view, saving changes to the table, and then view the default value in the **Status** field.

> Inserting quotation marks around *Not Started* informs Access that both words are part of the text expression.

More Knowledge | **Using the Current Date as a Default Value**

To use the current date as the default value for a Date/Time field, in the Default Value box, type date()

Activity 4.21 | Indexing Fields in a Table

An *index* is a special list created in Access to speed up searches and sorting—such as the index at the back of a book. The index is visible only to Access and not to you, but it helps Access find items much faster. You should index fields that you search frequently, fields that you sort, or fields used to join tables in relationships. Indexes, however, can slow down the creation and deletion of records because the data must be added to or deleted from the index.

1 ▶ Switch to **Design** view. Under **Field Name**, click **WO#**. Under **Field Properties**, locate the **Indexed** property box, and notice the entry of **Yes (No Duplicates)**.

By default, primary key fields are indexed. Because WO# is the primary key field, the field is automatically indexed, and no duplicate values are permitted in this field.

2 ▶ Under **Field Name**, click **Tech**. Under **Field Properties**, click in the **Indexed** property box, and then click the displayed **arrow**. Compare your screen with Figure 4.44.

Three options display for the Indexed property—No, Yes (Duplicates OK), and Yes (No Duplicates).

FIGURE 4.44

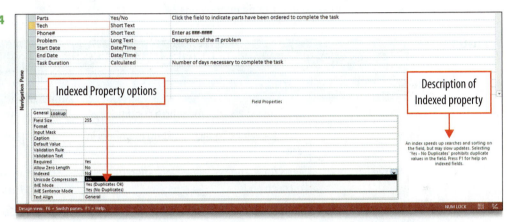

3 ▶ Click **Yes (Duplicates OK)**.

By adding an index to the field and allowing duplicates, you create faster searches and sorts on this field, while allowing duplicate data. Because a person may be assigned more than one task, allowing duplicate data is appropriate.

4 ▶ **Save** 🖫 the table design.

5 ▶ On the **TABLE TOOLS DESIGN tab**, in the **Show/Hide group**, click the **Indexes** button.

An Indexes dialog box displays the indexes in the current table. Opening the Indexes dialog box is an efficient way to determine the fields that have been indexed in a table.

6 ▶ In the **Indexes: 4B Tasks** dialog box, click **Close** ⊠.

Objective 8   Create Validation Rules and Validation Text

Video A4-8

You have practiced different techniques to help ensure that data entered into a field is valid. Data types restrict the type of data that can be entered into a field. Field sizes control the number of characters that can be entered into a field. Field properties further control how data is entered into a field, including the use of input masks to require individuals to enter data in a specific way.

Another way to ensure the accuracy of data is by using the Validation Rule property. A ***validation rule*** is an expression that precisely defines the range of data that will be accepted in a field. An ***expression*** is a combination of functions, field values, constants, and operators that brings about a result. ***Validation text*** is the error message that displays when an individual enters a value prohibited by the validation rule.

Activity 4.22 | Creating Data Validation Rules and Validation Text

In this activity, you will create data validation rules and validation text for the %Complete field, the Start Date field, and the Priority field.

1 ▶ Under **Field Name**, click **%Complete**. Under **Field Properties**, click in the **Validation Rule** box, and then click the **Build** button `...`.

The Expression Builder dialog box displays. Recall that the Expression Builder is a feature used to create formulas (expressions) in query criteria, form and report properties, and table validation rules. Take a moment to study the table shown in Figure 4.45, which describes the operators that can be used in building expressions.

FIGURE 4.45

OPERATORS USED IN EXPRESSIONS		
OPERATOR	**FUNCTION**	**EXAMPLE**
Not	Tests for values NOT meeting a condition.	**Not** >10 (the same as <=10)
In	Tests for values equal to existing members in a list.	**In** ("High","Normal","Low")
Between…And	Tests for a range of values, including the values on each end.	**Between** 0 **And** 100 (the same as >=0 **And** <=100)
Like	Matches pattern strings in Text and Memo fields.	**Like** "Car*"
Is Not Null	Requires individuals to enter values in the field. If used in place of the Required field, you can create Validation Text that better describes what should be entered in the field.	**Is Not Null** (the same as setting Required property to Yes)
And	Specifies that all of the entered data must fall within the specified limits.	>=#01/01/2016# **And** <=#03/01/2016# (Date must be between 01/01/2016 and 03/01/2016) Can use And to combine validation rules. For example, **Not** "USA" **And Like** "U*"
Or	Specifies that one of many entries can be accepted.	"High" **Or** "Normal" **Or** "Low"
<	Less than.	<100
<=	Less than or equal to.	<=100
>	Greater than.	>0
>=	Greater than or equal to.	>=0
=	Equal to.	=Date()
<>	Not equal to.	<>#12/24/53#

2 ▶ In the upper box of the **Expression Builder** dialog box, type **>=0 and <=1** Alternatively, type the expression in the Validation Rule property box. In the **Expression Builder** dialog box, click **OK**.

The %Complete field has a data type of Number and is formatted as a percent. Recall that the Format property changes the way the stored data displays. To convert the display of a number to a percent, Access multiplies the value by 100 and appends the percent sign (%). Therefore, 100% is stored as 1—Access multiples 1 by 100, resulting in 100. A job that is halfway completed—50%— has the value stored as .5 because .5 times 100 equals 50.

ANOTHER WAY   When using the Expression Builder to create an expression, you can either type the entire expression or, on the small toolbar in the dialog box, click an existing button, such as the > button, to insert operators into the expression.

3 ▶ Click in the **Validation Text** box, and then type **Enter a value between 0 and 100** so that the percentages are reflected accurately. Compare your screen with Figure 4.46.

FIGURE 4.46

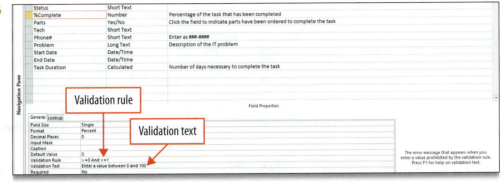

4 ▶ Under **Field Name**, click **Start Date** to make the field active. Under **Field Properties**, click in the **Validation Rule** box, and then type **>=3/15/2016** Click in the **Validation Text** box, and then type **You cannot enter a date prior to 3/15/2016** Compare your screen with Figure 4.47.

In expressions, Access inserts a number or pound sign (#) before and after a date. This validation rule ensures that the person entering data cannot enter a date prior to 3/15/2016.

FIGURE 4.47

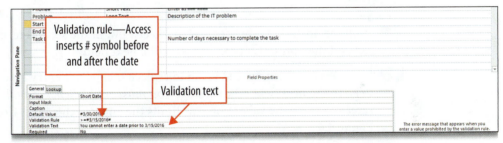

5 ▶ Under **Field Name**, click **Priority**. Under **Field Properties**, click in the **Validation Rule** box, and then type **in ("High","Normal","Low")** Click in the **Validation Text** box, and then type **You must enter High, Normal, or Low** Compare your screen with Figure 4.48.

The operators are not case sensitive; Access will capitalize the operators when you click in another property box. With the *In* operator, the members of the list must be enclosed in parentheses, and each member must be enclosed in quotation marks and separated from each other by commas. Another way to specify the same validation rule is: "High" Or "Normal" Or "Low".

FIGURE 4.48

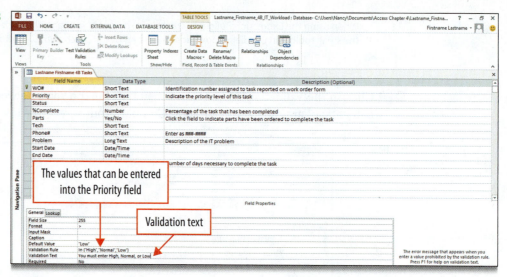

> **6** Save 🖫 the changes to the table. Switch to **Datasheet** view.
>
> A message displays stating that data integrity rules have changed. Even though you have clicked No in previous message boxes, click Yes. In a large database, you should click Yes to have Access check the data in all of the records before moving on.

Activity 4.23 | Testing Table Design and Field Properties

In this activity, you will add records to the *4B Tasks* table to test the design and field properties.

> **1** With the **4B Tasks** table open in **Datasheet** view, in the second record in the **WO#** field, type **sk1** and then press Tab or Enter to go to the next field.

> **2** In the **Priority** field, type **Medium** to replace the default entry *Low*, and then press Tab or Enter to go to the next field. The message *You must enter High, Normal, or Low* appears on your screen because the validation rule limits the entry in this field. Compare your screen with Figure 4.49.

FIGURE 4.49

> **3** Click **OK** and type **Normal** in the **Priority** field to replace *Medium*. Press Tab or Enter to go to the next field.

> **4** In the **Status** field, **Not Started** automatically appears because it is the default entry. Type **Backordered** and then press Tab or Enter to move to the next field.
>
> Recall that the Limit to List property setting is set to No for the lookup field, enabling you to type data other than that displayed in the list box. If the purpose of the lookup field is to restrict individuals to entering only certain data, then the Limit to List property setting should be set to Yes.

5 In the **%Complete** field, with the **0%** selected, type **50** and then press ⎡Tab⎤ or ⎡Enter⎤ to move to the next field.

6 In the **Parts** field, click in the **check box** to add a checkmark and indicate parts are on order to complete the task. Press ⎡Tab⎤ or ⎡Enter⎤ to move to the next field.

7 In the **Tech** field, select **William McCamara**. Press ⎡Tab⎤ or ⎡Enter⎤ to move to the next field.

> 🔄 **ANOTHER WAY**   You can locate an entry in a long list faster if you type the first letter of the data for which you are searching. For example, if you are searching for a last name that begins with the letter *m*, when the list displays, type m or M The selection will move down to the first entry that begins with the letter.

8 In the **Phone#** field, type **aaa** and notice that Access will not allow a letter entry because the input mask you just created requires numbers in this field. Type **5556798** and then press ⎡Tab⎤ or ⎡Enter⎤ to move to the next field.

9 In the **Problem** field, type **Printer B will not print** Press ⎡Tab⎤ or ⎡Enter⎤ to move to the next field

10 In the **Start Date** field, type **4/5/2016** Press ⎡Tab⎤ or ⎡Enter⎤ three times to move past **Task Duration** and move to the next record.

Notice the calendar icon that appears to the right of the date fields. Clicking the icon enables you to choose a date from a calendar.

End Date is not a required field, so it accepts a blank entry. Because End Date is blank, there is nothing to calculate in the Task Duration field.

11 In the third record, in the **WO#** field, type **da4** and then press ⎡Tab⎤ or ⎡Enter⎤ two times to move to the **Status** field.

12 In the **Status** field, select **Completed**. Press ⎡Tab⎤ or ⎡Enter⎤ to move to the next field.

13 In the **%Complete** field, with the *0%* selected, type **110** and then press ⎡Tab⎤ or ⎡Enter⎤ to move to the next field.

A message *Enter a value between 0 and 100* appears on your screen because the validation rule limits the entry in this field.

14 Click **OK** to close the dialog box. Select the *110%* and type **100** Press ⎡Tab⎤ or ⎡Enter⎤ two times. In the **Tech** field, type **Rukstad** Press ⎡Tab⎤ or ⎡Enter⎤ to move to the next field. Compare your screen with Figure 4.50.

A message *The text you entered isn't an item in the list* appears on your screen. Recall that the Limit to List property setting is set to Yes for the lookup field, which restricts you from entering anything that is not on the list.

FIGURE 4.50

Lookup list prohibits entries not on the lookup list

15 Click **OK** and select **Angelina Perry** from the lookup list. Press ⎡Tab⎤ or ⎡Enter⎤ to move to the next field.

16 In the **Phone#** field, type **5556313** Press `Tab` or `Enter` to move to the next field. In the **Description** field, type **Computer 3 needs updates** Press `Tab` or `Enter` to move to the next field

17 In the **Start Date** field, notice the default date of 3/30/2016, and press `Tab` or `Enter` to move to the next field. In the **End Date** field, type **4/2/2016** Press `Tab` or `Enter` to move to the next field.

18 Adjust all column widths, ensuring that all of the field names and all of the field data display. View the table in **Print Preview**, and then change the orientation to **Landscape**. If you are instructed to submit this result, create a paper or electronic printout. **Close Print Preview**.

19 Close `×` the table, saving changes. **Close** the database, and **Exit** Access.

20 As directed by your instructor, submit your database and the paper or electronic printout of the table that is the result of this project. Specifically, in this project, using your own name you created the following database and printout or electronic printout:

| 1. Lastname_Firstname_4B_IT_Workload | Database file |
| 2. Lastname Firstname 4B Tasks | Table (printed or electronic printout) |

END | You have completed Project 4B

END OF CHAPTER

SUMMARY

Backup files are copies of a database created to protect the data. Adding trustworthy storage locations to the Trust Center as secure locations allows the user full use of the content in the database.

Using existing tables as the basis to create new ones eliminates the chances of mistakes in table design, and they can be continually modified and updated to keep the data useful over time.

Creating a table in Design view allows control over the fields in the table, the choice of the data type based on the content, and the ability to set field properties to minimize errors in data entry.

Reducing errors starts with a lookup or calculated data type to minimize manual entry, formatting properties and input masks to ensure accurate presentation, and validation rules to restrict data entry.

GO! LEARN IT ONLINE

Review the concepts and key terms in this chapter by completing these online challenges, which you can find at **www.pearsonhighered.com/go**.

Matching and Multiple Choice: Answer matching and multiple choice questions to test what you learned in this chapter. MyITLab®

Crossword Puzzle: Spell out the words that match the numbered clues, and put them in the puzzle squares.

Flipboard: Flip through the definitions of the key terms in this chapter and match them with the correct term.

END OF CHAPTER

REVIEW AND ASSESSMENT GUIDE FOR ACCESS CHAPTER 4

Your instructor may assign one or more of these projects to help you review the chapter and assess your mastery and understanding of the chapter.

		Review and Assessment Guide for Access Chapter 4	
Project	**Apply Skills from These Chapter Objectives**	**Project Type**	**Project Location**
4C	Objectives 1–4 from Project 4A	**4C Skills Review** A guided review of the skills from Project 4A.	On the following pages
4D	Objectives 5–8 from Project 4B	**4D Skills Review** A guided review of the skills from Project 4B.	On the following pages
4E	Objectives 1–4 from Project 4A	**4E Mastery (Grader Project)** A demonstration of your mastery of the skills in Project 4A with extensive decision making.	In MyITLab and on the following pages
4F	Objectives 5–8 from Project 4B	**4F Mastery (Grader Project)** A demonstration of your mastery of the skills in Project 4B with extensive decision making.	In MyITLab and on the following pages
4G	Objectives 1–7 from Projects 4A and 4B	**4G Mastery (Grader Project)** A demonstration of your mastery of the skills in Projects 4A and 4B with extensive decision making.	In MyITLab and on the following pages
4H	Combination of Objectives from Projects 4A and 4B	**4H GO! Fix It** A demonstration of your mastery of the skills in Projects 4A and 4B by creating a correct result from a document that contains errors you must find.	Online
4I	Combination of Objectives from Projects 4A and 4B	**4I GO! Make It** A demonstration of your mastery of the skills in Projects 4A and 4B by creating a result from a supplied picture.	Online
4J	Combination of Objectives from Projects 4A and 4B	**4J GO! Solve It** A demonstration of your mastery of the skills in Projects 4A and 4B, your decision making skills, and your critical thinking skills. A task-specific rubric helps you self-assess your result.	Online
4K	Combination of Objectives from Projects 4A and 4B	**4K GO! Solve It** A demonstration of your mastery of the skills in Projects 4A and 4B, your decision making skills, and your critical thinking skills. A task-specific rubric helps you self-assess your result.	On the following pages
4L	Combination of Objectives from Projects 4A and 4B	**4L GO! Think** A demonstration of your understanding of the chapter concepts applied in a manner that you would use outside of college. An analytic rubric helps you and your instructor grade the quality of your work by comparing it to the work an expert in the discipline would create.	On the following pages
4M	Combination of Objectives from Projects 4A and 4B	**4M GO! Think** A demonstration of your understanding of the chapter concepts applied in a manner that you would use outside of college. An analytic rubric helps you and your instructor grade the quality of your work by comparing it to the work an expert in the discipline would create.	Online
4N	Combination of Objectives from Projects 4A and 4B	**4N You and GO!** A demonstration of your understanding of the chapter concepts applied in a manner that you would use in a personal situation. An analytic rubric helps you and your instructor grade the quality of your work.	Online

GLOSSARY

GLOSSARY OF CHAPTER KEY TERMS

Append A feature that allows you to add data to an existing table.

Back up A feature that creates a copy of the original database to protect against lost data.

Clipboard A temporary storage area in Windows that can hold up to 24 items.

Combo box A box that is a combination of a list box and a text box in a lookup field.

Copy A command that duplicates a selection and places it on the Clipboard.

Data validation Rules that help prevent invalid data entries and ensure data is entered consistently.

Default value A value displayed for new records.

Destination table The table to which records are appended.

Dynamic An attribute applied to data in a database that changes.

Expression A combination of functions, field values, constants, and operators that produces a result.

Expression Builder A feature used to create formulas (expressions) in calculated fields, query criteria, form and report properties, and table validation rules.

Field property An attribute or a characteristic of a field that controls the display and input of data.

Flagged A highlighted word that Spell Check does not recognize from the Office dictionary.

Index A special list created in Access to speed up searches and sorting.

Input mask A field property that determines the how the data displays and is stored.

Instance Each simultaneously running Access session.

List box A box containing a list of choices for a lookup field.

Lookup field A way to restrict data entered in a field.

Multivalued field A field that holds multiple values.

Paste An option that moves the copy of the selected table from the Clipboard into a new location.

Path The location of a folder or file on your computer or storage device.

Required A field property that ensures a field cannot be left empty.

Source table The table from which you are copying records.

System tables Tables used to keep track of multiple entries in an attachment field that you cannot view or work with.

Trust Center A security feature that checks documents for macros and digital signatures.

Trusted source A person or organization that you know will not send you databases with malicious content.

Validation rule An expression that precisely defines the range of data that will be accepted in a field.

Validation text The error message that displays when an individual enters a value prohibited by the validation rule.

Zero-length string An entry created by typing two quotation marks with no spaces between them ("") to indicate that no value exists for a required text or memo field.

CHAPTER REVIEW

Skills Review | Project 4C Commerce

Dario Soto, the city manager of Golden Grove, has a database of the city's industry information. This database has five tables. The Industries table contains summary information from the other four tables. Each update to an individual industry table would require updates to the summary table. In the following Skills Review, you will redesign the tables, taking advantage of table relationships to avoid entering and storing redundant data. Your completed tables and relationships will look similar to those in Figure 4.51.

PROJECT FILES

For Project 4C, you will need the following files:

a04C_Commerce
a04C_GCH_Contacts

You will save your databases as:

Lastname_Firstname_4C_Commerce
a04C_Commerce_2016-10-30 (date will vary)

PROJECT RESULTS

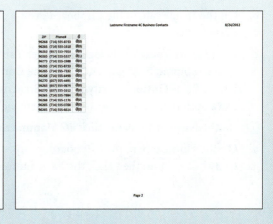

FIGURE 4.51

(Project 4C Commerce continues on the next page)

CHAPTER REVIEW

1 **Start** Access. Locate and open the **a04C_Commerce** database.

a. On the **FILE tab**, click **Save As**, and then, under **Save Database As**, double-click **Back Up Database**. In the **Save As** dialog box, navigate to the drive on which you will be storing your folders and projects for this chapter, and then click **Save** to accept the default name.

b. **Save** the database in the **Microsoft Access Database** format in your **Access Chapter 4** folder as **Lastname_Firstname_4C_Commerce**

2 In the **Navigation Pane**, double-click **4C Industries**. Take a moment to review the contents of the table. Close the **Navigation Pane**.

a. Click the **FILE tab,** and click **Save As**. Under **File Types**, double-click **Save Object As**.

b. In the displayed **Save As** dialog box, under **Save '4C Industries' to**, type **Lastname Firstname 4C Industries Revised** and then click **OK**.

3 Point to the **Business #5** field name until the pointer displays. Drag to the left to the **Business #1** field name to select the five fields. On the **Home tab**, in the **Records group**, click the **Delete** button. In the displayed message box, click **Yes** to permanently delete the fields and the data.

4 Switch to **Design** view. To the left of **Industry Code**, click the **row selector** box, and then in the **Tools group**, click the **Primary Key** button. **Close** the table, saving any changes. Open the **Navigation Pane**.

5 In the **Navigation Pane**, click **4C Agriculture**.

a. On the **Home tab**, in the **Clipboard group**, click the **Copy** button.

b. On the **Home tab**, in the **Clipboard group**, click the **Paste** button.

c. In the **Paste Table As** dialog box, under **Table Name**, type **Lastname Firstname 4C Business Contacts** Under **Paste Options**, verify that the **Structure and Data** option button is selected, and then click **OK**.

6 In the **Navigation Pane**, click **4C Manufacturing**.

a. On the **Home tab**, in the **Clipboard group**, click the **Copy** button, and then click the **Paste** button.

b. In the **Paste Table As** dialog box, under **Table Name**, type **Lastname Firstname 4C Business Contacts** Under **Paste Options**, click the **Append Data to Existing Table** option button, and then click **OK**.

c. Using the same procedure, append the **4C Medical Centers** table and the **4C E-Commerce** table to the **Lastname Firstname 4C Business Contacts** table.

7 Save the **4C Business Contacts** table as **Lastname Firstname 4C Business Stats** One table will contain only contact information, and the other table will contain only statistical information.

8 In the **4C Business Stats** table, select the **Business Name** field, and then press Delete. Click **Yes** to delete the field and data. If necessary, scroll to the right to display the **Address, City, State, ZIP, Contact,** and **Phone#** fields. Select all six fields, and then press Delete. Click **Yes** to delete the fields and data.

a. Switch to **Design** view, and click in the **Business ID** field. On the **TABLE TOOLS DESIGN tab**, in the **Tools group**, click the **Primary Key** button. Change the data type of the **First Year** field to **Number**. **Save** the changes, and then switch to **Datasheet** view.

b. Click in the **Employees** field in the first record. On the **HOME tab**, in the **Find group**, click the **Find** button. In the **Find What** box, type **12** In the **Look In** box, select Current field, if necessary. Click **Find Next** to select the next occurrence in the **current field**. Click **Cancel** in the **Find and Replace** dialog box.

c. Click the **Record Selector** box to select the record containing *12*. On the **HOME tab**, in the **Records group**, click the **Delete** button. In the displayed message box, click **Yes** to permanently delete the record.

d. Adjust all column widths to view the field names and data. View the table in **Print Preview**. If you are instructed to submit the results, create a paper or electronic printout. **Close Print Preview**.

9 Open the **4C Business Contacts** table. Close the **Navigation Pane**. Select the **Employees, Gross Sales,** and **First Year** fields. On the **Home tab**, in the **Records group**, click the **Delete** button. In the displayed message box, click **Yes** to permanently delete the fields and data.

(Project 4C Commerce continues on the next page)

CHAPTER REVIEW

10 Click the **Business Name** field name. On the **FIELDS tab**, in the **Add & Delete group**, click the **Short Text** button. Type **Industry Code** to replace **Field1,** and then press Enter. **Save** your work.

a. In the first record, click in the **Industry Code** field. Open the **Navigation Pane**, and open the **4C Industries Revised** table. Under **Industry Category**, locate the record for the **Agriculture**, and notice the **Industry Code** of AGR. On the **tab row**, click the **4C Business Contacts tab** to make the table active. In the **Business ID** of 189018, in the **Industry Code** field, type **AGR** Locate the **Business ID** of 675234, and then in the **Industry Code** field, type **AGR** Locate the **Business ID** of 234155, type **AGR**

b. Using the techniques you just practiced, locate the **Industry Codes** for the **Manufacturing, Medical Center**, and **E-Commerce** Industry Categories. In Business IDs **258679, 399740, 479728, 927685**, and **966657**, type **MAN** In Business IDs **252479, 295738, 362149**, and **420879**, type **MED** and then in Business IDs **129741, 329718**, and **420943**, type **INT**

11 In the **Search** box in the navigation area at the bottom of the window, type **adv** Click at the end of **AdventuCom**. Press the Spacebar and type **Resources** Move to the next record to save the changes.

12 Switch the **4C Business Contacts** table to **Design** view. With the insertion point in the **Business ID** field, on the **TABLE TOOLS DESIGN tab**, in the **Tools group**, click the **Primary Key** button. **Save** the changes.

13 To the left of **Contact**, click the **row selector** box. Drag the field up until you see a dark horizontal line between *Industry Code* and *Address*, and then release the mouse button. **Save** the changes.

14 Click in the blank field name box under **Phone#**, type **Contact List** and then press Tab to move to the **Data Type** box. Click the **Data Type arrow**, and click **Attachment**.

15 Switch to **Datasheet** view, saving changes to the table.

a. In the fourth record (Greater Community Hospital), double-click in the **Attachment** field. In the displayed **Attachments** dialog box, click **Add**.

b. Navigate to the location where the student data files for this textbook are stored. In the **Choose File** dialog box, double-click **a04C_GCH_Contacts**. In the **Attachments** dialog box, click **OK**.

16 On the **HOME tab**, in the **Records group**, click the **Spelling** button. Ignore the entries until it selects *Makets*, and **Change** the spelling to *Markets*. Ignore the other names it selects as the process continues.

17 Adjust all column widths to view the field names and data. View the table in **Print Preview**, and then change the orientation to **Landscape**. If you are instructed to submit the results, create a paper or electronic printout.

18 On the **tab row**, right-click any table tab, and then click **Close All**, saving changes if necessary. **Close** the database, and **Exit** Access.

19 As directed by your instructor, submit your database and the paper or electronic printout of the two tables that are the result of this project. Specifically, in this project, using your own name you created the following database and printouts or electronic printouts:

1. Lastname_Firstname_4C_Commerce	Database file
2. Lastname Firstname 4C Business Stats	Table (printed or electronic printout)
3. Lastname Firstname 4C Business Contacts	Table (printed or electronic printout)

END | You have completed Project 4C

CHAPTER REVIEW

Apply 4B skills from these Objectives:

5 Create a Table in Design View

6 Create a Lookup Field

7 Set Field Properties

8 Create Data Validation Rules and Validation Text

Skills Review | Project 4D City Airport

Dario Soto, city manager of Golden Grove, California, has created a table to keep track of airport personnel. In the following Skills Review, you will add a table that stores records about the employees, modify the properties, and customize the fields in the table. You will add features to the database table that will help to reduce data entry errors and that will make data entry easier. Your completed table will look similar to the table shown in Figure 4.52.

PROJECT FILES

For Project 4D, you will need the following files:

a04D_City_Airport

Two new blank Word documents

You will save your files as:

Lastname_Firstname_4D_City_Airport

Lastname_Firstname_4D_Indexes

Lastname_Firstname_4D_Validation

PROJECT RESULTS

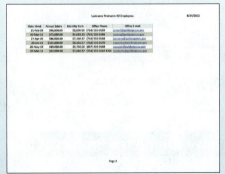

FIGURE 4.52

(Project 4D City Airport continues on the next page)

CHAPTER REVIEW

1 **Start** Access. Locate and open the **a04D_City_Airport** database. **Save** the database in the **Microsoft Access Database** format in your **Access Chapter 4** folder as **Lastname_Firstname_4D_City_Airport**

2 Close the **Navigation Pane**. On the **CREATE tab**, in the **Tables group**, click the **Table Design** button to open an empty table in **Design** view.

a. In the first **Field Name** box, type **Empl ID** and press Tab. On the **Table Tools DESIGN tab**, in the **Tools group**, click the **Primary Key** button. Press F6 to move to the **Field Properties** pane at the bottom of the screen. In the **Field Size** box, type **6** to replace the 255.

b. In the second **Field Name** box, type **Vacation** In the **Data Type** box, click the **arrow**, and then click **Number**. Press Tab to move to the **Description** box. Type **Indicate how many weeks of vacation the employee receives per year** Press Tab or Enter to move to the next field.

c. In the third **Field Name** box, type **Coverage** In the **Data Type** box, click the **arrow**, and from the displayed list of data types, click **Lookup Wizard**. In the first **Lookup Wizard** dialog box, click **I will type in the values that I want** option button, and then click **Next**. Verify the number of columns is **1**. Click in the first row under **Col1**, type **Emp** and then press Tab or ↓ to save the first item. In the next three rows type the following data: **Emp + C** and **Fam** and **None** and then click **Next**. In the final dialog box, click **Finish**.

d. Click in the **Description** box, and type **Indicate the type of insurance coverage the employee has selected**

e. Click in the fourth **Field Name** box, and type **LT Care** Click the **Data Type arrow**, and then click **Number**. Press Tab to move to the **Description** box.

Type **Indicate the benefit period option selected by the employee**

f. Press F6 to move to the **Field Properties** pane at the bottom of the screen, and then click in the **Validation Rule** box. Click the **Build** button. In the upper box of the **Expression Builder** dialog box, type **>=0 and <=2** and then click **OK**. Click in the **Validation Text** box, and then type **Enter a value between 0 and 2** Hold down Alt, and then press PrintScrn.

g. Start **Word 2013**. In a new, blank document, type your first and last names, press Enter, and then type **4D Validation** Press Enter, and then press Ctrl + V. **Save** the document in your **Access Chapter 4** folder as **Lastname_Firstname_4D_Validation** If you are instructed to submit this result, create a paper or electronic printout. **Exit** Word.

h. Click in the fifth **Field Name** box, and type **401K** Click the **Data Type arrow**, and then click **Yes/No**. Press Tab to move to the **Description** box. Type **Indicate whether or not the employee participates in the 401K plan**

i. Save the table as **Lastname Firstname 4D Employee Benefits** Switch to **Datasheet** view and enter the records in the table below.

If you are instructed to submit this result, create a paper or electronic printout of the **4D Employee Benefits** table. If you are to submit your work electronically, follow your instructor's directions. Close the table.

3 In the **Navigation Pane**, under **Tables**, rename the **4D Employees** table by adding your **Lastname Firstname** to the beginning of the table name. Double-click **4D Employees** to open the table. Close the **Navigation Pane**.

a. Switch to **Design** view. Make **Empl ID** the **Primary Key** field. Change the data type for the **Date Hired** field to **Date/Time**. Change the data type for the **Annual Salary** field to **Currency**. Change the data

Empl ID	Vacation	Coverage	LT Care	401K
589734	3	Emp	0	Yes
986458	2	None	1	No
564897	2	Emp + C	2	Yes
233311	4	Fam	1	Yes
722859	2	Fam	2	Yes

(Project 4D City Airport continues on the next page)

type for the **Office E-mail** field to **Hyperlink**. **Save** your work. You will see a message box warning that some data may be lost. Click **Yes** to continue.

b. In the **Dept** field, click in the **Data Type** box, click the **arrow**, and then click **Lookup Wizard**. In the first **Lookup Wizard** dialog box, verify that **I want the lookup field to get the values from another table or query** option button is selected. Click **Next**. Select the **4D Departments** table. Click **Next** to display the third **Lookup Wizard** dialog box. Under **Available Fields**, with **Department** selected, click the **Add Field** button to move the field to the **Selected Fields** box.

c. Click **Next** to display the fourth **Lookup Wizard** dialog box. In the **1** box, click the **arrow**, and then click **Department**. Leave the sort order as **Ascending**. Click **Next** to display the fifth **Lookup Wizard** dialog box. Click **Next** to display the sixth and final **Lookup Wizard** dialog box. Under **What label would you like for your lookup field?**, leave the default of **Dept** and be sure that **Allow Multiple Values** is *not* selected. Click **Finish**. Click **Yes** to save the table.

d. Under **Field Name**, click **Office Phone**. Under **Field Properties**, click in the **Input Mask** box and then click the **Build** button.

e. In the displayed **Input Mask Wizard** dialog box, with **Phone Number** selected, click **Edit List**. In the **Customize Input Mask Wizard** dialog box, click the **New (blank) record** button. In the **Description** box, type **Phone Number with Extension** In the **Input Mask** box, type **!(999) 000-0000 \X999** Click in the **Placeholder** box, and then change _ to # Click in the **Sample Data** box, and type **714 5551234236** In the **Customize Input Mask Wizard** dialog box, click **Close**.

f. Under **Input Mask**, scroll down, click **Phone Number with Extension**, and then click **Next**. Verify that # is displayed as the placeholder character, and then click **Next**. The next wizard screen enables you to decide how you want to store the data. Verify that the **Without the symbols in the mask, like this** option button is selected, and then click **Next**. In the final wizard screen, click **Finish**.

g. Click in the **Date Hired** field. Under **Field Properties**, click in the **Format** box, and then click the **Format arrow**. From the displayed list, click **Medium Date**. Click in the **Required** box. Click the **Required arrow**,

and then click **Yes**. Click in the **Monthly Earn** field. Under **Field Properties**, click in the **Expression** box, and edit the expression to read **[Annual Salary]/12** Click the **Format arrow**, and then select **Currency** from the displayed list.

h. Under **Field Name**, click **State**. Under **Field Properties**, click in the **Format** box, and then type **>** Click in the **Default Value** box, and then type **CA** Using the same technique, set the **Default Value** of the **City** field to **Golden Grove**

i. Under **Field Name**, click **Last Name**. Under **Field Properties**, click in the **Indexed** property box, and then click the displayed **arrow**. Click **Yes (Duplicates OK)**. **Save** your work. In the message box, click **Yes** to test the existing data with the new rules. On the **TABLE TOOLS DESIGN tab**, in the **Show/Hide group**, click the **Indexes** button. Hold down `Alt`, and then press `PrintScrn`.

j. Start **Microsoft Word**. In a new, blank document, type your first and last names, press `Enter`, and then type **4D Indexes** Press `Enter`, and then press `Ctrl` + `V`. **Save** the document in your **Access Chapter 4** folder as **Lastname_Firstname_4D_Indexes** If you are instructed to submit this result, create a paper or electronic printout. **Exit** Word. **Close** the **Indexes** dialog box.

4 Switch to **Datasheet** view, saving changes to the table if necessary.

a. Click the **New (blank) record** button. Type the following data:

Empl ID	543655
Title	Mr.
First Name	Mark
Last Name	Roberts
Street	1320 Woodbriar Court
City	Golden Grove
State	CA
ZIP	96265
Dept	Operations
Date Hired	3/9/2012
Salary	92000
Office Phone	714 555 0167 101
Office E-Mail	mroberts@goldengrove.gov

(Project 4D City Airport continues on the next page)

CHAPTER REVIEW

b. If you are instructed to submit this result, create a paper or electronic printout of the **4D Employees** table in **Landscape** orientation. This table will print on two pages. **Close 4D Employees**. If you are to submit your work electronically, follow your instructor's directions.

5 Open the **Navigation Pane**. **Close** the database, and **Exit** Access.

6 As directed by your instructor, submit your database and the paper or electronic printout of the four objects—two tables and two Word documents—that are the result of this project. Specifically, in this project, using your own name you created the following database and printouts or electronic printouts:

1. Lastname_Firstname_4D_City_Airport	Database file
2. Lastname_Firstname_4D_Validation	Word document (printed or electronic printout)
3. Lastname Firstname 4D Employee Benefits	Table (printed or electronic printout)
4. Lastname_Firstname_4D_Indexes	Word document (printed or electronic printout)
5. Lastname Firstname 4D Employees	Table (printed or electronic printout)

END | You have completed Project 4D

CONTENT-BASED ASSESSMENTS

In the following Mastering Access project, you will manage and modify tables in a database that contains cultural information about the city of Golden Grove. The database will be used by the arts council. Your completed tables and report will look similar to those in Figure 4.53.

Apply 4A skills from these Objectives:

1 Manage Existing Tables
2 Modify Existing Tables
3 Change Data Types
4 Attach Files to Records

PROJECT FILES

For Project 4E, you will need the following files:

a04E_Cultural_Events
a04E_Concert_Flyer
a04E_Quilts_Flyer

You will save your database as:

Lastname_Firstname_4E_Cultural_Events

PROJECT RESULTS

FIGURE 4.53

(Project 4E Cultural Events continues on the next page)

CONTENT-BASED ASSESSMENTS

1 **Start** Access. Locate and open the **a04E_Cultural_ Events** file. **Save** the database in the **Microsoft Access Database** format in your **Access Chapter 4** folder as **Lastname_Firstname_4E_Cultural_Events**

2 Open the **4E Cultural Events** table. From **Backstage** view, click **Save As**. Under **File Types**, double-click **Save Object As**. In the **Save As** dialog box, type **Lastname Firstname 4E Events Schedule** Click **OK**.

3 Make a second copy of the table. Name the table **Lastname Firstname 4E Event Sponsors**

4 Open the **4E Event Sponsors** table in **Datasheet** view. Select the first four columns, the **Event Name** field through the **Cost** field. Press [Delete], and then click **Yes** to delete the fields and data. Switch to **Design** view, and then make the **Org ID** field the **Primary Key** field.

5 Insert a row above the **Members** field, and add a field named **Chamber** with a data type of **Yes/No**. Switch to **Datasheet** view, saving the changes.

6 In **Datasheet** view, click the **Chamber** field to place a checkmark for the **Downtown Merchants Association**, **Quilt Guild**, and **Garden Club of Golden Grove**. If you are instructed to submit this result, create a paper or electronic printout of the **4E Event Sponsors** table in **Landscape** orientation. It will print on two pages. **Close Print Preview** and the table.

7 Open the **4E Events Schedule** table in **Datasheet** view. Close the **Navigation Pane**. Select and delete the following fields: **Civic Name**, **Org Type**, **Members**, **Address**, **City**, **State**, **Postal Code**, **Contact**, and **Phone#**.

8 Using **Find**, find **1876** in the **Event Name** field; in the **Match** field, select Any Part of Field, if necessary. Select and delete the record.

9 In the navigation area at the bottom of the window, search for *k* in the records. When it stops at *Make Golden Grove Beautiful*, delete the word **Make** and the space following the word from the **Event Name**.

10 Switch to **Design** view. Select the **Event Date** field, and drag it up until it is between **Event Name** and **Location**. Add a **Flyer** field at the bottom of the field list using an **Attachment** data type.

11 Switch to **Datasheet** view, saving the changes to the table design. Attach the **a04E_Concert_Flyer** to the *Beachside Singers Holiday Concert* record, and add the **a04E_Quilts_Flyer** to the *Annual Quilt Show* record.

12 On the **HOME tab**, in the **Records group**, click **Spelling**. Make any spelling corrections necessary in the table. If you are instructed to submit this result, create a paper or electronic printout of the **4E Events Schedule** table in **Landscape** orientation. Close the table.

13 **Close** the database, and **Exit** Access.

14 As directed by your instructor, submit your database and the paper or electronic printout of the two tables that are the result of this project. Specifically, in this project, using your own name you created the following database and printouts or electronic printouts:

1. Lastname_Firstname_4E_Cultural_Events	Database file
2. Lastname Firstname 4E Event Sponsors	Table (printed or electronic printout)
3. Lastname Firstname 4E Events Schedule	Table (printed or electronic printout)

END | You have completed Project 4E

CONTENT-BASED ASSESSMENTS

Mastering Access   Project 4F Library System

Dario Soto, city manager, has asked Ron Singer, database manager for the city, to improve the library database. In the following Mastering Access project, you will create a table that stores records about the library programs in Design view, and then modify the properties and customize the fields in the table. You will add features to the database table that will help to reduce data entry errors and that will make data entry easier. Your completed table will look similar to the table shown in Figure 4.54.

PROJECT FILES

For Project 4F, you will need the following file:

a04F_Library_System

You will save your database as:

Lastname_Firstname_4F_Library_System

PROJECT RESULTS

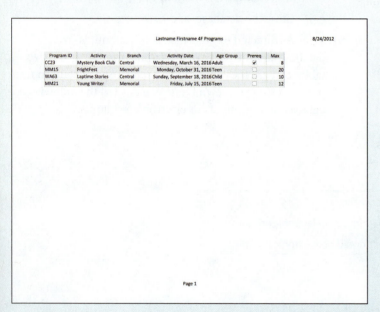

FIGURE 4.54

(Project 4F Library System continues on the next page)

CONTENT-BASED ASSESSMENTS

1 **Start** Access. Locate and open the **a04F_Library_ System** file. **Save** the database in the **Microsoft Access Database** format in your **Access Chapter 4** folder as **Lastname_Firstname_4F_Library_System** Rename the table by adding your **Lastname Firstname** to the beginning of the table name. Close the **Navigation Pane**.

2 Create a table in **Design** view. In the first **Field Name** box, type **Program ID** and set the field as the **Primary Key**. Change the **Field size** to **5**

3 In the second **Field Name** box, type **Activity** In the **Field Properties**, click the **Indexed down arrow**, and then select **Yes (Duplicates OK)**. Make it a **Required** field.

4 In the third **Field Name** box, type **Branch** and select **Lookup Wizard** as the data type. Verify that **I want the lookup field to get the values from another table or query** is selected. Click **Next**. There is only one other table in this database from which to choose—*4F Branches*—and it is selected. Click **Next**. Add **Branch** to the Selected Fields. Click **Next**. In the **1** box, click the **arrow**, and then click **Branch**. Leave the sort order as **Ascending**. Click **Next** two times. Under **What label would you like for your lookup field?**, accept the default of **Branch**, and then verify that **Allow Multiple Values** is *not* selected. Click **Finish**. In the message box, click **Yes**.

5 **Save** the table as **Lastname Firstname 4F Programs**

6 In the fourth **Field Name** box, type **Activity Date** and then select the **Date/Time** data type. Click in the **Format** box, and select **Long Date**.

7 In the fifth **Field Name** box, type **Age Group** Set the **Default Value** to **Teen** In the **Validation Rule** box, type **"Child" OR "Teen" OR "Adult"** For the **Validation Text**, type **Entry must be Child, Teen, or Adult**

8 In the sixth **Field Name** box, type **Prereq** Select the **Yes/No** data type. In the **Description** box, type **Click to indicate a prerequisite is required before enrolling in this activity**

9 In the seventh **Field Name** box, type **Max** and select **Number** data type. Change the **Field Size** to **Integer**. In the **Validation Rule** box, type **<=20** In the **Validation Text** box, type **Participation is limited to 20**

10 Switch to **Datasheet** view, saving the changes to the design. Populate the table with the data shown at the bottom of the page.

11 Adjust the column widths so all data is visible. If you are instructed to submit this result, create a paper or electronic printout of the **4F Programs** table in **Landscape** orientation. **Close** the table, saving the changes. Open the **Navigation Pane**.

12 Open the **4F Branches** table in **Design** view. In the **Postal Code** field, under **Input Mask**, click the **Build** button. If prompted, **Save** the table. From the **Input Mask Wizard**, under **Input Mask**, select **Zip Code**, and then click **Next**. Accept the default "_" as the placeholder character. Click **Next**. Store the data without the symbols in the mask, click **Next**, and then click **Finish**.

13 Switch to **Datasheet** view, saving the changes to the table design. Update the data for each branch.

Central	96265-0001
Memorial	96270-0030
West Side	96268-0010

14 Adjust column widths as needed to display all of the data and field names. **Save** the changes. If you are instructed to submit this result, create a paper or electronic printout of the **4F Branches** table. **Close** the table.

15 **Close** the database, and **Exit** Access.

Program ID	Activity	Branch	Activity Date	Age Group	Prereq	Max
CC23	Mystery Book Club	Central	3/16/16	Adult	Yes	8
MM15	FrightFest	Memorial	10/31/16	Teen	No	20
WA63	Laptime Stories	Central	9/8/16	Child	No	10
MM21	Young Writer	Memorial	7/15/16	Teen	No	12

(Project 4F Library System continues on the next page)

CONTENT-BASED ASSESSMENTS

16 As directed by your instructor, submit your database and the paper or electronic printout of the two tables that are the result of this project.

Specifically, in this project, using your own name you created the following database and printouts or electronic printouts:

1. Lastname_Firstname_4F_Library_System	Database file
2. Lastname Firstname 4F Programs	Table (printed or electronic printout)
3. Lastname Firstname 4F Branches	Table (printed or electronic printout)

END | You have completed Project 4F

CONTENT-BASED ASSESSMENTS

Mastering Access | Project 4G Parks and Recreation

Yvonne Guillen is the chair of the Parks & Recreation Commission for Golden Grove, California. The database she is using has separate tables that should be combined. In the following Mastering Access project, you will combine these tables into a facilities table. You will modify the existing tables, set field properties to ensure more accurate data entry, and add driving directions to the facilities as an attached document. You will also create a table to organize youth sports programs that use the facilities. Your completed work will look similar to Figure 4.55.

Apply 4A and 4B skills from these Objectives:

1. Manage Existing Tables
2. Modify Existing Tables
3. Change Data Types
4. Attach Files to Records
5. Create a Table in Design View
6. Create a Lookup Field
7. Set Field Properties
8. Create Data Validation Rules and Validation Text

PROJECT FILES

For Project 4G, you will need the following files:

a04G_Parks_and_Recreation
a04G_Biscayne_Park
a04G_Hugo_West
One blank Word document

You will save your files as:

Lastname_Firstname_4G_Parks_and_Recreation
Lastname_Firstname_4G_Phone_Properties

PROJECT RESULTS

FIGURE 4.55

(Project 4G Parks and Recreation continues on the next page)

CONTENT-BASED ASSESSMENTS

1 **Start** Access. Locate and open the **a04G_Parks_and_Recreation** file. **Save** the database in the **Microsoft Access Database** format in your **Access Chapter 4** folder as **Lastname_Firstname_4G_Parks_and_Recreation** Rename all tables by adding your **Lastname Firstname** to the beginning of each table name.

2 Select the **4G Community Centers** table. **Copy** and **Paste** the table. Name the table **Lastname Firstname 4G Facilities** In the **Paste Table As** dialog box, verify the **Structure and Data** option is selected. Click **OK**.

3 Select the **4G Parks** table. **Copy** and **Paste** the table. In the **Table Name** box, type **Lastname Firstname 4G Facilities** Under **Paste Options**, select **Append Data to Existing Table**, and then click **OK** to create one table that contains all of the facility information for the Parks & Recreation Department.

4 Open the **4G Facilities** table in **Design** view. Change the data type for the **Entry Fee** field to **Currency**. In the **Contact** field, change the field size to **20**

5 Add a new **Monthly Pass** field between the **Entry Fee** and **Contact** fields, and use a data type of **Calculated**. In the **Expression Builder** dialog box, type **[Entry Fee]*15** Change the **Result Type** to **Currency**.

6 Below the **Phone#** field add a new **Directions** field to the table and assign a data type of **Attachment**. In the description box, type **Directions to facility**

7 Select the **Phone#** field. In the **Input Mask** box, type **!000-0000** Change the field size to **8** Set the **Field Property** of **Required** to **Yes**. Using the Clipboard and Word, submit a printed copy of the **Phone#** Field Properties if you are requested to do so. **Save** the document as **Lastname_Firstname_4G_Phone_Properties** Switch to **Datasheet** view. Save your changes. You will see a message box warning that some data may be lost. Click **Yes** to continue. You will also see a message explaining that data integrity rules have changed, click **No** to testing the data with the new rules.

8 In the **Biscayne Park** record, in the **Attachment** field, double-click, and then from the student data files, attach **a04G_Biscayne_Park**. Click **OK**.

9 Using the same technique, for the **Hugo West Center**, add the directions that are in the **a04G_Hugo_West** file.

10 Create a table in **Design** view. In the first **Field Name** box, type **Sport ID** Select an **AutoNumber** data type. Set this as the primary key.

11 In the second **Field Name** box, type **Sport** In the third **Field Name** box, type **Season** and select a **Lookup Wizard** data type. Type the following four items into the lookup list: **Winter Spring Summer** and **Fall** Save the table as **Lastname Firstname 4G Youth Sports**

12 Switch to **Datasheet** view, and populate the table with the following data.

Sport ID	Sport	Season
1	t-ball	Spring
2	baseball	Summer
3	fast pitch softball	Fall
4	basketball	Winter
5	volleyball	Fall

13 Adjust the column widths as needed to display all of the data and field names.

14 If you are instructed to submit this result, create a paper or electronic printout of the **4G Facilities** table and **4G Youth Sports** table. Be sure that all field names and data display.

15 **Close** the tables, saving changes if necessary. **Close** the database, and **Exit** Access.

16 As directed by your instructor, submit your database and the paper or electronic printout of the three objects—two tables and one Word document—that are the result of this project. Specifically, in this project, using your own name you created the following database and printouts or electronic printouts:

1. Lastname_Firstname_4G_Parks_and_Recreation	Database file
2. Lastname_Firstname_4G_Phone_Properties	Word (printed or electronic printout)
3. Lastname Firstname 4G Facilities	Table (printed or electronic printout)
4. Lastname Firstname 4G Youth Sports	Table (printed or electronic printout)

END | You have completed Project 4G

CONTENT-BASED ASSESSMENTS

GO! Fix It	Project 4H Permit Applications	Online
GO! Make It	Project 4I Medical Centers	Online
GO! Solve It	Project 4J Fire Department	Online
GO! Solve It	Project 4K City Zoo	

Apply a combination of the 4A and 4B skills.

PROJECT FILES

For Project 4K, you will need the following files:

a04K_City_Zoo
a04K_Dragonfly

You will save your database as:

Lastname_Firstname_4K_City_Zoo

From the student files that accompany this textbook, open the a04K_City_Zoo database file, and then save the database in your Access Chapter 4 folder as **Lastname_Firstname_4K_City_Zoo**

Mandi Cartwright, public relations director of Golden Grove, California, and City Manager Dario Soto are meeting with the mayor, Sheila Kehoe, to discuss the funding for the city zoo. The Corporate and Foundation Council provides citizens and corporations with a partnering opportunity to support the city zoo. Mandi has outlined a database to organize the sponsorships.

In this project, you will open the a04K_City_Zoo database and examine the tables. Rename the tables by adding your **Lastname Firstname** to the beginning of each table name. Modify the 4K Sponsored Events table to eliminate redundancy between it and the 4K Sponsors table. Also, change data types to match the data, including a lookup field for the Sponsor field, and apply an applicable input mask to the Event Date. In the 4K Sponsors table, create data validation for sponsor type; it must be Individual, Family, or Corporate. In the 4K Sponsors table, use the 4K Sponsor Levels table as a lookup field. To the 4K Sponsor Levels table, add an attachment field named Logo. Add the a04K_Dragonfly file from the student data files to the appropriate record. If you are instructed to submit this result, create a paper or electronic printout of the tables and the Object Definition report.

(Project 4K City Zoo continues on the next page)

CONTENT-BASED ASSESSMENTS

Performance Element	Exemplary: You consistently applied the relevant skills	Proficient: You sometimes, but not always, applied the relevant skills	Developing: You rarely or never applied the relevant skills
Modify the 4K Sponsored Events table to eliminate redundancy	Table was modified with correct fields in easy-to-follow format.	Table was modified with no more than two missing elements.	Table was modified with more than two missing elements.
Change data types and field properties in the 4K Sponsored Events and 4K Sponsors tables	Data types and field properties were assigned effectively for the data that each field will hold.	Data types and field properties were assigned with no more than two missing or incorrect elements.	Data types and field properties were assigned with more than two missing or incorrect elements.
Add field to 4K Sponsor Levels and populate field	Field was added with correct data type and correct data was added to the table.	Field was added with no more than two missing or incorrect elements.	Field was added with more than two missing or incorrect elements.

END | You have completed Project 4K

OUTCOMES-BASED ASSESSMENTS

RUBRIC

The following outcomes-based assessments are open-ended assessments. That is, there is no specific correct result; your result will depend on your approach to the information provided. Make Professional Quality your goal. Use the following scoring rubric to guide you in how to approach the problem and then to evaluate how well your approach solves the problem.

The *criteria*—Software Mastery, Content, Format and Layout, and Process—represent the knowledge and skills you have gained that you can apply to solving the problem. The *levels of performance*—Professional Quality, Approaching Professional Quality, or Needs Quality Improvements—help you and your instructor evaluate your result.

	Your completed project is of Professional Quality if you:	Your completed project is Approaching Professional Quality if you:	Your completed project Needs Quality Improvements if you:
1-Software Mastery	Choose and apply the most appropriate skills, tools, and features and identify efficient methods to solve the problem.	Choose and apply some appropriate skills, tools, and features, but not in the most efficient manner.	Choose inappropriate skills, tools, or features, or are inefficient in solving the problem.
2-Content	Construct a solution that is clear and well organized, contains content that is accurate, appropriate to the audience and purpose, and is complete. Provide a solution that contains no errors in spelling, grammar, or style.	Construct a solution in which some components are unclear, poorly organized, inconsistent, or incomplete. Misjudge the needs of the audience. Have some errors in spelling, grammar, or style, but the errors do not detract from comprehension.	Construct a solution that is unclear, incomplete, or poorly organized; contains some inaccurate or inappropriate content; and contains many errors in spelling, grammar, or style. Do not solve the problem.
3-Format & Layout	Format and arrange all elements to communicate information and ideas, clarify function, illustrate relationships, and indicate relative importance.	Apply appropriate format and layout features to some elements, but not others. Overuse features, causing minor distraction.	Apply format and layout that does not communicate information or ideas clearly. Do not use format and layout features to clarify function, illustrate relationships, or indicate relative importance. Use available features excessively, causing distraction.
4-Process	Use an organized approach that integrates planning, development, self-assessment, revision, and reflection.	Demonstrate an organized approach in some areas, but not others; or, use an insufficient process of organization throughout.	Do not use an organized approach to solve the problem.

OUTCOMES-BASED ASSESSMENTS

Apply a combination of the 4A and 4B skills.

PROJECT FILES

For Project 4L, you will need the following files:

a04L_Streets_Department
a04L_Work_Order

You will save your database as:

Lastname_Firstname_4L_Streets_Department

In this project, you will examine the database that has been created to help the Deputy City Manager of Infrastructure Services organize and track the constituent work requests for the city street repairs. Save the database as **Lastname_Firstname_4L_Streets_Department** Rename all of the tables by adding your **Lastname_Firstname** to the beginning of each table name. Modify the design of the 4L Work Requests table. Set the Work Order # field as the primary key field, and then create an input mask to match the data for that field in the first record. For the Type field, create a lookup table using the 4L Repair Types table. In the Repair Team field, create a Lookup Wizard data type using the 4L Repair Teams table. In the Priority field, create a validation rule requiring an entry of 1, 2, or 3. Explain this rule with appropriate validation text. Add a long text field called Description between Type and Repair Team. Open a04L_Work_Order, and then use the data to add information to the first record in the table. Use today's date as the start date. Add an attachment field to the table, and then add a04L_Work_Order as the attachment. If you are instructed to submit this result, create a paper or electronic printout of the 4L Work Requests table.

END | You have completed Project 4L

GO! Think   Project 4M Police Department   **Online**

You and GO!   Project 4N Club Directory   **Online**

Enhancing Queries

GO! to Work
Video A5

5
ACCESS 2013

PROJECT 5A

OUTCOMES
Create special-purpose queries.

OBJECTIVES

1. Create Calculated Fields in a Query
2. Use Aggregate Functions in a Query
3. Create a Crosstab Query
4. Find Duplicate and Unmatched Records
5. Create a Parameter Query

PROJECT 5B

OUTCOMES
Create action queries and modify join types.

OBJECTIVES

6. Create a Make Table Query
7. Create an Append Query
8. Create a Delete Query
9. Create an Update Query
10. Modify the Join Type

Carlos Caetano/Fotolia

In This Chapter

Queries can do more than extract data from tables and other queries. You can create queries to perform special functions, such as calculate and summarize numeric data. Queries can also be used to find duplicate and unmatched records in tables, which is useful for maintaining data integrity. You can create a parameter query, where an individual is prompted for the criteria each time the query is run, for more flexibility in the data extracted. Queries can create additional tables in the database, append records to an existing table, delete records from a table, and modify data in the tables based on specific criteria.

S-Boards, Inc., a snowboard and surf shop, combines the expertise and favorite sports of two friends after they graduated from college. Gina Pollard and Steven Michaels grew up in the sun of Southern California, but they also spent time in the mountain snow. The store carries top brands of men's and women's apparel, goggles and sunglasses, boards and gear. The surfboard selection includes both classic boards and the latest high-tech boards. Snowboarding gear can be purchased in packages or customized for the most experienced boarders. Pollard and Michaels are proud to serve Southern California's board enthusiasts.

PROJECT ACTIVITIES

In Activities 5.01 through 5.10, you will help Miles Gorden, purchasing manager of S-Boards, Inc. Surf and Snowboard Shop, create special-purpose queries to calculate data, summarize and group data, display data in a spreadsheet-like format, and find duplicate and unmatched records. You will also create a query that prompts individuals to enter the criteria. Your completed queries will look similar to Figure 5.1.

PROJECT FILES

For Project 5A, you will need the following file:

a05A_Store_Inventory

You will save your database as:

Lastname_Firstname_5A_Store_Inventory

PROJECT RESULTS

FIGURE 5.1 Project 5A Store Inventory

Video A5-1

Queries can be used to create a *calculated field*—a field that obtains its data by performing a calculation or computation, using a formula. For example, to determine the profit that will be made from the sale of an item, subtract the cost of the item from the sale price of the item. Another example is to create a calculated field that computes the gross pay for an employee. There are two steps needed to produce a calculated field in a query. First, in the design grid of the query, in a blank column, type the name of the field that will store the results of the calculated field—the name must be followed by a colon (:). Second, type the *expression*—the formula—that will perform the calculation. *Each field name* used in the expression must be enclosed within *its own pair* of square brackets, []. If you are using a number in the expression—for example, a decimal—type only the decimal; do not enclose it in brackets.

Activity 5.01 | Creating a Calculated Field Based on Two Existing Fields

In this activity, you will create a calculated field to determine the profit for each item in the inventory database.

1 **Start** Access. Navigate to the location where the student data files for this textbook are saved. Locate and open the **a05A_Store_Inventory** file. Display **Backstage** view. Click **Save As**, and then, under *File Types*, double-click **Save Database As**. In the **Save As** dialog box, navigate to the drive on which you will be saving your folders and projects for this chapter. Create a new folder named **Access Chapter 5** and then save the file as **Lastname_Firstname_5A_Store_Inventory** in the folder.

2 If necessary, enable the content or add the Access Chapter 5 folder to the Trust Center. In the **Navigation Pane**, rename each table by adding your **Lastname Firstname** to the beginning of each table name. Resize the **Navigation Pane** so all table names are visible.

3 In the **Navigation Pane**, double-click **5A Inventory**. If the Field List pane opens, close it. Take a moment to study the fields in the table.

> Snowboarding items have a catalog number beginning with 8; surfing items have a catalog number beginning with 9. The Category field is a Lookup column. If you click in the Category field, and then click the arrow, a list of category numbers and their descriptions display. The Supplier field identifies the supplier numbers. Cost is the price the company pays to a supplier for each item. Selling Price is what the company will charge its customers for each item. On Hand refers to the current inventory for each item.

4 Switch to **Design** view, and then take a moment to study the data structure. Notice the Category field has a data type of Number; this reflects the autonumber field (ID field) in the Category table used in the Lookup field. When you are finished, **Close** ☒ the table, and then **Close** ☒ the **Navigation Pane**.

5 On the Ribbon, click the **CREATE tab**. In the **Queries group**, click the **Query Design** button. In the **Show Table** dialog box, double-click **5A Inventory** to add the table to the Query design workspace, and then click **Close**. Resize the list so the table name and all fields are visible.

> If you add the wrong table to the workspace or have two copies of the same table, right-click the extra table, and click Remove Table.

 BY TOUCH   To resize the file list, touch the file list with two or more fingers and then stretch your fingers apart to zoom out.

6 From the **5A Inventory** field list, add the following fields, in the order specified, to the design grid: **Catalog#**, **Item**, **Cost**, and **Selling Price**.

Recall that you can double-click a field name to add it to the design grid, or you can drag the field name to the field box on the design grid. You can also click in the field box, click the arrow, and click the field name from the displayed list.

7 On the **QUERY TOOLS DESIGN tab**, in the **Results group**, click the **Run** button to display the four fields used in the query, and then compare your screen with Figure 5.2.

FIGURE 5.2

8 Switch to **Design** view. In the **Field row**, right-click in the first empty column—the fifth column—to display a shortcut menu, and then click **Zoom**. *Arithmetic operators* are mathematical symbols used to build expressions in calculated fields. Take a moment to study the arithmetic operators as described in Figure 5.3.

FIGURE 5.3

ARITHMETIC OPERATORS			
OPERATOR	**DESCRIPTION**	**EXAMPLE**	**RESULT**
+	Addition	Cost:[Price]+[Tax]	Adds the value in the Price field to the value in the Tax field and displays the result in the Cost field.
−	Subtraction	Cost:[Price]-[Markdown]	Subtracts the value in the Markdown field from the value in the Price field and displays the result in the Cost field.
*	Multiplication	Tax:[Price]*.05	Multiplies the value in the Price field by .05 (5%) and displays the result in the Tax field. (Note: This is an asterisk, not an x.)
/	Division	Average:[Total]/3	Divides the value in the Total field by 3 and displays the result in the Average field.
^	Exponentiation	Required:2^[Bits]	Raises 2 to the power of the value in the Bits field and stores the result in the Required field.
\	Integer division	Average:[Children]\[Families]	Divides the value in the Children field by the value in the Families field and displays the integer portion—the digits to the left of the decimal point—in the Average field.

9 In the **Zoom** dialog box, type **Per Item Profit:[Selling Price]-[Cost]** and then compare your screen with Figure 5.4.

The first element of the calculated field—Per Item Profit—is the new field name that will display the calculated value. The field name must be unique for the table being used in the query. Following the new field name is a colon (:). A colon in a calculated field separates the new field name from the expression. Selling Price is enclosed in square brackets because it is an existing field name in the 5A Inventory table and contains data that will be used in the calculation. Following [Selling Price] is a hyphen (-), which, in math calculations, signifies subtraction. Finally, Cost, an existing field in the 5A Inventory table, is enclosed in square brackets. This field also contains data that will be used in the calculation.

FIGURE 5.4

NOTE | **Using Square Brackets Around Field Names in Expressions**

Square brackets are not required around a field name in an expression if the field name is only one word. For example, if the field name is Cost, it is not necessary to type brackets around it—Access will automatically insert the square brackets. If a field name has a space in it, however, you must type the square brackets around the field name. Otherwise, Access will display a message stating that the expression you entered contains invalid syntax.

---

10 In the **Zoom** dialog box, click **OK**, and then **Run** the query. Adjust the column width of the *Per Item Profit* field to display the entire field name, and then compare your screen with Figure 5.5.

A fifth column—the calculated field—with a field name of Per Item Profit displays. For each record, the value in the Per Item Profit field is calculated by subtracting the value in the Cost field from the value in the Selling Price field.

FIGURE 5.5

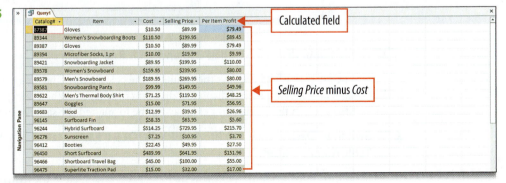

11 On the **tab row**, right-click the **Query1 tab**, and then click **Save** 🖫. In the **Save As** dialog box, under **Query Name**, type **Lastname Firstname 5A Per Item Profit** and then click **OK**. View the query in **Print Preview**, ensuring that the query prints on one page; if you are instructed to submit this result, create a paper or electronic printout. **Close** Print Preview. **Close** ✕ the query.

Activity 5.02 | Creating a Calculated Field Based on One Existing Field and a Number

In this activity, you will calculate the sale prices of each surfboarding item for the annual sale. During this event, all surfboarding supplies are discounted by 15 percent.

1 On the Ribbon, click the **CREATE tab**. In the **Queries group**, click the **Query Design** button. Add the **5A Inventory** table to the Query design workspace, and then **Close** the **Show Table** dialog box. Resize the field list.

2 From the **5A Inventory** field list, add the following fields, in the order specified, to the design grid: **Catalog#**, **Item**, and **Selling Price**.

3 In the **Field row**, right-click in the field cell in the first empty column—the fourth column—to display a shortcut menu, and then click **Zoom**. In the **Zoom** dialog box, type **Discount:[Selling Price]*.15** and then compare your screen with Figure 5.6.

The value in the Discount field is calculated by multiplying the value in the Selling Price field by .15—15%. Recall that only field names are enclosed in square brackets.

FIGURE 5.6

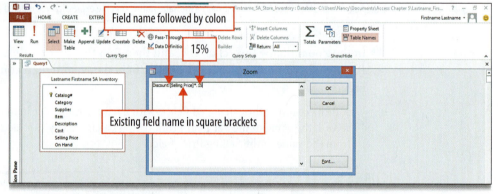

4 In the **Zoom** dialog box, click **OK**, and then **Run** the query.

The Discount field displays the results of the calculation. The data is not formatted with a dollar sign, and the first record displays a discount of 13.4985. When using a number in an expression, the values in the calculated field may not be formatted the same as in the existing field.

5 Switch to **Design** view. On the **QUERY TOOLS DESIGN tab**, in the **Show/Hide group**, click the **Table Names** button.

In the design grid, the Table row no longer displays. If all of the fields in the design grid are from one table, you can hide the Table row. The Table Names button is a toggle button; if you click it again, the Table row displays in the design grid.

6 Click in the **Field row**, in the **Discount** field box. On the **QUERY TOOLS DESIGN tab**, in the **Show/Hide group**, click the **Property Sheet** button. Alternatively, right-click in the field box and click Properties, or hold down [Alt] and press [Enter].

The Property Sheet for the selected field—Discount—displays on the right side of the screen. In the Property Sheet, under the title of Property Sheet, is the subtitle—Selection type: Field Properties.

ALERT! **Does the Property Sheet Display a Subtitle of Selection Type: Query Properties?**

To display the Property Sheet for a field, you must first click in the field; otherwise, the Property Sheet for the query might display. If this occurs, in the Field row, click the Discount field box to change the Property Sheet to this field.

7 In the **Property Sheet**, on the **General tab**, click in the **Format** box, and then click the displayed **arrow**. Compare your screen with Figure 5.7.

FIGURE 5.7

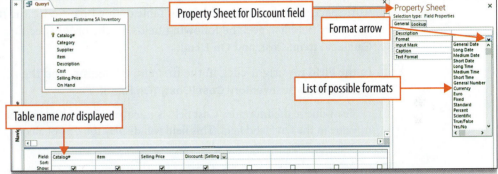

8 From the list of formats, click **Currency**. On the **Property Sheet** title bar, click the **Close** button. **Run** the query to display the results.

The values in the Discount field now display with a dollar sign, and the first record's discount—$13.50—displays with two decimal places.

9 Switch to **Design** view. In the **Field row**, right-click in the first empty column, and then click **Zoom**. In the **Zoom** dialog box, type **Sale Price:[Selling Price]-[Discount]** and then click **OK**. **Run** the query to display the results.

The Sale Price for Catalog #87387, Gloves, is $76.49. The value in the Sale Price field is calculated by subtracting the value in the Discount field from the value in the Selling Price field. The field names are not case sensitive—you can type a field name in lower case, such as [selling price]. Because you used only existing fields in the expression that were formatted as currency, the values in the Sale Price field are formatted as currency.

10 Switch to **Design** view. In the design grid, click in the **Criteria row** under **Catalog#**, type **9*** and then press [Enter].

Recall that the asterisk (*) is a wildcard. With the criteria, Access will extract those records where the catalog number begins with 9 followed by one or more characters. Also, recall that Access formats the criteria. For example, you typed 9*, and Access formatted the criteria as Like "9*".

11 **Run** the query. Notice that only the records with a **Catalog#** beginning with a **9** display—surfboarding items.

12 **Save** 🖫 the query as **Lastname Firstname 5A Surfboarding Sale** View the query in **Print Preview**, ensuring that the query prints on one page. If you are instructed to submit this result, create a paper or electronic printout. **Close** Print Preview. **Close** ⟦×⟧ the query.

Video A5-2

In Access queries, you can use **aggregate functions** to perform a calculation on a column of data and return a single value. Examples are the Sum function, which adds a column of numbers, and the Average function, which adds a column of numbers and divides by the number of records with values, ignoring null values. Access provides two ways to use aggregate functions in a query— you can add a total row in Datasheet view or create a totals query in Design view.

Activity 5.03 | Adding a Total Row to a Query

In this activity, you will create and run a query. In Datasheet view, you will add a Total row to insert an aggregate function in one or more columns without having to change the design of the query.

1 Create a new query in **Query Design**. Add the **5A Inventory** table to the Query design workspace, and then **Close** the **Show Table** dialog box. Resize the field list. From the **5A Inventory** field list, add the following fields, in the order specified, to the design grid: **Catalog#**, **Item**, **Cost**, and **On Hand**.

2 In the **Field row**, right-click in the first empty column, and then click **Zoom**. In the **Zoom** dialog box, type **Inventory Cost:[Cost]*[On Hand]**

The value in the Inventory Cost field is calculated by multiplying the value in the Cost field by the value in the On Hand field. This field will display the cost of all of the inventory items, not just the cost per item.

3 In the **Zoom** dialog box, click **OK**, and then **Run** the query to display the results in **Datasheet** view. Adjust the column width of the **Inventory Cost** field to display the entire field name, and then compare your screen with Figure 5.8.

If the *Inventory Cost* for Catalog #87387, Gloves, is not $525.00, switch to Design view and edit the expression you entered for the calculated field.

FIGURE 5.8

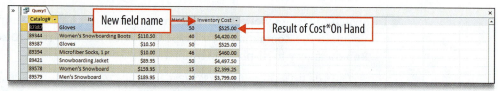

4 On the **HOME tab**, in the **Records group**, click the **Totals** button. If necessary, scroll down until the newly created Total row displays. In the **Total row** under **Inventory Cost**, click in the empty box to display an arrow at the left edge. Click the **arrow**, and then compare your screen with Figure 5.9. Take a moment to study the aggregate functions that can be used with both the **Total row** and the design grid, as described in the table in Figure 5.10.

The Total row displays after the New record row. The first field in a Total row contains the word Total. The Total row is not a record. The list of aggregate functions displayed will vary depending on the data type for each field or column; for example, number types display a full list of functions, whereas a text field will display only the Count function.

FIGURE 5.9

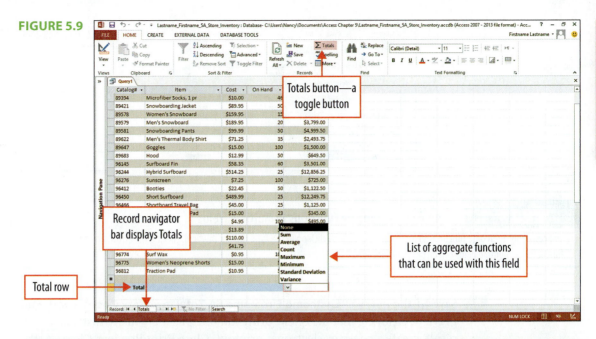

Totals button—a toggle button

Record navigator bar displays Totals

Total row

List of aggregate functions that can be used with this field

FIGURE 5.10

AGGREGATE FUNCTIONS		
FUNCTION	**DESCRIPTION**	**CAN BE USED WITH DATA TYPE(S)**
Sum	Adds the values in a column.	Currency, Decimal, Number
Average	Calculates the average value for a column, ignoring null values.	Currency, Date/Time, Decimal, Number
Count	Counts the number of items in a column, ignoring null values.	All data types, except complex repeating scalar data, such as a column of multivalued lists
Maximum	Displays the item with the highest value. Can be used with text data only in Design view. With text data, the highest value is *Z*. Case and null values are ignored.	Currency, Date/Time, Decimal, Number, Text
Minimum	Displays the item with the lowest value. Can be used with text data only in Design view. For text data, the lowest value is *A*. Case and null values are ignored.	Currency, Date/Time, Decimal, Number, Text
Standard Deviation	Measures how widely values are dispersed from the mean value.	Currency, Decimal, Number
Variance	Measures the statistical variance of all values in the column. If the table has less than two rows, a null value is displayed.	Currency, Decimal, Number

5 From the displayed list, click **Sum**, and then compare your screen with Figure 5.11.

A sum of $67,186.25 displays, which is the total of all the data in the Total Cost On Hand field.

FIGURE 5.11

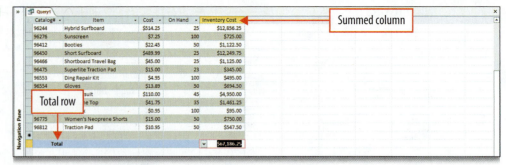

Catalog#	Item	Cost	On Hand	Inventory Cost
96244	Hybrid Surfboard	$514.25	25	$12,856.25
96276	Sunscreen	$7.25	100	$725.00
96412	Booties	$22.45	50	$1,122.50
96450	Short Surfboard	$489.99	25	$12,249.75
96466	Shortboard Travel Bag	$45.00	25	$1,125.00
96475	Superlite Traction Pad	$15.00	23	$345.00
96553	Ding Repair Kit	$4.95	100	$495.00
96554	Gloves	$13.89	50	$694.50
	suit	$110.00	45	$4,950.00
	e Top	$41.75	35	$1,461.25
		$0.95	100	$95.00
96775	Women's Neoprene Shorts	$15.00	50	$750.00
96812	Traction Pad	$10.95	50	$547.50
Total				$67,186.25

Summed column — Total row

> **N O T E** Applying Aggregate Functions to Multiple Fields
>
> You can apply aggregate functions to more than one field by clicking in the Total row for the field, clicking the arrow, and then clicking the function. The functions for multiple fields can be different functions.

6 ▸ Save the query as **Lastname Firstname 5A Total Inventory Cost** View the query in **Print Preview**, ensuring that the query prints on one page; if you are instructed to submit this result, create a paper or electronic printout. **Close** Print Preview. **Close** × the query.

> *More* **Knowledge** Removing the Aggregate Function and Removing the Total Row
>
> To remove an aggregate function from a column, on the Total row under the field, click the arrow and then click None. To remove the Total row, on the HOME tab, in the Records group, click the Totals button. You cannot cut or delete a Total row; you can only turn it on or off. You can copy a Total row and paste it into another file—for example, an Excel worksheet or a Word document.

Activity 5.04 | Creating a Totals Query

In this activity, you will create a *totals query*—a query that calculates subtotals across groups of records. For example, to subtotal the number of inventory items by suppliers, use a totals query to group the records by the supplier and then apply an aggregate function to the On Hand field. In the previous activity, you created a Total row, which applied an aggregate function to one column—field—of data. A totals query is used when you need to apply an aggregate function to some or all of the records in a query. A totals query can then be used as a source for another database object, such as a report.

1 ▸ Create a new query in **Query Design**. Add the **5A Suppliers** table and the **5A Inventory** table to the Query design workspace, and then **Close** the **Show Table** dialog box. Resize both field lists. Notice that there is a one-to-many relationship between the tables—*one* supplier can supply *many* items. From the **5A Inventory** field list, add **On Hand** to the first field box in the design grid.

2 ▸ On the **QUERY TOOLS DESIGN tab**, in the **Show/Hide group**, click the **Totals** button.

Like the Totals button on the HOME tab, this button is a toggle button. In the design grid, a Total row displays under the Table row, and Group By displays in the box.

3 ▸ In the design grid, click in the **Total row** under **On Hand** to display the arrow. Click the **arrow**, and then compare your screen with Figure 5.12.

A list of aggregate functions displays. This list displays more functions than the list in Datasheet view, and the function names are abbreviated.

FIGURE 5.12

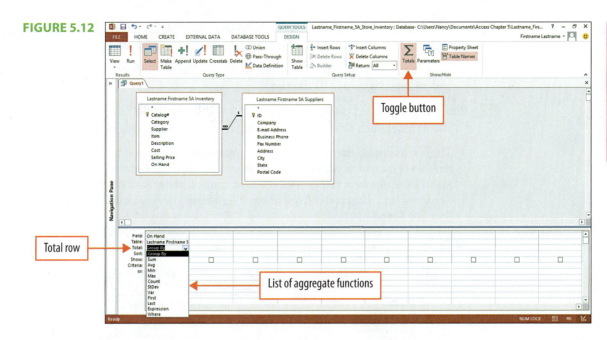

Toggle button

Total row

List of aggregate functions

4 From the displayed list, click **Sum**. **Run** the query, and then adjust the width of the column to display the entire field name. Compare your screen with Figure 5.13.

When you run a totals query, the result—*1244*—of the aggregate function is displayed; the records are not displayed. The name of the function and the field used are displayed in the column heading.

FIGURE 5.13

Field name displays the function used—Sum

Only the sum is displayed in the totals query

More Knowledge   **Changing the Name of the Totals Query Result**

To change the name from the combination aggregate function and field name to something more concise and descriptive, in Design view, in the Field row, click in the On Hand field box. On the DESIGN tab, in the Show/Hide group, click the Property Sheet button. In the Property Sheet, on the General tab, click in the Caption box, and type the new name for the result.

---

5 Switch to **Design** view. In the **5A Inventory** field list, double-click **Item** to insert the field in the second column in the design grid. In the design grid, click in the **Total row** under **Item**, click the displayed **arrow**, and then click **Count**. **Run** the query. Adjust the width of the second column to display the entire field name.

The number of records—25—displays. You can include multiple fields in a totals query, but each field in the query must have an aggregate function applied to it. If you include a field but do not apply an aggregate function, the query results will display every record and will not display a single value for the field or fields. The exception to this is when you group records by a category, such as supplier name.

6 Switch to **Design** view. From the **5A Suppliers** field list, drag **Company** to the design grid until the field is on top of **On Hand** and then release the mouse button.

Company is inserted as the first field, and the On Hand field moves to the right. In the Total row under Company, Group By displays.

7 **Run** the query. If necessary, adjust column widths to display all of the field names and all of the data under each field, and then compare your screen with Figure 5.14.

The results display the total number of inventory items on hand from each supplier and the number of individual items purchased from each supplier. By using this type of query, you can identify the suppliers that provide the most individual items—Bob's Sporting Shop and Wetsuit Country—and the supplier from whom the company has the most on-hand inventory items—Bob's Sporting Shop.

FIGURE 5.14

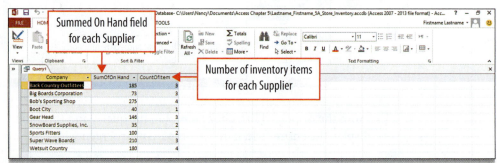

8 **Save** 💾 the query as **Lastname Firstname 5A Inventory By Supplier** View the query in **Print Preview**, ensuring that the query prints on one page. If you are instructed to submit this result, create a paper or electronic printout. **Close** Print Preview. **Close** ✕ the query.

Objective 3   Create a Crosstab Query

Video A5-3

A ***crosstab query*** uses an aggregate function for data that is grouped by two types of information and displays the data in a compact, spreadsheet-like format. A crosstab query always has at least one row heading, one column heading, and one summary field. Use a crosstab query to summarize a large amount of data in a small space that is easy to read.

Activity 5.05 │ Creating a Select Query as the Source for a Crosstab Query

In this activity, you will create a select query displaying suppliers, the category of the inventory item, the inventory item, and the number on hand. Recall that a select query is the most common type of query, and it extracts data from one or more tables or queries, displaying the results in a datasheet. After creating the select query, you will use it to create a crosstab query to display the data in a format that is easier to analyze. Because most crosstab queries extract data from more than one table or query, it is best to create a select query containing all of the fields necessary for the crosstab query.

1 Create a new query in **Query Design**. Add the following tables to the Query design workspace: **5A Category**, **5A Inventory**, and **5A Suppliers**. In the **Show Table** dialog box, click **Close**. Resize the field lists.

2 In the **5A Suppliers** field list, double-click **Company** to add it to the first field box in the design grid. In the **5A Category** field list, double-click **CatName** to add it to the second field box in the design grid. In the **5A Inventory** field list, double-click **On Hand** to add it to the third field box in the design grid. In the design grid, click in the **Sort** box under **Company**. Click the **arrow**, and then click **Ascending**. Sort the **CatName** field in **Ascending** order.

3 On the **DESIGN tab**, in the **Show/Hide group**, click the **Totals** button. Click in the **Total row** under **On Hand**, click the **arrow**, and then click **Sum**. Compare your screen with Figure 5.15.

FIGURE 5.15

Three fields added to design grid

First two fields sorted

Aggregate function—sums On Hand field

4 **Run** the query. In the datasheet, adjust all column widths to display the entire field name and the data for each record, and then compare your screen with Figure 5.16.

The select query groups the totals vertically by company and then by category.

FIGURE 5.16

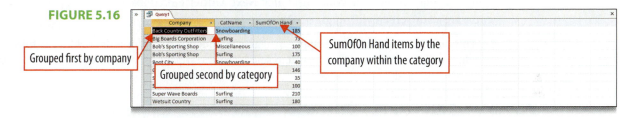

Grouped first by company

Grouped second by category

SumOfOn Hand items by the company within the category

5 Switch to **Design** view. On the **DESIGN tab**, in the **Show/Hide group**, click the **Totals** button to remove the **Total row** from the design grid.

This select query will be used to create the crosstab query. When you create a crosstab query, you will be prompted to use an aggregate function on a field, so it should not be summed prior to creating the query.

6 Save 🖫 the query as **Lastname Firstname 5A On Hand Per Company and Category** and then Close ⌧ the query.

Activity 5.06 | Creating a Crosstab Query

In this activity, you will create a crosstab query using the 5A Cost Per Company and Category query as the source for the crosstab query.

1 On the Ribbon, click the **CREATE tab**. In the **Queries group**, click the **Query Wizard** button. In the **New Query** dialog box, click **Crosstab Query Wizard**, and then click **OK**.

In the first Crosstab Query Wizard dialog box, you select the table or query to be used as the source for the crosstab query.

2 In the middle of the dialog box, under **View**, click the **Queries** option button. In the list of queries, click **Query: 5A On Hand Per Company and Category**, and then click **Next**.

In the second Crosstab Query Wizard dialog box, you select the fields with data that you want to use as the row headings.

3 Under **Available Fields**, double-click **Company**, and then compare your screen with Figure 5.17.

Company displays under Selected Fields. At the bottom of the dialog box, in the Sample area, a preview of the row headings displays. Each company name will be listed on a separate row in the first column.

FIGURE 5.17

4 In the **Crosstab Query Wizard** dialog box, click **Next**.

In the third dialog box, you select the fields with data that you want to use as column headings.

5 In the displayed list of fields, **CatName** is selected; notice in the sample area that the category names display in separate columns. Click **Next**. Under **Functions**, click **Sum**, and then compare your screen with Figure 5.18.

This dialog box enables you to apply an aggregate function to one or more fields. The function will add the number on hand for every item sold by each company for each category. Every row can also be summed.

FIGURE 5.18

6 On the left side of the **Crosstab Query Wizard** dialog box, above the **Sample** area, clear the **Yes, include row sums** check box, and then click **Next**.

If the check box is selected, a column will be inserted between the first and second column that sums all of the numeric data per row.

7 Under **What do you want to name your query?**, select the existing text, type **Lastname Firstname 5A Crosstab Query** and then click **Finish**. Adjust all of the column widths to display the entire field name and the data in each field, and then compare your screen with Figure 5.19. Then take a moment to compare this screen with Figure 5.16, the select query you created with the same extracted data.

The same data is extracted using the select query as shown in Figure 5.16; however, the crosstab query displays the data differently. A crosstab query reduces the number of records displayed as shown by the entry for Bob's Sporting Shop. In the select query, there are two records displayed, one for the Miscellaneous category and one for the Surfing category. The crosstab query combines the data into one record.

FIGURE 5.19

Categories—column headings

Company—row headings

On Hand summed per company, per category

NOTE | **Including Row Sums**

If you include row sums in a crosstab query, the sum will display in a column following the column for the row headings. In this activity, the row sums column would display following the Company column. For Bob's Sporting Shop, the row sum would be 275—100 plus 175.

---

8 View the query in **Print Preview**, ensuring that the query prints on one page. If you are instructed to submit this result, create a paper or electronic printout. **Close** Print Preview. **Close** ☒ the query, saving changes—you adjusted the column widths.

Objective 4 Find Duplicate and Unmatched Records

Video A5-4

Even when a table contains a primary key, it is still possible to have duplicate records in a table. For example, the same inventory item can be entered with different catalog numbers. You can use the **Find Duplicates Query** Wizard to locate duplicate records in a table. As databases grow, you may have records in one table that have no matching records in a related table; these are **unmatched records**. For example, there may be a record for a supplier in the Suppliers table, but no inventory items are ordered from that supplier. You can use the **Find Unmatched Query** Wizard to locate unmatched records.

Activity 5.07 | Finding Duplicate Records

In this activity, you will find duplicate records in the *5A Inventory* table by using the Find Duplicates Query Wizard.

1 On the **CREATE tab**, in the **Queries group**, click the **Query Wizard** button. In the **New Query** dialog box, click **Find Duplicates Query Wizard**, and then click **OK**.

2 In the first **Find Duplicates Query Wizard** dialog box, in the list of tables, click **Table: 5A Inventory**, and then click **Next**.

The second dialog box displays, enabling you to select the field or fields that may contain duplicate data. If you select all of the fields, then every field must contain the same data, which cannot be the case for a primary key field.

3 Under **Available fields**, double-click **Item** to move it under **Duplicate-value fields**, and then click **Next**.

The third dialog box displays, enabling you to select one or more fields that will help you distinguish duplicate from nonduplicate records.

4 Under **Available fields**, add the following fields, in the order specified, to the **Additional query fields** box: **Catalog#**, **Category**, **Supplier**, **Cost**, and **Selling Price**. Compare your screen with Figure 5.20.

FIGURE 5.20

5 Click **Next**. Click **Finish** to accept the suggested query name—*Find duplicates for Lastname Firstname 5A Inventory*—and then compare your screen with Figure 5.21.

Three records display with a duplicate value in the *Item* field. Using the displayed fields, you can determine that the second and third records are duplicates; the *Catalog#* was entered incorrectly for one of the records. By examining the *5A Inventory* table, you can determine that Category 1 is Snowboarding and Category 2 is Surfing. You must exercise care when using the Find Duplicates Query Wizard. If you do not include additional fields to help determine whether the records are duplicates or not, you might mistakenly determine that they are duplicates.

FIGURE 5.21

6 Adjust all column widths, as needed. View the query in **Print Preview**, ensuring that the query prints on one page. If you are instructed to submit this result, create a paper or electronic printout. **Close** ⊠ the query, saving changes.

Normally, you would delete the duplicate record, but your instructor needs to verify that you have found the duplicate record by using a query.

More Knowledge | **Removing Duplicate Records**

If you choose to delete duplicate records, you must first deal with existing table relationships. If the record you want to delete exists in the table on the *many* side of the relationship, you can delete the record without taking additional steps. If the record exists in the table on the *one* side of the relationship, you must first delete the relationship, and then delete the record. You should then re-create the relationship between the tables. You can either manually delete the duplicate records or create a delete query to remove the duplicate records.

Activity 5.08 | Finding Unmatched Records

In this activity, you will find unmatched records in related tables—*5A Suppliers* and *5A Inventory*—by using the Find Unmatched Query Wizard.

1 On the **CREATE tab**, in the **Queries group**, click the **Query Wizard** button. In the **New Query** dialog box, click **Find Unmatched Query Wizard**, and then click **OK**.

2 In the first **Find Unmatched Query Wizard** dialog box, in the list of tables, click **Table: 5A Suppliers**, and then click **Next**.

The second dialog box displays, enabling you to select the related table or query that you would like Access to compare to the first table to find unmatched records.

3 In the list of tables, click **Table: 5A Inventory**, and then click **Next**.

The third dialog box displays, enabling you to select the matching fields in each table.

4 Under **Fields in '5A Suppliers'**, if necessary, click ID. Under **Fields in '5A Inventory'**, if necessary, click **Supplier**. Between the two fields columns, click the button that displays <=>. Click **Next**.

At the bottom of the dialog box, Access displays the matching fields of ID and Supplier.

5 Under **Available fields**, double-click **ID**, and then double-click **Company** to move the field names under **Selected fields**. Notice that these fields will display in the query results, and then compare your screen with Figure 5.22.

FIGURE 5.22

Find Unmatched Query Wizard dialog box

Common field in 5A Inventory table

Additional field displayed in results

6 Click **Next**. In the last dialog box, under **What would you like to name your query?**, type **Lastname Firstname 5A Find Unmatched Query** and then click **Finish**. Compare your screen with Figure 5.23.

The query results display one company—*Cold Sports Club*—that has no inventory items in the *5A Inventory* table. Normally, you would either delete the Cold Sports Club record from the *5A Suppliers* table or add inventory items in the related *5A Inventory* for the Cold Sports Club, but your instructor needs to verify that you have located an unmatched record by using a query.

FIGURE 5.23

Supplier with no inventory items

7 Adjust all column widths. View the query in **Print Preview**, ensuring that the query prints on one page. If you are instructed to submit this result, create a paper or electronic printout. **Close** Print Preview. **Close** ☒ the query, saving changes.

More Knowledge | **Finding Unmatched Records in a Table with Multivalued Fields**

You cannot use the Find Unmatched Query Wizard with a table that has *multivalued fields*—fields that appear to hold multiple values. If your table contains multivalued fields, you must first create a query, extracting all of the fields except the multivalued fields, and then create the query to find unmatched records.

Video A5-5

A *parameter query* prompts you for criteria before running the query. For example, if you had a database of snowboarding events, you might need to find all of the snowboarding events in a particular state. You can create a select query for a state, but when you need to find information about snowboarding events in another state, you must open the original select query in Design view, change the criteria, and then run the query again. With a parameter query, you can create one query—Access will prompt you to enter the state and then display the results based upon the criteria you enter in the dialog box.

Activity 5.09 | Creating a Parameter Query Using One Criterion

In this activity, you will create a parameter query to display a specific category of inventory items. You can enter a parameter anywhere you use text, number, or date criteria.

1 **Open** » the **Navigation Pane**. Under **Tables**, double-click **5A Inventory** to open the table in **Datasheet** view. In any record, click in the **Category** field, and then click the **arrow** to display the list of categories. Take a moment to study the four categories used in this table. Be sure you do not change the category for the selected record. **Close** × the table, and **Close** « the **Navigation Pane**.

2 Create a new query in **Query Design**. Add the **5A Category** table, the **5A Inventory** table, and the **5A Suppliers** table to the Query design workspace, and then **Close** the **Show Table** dialog box. Resize the field lists. From the **5A Category** field list, add **CatName** to the first column in the design grid. From the **5A Inventory** field list, add **Catalog#** and **Item** to the second and third columns in the design grid. From the **5A Suppliers** field list, add **Company** to the fourth column in the design grid.

3 In the **Criteria row** under **CatName**, type **[Enter a Category]** and then compare your screen with Figure 5.24.

The brackets indicate a *parameter*—a value that can be changed—rather than specific criteria. When you run the query, a dialog box will display, prompting you to *Enter a Category*. The category you type will be set as the criteria for the query. Because you are prompted for the criteria, you can reuse this query without resetting the criteria in Design view.

FIGURE 5.24

Parameter entered in Criteria row

4 **Run** the query. In the **Enter Parameter Value** dialog box, type **Surfing** and then compare your screen with Figure 5.25.

FIGURE 5.25

Type *Surfing* as the criteria—spell it correctly

A L E R T !   **Does Your Screen Differ?**

If the Enter Parameter Value dialog box does not display, you may have typed the parameter incorrectly in the design grid. Common errors include using parentheses or curly braces instead of square brackets around the parameter text, causing Access to interpret the text as specific criteria. If you use parentheses, when you run the query, there are no records displayed. If you use curly braces, the query will not run. To correct, display the query in Design view, and then correct the parameter entered in the criteria row.

---

5   In the **Enter Parameter Value** dialog box, click **OK**.

Thirteen records display where the CatName field is Surfing.

6   Adjust column widths, if necessary, and **Save** 🔲 the query as **Lastname Firstname 5A Category Parameter Query Close** ✕ the query, and then **Open** » the **Navigation Pane**.

7   In the **Navigation Pane**, under **Queries**, double-click **5A Category Parameter Query**. In the **Enter Parameter Value** dialog box, type **Snowboarding** and then click **OK**.

Eleven items categorized as Snowboarding display. Recall that when you open a query, Access runs the query so that the most up-to-date data is extracted from the underlying table or query. When you have entered a parameter as the criteria, you will be prompted to enter the criteria every time you open the query.

8   Switch to **Design** view. Notice that the parameter—[**Enter a Category**]—is stored with the query. Access does not store the criteria entered in the **Enter Parameter Value** dialog box.

9   **Run** the query, and in the **Enter Parameter Value** dialog box, type **Miscellaneous** being careful to spell it correctly. Click **OK** to display one record. Adjust all column widths.

10   View the query in **Print Preview**, ensuring that the query prints on one page. If you are instructed to submit this result, create a paper or electronic printout. **Close** Print Preview. **Close** ✕ the query, saving changes, and then **Close** « the **Navigation Pane**.

More **Knowledge**   **Parameter Query Prompts**

When you enter the parameter in the criteria row, make sure that the prompt—the text enclosed in the square brackets—is not the same as the field name. For example, if the field name is Category, do not enter [Category] as the parameter. Because Access uses field names in square brackets for calculations, no prompt will display. If you want to use the field name by itself as a prompt, type a question mark at the end of the prompt; for example, [Category?]. You cannot use a period, exclamation mark (!), square brackets ([ ]), or the ampersand (&) as part of the prompt.

Activity 5.10 | Creating a Parameter Query Using Multiple Criteria

In this activity, you will create a parameter query to display the inventory items that fall within a certain range in the On Hand field.

1   Create a new query in **Query Design**. Add the **5A Suppliers** table and the **5A Inventory** table to the Query design workspace, and then **Close** the **Show Table** dialog box. Resize the field lists. From the **5A Inventory** field list, add **Item** and **On Hand** to the first and second columns in the design grid. From the **5A Suppliers** field list box, add **Company** to the third column in the design grid.

2 In the **Criteria row**, right-click in the **On Hand** field, and then click **Zoom**. In the **Zoom** dialog box, type **Between [Enter the lower On Hand number] and [Enter the higher On Hand number]** and then compare your screen with Figure 5.26.

> The Zoom dialog box enables you to see the entire parameter. The parameter includes *Between* and *And*, which will display a range of data. Two dialog boxes will display when you run the query. You will be prompted first to enter the lower number and then the higher number.

FIGURE 5.26

3 After verifying that you have entered the correct parameter, in the **Zoom** dialog box, click **OK**, and then **Run** the query. In the first **Enter Parameter Value** dialog box, type **10** and then click **OK**. In the second **Enter Parameter Value** dialog box, type **25** and then click **OK**. Compare your screen with Figure 5.27.

> Six records have On Hand items in the range of 10 to 25. These might be inventory items that need to be ordered soon.

FIGURE 5.27

More Knowledge   **Creating a Parameter Query Using Multiple Criteria**

When you create a query using more than one field with parameters, the individual sees the prompts in the order that the fields are arranged from left to right in the design grid. When you create a query using more than one parameter in a single field, the individual sees the prompts in the order displayed, from left to right, in the Criteria box.

    If you want the prompts to display in a different order, on the DESIGN tab, in the Show/Hide group, click the Parameters button. In the Parameter column, type the prompt for each parameter exactly as it was typed in the design grid. Enter the parameters in the order you want the dialog boxes to display when the query is run. In the Data Type column, next to each entered parameter, specify the data type by clicking the arrow and displaying the list of data types. Click OK, and then run the query.

---

4 Adjust all column widths, and **Save** 💾 the query as **Lastname Firstname 5A On Hand Parameter Query**

5 View the query in **Print Preview**, ensuring that the query prints on one page. If you are instructed to submit this result, create a paper or electronic printout. **Close** Print Preview. **Close** ⊠ the query.

6 **Open** » the **Navigation Pane**. **Close** the database, and **Exit** ⊠ Access.

7 As directed by your instructor, submit your database and the paper or electronic printouts of the nine queries that are the result of this project. Specifically, in this project, using your own name you created the following database and printouts or electronic printouts:

1. Lastname_Firstname_5A_Store_Inventory	Database file
2. Lastname Firstname 5A Per Item Profit	Query (printed or electronic printout)
3. Lastname Firstname 5A Surfboarding Sale	Query (printed or electronic printout)
4. Lastname Firstname 5A Total Inventory Cost	Query (printed or electronic printout)
5. Lastname Firstname 5A Inventory by Supplier	Query (printed or electronic printout)
6. Lastname Firstname 5A Crosstab Query	Query (printed or electronic printout)
7. Find duplicates for Lastname Firstname 5A Inventory	Query (printed or electronic printout)
8. Lastname Firstname 5A Find Unmatched Query	Query (printed or electronic printout)
9. Lastname Firstname 5A Category Parameter Query	Query (printed or electronic printout)
10. Lastname Firstname 5A On Hand Parameter Query	Query (printed or electronic printout)

END | You have completed Project 5A

Customer Orders

PROJECT ACTIVITIES

In Activities 5.11 through 5.19, you will help Miko Adai, sales associate for S-Boards, Inc. Surf and Snowboard Shop, keep the tables in the database up-to-date and ensure that the queries display pertinent information. You will create action queries that will create a new table, update records in a table, append records to a table, and delete records from a table. You will also modify the join type of relationships to display different subsets of the data when the query is run. Your completed queries will look similar to Figure 5.28.

PROJECT FILES

For Project 5B, you will need the following files:

a05B_Customer_Orders
a05B_Potential_Customers

You will save your databases as:

Lastname_Firstname_5B_Customer_Orders
Lastname_Firstname_5B_Potential_Customers

PROJECT RESULTS

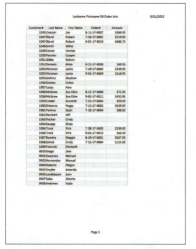

FIGURE 5.28 Project 5B Customer Orders

Video A5-6

An *action query* enables you to create a new table or change data in an existing table. A *make table query* is an action query that creates a new table by extracting data from one or more tables. Creating a new table from existing tables is useful when you need to copy or back up data. For example, you may wish to create a table that displays the orders for the past month. You can extract that data and store it in another table, using the new table as a source for reports or queries. Extracting data and storing it in a new table reduces the time to retrieve *static data*—data that does not change—and creates a convenient backup of the data.

Activity 5.11 | Creating a Select Query

In this activity, you will create a select query to extract the fields you wish to store in the new table.

1 **Start** Access. Navigate to the location where the student data files for this textbook are saved. Locate and open the **a05B_Customer_Orders** file. **Save** the database in your **Access Chapter 5** folder as **Lastname_Firstname_5B_Customer_Orders**

2 If you did not add the **Access Chapter 5** folder to the Trust Center, enable the content. In the **Navigation Pane**, under **Tables**, rename the four tables by adding **Lastname Firstname** to the beginning of each table name. Resize the **Navigation Pane** so all table names are visible. Take a moment to open each table and observe the data in each. In the **5B Orders** table, make a note of the data type for the **Order#** field and the pattern of data entered in the field. When you are finished, close all of the tables, and **Close** ⏴ the **Navigation Pane**.

In the *5B Orders* table, the first record contains an Order# of 7-11-17-0002. The first section of the order number is the month of the order, the second section is the day of the month, and the third section is the year. The fourth section is a sequential number. Records with orders for July, August, and September are contained in this table.

> **ALERT!** **Action Queries and Trusted Databases**
>
> To run an action query, the database must reside in a trusted location, or you must enable the content. If you try running an action query and nothing happens, check the status bar for the following message: *This action or event has been blocked by Disabled Mode.* Either add the storage location to Trusted Locations or enable the content. Then, run the query again.

3 Create a new query in **Query Design**. From the **Show Table** dialog box, add the following tables to the Query design workspace: **5B Customers**, **5B Orders**, and **5B Shippers**. **Close** the **Show Table** dialog box, and then resize the field lists. Notice the relationships between the tables.

The *5B Customers* table has a one-to-many relationship with the *5B Orders* table—*one* customer can have *many* orders. The *5B Shippers* table has a one-to-many relationship with the *5B Orders* table—*one* shipper can ship *more* than one order.

4 From the **5B Orders** field list, add **Order#** to the first column of the design grid. From the **5B Customers** field list, add **Last Name** and **First Name** to the second and third columns of the design grid. From the **5B Shippers** field list, add **Shipping Company** to the fourth column of the design grid.

5 In the design grid, click in the **Criteria row** under **Order#**, type **9*** and then compare your screen with Figure 5.29.

> Recall that the asterisk is a wildcard that stands for one or more characters—Access will extract the records where the Order# starts with a 9, and it does not matter what the following characters are. The first section of the Order# contains the month the order was placed without any regard for the year; all September orders will display whether they were placed in 2016, 2017, or any other year. You do not need criteria in a select query to convert it to a make table query.

FIGURE 5.29

N O T E   **Using Expressions and Aggregate Functions in a Make Table Query**

In addition to using criteria in a select query upon which a make table query is based, you can use expressions to create a calculated field; for example, *Gross Pay:[Hourly Wage]*[Hours Worked]*. You can also use aggregate functions; for example, you may want to sum the *Hours Worked* field.

---

6 **Run** the query, and notice that four orders were placed in September.

> The select query displays the records that will be stored in the new table.

Activity 5.12 | Converting a Select Query to a Make Table Query

In this activity, you will convert the select query you just created to a make table query.

1 Switch to **Design** view. On the **QUERY TOOLS DESIGN tab**, in the **Query Type group**, click the **Make Table** button. Notice the exclamation point (!) in several of the buttons in the Query Type group—these are action queries. In the **Make Table** dialog box, in the **Table Name** box, type **Lastname Firstname 5B September Orders** and then compare your screen with Figure 5.30.

> The table name should be a unique table name for the database in which the table will be saved. If it is not, you will be prompted to delete the first table before the new table can be created. You can save a make table query in the current database or in another existing database.

FIGURE 5.30

2 In the **Make Table** dialog box, be sure that **Current Database** is selected, and then click **OK**. **Run** the query.

> A message displays indicating that *You are about to paste 4 row(s) into a new table* and that you cannot use the Undo command.

3 In the displayed message box, click **Yes**. **Close** ☒ the query, click **Yes** in the message box prompting you to save changes, and then name the query **Lastname Firstname 5B Make Table Query**

4 **Open** ⟩⟩ the **Navigation Pane**. Notice that under **Tables**, the new table you created—**5B September Orders**—is displayed. Under **Queries**, the **5B Make Table Query** is displayed.

5 In the **Navigation Pane**, click the title—**All Access Objects**. Under **Navigate To Category**, click **Tables and Related Views**, widen the **Navigation Pane**, and then compare your screen with Figure 5.31.

> The Navigation Pane is grouped by tables and related objects. Because the 5B Make Table Query extracted records from three tables—*5B Customers*, *5B Orders*, and *5B Shippers*—it is displayed under all three tables. Changing the grouping in the Navigation Pane to Tables and Related Views enables you to easily determine which objects are dependent upon other objects in the database.

FIGURE 5.31

6 In the **Navigation Pane**, double-click **5B September Orders** to open the table in **Datasheet** view.

> If you click the category title instead of the table, the category will close—if that happens, double-click the category title to redisplay the table, and then double-click the table.

7 Switch to **Design** view. Notice that the **Order#** field does not have an input mask associated with it and that there is no **Primary Key** field for this table.

> When using a make table query to create a new table, the data in the new table does not inherit the field properties or the Primary Key field setting from the original table.

8 Switch to **Datasheet** view, and then adjust all column widths. **Close** ☒ the table, saving changes.

NOTE	Updating a Table Created with a Make Table Query

The data stored in a table created with a make table query is not automatically updated when records in the original tables are modified. To keep the new table up-to-date, you must run the make table query periodically to be sure the information is current.

Objective 7 Create an Append Query

Video A5-7

An ***append query*** is an action query that adds new records to an existing table by adding data from another Access database or from a table in the same database. An append query can be limited by criteria. Use an append query when the data already exists and you do not want to manually enter it into an existing table. Like the make table query, you first create a select query and then convert it to an append query.

Activity 5.13 | Creating an Append Query for a Table in the Current Database

In this activity, you will create a select query to extract the records for customers who have placed orders in August and then append the records to the *5B September Orders* table.

1 **Close** « the **Navigation Pane**. Create a new query in **Query Design**. From the **Show Table** dialog box, add the following tables to the Query design workspace: **5B Customers**, **5B Orders**, and **5B Shippers**. **Close** the **Show Table** dialog box, and then resize the field lists.

2 From the **5B Customers** field list, add **First Name** and **Last Name**, in the order specified, to the first and second columns of the design grid. From the **5B Orders** field list, add **Order#** and **Shipping Cost**, in the order specified, to the third and fourth columns of the design grid. From the **5B Shippers** field list, add **Shipping Company** to the fifth column of the design grid.

3 In the design grid, click in the **Criteria row** under **Order#**, type **8*** and then press ↓. Compare your screen with Figure 5.32.

FIGURE 5.32

4 **Run** the query, and notice that four customers placed orders in August.

5 Switch to **Design** view. On the **QUERY TOOLS DESIGN tab**, in the **Query Type group**, click the **Append** button. In the **Append** dialog box, click the **Table Name arrow**, and from the displayed list, click **5B September Orders**, and then click **OK**. Compare your screen with Figure 5.33.

In the design grid, Access inserts an *Append To* row above the Criteria row. Access compares the fields in the query with the fields in the ***destination table***—the table to which you are appending the fields—and attempts to match fields. If a match is found, Access adds the name of the destination field to the Append To row in the query. If no match is found, Access leaves the destination field blank. You can click the box in the Append To row and select a destination field.

FIGURE 5.33

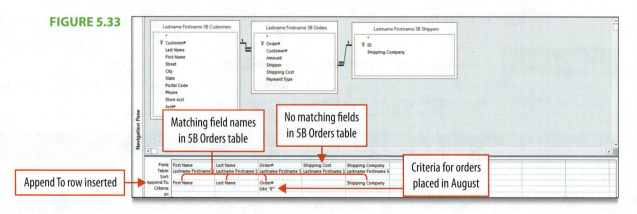

6 **Run** the query. In the displayed message box, click **Yes** to append the four rows to the *5B September Orders* table.

7 ▸ **Close** ☒ the query, and then save it as **Lastname Firstname 5B Append August Orders**

8 ▸ **Open** ⏵ the **Navigation Pane**. Notice that **5B Append August Orders** displays under the three tables from which data was extracted.

9 ▸ In the **Navigation Pane**, click the title—**All Tables**. Under **Navigate To Category**, click **Object Type** to group the **Navigation Pane** objects by type. Under **Queries**, notice the icon that displays for **5B Append August Orders**. Recall that this icon indicates the query is an action query.

10 ▸ Under **Tables**, double-click **5B September Orders** to open the table in **Datasheet** view, and then compare your screen with Figure 5.34.

> Four orders for August are appended to the *5B September Orders* table. Because there is no match in the *5B September Orders* table for the Shipping Cost field in the 5B Append August Orders query, the field is ignored when the records are appended.

FIGURE 5.34

11 ▸ **Close** ☒ the table. In the **Navigation Pane**, under **Tables**, right-click **5B September Orders**, and then click **Rename**. **Rename** the table as **Lastname Firstname 5B August & September Orders**

12 ▸ With **5B August & September Orders** selected, display **Backstage** view and view the table in **Print Preview**. If you are instructed to submit this result, create a paper or electronic printout of the table, and then **Close** the **Print Preview** window.

Activity 5.14 | Creating an Append Query for a Table in Another Database

Miko Adai recently discovered that the marketing manager has been keeping a database of persons who have requested information about the S-Boards, Inc. Surf and Snowboard Shop. These names need to be added to the *5B Customers* table so those potential clients can receive catalogs when they are distributed. In this activity, you will create an append query to add the records from the marketing manager's table to the *5B Customers* table.

1 ▸ On the Access window title bar, click the **Minimize** 🔲 button. Display the **Start screen**, and then open **Access**. Navigate to the location where the student data files for this textbook are saved. Locate and open the **a05B_Potential_Customers** file. **Save** the database in your **Access Chapter 5** folder as **Lastname_Firstname_5B_Potential_Customers**

🔁 **BY TOUCH**   To display the Start screen, always swipe in from the right and tap Start. To scroll, slide your finger to the left to scroll to the right.

2 If you did not add the **Access Chapter 5** folder to the Trust Center, enable the content. In the **Navigation Pane**, under **Tables**, rename the table by adding **Lastname Firstname** to the beginning of **5B Potential Customers**. Take a moment to open the table, noticing the fields and field names. When you are finished, **Close** ⊠ the table, and **Close** « the **Navigation Pane**.

> The *5B Potential Customers* table in this database contains similar fields to the *5B Customers* table in the 5B_Customer_Orders database.

3 Create a new query in **Query Design**. From the **Show Table** dialog box, add the **5B Potential Customers** table to the Query design workspace, and then **Close** the **Show Table** dialog box. Resize the field list.

4 In the **5B Potential Customers** field list, click **Customer#**, hold down Shift, and then click **Phone** to select all of the fields. Drag the selection down into the first column of the design grid.

> Although you could click the asterisk (*) in the field list to add all of the fields to the design grid, it is easier to detect which fields have no match in the destination table when the field names are listed individually in the design grid.

5 On the **QUERY TOOLS DESIGN tab**, in the **Query Type group**, click the **Append** button. In the **Append** dialog box, click the **Another Database** option button, and then click the **Browse** button. Navigate to your **Access Chapter 5** folder, and then double-click **5B Customer Orders**.

> The 5B Customer Orders database contains the destination table.

6 In the **Append** dialog box, click the **Table Name arrow**, click **5B Customers**, and then compare your screen with Figure 5.35.

> Once you select the name of another database, the tables contained in that database display.

FIGURE 5.35

7 Click **OK**. In the design grid, notice that in the **Append To row**, Access found field name matches for all fields, except **LName** and **FName**.

8 In the design grid, click in the **Append To row** under **LName**, click the **arrow**, and then compare your screen with Figure 5.36.

> A list displays the field names contained in the *5B Customers* table. If the field names are not exactly the same in the source and destination tables, Access will not designate them as matched fields. A *source table* is the table from which records are being extracted.

FIGURE 5.36

9 From the displayed list, click **Last Name**. Click in the **Append To** row under **FName**, and then click the **arrow**. In the displayed list, click **First Name**.

10 Save 💾 the query as **Lastname Firstname 5B Append to 5B Customers** and then **Run** the query, clicking **Yes** to append 9 rows. **Close** ✕ the query, and then **Open** » the **Navigation Pane**. **Close** the database, and then **Exit** ❎ this instance of Access.

ALERT!   **To Trust or Not to Trust? That Is the Question!**

When you allow someone else to run an action query that will modify a table in your database, be sure that you can trust that individual. One mistake in the action query could destroy your table. A better way of running an action query that is dependent upon someone else's table is to obtain a copy of the table, place it in a database that you have created, and examine the table for malicious code. Once you are satisfied that the table is safe, you can create the action query to modify the data in your tables. Be sure to make a backup copy of the destination database before running action queries.

---

11 If necessary, on the taskbar, click the button for your 5B_Customer_Orders database. If you mistakenly closed the 5B_Customer_Orders database, reopen it. In the **Navigation Pane**, under **Tables**, double-click **5B Customers** to open the table in **Datasheet** view. **Close** « the **Navigation Pane**. Scroll down until **Customer# 9908** is displayed, and then compare your screen with Figure 5.37.

The last nine records—Customer#s 9900 through 9908—have been appended to the *5B Customers* table. The last two fields—Store Acct and Acct#—are blank because there were no corresponding fields in the *5B Potential Customers* table.

FIGURE 5.37

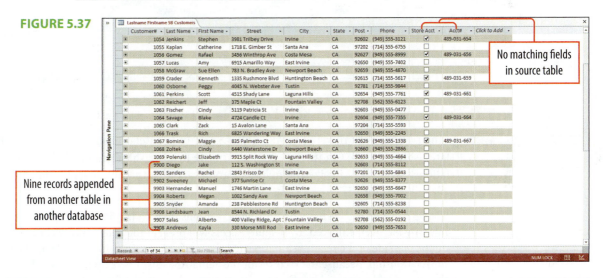

More Knowledge   **Running the Same Append Query a Second Time**

If you run the same append query a second time with the same records in the source table and no primary key field is involved in the appending of records, you will have duplicate records in the destination table. If a primary key field is part of the records being duplicated, a message will display stating that Access cannot append all of the records due to one of several rule violations. If new records were added to the source table that were not originally appended to the destination table, clicking Yes in the message dialog box will enable those records to be added without adding duplicate records.

Objective 8   Create a Delete Query

Video A5-8

A **delete query** is an action query that removes records from an existing table in the same database. When information becomes outdated or is no longer needed, the records should be deleted from your database. Recall that one method you can use to find unnecessary records is to create a find unmatched query. Assuming outdated records have common criteria, you can create a select query, convert it to a delete query, and then delete all of the records at one time rather than deleting the records one by one. Use delete queries only when you need to remove many records quickly. Before running a delete query, you should back up the database because you cannot undo the deletion.

Activity 5.15 | Creating a Delete Query

A competing store has opened in Santa Ana, and the former customers living in that city have decided to do business with that store. In this activity, you will create a select query and then convert it to a delete query to remove records for clients living in Santa Ana.

1 With the **5B Customers** table open in **Datasheet** view, under **City**, click in any row. On the **HOME tab**, in the **Sort & Filter group**, click the **Descending** button to arrange the cities in descending alphabetical order.

2 At the top of the datasheet, in the record for **Customer# 1060**, click the **plus (+) sign** to display the subdatasheet. Notice that this customer has placed one order that has been shipped.

3 Display the subdatasheets for the four customers residing in Santa Ana, and then compare your screen with Figure 5.38.

The four customers residing in Santa Ana have not placed orders.

FIGURE 5.38

4 Collapse all of the subdatasheets by clicking each **minus (–) sign**.

5 On the ribbon, click the **DATABASE TOOLS tab**. In the **Relationships group**, click the **Relationships** button. On the **DESIGN tab**, in the **Relationships group**, click the **All Relationships** button. Resize the field lists and rearrange the field lists to match the layout displayed in Figure 5.39.

The *5B Customers* table has a one-to-many relationship with the *5B Orders* table, and referential integrity has been enforced. By default, Access will prevent the deletion of records from the table on the *one* side of the relationship if related records are contained in the table on the *many* side of the relationship. Because the records for the Santa Ana customers do not have related records in the related table, you will be able to delete the records from the *5B Customers* table, which is on the *one* side of the relationship.

To delete records from the table on the *one* side of the relationship that have related records in the table on the *many* side of the relationship, you must either delete the relationship or enable Cascade Delete Related Records. If you need to delete records on the *many* side of the relationship, you can do so without changing or deleting the relationship.

FIGURE 5.39

6 ▶ On the **tab row**, right-click any tab, and then click **Close All**, saving changes to the table and to the layout of the **Relationships** window.

7 ▶ Create a new query in **Query Design**. Add the **5B Customers** table to the Query design workspace, and then **Close** the **Show Table** dialog box. Resize the field list. From the field list, add **Customer#** and **City**, in the order specified, to the first and second columns in the design grid.

> Since you are deleting existing records based on criteria, you need to add only the field that has criteria attached to it—the City field. However, it is easier to analyze the results if you include another field in the design grid.

8 ▶ In the design grid, click in the **Criteria** row under **City**, type **Santa Ana** and then press ⬇.

> Access inserts the criteria in quotation marks because this is a Text field.

9 ▶ **Run** the query, and then compare your screen with Figure 5.40.

> Four records for customers in Santa Ana are displayed. If your query results display an empty record, switch to Design view and be sure that you typed the criteria correctly.

FIGURE 5.40

10 ▶ Switch to **Design** view. In the Query design workspace, to the right of the field list, right-click in the empty space. From the displayed shortcut menu, point to **Query Type**, and click **Delete Query**. Compare your screen with Figure 5.41. Alternatively, on the QUERY TOOLS DESIGN tab, in the Query Type group, click the Delete button.

> In the design grid, a Delete row is inserted above the Criteria row with the word *Where* in both columns. Access will delete all records *Where* the City is Santa Ana. If you include all of the fields in the query using the asterisk (*), Access inserts the word *From* in the Delete row, and all of the records will be deleted.

FIGURE 5.41

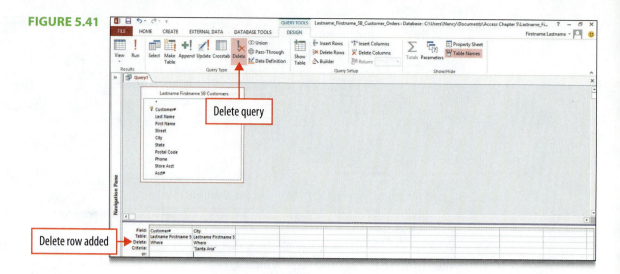

Delete row added

11 Save 💾 the query as **Lastname Firstname 5B Delete Santa Ana Customers** and then **Run** the query. In the message box stating that *You are about to delete 4 row(s) from the specified table*, click **Yes**.

12 Close ✕ the query, and then **Open** 》 the **Navigation Pane**. Under **Queries**, notice the icon that is associated with a delete query—**5B Delete Santa Ana Customers**. Under **Tables**, open the **5B Customers** table in **Datasheet** view. Notice that the records are still in descending order by the **City** field, and notice that the four records for customers living in **Santa Ana** have been deleted from the table.

13 Close 《 the **Navigation Pane**, leaving the table open for the next activity. On the **HOME tab**, in the **Sort & Filter group**, click the **Remove Sort** button to clear all sorts from the **City** field.

Objective 9 Create an Update Query

Video A5-9

An ***update query*** is an action query that is used to add, change, or delete data in fields of one or more existing records. Combined with criteria, an update query is an efficient way to change data for a large number of records at one time, and you can change records in more than one table at a time. If you need to change data in a few records, you can use the Find and Replace dialog box. You are unable to use update queries to add or delete records in a table; use an append query or delete query as needed. Because you are changing data with an update query, you should back up your database before running one.

Activity 5.16 | Creating an Update Query

The postal codes are changing for all of the customers living in Irvine or East Irvine to a consolidated postal code. In this activity, you will create a select query to extract the records from the *5B Customers* table for customers living in these cities and then convert the query to an update query so that you change the postal codes for all of the records at one time.

1 With the **5B Customers** table open in **Datasheet** view, click in the **City** field in any row. Sort the **City** field in **Ascending** order. Notice that there are five customers living in East Irvine with postal codes of 92650 and five customers living in Irvine with postal codes of 92602, 92603, and 92604.

2 Close ✕ the table, saving changes. Create a new query in **Query Design**. Add the **5B Customers** table to the Query design workspace, and then close the **Show Table** dialog box. Resize the field list.

3 In the **5B Customers** field list, double-click **City** to add the field to the first column of the design grid. Then add the **Postal Code** field to the second column of the design grid. In the design grid, click in the **Criteria row** under **City**, and then type **Irvine or East Irvine** Alternatively, type **Irvine** in the Criteria row, and then type **East Irvine** in the Or row. **Run** the query.

> Ten records display for the cities of Irvine or East Irvine. If your screen does not display ten records, switch to Design view and be sure you typed the criteria correctly. Then run the query again.

4 Switch to **Design** view, and then notice how Access changed the criteria under the **City** field, placing quotation marks around the text and capitalizing *or*. On the **QUERY TOOLS DESIGN tab**, in the **Query Type group**, click the **Update** button.

> In the design grid, an Update To row is inserted above the Criteria row.

5 In the design grid, click in the **Update To** row under **Postal Code**, type **92601** and then compare your screen with Figure 5.42.

FIGURE 5.42

6 Save 💾 the query as **Lastname Firstname 5B Update Postal Codes** and then **Run** the query. In the message box stating that *You are about to update 10 row(s)*, click **Yes**.

7 Close ✕ the query, and then **Open** » the **Navigation Pane**. Under **Queries**, notice the icon that is associated with an update query—**5B Update Postal Codes**. Under **Tables**, open the **5B Customers** table in **Datasheet** view. Notice that the 10 records for customers living in **East Irvine** and **Irvine** have **Postal** codes of **92601**.

8 View the table in **Print Preview**. Change the orientation to **Landscape**, and, if necessary, change the margins to ensure that the table prints on one page. If you are instructed to submit this result, create a paper or electronic printout, and then **Close** the **Print Preview** window. **Close** ✕ the table.

Activity 5.17 | Creating an Update Query with an Expression

There was a computer problem, and customers were overcharged for items shipped by FedEx. In this activity, you will create an update query to correct the field to reflect an accurate shipping cost. Any item shipped by FedEx will be discounted 7 percent.

1 ▶ Open the **5B Orders** table in **Datasheet** view, and **Close** `«` the **Navigation Pane**. Click the right side of the **Shipper** field to see the lookup list. Notice an entry of **1** means the order was shipped using FedEx. Press `Esc` to return to the field box. Sort the **Shipper** field from **Smallest to Largest**. Notice that there are five orders that were shipped using FedEx. Make note of the shipping cost for each of those items.

2 ▶ **Close** `×` the table, saving changes. Create a new query in **Query Design**. From the **Show Table** dialog box, add the **5B Shippers** table and the **5B Orders** table to the Query design workspace, and then **Close** the **Show Table** dialog box. Resize the field lists.

3 ▶ From the **5B Shippers** field list, add **Shipping Company** to the design grid. From the **5B Orders** field list, add **Shipping Cost** to the design grid. In the **Criteria row** under **Shipping Company**, type **FedEx Run** the query.

> Five records display for FedEx. If your screen does not display five records, switch to Design view and be sure you typed the criteria correctly. Then run the query again.

4 ▶ Switch to **Design** view. On the **QUERY TOOLS DESIGN tab**, in the **Query Type group**, click the **Update** button.

> In the design grid, an Update To row is inserted above the Criteria row.

5 ▶ In the design grid, under **Shipping Cost**, click in the **Update To row**, type **[Shipping Cost]*.93** and then compare your screen with Figure 5.43.

> Recall that square brackets surround existing fields in an expression, and numbers do not include any brackets. This expression will reduce the current shipping cost by 7%, so the customers will pay 93% of the original cost. Currency, Date/Time, and Number fields can be updated using an expression. For example, a selling price field can be increased by 15% by keying [selling price]*1.15 in the Update To box, and an invoice due date can be extended by 3 days by keying [invoice date]+3 in the Update To box.

FIGURE 5.43

Criteria for records to be updated

Expression to update shipping cost

6 ▶ **Save** 🖫 the query as **Lastname Firstname 5B Update FedEx Shipping Costs** and then **Run** the query. In the message box stating that *You are about to update 5 row(s)*, click **Yes**.

> The update query runs every time the query is opened, unless it is opened directly in Design view. To review or modify the query, right-click the query name, and then click Design view.

7 ▶ **Close** `×` the query, and then **Open** `»` the **Navigation Pane**. Under **Tables**, open the **5B Orders** table in **Datasheet** view. Notice that the five records for orders shipped FedEx have lower shipping costs than they did prior to running the query, 93 percent of the original cost.

8 ▶ View the table in **Print Preview**. If you are instructed to submit this result, create a paper or electronic printout and then **Close** the **Print Preview** window. **Close** `×` the **5B Orders** table.

More Knowledge | **Restrictions for Update Queries**

It is not possible to run an update query with these types of table fields:

- Calculated fields, created in a table or in a query
- Fields that use total queries or crosstab queries as their source
- AutoNumber fields, which can change only when you add a record to a table
- Fields in union queries
- Fields in unique-values or unique-records queries
- Primary key fields that are common fields in table relationships, unless you set Cascade Update Related Fields

You cannot cascade updates for tables that use a data type of AutoNumber to generate the primary key field.

Objective 10 Modify the Join Type

Video A5-10

When multiple tables are included in a query, a *join* helps you extract the correct records from the related tables. The relationship between the tables, based upon common fields, is represented in a query by a join, which is displayed as the join line between the related tables. When you add tables to the Query design workspace, Access creates the joins based on the defined relationships. If you add queries to the Query design workspace or tables where the relationship has not been defined, you can manually create joins between the objects by dragging a common field from one object to the common field in the second. Joins establish rules about records to be included in the query results and combine the data from multiple sources on one record row in the query results.

Activity 5.18 | Viewing the Results of a Query Using an Inner Join

The default join type is the *inner join*, which is the most common type of join. When a query with an inner join is run, only the records where the common field exists in both related tables are displayed in the query results. All of the queries you have previously run have used an inner join. In this activity, you will view the results of a query that uses an inner join.

1 Close ⫷ the **Navigation Pane**. On the Ribbon, click the **DATABASE TOOLS tab**, and then in the **Relationships group** click the **Relationships** button. Notice the relationship between the **5B Customers** table and the **5B Orders** table.

Because referential integrity has been enforced, it is easy to determine that the *5B Customers* table is on the *one* side of the relationship, and the *5B Orders* table is on the *many* side of the relationship. *One* customer can have *many* orders. The common field is Customer#.

2 In the **Relationships** window, double-click the **join line** between the **5B Customers** table and the **5B Orders** table. Alternatively, right-click the join line, and then click Edit Relationship, or click the line, and then in the Tools group, click the Edit Relationships button. Compare your screen with Figure 5.44.

The Edit Relationships dialog box displays, indicating that referential integrity has been enforced and that the relationship type is *One-to-Many*. Because the relationship has been established for the tables, you can view relationship properties in the Relationships window.

> **ALERT!** **Is Your Edit Relationships Dialog Box Empty?**
>
> If your Edit Relationships dialog box does not display as shown in Figure 5.44, you may have double-clicked near the join line and not on the join line. In the Edit Relationships dialog box, click Cancel, and then try again.

FIGURE 5.44

3 In the **Edit Relationships** dialog box, click **Join Type**, and then compare your screen with Figure 5.45. In the displayed **Join Properties** dialog box, notice that option **1** is selected—*Only include rows where the joined fields from both tables are equal.*

Option 1 is the default join type, which is an inner join. Options 2 and 3 are outer join types.

4 In the **Join Properties** dialog box, click **Cancel**. In the **Edit Relationships** dialog box, click **Cancel**. **Close** the **Relationships** window.

Because the relationships have been established and saved in the database, you should not change the join properties in the Relationships window. You should only change join properties in the Query design workspace.

5 **Open** » the **Navigation Pane**. In the **Navigation Pane**, open the **5B Orders** table and the **5B Customers** table, in the order specified, and then **Close** « the **Navigation Pane**.

🔄 BY TOUCH   If tables are not displayed in the order specified, slide to rearrange—similar to dragging with a mouse.

6 With the **5B Customers** table active, on the **HOME tab**, in the **Sort & Filter group**, click the **Remove Sort** button to remove the ascending sort from the **City** field. Notice that the records are now sorted by the **Customer#** field—the primary key field.

7 In the third record, click the **plus (+) sign** to expand the subdatasheet—the related record in the *5B Orders* table—and then notice that Willie Smith has no related records—he has not placed any orders. Click the **minus (–) sign** to collapse the subdatasheets.

8 Expand the subdatasheet for **Customer# 1045**, and then notice that Joe Crocker has one related record in the *5B Orders* table—he has placed one order. Collapse the subdatasheet.

9 Expand the subdatasheet for **Customer# 1047**, and then notice that Robert Bland has two related records in the *5B Orders* table—he has placed *many* orders. Collapse the subdatasheet.

10 On the **tab row**, click the **5B Orders tab** to make the datasheet active, and then notice that **15** orders have been placed. On the **tab row**, right-click any tab, and then click **Close All**, saving changes, if prompted.

11 Create a new query in **Query Design**. From the **Show Table** dialog box, add the **5B Customers** table and the **5B Orders** table to the Query design workspace, and then close the **Show Table** dialog box. Resize both field lists.

374   **Access** | Chapter 5: ENHANCING QUERIES

12 ▶ From the **5B Customers** field list, add **Customer#**, **Last Name**, and **First Name**, in the order specified, to the design grid. In the design grid, under **Customer#**, click in the **Sort row**, click the **arrow**, and then click **Ascending**. **Run** the query, and then compare your screen with Figure 5.46. There is no record for **Willie Smith**, there is one record for **Customer# 1045**—Joe Crocker—and there are two records for **Customer# 1047**—Robert Bland.

Because the default join type is an inner join, the query results display records only where there is a matching Customer#—the common field—in both related tables, even though you did not add any fields from the *5B Orders* table to the design grid. All of the records display for the table on the *many* side of the relationship—*5B Orders*. For the table on the *one* side of the relationship—*5B Customers*—only those records that have matching records in the related table display. Recall that there were 30 records in the *5B Customers* table and 15 records in the *5B Orders* table.

FIGURE 5.46

13 ▶ Switch to **Design** view. From the **5B Orders** field list, add **Order#** to the fourth column of the design grid, and then add **Amount** to the fifth column of the design grid. **Run** the query to display the results.

The same 15 records display but with two additional fields.

Activity 5.19 | Changing the Join Type to an Outer Join

An **outer join** is typically used to display records from both tables, regardless of whether there are matching records. In this activity, you will modify the join type to display all of the records from the *5B Customers* table, regardless of whether the customer has placed an order.

1 ▶ Switch to **Design** view. In the Query design workspace, double-click the **join line** to display the **Join Properties** dialog box. Alternatively, right-click the join line, and then click Join Properties. Compare your screen with Figure 5.47.

The Join Properties dialog box displays the tables used in the join and the common fields from both tables. Option 1—inner join type—is selected by default. Options 2 and 3 are two different types of outer joins.

Option 2 is a **left outer join**. Select a left outer join when you want to display all of the records on the *one* side of the relationship, whether or not there are matching records in the table on the *many* side of the relationship. Option 3 is a **right outer join**. Selecting a right outer join will display all of the records on the *many* side of the relationship, whether or not there are matching records in the table on the *one* side of the relationship. This should not occur if referential integrity has been enforced because all orders should have a related customer.

FIGURE 5.47

2 In the **Join Properties** dialog box, click the option button next to **2**, and then click **OK**. **Run** the query, and then compare your screen with Figure 5.48.

> Thirty-four records display. There are thirty records in the *5B Customers* table; however, four customers have two orders, so there are two separate records for each of these customers. If a customer does not have a matching record in the *5B Orders* table, the Order# and Amount fields are left empty in the query results.

FIGURE 5.48

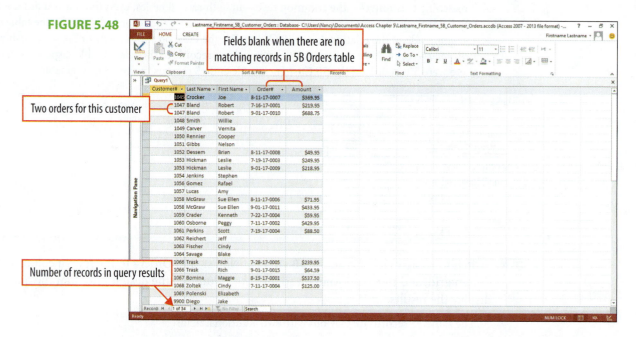

3 Save 🖫 the query as **Lastname Firstname 5B Outer Join** View the query in **Print Preview**, ensuring that the table prints on one page. If you are instructed to submit this result, create a paper or electronic printout. **Close** the **Print Preview** window.

4 **Close** ✕ the query, and then **Open** » the **Navigation Pane**. **Close** the database, and then **Exit** Access.

5 As directed by your instructor, submit your database and the paper or electronic printouts of the four objects—three tables and a query—that are the result of this project. Specifically, in this project, using your own name you created the following database and printouts or electronic printouts:

1. Lastname_Firstname_5B_Customer_Orders	Database file
2. Lastname Firstname 5B August & September Orders	Table (printed or electronic printout)
3. Lastname Firstname 5B Customers	Table (printed or electronic printout)
4. Lastname Firstname 5B Orders	Table (printed or electronic printout)
5. Lastname Firstname 5B Outer Join	Query (printed or electronic printout)

0

More Knowledge — Other Types of Joins

There are two other types of joins: cross joins and unequal joins. A *cross join* is not explicitly set in Access 2013. In a cross join, each row from one table is combined with each row in a related table. Cross joins are usually created unintentionally when you do not create a join line between related tables. In fact, the results of the query will probably not make much sense. In the previous query, you would create a cross join by deleting the join line between the 5B Customers table and the 5B Orders table. A cross join produces many records; depending on the number of records in both tables, the cross join can take a long time to run. A cross join using the aforementioned tables would result in 348 displayed records when the query is run (29 customers × 12 orders = 348 records).

An *unequal join* is used to combine rows from two data sources based on field values that are not equal. The join can be based on any comparison operator, such as greater than (>), less than (<), or not equal to (<>). The results in an unequal join using the not equal to comparison operator are difficult to interpret and can display as many records as those displayed in a cross join. Unequal joins cannot be created in Design view; they can be created only in SQL view.

END | You have completed Project 5B

END OF CHAPTER

SUMMARY

Queries are powerful database objects created to do more than extract data from tables and other queries; results can provide tools for analyzing, updating, and maintaining the integrity of the data.

Special-purpose queries are created to calculate fields, use aggregate functions, display data for easier analysis, find duplicate and unmatched records to avoid problems, and create prompts to use.

Action queries are used to create new tables, append and delete records, and update data in tables. Query results can be modified by changing from the default inner join to an outer join between tables.

GO! LEARN IT ONLINE

Review the concepts and key terms in this chapter by completing these online challenges, which you can find at **www.pearsonhighered.com/go.**

Matching and Multiple Choice:
Answer matching and multiple choice questions to test what you learned in this chapter. MyITLab®

Crossword Puzzle:
Spell out the words that match the numbered clues, and put them in the puzzle squares.

Flipboard:
Flip through the definitions of the key terms in this chapter and match them with the correct term.

END OF CHAPTER

REVIEW AND ASSESSMENT GUIDE FOR ACCESS CHAPTER 5

Your instructor may assign one or more of these projects to help you review the chapter and assess your mastery and understanding of the chapter.

Project	Apply Skills from These Chapter Objectives	Project Type	Project Location
	Review and Assessment Guide for Access Chapter 5		
5C	Objectives 1–5 from Project 5A	**5C Skills Review** A guided review of the skills from Project 5A.	On the following pages
5D	Objectives 6–10 from Project 5B	**5D Skills Review** A guided review of the skills from Project 5B.	On the following pages
5E	Objectives 1–5 from Project 5A	**5E Mastery (Grader Project)** A demonstration of your mastery of the skills in Project 5A with extensive decision making.	In MyITLab and on the following pages
5F	Objectives 6–10 from Project 5B	**5F Mastery (Grader Project)** A demonstration of your mastery of the skills in Project 5B with extensive decision making.	In MyITLab and on the following pages
5G	Objectives 1–3, 9 from Projects 5A and 5B	**5G Mastery (Grader Project)** A demonstration of your mastery of the skills in Projects 5A and 5B with extensive decision making.	In MyITLab and on the following pages
5H	Combination of Objectives from Projects 5A and 5B	**5H GO! Fix It** A demonstration of your mastery of the skills in Projects 5A and 5B by creating a correct result from a document that contains errors you must find.	Online
5I	Combination of Objectives from Projects 5A and 5B	**5I GO! Make It** A demonstration of your mastery of the skills in Projects 5A and 5B by creating a result from a supplied picture.	Online
5J	Combination of Objectives from Projects 5A and 5B	**5J GO! Solve It** A demonstration of your mastery of the skills in Projects 5A and 5B, your decision-making skills, and your critical thinking skills. A task-specific rubric helps you self-assess your result.	Online
5K	Combination of Objectives from Projects 5A and 5B	**5K GO! Solve It** A demonstration of your mastery of the skills in Projects 5A and 5B, your decision-making skills, and your critical thinking skills. A task-specific rubric helps you self-assess your result.	On the following pages
5L	Combination of Objectives from Projects 5A and 5B	**5L GO! Think** A demonstration of your understanding of the chapter concepts applied in a manner that you would use outside of college. An analytic rubric helps you and your instructor grade the quality of your work by comparing it to the work an expert in the discipline would create.	On the following pages
5M	Combination of Objectives from Projects 5A and 5B	**5M GO! Think** A demonstration of your understanding of the chapter concepts applied in a manner that you would use outside of college. An analytic rubric helps you and your instructor grade the quality of your work by comparing it to the work an expert in the discipline would create.	Online
5N	Combination of Objectives from Projects 5A and 5B	**5N You and GO!** A demonstration of your understanding of the chapter concepts applied in a manner that you would use in a personal situation. An analytic rubric helps you and your instructor grade the quality of your work.	Online

GLOSSARY

GLOSSARY OF CHAPTER KEY TERMS

Action query A query that creates a new table or changes data in an existing table.

Aggregate function Performs a calculation on a column of data and returns a single value.

Append query An action query that adds new records to an existing table by adding data from another Access database or from a table in the same database.

Arithmetic operators Mathematical symbols used in building expressions.

Calculated field A field that obtains its data by using a formula to perform a calculation or computation.

Cross join A join that displays when each row from one table is combined with each row in a related table, usually created unintentionally when you do not create a join line between related tables.

Crosstab query A query that uses an aggregate function for data that is grouped by two types of information and displays the data in a compact, spreadsheet-like format. A crosstab query always has at least one row heading, one column heading, and one summary field.

Delete query An action query that removes records from an existing table in the same database.

Destination table The table to which you are appending records, attempting to match the fields.

Expression The formula that will perform a calculation.

Find Duplicates Query A query used to locate duplicate records in a table.

Find Unmatched Query A query used to locate unmatched records so they can be deleted from the table.

Inner join A join that allows only the records where the common field exists in both related tables to be displayed in query results.

Join A relationship that helps a query return only the records from each table you want to see, based on how those tables are related to other tables in the query.

Left outer join A join used when you want to display all of the records on the *one* side of a one-to-many relationship, whether or not there are matching records in the table on the *many* side of the relationship.

Make table query An action query that creates a new table by extracting data from one or more tables.

Multivalued fields Fields that hold multiple values.

Outer join A join that is typically used to display records from both tables, regardless of whether there are matching records.

Parameter A value that can be changed.

Parameter query A query that prompts you for criteria before running.

Right outer join A join used when you want to display all of the records on the *many* side of a one-to-many relationship, whether or not there are matching records in the table on the *one* side of the relationship.

Source table The table from which records are being extracted.

Static data Data that does not change.

Totals query A query that calculates subtotals across groups of records.

Unequal join A join used to combine rows from two data sources based on field values that are not equal; can be created only in SQL view.

Unmatched records Records in one table that have no matching records in a related table.

Update query An action query used to add, change, or delete data in fields of one or more existing records.

CHAPTER REVIEW

Apply 5A skills from these Objectives:

1 Create Calculated Fields in a Query

2 Use Aggregate Functions in a Query

3 Create a Crosstab Query

4 Find Duplicate and Unmatched Records

5 Create a Parameter Query

Skills Review | Project 5C Employee Payroll

Derek Finkel, human resource specialist at S-Boards, Inc. Surf and Snowboard Shop, has a database containing employee data and payroll data. In the following Skills Review, you will create special-purpose queries to calculate data, summarize and group data, display data in a spreadsheet-like format, and find duplicate and unmatched records. You will also create a query that prompts an individual to enter the criteria. Your completed queries will look similar to Figure 5.49.

PROJECT FILES

For Project 5C, you will need the following file:

a05C_Employee_Payroll

You will save your database as:

Lastname_Firstname_5C_Employee_Payroll

PROJECT RESULTS

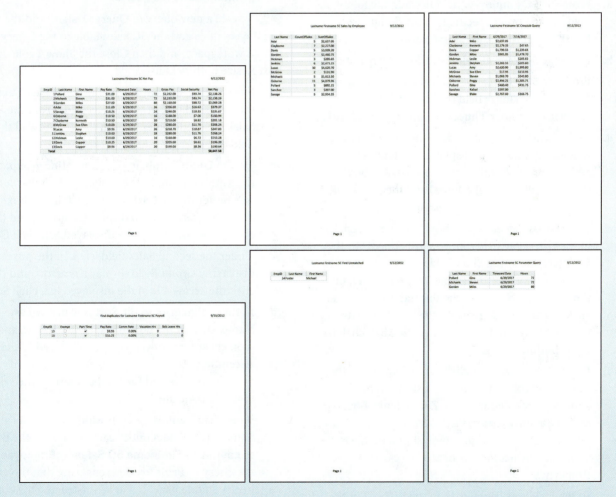

FIGURE 5.49

(Project 5C Employee Payroll continues on the next page)

CHAPTER REVIEW

1 **Start** Access. Locate and open the **a05C_Employee_Payroll** file. Display **Backstage** view. **Save** the database in your **Access Chapter 5** folder as **Lastname_Firstname_5C_Employee_Payroll**

a. If necessary, enable the content or add the Access Chapter 5 folder to the Trust Center.

b. Rename the tables by adding your **Lastname Firstname** to the beginning of each table name. **Close** the **Navigation Pane**.

2 On the Ribbon, click the **CREATE tab**. In the **Queries group**, click the **Query Design** button. In the **Show Table** dialog box, select the following three tables— **5C Employees**, **5C Payroll**, and **5C Timecard**. **Add** the tables to the Query design workspace, and then click **Close**. Resize the field lists.

a. From the **5C Employees** field list, add the following fields, in the order specified, to the design grid: **EmpID**, **Last Name**, and **First Name**.

b. From the **5C Payroll** field list, add the **Pay Rate** field.

c. From the **5C Timecard** field list, add the **Timecard Date** and the **Hours** field in this order. In the **Criteria row** under **Timecard Date**, type **6/29/2017**

d. In the **Field row**, right-click in the first cell in the first empty column to display a shortcut menu, and then click **Zoom**. In the **Zoom** dialog box, type **Gross Pay:[Pay Rate]*[Hours]** and then click **OK**. Run the query. Return to **Design** view.

e. If the **Gross Pay** does not show as currency, click in the **Gross Pay** field that you just added. On the **DESIGN tab**, in the **Show/Hide group**, click the **Property Sheet** button. In the **Property Sheet**, on the **General tab**, click in the **Format** box, and then click the displayed **arrow**. In the list of formats, click **Currency**. On the **Property Sheet** title bar, click the **Close** button.

f. In the **Field row**, right-click in the first cell in the first empty column to display a shortcut menu, and then click **Zoom**. In the **Zoom** dialog box, type **Social Security:[Gross Pay]*0.042** and then click **OK**. Using the technique you just practiced, set a Currency format for this field if necessary. **Close** the Property Sheet.

g. In the **Field row**, right-click in the first cell in the first empty column to display a shortcut menu, and then click **Zoom**. In the **Zoom** dialog box,

type **Net Pay:[Gross Pay]-[Social Security]** and then click **OK**. **Run** the query to display the payroll calculations. Adjust column widths to display all field names and all data under each field.

h. In the **Records group**, click the **Totals** button. In the **Total row** under **Net Pay**, click in the empty box, and then click the **arrow** at the left edge. From the displayed list, click **Sum**.

i. On the **tab row**, right-click the **Query1 tab**, and then click **Save**. In the **Save As** dialog box, under **Query Name**, type **Lastname Firstname 5C Net Pay** and then click **OK**. View the query in **Print Preview**. Change the orientation to **Landscape** to ensure the table prints on one page. If you are instructed to submit this result, create a paper or electronic printout. **Close** the query.

3 Create a new query in **Query Design**. Add the 5C **Employees** table and the **5C Sales** table to the Query design workspace, and then **Close** the **Show Table** dialog box. Resize both field lists.

a. From the **5C Employees** field list, add **Last Name** to the first field box in the design grid. From the **5C Sales** table, add **Sales** to both the second and third field boxes.

b. On the **DESIGN tab**, in the **Show/Hide group**, click the **Totals** button. In the design grid, in the **Total row** under the first **Sales** field, click in the box displaying *Group By* to display the arrow, and then click the **arrow**. From the displayed list, click **Count**.

c. Under the second **Sales** field, click in the box displaying *Group By* to display the arrow, and then click the **arrow**. From the displayed list, click **Sum**.

d. In the design grid, in the **Sort row** under **Last Name**, click in the box to display the arrow, and then click the **arrow**. From the displayed list, click **Ascending**. **Run** the query to display the total number of sales and the total amount of the sales for each associate.

e. If necessary, adjust column widths to display all field names and all data under each field. **Save** the query as **Lastname Firstname 5C Sales by Employee** View the query in **Print Preview**, ensuring that the query prints on one page. If you are instructed to submit this result, create a paper or electronic printout. **Close** the query.

(Project 5C Employee Payroll continues on the next page)

5 | ACCESS

4 **Create** a new query in **Query Design**. Add the following tables to the Query design workspace: **5C Employees** and **5C Sales**. In the **Show Table** dialog box, click **Close**. Resize the field lists.

a. From the **5C Employees** table, add the **Last Name** and **First Name** fields. From the **5C Sales** table, add the **Timecard Date** and **Sales** fields. **Run** the query to display the sales by date. **Save** the query as **Lastname Firstname 5C Sales by Date** and then **Close** the query.

b. On the Ribbon, click the **CREATE tab**. In the **Queries group**, click the **Query Wizard** button. In the **New Query** dialog box, click **Crosstab Query Wizard**, and then click **OK**. In the middle of the dialog box, under **View**, click the **Queries** option button. In the list of queries, click **Query: 5C Sales by Date**, and then click **Next**.

c. Under **Available Fields**, double-click **Last Name** and **First Name**, and then click **Next**. In the displayed list of fields, double-click **Timecard Date**. Select an interval of **Date**. Click **Next**. Under **Functions**, click **Sum**. On the left side of the **Crosstab Query Wizard** dialog box, above the **Sample** area, clear the **Yes, include row sums** check box, and then click **Next**.

d. Under **What do you want to name your query?**, select the existing text, type **Lastname Firstname 5C Crosstab Query** and then click **Finish**. Adjust all of the column widths to display the entire field name and the data in each field. The result is a spreadsheet view of total sales by employee by payroll date. View the query in **Print Preview**, ensuring that the query prints on one page. If you are instructed to submit this result, create a paper or electronic printout. **Close** the query, saving changes.

5 On the **CREATE tab**, in the **Queries group**, click the **Query Wizard** button. In the **New Query** dialog box, click **Find Duplicates Query Wizard**, and then click **OK**.

a. In the first **Find Duplicates Query Wizard** dialog box, in the list of tables, click **Table: 5C Payroll**, and then click **Next**. Under **Available fields**, double-click **EmpID** to move it under **Duplicate-value fields**, and then click **Next**.

b. Under **Available fields**, add all of the fields to the **Additional query fields** box. Click **Next**. Click

Finish to accept the suggested query name—*Find duplicates for Lastname Firstname 5C Payroll*. Adjust all column widths. View the query in **Print Preview**, ensuring that the query prints on one page. If you are instructed to submit this result, create a paper or electronic printout. **Close** the query, saving changes.

6 On the **CREATE tab**, in the **Queries group**, click the **Query Wizard** button. In the **New Query** dialog box, click **Find Unmatched Query Wizard**, and then click **OK**.

a. In the first **Find Unmatched Query Wizard** dialog box, in the list of tables, click Table: 5C Employees, if necessary, and then click **Next**. In the list of tables, click **Table: 5C Payroll**, and then click **Next**. Under **Fields in '5C Employees'**, if necessary, click EmpID. Under **Fields in 5C Payroll**, if necessary, click EmpID. Click the **<=>** button. Click **Next**.

b. Under **Available fields**, double-click **EmpID**, **Last Name**, and **First Name** to move the field names under **Selected fields**. Click **Next**. In the last dialog box, under **What would you like to name your query?**, type **Lastname Firstname 5C Find Unmatched** and then click **Finish**.

c. Adjust all column widths. View the query in **Print Preview**, ensuring that the query prints on one page. If you are instructed to submit this result, create a paper or electronic printout. **Close** the query, saving changes if necessary.

7 **Create** a new query in **Query Design**. Add the **5C Employees** table and the **5C Timecard** table to the Query design workspace, and then **Close** the **Show Table** dialog box. Resize the field lists.

a. From the **5C Employees** field list, add **Last Name** and **First Name** to the first and second columns in the design grid. From the **5C Timecard** field list, add **Timecard Date** and **Hours** to the third and fourth columns in the design grid.

b. In the **Criteria row** under **Timecard Date** field, type **[Enter Date]**

c. In the **Criteria row**, right-click in the **Hours** field, and then click **Zoom**. In the **Zoom** dialog box, type **Between [Enter the minimum Hours] And [Enter the maximum Hours]** and then click **OK**.

(Project 5C Employee Payroll continues on the next page)

CHAPTER REVIEW

d. **Run** the query. In the **Enter Parameter Value** dialog box, type **6/29/17** and then click **OK**. Type **60** and then click **OK**. Type **80** and then click **OK**. Three employees have worked between 60 and 80 hours during the pay period for 6/29/17. They have earned vacation hours.

e. Adjust all column widths, and **Save** the query as **Lastname Firstname 5C Parameter Query** View the query in **Print Preview**, ensuring that the query prints on one page. If you are instructed to submit this result, create a paper or electronic printout. **Close** the query.

8 Open the **Navigation Pane**, **Close** the database, and then **Exit** Access.

9 As directed by your instructor, submit your database and the paper or electronic printouts of the six queries that are the result of this project. Specifically,

in this project, using your own name you created the following database and printouts or electronic printouts:

1. Lastname_Firstname_5C_ Employee_Payroll	Database file
2. Lastname Firstname 5C Net Pay	Query (printed or electronic printout)
3. Lastname Firstname 5C Sales by Employee	Query (printed or electronic printout)
4. Lastname Firstname 5C Crosstab Query	Query (printed or electronic printout)
5. Find duplicates for Lastname Firstname 5C Payroll	Query (printed or electronic printout)
6. Lastname Firstname 5C Find Unmatched	Query (printed or electronic printout)
7. Lastname Firstname 5C Parameter Query	Query (printed or electronic printout)

END | You have completed Project 5C

CHAPTER REVIEW

Skills Review | Project 5D Clearance Sale

Apply **5B** skills from these Objectives:

6 Create a Make Table Query
7 Create an Append Query
8 Create a Delete Query
9 Create an Update Query
10 Modify the Join Type

Miles Gorden, purchasing manager for S-Boards, Inc. Surf and Snowboard Shop, must keep the tables in the database up to date and ensure that the queries display pertinent information. Two of the suppliers, Super Wave Boards and Boot City, will no longer provide merchandise for S-Boards, Inc. Surf and Snowboard Shop. This merchandise must be moved to a new discontinued items table. In the following Skills Review, you will create action queries that will create a new table, update records in a table, append records to a table, and delete records from a table. You will also modify the join type of relationships to display different subsets of the data when the query is run. Your completed queries will look similar to Figure 5.50.

PROJECT FILES

For Project 5D, you will need the following files:

a05D_Store_Items
a05D_Warehouse_Items

You will save your databases as:

Lastname_Firstname_5D_Store_Items
Lastname_Firstname_5D_Warehouse_Items

PROJECT RESULTS

FIGURE 5.50

(Project 5D Clearance Sale continues on the next page)

CHAPTER REVIEW

1 **Start** Access. Locate and open the **a05D_Store_Items** file. Display **Backstage** view. **Save** the database in your **Access Chapter 5** folder as **Lastname_Firstname_5D_Store_Items**

a. If necessary, enable the content or add the Access Chapter 5 folder to the Trust Center.

b. Rename the tables by adding your **Lastname Firstname** to the beginning of each table name. **Close** the **Navigation Pane**.

2 Create a new query in **Query Design**. From the **Show Table** dialog box, add the following tables to the Query design workspace: **5D Suppliers** and **5D Inventory**. **Close** the **Show Table** dialog box, and then Resize the field lists.

a. From the **5D Suppliers** field list, add **Company** to the first column of the design grid. From the **5D Inventory** field list, double-click each field to add them all to the design grid.

b. In the design grid, click in the **Criteria row** under **Supplier**, type **8** and then **Run** the query. Notice that three items are supplied by *Super Wave Boards*.

c. Switch to **Design** view. On the **DESIGN tab**, in the **Query Type group**, click the **Make Table** button. In the **Make Table** dialog box, in the **Table Name** box, type **Lastname Firstname 5D Discontinued Items** In the **Make Table** dialog box, be sure that **Current Database** is selected, and then click **OK**. **Run** the query. In the displayed message box, click **Yes** to paste the rows to the new table.

d. **Close** the query, click **Yes** in the message box asking if you want to save changes, and then name the query **Lastname Firstname 5D SWB Items**

3 Create a new query in **Query Design**. From the **Show Table** dialog box, add the following tables, in the order specified, to the Query design workspace: **5D Suppliers** and **5D Inventory**. **Close** the **Show Table** dialog box, and then Resize the field lists.

a. From the **5D Suppliers** field list, add **Company** to the first column of the design grid. From the **5D Inventory** field list, add all fields in the field list to the design grid.

b. In the design grid, click in the **Criteria row** under **Supplier**, type **3** and then **Run** the query. Notice that one item is supplied by *Boot City*.

c. Switch to **Design** view. On the **DESIGN tab**, in the **Query Type group**, click the **Append** button. In the **Append** dialog box, click the **Table Name arrow**, and from the displayed list, click **5D Discontinued Items**, and then click **OK**.

d. **Run** the query. In the displayed message box, click **Yes** to append one row. **Close** the query, and then save it as **Lastname Firstname 5D Append Items**

4 On the Access window title bar, click the **Minimize** button. **Start** a second instance of Access. Navigate to the location where the student data files for this textbook are saved. Locate and open the **a05D_Warehouse_Items** file. Save the database in your **Access Chapter 5** folder as **Lastname_Firstname_5D_Warehouse_Items** If necessary, enable the content or add the Access Chapter 5 folder to the Trust Center.

5 Create a new query in **Query Design**. From the **Show Table** dialog box, add the **5D Suppliers** table and the **5D Discontinued Items** table to the Query design workspace, and then close the **Show Table** dialog box. Resize the field lists. From the **5D Suppliers** field list, add **Company** to the first column of the design grid. From the **5D Discontinued Items** field list, add all of the fields to the design grid in the order listed.

a. On the **DESIGN tab**, in the **Query Type group**, click the **Append** button. In the **Append** dialog box, click the **Another Database** option button, and then click the **Browse** button. Navigate to your **Access Chapter 5** folder, and then double-click **Lastname_Firstname_5D_Store_Items**.

b. In the **Append** dialog box, click the **Table Name arrow**, click **5D Discontinued Items**, and then click **OK**. **Save** the query as **Lastname Firstname 5D Append Warehouse** and then **Run** the query. In the displayed message box, click **Yes** to append three rows. **Close** the query. **Close** the database, and then **Exit** this instance of Access.

c. If necessary, from the Windows taskbar, click the 5D_Store_Items database. Verify that the **5D Discontinued Items** table now contains seven rows, and then close the table. Create a new query in **Query Design**. Add the **5D Inventory** table to the Query design workspace, and then **Close** the **Show Table** dialog box.

(Project 5D Clearance Sale continues on the next page)

d. Resize the field list. From the field list, add **Catalog#** and **On Hand**, in this order, to the first and second columns in the design grid. In the design grid, click in the **Criteria row** under **On Hand**, type **0** and then **Run** the query to display one record.

e. Switch to **Design** view. In the Query design workspace, right-click in the empty space. From the displayed shortcut menu, point to **Query Type**, and then click **Delete Query**.

f. **Save** the query as **Lastname Firstname 5D Delete Zero Inventory** and then **Run** the query. In the message box stating that *You are about to delete 1 row(s) from the specified table*, click **Yes**. **Close** the query. You have removed this item from the inventory.

6 Create a new query in **Query Design**. Add the **5D Discontinued Items** table to the Query design workspace, and then **Close** the **Show Table** dialog box. Resize the field list.

a. In the **5D Discontinued Items** field list, double-click **Catalog#** to add the field to the first column of the design grid. Then add the **Selling Price** field to the second column of the design grid.

b. On the **DESIGN tab**, in the **Query Type group**, click the **Update** button. In the design grid, click in the **Update To row** under **Selling Price**, and then type **[Selling Price]*0.75**

c. **Save** the query as **Lastname Firstname 5D Discounted Selling Prices** and then **Run** the query. In the message box stating that *You are about to update 7 row(s)*, click **Yes**. **Close** the query.

d. Open the **Navigation Pane**, and then double-click the **5D Discontinued Items** table to open it in **Datasheet** view. Close the **Navigation Pane**. Adjust all column widths. View the table in **Print Preview**. If you are instructed to submit this result, create a paper or electronic printout to fit on one page in **Landscape** orientation. **Close** the table, saving changes.

7 Create a new query in **Query Design**. From the **Show Table** dialog box, add the **5D Suppliers** table and the **5D Discontinued Items** table to the Query design workspace, and then **Close** the **Show Table** dialog box.

a. Resize both field lists. From the **5D Suppliers** table, drag the **ID** field to the **5D Discontinued Items** table **Supplier** field to create a join between the tables.

b. From the **5D Suppliers** field list, add **Company** and **Business Phone** to the first and second columns in the design grid. From the **5D Discontinued Items** field list, add **Catalog#**, **Item**, and **On Hand**, in this order, to the design grid. In the design grid, click in the **Sort row** under **Company**, click the **arrow**, and then click **Ascending**. **Run** the query.

c. Switch to **Design** view. Verify that the **5D Suppliers** table appears on the left, and the **5D Discontinued Items** table is on the right. Correct as necessary. In the Query design workspace, double-click the **join line** to display the **Join Properties** dialog box. Click the option button next to **2**, and then click **OK**. **Run** the query. Adjust all column widths. This query displays all of the supplier companies used by the shop, not just those with discontinued items.

d. **Save** the query as **Lastname Firstname 5D Outer Join** View the query in **Print Preview** in **Landscape** orientation. If you are instructed to submit this result, create a paper or electronic printout. **Close** the query.

8 Open the **Navigation Pane**, **Close** the database, and then **Exit** Access.

9 As directed by your instructor, submit your databases and the paper or electronic printouts of the two objects—one table and one query—that are the result of this project. Specifically, in this project, using your own name you created the following databases and printouts or electronic printouts:

1. Lastname_Firstname_5D_Store_Items	Database file
2. Lastname_Firstname_5D_Warehouse_Items	Database file
3. Lastname Firstname 5D Discontinued Items	Table (printed or electronic printout)
4. Lastname Firstname 5D Outer Join	Query (printed or electronic printout)

END | You have completed Project 5D

CONTENT-BASED ASSESSMENTS

Mastering Access Project 5E Surfing Lessons

Gina Pollard, one of the owners of S-Boards, Inc. Surf and Snowboard Shop, has a database containing student, instructor, and surfing lesson data. In the following Mastering Access project, you will create special-purpose queries to calculate data, summarize and group data, display data in a spreadsheet-like format, and find duplicate and unmatched records. You will also create a query that prompts an individual to enter the criteria. Your completed queries will look similar to Figure 5.51.

Apply 5A skills from these Objectives:

1 Create Calculated Fields in a Query

2 Use Aggregate Functions in a Query

3 Create a Crosstab Query

4 Find Duplicate and Unmatched Records

5 Create a Parameter Query

PROJECT FILES

For Project 5E, you will need the following file:

a05E_Surfing_Lessons

You will save your database as:

Lastname_Firstname_5E_Surfing_Lessons

PROJECT RESULTS

FIGURE 5.51

(Project 5E Surfing Lessons continues on the next page)

CONTENT-BASED ASSESSMENTS

1 **Start** Access. Locate and open the **a05E_Surfing_Lessons** file. Display **Backstage** view. Save the database in your **Access Chapter 5** folder as **Lastname_Firstname_5E_Surfing_Lessons** If necessary, enable the content or add the Access Chapter 5 folder to the Trust Center. Rename the tables by adding your **Lastname Firstname** to the beginning of each table name.

2 **Create** a query in **Query Design** using the **5E Surfing Lessons** table and the **5E Students** table. From the **5E Surfing Lessons** table, add the **Instructor** field, the **Lesson Time** field, and the **Duration** field to the first, second, and third columns of the design grid. From the **5E Students** table, add the **Last Name** and **First Name** fields to the fourth and fifth columns.

3 In the sixth column of the design grid, add a calculated field. In the **field name row**, type **End Time:[Duration]/24+[Lesson Time]** Display the field properties sheet, and then format this field as **Medium Time**. This field will display the time the lesson ends.

4 In the first blank column, in the **field name row**, add the calculated field **Fee:[Duration]*80** from the field properties sheet, and then format this field as **Currency**. Surfing lessons cost $80.00 an hour.

5 In the **Instructor** field, in the **Sort row**, click **Ascending**. In the **Lesson Time** field, in the **Sort row**, click **Ascending**. **Run** the query.

6 On the **HOME tab**, in the **Records group**, click the **Totals** button. In the **Fee** column, in the **Total row**, click the **down arrow**, and then click **Average**. Adjust field widths as necessary.

7 **Save** the query as **Lastname Firstname 5E Student Lessons** View the query in **Print Preview**, ensuring that the query prints on one page in **Landscape** orientation. If you are instructed to submit this result, create a paper or electronic printout. **Close** the query.

8 **Create** a new query using the **Crosstab Query Wizard**. Select the **Query: 5E Student Lessons**. Click **Next**. From the **Available Fields**, add **Instructor** to the **Selected Fields** column. Click **Next**. Double-click **Lesson Time**, and then click **Date**. Click **Next**. From the **Fields column**, select **Duration**, and then from **Functions**, select **Sum**. Clear the **Yes, include row sums** check box.

9 Click **Next**. Name the query **Lastname Firstname 5E Crosstab Query** Select **View the query**, and then click

Finish. This query displays the instructor and the number of hours he or she taught by date. Adjust field widths as necessary.

10 View the query in **Print Preview**, ensuring that the query prints on one page. If you are instructed to submit this result, create a paper or electronic printout. **Close** the query, saving changes.

11 Click the **Query Wizard** button. In the **New Query** dialog box, click **Find Duplicates Query Wizard**. Search the **Table: 5E Surfing Lessons**, and select the **Lesson Time** field for duplicate information. Click **Next**. From **Available fields**, add the **Instructor** and **Duration** fields to the **Additional query fields** column. Accept the default name for the query. Click **Finish**. The query results show that there are duplicate lesson times. Adjust field widths as necessary.

12 View the query in **Print Preview**, ensuring that the query prints on one page. If you are instructed to submit this result, create a paper or electronic printout. **Close** and **Save** the query.

13 Click the **Query Wizard** button. In the **New Query** dialog box, click **Find Unmatched Query Wizard**. Select **Table: 5E Surfing Instructors**. From the **Which table or query contains the related records?** dialog box, click **Table: 5E Surfing Lessons**. Click **Instructor** as the **Matching** field. Display the one field **Instructor** in the query results. Name the query **Lastname Firstname 5E Unmatched Instructors** and then click **Finish**. Ralph is the only instructor who has no students.

14 View the query in **Print Preview**. If you are instructed to submit this result, create a paper or electronic printout. **Close** the query.

15 **Create** a query in **Design** view using the **5E Surfing Lessons** table and the **5E Students** table. From the **5E Surfing Lessons** table, add the **Instructor** field. From the **5E Students** table, add the **Last Name**, **First Name**, and **Phone#** fields in that order to the design grid. In the **Criteria row** under **Instructor**, type **[Enter Instructor's First Name]**

16 **Run** the query. In the **Enter Parameter Value** dialog box, type **Andrea** and then press Enter. The query displays Andrea's students and their phone numbers.

17 **Save** the query as **Lastname Firstname 5E Parameter Query** Adjust field widths as necessary.

(Project 5E Surfing Lessons continues on the next page)

18 View the query in **Print Preview**, ensuring that the query prints on one page. If you are instructed to submit this result, create a paper or electronic printout. **Close** the query.

19 Open the **Navigation Pane**, **Close** the database, and then **Exit** Access.

20 As directed by your instructor, submit your database and the paper or electronic printouts of the five queries that are the result of this project. Specifically, in this project, using your own name you created the following database and printouts or electronic printouts:

1. Lastname_Firstname_5E_Surfing_Lessons	Database file
2. Lastname Firstname 5E Student Lessons	Query (printed or electronic printout)
3. Lastname Firstname 5E Crosstab Query	Query (printed or electronic printout)
4. Lastname Firstname Find duplicates…	Query (printed or electronic printout)
5. Lastname Firstname 5E Unmatched Instructors	Query (printed or electronic printout)
6. Lastname Firstname 5E Parameter Query	Query (printed or electronic printout)

END | You have completed Project 5E

CONTENT-BASED ASSESSMENTS

Apply 5B skills from these Objectives:

6 Create a Make Table Query

7 Create an Append Query

8 Create a Delete Query

9 Create an Update Query

10 Modify the Join Type

Mastering Access | Project 5F Gift Cards

Karen Walker, sales manager for S-Boards, Inc. Surf and Snowboard Shop, has decided to offer gift cards for purchase at the shop. She has a database of the employees and the details of the cards they have sold. In the following Mastering Access project, you will create action queries that will create a new table, update records in a table, append records to a table, and delete records from a table. You will also modify the join type of the relationship to display a different subset of the data when the query is run. Your completed queries will look similar to Figure 5.52.

PROJECT FILES

For Project 5F, you will need the following file:

a05F_Gift_Cards

You will save your database as:

Lastname_Firstname_5F_Gift_Cards

PROJECT RESULTS

FIGURE 5.52

(Project 5F Gift Cards continues on the next page)

Project 5F: Gift Cards | Access 391

1 **Start** Access. Locate and open the **a05F_Gift_Cards** file. Display **Backstage** view. Save the database in your **Access Chapter 5** folder as **Lastname_Firstname_5F_Gift_ Cards** If necessary, enable the content or add the Access Chapter 5 folder to the Trust Center. Rename the tables by adding your **Lastname Firstname** to the beginning of each table name.

2 Create a new query in **Query Design**. To the Query design workspace, add the **5F Employees**, **5F Sales**, and the **5F Inventory** tables. From the **5F Employees** table, add the **First Name** and **Last Name** fields to the first and second columns of the design grid. From the **5F Sales** table, add the following fields to the design grid in the order specified: **Sales Date** and **Quantity**. From the **5F Inventory** table, add the **Item** and **Cost** fields.

3 In the **Criteria row** under **Item**, type **Gift Cards** In the **Criteria row** under **Cost**, type **25 Or 50 Sort** the **Last Name** field in **Ascending** order.

4 On the **DESIGN tab**, click the **Make Table** button. Name the table **Lastname Firstname 5F $25 or $50 Gift Cards** Select **Current Database**, click **OK**, and then **Run** the query. **Close** the query, saving it as **Lastname Firstname 5F Make Table Query** Open the 5F $25 or $50 Gift Cards table to display the two gift card purchases. **Close** the table.

5 Create a new query in **Query Design**. To the Query design workspace, add the **5F Employees**, **5F Sales**, and the **5F Inventory** tables. From the **5F Employees** table, add the **First Name** and **Last Name** fields to the first and second columns of the design grid. From the **5F Sales** table, add the following fields to the design grid in the following order: **Sales Date** and **Quantity**. From the **5F Inventory** table, add the **Item** and **Cost** fields.

6 In the **Criteria row** under **Item**, type **Gift Cards** In the **Criteria row** under **Cost**, type **100 Or 250 Sort** the **Last Name** field in **Ascending** order.

7 Click the **Append** button, and then append the records to the **5F $25 or $50 Gift Cards** table. Click **OK**. **Run** the query. Click **Yes** to append three rows. **Close** the query, saving it as **Lastname Firstname 5F Append Query** Open the **5F $25 or $50 Gift Cards** table to display all gift card purchases. **Close** the table, and then rename it **Lastname Firstname 5F Gift Cards**

8 View the table in **Print Preview**, ensuring that the table prints on one page. If you are instructed to submit this result, create a paper or electronic printout. **Close** the table.

9 Create a new query in **Query Design**. Add the **5F Inventory** table to the Query design workspace. From the **5F Inventory** table, add the **Catalog#** and **Item** fields to the first and second columns of the design grid. In the design grid, click in the **Criteria row** under **Item**, and type **Gift Cards**

10 **Run** the query to view the results. Switch to **Design** view, click the **Query Type: Delete** button, and then **Run** the query. Click **Yes** to delete five gift cards from the **5F Inventory** table. The gift cards are not to be counted as inventory items. **Close** and **Save** the query, naming it **Lastname Firstname 5F Delete Query**

11 Open the **5F Inventory** table. If you are instructed to submit this result, create a paper or electronic printout in **Landscape** orientation. **Close** the table.

12 Create a new query in **Query Design**. Add the **5F Employees** table to the Query design workspace. From the **5F Employees** table, add **Postal Code** to the first column of the design grid. In the design grid, click in the **Criteria row** under **Postal Code**, and then type **972*** **Run** the query to view the results. Switch to **Design** view. Click the **Query Type: Update** button.

13 In the design grid, click in the **Update To row** under **Postal Code**, and then type **92710**

14 **Run** the query. Click **Yes** to update two rows. **Close** the query, saving it as **Lastname Firstname 5F Update Postal Code** Open the **5F Employees** table. View the table in **Print Preview**, ensuring that the table prints on one page. If you are instructed to submit this result, create a paper or electronic printout. **Close** the table.

15 Create a new query in **Query Design**. Add the **5F Employees** and **5F Gift Cards** tables to the Query design workspace. From the **5F Employees** field list, click **Last Name**, and then drag to the **5F Gift Cards Last Name** field. Double-click the **join line**, and then select option **2**.

16 From the **5F Employees** field list, add **First Name** and **Last Name** to the first two columns of the design grid. From the **5F Gift Cards** field list, add **Cost** and **Quantity** field, in this order, to the design grid. **Run** the query to

(Project 5F Gift Cards continues on the next page)

display the results, which include all 14 employees and not just gift card sellers. **Save** the query as **Lastname Firstname 5F Modified Join**

17 View the table in **Print Preview**, ensuring that the table prints on one page. If you are instructed to submit this result, create a paper or electronic printout. **Close** the query.

18 **Close** the database, and then **Exit** Access.

19 As directed by your instructor, submit your database and the paper or electronic printouts of the four objects—three tables and one query—that are the result of this project. Specifically, in this project, using your own name you created the following database and printouts or electronic printouts:

1. Lastname_Firstname_5F_Gift_Cards	Database file
2. Lastname Firstname 5F Gift Cards	Table (printed or electronic printout)
3. Lastname Firstname 5F Inventory	Table (printed or electronic printout)
4. Lastname Firstname 5F Employees	Table (printed or electronic printout)
5. Lastname Firstname 5F Modified Join	Query (printed or electronic printout)

END | You have completed Project 5F

CONTENT-BASED ASSESSMENTS

Apply 5A and 5B skills from these Objectives:

1 Create Calculated Fields in a Query
2 Use Aggregate Functions in a Query
3 Create a Crosstab Query
9 Create an Update Query

Steven Michaels, one of the owners of S-Boards, Inc., is responsible for all of the advertising for the business. In the following Mastering Access project, you will create special-purpose queries to calculate data, and then summarize and group data for advertising cost analysis. You will also create a query that prompts an individual to enter the criteria for a specific type of advertisement media. Your completed queries will look similar to Figure 5.53.

PROJECT FILES

For Project 5G, you will need the following file:

a05G_Advertising_Options

You will save your database as:

Lastname_Firstname_5G_Advertising_Options

PROJECT RESULTS

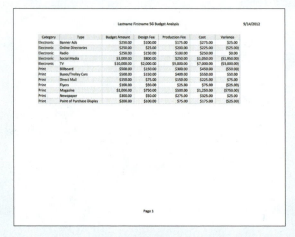

FIGURE 5.53

(Project 5G Advertising Options continues on the next page)

CONTENT-BASED ASSESSMENTS

1 **Start** Access. Locate and open the **a05G_Advertising_Options** file. Display **Backstage** view. Save the database in your Access Chapter 5 folder as **Lastname_Firstname_5G_Advertising_Options** If necessary, enable the content or add the Access Chapter 5 folder to the Trust Center. Rename the table by adding your **Lastname Firstname** to the beginning of the table names. Close the **Navigation Pane**.

2 Create a new query in **Query Design**. From the **5G Categories** table, add the **Category** field to the design grid. From the **5G Advertisements** table, add the **Type**, **Budget Amount**, **Design Fee**, and **Production Fee** fields to the design grid in this order.

3 In the first blank field column, add a calculated field. Type **Cost:[Design Fee]+[Production Fee]** In the next blank field column, add a second calculated field: **Variance:[Cost]-[Budget Amount]**

4 **Run** the query. Save it as **Lastname Firstname 5G Budget Analysis.** View the results in **Print Preview**, ensuring that it fits on one page in **Landscape** orientation. If you are instructed to submit this result, create a paper or electronic printout. **Close** the query.

5 Create a new query in **Query Design**. From the **5G Categories** table, add the **Category** field to the design grid. From the **5G Advertisements** table, add the **Objective** and **Budget Amount** fields to the design grid. On the **DESIGN tab**, in the **Show/Hide group**, click the **Totals** button. In the design grid, in the **Total row** under **Budget Amount**, click **Sum**.

6 **Run** the query. Save it as **Lastname Firstname 5G Budget by Category and Objective** View the results in **Print Preview**, ensuring that it fits on one page. If you are instructed to submit this result, create a paper or electronic printout. **Close** the query.

7 Create a new crosstab query using the **Query Wizard**. Select the **Query: 5G Budget Analysis**. For row headings, use **Type**, and for column headings, use **Category**. Select **Cost** for the calculated field, using the **Sum** function. Do not summarize each row. Save it as **Lastname Firstname 5G Crosstab Query**

8 Click **Finish** to view the cost in relation to the response rate for each type of advertisement.

9 View the query in **Print Preview**, ensuring that the query prints on one page. If you are instructed to submit this result, create a paper or electronic printout. **Close** the query.

10 Create a new query in **Query Design**. From the **5G Categories** table, add the **Category** field to the design grid. From the **5G Advertisements** table, add the **Budget Amount** field to the design grid. In the design grid, click in the **Criteria row** under **Category**, and type **Electronic**

11 Click the **Query Type: Update** button. In the design grid, click in the **Update To row** under **Budget Amount**, and type **[Budget Amount]*1.15**

12 **Run** the query. Click **Yes** to update five rows. **Close** the query, saving it as **Lastname Firstname 5G Update Electronics Budget** Open the **Navigation Pane**. Open the **5G Advertisements** table. View the table in **Print Preview**, ensuring that the table prints on one page. If you are instructed to submit this result, create a paper or electronic printout. **Close** the table.

13 **Close** the database, and then **Exit** Access.

14 As directed by your instructor, submit your database and the paper or electronic printouts of the four objects—three queries and one table—that are the result of this project. Specifically, in this project, using your own name you created the following database and printouts or electronic printouts:

1. Lastname_Firstname_5G_Advertising_Options	Database file
2. Lastname Firstname 5G Budget Analysis	Query (printed or electronic printout)
3. Lastname Firstname 5G Budget by Category and Objective	Query (printed or electronic printout)
4. Lastname Firstname 5G Crosstab Query	Query (printed or electronic printout)
5. Lastname Firstname 5G Advertisements	Table (printed or electronic printout)

END | You have completed Project 5G

CONTENT-BASED ASSESSMENTS

GO! Fix It	Project 5H Contests	Online

GO! Make It	Project 5I Ski Trips	Online

GO! Solve It	Project 5J Applications	Online

GO! Solve It	Project 5K Ski Apparel	

Apply a combination of the 5A and 5B skills.

PROJECT FILES

For Project 5K, you will need the following file:

a05K_Ski_Apparel

You will save your database as:

Lastname_Firstname_5K_Ski_Apparel

Miles Gorden is the purchasing manager for S-Boards, Inc. It is his responsibility to keep the clothing inventory current and fashionable. You have been asked to help him with this task. From the student files that accompany this textbook, open the **a05K_Ski_Apparel** database file, and then save the database in your **Access Chapter 5** folder as **Lastname_Firstname_5K_Ski_Apparel**

The database consists of a table of ski apparel for youth, women, and men. Create a query to identify the inventory by status of the items (promotional, in stock, and discontinued clothing), and the number of items that are in each category. Update the selling price of the discontinued items to 80 percent of the current selling price. Use a make table query to place the promotional items into their own table and use a delete query to remove those items from the *5K Ski Apparel* table. Save your queries using your last and first names followed by the query type. View the queries in Print Preview, ensuring that each query prints on one page. If you are instructed to submit this result, create a paper or electronic printout. Close the queries, and then close the database.

Performance Level

Performance Criteria		Exemplary	Proficient	Developing
	Create 5K Totals Query	Query created to display inventory by status	Query created with no more than two missing elements	Query created with more than two missing elements
	Create 5K Update Query	Query created to update clearance sale prices	Query created with no more than two missing elements	Query created with more than two missing elements
	Create 5K Make Table Query	Query created to make a table for promotional items	Query created with no more than two missing elements	Query created with more than two missing elements
	Create 5K Delete Query	Query created to delete promotional items from the Ski Apparel table	Query created with no more than two missing elements	Query created with more than two missing elements

END | You have completed Project 5K

OUTCOMES-BASED ASSESSMENTS

RUBRIC

The following outcomes-based assessments are open-ended assessments. That is, there is no specific correct result; your result will depend on your approach to the information provided. Make Professional Quality your goal. Use the following scoring rubric to guide you in how to approach the problem and then to evaluate how well your approach solves the problem.

The *criteria*—Software Mastery, Content, Format and Layout, and Process—represent the knowledge and skills you have gained that you can apply to solving the problem. The *levels of performance*—Professional Quality, Approaching Professional Quality, or Needs Quality Improvements—help you and your instructor evaluate your result.

	Your completed project is of Professional Quality if you:	Your completed project is Approaching Professional Quality if you:	Your completed project Needs Quality Improvements if you:
1-Software Mastery	Choose and apply the most appropriate skills, tools, and features and identify efficient methods to solve the problem.	Choose and apply some appropriate skills, tools, and features, but not in the most efficient manner.	Choose inappropriate skills, tools, or features, or are inefficient in solving the problem.
2-Content	Construct a solution that is clear and well organized, contains content that is accurate, appropriate to the audience and purpose, and is complete. Provide a solution that contains no errors in spelling, grammar, or style.	Construct a solution in which some components are unclear, poorly organized, inconsistent, or incomplete. Misjudge the needs of the audience. Have some errors in spelling, grammar, or style, but the errors do not detract from comprehension.	Construct a solution that is unclear, incomplete, or poorly organized; contains some inaccurate or inappropriate content; and contains many errors in spelling, grammar, or style. Do not solve the problem.
3-Format & Layout	Format and arrange all elements to communicate information and ideas, clarify function, illustrate relationships, and indicate relative importance.	Apply appropriate format and layout features to some elements, but not others. Overuse features, causing minor distraction.	Apply format and layout that does not communicate information or ideas clearly. Do not use format and layout features to clarify function, illustrate relationships, or indicate relative importance. Use available features excessively, causing distraction.
4-Process	Use an organized approach that integrates planning, development, self-assessment, revision, and reflection.	Demonstrate an organized approach in some areas, but not others; or, use an insufficient process of organization throughout.	Do not use an organized approach to solve the problem.

OUTCOMES-BASED ASSESSMENTS

PROJECT FILES

For Project 5L, you will need the following file:

a05L_Surfboards

You will save your document as:

Lastname_Firstname_5L_Surfboards

Miles Gorden, Purchasing Manager for S-Boards, Inc., is stocking the shop with a variety of surfboards and accessories for the upcoming season. In this project, you will open the **a05L_Surfboards** database and create queries to perform special functions. Save the database as **Lastname_Firstname_5L_Surfboards** Create a query to display the item, cost, selling price, on hand, and two calculated fields: Item Profit by subtracting the cost from the selling price, and Inventory Profit by multiplying Item Profit by the number on hand for each item. Be sure both fields display as Currency. Include a sum for the Inventory Profit column at the bottom of the query results. Check the supplier against the inventory using a find unmatched records query; display all fields in the supplier table. Create a query to show the organization that supplies each item, its email address, and then the item and on hand fields for each item in the inventory. Before running the query, create an outer join query using the *5L Suppliers* table and the *5L Inventory* table. Save your queries using your last and first names followed by the query type. View the queries in Print Preview, ensuring that the queries print on one page. If you are instructed to submit this result, create a paper or electronic printout. Close the queries.

END | You have completed Project 5L

Customizing Forms and Reports

GO! to Work
Video A6

6

ACCESS 2013

PROJECT 6A

OUTCOMES
Customize forms.

OBJECTIVES
1. Create a Form in Design View
2. Change and Add Controls
3. Format a Form
4. Make a Form User Friendly

PROJECT 6B

OUTCOMES
Customize reports.

OBJECTIVES
5. Create a Report Based on a Query Using a Wizard
6. Create a Report in Design View
7. Add Controls to a Report
8. Group, Sort, and Total Records in Design View

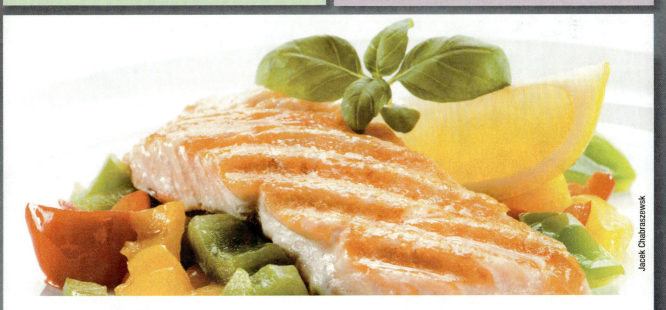

Jacek Chabraszewsk

In This Chapter

Forms provide a way to enter, edit, and display data from underlying tables. You have created forms using the Form button and wizard. Forms can also be created in Design view. Access provides tools to enhance the appearance of forms, like adding color, backgrounds, borders, or instructions to the person using the form. Forms can also be created from multiple tables if a relationship exists between the tables.

Reports display data in a professional-looking format. Like forms, reports can be created using a wizard or in Design view, and they can all be enhanced using Access tools. Reports can be based on tables or queries.

Rosebud Cafe is a "quick, casual" franchise restaurant chain with headquarters in Florida and locations throughout the United States. The founders wanted to create a restaurant where fresh flavors would be available at reasonable prices in a bright, comfortable atmosphere. The menu features quality ingredients in offerings like grilled meat and vegetable skewers, wraps, salads, frozen yogurt, smoothies, coffee drinks, and seasonal favorites. All 81 outlets offer wireless Internet connections and meeting space, making Rosebud Cafe the perfect place for groups and people who want some quiet time or to work with others.

PROJECT ACTIVITIES

In Activities 6.01 through 6.10, you will help Linda Kay, president, and James Winchell, vice president of franchising, create robust forms to match the needs of Rosebud Cafe. For example, the forms can include color and different types of controls and can manipulate data from several tables. You will customize your forms to make them easier to use and more attractive. Your completed form will look similar to Figure 6.1.

PROJECT FILES

For Project 6A, you will need the following files:

a06A_Locations
a06A_Logo
a06A_Background

You will save your database as:

Lastname_Firstname_6A_Locations

PROJECT RESULTS

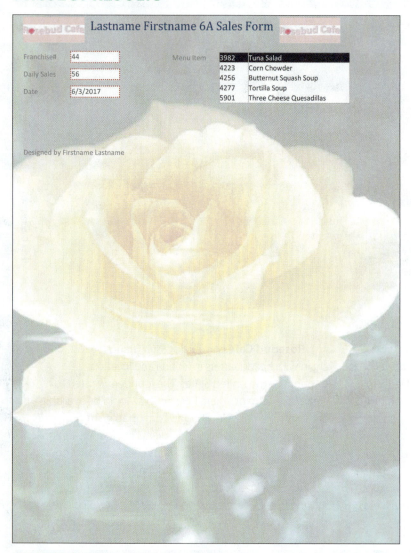

FIGURE 6.1 Project 6A Locations

Video A6-1

Forms are usually created using the Form tool or the Form Wizard and then modified in Design view to suit your needs. Use Design view to create a form when these tools do not meet your needs, or if you want more control in the creation of a form. Creating or modifying a form in Design view is a common technique when additional controls, such as combo boxes or images, need to be added to the form.

Activity 6.01 | Creating a Form in Design View

In this activity, you will create a form in Design view that will enable employees to enter the daily sales data for each franchise of Rosebud Cafe.

1 **Start** Access. Navigate to the location where the student data files for this textbook are saved. Locate and open the **a06A_Locations** file. Display **Backstage** view. Click **Save As**, and then, under *File Types*, double-click **Save Database As**. In the **Save As** dialog box, navigate to the drive on which you will be saving your folders and projects for this chapter. Create a new folder named **Access Chapter 6** and then save the database as **Lastname_Firstname_6A_ Locations** in the folder.

2 Enable the content or add the **Access Chapter 6** folder to the Trust Center.

3 In the **Navigation Pane**, double-click **6A Sales** to open the table in **Datasheet** view. Take a moment to examine the fields in the table. In any record, click in the **Franchise#** field, and then click the **arrow**. This field is a Lookup field—the values are looked up in the *6A Franchises* table. The **Menu Item** field is also a Lookup field—the values are looked up in the *6A Menu Items* table.

4 **Close** ⊗ the table, and then **Close** « the **Navigation Pane**. On the **CREATE tab**, in the **Forms group**, click the **Form Design** button.

The design grid for the Detail section displays.

5 On the **FORM DESIGN TOOLS DESIGN tab**, in the **Tools group**, click the **Property Sheet** button. Compare your screen with Figure 6.2. Notice that the *Selection type* box displays *Form*—this is the Property Sheet for the entire form.

Every object on a form, including the form itself, has an associated *Property Sheet* that can be used to further enhance the object. *Properties* are characteristics that determine the appearance, structure, and behavior of an object. This Property Sheet displays the properties that affect the appearance and behavior of the form. The left column displays the property name, and the right column displays the property setting. Some of the text in the property setting boxes may be truncated.

FIGURE 6.2

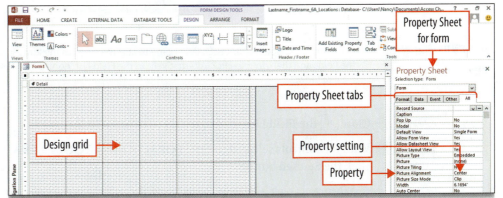

6 On the **Property Sheet**, click the **Format tab**, and then scroll down, if necessary, to display the **Split Form Orientation** property box. Point to the left edge of the **Property Sheet** until the ⟷ pointer displays, and then drag to the left until the setting in the **Split Form Orientation** property box—**Datasheet on Top**—displays entirely.

7 On the **Property Sheet**, click the **Data tab**. Click the **Record Source property setting box arrow**, and then click **6A Sales**.

> The *Record Source property* enables you to specify the source of the data for a form or a report. The property setting can be a table name, a query name, or an SQL statement.

8 Close ⊠ the **Property Sheet**. On the **FORM DESIGN TOOLS DESIGN tab**, in the **Tools group**, click the **Add Existing Fields** button, and then compare your screen with Figure 6.3.

> The Field List for the record source—6A Sales—displays.

FIGURE 6.3

9 In the **Field List**, click **Franchise#**. To select multiple fields, hold down Shift, and then click **Date**. Drag the selected fields onto the design grid until the top of the arrow of the pointer is **three dots** below the bottom edge of the **Detail section bar** and aligned with the **1.5-inch mark on the horizontal ruler**, as shown in Figure 6.4, and then release the mouse button.

> Drag the fields to where the text box controls should display. If you drag to where the label controls should display, the label controls and text box controls will overlap. If you move the controls to an incorrect position, click the Undo button before moving them again.

FIGURE 6.4

 ANOTHER WAY   In the Field List, double-click each field name to add the fields to the form. It is not possible to select all the fields and then double-click. Alternatively, in the Field List, right-click a field name, and then click Add Field to View.

10 Close ⊠ the **Field List**.

11 With all controls selected, on the **FORM DESIGN TOOLS ARRANGE tab**, in the **Table group**, click the **Stacked** button.

> When you create a form in Design view, the controls are not automatically grouped in a stacked or tabular layout. Grouping the controls makes it easier to format the controls and keeps the controls aligned.

12 ▸ Save 💾 the form as **Lastname Firstname 6A Sales Form**

Activity 6.02 | Adding Sections to a Form

The only section that is automatically added to a form when it is created in Design view is the Detail section. In this activity, you will add a Form Header section and a Form Footer section.

1 ▸ Switch to **Form** view, and notice that the form displays only the data. There is no header section with a logo or name of the form.

2 ▸ Switch to **Design** view. On the **FORM DESIGN TOOLS DESIGN tab**, in the **Header/Footer group**, click the **Logo** button. Navigate to the location where the student data files for this textbook are saved. Locate and double-click **a06A_Logo** to insert the logo in the **Form Header** section.

Two sections—the Form Header and the Form Footer—are added to the form along with the logo. Sections can be added only in Design view.

3 ▸ On the selected logo, point to the right middle sizing handle until the ↔ pointer displays. Drag to the right until the right edge of the logo is aligned with the **1.5-inch mark on the horizontal ruler**.

4 ▸ In the **Header/Footer group**, click the **Title** button to insert the title in the **Form Header** section. Compare your screen with Figure 6.5.

The name of the form is inserted as a title into the Form Header section, and the label control is the same height as the logo.

FIGURE 6.5

5 ▸ Scroll down until the **Form Footer** section bar displays. Point to the top of the **Form Footer** section bar until the ✛ pointer displays. Drag upward until the top of the **Form Footer** section bar aligns with the **2-inch mark on the vertical ruler**.

The height of the Detail section is decreased. Extra space at the bottom of the Detail section will cause blank space to display between records if the form is printed.

6 ▸ On the **FORM DESIGN TOOLS DESIGN tab**, in the **Controls group**, click the **Label** button *Aa*. Point to the **Form Footer** section until the plus sign (+) of the pointer aligns with the bottom of the **Form Footer** section bar and with the left edge of the **Date label control** in the **Detail** section. Drag downward to the bottom of the **Form Footer** section and to the right to **3 inches on the horizontal ruler**. Using your own first name and last name, type **Designed by Firstname Lastname** Press Enter, and then compare your screen with Figure 6.6.

FIGURE 6.6

Label button

Label control

7 ▶ With the **label control** in the **Form Footer** section selected, hold down Shift, and then click each of the label controls in the **Detail** section. On the **FORM DESIGN TOOLS ARRANGE tab**, in the **Sizing & Ordering group**, click the **Align** button, and then select **Left. Save** 🔲 the form, and then switch to **Form** view.

> The Form Header section displays the logo and the title of the form. The Form Footer section displays the label control that is aligned with the label controls in the Detail section. Both the Form Header and Form Footer sections display on every form page.

Objective 2 | Change and Add Controls

Video A6-2

A *control* is an object, such as a label or text box, in a form or report that enables you to view or manipulate information stored in tables or queries. You have worked with label controls, text box controls, and, earlier in the chapter, logo controls, but there are more controls that can be added to a form. More controls are available in Design view than in Layout view. By default, when you create a form, Access uses the same field definitions as those in the underlying table or query.

Activity 6.03 | Changing Controls on a Form

In this activity, you will change a combo box control to a list box control.

1 ▶ Click the **Menu Item field arrow**.

> Because the underlying table—*6A Sales*—designated this field as a lookup field, Access inserted a combo box control for this field instead of a text box control. The Franchise# field is also a combo box control. A *combo box* enables individuals to select from a list or to type a value.

2 ▶ Switch to **Design** view. In the **Detail** section, click the **Menu Item label control**, hold down Shift, and then click the **Menu Item combo box control**. On the **FORM DESIGN TOOLS ARRANGE tab**, in the **Table group**, click the **Remove Layout** button.

> The Remove Layout button is used to remove a field from a stacked or tabular layout—it does not delete the field or remove it from the form. If fields are in the middle of a stacked layout column and are removed from the layout, the remaining fields in the column will display over the removed field. To avoid the clutter, first move the fields that you want to remove from the layout to the bottom of the column.

3 ▶ Click the **Undo** button 🔄. Point to the **Menu Item label control** until the ⬚ pointer displays. Drag downward until a thin orange line displays on the bottom edges of the **Date** controls.

ALERT!   **Did the Control Stay in the Same Location?**

In Design view, the orange line that indicates the location where controls will be moved is much thinner than—and not as noticeable as—the line in Layout view. If you drag downward too far, Access will not move the selected fields.

---

4 ▷ In the **Table group**, click the **Remove Layout** button to remove the **Menu Item** field from the stacked layout. Point to the selected controls, and then drag to the right and upward until the **Menu Item label control** is aligned with the **Franchise#** controls and with the **3.25-inch mark on the horizontal ruler**. Compare your screen with Figure 6.7.

FIGURE 6.7

5 ▷ With the **Menu Item controls** selected, in the **Table group**, click the **Stacked** button. Click anywhere in the **Detail** section to deselect the second column.

> The Menu Item controls display in the second column and are grouped in a stacked layout. Recall that a stacked layout keeps the controls aligned and makes it easier to edit and move the controls.

6 ▷ Right-click the **Menu Item combo box control**. From the shortcut menu, point to **Change To**, and then click **List Box**.

> A *list box* enables individuals to select from a list but does not enable individuals to type anything that is not in the list. Based on the data in the underlying table or query, Access displays the control types to which you can change a field. The control type can be changed in Design view only.

7 ▷ Save 🖫 the form, and then switch to **Form** view. Notice the **Menu Item list box control** is not wide enough to display both columns and that there are horizontal and vertical scroll bars to indicate there is more data. Press Esc.

8 ▷ Click the **Menu Item list box control**. Scroll down until Menu Item *7839* displays. Switch to **Layout** view. Point to the right edge of the control until the ↔ pointer displays. Drag to the right until all of the Menu Item *7839* displays. Release the mouse button to display the resized list box.

9 ▷ Save 🖫 the form, and switch to **Design** view.

More Knowledge **Validate or Restrict Data in Forms**

When you design tables, set field properties to ensure the entry of valid data by using input masks, validation rules, and default values. Any field in a form created with a table having these properties inherits the validation properties from the underlying table. Setting these properties in the table is the preferred method; however, you can also set the properties on controls in the form. If conflicting settings occur, the setting on the bound control in the form will override the field property setting in the table.

Activity 6.04 | Adding Controls to a Form

In this activity, you will add an image control and button controls to the form. An *image control* enables individuals to insert an image into any section of a form or report. A *button control* enables individuals to add a command button to a form or report that will perform an action when the button is clicked.

1 ▷ On the **FORM DESIGN TOOLS DESIGN tab**, in the **Controls group**, click the **Insert Image** button, and then click **Browse**. In the displayed **Insert Picture** dialog box, navigate to the location where the student data files for this textbook are saved and double-click **a06A_Logo**. Align the plus sign (+) of the pointer with the bottom of the **Form Header** section bar at **5.5-inches on the horizontal ruler**, as shown in Figure 6.8.

FIGURE 6.8

2 ▶ Drag the pointer downward to the lower right of the **Form Header** section to **6.75 inches on the horizontal ruler**. Release the mouse button to insert the picture in the **Form Header** section.

Using the logo control inserts a picture in a predetermined location—the left side—of the Form Header section. The image control is used to insert a picture anywhere in the form. There is a second image control in the Controls gallery on the FORM DESIGN TOOLS DESIGN tab.

3 ▶ Click the **title's label control**. Point to the right edge of the **label control** until the [🔼] pointer displays. Drag to the left until there is **one dot** between the right edge of the **label control** and the left edge of the **image control**. On the **FORM DESIGN TOOLS FORMAT tab**, in the **Font group**, click the **Center** button [≡]. Switch to **Form** view, and then compare your screen with Figure 6.9.

The title is centered between the logo on the left and the image on the right, but the logo and the image are not the same size.

FIGURE 6.9

4 ▶ Switch to **Design** view, and then click the **image control**—the Rosebud Cafe image on the right side in the **Form Header** section. On the **FORM DESIGN TOOLS DESIGN tab**, in the **Tools group**, click the **Property Sheet** button. If necessary, on the Property Sheet, click the Format tab, and then compare your screen with Figure 6.10. Notice the **Width** and **Height** property settings.

Your Width property setting and Height property setting may differ.

FIGURE 6.10

5 If necessary, change the Width property setting to 1.25 and then change the Height property setting to 0.5 In the **Form Header** section, on the left side, click the **logo control**, and then notice that the Property Sheet for the logo control displays. On the **Property Sheet**, change the **Width** property setting to **1.25** and then change the **Height** property setting to **0.5 Close** ⌧ the **Property Sheet**.

> The width and height of the two controls are now the same.

6 With the logo control selected, hold down Shift, and then click the **image control**. On the **FORM DESIGN TOOLS ARRANGE tab**, in the **Sizing & Ordering group**, click the **Align** button, and then click **Bottom**. Click the **title's label control**. In the **Table group**, click **Remove Layout**, and then point to the left middle sizing handle until the ↔ pointer displays. Drag to the right until there is **one dot** between the right edge of the **logo control** and the left edge of the **title's label control**.

> The logo control and the image control are aligned at the bottom, and the title's label control is resized.

7 On the **FORM DESIGN TOOLS DESIGN tab**, at the right edge of the **Controls gallery**, click the **More** button ⌄, and verify that the **Use Control Wizards** option is active. Click the **Button** button ▭. Move the mouse pointer down into the **Detail** section. Align the plus sign (+) of the pointer at **1.5 inches on the vertical ruler** and **1.5 inches on the horizontal ruler**, and then click. Compare your screen with Figure 6.11.

> The Command Button Wizard dialog box displays. The first dialog box enables you to select an action for the button based on the selected category.

FIGURE 6.11

8 Take a moment to click the different categories to display the actions associated with each category. When you are finished, under **Categories**, click **Record Navigation**. Under **Actions**, click **Go to Previous Record**, and then click **Next**.

> The second Command Button Wizard dialog box displays, which enables you to select what will display on the button—either text or a picture. If you select picture, you can then click Browse to navigate to a location on your computer where pictures are saved, and then select any picture. If you select text, accept the default text or type new text. A preview of the button displays on the left side of the dialog box.

9 Next to **Picture**, verify **Go to Previous** is selected, and then click **Next**.

> The third Command Button Wizard dialog box displays, which enables you to name the button. If you need to refer to the button later—usually in creating macros—a meaningful name is helpful. The buttons created with the Command Button Wizard are linked to macros or programs.

10 In the text box, type **btnPrevRecord** and then click **Finish**.

> When creating controls that can later be used in programming, it is a good idea to start the name of the control with an abbreviation of the type of control—btn—and then a descriptive abbreviation of the purpose of the control.

11 Using the techniques you have just practiced, add a **button control** about **1 inch** to the right of the **Previous Record button control**. Under **Categories**, click **Record Navigation**, if necessary. Under **Actions**, click **Go to Next Record**. For **Picture**, click **Go to Next**, and then name the button **btnNxtRecord** and then click **Finish**. Do not be concerned if the button controls are not exactly aligned.

12 With the **Next Record button control** selected, hold down Shift, and then click the **Previous Record button control**. On the **FORM DESIGN TOOLS ARRANGE tab**, in the **Sizing & Ordering group**, click the **Align** button, and then click **Top**. Click the **Size/Space** button, and then click either **Increase Horizontal Spacing** button or **Decrease Horizontal Spacing** until there is approximately **1 inch** of space between the two controls. Compare your screen with Figure 6.12.

FIGURE 6.12

13 **Save** 🖫 the form, and then switch to **Form** view. Experiment by clicking the **Next Record** button and the **Previous Record** button, and notice in the record navigator that you are displaying different records.

14 Switch to **Design** view. On the **FORM DESIGN TOOLS DESIGN tab**, in the **Controls group**, click the **Button** button ⌷. Align the plus sign (+) of the pointer at **1.5 inches on the vertical ruler** and at **5.5 inches on the horizontal ruler**, and then click.

15 In the **Command Button Wizard** dialog box, under **Categories**, click **Form Operations**. Under **Actions**, click **Print Current Form**, and then click **Next**. Click the **Text** option button to accept *Print Form*, and then click **Next**. Name the button **btnPrtForm** and then click **Finish**.

You will use this button to print one form when you are finished formatting the form.

16 **Save** 🖫 the form.

More Knowledge   **Remove Form Controls**

To remove any control from a form, click the control to select it, and then press Del. To select more than one control at a time before deleting, select the controls by pressing Ctrl when you click each item.

Objective 3 Format a Form

Video A6-3

There are several methods you can use to modify the appearance of a form. Each section and control on a form has properties. Some properties can be modified by using buttons in the groups on a tab or by changing the property setting on the Property Sheet.

Activity 6.05 | Adding a Background Color

1 With **6A Sales Form** open in **Design** view, click the **Form Header** section bar.

The darkened bar indicates that the entire Form Header section of the form is selected.

2 On the **FORM DESIGN TOOLS FORMAT tab**, in the **Control Formatting group**, click the **Shape Fill** button. Under **Theme Colors**, in the second row, click the sixth color—**Red, Accent 2, Lighter 80%**.

The background color for the Form Header section changes to a light shade of red.

3 Double-click the **Form Footer** section bar to display the **Property Sheet** for the **Form Footer** section. On the **Property Sheet**, click the **Format tab**, if necessary, and then click in the **Back Color** property setting box—it displays Background 1. Click the **Build** button ⸭.

The color palette displays. Background 1 is a code used by Access to represent the color white. You can select an Access Theme Color, a Standard Color, a Recent Color, or click More Colors to select shades of colors.

4 Click **More Colors**. In the displayed **Colors** dialog box, click the **Custom tab**.

All colors use varying shades of Red, Green, and Blue.

5 In the **Colors** dialog box, click **Cancel**. On the **Property Sheet**, click the **Back Color property setting arrow**.

A list of color schemes display. These colors also display on the color palette under Access Theme Colors.

6 From the displayed list, experiment by clicking on different color schemes and viewing the effects of the background color change. You will have to click the **property setting arrow** each time to select another color scheme. When you are finished, click the **Build** button ⸭. Under **Theme Colors**, in the second row, click the sixth color—**Red, Accent 2, Lighter 80%**. **Close** ⨯ the **Property Sheet**.

You can change the background color either by using the Background Color button in the Font group or by changing the Back Color property setting on the Property Sheet.

🔄 ANOTHER WAY   Open the form in Layout view. To select a section, click in an empty area of the section. On the HOME tab, in the Text Formatting group, click the Background Color button.

7 Using one of the techniques you have just practiced, change the background color of the **Detail** section to **Red, Accent 2, Lighter 80%**. Switch to **Form** view, and then compare your screen with Figure 6.13.

FIGURE 6.13

Background color set to Red, Accent 2, Lighter 80%

8 Save 🖫 the form, and then switch to **Design** view.

Activity 6.06 | Adding a Background Picture to a Form

In this activity, you will add a picture to the background of *6A Sales Form*.

1 With **6A Sales Form** open in **Design** view, locate the **Form selector**, as shown in Figure 6.14.

The *Form selector* is the box where the rulers meet, in the upper left corner of a form in Design view. Use the Form selector to select the entire form.

FIGURE 6.14

2 Double-click the **Form selector** to open the **Property Sheet** for the form.

3 On the **Property Sheet**, on the **Format tab**, click in the **Picture** property setting box. Click the **Build** button ⋯ . Navigate to the location where the student data files for this textbook are saved. Locate and double-click **a06A_Background** to insert the picture in the form, and then compare your screen with Figure 6.15.

FIGURE 6.15

4 Click in the **Picture Alignment** property setting box, click the **arrow**, and then click **Form Center**.

The *Picture Alignment property* determines where the background picture for a form displays on the form. Center places the picture in the center of the page when the form is printed. Form Center places the picture in the center of the form data when the form is printed.

5 Click in the **Picture Size Mode** property setting box, and then click the **arrow** to display the options. From the displayed list, click **Stretch**.

The *Picture Size Mode property* determines the size of the picture in the form. The Clip setting retains the original size of the image. The Stretch setting stretches the image both vertically and horizontally to match the size of the form—the image may be distorted. The Zoom setting adjusts the image to be as large as possible without distorting the image. Both Stretch Horizontal and Stretch Vertical can distort the image. If you have a background color and set the Picture Type property setting to Stretch, the background color will not display.

6 Close ✕ the **Property Sheet**, Save 💾 the form, and then switch to **Layout** view. Compare your screen with Figure 6.16.

FIGURE 6.16

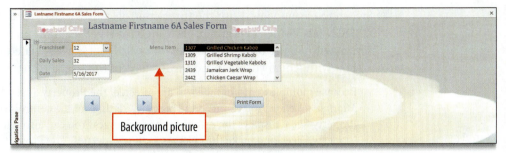

Activity 6.07 | Modifying the Borders of Controls

In this activity, you will modify the borders of some of the controls on *6A Sales Form*. There are related property settings on the Property Sheet.

1 With **6A Sales Form** open in **Layout** view, click the **Franchise#** combo box control. Holding down Shift, click the **Daily Sales** text box control, and then click the **Date text box control**. On the **FORM LAYOUT TOOLS FORMAT tab**, in the **Control Formatting group**, click the **Shape Outline** button. Notice the options that are used to modify borders—Colors, Line Thickness, and Line Type. Compare your screen with Figure 6.17.

FIGURE 6.17

2 Point to **Line Type** and point to each line type to display the **ScreenTip**. The second line type—**Solid**—is the default line type. Click the fifth line type—**Dots**—and then switch to **Form** view to display the results. Notice that the borders of the three controls display a line type of Dots. Switch to **Layout** view.

You can review the results in Layout view, but you would have to deselect the three controls.

3 With the three controls still selected, on the **FORM LAYOUT TOOLS FORMAT tab**, in the **Control Formatting group**, click the **Shape Outline** button. Point to **Line Thickness** and point to each line thickness to display the **ScreenTip**. The first line thickness—**Hairline**—is the default line thickness. Click the second line type—**1 pt**.

4 In the **Control Formatting group, click** the **Shape Outline** button. Under **Theme Colors**, point to each color to display the **ScreenTip**, and then in the first row, click the sixth color—**Red, Accent 2**. Switch to **Form** view to display the results.

The borders of the three controls display a line thickness of 1 point, and the color of the borders is a darker shade. A **point** is 1/72 of an inch.

5 Switch to **Layout** view. With the three controls still selected, on the **FORM LAYOUT TOOLS DESIGN tab**, in the **Tools group**, click the **Property Sheet** button, and then compare your screen with Figure 6.18. Notice the properties that are associated with the buttons on the ribbon with which you changed the borders of the selected controls.

Because multiple items on the form are selected, the Property Sheet displays Selection type: *Multiple selection*. You changed the property settings of the controls by using buttons, and the Property Sheet displays the results of those changes. You can also select multiple controls, open the Property Sheet, and make the changes to the properties. The Property Sheet displays more settings than those available through the use of buttons.

FIGURE 6.18

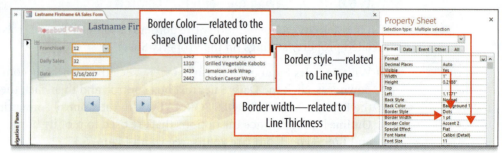

6 **Close** ☒ the **Property Sheet**, and then **Save** 🖫 the form. Switch to **Form** view.

More Knowledge   **Adding Borders to Label Controls**

By default, the border style—line style—of a Label control is transparent, effectively hiding the border from the display. Because borders display around bound controls that contain data, it is recommended that you do not add borders to label controls so that individuals can easily distinguish the control that holds data.

Objective 4   Make a Form User Friendly

Video A6-4

To make forms easy to use, you can add instructions to the status bar while data is being entered and custom *ControlTips* that display when an individual pauses the mouse pointer over a control on a form. Additionally, you can change the tab order of the fields on a form. *Tab order* refers to the order in which the fields are selected when the Tab key is pressed. By default, the tab order is created based on the order in which the fields are added to the form.

Activity 6.08 │ Adding a Message to the Status Bar

When you created tables, you may have added a description to the field, and the description displayed in the status bar of the Access window. If a description is included for a field in the underlying table of a form, the text of the description will also display in the status bar when an individual clicks in the field on the form. In this activity, you will add a description to the Daily Sales field in the *6A Sales* table, and then *propagate*—disseminate or apply—the changes to *6A Sales Form*. You will also add status bar text to a field on a form using the Property Sheet of the control.

1 With **6A Sales Form** open in **Form** view, click in the **Daily Sales** field. On the left side of the status bar, *Form View* displays—there is no text that helps an individual enter data.

2 Close ☒ the form, and then **Open** ⸌«⸍ the **Navigation Pane**. Under **Tables**, right-click **6A Sales**, and then from the shortcut menu, click **Design View**. In the **Daily Sales** field, click in the **Description** box. Type **How many items were sold?** and then press Enter. Compare your screen with Figure 6.19.

A *Property Update Options button* displays in the Description box for the Date field. When you make changes to the design of a table, Access displays this button, which enables individuals to update the Property Sheet for this field in all objects that use this table as the record source.

FIGURE 6.19

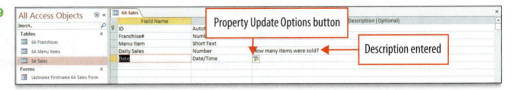

3 Click the **Property Update Options** button 🖉, and then click **Update Status Bar Text everywhere Daily Sales is used**. In the displayed **Update Properties** dialog box, under **Update the following objects?**, notice that only one object—*Form: 6A Sales Form*—displays, and it is selected. In the **Update Properties** dialog box, click **Yes**. Close ☒ the table, saving changes.

The changes in the Description field in the table will be propagated to *6A Sales Form*. If multiple objects use the *6A Sales* table as the underlying object, you can propagate the change to all of the objects.

4 In the **Navigation Pane**, under **Forms**, double-click **6A Sales Form** to open it in **Form** view. Close ⸌«⸍ the **Navigation Pane**. Click in the **Daily Sales** field, and then notice that on the left side of the status bar, *How many items were sold?* displays.

Access propagated the change made in the underlying table to the form.

5 Switch to **Design** view. Click the **Daily Sales text box control**. On the **FORM DESIGN TOOLS DESIGN tab**, in the **Tools group**, click the **Property Sheet** button.

6 On the **Property Sheet**, click the **Other tab**. Locate the **Status Bar Text** property, and notice the setting *How many items were sold?*

When Access propagated the change to the form, it populated the Status Bar Text property setting. The *Status Bar Text property* enables individuals to add descriptive text that will display in the status bar for a selected control.

7 In the **Detail** section, click the **Date text box control**, and then notice that the **Property Sheet** changes to display the properties for the **Date text box control**. Click in the **Status Bar Text** property setting box, type **Enter the date of sales report** and then Press Enter.

Entering a Status Bar Text on the Text Box Property Sheet does not display a Property Update Options button to propagate changes to the underlying table or add the information to the Description box for the field in the table.

8 Save 🖫 the form, and then switch to **Form** view. Click in the **Date** field, and then compare your screen with Figure 6.20.

The status bar displays the text you entered in the Status Bar Text property setting box.

FIGURE 6.20

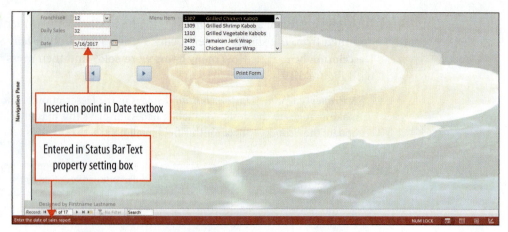

9 ▸ Switch to **Design** view.

Conflicting Field Description and Status Bar Text Property Setting

When you create a form, the fields inherit the property settings from the underlying table. You can change the Status Bar Text property setting for the form, and it will override the setting that is inherited from the table. If you later change field properties in Table Design view, the Property Update Options button displays—you must manually propagate those changes to the table's related objects; propagation is not automatic. An exception to this is entering Validation Rules—changes are automatically propagated.

Activity 6.09 | Creating Custom ControlTips

Another way to make a form easier to use is to add custom ControlTips to objects on the form. A ControlTip is similar to a ScreenTip, and temporarily displays descriptive text while the mouse pointer is paused over the control. This method is somewhat limited because most individuals press Tab or Enter to move from field to field and thus do not see the ControlTip. However, a ControlTip is a useful tool in a training situation when an individual is learning how to use the data entry form. In this activity, you will add a ControlTip to the Print Form button control.

1 ▸ With **6A Sales Form** open in **Design** view and the **Property Sheet** displayed, click the **Print Form** button. If necessary, click the Other tab to make it active. Notice the **Property Sheet** displays *Selection type: Command Button* and the **Selection type** box displays *btnPrtForm*, the name you gave to the button when you added it to the form.

2 ▸ Click in the **ControlTip Text** property setting box, type **Prints the selected record** and then press Enter. Compare your screen with Figure 6.21.

FIGURE 6.21

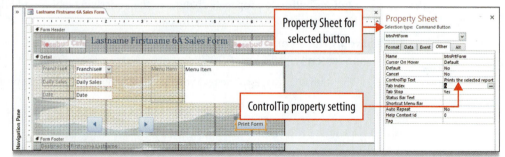

3 ▸ **Close** ☒ the **Property Sheet**, **Save** 🖫 the form, and then switch to **Form** view. Point to the **Print Form** button, and then compare your screen with Figure 6.22.

A ControlTip displays the message you typed for the ControlTip Text property setting.

FIGURE 6.22

Activity 6.10 | Changing the Tab Order

You can customize the order in which you enter data on a form by changing the tab order. Recall that tab order refers to the order in which the fields are selected each time [Tab] is pressed. As you press [Tab], the focus of the form changes from one control to another control. *Focus* refers to the object that is selected and currently being acted upon.

> **1** With **6A Sales Form** open in **Form** view, in the record navigator, click the **New (blank) record** button. If necessary, click in the Franchise# combo box. Press [Tab] three times, and then notice that the insertion point moves from field to field, ending with the **Date** text box. Press [Tab] three more times, and then notice the **Print Form** button is the focus. The button displays with a darker border. Press [Enter].

Because the focus is on the Print Form button, the Print dialog box displays.

> **2** In the **Print** dialog box, click **Cancel**. Switch to **Design** view.

> **3** On the **FORM DESIGN TOOLS DESIGN tab**, in the **Tools group**, click the **Tab Order** button, and then compare your screen with Figure 6.23.

The Tab Order dialog box displays. Under Section, Detail is selected. Under Custom Order, the fields and controls display in the order they were added to the form. To the left of each field name or button name is a row selector button.

As you rearrange fields on a form, the tab order does not change from the original tab order. This can make data entry chaotic because the focus is changed in what appears to be an illogical order. The Auto Order button will change the tab order based on the position of the controls in the form from left to right and top to bottom.

FIGURE 6.23

> **4** To the left of **Menu Item**, click the **row selector** box. Point to the **row selector** box, and then drag downward until a dark horizontal line displays between **Date** and **btnPrevRecord**.

The Menu Item field will now receive the focus after the Date field.

ALERT! **Did the Field Stay in the Same Location?**

You must point to the row selector box before dragging the field. If you point to the field name, the field will not be moved.

5 In the **Tab Order** dialog box, click **OK. Save** 🖫 the form, and then switch to **Form** view. In the record navigator, click the **Last Record** button. When the **Menu Item** field has the focus, it is easier to see it on a blank record. In the record navigator, click the **New (blank) record** button.

The insertion point displays in the Franchise# field.

6 Press Tab three times. Even though it is difficult to see, the focus changes to the **Menu Item** list box. Press Tab again, and then notice that the focus changes to the **btnPrevRecord** button.

Before allowing individuals to enter data into a form, you should always test the tab order to ensure that the data will be easy to enter.

7 Switch to **Design** view. In the **Detail** section, right-click the **Date text box control**, click **Properties**. If necessary, click the Other tab, and then compare your screen with Figure 6.24.

Text box controls have three properties relating to tab order: Tab Index, Tab Stop, and Auto Tab. Combo box controls and list box controls do not have an Auto Tab property.

FIGURE 6.24

8 On the **Property Sheet**, click in the **Tab Index property setting box**, which displays *2*. Click the **Build** button ⌷.

Tab Index settings begin with 0. Franchise# has a Tab Index setting of 0, which indicates that this field has the focus when the form is opened. Daily Sales has a Tab Index setting of 1—it will receive the focus when Tab is pressed one time. Date has a Tab Index setting of 2—it will receive the focus when Tab is pressed a second time. Menu Item has a Tab Index setting of 3—it will receive the focus when Tab is pressed a third time.

9 In the **Tab Order** dialog box, click **Cancel**. On the **Property Sheet**, notice that the **Tab Stop** property setting is **Yes**, which means individuals can press Tab to move to this field.

The Auto Tab property setting is No. It should be changed to Yes only when a text field has an input mask. Recall that an input mask controls how the data is entered into a field; for example, the formatting of a phone number.

10 In the **Detail** section, click the **Franchise# combo box control**, and then on the **Property Sheet**, notice the settings for the **Tab Index** and **Tab Stop** properties.

The Tab Index setting is 0, which means this field has the focus when the form page is displayed—it is first on the tab order list. The Tab Stop setting is Yes. Because an input mask cannot be applied to a combo box, there is no Auto Tab property. The Auto Tab property applies only to a text box control.

11 In the **Detail** section, click the **Previous Record button control**. On the **Property Sheet**, click in the **Tab Stop** property setting box, click the **arrow**, and then click **No**.

Changing the Tab Stop property setting to No means that the focus will not be changed to the button by pressing Tab.

12 **Save** 🖫 the form, and then switch to **Form** view. In the record navigator, click the **Last record** button. Press Tab two times, watching the focus change from the **Franchise#** field to the **Date** field. Press Tab two more times, and then compare your screen with Figure 6.25.

Because the Tab Stop property setting for the Previous Record button control was changed to No, the button does not receive the focus by pressing the Tab key.

FIGURE 6.25

13 In the **Detail** section, click the **Previous Record** button.

The previous record displays—you can still use the button by clicking on it.

14 Switch to **Design** view. Using the techniques you have just practiced, for the **Next Record** button and the **Print Form** button, change the **Tab Stop** property setting to **No**.

15 **Close** ☒ the **Property Sheet**. **Save** 🖫 the form, and then switch to **Form** view. Test the tab order by pressing Tab, making sure that the focus does not change to the **Next Record** button or the **Print Form** button.

When the focus is on the Date field, pressing the Tab key moves the focus to the Franchise# field in the next record.

16 Navigate to **Record 5**—Franchise# 44. Unless you are required to submit your database electronically, in the **Detail** section, click the **Print Form** button. In the **Print** dialog box, under **Print Range**, click **Selected Record(s)**, and then click **OK**. If you are instructed to submit this result as an electronic printout, select the record using the selector bar, and then from **Backstage** view, click **Save As**. Click the **Save Object As** button, and double-click **PDF or XPS**. Navigate to the folder where you store your electronic printouts. Click the **Options** button, click **Selected records**, and then click **OK**. Click **Publish**.

17 **Close** ☒ the form, and then **Close** « the **Navigation Pane**. **Close** the database, and then **Exit** ☒ Access.

18 As directed by your instructor, submit your database and the paper or electronic printout of the form that is the result of this project. Specifically, in this project, using your own name you created the following database and printout or electronic printout:

| 1. Lastname_Firstname_6A_Locations | Database file |
| 2. Lastname_Firstname_6A_Sales_Form | Form (printed or electronic printout) |

END | You have completed Project 6A

PROJECT ACTIVITIES

In Activities 6.11 through 6.18, you will create customized reports. The corporate office of Rosebud Cafe (RBC) maintains a database about the franchises, including daily sales of menu items per franchise, the franchise owners, and franchise fees and payments. Reports are often run to summarize data in the tables or queries. Creating customized reports will help the owners and officers of the company view the information in the database in a meaningful way. Your completed reports will look similar to Figure 6.26.

PROJECT FILES

For Project 6B, you will need the following files: You will save your database as:

a06B_RBC   **Lastname_Firstname_6B_RBC**
a06B_Logo

PROJECT RESULTS

FIGURE 6.26 Project 6B Rosebud Cafe

Video A6-5

A report wizard is a more efficient way to start a report, although Design view does offer you more control as you create your report. Once the report has been created, its appearance can be modified in Design or Layout view.

Activity 6.11 | Creating a Report Using a Wizard

In this activity, you will use a wizard to create a report for Rosebud Cafe that displays the data from the 6B Total Daily Sales Crosstab Query.

1   **Start** Access. Navigate to the location where the student data files for this textbook are saved. Locate and open the **a06B_RBC** file. Save the database in your **Access Chapter 6** folder as **Lastname_Firstname_6B_RBC**

2   If you did not add the **Access Chapter 6** folder to the Trust Center, enable the content. In the **Navigation Pane**, under **Queries**, double-click **6B Total Daily Sales Crosstab Query**. Take a moment to study the data in the query, as shown in Figure 6.27.

> The data is grouped by Item Name and Month. The sum function calculates the total daily sales for each item per month.

FIGURE 6.27

3   **Close** ⊠ the query. With **6B Total Daily Sales Crosstab Query** still selected, **Close** « the **Navigation Pane**.

4   On the **CREATE tab**, in the **Reports group**, click the **Report Wizard** button.

5   Because the crosstab query was selected in the **Navigation Pane**, in the **Report Wizard** dialog box, in the **Tables/Queries** box, **Query: 6B Total Daily Sales Crosstab Query** displays. If it does not display, click the Tables/Queries arrow, and then click Query: 6B Total Daily Sales Crosstab Query.

6   Under **Available Fields**, notice there are more months than those that were displayed in **6B Total Daily Sales Crosstab Query**.

> Because there was data for the months of May, June, and July only, the other months were hidden from the display in the query. To hide a column in Datasheet view, right-click the column header, and then from the shortcut menu, click Hide Fields.

7   Under **Available Fields**, double-click each field name, in the order specified, to add the field names to the **Selected Fields** box: **Item Name**, **May**, **Jun**, and **Jul**.

8   In the **Report Wizard** dialog box, click **Next**. Because no grouping levels will be used, click **Next**.

9   To sort the records within the report by Item Name, click the **arrow** next to the **1** box. From the displayed list, click **Item Name**. Leave the sort order as **Ascending**, and then click **Next**.

10 Under **Layout**, verify the **Tabular** option button is selected. Under **Orientation**, verify the **Portrait** option button is selected, and then click **Next**.

11 In the **What title do you want for your report?** box, type **Lastname Firstname 6B Monthly Sales** and then click **Finish**. Compare your screen with Figure 6.28.

The report displays in Print Preview. Because this report uses a crosstab query as the record source, it displays calculated data grouped by two different types of information.

FIGURE 6.28

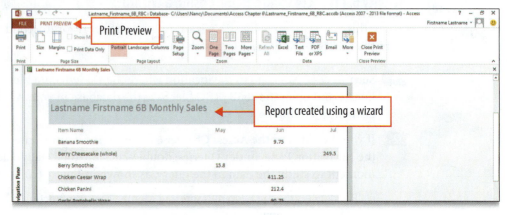

Activity 6.12 | Modifying a Report Created Using a Wizard

In this activity, you will modify controls in the report to change its appearance. Although the report was created using a wizard, its appearance can be modified in Design view and Layout view.

1 On the **Print Preview tab**, in the **Close Preview group**, click the **Close Print Preview** button. If the Field List or Property Sheet displays, close it.

2 On the **REPORT DESIGN TOOLS DESIGN tab**, in the **Themes group**, click the **Themes** button to display a list of available themes. Under **Office**, on the second row, click the second theme—**Organic**.

Themes simplify the process of creating professional-looking objects within one program or across multiple programs. A theme includes theme colors and theme fonts that will be applied consistently throughout the objects in the database. It is a simple way to provide professional, consistent formatting in a database.

3 If necessary, click anywhere in an empty area of the report to deselect the Item Name column. Click the **Report title text box control**. On the **REPORT DESIGN TOOLS FORMAT tab**, in the **Font group**, click the **Font Color button arrow** [A ▾]. Under **Theme Colors**, in the first row, click the eighth color—**Red, Accent 4**. If necessary, resize the title text box so the entire title is visible.

4 Select all of the controls in the **Page Header** section by pointing to the top left of the **Page Header** section, holding down your mouse button, dragging the mouse across the **Page Header controls** and to the bottom of the **Page Header** section, and then releasing the mouse button. Use the techniques you have practiced to change the font color to **Red, Accent 4**.

Any group of controls can be selected using this lasso method. It can be more efficient than holding down [Shift] while clicking each control.

🔁 **BY TOUCH**   Use your finger to draw the circle and to highlight text.

5 Save the report, and then switch to **Layout** view.

6 ▶ In the **Item Name** column, select any **text box control**. Hold down ⬒Shift⬓ and click the **Item Name label control** to select the entire column. Point to the right edge of the control until the ↔ pointer displays. Drag to the left until the box is approximately **2.5 inches** wide; be sure none of the data in the column is cut off.

7 ▶ To select all of the text box controls, in the **May** column, click **15.8**. Holding down ⬒Shift⬓, in the **Jun** and **Jul** columns, click a **text box control**. Compare your screen with Figure 6.29.

FIGURE 6.29

Item Name	May	Jun	Jul
Banana Smoothie		9.75	
Berry Cheesecake (whole)			249.5
Berry Smoothie	15.8		
Chicken Caesar Wrap		411.25	
Chicken Panini		212.4	
Garlic Portobello Wrap		90.75	
Grilled Chicken Kabob	318.4		398

Lastname Firstname 6B Monthly Sales

Selected text box controls

8 ▶ On the **REPORT LAYOUT TOOLS DESIGN tab**, in the **Tools group**, click the **Property Sheet** button. Notice that the selection type is *Multiple selection*.

9 ▶ On the **Property Sheet**, click the **Format tab**. Click the **Format property setting arrow**. From the displayed list, select **Currency**. Click the **Border Style property setting arrow**, and click **Short Dashes**. **Close** ✕ the **Property Sheet**.

10 ▶ **Save** 🖫 the report, and then switch to **Print Preview** view. If you are instructed to submit this result, create a paper or electronic printout. On the **Print Preview tab**, in the **Close Preview group**, click the **Close Print Preview** button.

11 ▶ **Close** ✕ the report, and then **Open** » the **Navigation Pane**.

Objective 6 Create a Report in Design View

Video A6-6

You usually create a report using the Report tool or the Report Wizard, and then modify the report in Design view to suit your needs. Use Design view to create a report when these tools do not meet your needs or if you want more control in the creation of a report. Creating or modifying a report in Design view is a common technique when additional controls, such as calculated controls, need to be added to the report or properties need to be changed.

Activity 6.13 │ Creating a Report in Design View

Creating a report with the Report tool or the Report Wizard is the easiest way to start the creation of a customized report, but you can also create a report from scratch in Design view. Once you understand the sections of a report and how to manipulate the controls within the sections, it is easier to modify a report that has been created using the report tools.

1 ▶ In the **Navigation Pane**, open **6B Total Daily Sales Query** in **Design** view, and then notice the underlying tables that were used in the creation of the query. Notice the calculated field— *Total Cost*.

> Recall that a calculated field contains the field name, followed by a colon, and then an expression. In the expression, the existing field names must be enclosed in square brackets. The Total Cost was calculated by multiplying the value in the Cost field by the value in the Daily Sales field.

2 When you are finished, **Close** ⊠ the query, and **Close** « the **Navigation Pane**. On the **CREATE tab**, in the **Reports group**, click the **Report Design** button. When the design grid displays, scroll down to display all of the report sections.

> Three sections are included in the blank design grid: the Page Header section, the Detail section, and the Page Footer section. A page header displays at the top of every printed page, and a page footer displays at the bottom of every printed page.

3 Select the report using the report selector, if necessary. On the **REPORT DESIGN TOOLS DESIGN tab**, in the **Tools group**, click the **Property Sheet** button, if necessary. On the **Property Sheet**, click the **Data tab**. Click the **Record Source property setting box arrow**, and then compare your screen with Figure 6.30. If necessary, increase the width of the Property Sheet.

FIGURE 6.30

4 From the displayed list of tables and queries, click **6B Total Daily Sales Query**, and then **Close** ⊠ the **Property Sheet**.

> 6B Total Daily Sales Query is the record source—underlying query—for this report.

5 On the **REPORT DESIGN TOOLS DESIGN tab**, in the **Tools group**, click the **Add Existing Fields** button to display the fields in **6B Total Daily Sales Query.**

6 In the **Field List**, click **Date**. Hold down Shift, and then click **Franchise#** to select all of the fields.

ALERT! **Are multiple tables displayed in the field list?**

If all tables display in the field list, click Show only fields in the current record source at the bottom of the Field List box.

7 Drag the selected fields into the **Detail** section of the design grid until the top of the arrow of the pointer is **one dot** below the bottom edge of the **Detail** section bar and aligned with the **3-inch mark on the horizontal ruler**. **Close** ⊠ the **Field List**, and then compare your screen with Figure 6.31.

FIGURE 6.31

8 With the label controls and text box controls for the fields selected, click the **REPORT DESIGN TOOLS ARRANGE tab**. In the **Table group**, click the **Stacked** button to group the fields together for easier formatting.

9 On the **REPORT DESIGN TOOLS DESIGN tab**, in the **Themes group**, click the **Themes** button. Under **In This Database**, notice the theme used in this database—**Organic**. Press [Esc] to close the gallery.

10 Save 🖫 the report as **Lastname Firstname 6B Total Daily Sales**.

Activity 6.14 | Modifying the Sections of a Report

By default, a report created in Design view includes a Page Header section and a Page Footer section. Reports can also include a Report Header section and a Report Footer section. In this activity, you will add the Report Header and Report Footer sections and hide the Page Header section. Recall that a Report Header displays at the top of the first printed page of a report, and the Report Footer displays at the bottom of the last printed page of a report.

1 Right-click in the **Detail** section of the report, and click **Report Header/Footer**. Notice that the **Report Header** section displays at the top of the design grid. Scroll down to display the **Report Footer** section.

2 Scroll up to display the **Report Header** section. On the **REPORT DESIGN TOOLS DESIGN tab**, in the **Header/Footer group**, click the **Logo** button. Locate and double-click **a06B_Logo** to insert the logo in the **Report Header** section. On the selected logo, point to the right middle sizing handle until the ↔ pointer displays. Drag to the right until the right edge of the logo is aligned with the **1.5-inch mark on the horizontal ruler**.

3 On the **REPORT DESIGN TOOLS DESIGN tab**, in the **Header/Footer group**, click the **Title** button. In the **title's label control**, click to the left of your **Lastname**, delete your **Lastname Firstname** and the space, and then press [Enter]. On the **title's label control**, point to the right middle sizing handle until the ↔ pointer displays, and then double-click to adjust the size of the **label control** to fit the text. Alternatively, drag the right middle sizing handle to the left.

4 Scroll down until the **Page Footer** section bar displays. Point to the top edge of the **Page Footer** section bar until the ⊹ pointer displays. Drag upward until the top of the **Page Footer** section bar aligns with the **2.25-inch mark on the vertical ruler**.

This prevents extra blank space from printing between the records.

5 Scroll up until the **Report Header** section displays. Point to the top edge of the **Detail** section bar until the ⊹ pointer displays. Drag upward until the top edge of the **Detail** section bar aligns with the bottom edge of the **Page Header** section bar, and then compare your screen with Figure 6.32.

The Page Header and Page Footer sections are paired together. Likewise, the Report Header and Report Footer sections are paired together. You cannot remove only one section of the pair. If you wish to remove one section of a paired header/footer, decrease the height of the section. Alternatively, set the Height property for the section to 0. Because there is no space in the Page Header section, nothing will print at the top of every page. To remove both of the paired header/footer sections, right-click in the Detail section, and click the Page Header/Footer to deselect it.

FIGURE 6.32

Report Header section with logo and title

Paired sections

Label control sized to fit text

Height of 0

Paired sections

6 ▶ Drag the right edge of the design grid to the left until it aligns with the **6.5-inch mark on the horizontal ruler**. **Save** 💾 the report.

> The width of the report page is decreased, which will enable the report to fit within the margins of paper in portrait orientation.

Objective 7 | Add Controls to a Report

Video A6-7

Reports are not used to manipulate data in the underlying table or query, so they contain fewer types of controls. You can add label controls, text box controls, images, hyperlinks, or calculated controls to a report.

Activity 6.15 | Adding Label and Text Box Controls to a Report

In this activity, you will add controls to the report that will contain the page number, the date, and your first name and last name.

1 ▶ On the **REPORT DESIGN TOOLS DESIGN tab**, in the **Header/Footer group**, click the **Page Numbers** button. In the displayed **Page Numbers** dialog box, under **Format**, click **Page N of M**. Under **Position**, click **Bottom of Page [Footer]**. Alignment should remain **Center**; click **OK**.

> A text box control displays in the center of the Page Footer section. The control displays an expression that will display the page number. Every expression begins with an equal sign (=). "Page" is enclosed in quotation marks. Access interprets anything enclosed in quotation marks as text and will display it exactly as it is typed within the quotation marks, including the space. The & symbol is used for *concatenation*—linking or joining—of strings. A *string* is a series of characters. The word *Page* followed by a space will be concatenated—joined—to the string that follows the & symbol. [Page] is a reserved name that retrieves the current page number. This is followed by another & symbol that concatenates the page number to the next string—"of ". The & symbol continues concatenation of [Pages], a reserved name that retrieves the total number of pages in the report.

2 ▶ **Save** 💾 the report. On the **REPORT DESIGN TOOLS DESIGN tab**, in the **Views group**, click the **View button arrow**, and then click **Print Preview**. On the **Print Preview tab**, in the **Zoom group**, click the **Two Pages** button. Notice at the bottom of each page the format of the page number.

3 ▶ In the **Close Preview group**, click the **Close Print Preview** button.

4 ▶ On the **REPORT DESIGN TOOLS DESIGN tab**, in the **Controls group**, click the **Label** button **Aa**. Point to the **Report Footer** section until the plus sign (+) of the pointer aligns with the bottom edge of the **Report Footer** section bar and with the left edge of the **Report Footer** section. Drag downward to the bottom of the **Report Footer** section and to the right to the **2.5-inch mark on the horizontal ruler**. Using your own first name and last name, type **Submitted by Firstname Lastname** and then compare your screen with Figure 6.33.

FIGURE 6.33

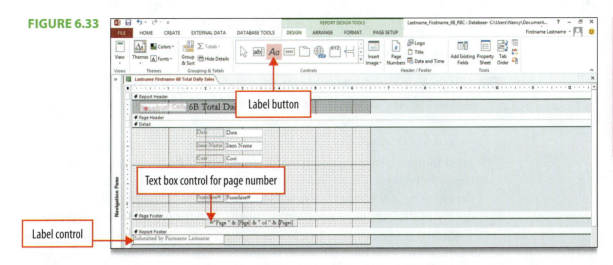

5 Click away from the **label box**, and then **Save** 🔲 the report. On the **REPORT DESIGN TOOLS DESIGN tab**, in the **Header/Footer group**, click the **Date and Time** button. In the **Date and Time** dialog box, under **Include Date**, click the third option button, which displays the date as mm/dd/yyyy. Clear the **Include Time** check box, and then click **OK**.

A text box control with an expression for the current date displays in the Report Header section. It may display over the Report title.

6 In the **Report Header**, click the **Date text box control** to select it. On the **REPORT DESIGN TOOLS ARRANGE tab**, in the **Table group**, click the **Remove Layout** button so the **Date text box control** can be moved. Right-click the selected control, and click **Cut**. Point to the **Report Footer** section bar, right-click, and then click **Paste**. Drag the text box control until the right edge of the text box control aligns with the **6.25-inch mark on the horizontal ruler**. Click the **Title label control** to select it, point to the right middle sizing handle until the ↔ pointer displays, and then drag to the right until the right edge of the text box control aligns with the **4.5-inch mark on the horizontal ruler**.

7 **Save** 🔲 the report, and then switch to **Layout** view. Notice that, for the first record, the data for the **Item Name** field does not fully display. Click the **Item Name text box control**, which partially displays *Banana Smoothie*. Point to the right edge of the **Item Name text box control** until the ↔ pointer displays. Drag to the right approximately **1.5 inches**. Because no ruler displays in Layout view, you will have to estimate the distance to drag.

Because the controls are in a stacked layout, the widths of all of the text box controls are increased.

8 Scroll down, observing the data in the **Item Name** field. Ensure that all of the data displays. If the data is not all visible in a record, use the technique you just practiced to increase the width of the text box control until all of the data displays.

9 Switch to **Design** view. Point to the right edge of the design grid until the ✛ pointer displays. If necessary, drag to the left until the right edge of the design grid aligns with the 6.5-inch mark on the horizontal ruler. Save 🔲 the report.

The width of the report page will change with the addition of more text boxes, making it necessary to readjust the width so the report will fit within the margins of paper in portrait orientation.

More Knowledge | **Adding a Hyperlink to a Report**

Add a hyperlink to a report in Design view by clicking the Insert Hyperlink button in the Controls group and then specifying the complete URL. To test the hyperlink, in Design view, right-click the hyperlink, click Hyperlink, and then click Open Hyperlink. The hyperlink is active—jumps to the target—in Design view, Report view, and Layout view. The hyperlink is not active in Print Preview view. If the report is exported to another Office application, the hyperlink is active when it is opened in that application. An application that can export data can create a file in a format that another application understands, enabling the two programs to share the same data.

Activity 6.16 | Adding an Image Control to a Report

In this activity, you will add image controls to the report header.

1 In **Design view**, in the **Report Header** section, right-click the **logo control**. From the displayed shortcut menu, click **Copy**. Right-click anywhere in the **Report Header** section, and then from the shortcut menu, click **Paste**.

> A copy of the image displays on top and slightly to the left of the original logo control.

2 Point to the selected logo until the ⬚ pointer displays. Drag to the right until the left edge of the outlined control is the same distance from the title as the logo control on the left. Point to the top edge of the **Page Header** section bar until the ⊥ pointer displays. Drag upward until the top of the **Page Header** section bar aligns with the **0.5-inch mark on the vertical ruler**.

> Recall that when you created a form in Design view, you clicked the Insert Image button and selected the location in the header section. You then had to change the properties of the image to match the size of the image in the logo control. Because you copied the original image from the logo, the images are the same size.

3 With the image control on the right selected, hold down Ctrl, and then click the **logo control**. On the **REPORT DESIGN TOOLS ARRANGE tab**, in the **Sizing & Ordering group**, click the **Align button**, and select **Bottom**. Compare your screen with Figure 6.34.

> Both the logo control and the image control are aligned along the bottom edges.

FIGURE 6.34

4 On the **REPORT DESIGN TOOLS DESIGN tab**, in the **Controls group**, click the **More** button ▼, and then click the **Line** button ╲. Point to the **Detail** section until the middle of the plus sign (+) of the pointer aligns at **2 inches on the vertical ruler** and **0 inches on the horizontal ruler**, as shown in Figure 6.35.

> A *line control* enables an individual to insert a line in a form or report.

FIGURE 6.35

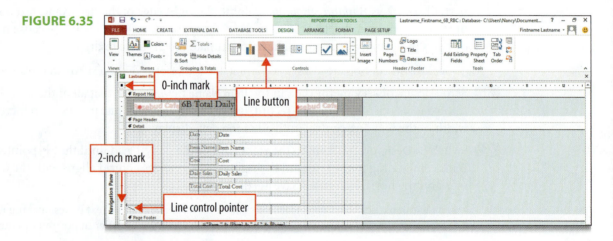

5 Hold down Shift, click and then drag to the right to **6.5 inches on the horizontal ruler**, and then release the mouse button.

> An orange line control displays. Holding down the Shift key ensures that the line will be straight.

6 On the **REPORT DESIGN TOOLS FORMAT tab**, in the **Control Formatting group**, click the **Shape Outline** button. Point to **Line Thickness** and then click the third line—**2 pt**. In the **Control Formatting group**, click the **Shape Outline** button. Under **Theme Colors**, on the fifth row, click the sixth color—**Teal, Accent 2, Darker 25%**.

7 Save the report, and then switch to **Report** view. Compare your screen with Figure 6.36. Notice the horizontal line that displays between the records.

FIGURE 6.36

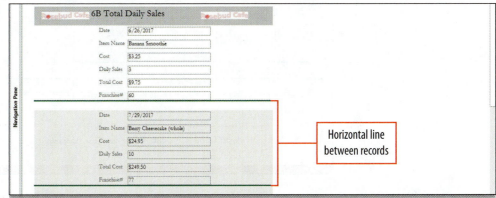

8 Switch to **Design** view.

Objective 8 | Group, Sort, and Total Records in Design View

Video A6-8

Although it is much easier to create a report that is grouped and sorted using the Report Wizard, the same tasks can be completed in Design view. If a report has been created that was not grouped, you can modify the report in Design view to include grouping and summary data. Calculated controls are often added to reports to display summary information in reports with grouped records.

Activity 6.17 | Adding a Grouping and Sort Level to a Report

In this activity, you will add a grouping and sort order to the report, and then move a control from the Detail section to the Header section.

1 On the **REPORT DESIGN TOOLS DESIGN tab**, in the **Grouping & Totals group**, click the **Group & Sort** button, and then compare your screen with Figure 6.37.

The Group, Sort, and Total pane displays at the bottom of the screen. Because no grouping or sorting has been applied to the report, two buttons relating to these functions display in the Group, Sort, and Total pane.

FIGURE 6.37

2 In the **Group, Sort, and Total pane**, click the **Add a group** button. A list of fields that are used in the report displays, as shown in Figure 6.38.

FIGURE 6.38

3 From the displayed list, click **Item Name**.

An empty Item Name Header section is inserted above the Detail section. The report will be grouped by the Item Name, and the Item Names will be sorted in ascending order.

4 In the **Detail** section, click the **Item Name text box control**. Point to the selected text box control until the pointer displays. Drag downward until a thin orange line displays below the **Franchise#** controls.

The text box control for this field will be moved to the Item Name Header section in the report. Recall that moving the controls to the bottom of the stacked layout makes it easier to remove the controls from the stacked layout.

5 On the **REPORT DESIGN TOOLS ARRANGE tab**, in the **Table group**, click the **Remove Layout** button.

The label control and the text box control for the Item Name field are removed from the stacked layout.

6 Right-click the selected **Item Name text box control** to display the shortcut menu, and click **Cut**. Click the **Item Name Header** section bar to select it, right-click to display the shortcut menu, and click **Paste**.

The controls for the Item Name are moved from the Detail section to the Item Name Header section. Because the report is being grouped by this field, the controls should be moved out of the Detail section.

7 In the **Item Name Header** section, click the **Item Name label control**, and then press ⌨Delete⌨. Click the **Item Name text box control** to select it, and then drag it to the right until the left edge of the control aligns with the **1-inch mark on the horizontal ruler**. Compare your screen with Figure 6.39.

> Because the records are grouped by the data in the Item Name field, the name of the field is unnecessary.

FIGURE 6.39

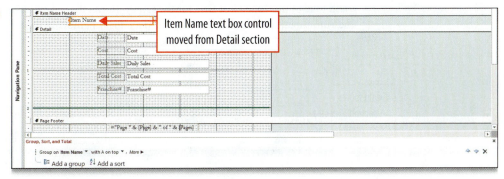

8 Save 🖫 the report, and then switch to **Report** view. Scroll down, noticing the grouping of records, until the grouping for **Grilled Chicken Kabob** displays. Notice that there are two records, one for Franchise# 62 and another for Franchise# 12. For these two records, notice the dates.

9 Switch back to **Design** view. In the **Group, Sort, and Total pane**, click the **Add a sort** button, and then click **Date**. Notice that the date will be sorted from oldest to newest.

10 Save 🖫 the report, and then switch to **Report** view. Scroll down until the **Grilled Chicken Kabob** grouping displays. Within the grouping, the two records are arranged in order by the date with the oldest date listed first.

11 Switch to **Design** view, and then **Close** ☒ the **Group, Sort, and Total pane**. Be sure to click the **Close** button located in the title bar and not the **Delete** button that is inside the pane.

Activity 6.18 | Adding Calculated Controls to a Report

In this activity, you will add an aggregate function and appropriate section to the report.

1 In the **Detail** section, click the **Total Cost text box control**. On the **REPORT DESIGN TOOLS DESIGN tab**, in the **Grouping & Totals group**, click the **Totals** button, and then compare your screen with Figure 6.40.

> A list of *aggregate functions*—functions that group and perform calculations on multiple fields—displays. Before selecting the Totals button, the field that will be used in the aggregate function must be selected. If you wish to perform aggregate functions on multiple fields, you must select each field individually, and then select the aggregate function to apply to the field.

FIGURE 6.40

2 In the displayed list of aggregate functions, click **Sum**, and then compare your screen with Figure 6.41.

> The Item Name Footer section is added to the report. A calculated control is added to the section that contains the expression that will display the sum of the Total Cost field for each grouping. A calculated control is also added to the Report Footer section that contains the expression that will display the grand total of the Total Cost field for the report. Recall that an expression begins with an equal sign (=). The Sum function adds or totals numeric data. Field names are included in square brackets.

FIGURE 6.41

3 Save 💾 the report, and then switch to **Report** view. Notice that for the first grouping—**Banana Smoothie**—which only contains one record, the sum of the grouping displays below the horizontal line. Scroll down to the **Grilled Chicken Kabob** grouping, and then notice that the total for the grouping—**$716.40**—displays below the horizontal line for the second record in the grouping.

> The placement of the horizontal line is distracting in the report, and there is no label attached to the grouping total.

4 Switch to **Design** view. On the **REPORT DESIGN TOOLS DESIGN tab**, in the **Controls group**, click the **Text Box** button 🔲. Point to the **Item Name Footer** section until the plus sign (+) of the pointer aligns with the lower edge of the **Item Name Footer** section bar and with the **0.25-inch mark on the horizontal ruler**. Drag downward to the lower right of the **Item Name Footer** section and to the **2.5-inch mark on the horizontal ruler**.

5 Click inside the text box, and type **=[Item Name] & " Total Cost:"** ensuring that you include a space between the quotation mark and *Total* and that *Item Name* is enclosed in square brackets. Compare your screen with Figure 6.42.

> Because a field name is included in the description of the total, a text box control must be used. This binds the control to the Item Name field in the underlying query, which makes this control a bound control. If you wish to insert only string characters as a description—for example, Total Cost—add a label control, which is an unbound control.

FIGURE 6.42

6 In the **Item Name Footer** section, click the **label control** that displays to the left of the text box control where you typed the expression. Press Delete to delete the text box control's associated **label control**.

> The data in the text box control is descriptive and does not require an additional label control.

7 In the **Item Name Footer** section, click the **text box control** that contains the expression you typed. Point to the left middle sizing handle until the ↔ pointer displays. Drag to the left until the left edge of the text box control aligns with the left edge of the design grid. With the text box control selected, hold down Shift. In the **Item Name Footer** section, click the **calculated control** for the sum. On the **REPORT DESIGN TOOLS ARRANGE tab**, in the **Sizing & Ordering group**, click the **Size/Space** button, and then click **To Tallest**. In the **Sizing & Ordering group**, click the **Align** button, and then click **Top** to align both controls at the top.

> The two controls are now the same height and aligned at the top edges of the controls.

8 Point to the top of the **Page Footer** section bar until the ✛ pointer displays. Drag downward to the top of the **Report Footer** section bar to increase the height of the **Item Name Footer** section so **four dots** display below the **Total Cost** controls.

9 In the **Detail** section, click the **line control**. Point to the **line control** until the ☝ pointer displays. Drag downward into the **Item Name Footer** section under the controls until there are approximately **two dots** between the **text box controls** and the **line control**, and then release the mouse button.

The line control is moved from the Detail section to the Item Name Footer section.

10 Point to the top of the **Item Name Footer** section bar until the ✛ pointer displays. Drag upward until approximately **two dots** display between the **Franchise#** controls and the top edge of the **Item Name Footer** section bar. Compare your screen with Figure 6.43.

The height of the Detail section is changed.

FIGURE 6.43

11 Save 💾 the report, and then switch to **Report** view. Scroll down until the **Grilled Chicken Kabob** grouping displays, and then compare your screen with Figure 6.44.

The report is easier to read with the horizontal line moved to the grouping footer section and with an explanation of the total for the grouping.

FIGURE 6.44

12 Hold down Ctrl, and then press End to move to the end of the report. Notice the sum of **$3,154.80**.

By default, when you insert an aggregate function into a report, a calculated control for the grand total is inserted in the Report Footer section. The control is aligned with the text box control that is being used in the aggregate function. If the Report Footer section is not tall enough and multiple aggregate functions are used, the controls will display on top of one another.

13 Switch to **Design** view. In the **Report Footer** section, the calculated control displays *=Sum([Total Cost])*. Point to the bottom of the **Report Footer** section—not the section bar—until the ✛ pointer displays. Drag downward until the height of the **Report Footer** section is approximately **1 inch**.

14 Click the label control that displays **Submitted by Firstname Lastname**. Hold down Shift, and then click the text box control that displays the **Date** expression. On the **REPORT DESIGN TOOLS ARRANGE tab**, in the **Sizing & Ordering group**, click the **Size/Space** button, and then click **To Tallest**. In the **Sizing & Ordering group**, click the **Align** button, and then click **Bottom**.

The two controls are the same height and aligned at the bottom edges of the controls.

15 Point to either of the selected controls until the ⊕ pointer displays. Drag downward until the bottom edges of the controls align with the bottom edge of the Report Footer section, and then compare your screen with Figure 6.45.

The controls are moved to the bottom of the Report Footer section to increase readability and to make space to insert a label control for the grand total.

FIGURE 6.45

Height of Report Footer section increased

Calculated control for grand total

Controls aligned, resized, and moved down

16 Click the **REPORT DESIGN TOOLS DESIGN tab**. Use the techniques you have practiced previously to add a **label control** in the **Report Footer section** to the left of the calculated control—the left edge of the control should be aligned with the **0-inch mark on the horizontal ruler** and the right edge should be **one dot** to the left of the calculated control. In the label control, type **Grand Total Cost of All Items:** Align the label control with the calculated control and be sure that the controls are the same height. Compare your screen with Figure 6.46.

FIGURE 6.46

Label control

Controls aligned and same height

ALERT!   **Does Your Control Display with Two Boxes?**

If your control displays with two boxes—one that displays text and a number; for example Text35, and one that displays Unbound—you selected the Text Box button instead of the Label button. If that happens, click the Undo button, and then begin again

---

17 **Save** 🔲 the report, and then switch to **Report** view. Hold down Ctrl, and then press End to move to the end of the report. Notice that the grand total is now easier to distinguish because a description of the control has been added and the other controls are moved down.

18 Switch to **Print Preview** view. If necessary, on the PRINT PREVIEW tab, in the Zoom group, click the Two Pages button. Look at the bottom of Page 1 and the top of Page 2, and notice that the grouping breaks across two pages. In the navigation area, click the **Next Page** button to display pages 3 and 4. Groupings are split between these pages. Compare your screen with Figure 6.47.

For a more professional-looking report, avoid splitting groupings between pages.

FIGURE 6.47

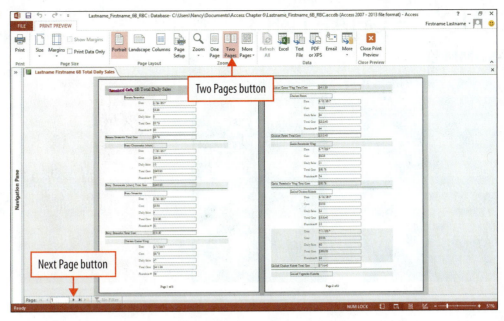

Two Pages button

Next Page button

19 ▶ In the **Close Preview group**, click the **Close Print Preview** button. Switch to **Design** view. On the **DESIGN tab**, in the **Grouping & Totals group**, click the **Group & Sort** button.

20 ▶ In the displayed **Group, Sort, and Total pane**, on the **Group on Item Name** bar, click **More**. Click the **do not keep group together on one page arrow**, and then click **keep whole group together on one page**. **Close** ☒ the **Group, Sort, and Total pane**—do not click the **Delete** button.

21 ▶ **Save** 🖫 the report, and then switch to **Print Preview** view. In the navigation area, click the buttons to display pages in the report, and then notice that groupings are no longer split between pages. Also notice that more blank space displays at the bottom of some pages.

22 ▶ If you are instructed to submit this result, create a paper or electronic printout. On the **Print Preview tab**, in the **Close Preview group**, click the **Close Print Preview** button. **Close** ☒ the report. **Close** the database, and **Exit** ☒ Access.

More Knowledge **Formatting a Report**

You can add a background picture to a report or change the background color of a report using the same techniques you used for forms.

---

23 ▶ As directed by your instructor, submit your database and the paper or electronic printouts of the two reports that are the result of this project. Specifically, in this project, using your own name you created the following database and printouts or electronic printouts:

1. Lastname_Firstname_6B_RBC	Database file
2. Lastname Firstname 6B Monthly Sales	Report (printed or electronic printout)
3. Lastname Firstname 6B Total Daily Sales	Report (printed or electronic printout)

END | You have completed Project 6B

END OF CHAPTER

SUMMARY

Forms are database objects used to interact with the data in tables. A form can be created in Design view. Sections and controls can be added, formatted, and modified to make the form user friendly.

Reports are database objects used to present data from tables or queries in a professional format. Grouping and sorting levels are added for organization, and then aggregate functions can summarize the data.

Controls added to forms and reports include label controls, image controls, command button controls, and line controls. Text box controls with expressions and concatenated strings are used to clarify data.

GO! LEARN IT ONLINE

Review the concepts and key terms in this chapter by completing these online challenges, which you can find at **www.pearsonhighered.com/go**.

Matching and Multiple Choice: Answer matching and multiple choice questions to test what you learned in this chapter. **MyITLab®**

Crossword Puzzle: Spell out the words that match the numbered clues, and put them in the puzzle squares.

Flipboard: Flip through the definitions of the key terms in this chapter and match them with the correct term.

END OF CHAPTER

REVIEW AND ASSESSMENT GUIDE FOR ACCESS CHAPTER 6

Your instructor may assign one or more of these projects to help you review the chapter and assess your mastery and understanding of the chapter.

		Review and Assessment Guide for Access Chapter 6	
Project	**Apply Skills from These Chapter Objectives**	**Project Type**	**Project Location**
6C	Objectives 1–4 from Project 6A	**6C Skills Review** A guided review of the skills from Project 6A.	On the following pages
6D	Objectives 5–8 from Project 6B	**6D Skills Review** A guided review of the skills from Project 6B.	On the following pages
6E	Objectives 1–4 from Project 6A	**6E Mastery (Grader Project)** A demonstration of your mastery of the skills in Project 6A with extensive decision making.	In MyITLab and on the following pages
6F	Objectives 5–8 from Project 6B	**6F Mastery (Grader Project)** A demonstration of your mastery of the skills in Project 6B with extensive decision making.	In MyITLab and on the following pages
6G	Objectives 1–8 from Projects 6A and 6B	**6G Mastery (Grader Project)** A demonstration of your mastery of the skills in Projects 6A and 6B with extensive decision making.	In MyITLab and on the following pages
6H	Combination of Objectives from Projects 6A and 6B	**6H GO! Fix It** A demonstration of your mastery of the skills in Projects 6A and 6B by creating a correct result from a document that contains errors you must find.	Online
6I	Combination of Objectives from Projects 6A and 6B	**6I GO! Make It** A demonstration of your mastery of the skills in Projects 6A and 6B by creating a result from a supplied picture.	Online
6J	Combination of Objectives from Projects 6A and 6B	**6J GO! Solve It** A demonstration of your mastery of the skills in Projects 6A and 6B, your decision-making skills, and your critical thinking skills. A task-specific rubric helps you self-assess your result.	Online
6K	Combination of Objectives from Projects 6A and 6B	**6K GO! Solve It** A demonstration of your mastery of the skills in Projects 6A and 6B, your decision-making skills, and your critical thinking skills. A task-specific rubric helps you self-assess your result.	On the following pages
6L	Combination of Objectives from Projects 6A and 6B	**6L GO! Think** A demonstration of your understanding of the chapter concepts applied in a manner that you would use outside of college. An analytic rubric helps you and your instructor grade the quality of your work by comparing it to the work an expert in the discipline would create.	On the following pages
6M	Combination of Objectives from Projects 6A and 6B	**6M GO! Think** A demonstration of your understanding of the chapter concepts applied in a manner that you would use outside of college. An analytic rubric helps you and your instructor grade the quality of your work by comparing it to the work an expert in the discipline would create.	Online
6N	Combination of Objectives from Projects 6A and 6B	**6N You and GO!** A demonstration of your understanding of the chapter concepts applied in a manner that you would use in a personal situation. An analytic rubric helps you and your instructor grade the quality of your work.	Online

GLOSSARY

GLOSSARY OF CHAPTER KEY TERMS

Aggregate function A function that groups and performs calculations on multiple fields.

Button control A control that enables individuals to add a command button to a form or report that will perform an action when the button is clicked.

Combo box A control that enables individuals to select from a list or to type a value.

Concatenation Linking or joining strings.

Control An object, such as a label or text box, in a form or report that enables individuals to view or manipulate information stored in tables or queries.

ControlTip Displays descriptive text when the mouse pointer is paused over the control.

Focus An object that is selected and currently being acted upon.

Form selector The box in the upper left corner of a form in Design view where the rulers meet; used to select the entire form.

Image control A control that enables individuals to insert an image into any section of a form or report.

Line control A control that enables an individual to insert a line into a form or report.

List box A control that enables individuals to select from a list but does not enable individuals to type anything that is not in the list.

Picture Alignment property A property that determines where the background picture for a form displays on the form.

Picture Size Mode property A property that determines the proportion of a picture in a form.

Point A measurement that is 1/72 of an inch.

Propagate To disseminate or apply changes to an object.

Properties The characteristics that determine the appearance, structure, and behavior of an object.

Property Sheet A sheet that is available for every object on a form, including the form itself, to further enhance the object.

Property Update Options button An option button that displays when you make changes to the design of a table; it enables individuals to update the Property Sheet for a field in all objects that use a table as the record source.

Record Source property A property that enables you to specify the source of the data for a form or a report. The property setting can be a table name, a query name, or an SQL statement.

Status Bar Text property A form property that enables individuals to enter text that will display in the status bar for a selected control.

String A series of characters.

Tab order A setting that refers to the order in which the fields are selected when the Tab key is pressed.

Theme A design tool that simplifies the process of creating professional-looking objects within one program or across multiple programs; includes theme colors and theme fonts that will be applied consistently throughout the objects in a database.

CHAPTER REVIEW

Skills Review   Project 6C Party Orders

Apply **6A** skills from these Objectives:

1 Create a Form in Design View

2 Change and Add Controls

3 Format a Form

4 Make a Form User Friendly

Marty Kress, vice president of marketing for the Rosebud Cafe franchise restaurant chain, wants to expand the chain's offerings to include party trays for advance order and delivery. In the following project, you will create a form to use for the data entry of these party order items. Your completed form, if printed, will look similar to Figure 6.48. An electronic version of the form will look slightly different.

PROJECT FILES

For Project 6C, you will need the following files:

a06C_Party_Orders
a06C_Logo
a06C_Rose

You will save your database as:

Lastname_Firstname_6C_Party_Orders

PROJECT RESULTS

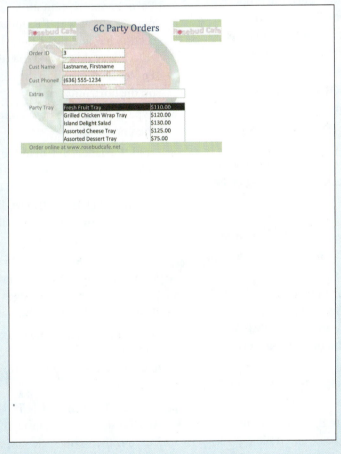

FIGURE 6.48

(Project 6C Party Orders continues on the next page)

CHAPTER REVIEW

1 **Start** Access. Locate and open the **a06C_Party_Orders** file. Save the database in your **Access Chapter 6** folder as **Lastname_Firstname_6C_Party_Orders** If necessary, click Enable Content.

2 Double-click **6C Party Orders** to open the table in **Datasheet** view. Take a moment to examine the fields in the table.

   a. In any record, click in the **Party Tray** field, and then click the **arrow**. This field is a Lookup field in the *6C Trays* table. In any record, click in the **Extras** field, and then click the **arrow**. This field is a Lookup field in the *6C Menu Items* table.

   b. **Close** the table, and then **Close** the **Navigation Pane**.

3 On the **CREATE tab**, in the **Forms group**, click the **Form Design** button.

   a. If necessary, on the FORM DESIGN TOOLS DESIGN tab, in the Tools group, click the Property Sheet button. On the **Property Sheet**, click the **Data tab**. Click the **Record Source property setting box arrow**, and then click **6C Party Orders**. Close the **Property Sheet**.

4 On the **FORM DESIGN TOOLS DESIGN tab**, in the **Tools group**, click the **Add Existing Fields** button.

   a. In the **Field List**, click **Order ID**, hold down Shift, and then click **Extras**. Drag the selected fields onto the design grid until the top of the pointer arrow is aligned at **0.25 inch on the vertical ruler** and **2 inches on the horizontal ruler**, and then release the mouse button. **Close** the **Field List**.

   b. With all of the controls still selected, on the **FORM DESIGN TOOLS ARRANGE tab**, in the **Table group**, click the **Stacked** button.

   c. Drag the left edge of the selected text box controls to the **0.5-inch mark on the horizontal ruler**. Increase the width of the text boxes by approximately **0.5 inches**. **Save** the form as **Lastname Firstname 6C Party Orders Form**

5 On the **FORM DESIGN TOOLS DESIGN tab**, in the **Header/Footer group**, click the **Logo** button.

   a. Navigate to the location where the student data files for this textbook are saved. Locate and double-click **a06C_Logo** to insert the logo in the **Form Header**.

   b. On the selected logo, point to the right middle sizing handle until the pointer displays. Drag to the right until the right edge of the logo is aligned with the **1.5-inch mark on the horizontal ruler**.

6 In the **Header/Footer group**, click the **Title** button.

   a. In the **label control** for the title, replace the text with **6C Party Orders** and then press Enter.

   b. Drag the right edge of the title to align it with the **4-inch mark on the horizontal ruler**.

   c. With the title selected, on the **FORMAT tab**, in the **Font group**, click the **Center** button.

7 Scroll down until the **Form Footer** section bar displays. Point to the top of the **Form Footer** section bar until the pointer displays. Drag upward until the top of the **Form Footer** section bar aligns with the **2.5-inch mark on the vertical ruler**.

   a. On the **FORM DESIGN TOOLS DESIGN tab**, in the **Controls group**, click the **Label** button. Point to the **Form Footer** section until the plus sign (+) of the pointer aligns with the bottom of the **Form Footer** section bar and the **0.25-inch mark on the horizontal ruler**. Drag downward to the bottom of the **Form Footer** section and to the right to the **3.25-inch mark on the horizontal ruler**.

   b. Type **Order online at www.rosebudcafe.net** and then press Enter.

   c. With the **label control** in the **Form Footer** section selected, hold down Shift, and then click the **Logo control** and the **Extras label control**. On the **FORM DESIGN TOOLS ARRANGE tab**, in the **Sizing & Ordering group**, click the **Align** button, and then click **Left**. **Save** the form.

8 Click and hold the **Party Tray text box control** until the pointer displays. Drag downward until a thin orange line displays on the bottom edges of the **Extras** controls and then release the mouse button.

   a. With the **Party Tray text box control** selected, hold down Shift, and then click the **Party Tray label control**, **Extras text box control**, and **Extras label control**.

   b. On the **FORM DESIGN TOOLS ARRANGE tab**, in the **Table group**, click the **Remove Layout** button to remove the *Extras* field and the *Party Tray* field from the stacked layout.

   c. Click in the **Detail** section to deselect the controls. Right-click the **Party Tray combo box control**. From

(Project 6C Party Orders continues on the next page)

CHAPTER REVIEW

the shortcut menu, point to **Change To**, and then click **List Box**.

d. **Save** the form, and then switch to **Form** view. Notice that the **Party Tray list box control** is not wide enough to display all columns and that there are horizontal and vertical scroll bars to indicate there is more data. Click the **Extras combo box arrow** to see if any menu item names or prices are cut off. Press Esc.

e. Switch to **Design** view, and click the **Party Tray list box control**, if necessary. Point to the right edge of the control until the pointer displays. Drag to the right until the right edge of the control aligns with the **4.25-inch mark on the horizontal ruler**.

f. Switch to **Layout** view. Resize the **Extras combo box control** to be the same size as the **Party Tray list box control**. **Save** the form and switch to **Design** view. Click the **Form Header section bar**.

9 ▶ On the **FORM DESIGN TOOLS DESIGN tab**, in the **Controls group**, click the **Insert Image** button, and then click **Browse**. In the displayed **Insert Picture** dialog box, navigate to the location where the student data files for this textbook are saved.

a. Locate and double-click **a06C_Logo**.

b. Align the plus sign (+) with the bottom of the **Form Header** section bar and with the **4-inch mark on the horizontal ruler**. Drag downward to the top of the **Detail** section bar and to the right to the **5.25-inch mark on the horizontal ruler**.

c. Click the **image control**—the Rosebud Cafe image on the right side in the **Form Header** section—if necessary. On the **DESIGN tab**, in the **Tools group**, click the **Property Sheet** button. If necessary, on the Format tab, change the Width property setting to 1.25 and then change the Height property setting to 0.5.

d. In the **Form Header** section, click the **logo control**. On the **Property Sheet**, change the **Width** property setting to **1.25** and change the **Height** property setting to **0.5**. **Close** the **Property Sheet**.

e. With the logo control selected, hold down Shift, and then click the **image control**. On the **ARRANGE tab**, in the **Sizing & Ordering group**, click the **Align** button, and then click **Top**.

10 ▶ On the **FORM DESIGN TOOLS DESIGN tab**, in the **Controls group**, click the **Button** button.

a. Move the mouse pointer down into the **Detail** section. Align the plus sign (+) of the pointer at **0.25 inches on the vertical ruler** and **3.25 inches on the horizontal ruler**, and then click.

b. Under **Categories**, verify **Record Navigation** is selected. Under **Actions**, click **Find Record**, and then click **Next** two times. In the text box, type **btnFindRcrd** and then click **Finish**.

c. Using the technique you just practiced, add a **button control** right next to the **Find Record button**. Under **Categories**, click **Form Operations**. Under **Actions**, click **Print Current Form**, and then click **Next** two times. Name the button **btnPrtForm** Click **Finish**.

d. With the **Print Current Form button control** selected, hold down Shift, and then click the **Find Record button control**. On the **ARRANGE tab**, in the **Sizing & Ordering group**, click the **Align** button, and then click **Top**.

11 ▶ Switch to **Layout** view. Click in the **Form Footer** section to the right of the **label control**.

a. On the **FORMAT tab**, in the **Control Formatting group**, click the **Shape Fill** button. Under **Theme Colors**, in the third row, click the seventh color—**Olive Green, Accent 3, Lighter 60%**.

b. Using the technique you just practiced, change the color of the **Form Header** section to match the **Form Footer** section.

12 ▶ Switch to **Design** view, and then double-click the **Form selector** to open the **Property Sheet** for the form.

a. On the **Property Sheet**, on the **Format tab**, click in the **Picture** property setting box, and then click the **Build** button. Navigate to where the student data files for this textbook are saved. Locate and double-click **a06C_Rose** to insert the picture in the form.

b. Click in the **Picture Alignment** property setting box, click the **arrow**, and then click **Form Center**. **Close** the **Property Sheet**, and then **save** the form.

13 ▶ Switch to **Layout** view, click the **Order ID text box control**, hold down Shift, and then click the **Cust Name text box control** and the **Cust Phone# text box control**.

(Project 6C Party Orders continues on the next page)

CHAPTER REVIEW

a. On the **FORM LAYOUT TOOLS FORMAT tab**, in the **Control Formatting group**, click the **Shape Outline** button. Point to **Line Type**, and click the fifth line type—**Dots**.

b. On the **FORM LAYOUT TOOLS FORMAT tab**, in the **Control Formatting group**, click the **Shape Outline** button. Point to **Line Thickness**, and then click the second line type—**1 pt**.

c. In the **Control Formatting group**, click the **Shape Outline** button. Under **Theme Colors**, in the fifth row, click the seventh color—**Olive Green, Accent 3, Darker 25%**.

14 Switch to **Form** view, and then click in the **Cust Phone# text box control**. On the left side of the status bar, *Form View* displays—there is no text that helps an individual enter data. **Close** the form, **Save** your changes, and open the **Navigation Pane**.

a. Under **Tables**, right-click **6C Party Orders**; from the shortcut menu, click **Design View**. In the **Cust Phone#** field, click in the **Description** box. Type **Include area code for 10-digit dialing** and then press Enter.

b. Click the **Property Update Options** button, and then click **Update Status Bar Text everywhere Cust Phone# is used**. In the displayed **Update Properties** dialog box, click **Yes**. **Close** the table, saving changes.

15 Open **6C Party Order Form** in **Design** view. **Close** the **Navigation Pane**. On the **DESIGN tab**, in the **Tools** group, click the **Property Sheet** button.

a. In the **Detail** section, click the **Print Form** button. Notice that the **Property Sheet** is displayed for the button you selected.

b. On the **Other tab**, click in the **ControlTip Text** property setting box, type **Prints the Current Form** to replace the existing **Print Form** text, and then press Enter.

c. **Close** the **Property Sheet**, **Save** the form, and then switch to **Form** view. Point to the **Print Form** button to display the **ControlTip**.

16 Switch to **Design** view. In the **Detail** section, click the **Order ID text box control**, hold down Shift, and then click the **Find Record button control** and the **Print Current Form button control**.

a. On the **FORM DESIGN TOOLS DESIGN tab**, in the **Tools group**, click the **Property Sheet** button. If necessary, on the Property Sheet, click the Other tab. On the **Property Sheet**, click in the **Tab Stop** property setting box, click the **arrow**, and then click **No**.

b. Click the **Cust Name text box control**. Click in the **Tab Index** property setting box, and then type **0 Close** the **Property Sheet**.

17 Switch to **Form** view. With the **Cust Name** control selected, click the **Find Record** button.

a. In the **Find and Replace** dialog box, in the **Find What** box, type **Gonzalez, Ricardo** Click **Find Next**. **Close** the **Find and Replace** dialog box.

b. In the **Cust Name text box**, type your **Lastname, Firstname** replacing Ricardo's name. Press Tab. In the **Cust Phone#** field, enter your phone number, and then press Enter. **Save** the form.

18 If you are instructed to submit this result, click the **Print Current Form** button to create a paper or electronic printout. If you are to submit your work electronically, follow your instructor's directions.

19 **Close** the form, **Close** the **Navigation Pane**, **Close** the database, and then **Exit** Access.

20 As directed by your instructor, submit your database and the paper or electronic printout of the one form that is the result of this project. Specifically, in this project, using your own name you created the following database and printout or electronic printout:

1. Lastname_Firstname_6C_Party_Orders	Database file
2. Lastname Firstname 6C Party Orders	Form (printed or electronic printout)

END | You have completed Project 6C

CHAPTER REVIEW

Skills Review | Project 6D Catering

Apply **6B skills from these Objectives:**

5 Create a Report Based on a Query Using a Wizard

6 Create a Report in Design View

7 Add Controls to a Report

8 Group, Sort, and Total Records in Design View

Each Rosebud Cafe location maintains a database about the orders that are placed for the catering entity of the business. Reports are run to summarize data in the tables or queries. Creating customized reports will help the managers of each location view the information in the database in a meaningful way. In this project, you will create customized reports. Your completed reports will look similar to Figure 6.49.

PROJECT FILES

For Project 6D, you will need the following files:

a06D_Catering

a06D_Logo

You will save your database as:

Lastname_Firstname_6D_Catering

PROJECT RESULTS

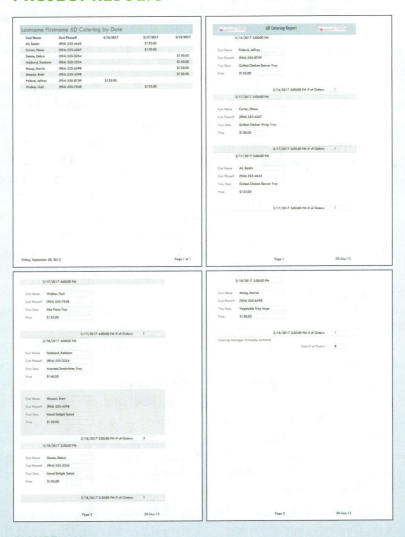

FIGURE 6.49

(Project 6D Catering continues on the next page)

CHAPTER REVIEW

1 **Start** Access. Locate and open the **a06D_Catering** file. Save the database in your **Access Chapter 6** folder as **Lastname_Firstname_6D_Catering** If necessary, click Enable Content.

2 In the Navigation Pane, under **Queries**, double-click **6D Catering Crosstab Query**. Take a moment to study the data in the query. **Close** the query, and then **Close** the **Navigation Pane**.

3 On the **CREATE tab**, in the **Reports group**, click the **Report Wizard** button.

  a. Under **Tables/Queries**, verify **Query: 6D Catering Crosstab Query** is displayed. Under **Available Fields**, add all of the field names to the **Selected Fields** box. Click **Next** twice.

  b. Click the **arrow** next to the **1** box, and then click **Cust Name**. Leave the sort order as **Ascending**, and then click **Next**.

  c. Under **Layout**, verify the **Tabular** option button is selected. Under **Orientation**, verify the **Portrait** option button is selected. Verify the **Adjust the field width so all fields fit on a page** check box is selected. Click **Next**.

  d. For the title of the report, type **Lastname Firstname 6D Catering by Date** Select **Modify the report's design**, and then click **Finish**.

4 On the **REPORT DESIGN TOOLS DESIGN tab**, in the **Themes group**, click the **Themes** button, and then in the first row click the third theme—**Integral**.

5 Switch to **Layout** view. If necessary, in the 3/16/2017 column, point to the left edge of the column and drag to the right approximately 0.5 inches. Point to the right edge of the **Cust Phone#** column and drag to the left until all of the data in the **Cust Phone#** column displays. Click in a blank area of the report to deselect the column. Switch to **Design** view. Drag the right edge of the report to the **7.75-inch mark on the horizontal ruler**, resizing the right column as necessary.

6 Select all of the controls in the **Page Header** section by pointing to the top left of the **Page Header** section, holding down your mouse button, and then dragging the mouse across the **Page Header controls** and to the bottom of the **Page Header** section. Release the mouse button.

  a. On the **REPORT DESIGN TOOLS FORMAT tab**, in the **Font group**, click the **Font color button arrow**.

Under **Theme Colors**, on the first row, click the fourth color—**Dark Teal, Text 2**. In the **Font group**, click the **Bold button**.

7 **Save** the report, and then switch to **Print Preview**. If you are instructed to submit this result, create a paper or electronic printout. **Close Print Preview**. **Close** the report.

8 On the **CREATE tab**, in the **Reports group**, click the **Report Design** button.

  a. On the **REPORT DESIGN TOOLS DESIGN tab**, in the **Tools group**, click the **Property Sheet** button. On the **Property Sheet**, click the **Data tab**. Click the **Record Source arrow**, click **6D Catering**, and then **Close** the **Property Sheet**.

  b. On the **REPORT DESIGN TOOLS DESIGN tab**, in the **Tools group**, click the **Add Existing Fields** button.

  c. In the **Field List**, click **Pickup Time**. Hold down Shift, and then click **Price** to select all of the fields. Drag the selected fields into the **Detail** section until the top of the arrow of the pointer is aligned with the **0.25-inch mark on the vertical ruler** and with the **1.5-inch mark on the horizontal ruler**.

  d. With the controls still selected, on the **REPORT DESIGN TOOLS ARRANGE tab**, in the **Table group**, click the **Stacked** button. **Close** the **Field List**, and then **Save** the report as **Lastname Firstname 6D Catering Report**

9 On the **REPORT DESIGN TOOLS DESIGN tab**, in the **Header/Footer group**, click the **Logo** button.

  a. Locate and double-click **a06D_Logo** to insert the logo in the **Report Header** section.

  b. On the selected logo, point to the right middle sizing handle until the pointer displays. Drag to the right until the right edge of the logo is aligned with the **1.5-inch mark on the horizontal ruler**.

10 On the **REPORT DESIGN TOOLS DESIGN tab**, in the **Header/Footer group**, click the **Title** button. In the **title's label control**, select **Lastname Firstname**, and then press Delete.

11 Point to the top edge of the **Page Footer** section bar until the pointer displays. Drag upward until the top of the **Page Footer** section bar aligns with the **2-inch mark on the vertical ruler**.

12 Point to the top edge of the **Detail** section bar until the pointer displays. Drag upward until the top edge of

(Project 6D Catering continues on the next page)

CHAPTER REVIEW

the **Detail** section bar aligns with the bottom edge of the **Page Header** section bar. **Save** the report.

13 On the **REPORT DESIGN TOOLS DESIGN tab**, in the **Header/Footer group**, click the **Page Numbers** button.

a. In the displayed **Page Numbers** dialog box, under **Format**, click **Page N**, if necessary. Under **Position**, click **Bottom of Page [Footer]**, and then click **OK**.

b. Resize and move the **Page Number control box** until it fits between the **2-inch and 4-inch marks on the horizontal ruler**.

14 On the **REPORT DESIGN TOOLS DESIGN tab**, in the **Controls group**, click the **Label** button.

a. Drag the plus sign (+) from the bottom edge of the **Report Footer** section bar at the **0.25-inch mark on the horizontal ruler** to the bottom of the **Report Footer** section at the **3-inch mark on the horizontal ruler**.

b. Using your own first and last names, type **Catering Manager: Firstname Lastname** Press Enter.

15 On the **REPORT DESIGN TOOLS DESIGN tab**, in the **Header/Footer group**, click the **Date & Time** button. In the **Date and Time** dialog box, under **Include Date**, click the second option button. Under **Include Time**, remove the check mark, and then click **OK**. **Save** the report.

a. Click the **Date text box control**. On the **ARRANGE tab**, in the **Table group**, click the **Remove Layout** button.

b. Right-click the selected control, and click **Cut**. Right-click the **Page Footer** section, and click **Paste**.

c. Move the **Date text box control** and resize it until the right edge of the **text box control** aligns with the **6.25-inch mark on the horizontal ruler**.

d. Click the **Title text box control** to select it, point to the right middle sizing handle until the pointer displays, and then drag to the left until the right edge of the text box control aligns with the **4.75-inch mark on the horizontal ruler**.

16 Drag the right edge of the design grid to the left until it aligns with the **6.5-inch mark on the horizontal ruler**. **Save** the report.

a. Switch to **Layout** view. In the first record, click the **Tray Desc text box control**, and then point to the right edge of the control until the pointer displays. Drag to the right until all of the text displays in

the **Tray Desc text box control**—*Grilled Chicken Skewer Tray*.

17 Switch to **Design** view. In the **Report Header** section, right-click the **logo control**. From the displayed shortcut menu, click **Copy**. Right-click anywhere in the **Report Header** section, and then from the shortcut menu, click **Paste**.

a. Point to the selected logo, and then drag to the right until the left edge of the outlined control aligns with the **4.75-inch mark on the horizontal ruler**.

b. With the image control on the right selected, hold down Ctrl, and then click the **logo control**. On the **ARRANGE tab**, in the **Sizing & Ordering group**, click the **Align** button, and then click **Bottom**.

c. Resize the **Title text box control** so the right edge is **one dot** away from the image on its right. **Center** the title in the control. Drag the **Page Header section bar** up to the **0.5-inch mark on the vertical ruler**.

18 On the **REPORT DESIGN TOOLS DESIGN tab**, in the **Grouping & Totals group**, click the **Group & Sort** button.

a. In the **Group, Sort, and Total Pane**, click the **Add a group** button. From the displayed list, click **Pickup Time**.

b. Click the **by quarter arrow** that displays after **from oldest to newest**, and then click **by entire value**. Click in a blank area of the **Group, Sort, and Total Pane**. Click the **More arrow**, click the **do not keep group together on one page arrow**, and then click **keep whole group together on one page**.

c. In the **Group, Sort, and Total Pane**, click the **Add a sort** button, and then click **Cust Name**. **Close** the **Group, Sort, and Total Pane**.

19 In the **Detail** section, click the **Pickup Time text box control**. Drag downward until a thin orange line displays at the bottom of the **Price** controls, and then release the mouse button.

a. On the **ARRANGE tab**, in the **Table group**, click the **Remove Layout** button.

b. Move the **Pickup Time text box control** into the **Pickup Time Header** section so the left edge of the **text box control** aligns with the **1-inch mark on the horizontal ruler**.

c. In the **Pickup Time Header** section, click the **Pickup Time label control**, and then press Delete.

(Project 6D Catering continues on the next page)

CHAPTER REVIEW

20 In the **Detail** section, click the **Tray Desc text box control**. On the **DESIGN tab**, in the **Grouping & Totals group**, click the **Totals** button. In the displayed list of aggregate functions, click **Count Records**.

21 In the **Pickup Time Footer** section, select the **Count text box control**, and then holding down Shift, in the **Report Footer** select the **Count text box control**.

a. On the **REPORT DESIGN TOOLS ARRANGE tab**, in the **Table group**, click the **Remove Layout** button.

b. Align and resize the control so the left edge of each control is even with the **5.5-inch marker on the horizontal ruler** and the right edge of each control is even with the **6-inch marker on the horizontal ruler**.

c. On the **REPORT DESIGN TOOLS DESIGN tab**, in the **Controls group**, click the **Text Box** button. Drag the plus sign (+) from the bottom edge of the **Pickup Time Footer** section bar at the **2.75-inch mark on the horizontal ruler** to the bottom of the **Pickup Time Footer** section and to the right to the **5.5-inch mark on the horizontal ruler**.

d. In the Unbound text box, type **=[Pickup Time] & " # of Orders:"** In the **Pickup Time Footer** section, click the **label control** that displays to the left of the **text box control**, and then press Delete.

e. In the **Pickup Time Footer** section, click the **text box control** that contains the expression you typed. Hold down Shift and click the **count calculated control** in the **Pickup Time Footer**. On the **ARRANGE tab**, in the **Sizing & Ordering group**, click **Size/Space**, and then click **To Tallest**. In the **Sizing & Ordering group**, click the **Align** button, and then click **Top**.

22 Drag the right edge of the design grid to the left until it aligns with the **6.5-inch mark on the horizontal ruler**. Switch to **Report** view. Hold down Ctrl, and then press End to move to the end of the report.

23 Switch to **Design** view. Point to the bottom of the **Report Footer** section, and then drag downward until it reaches the **0.5-inch mark on the vertical ruler**.

a. In the **Report Footer** section, click the **Count text box control**, and then drag downward until the bottom edge of the control aligns with the bottom edge of the **Report Footer** section.

b. Use the techniques you have practiced to add a label control in the **Report Footer** section to the left of the calculated control—the left edge of the control should be aligned with the **4-inch mark on the horizontal ruler**. In the **label control**, type **Total # of Orders:**

c. Align the label control with the calculated control and then be sure that the controls are the same height.

24 On the **REPORT DESIGN TOOLS DESIGN tab**, in the **Controls group**, click the **Line** button. Point to the bottom of the **Pickup Time Footer** section until the middle of the plus sign (+) of the pointer aligns with the top of the **Page Footer** section bar and the **0-inch mark on the horizontal ruler**. Hold down Shift, drag to the right to the **6.5-inch mark on the horizontal ruler**, and then release the mouse button and Shift.

25 On the **FORMAT tab**, in the **Control Formatting group**, click the **Shape Outline** button. Click **Line Thickness**, and then click the third line—**2 pt**. In the **Control Formatting group**, click the **Shape Outline** button. Under **Theme Colors**, in the first row, click the eighth color—**Green, Accent 4**. **Save** the report.

26 Switch to **Print Preview**. Adjust the margins or report width as needed. If you are instructed to submit this result, create a paper or electronic printout. **Close Print Preview**.

27 **Close** the report, and then **Close** the **Navigation Pane**. **Close** the database, and then **Exit** Access.

28 As directed by your instructor, submit your database and the paper or electronic printouts of the two reports that are the result of this project. Specifically, in this project, using your own name you created the following database and printouts or electronic printouts:

1. Lastname_Firstname_6D_Catering	Database file
2. Lastname Firstname 6D Catering by Date	Report (printed or electronic printout)
3. Lastname Firstname 6D Catering Report	Report (printed or electronic printout)

END | You have completed Project 6D

CONTENT-BASED ASSESSMENTS

In the following project, you will create a form that will be used to enter the data for the monthly promotions that are offered to guests at the Rosebud Cafe restaurant franchise. Your task includes designing a form that will be attractive and provide easy data entry for the staff. Your completed form will look similar to Figure 6.50.

Apply 6A skills from these Objectives:

1 Create a Form in Design View
2 Change and Add Controls
3 Format a Form
4 Make a Form User Friendly

PROJECT FILES

For Project 6E, you will need the following files:

a06E_Monthly_Promotions
a06E_Logo
a06E_Dollar

You will save your database as:

Lastname_Firstname_6E_Monthly_Promotions

PROJECT RESULTS

FIGURE 6.50

(Project 6E Monthly Promotions continues on the next page)

CONTENT-BASED ASSESSMENTS

1 **Start** Access. Locate and open the **a06E_Monthly_Promotions** file. Save the database in your **Access Chapter 6** folder as **Lastname_Firstname_6E_Monthly_Promotions** If necessary, click Enable Content.

2 Create a form in **Form Design**. For the **Record Source**, use the **6E Monthly Results** table. Select all of the fields, and then drag them onto the design grid until the top of the arrow is aligned with the **1-inch mark on the horizontal ruler** and the **0.25-inch mark on the vertical ruler**. **Save** the form as **Lastname Firstname 6E Promo Form**

3 With all of the text box controls selected, display the **Property Sheet**, and then click the **Format tab**. In the **Left** property box, type **1.5** and press Enter. Click anywhere in the **Detail** section to deselect the controls. Select the **Franchise text box control**, and then drag the right edge to the **3-inch mark on the horizontal ruler**. Select the **# Redeemed text box control**, and in the **Property Sheet**, change the **Width** to **0.75** Close the Property Sheet. **Save** the form. Switch to **Form** view, and then click the **Promo Month text box control** to view the entries. Switch to **Design** view.

4 In the **Form Header**, insert the **a06E_Logo**. Widen the selected logo to the **1.5-inch mark on the horizontal ruler**.

5 In the **Header/Footer group**, add a **Title**, and then, if necessary, resize the **Title label control** so the entire title is visible. With the title selected, select all of the label controls. On the **FORMAT tab**, in the **Font group**, under **Theme Colors**, in the fifth row click the sixth color—**Red, Accent 2, Darker 25%**.

6 Scroll down until the **Form Footer** section bar displays. Point to the top of the **Form Footer**, and drag up until the top of the **Form Footer** section bar aligns with the **1.5-inch mark on the vertical ruler**.

7 In the **Form Footer**, insert a **Label** control so the left aligns with the **0-inch mark on the horizontal ruler** and

the right aligns with the **4-inch mark on the horizontal ruler**. Type **Coupons may be redeemed at any Rosebud Cafe location** Press Enter. Change the font color to **Red, Accent 2, Darker 25%**.

8 In the **Form Footer**, insert the **a06E_Dollar** image at the top of the **Form Footer** section and at the **4.25-inch mark on the horizontal ruler**.

9 Display the **Property Sheet**, and change the **Width** and **Height** to **0.35** Point to the bottom of the **Form Footer**; drag up until the bottom of the **Form Footer** section bar aligns with the **0.5-inch mark on the vertical ruler**. **Close** the **Property Sheet**.

10 In the **Detail** section, insert a **Button** control aligning the plus sign (+) of the pointer with the **0.5-inch mark on the vertical ruler** and the **3.5-inch mark on the horizontal ruler**.

11 Under **Categories**, click **Form Operations**. Under **Actions**, click **Close Form**. Select the **Text** option button. Name the button **btnCloseFrm** With the button selected, change the **Font Color** to **Red, Accent 2, Darker 25%**.

12 With the **Close Form** button selected, open the **Property Sheet**. Change the **Tab Stop** property to **No**. **Close** the **Property Sheet**.

13 If you are instructed to submit this result, create a paper or electronic printout of **record 8**. If you are to submit your work electronically, follow your instructor's directions.

14 Click the **Close Form** button, saving changes. **Close** the database, and then **Exit** Access.

15 As directed by your instructor, submit your database and the paper or electronic printout of the report that is the result of this project. Specifically, in this project, using your own name you created the following database and printout or electronic printout:

1. Lastname_Firstname_6E_Monthly_Promotions	Database file
2. Lastname Firstname 6E Promo Form	Report (printed or electronic printout)

END | You have completed Project 6E

CONTENT-BASED ASSESSMENTS

Mastering Access   Project 6F Promotional Results

In the following project, you will create a report that will display the promotions that are offered to guests of the Rosebud Cafe restaurant franchise. You will also create a crosstab report that will summarize the results of the promotions. Creating customized reports will help the managers of each location view the information in the database in a meaningful way. Your completed reports will look similar to Figure 6.51.

Apply 6B skills from these Objectives:

5 Create a Report Based on a Query Using a Wizard

6 Create a Report in Design View

7 Add Controls to a Report

8 Group, Sort, and Total Records in Design View

PROJECT FILES

For Project 6F, you will need the following files:

a06F_Promotional_Results
a06F_Logo

You will save your database as:

Lastname_Firstname_6F_Promotional_Results

PROJECT RESULTS

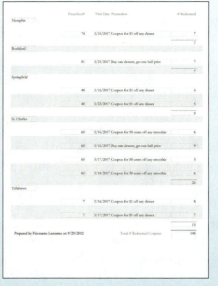

FIGURE 6.51

(Project 6F Promotional Results continues on the next page)

CONTENT-BASED ASSESSMENTS

1 **Start** Access. Locate and open the **a06F_ Promotional Results** file. Save the database in your **Access Chapter 6** folder as **Lastname_Firstname_6F_ Promotional_Results** If necessary, click Enable Content.

2 Under **Queries**, open the **6F Coupons Crosstab Query**. Take a moment to study the data in the query. **Close** the query, and then **Close** the **Navigation Pane**.

3 **Create** a report using the **Report Wizard**. From the **Query: 6F Coupons Crosstab Query**, select all of the fields. Under **Do you want to add any grouping levels?**, select **City**. **Sort** the records within the report by **Franchise#** in **Ascending** order. Under **Layout**, be sure the **Stepped** option button is selected. Under **Orientation**, click the **Landscape** option button. Be sure the **Adjust the field width so all fields fit on a page** check box is selected. For the title of the report, type **Lastname Firstname 6F Coupons Redeemed** Select **Modify the report's design**, and then click **Finish**.

4 Switch to **Layout** view. On the **DESIGN tab**, click the **Themes** button, and then apply the **Organic** theme. If any data is cut off, select the label control, and drag to the right to widen the column to display all data. Reduce the width of any columns that display a lot of blank space to allow for the widened columns.

5 Switch to **Design** view. Insert the **a06F_Logo** image so it appears from the **5.25-inch mark on the horizontal ruler** to the **7-inch mark**, and is the height of the **Report Header** section.

6 Select the five **Date label controls and textbox controls**. Change the width to **0.8**. Change the **Font Color** to **Teal, Accent 2, Darker 50%**—the sixth option in the sixth row under **Theme Colors**.

7 If necessary, resize and move controls so you can resize the report to print on one landscape page. **Save** the report. If you are instructed to submit this result, create a paper or electronic printout. **Close** the report.

8 Open the **6F Coupons** query. Switch to **Design** view, and then notice the underlying tables that were used in the creation of the query. **Close** the query, and then **Close** the **Navigation Pane**.

9 Create a new report using **Report Design**. Display the **Property Sheet**. On the **Data tab**, click the **Record Source property setting box arrow**, and then click **6F Coupons**. **Close** the **Property Sheet**. Display the **Field List**.

10 From the **Field List**, select all fields included in the query. Drag the selected fields into the **Detail** section of the design grid until the top of the pointer is aligned with the **0.25-inch mark on the vertical ruler** and the **1-inch mark on the horizontal ruler**. With the controls selected, on the **REPORT DESIGN TOOLS ARRANGE tab**, in the **Table group**, click the **Tabular** button. **Close** the **Field List**. Drag the **Page Footer section bar** up to the **0.5-inch mark on the vertical ruler**.

11 **Save** the report as **Lastname Firstname 6F Promotions** Switch to **Layout** view to be sure all data is visible in the report. If necessary, adjust the width of any columns where data is cut off. Switch to **Design** view.

12 On the **REPORT DESIGN TOOLS DESIGN tab**, click the **Group & Sort** button. Click the **Add a group** button, and then from the displayed list, click **City**. Apply **Keep whole group together on one page**. Click the **Add a sort** button, and then click **Visit Date**. **Close** the **Group, Sort, and Total Pane**.

13 In the **Page Header** section, click the **City** label control, and then press Delete. In the **Detail** section, delete the **City text box control**. Click the **City Header** section bar to select it, right-click to display the shortcut menu, and click **Paste**.

14 In the **Detail** section, click the **# Redeemed text box control**. On the **DESIGN tab**, click the **Totals** button, and then click **Sum**.

15 Insert the **a06F_Logo**. On the **Property Sheet**, increase the width to **1.75 inches** and the height to **0.5 inches**. Insert a **Title**. Delete your Lastname Firstname from the beginning of the title.

16 Add a **label control** to the **Report Footer**. Position the plus sign of the pointer at the bottom of the **Report Footer** section bar and the **4.5-inch mark on the horizontal ruler**. Drag upward to the top of the **Report Footer** section and to the right to the left edge of the Sum control box. Type **Total # Redeemed Coupons**

17 Click the **Date & Time** button. Under **Include Date**, click the second option button. Do not **Include Time**. Remove the **Date text box control** from the **Layout**.

18 Move the control to the left edge of the **Report Footer**. Click the **Date text box control** two times. Position the insertion point between the equal sign and the **D**. Type **"Prepared by Firstname Lastname on "& and**

(Project 6F Promotional Results continues on the next page)

Mastering Access   Project 6F Promotional Results (continued)

then Press [Enter]. Click the **Title label control**, and resize it so the right edge aligns with the **4-inch mark on the horizontal ruler**. **Center** the text in the control. Resize the report to **7.75 inches wide**.

19 Select all of the controls in the **Report Footer**. Be sure they are all the same height and aligned at the bottom.

20 Switch to **Layout** view, and then adjust all controls to fit the data without extending beyond the right margin.

Save the report. If you are instructed to submit this result, create a paper or electronic printout. **Close** the report.

21 **Close** the database, and then **Exit** Access.

22 As directed by your instructor, submit your database and the paper or electronic printouts of the two reports that are the result of this project. Specifically, in this project, using your own name you created the following database and printouts or electronic printouts:

1. Lastname_Firstname_6F_Promotional Results	Database file
2. Lastname Firstname 6F Coupons Redeemed	Report (printed or electronic printout)
2. Lastname Firstname 6F Promotions	Report (printed or electronic printout)

END | You have completed Project 6F

CONTENT-BASED ASSESSMENTS

Apply 6A and 6B skills from these Objectives:

1 Create a Form in Design View

2 Add and Change Controls

3 Format a Form

4 Make a Form User Friendly

5 Create a Report Based on a Query Using a Wizard

Marty Kress, vice president of marketing for Rosebud Cafe franchises, keeps a database on the wireless usage per franchise on a monthly basis. The individual restaurants report the number of customers using the wireless connections and the average length of usage per customer. In this project, you will design a form for the data entry of this data and design a report that can be used by Mr. Kress to plan next year's marketing strategies. Your completed work will look similar to Figure 6.52.

PROJECT FILES

For Project 6G, you will need the following files:

a06G_Wireless_Usage

a06G_Logo

You will save your database as:

Lastname_Firstname_6G_Wireless_Usage

PROJECT RESULTS

FIGURE 6.52   (Project 6G Wireless Usage continues on the next page)

1 **Start** Access. Locate and open the **a06G_ Wireless_ Usage** file. Save the database in your **Access Chapter 6** folder as **Lastname_Firstname_6G_Wireless_Usage** If necessary, Enable Content.

2 Create a form in **Form Design**. For the **Record Source**, use the **6G Wireless Usage** table. Select all of the fields, and then drag them onto the design grid until the top of the arrow is aligned with the **1-inch mark on the horizontal ruler** and the **0.25-inch mark on the vertical ruler**. Save the form as **Lastname Firstname 6G Wireless Usage**

3 Apply a **Stacked** layout. Add a **Red, Accent 2** dashed outline to the **text box controls** in the **Detail** section.

4 Insert **a06G_Logo**. Widen the selected logo to the **1.5-inch mark on the horizontal ruler**.

5 Insert a **Title**. Delete Lastname Firstname and the following space, and then press Enter. Adjust the right edge of the title label control to just fit the text.

6 Add a **Button** in the **Detail** section at the **0.5-inch mark on the vertical ruler** and the **2.5-inch mark on the horizontal ruler**. Click **Record Operations**, and then **Add New Record**. Apply the **Go To New Picture**, and then name the button **btnNewRcrd** Add a button to print the record below the **Add New Record** button. Place a picture on it, and name it **btnPrtRcrd**

7 With the **New Record** and **Print Record** buttons selected, change the **Tab Stop** property to **No**. If necessary, Align the buttons at the Right.

8 Drag the top of the **Form Footer** section bar until it aligns with the **0.5-inch mark on the vertical ruler**. In the **Form Footer** section, insert a label aligned with the bottom of the **Form Footer** section bar and the left edge of the form. Type **Created by Firstname Lastname** and then press Enter.

9 Switch to **Form** view. Click the **New Record** button. From the list of **Franchises**, select **Holland MI**. In the **Wireless Month text box control**, select **June 1** of the current year. In the **# of Customers text box control**, type **757** In the **Avg Minutes text box control**, type **25**

10 If you are instructed to submit this result, create a paper or electronic printout of the new, selected record only. **Close** the form and **Save** changes.

11 **Create** a report using the **Report Wizard**. From the **Query: 6G Wireless Crosstab Query**, select the **City, Total Of # of Customers, Jul, Aug,** and **Sep** fields. Do not add any grouping levels. **Sort** records within the report by **City**, in **Ascending** order. Use a **Tabular** layout and a **Landscape** orientation. Title your report as **6G Wireless Usage by Month**

12 Switch to **Design** view. Select the **Title** label control and all of the label controls in the **Page Header** section. Change the font color to **Orange, Accent 6, Darker 50%**. Reduce the width of the **Page # control** so the right edge aligns with the **8-inch mark on the horizontal ruler**.

13 Resize the **Jul, Aug,** and **Sep textbox controls** and **label controls** to **1 inch**. Move the controls so there is one dot between the monthly columns. Resize the report to **9.5 inches** wide.

14 Modify the **Page Footer** by adding **Prepared by Firstname Lastname on** before **Now()**. Widen the control to the **5-inch mark on the horizontal ruler**. Switch to **Print Preview**.

15 If you are instructed to submit this result, create a paper or electronic printout. **Close** the report and **Save** changes.

16 Close the **Navigation Pane**, **Close** the database, and then **Exit** Access.

17 As directed by your instructor, submit your database and the paper or electronic printouts of the two objects—one form and one report—that are the result of this project. Specifically, in this project, using your own name you created the following database and printouts or electronic printouts:

1. Lastname_Firstname_6G_Wireless_Usage	Database file
2. Lastname Firstname 6G Wireless Usage	Form (printed or electronic printout)
3. Lastname Firstname 6G Wireless Usage by Month	Report (printed or electronic printout)

END | You have completed Project 6G

CONTENT-BASED ASSESSMENTS

GO! Fix It	Project 6H Advertising Contracts	Online

GO! Make It	Project 6I Supply Orders	Online

GO! Solve It	Project 6J Menu Items	Online

GO! Solve It	Project 6K Birthday Coupons	

Apply a combination of the **6A** and **6B** skills.

PROJECT FILES

For Project 6K, you will need the following files:

a06K_Birthday_Coupons
a06K_Rose
a06K_Birthday
a06K_Cupcake

You will save your database as:

Lastname_Firstname_6K_Birthday_Coupons

The Vice President of Marketing, Marty Kress, encourages each location of the Rosebud Cafe franchise to offer birthday coupons to its customers as a promotional venture. Open the a06K_Birthday_Coupons database, and then save it as **Lastname_Firstname_6K_Birthday_Coupons** Use the 6K Birthdates table to create a form to enter the names, birthday months, and email addresses of the customers visiting one of the restaurants. Save the form as **Lastname Firstname 6K Birthday Form** Add a button control to print the current form. Include the Rose image as the logo and title the form **6K Happy Birthday** Remove the background from the Form Header. Resize the Detail area to 1 inch. Be sure all data is visible on the form. Add a new record using the form and your own information.

Create a report to display the customer name and email address grouped by birthday month using the months as a section header and sorted by customer name. Add the **a06K_Birthday** image as the logo, resized to 1 inch tall and wide. Add a title. Draw a line above the Birthday Month header control to separate the months; apply a Line Color and Line Type. Save the report as **Lastname Firstname 6K Birthdate Report**

Create a report based on the 6K First Quarter Birthdays query. Include both of the fields arranged in a tabular format. Save the report as **Lastname Firstname 6K First Quarter Birthdays** Add a title to the report, **Lastname Firstname 6K First Quarter Birthdays** Add the current date and time to the Report Header section. Delete the Page Footer controls, and resize the Page Footer section to 0. Apply a dotted outline to the label controls in the Page Header section; choose a Line Color and Line Thickness. Add a count of how many first quarter birthdays there are to the Report Footer. Include a descriptive label to the right of the count. Be sure the controls are sized the same and aligned. Adjust the width of the report to 7.5 inches, making necessary adjustments to textbox controls. Add the **a06K_Cupcake** image and place it in the lower right of the Report Footer. Resize it to 1 inch tall and wide. Save the changes. If you are instructed to submit the results, create a paper or electronic printout of the objects created.

(Project 6K Birthday Coupons continues on the next page)

GO! Solve It | Project 6K Birthday Coupons (continued)

Performance Level

	Exemplary	Proficient	Developing
Create 6K Birthday Form	Form created with the correct fields and formatted as directed.	Form created with no more than two missing elements.	Form created with more than two missing elements.
Create 6K Birthdate Report	Report created with the correct fields and formatted as directed.	Report created with no more than two missing elements.	Report created with more than two missing elements.
Create 6K First Quarter Birthdays Report	Report created with the correct fields and formatted as directed.	Report created with no more than two missing elements.	Report created with more than two missing elements.

Performance Criteria (left side label)

END | You have completed Project 6K

OUTCOMES-BASED ASSESSMENTS

RUBRIC

The following outcomes-based assessments are open-ended assessments. That is, there is no specific correct result; your result will depend on your approach to the information provided. Make Professional Quality your goal. Use the following scoring rubric to guide you in how to approach the problem and then to evaluate how well your approach solves the problem.

The *criteria*—Software Mastery, Content, Format and Layout, and Process—represent the knowledge and skills you have gained that you can apply to solving the problem. The *levels of performance*—Professional Quality, Approaching Professional Quality, or Needs Quality Improvements—help you and your instructor evaluate your result.

	Your completed project is of Professional Quality if you:	Your completed project is Approaching Professional Quality if you:	Your completed project Needs Quality Improvements if you:
1-Software Mastery	Choose and apply the most appropriate skills, tools, and features and identify efficient methods to solve the problem.	Choose and apply some appropriate skills, tools, and features, but not in the most efficient manner.	Choose inappropriate skills, tools, or features, or are inefficient in solving the problem.
2-Content	Construct a solution that is clear and well organized, contains content that is accurate, appropriate to the audience and purpose, and is complete. Provide a solution that contains no errors in spelling, grammar, or style.	Construct a solution in which some components are unclear, poorly organized, inconsistent, or incomplete. Misjudge the needs of the audience. Have some errors in spelling, grammar, or style, but the errors do not detract from comprehension.	Construct a solution that is unclear, incomplete, or poorly organized; contains some inaccurate or inappropriate content; and contains many errors in spelling, grammar, or style. Do not solve the problem.
3-Format & Layout	Format and arrange all elements to communicate information and ideas, clarify function, illustrate relationships, and indicate relative importance.	Apply appropriate format and layout features to some elements, but not others. Overuse features, causing minor distraction.	Apply format and layout that does not communicate information or ideas clearly. Do not use format and layout features to clarify function, illustrate relationships, or indicate relative importance. Use available features excessively, causing distraction.
4-Process	Use an organized approach that integrates planning, development, self-assessment, revision, and reflection.	Demonstrate an organized approach in some areas, but not others; or, use an insufficient process of organization throughout.	Do not use an organized approach to solve the problem.

OUTCOMES-BASED ASSESSMENTS

GO! Think   Project 6L Vacation Days

PROJECT FILES

For Project 6L, you will need the following files:

a06L_Vacation_Days
a06L_Logo

You will save your database as:

Lastname_Firstname_6L_Vacation_Days

In this project, you will create a report to display the information for the Rosebud Cafe employees and their vacation days. Open the **a06L_Vacation_Days** database and save it as **Lastname_Firstname_6L_Vacation_Days** From the *6L Vacation Days* table, add the following fields to the report: Employee Name, Days Allotted, and Days Taken. Add a calculated text box control to display the number of vacation days each employee has remaining (Days Allotted-Days Taken) with a label control to describe the field, and format the result as a General Number. Change the Theme to Ion. In the Report Header section, add the Rosebud Cafe logo and a descriptive title. Add a label control to the Report Footer section that reads **Report Designed by Firstname Lastname** Align the left edge with the label controls in the Detail section. Change the background color used in the Report Header and Report Footer sections, and change the font color so they are easy to read. Sort the report on Employee Name. Adjust all label and text controls to display all field names and data. Adjust the width of the report so it is 6 inches wide. Add a dotted line between employees to make it easier to read. Center page numbers in the page footer. Resize the Detail section to reduce the blank space. Close the space for the Page Header. Save the report as **Lastname Firstname 6L Vacation Information** If you are instructed to submit this result, create a paper or electronic printout.

END | You have completed Project 6L

OUTCOMES-BASED ASSESSMENTS

GO! Think	Project 6M Seasonal Items	Online

| **You and GO!** | Project 6N Club Directory | Online |

Creating Advanced Forms and Reports

GO! to Work
Video A7

PROJECT 7A

OUTCOMES
Create advanced forms.

OBJECTIVES

1. Create a Split Form
2. Create a Form and a Subform
3. Create a Multi-Page Form

PROJECT 7B

OUTCOMES
Create advanced reports.

OBJECTIVES

4. Create and Modify a Subreport
5. Create a Report Based on a Parameter Query
6. Create an Alphabetic Index

Igor Sokolov

In This Chapter

Forms provide a way to enter, edit, and display data; reports display the data in a professional manner. Access 2013 enables you to create a form that also displays the data in Datasheet view or to create multiple-page forms. If a one-to-many relationship exists between the underlying tables, forms can be used to manipulate data from multiple tables, and reports can display data from multiple tables. You have also practiced creating a parameter query, which, in turn, can be used to create a report based on the criteria entered when the report is opened. Specialty reports, like an alphabetic index, can also be created.

Recently, gardening has increased in popularity in many areas of the country. The stylish simplicity and use of indigenous, hardy plants make for beautiful, environmentally friendly gardens in any region of the country. Gardeners also enjoy learning about plants and gardens in other parts of the country and the world. Produced by MWB Productions, **Midwest Botanicals** is a syndicated television show that is broadcast nationwide. The show and its website provide tips and tricks for beautiful plants and gardens, highlight new tools and techniques, and present tours of public and private gardens to inspire home gardeners.

PROJECT 7A MWB Schedule

PROJECT ACTIVITIES

In Activities 7.01 through 7.08, you will help Gina Donaldson, office manager of MWB Productions, customize the company's forms. She wants the database forms to display related data. For example, she is interested in displaying the advertisers of the television shows on one form. You will display data in two ways on the same form, display data from multiple tables on one form, and display data on multiple pages on a form. Your completed forms will look similar to Figure 7.1.

PROJECT FILES

For Project 7A, you will need the following files:

a07A_MWB_Schedule
a07A_MWB_Logo
A blank Word document

You will save your files as:

Lastname_Firstname_7A_MWB_Schedule
Lastname_Firstname_7A_Tab_Control_Form

PROJECT RESULTS

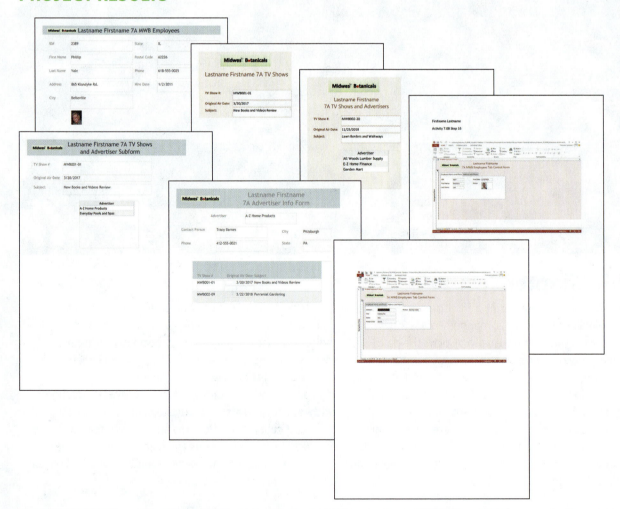

FIGURE 7.1 Project 7A MWB Schedule

Video A7-1

A *split form* displays data in two views—Form view and Datasheet view—on a single form. The two views display data from the same source and are synchronized with each other at all times. When you select a field in one of the views, the same field displays in the other view. You can add, delete, or edit data in either view. An advantage of displaying data in a split form is the flexibility of finding a record in Datasheet view and then editing the same record in Form view.

Activity 7.01 | Creating a Split Form Using the Split Form Tool

In this activity, you will create a split form from scratch.

1 Start Access. Navigate to the location where the student data files for this textbook are saved. Locate and **Open** the **a07A_MWB_Schedule** file. Display **Backstage** view, and click **Save Database As** and then, under File Types, double-click **Save Database As**. In the **Save As** dialog box, navigate to the drive on which you will be saving your folders and projects for this chapter. Create a new folder named **Access Chapter 7** and **Save** the database as **Lastname_ Firstname_7A_MWB_Schedule** in the folder. Enable the content or add the Access Chapter 7 folder to the Trust Center.

2 In the **Navigation Pane**, double-click **7A TV Show Advertisers** to open the table in Datasheet view. In the first record, in the **TV Show #** field, click the **arrow** to the right of *MWB001-01* to display a list of television show codes. In the first record, click in the **Advertiser** field, and then click the **arrow** to the right of *A-Z Home Products* to display a list of advertisers.

> Both of these fields are lookup fields. The TV Show # field looks up data in the 7A TV Shows table. The Advertiser field looks up data in the 7A Advertiser Info table. Because these fields look up data in specific tables, you will not change the names of the existing tables and forms in this database. If you did rename the tables, the lookup fields would not be able to locate the related tables.

3 Press [Esc] to close the list. If the small pencil displays in the record selector box, press [Esc] one more time. **Close** [×] the table.

4 In the **Navigation Pane**, double-click **7A MWB Employees** to open the table in Datasheet view. Take a moment to review the fields in the table. Scroll to the right, if necessary, until the Attachment field displays. In the **Attachment** field, double-click any record. In the displayed **Attachments** dialog box, click **Open** to display a photograph of the employee. **Close** [×] the window with the picture, and then **Close** [×] the **Attachments** dialog box. **Close** [×] the table.

5 With the **7A MWB Employees** table selected, **Close** [«] the **Navigation Pane**. On the **CREATE tab**, in the **Forms group**, click the **More Forms** button, and then click **Split Form**. Compare your screen with Figure 7.2.

> The underlying table or query does not need to be open to create a split form as long as it is selected before clicking the CREATE tab on the Ribbon.

> The split form displays in Layout view. The top section of the split form displays the data in Form view, and the bottom section of the split form displays the data in Datasheet view.

FIGURE 7.2

In the datasheet section of the split form, click anywhere in the first record, and then press ↓. Notice that the form section displays the data and photograph for the second record—the two sections are synchronized.

Save the split form as **Lastname Firstname 7A MWB Employees Split Form**

Activity 7.02 | Formatting a Split Form

In this activity, you will enhance the split form by modifying the fields and form properties.

In the datasheet section of the split form, click anywhere in the first record. In the form section of the split form, click the **Photo** for *Andi Shell*, and then compare your screen with Figure 7.3.

A mini toolbar displays above Andi's photograph. If the mini toolbar does not display, point to the picture. A *mini toolbar* is a miniature, semitransparent toolbar that is used to work with objects on the screen. In this case, the mini toolbar displays a Back button, a Forward button, and a Manage Attachments button. If there were multiple attachments for this record, clicking the Forward button would display the next attachment, and clicking the Back button would display the previous attachment. Clicking the Manage Attachments button would display the Attachments dialog box.

Recall that the Layout Selector is used to select all of the fields in the column. Clicking any field in a column displays the Layout Selector for the column.

FIGURE 7.3

2 Select the **Photo attachment control**—the box displaying the photograph—and **Photo label control**, and then on the ribbon, click the **FORM LAYOUT TOOLS ARRANGE tab**. In the **Table group**, click the **Stacked** button. Notice that both controls have been removed from the stacked layout.

The Photo field is moved outside of the form, to the left margin, because it was removed from the stacked layout. A dotted placeholder displays the original position in the stacked layout.

3 Click in the **Photo attachment control**. On the **FORM LAYOUT TOOLS DESIGN tab**, in the **Tools group**, click the **Property Sheet** button. Verify the **Property Sheet** displays *Selection type: Attachment*. On the **Property Sheet Format tab**, click in the **Picture Alignment** property setting box, and then click the **arrow** to review the options. Click **Bottom Left**, and then **Close** ⊠ the **Property Sheet**.

Aligning the photograph at the left edge of the attachment control makes it easier to adjust the width of the control. Recall that you must remove a field from the predefined layout to resize only that field.

4 Point to the right edge of the **Photo attachment control** until the ↔ pointer displays. Drag to the left until the border aligns with the right edge of the photograph, and then compare your screen with Figure 7.4.

FIGURE 7.4

Layout Selector for Photo control

Attachment control resized (width decreased)

5 Press PageDown to display the second record. Scroll down, if necessary, and notice that the width of the attachment control is also decreased for this record.

6 Save 🖫 the split form. With the **Photo attachment control** selected, right-click and click **Form Properties** to display the form's **Property Sheet**.

7 On the **Property Sheet Format tab**, scroll down, if necessary, until the properties that relate to split forms display, and then compare your screen with Figure 7.5. Take a moment to study the six properties that directly relate to split forms, as described in the table in Figure 7.6.

FIGURE 7.5

FIGURE 7.6

SPLIT FORM PROPERTIES		
PROPERTY	**DESCRIPTION**	**VIEW(S) IN WHICH THE PROPERTY CAN BE SET**
Split Form Size	Specify an exact height or width, depending on whether the form is split vertically or horizontally, for the form section of the split form. For example, type *1* to set the form height or width to 1 inch. Type *Auto* to set the size by other means, such as dragging the splitter bar in Layout view. The default is *Auto*.	Design or Layout
Split Form Orientation	Define whether the datasheet displays above, below, to the left, or to the right of the form. The default is *Datasheet on Bottom*.	Design
Split Form Splitter Bar	If set to *Yes*, the form and datasheet can be resized by moving the splitter bar that separates the two sections. If set to *No*, the splitter bar is hidden, and the form and datasheet cannot be resized. The default is *Yes*.	Design
Split Form Datasheet	If set to *Allow Edits* and the form's source can be updated, editing can be done in the datasheet section. If set to *Read Only*, editing cannot be done in the datasheet section. The default is *Allow Edits*.	Design or Layout
Split Form Printing	Define which section of the form is printed. If set to *Form Only*, only the form section is printed. If set to *Datasheet Only*, only the datasheet section is printed. The default is *Datasheet Only*.	Design or Layout
Save Splitter Bar Position	If set to *Yes*, the form opens with the splitter bar in the same position in which it was saved. If set to *No*, the form and datasheet cannot be resized, and the splitter bar is hidden. The default is *Yes*.	Design

8 On the **Property Sheet**, click in the **property setting** box for **Split Form Printing**, click the **arrow**, and then click **Form Only**. Notice that you can print either the Form or the Datasheet, but not both.

9 On the **tab row**, right-click **7A MWB Employees Split Form**, and then click **Design View**. On the **Property Sheet** for the form, click in the **Split Form Orientation** property setting box, and then click the **arrow**. Compare your screen with Figure 7.7. If necessary, increase the width of the Property Sheet to display all four of the property settings.

FIGURE 7.7

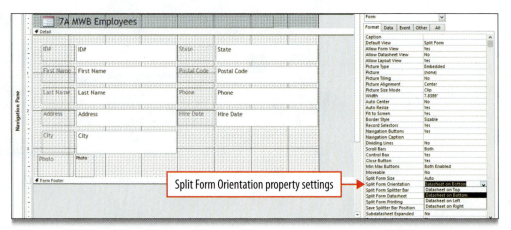

Split Form Orientation property settings

10 Click **Datasheet on Top**, and then **Close** ☒ the **Property Sheet**.

11 Switch to **Layout** view. Click the **Photo label control**, and press Delete. Click the **Photo attachment control**, and drag it to the right until the left edge aligns with the left edge of the **City text box control**.

Some editing in the Form can be done in Layout view. The datasheet section displays above the form section of the split form. A splitter bar divides the two sections.

12 Point to the **splitter bar** until the pointer displays. Drag upward until the dark horizontal line displays between the records with an **ID#** of **0855** and **1047**.

In the datasheet section, Records 1 through 3 display, and the height of the form section is increased.

13 Switch to **Design** view. On the **FORM DESIGN TOOLS DESIGN tab**, in the **Header/Footer group**, click the **Logo** button. Navigate to the location where the student data files are saved, and then double-click **a07A_MWB_Logo**. In the **Tools group**, click the **Property Sheet** button to display the **Property Sheet** for the logo. Click in the **Size Mode** setting box—*Clip* is displayed. Click the **arrow**, and then click **Zoom**. **Close** ☒ the **Property Sheet**.

When a logo is inserted in a form or report that includes a logo placeholder, the Size Mode property is set to *Clip*, and the image may be too large to display in the control. By setting the property to *Zoom*, the image is resized to fit the control while maintaining the proportions of the object.

14 Increase the width of the **logo control** to the **1.5-inch mark on the horizontal ruler**. Click in the title's **label control**, and then click at the beginning of the line. Using your own first and last names, type **Lastname Firstname** and press Spacebar to add your name before the title of the form and press Enter to accept the changes. Switch to **Form** view, and then compare your screen with Figure 7.8.

FIGURE 7.8

15 Save 🖫 the form. Press PageDown to display **Record 6**. In the form section, change the **First Name** from *Elliott* to **Phillip** and then press Tab. Notice that in the **datasheet section**, the same record—*ID# 2389*—is selected and is in the editing mode. Also notice that the **First Name** field has been updated in the datasheet section.

Recall that you can only make changes to the data in the fields with the form displayed in Form view.

16 In the form section, on the left side, click the **Record Selector** ▶ bar. If you are instructed to submit this result, create a paper or electronic printout of the selected record. **Close** ✕ the form. **Open** » the **Navigation Pane**.

> The form section prints because you set the Split Form Printing property to Form Only.

More Knowledge   **Adding or Deleting a Field**

To add a field to a split form in Layout view, display the Field List—on the DESIGN tab, in the Tools group, click the Add Existing Fields button. Drag the field from the Field List to the datasheet section or the form section. The field will be added to both sections of the split form.

To delete a field from a split form, you must delete it from the form section. The field will then be removed automatically from the datasheet section.

Activity 7.03 | Converting an Existing Form into a Split Form

In this activity, you will convert the 7A TV Shows Form into a split form.

1 In the **Navigation Pane**, under **Forms**, right-click **7A TV Shows Form**, and then click **Design View**. **Close** « the **Navigation Pane**. On the **FORM DESIGN TOOLS DESIGN tab**, in the **Tools** group, click the **Property Sheet** button to display the **Property Sheet** for the form. If the Property Sheet does not display *Selection type: Form*, click the **Selection type arrow**, and then click **Form**.

> To convert an existing form to a split form, the form must be open in Design view.

2 On the **Property Sheet Format tab**, click in the **Default View** property setting box—*Single Form* is displayed. Click the **arrow**, and then click **Split Form**. **Close** ✕ the **Property Sheet**, and then switch to **Layout** view.

> The split form displays with the datasheet section on top; Access applied the same Split Form Orientation to this split form as the previous split form.

3 Switch to **Design** view, and then using the techniques you practiced in Activity 7.02, change the **Split Form Orientation** to display the **Datasheet on Bottom**. **Close** ✕ the **Property Sheet**, display the split form in **Layout** view, and then compare your screen with Figure 7.9.

FIGURE 7.9

Datasheet section on bottom

4 In the form section, click the **title's label control**, and then click at the beginning of the line. Using your own first and last names, type **Lastname Firstname** and then press ⎵Spacebar⎵.

5 Switch to **Design** view. Hold down Shift, click the **title's label control**, and then click the **label control** for **TV Show #**. On the **FORM DESIGN TOOLS ARRANGE tab**, in the **Sizing & Ordering group**, click the **Align** button, and then click **Left**.

> The left edge of the title's label control is aligned with the left edge of the TV Show # label control.

6 Click in an empty area of the design grid to deselect the controls, and then click the **title's label control**. Point to the right edge of the **title's label control** until the ↔ pointer displays. Drag to the right until the right edge of the label control aligns with the right edges of the text box controls in the **Detail** section. If your entire name does not display within the title's label control, click the **HOME tab**, and in the **Text Formatting group**, reduce the font size of the text.

> Even though the entire title displays in Layout view and in Form view, if the title is truncated in Design view, it will be truncated when you print the form.

7 Save 🖫 and **Close** ✕ the form. **Open** » the **Navigation Pane**. Under **Forms**, right-click **7A TV Shows Form**, and then click **Rename**. Type **Lastname Firstname 7A TV Shows Split Form** and then press Enter.

> Recall that an object must be closed before you can rename it.

8 Double-click **7A TV Shows Split Form** to open it in **Form** view. Be sure that **Record 1** is displayed. In the form section, on the left side, click the **Record Selector** bar. If you are instructed to submit this result, create a paper or electronic printout of the selected record.

9 **Close** ✕ the form, and then **Close** « the **Navigation Pane**.

Objective 2   Create a Form and a Subform

Video A7-2

In the previous activities, you created a split form that displayed the datasheet of the underlying table—the data in the form section was the same data as that displayed in the datasheet section. A *subform* is a form that is embedded within another form—the *main form*—and is used to view, enter, and edit data that is related to data in the main form. A subform is similar to a subdatasheet—the data in the related table is displayed without having to open another table or form.

Activity 7.04 | Creating a Form and a Subform Using the Form Tool

If Access finds a single table that has a one-to-many relationship with the table used to create a form, Access adds the datasheet as a subform to display the related records. In this activity, you will create the main form using the 7A TV Shows table. Because a one-to-many relationship has been created between this table and the 7A TV Show Advertisers table, the datasheet for the 7A TV Show Advertisers table will be inserted as a subform.

1 Click the **DATABASE TOOLS tab**, and then in the **Relationships group**, click the **Relationships** button. If the tables do not display in the Relationships window, on the **RELATIONSHIP TOOLS DESIGN tab**, in the **Relationships group**, click the **All Relationships** button. If necessary, expand the table boxes and rearrange them so that it is easier to view the relationships as shown in Figure 7.10. Take a moment to study the established relationships.

> This is an example of a *many-to-many relationship* between the *7A TV Shows* table and the *7A Advertiser Info* table. *Many* television shows can have *many* advertisers. Conversely, *many* advertisers can advertise on *many* television shows.

> To create the *many-to-many relationship* between *7A TV Shows* and *7A Advertiser Info*, the *7A TV Show Advertisers* table was created. This table is known as a *junction table*. It breaks down the many-to-many relationship into two *one-to-many relationships*. The data from the primary key fields—*TV Show #* and *Advertiser*—from the two tables are added to the junction table, which records each instance of the relationship. The primary key fields from the two tables are connected to the foreign key fields in the junction table.

FIGURE 7.10

One-to-many relationships

Junction table

Many-to-many relationships

NOTE   Specifying Multiple Primary Key Fields

A junction table contains data from the primary key fields in two tables. The fields in the junction table are designated as primary key fields. In Design view, to specify multiple fields as primary key fields, hold down the Ctrl key, and then click the row selector boxes for each primary key field. On the TABLE TOOLS DESIGN tab, in the Tools group, click the Primary Key button. A junction table can include fields other than the common fields from the two related tables.

---

2 ▶ **Close** ☒ the Relationships window, saving changes if prompted. **Open** » the **Navigation Pane**. Under **Tables**, click **7A TV Shows**. On the **CREATE tab**, in the **Forms group**, click the **Form** button. **Close** « the **Navigation Pane**, and then compare your screen with Figure 7.11.

The data in the *7A TV Shows* table displays in the main form and the subform displays the Advertiser information from the related table, *7A TV Show Advertisers*.

FIGURE 7.11

Main form—7A TV Shows table

Subform—7A TV Show Advertisers table

Navigation area for subform

Navigation area for main form

3 ▶ In the main form, click the **TV Show # text box control**, if necessary, and then press PageDown until **Record 5** is displayed, observing changes in the subform and in the two record navigators.

As you scroll through the records in the *7A TV Shows* table, the subform displays the related records for each television show. For example, in Record 5, the TV Show # is *MWB001-06*, and three advertisers support this show.

4 ▶ In the main form, click the **Subject text box control**. Point to the right edge of the text box control until the pointer displays, and then drag the right edge of the text box control to the left until there is approximately **1 inch** of space between *Devices* and the right edge of the text box control.

Because the controls are part of the same stacked layout, the width of all of the text box controls is decreased.

5 ▶ Click anywhere in the subform. Notice that the **Layout Selector** ⊞ displays above the upper left corner of the subform and the datasheet is selected with a border around it. The **Layout Selector** also displays above the upper left corner of the main form because the forms are stacked. Switch to **Design** view. Click in the Table.7A TV Show Advertisers subform placeholder. On the **FORM LAYOUT TOOLS ARRANGE tab**, in the **Table group**, click **Remove Layout** to remove the **subform** from the stacked layout.

6 ▶ Switch to **Layout** view. Click the **subform**, and then compare your screen with Figure 7.12.

Notice that the Layout Selector only displays above the upper left corner of the form because the forms are no longer stacked.

FIGURE 7.12

> Separate Layout Selector because forms are no longer stacked

---

More Knowledge **Sort Records in a Form**

In a form or subform, records are sorted by the primary key field. To modify the sort order, click the text box control for the field for the sort. On the HOME tab, in the Sort & Filter group, click the Ascending or Descending button (depending on the sort you want to perform). To remove the sort, on the HOME tab, in the Sort & Filter group, click the Remove Sort button.

---

7 ▶ Click the **subform** to select it, if necessary. Point to the right edge of the subform until the ↔ pointer displays, and then drag the right edge of the subform to the left until it aligns with the right edge of the **Advertiser** control box. Point to the subform **Layout Selector** ⊞ until the pointer displays, and then drag to the right until the subform is centered under the text box controls in the main form. **Save** 🖫 the form as **Lastname Firstname 7A TV Shows and Advertisers**

Be sure to leave some space between the main form and the subform so it is not returned to the Stacked Layout. If it returns to that layout, click Undo, and move the subform again.

8 ▶ Switch to **Design** view. On the **FORM DESIGN TOOLS DESIGN tab**, in the **Header/Footer group**, click the **Logo** button. Navigate to the location where the student data files for this textbook are saved. Locate and double-click **a07A_MWB_Logo** to insert the logo in the form header. In the **Tools group**, click the **Property Sheet** button to display the **Property Sheet** for the logo. Click in the **Size Mode** property box, click the **arrow**, and then click **Zoom**. Close ✕ the **Property Sheet**. Point to the center right edge of the control until the ↔ pointer displays; drag to the right until it is between the *S* and *h* in *Shows*, and then compare your screen to Figure 7.13.

FIGURE 7.13

> Logo inserted and resized

> Subform control is centered under the text box controls

9 Click at the beginning of the title label control, and type **Lastname Firstname** and then press Spacebar once. To the right of *Shows*, press Spacebar one time, hold down Shift, and then press Enter. Type **and Advertiser Subform** Press Enter.

> The title now displays on two lines in the label control.

10 Point to the right edge of the **title's label control** until the ↔ pointer displays—the right edge may display at the very right side of your screen. Drag to the left until the right edge aligns with the **5.75-inch mark on the horizontal ruler**. With the **title's label control** selected, on the **FORM DESIGN TOOLS FORMAT tab**, in the **Font group**, click the **Center** button ☰.

11 Resize the width of the form to **7 inches**. Compare your screen with Figure 7.14. Notice that the subform control displays the related table's name—*Table.7A TV Show Advertisers*. Also, notice that the title's label control may not display the entire title. Be sure it is visible before moving on.

> Although you can make most adjustments to a form in Layout view, you should adjust the title's control in Design view to ensure the form's title will print as desired. With narrow margins for a form and with Portrait orientation, the right edge of the form should not exceed 7.5 inches on the horizontal ruler; otherwise, pages will print with only the background color in the form header.

FIGURE 7.14

12 **Save** 🖫 the form, and then switch to **Form** view. On the left side of the form, click the **Record Selector** bar, and then if you are instructed to submit this result, create a paper or electronic printout of only Record 1—the selected record. Notice that both the main form and the subform print. **Close** ⊠ the form.

More Knowledge   **Create Forms with Application Parts**

Create a form using application parts by clicking the CREATE tab. In the Templates group, click the Application Parts arrow, and then click the template you want to use for the form. Once you assign the Record Source to the form, you can add fields to the form.

Activity 7.05 │ Creating a Form and a Subform Using the Form Wizard

Use the Form Wizard to create a form and a subform when you want to have more control over the design of the subform, or if the underlying table or query has more than one relationship established. If the underlying table or query that is on the *one* side of the relationship is related to more than one table or query on the *many* side of the relationship, the subform will not automatically be created when the form is created. The same technique can be used to create a split form between two tables that have a many-to-many relationship.

1 On the **CREATE tab**, in the **Forms group**, click the **Form Wizard** button. In the **Form Wizard** dialog box, click the **Tables/Queries arrow**, and then, if necessary, click **Table: 7A TV Shows**, which is on the *one* side of the relationship with the **7A Advertiser Info** using the junction table.

> It does not matter which table you select first; in a later dialog box, you can select the table that displays in the main form and the table that displays in the subform.

2 Under **Available Fields**, click the **All Fields** >> button to add all of the fields to the **Selected Fields** box. In the same dialog box, click the **Tables/Queries arrow**, and from the displayed list, click **Table: 7A Advertiser Info**, which is on the *many* side of the relationship with the **7A TV Shows** table. Again, add **All Fields** to the **Selected Fields** box. Click **Next**, and then compare your screen with Figure 7.15.

> The second Form Wizard dialog box displays with a preview of how the data will be arranged. The order in which you select the tables or queries to be included in the main form and subform does not matter because you can change the way the data is displayed in this Form Wizard dialog box. If a relationship between the tables has not been established, this Form Wizard dialog box will not display.

FIGURE 7.15

3 Under **How do you want to view your data?**, click **by 7A Advertiser Info**, and notice that the form will display with the *7A Advertiser Info* table as the main form and the *7A TV Shows* table as the subform. Under the preview of the form, click **Linked forms**, and notice the preview displays two separate forms with a button on the main form that represents the link between the two forms.

> A *linked form* is a related form that is not stored within the main form. To view the data in a linked form, click on the link that is displayed on the main form.

N O T E | **Switching Main Form and Subform Tables**

If the tables have a one-to-many relationship, and you switch the view to display the many side as the main form and the one side as the subform, the form will display as a single form instead of a main form with a subform. With a one-to-many relationship, the main form should display the table on the one side of the relationship, and the subform should display the table on the many side of the relationship.

---

4 Click **Form with subform(s)**, and then click **Next** to display the third **Form Wizard** dialog box, where you can select the subform layout. Notice the two layouts are **Tabular** and **Datasheet**, with **Datasheet** being the default layout.

> Both layouts arrange the subform data in rows and columns, but the tabular layout is more customizable. You can add color, graphics, and other elements to a tabular subform. The subform you created in the previous activity used the datasheet layout, which is more compact than the tabular layout.

5 Click **Tabular**, and then click **Next** to display the last **Form Wizard** dialog box. In the **Form** text box, select the existing text, and then type **Lastname Firstname 7A Advertiser Info Form** In the **Subform** text box, select the existing text, type **Lastname Firstname 7A TV Shows Subform** and then click **Finish**. Compare your screen to Figure 7.16.

> The form and subform display in Form view. Notice that all of the fields and data are not visible in the subform.

FIGURE 7.16

Main Form—fields from
7A Advertiser Info table

Subform—fields from
7A TV Shows table

6 Switch to **Design** view. Using the lasso technique you have practiced, select all of the controls in the main form. On the **FORM DESIGN TOOLS ARRANGE tab**, in the **Table** group, click the **Stacked** button.

 BY TOUCH   Use your finger to draw the circle and to highlight text.

7 Save 💾 the form.

Activity 7.06 | Modifying a Form and a Subform

1 Switch the **7A Advertiser Info form** to **Layout** view. In the subform, click the **TV Show # label control**. Hold down Shift, and then click the **TV Show # text box control** to select both controls. Point to the right edge of the **TV Show # text box control** until the ↔ pointer displays. Drag the right edge of the control to the left until there are approximately **0.25 inches** of space between the first show # and the right edge of the **TV Show # text box control**.

2 Click the **Subject label control**; hold down Shift and click the **Subject text box control**, scrolling to the right if necessary. On the **FORM LAYOUT TOOLS DESIGN tab**, in the **Tools** group, click the **Property Sheet** button to display the **Property Sheet** for *Multiple selection*. On the **Format tab**, select the **Width** property. Type **3** and press Enter. Hold down Shift and click the **Original Air Date text box** and **label controls**. Drag the controls to the left until the **Original Air Date** appears immediately to the right of **TV Show #**.

> The widths of the controls are decreased and the controls are all right next to one another.

3 In the upper left corner of the subform, click the **Layout Selector** ⊞. On the **Property Sheet**, the **Selection Type** should now read *Subform/Subreport*. Select the **Width** property setting, and then type **6.15** Press Enter, and then type **3.5** in the **Height** property setting. **Close** ☒ the **Property Sheet**. Compare your screen with Figure 7.17.

> The width and height of the subform are adjusted, and the vertical and horizontal scroll bars in the subform do not display.

FIGURE 7.17

Scroll bars no longer appear

4 ▶ Click the main form, and navigate to **Record 17**—*Advertiser* of *Very Green Lawns Inc*. In the main form, click the **Advertiser text box control**. Point to the right edge of the text box control until the ↔ pointer displays. Drag to the left until there is approximately **0.5 inches** of space between the data in the **Advertiser** field and the right edge of the text box control. Recall that the controls are grouped together in a stacked layout, so adjusting the size of one control adjusts the size of all of the controls.

5 ▶ Click the **Phone text box control**; hold down Shift and click the **Phone label control**. Point to the **Phone text box control** until the 🔀 pointer displays. Drag upward until an orange horizontal line displays between the **Contact Person** field and the **City** field. Click the **City text box control**. Hold down Shift, and then click the **City label control**, the **State text box control**, and the **State label control** to select all four controls. On the **FORM LAYOUT TOOLS ARRANGE tab**, in the **Table group**, click the **Stacked** button to remove the controls from the Stacked Layout. Click the original location of the **City text box control**. Hold down Shift, and then click the original location of the **City label control**, the **State text box control**, and the **State label control** to select all four placeholders. Press Delete to remove the placeholders from the stacked layout.

Recall that it is easier to remove fields from a stacked layout when they are at the bottom of the layout, but the placeholders remain once the controls are removed from the stacked layout.

6 ▶ Click the **City label control** to display the **Layout Selector** ⊞ for the controls. Point to the **Layout Selector** until the 🔀 pointer displays, and then drag upward and to the right until the **City** field aligns with the **Contact Person** field and there is approximately **0.5 inches** of space between the **Contact Person text box control** and the **City label control**. Click in a blank area of the form to deselect the controls. Click the **City label control**, and then point to the right edge of the **City label control** until the ↔ pointer displays. Drag the right edge of the **City label control** to the left until there is approximately **0.5 inches** of space between the word *City* and the right edge of the **City label control**. Using the same technique, resize the **City text box control**. Save 🖫 the form. Compare your screen with Figure 7.18.

After removing the fields from the stacked layout, they are grouped as a separate layout for ease in making adjustments to the controls. The widths of the City and State label controls are decreased so that the text box controls will not exceed the allowable width when printed.

FIGURE 7.18

Fields moved from the first column

Widths of controls decreased

7 ▸ Using the techniques you have practiced, remove the **Advertiser textbox control** and the **Advertiser label control** from the stacked layout, and then delete the placeholders from the stacked layout. Move the left column down so the **Contact Person** field aligns with the **City** field. Click the **Advertiser label control**. Hold down ⇧Shift, and then click the **Advertiser text box control** to select both controls. Point to one of the selected controls until the ▨ pointer displays. Drag upward and to the right until the controls are approximately centered above the controls on the left and the controls on the right.

The Advertiser field is contained in its own stacked layout.

8 ▸ Click the **subform label control**—*Lastname Firstname 7A TV Shows*—and press ⌦Delete to remove the label from the subform control. Click the **subform** to display the **Layout Selector** for the subform. Point to the **Layout Selector** until the ▨ pointer displays. Drag the subform upward until there is approximately **0.5 inches** of space between the **Phone** field and the **subform**, and the right edge of the subform aligns with the right edge of the **State text box control**. Compare your screen with Figure 7.19.

FIGURE 7.19

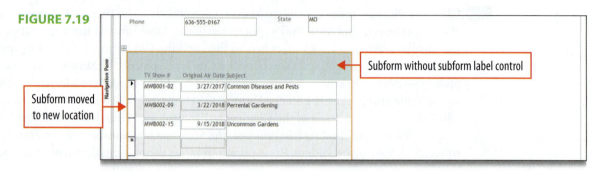

9 ▸ **Save** 🖫 the form, and switch to **Design** view. Using the techniques you have practiced, in the main form, add a **Logo** to the **Form Header** section using **a07A_MWB_Logo**, and then **Delete** the accompanying label control. Move the **form title's label control** so the left edge aligns with the **2-inch mark on the horizontal ruler**, and place *7A Advertiser Info Form* on the second line of the title. Align the right edge of the form title's label control with the right edge of the subform. **Center** the text in the **form title's label control**. Adjust the size of the logo so there is **one dot** between it and the **title label control** and it is the same height as the title. If necessary, resize the form width to **7.25 inches** so no extraneous pages print when the form is printed. Compare your screen with Figure 7.20.

FIGURE 7.20

10 ▸ Switch to **Form** view. Press PageDown until the record for **A-Z Home Products**—*Record 4*—displays. If you are instructed to submit this result, create a paper or electronic printout of only this record.

11   **Close** ☒ the form, saving changes. **Open** ⟩⟩ the **Navigation Pane**. Under **Forms**, **7A Advertiser Info Form** and **7A TV Shows Subform** display. Double-click **7A Advertiser Info Form** to open it in **Form** view. The subform is embedded in the form. Double-click **7A TV Shows Subform** to open it in **Form** view. This form displays the fields from the *7A TV Shows* table that are used in the subform of *7A Advertiser Info Form*.

When a subform is created in a main form, a separate form object is created and displays in the Navigation Pane under Forms.

12   **Close** all forms.

> **More Knowledge**   **Adding the Table Name to the Subform**
>
> To add the name of the table used to create the subform at the top of the subform, add a label control to the Form Header section of the subform, and then type the name of the table. If the table name is added to the Form Header section, the label control with the table name that displays to the left of the subform should be deleted.

Activity 7.07 | Creating a Subform by Dragging a Related Table onto an Existing Form

In this activity, you will create a subform by dragging an existing table—*7A TV Show Advertisers*—on the *many* side of the relationship onto an existing form—*7A TV Shows Main Form*—on the *one* side of the relationship. When a table has more than one relationship with other tables, this method is helpful in adding a subform to a form.

1   In the **Navigation Pane**, under **Forms**, open **7A TV Shows Main Form** in **Design** view. On the **FORM DESIGN TOOLS DESIGN tab**, in the **Controls group**, click the **More** ▾ arrow, and verify that the **Use Control Wizards** ⬚ option is active.

The existing form must be open in Design view before dragging a related table onto it. If you try to drag a related table onto a form in Layout view, an error message displays.

2   In the form, point to the top of the **Form Footer section bar** until the pointer displays. Drag downward until the **Detail** section is **3 inches** high.

3   In the **Navigation Pane**, under **Tables**, drag **7A TV Show Advertisers** onto *7A TV Shows Main Form* to the **1.75-inch mark on the vertical ruler** and **0.25-inch mark on the horizontal ruler**. The first **SubForm Wizard** dialog box displays. Compare your screen with Figure 7.21.

Notice at the bottom of the dialog box that Access will display records from the *7A TV Show Advertisers* table for each record in the *7A TV Shows* table using the *TV Show #* field—the common field.

FIGURE 7.21

4   In the **SubForm Wizard** dialog box, click **Define my own**.

The SubForm Wizard dialog box changes to display list boxes in which you can select the fields that link the main form to the subform.

5 Under **Form/report fields**, in the **first list box**, click the **arrow**, and then click **TV Show #**. Under **Subform/subreport fields**, in the **first list box**, click the **arrow**, and then click **TV Show #**. Compare your screen with Figure 7.22.

> The same field is used to link the form and the subform as when *Choose from a list* was selected. By default, Access uses the fields that are used to create the join line in the relationship between the tables. You should select *Define my own* when you want to use fields other than the common fields as defined in the relationship.

FIGURE 7.22

6 Click **Next**. Under **What name would you like for your subform or subreport?**, type **Lastname Firstname 7A TV Show Advertisers Subform** and then click **Finish**. Compare your screen with Figure 7.23.

> The subform displays under the label and text box controls of the main form, and a subform label control displays above the subform.

FIGURE 7.23

7 With the subform control selected, point to the **bottom middle sizing handle** of the subform control until the ⬍ pointer displays. If the subform is not selected, point to the bottom edge of the subform control, and then click to display the sizing handles. Drag downward about one-half inch. If necessary, point to the top of the **Form Footer section bar** until the pointer displays, and then drag upward to the bottom of the subform control. **Close** ⊠ the **Field List**. **Save** 🖬 the form, and then **Close** « the **Navigation Pane**.

8 Switch to **Layout** view. If necessary, resize controls so both fields are visible in the subform. Press PageDown to display the record for each television show and the related record(s) in the subform. Notice that the **TV Show #** field displays in both the main form and the subform.

9 In the record navigator for the main form, click the **First Record** button. Switch to **Design** view. In the subform control, click the **TV Show # label control**, hold down Shift and click the **TV Show # text box control**. Press Delete, and then switch to **Layout** view. Press PageDown until the record for **MWB001-09**—*Record 7*—displays. Double-click the right edge of the **Advertiser label control** to resize for the longest item in the list.

The *TV Show #* field is removed from the subform.

10 Click the **subform control** and then click the displayed **Layout Selector** ⊞. Point to the bottom right corner of the **subform control** until the pointer displays. Drag upward and to the left until there is approximately **0.25 inches** of blank space between the **Advertiser** controls and the bottom and right edges of the subform. Compare your screen with Figure 7.24.

FIGURE 7.24

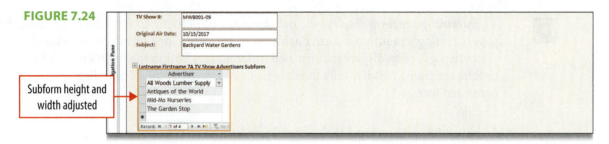

Subform height and width adjusted

11 Click the **subform label control**, which displays *Lastname Firstname 7A Show Advertisers Subform*, and then press Delete to remove the label control from the subform.

12 Click anywhere in the subform, and then point to the displayed **Layout Selector** ⊞ until the pointer displays. Drag to the right until the subform is centered under the form text box controls.

13 Switch to **Design** view, saving changes to both objects. Change the title of the form to **Lastname Firstname 7A TV Shows and Advertisers** and then move **7A TV Shows and Advertisers** onto the second line. Adjust the width of the **title's label control** so that the left edge of the label control aligns with the left edge of the field label controls and the right edge of the label control aligns with the right edge of the field text box controls. In the **title's label control**, **Center** the text, and then compare your screen with Figure 7.25.

FIGURE 7.25

Form title

Subform control without subform label control

14 Save 🖫 the form, and in the **Microsoft Access** dialog box, click **Yes**. Switch to **Form** view. If you are instructed to submit this result, create a paper or electronic printout of only the last record.

15 **Close** ✕ the form and **Open** » the **Navigation Pane**. Under **Forms**, **Rename** *7A TV Shows Main Form* as **Lastname Firstname 7A TV Shows Main Form and Advertisers Subform**

Objective 3 | Create a Multi-Page Form

Video A7-3

A *multi-page form* displays the data from the underlying table or query on more than one page. Creating a multi-page form enables you to divide a long form into sections that display on separate pages or to display subforms on different tabs within the main form. A multi-page form enables the user to display only the data that needs to be accessed and displays the form in a more organized format.

Activity 7.08 | Creating a Multi-Page Form Using the Tab Control

In this activity, you will modify a form to create a multi-page form using the tab control. A *tab control* is used to display data on the main form on different tabs, similar to the way database objects, such as forms and tables, display on different tabs.

1 In the **Navigation Pane**, under **Forms**, open **7A MWB Employees TC Form** in **Design** view, and then **Close** [«] the **Navigation Pane**. Point to the top of the **Form Footer section bar** until the pointer displays. Drag downward to the **2.25-inch mark on the vertical ruler** to increase the height of the **Detail** section.

2 On the **FORM DESIGN TOOLS DESIGN tab**, in the **Controls group**, click the **Tab Control** button [▯]. Move the pointer into the **Detail** section until the plus (+) sign of the pointer is aligned approximately with the **0.25-inch mark on the horizontal ruler** and with the **0.25-inch mark on the vertical ruler**. Click one time, and then compare your screen with Figure 7.26.

A tab control is inserted into the Detail section of the form. There are two tabs on the tab control. Each tab represents a separate page on the form. Do not be concerned if the page numbers on your tabs differ from those displayed in Figure 7.26.

FIGURE 7.26

3 In the selected **tab control**, point to the **right middle sizing handle** until the ↔ pointer displays. Drag to the right until the right edge of the **tab control** aligns with the **6-inch mark on the horizontal ruler**.

4 On the **FORM DESIGN TOOLS DESIGN tab**, in the **Tools group**, if necessary, click the **Add Existing Fields** button.

The Field List for the *7A MWB Employees* table displays.

5 In the **Field List**, click **ID#**. Hold down Shift, and then click **Last Name** to select three fields. Hold down Ctrl, click **Hire Date**, and then click **Photo** to select two additional fields. Point to a selected field, and then drag downward and to the left onto the first tab until the top of the arrow of the pointer aligns with the **1.5-inch mark on the horizontal ruler** and with the **0.75-inch mark on the vertical ruler**. Release the mouse button. Compare your screen with Figure 7.27.

The controls for the fields are arranged in a column on the first tab in the tab control, and Access automatically adjusts the height of the tab control so that all of the controls display. The controls are not grouped together.

FIGURE 7.27

Fields dragged to first tab

7A MWB Employees Field List

6 **Close** ☒ the **Field List**. Click in an empty area of the tab control to deselect the controls. Hold down Shift, and then click the **label controls** for the **Hire Date** and **Photo** fields, the **text box control** for **Hire Date**, and the **control** for the **Photo**. Point to the selected controls until the ⇱ pointer displays. Drag to the right and upward until the *Hire Date* controls align with the *ID#* controls and there is approximately **0.5 inches** of space between the two columns. Do not be concerned if the controls do not exactly align.

7 With the controls selected, on the **FORM DESIGN TOOLS ARRANGE tab**, in the **Table group**, click the **Stacked** button to group the controls together. Click the **ID# label control** to deselect the controls in the second column. Using the techniques you have just practiced, select all of the controls in the first column, and then group them together in a **Stacked** layout.

8 Click the **Layout Selector** ⊞ for the first column. Hold down Shift, click the **Hire Date label control**, and then click the **Layout Selector** ⊞ above the second column to select both columns. On the **FORM DESIGN TOOLS ARRANGE tab**, in the **Sizing & Ordering group**, click the **Align** button, and then click **Top**. Compare your screen with Figure 7.28.

FIGURE 7.28

Columns aligned at top edges

9 Save 🖫 the form, and then switch to **Layout** view. Press ⌨PageDown⌨ several times to display the other records in the table, ensuring that all of the data displays in all of the fields.

10 Switch to **Design** view. In the **Detail** section, click the **tab control** to select it, and then click the **second tab**, which has no controls added to it. On the **FORM DESIGN TOOLS DESIGN tab**, in the **Tools group**, click the **Add Existing Fields** button. In the **Field List**, click **Address**. Hold down ⌨Shift⌨, and then click **Phone** to select five fields. Point to the selected fields, and then drag downward and to the left onto the second tab until the top of the arrow of the pointer aligns with the **1.5-inch mark on the horizontal ruler** and with the **0.75-inch mark on the vertical ruler**.

11 Using the techniques you have practiced, move the **Phone label control** and **Phone text box control** upward and to the right until the controls are aligned with the **Address** controls. Arrange the **Phone controls** in a **Stacked** layout. Arrange the eight controls in the first column in a **Stacked** layout. Align the tops of both columns, **Close** ⌧ the **Field List**, and then compare your screen with Figure 7.29.

FIGURE 7.29

12 Save 🖫 the form, and then switch to **Layout** view. Click the **second tab** and notice that the data in the **Address** field is truncated. Press ⌨PageDown⌨ three times to display **Record 4**. Point to the right edge of the **Address text box control** until the ↔ pointer displays, and then drag to the right until the entire address displays in the **text box control**. Move the **Phone label control** to the right, if necessary. Click the **first tab** of the form.

13 Right-click the **first page** of the form, and then click **Properties**. The **Property Sheet** should display *Selection type: Page*, and the **Selection type** box should display the tab's page number. If necessary, change the *Selection type*. On the **Property Sheet Format tab**, click in the **Caption** property setting box, type **Employee Name and Photo** and then press ⌨Enter⌨.

The first tab displays the text you entered in the Caption property setting box.

14 In the form, click the **second tab** to display the **Property Sheet** for the second tab. Click in the **Caption** property setting box, type **Address and Phone** and then press ⌨Enter⌨ to change the text on the second tab. **Close** ⌧ the **Property Sheet**. In the form, click the **Employee Name and Photo tab** to display the first page of the form.

15 Change the **title** of the form to **Lastname Firstname 7A Employees Tab Control Form** and then place **7A Employees Tab Control Form** on the second line of the title. Switch to **Form** view.

16 Save the form, and navigate to **Record 5**. Press ⌨Alt⌨ + ⌨PrintScrn⌨ to place a copy of the screen into the clipboard. Open **Microsoft Office Word 2013**. In a New, Blank document, type your **Firstname Lastname** and press ⌨Enter⌨. Type **Activity 7.08 Step 16** and press ⌨Enter⌨. On the **HOME tab**, in the **Clipboard group**, click the **Paste** button to place the screenshot in the Word document window. Press ⌨Ctrl⌨ + ⌨End⌨ to move to the end of the Word document, and press ⌨Ctrl⌨ + ⌨Enter⌨ to move to the next page. **Minimize** the Word window.

Because it takes a long time for Access to format a form that contains a tab control for printing, you are copying the screens displaying the data on the tabs into Word, and then printing the Word document.

17 In the **Access** window, on the form, click the **Address and Phone tab**. Press [Alt] + [PrintScrn] to place a copy of the screen into the clipboard. On the taskbar, click the **Microsoft Word** button to display the Word document. In the **Word** window, on the **HOME tab**, in the **Clipboard group**, click the **Paste** button to place the second page of the form in the Word document window.

18 In the **Word** window, on the **Quick Access Toolbar**, click the **Save** 🖫 button. Under *Save As*, double-click **Computer**, navigate to the **Access Chapter 7** folder, and then save the file as **Lastname_Firstname_7A_Tab_Control_Form** If you are instructed to submit this result, create a paper or electronic printout of the document.

> The screen copy of the first tab prints on the first page, and the screen copy of the second tab prints on the second page.

19 **Close** [×] **Word**. If necessary, on the taskbar, click the **Access** button. In **Access**, **Close** [×] the form, saving changes. **Open** [»] the **Navigation Pane**. Under **Forms**, **Rename** *7A MWB Employees TC Form* as **Lastname Firstname 7A Employees Tab Control Form**. **Close** the database, and then **Exit** Access.

20 As directed by your instructor, submit your database and the paper or electronic printouts of the six objects—five forms and one Word document—that are the result of this project. Specifically, in this project, using your own name you created the following database and printouts or electronic printouts:

1. Lastname_Firstname_7A_MWB_Schedule	Database file
2. Lastname Firstname 7A MWB Employees Split Form	Form (printed or electronic printout)
3. Lastname Firstname 7A TV Shows Form	Form (printed or electronic printout)
4. Lastname Firstname 7A TV Shows Main Form	Form (printed or electronic printout)
5. Lastname Firstname 7A Advertiser Info Form	Form (printed or electronic printout)
6. Lastname Firstname 7A TV Shows and Advertisers	Form (printed or electronic printout)
7. Lastname_Firstname_7A_Tab_Control_Form	Word document (printed or electronic printout)

END | You have completed Project 7A

PROJECT ACTIVITIES

In Activities 7.09 through 7.15, you will create advanced reports that will help the president and officers of the production company view the information in a database in a different way. MWB Productions maintains a website where customers can order gardening supplies that are featured in the *Midwest Botanicals* television show. You will create advanced reports that display data from multiple tables and from a parameter query. You will also create an alphabetic index of garden suppliers. Your completed reports will look similar to Figure 7.30.

PROJECT FILES

For Project 7B, you will need the following file:

a07B_Online_Orders

You will save your database as:

Lastname_Firstname_7B_Online_Orders

PROJECT RESULTS

FIGURE 7.30 Project 7B Online Orders

Video A7-4

A *subreport* is a report that is embedded within another report—the *main report*. The main report is either bound or unbound. A *bound report* displays data from an underlying table, query, or SQL statement as specified in the report's Record Source property; an *unbound report* does not. An *SQL statement* is an instruction using Structured Query Language. An example of an unbound report being used as the main form would be a report that displays a title, logo, and date, similar to a report header. A main report can also contain a subform instead of a subreport. A main report can contain up to seven levels of subforms and subreports.

Activity 7.09 | Using the SubReport Wizard to Create a Subreport

In this activity, you will create a subreport using the SubReport Wizard. The main report will display the online orders, and the subreport will display the products that were ordered. Before creating a subreport using the SubReport Wizard, the underlying tables or queries should have established relationships.

1 Start Access. Navigate to the location where the student data files for this textbook are saved. Locate and open the **a07B_Online_Orders** file. Save the database in your **Access Chapter 7** folder as **Lastname_Firstname_7B_Online_Orders** If you did not add the **Access Chapter 7** folder to the Trust Center, enable the content.

2 Because some of the fields in the tables are lookup fields, you will not rename any of the tables. **Close** 〈«〉 the **Navigation Pane**.

3 On the **DATABASE TOOLS tab**, in the **Relationships group**, click the **Relationships** button. Take a moment to review the relationships between the tables.

> There is a *one-to-many* relationship between the *7B MWB Suppliers* table and the *7B Online Orders* table. There is a *one-to-many* relationship between the *7B Online Orders* table and the *7B Online Order Detail* table. There is a *one-to-many* relationship between the *7B Online Garden Supplies* table and the *7B Online Order Detail* table. The *7B Online Order Detail* table is a junction table that is used to create a *many-to-many* relationship between the *7B Online Orders* table and the *7B Online Garden Supplies* table.

4 **Close** 〈×〉 the **Relationships tab**, and then **Open** 〈»〉 the **Navigation Pane**. Under **Reports**, right-click **7B Orders Report**, and then click **Copy**. On the **HOME tab**, in the **Clipboard group**, click the **Paste** button. In the **Paste As** dialog box, under **Report Name**, and with the existing text selected, type **Lastname Firstname 7B Orders Main Report** and then click **OK**.

> In the Navigation Pane under Reports, the newly named copy of the *7B Orders Report* displays.

5 Open **7B Orders Main Report** in **Design** view, and then **Close** 〈«〉 the **Navigation Pane**. Click the **small box** in the upper left corner of the report, where the top and left margins intersect. Recall that clicking this box selects the report. On the **REPORT DESIGN TOOLS DESIGN tab**, in the **Tools group**, click the **Property Sheet** button.

> The Property Sheet should display *Selection type: Report*.

6 Click the **Property Sheet Data tab**. Notice that the **Record Source** property setting is *7B Online Orders*. **Close** 〈×〉 the **Property Sheet**.

> *7B Orders Main Report* is bound to the *7B Online Orders* table.

7 In the **Report Header** section, click the **title's label control**, and change *Lastname Firstname* to your own last and first names, and then press 〈Enter〉. In the report, point to the top of the **Page Footer section bar** until the pointer displays. Drag downward to the **1-inch mark on the vertical ruler** to make room in the **Detail** section for the subreport.

8 On the **REPORT DESIGN TOOLS DESIGN tab**, in the **Controls group**, click the **More** arrow, and verify that the **Use Control Wizards** option is active. In the **Controls group**, click the **Subform/Subreport** 🔲 button. Move the mouse pointer down into the **Detail** section until the top of the plus (+) sign of the pointer aligns with the **1-inch mark on the horizontal ruler** and with the **0.5-inch mark on the vertical ruler**, and then click. Compare your screen with Figure 7.31.

A subreport control is inserted into the Detail section of the report, and the SubReport Wizard dialog box displays. The control displays *Unbound* because the control has not yet been linked to a record source.

FIGURE 7.31

9 In the **SubReport Wizard** dialog box, verify that **Use existing Tables and Queries** is selected, and then click **Next**.

The second SubReport Wizard dialog box enables you to select the table or query and the fields to use in the subreport.

10 Click the **Tables/Queries box arrow**, and from the displayed list, click **Table: 7B Online Order Detail**. Under **Available Fields**, double-click **Product**, and then double-click **Quantity** to move the fields to the **Selected Fields** box. Click **Next**.

The third SubReport Wizard dialog box enables you to define the fields that link the main form to the subreport. Because there is a one-to-many relationship between the two tables, the default setting is to show the data in the *7B Online Order Detail* table for each record in the *7B Online Orders* table.

11 Click **Next**, name the report **Lastname Firstname 7B Products Ordered Subreport** and then click **Finish**. Save 🔲 the Main report. Switch to **Report** view, and then compare your screen with Figure 7.32.

The subreport data displays under each record from the *7B Online Orders* table. For example, for *Order # MWB100*, two Border Rakes were ordered.

FIGURE 7.32

Activity 7.10 | Modifying a Subreport

Just like the main report, the subreport can be modified. In this activity, you will remove the name of the subreport, apply conditional formatting in the subreport, and change the border color of the subreport. You can modify the subreport in either Layout view or Design view.

1 Switch to **Layout** view. **Close** ☒ the **Field List**, if necessary. In any subreport control, click the **subreport label control**, which displays *7B Products Ordered Subreport*, and then press ⌨Delete.

The label control for the subreport no longer displays.

2 In any subreport control, click the **Quantity text box control**. On the **REPORT LAYOUT TOOLS FORMAT tab**, in the **Control Formatting** group, click the **Conditional Formatting** button. The **Conditional Formatting Rules Manager** dialog box displays to show formatting rules for the *Quantity* field. Click the **New Rule** button, and compare your screen with Figure 7.33.

Conditional formatting is a way to apply formatting to specific controls based on a comparison to a rule set in the New Rule dialog box. It is one way to draw attention to an entry that might require additional action.

FIGURE 7.33

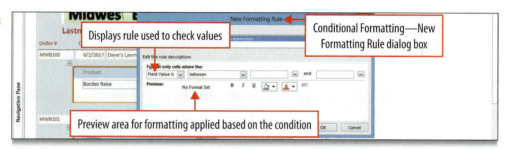

3 Click the arrow to the right of the box that displays *between*, and select **less than or equal to**. Click in the empty text box, and type **3** The rule will format only cells where the *Field Value is less than or equal to 3*.

The rule has now been set; however, no format options have been set. These settings are applied using the buttons below the rule.

4 Click the **Bold** B button, and then click the **Background color** 🎨 ▾ button arrow. Under **Standard Colors**, on the fourth row, click the sixth color—**Maroon 3**. Click **OK** to close the **New Formatting Rule** dialog box. Click **OK** to close the **Conditional Formatting Rules Manager**.

For any items ordered, if the quantity is 3 or less, the quantity will display bold with a light maroon background. This will alert the staff to determine if special marketing strategies might be helpful to increase sales.

5 Click anywhere in the subreport, and then click the **Layout Selector**. On the **REPORT LAYOUT TOOLS FORMAT tab**, in the **Control Formatting group**, click the **Shape Outline button arrow**. Under **Theme Colors**, on the first row, click the sixth color—**Red, Accent 2**. Again, click the **Shape Outline button arrow**, and then point to **Line Thickness**. In the displayed list, click the third line—**2 pt**—and then click anywhere in the main form to display the results of the formatting. Switch to **Report** view. Compare your screen with Figure 7.34.

The subreport displays with a thicker maroon border.

FIGURE 7.34

Subreport control border formatted

Conditional formatting applied to quantities less than or equal to 3

N O T E | **Removing a Horizontal Scroll Bar**

Adding the thicker border decreased the area where the data displays, and it may cause a horizontal scroll bar to display at the bottom of the subreport. If so, in Layout view, click the subreport control—not a field label control or text box control in the subreport—and then point to the right edge of the subreport control until the pointer displays. Drag the right edge of the subreport control to the right until the horizontal scroll bar no longer displays.

---

6 Save 💾 the report. If you are instructed to submit this result, view the report in **Print Preview**, and then create a paper or electronic printout.

7 Close the **Print Preview** window and the **report**, and then Open 〉〉 the **Navigation Pane**.

Activity 7.11 | Creating a Subreport by Adding an Object to an Existing Report

In this activity, you will drag the *7B Online Orders* table onto the *7B MWB Suppliers Report* to create a subreport. For the subreport to be linked to the main report, the underlying tables should have an established relationship. You can also create a subreport by dragging an existing form, subform, query, report, or subreport onto a report.

1 In the **Navigation Pane**, under **Reports**, locate **7B MWB Suppliers Report**, and then open the report in **Design** view. In the report, point to the top of the **Page Footer section bar** until the pointer displays. Drag downward to the **1.25-inch mark on the vertical ruler** to make room in the **Detail section** for the subreport.

2 In the **Navigation Pane**, under **Tables**, click **7B Online Orders**, and then drag the table to the right onto the **Detail** section until the top of the pointer aligns with the **1-inch mark on the horizontal ruler** and the **0.5-inch mark on the vertical ruler**. The **SubReport Wizard** dialog box displays, as shown in Figure 7.35.

The SubReport Wizard suggests that the report shows the Online Orders for each record in the Suppliers using Supplier Name. If you were dragging an existing report onto this report that had an established relationship between the underlying tables, the SubReport Wizard dialog box would not display.

FIGURE 7.35

SubReport Wizard dialog box

3 ▶ In the **SubReport Wizard** dialog box, verify that **Choose from a list** is selected, and then click **Next**. Name the subreport **Lastname Firstname 7B Orders Subreport** and then click **Finish**. **Save** the report. In the **Navigation Pane**, notice that the newly created subreport displays under **Reports**.

4 ▶ If necessary, Close the Field List. Press F4 to display the Property Sheet for the subreport, and then **Close** « the **Navigation Pane**. If necessary, click the **Property Sheet Data tab**, click in the **Link Master Fields** property setting box, and then click the **Build** button ⋯.

> The Subreport Field Linker dialog box displays. The fields that are used to link the two underlying record sources are displayed; the Master Fields property setting box displays the linked field in the main report, and the Child Fields property setting box displays the linked field in the subreport. Use the Subreport Field Linker dialog box to change the linked fields if the subreport does not display the data in the manner you intended. If you are unsure of which fields to link, click the Suggest button.

5 ▶ In the **Subreport Field Linker** dialog box, click **OK**. **Close** × the **Property Sheet**, and then switch to **Layout** view. Notice that **Record 1** displays no data in the subreport; no orders have been placed with A&S Garden Supply.

6 ▶ In the main report, locate Record 2—**Martinez Nurseries**. Notice that Record 2 displays one order in the subreport and displays the name of the supplier in the third field. In the **subreport control** for **Record 2**, click **Martinez Nurseries**, press Shift, and click the **Supplier Name label control**. Press Delete to remove the label and text box controls and the redundant data. Resize the other three controls so they are wide enough to just view the data. Move the controls to close large gaps between fields.

7 ▶ Click the **subreport's Layout Selector** ⊞, and then press F4 to display the Property Sheet for the subreport. Click the **Property Sheet Format tab**, select the text in the **Width** property setting box, type **3.5** and then press Enter to change the width of the subreport control. **Close** × the **Property Sheet**.

8 ▶ Click the **subreport label control**—*Lastname Firstname 7B Orders Subreport*. Change the **Font Color** of the text in the selected label control to **Red, Accent 2**, and then add **Bold** formatting to the text. Point to the selected label control until the pointer displays, and then drag the control to the right until it is approximately centered between the margins of the subreport control.

> The subreport has been modified, and the redundant field has been removed. A horizontal scroll bar displays in the subreport.

9 ▶ Switch to **Design** view, saving changes to the main report and subreport. Select the **Subreport Header**, and on the **REPORT DESIGN TOOLS FORMAT tab**, click the **Background color** 🎨 ▾ button arrow. Under **Standard Colors**, on the third row, click the sixth color—**Maroon 2**. Click the **Order # label control**, hold down Shift, click the **Order Date label control**, and then click the **Amount label control** to select all three label controls, scrolling to the right as necessary. Change the **Font Color** to **Red, Accent 2**. Switch to **Layout** view. If necessary, adjust the width of the phone number text box control to keep the number on one line, and then compare your screen with Figure 7.36.

FIGURE 7.36

10 ▸ **Save** 🖫 the report, and then switch to **Design** view.

Activity 7.12 | Displaying a Total from a Subreport on the Main Report

In this activity, you will display a total from the subreport on the main report.

1 ▸ Click the subreport to select it. On the **REPORT DESIGN TOOLS DESIGN tab**, in the **Tools** group, click the **Subreport in New Window** button 🖾.

The subreport displays on its own tab, and all of the controls are displayed, which makes it easier to edit.

2 ▸ On the **REPORT DESIGN TOOLS DESIGN tab**, in the **Tools group**, click the **Property Sheet** button. Verify that the **Property Sheet** displays *Selection type: Report*. On the **Property Sheet Format tab**, change the **Width** property setting to **3.45** and press Enter. Compare your screen with Figure 7.37.

Recall that the subreport control displayed a horizontal scroll bar—this is because the actual subreport's width was wider than the size of the control. By making the width of the report smaller than the width of the subreport control, the scroll bar will no longer display in the *7B MWB Suppliers Report* because it is not really necessary to view data.

FIGURE 7.37

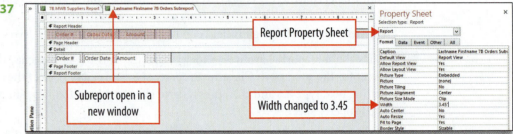

3 ▸ **Close** ⊠ the **Property Sheet**. In the **Detail** section, click the **Amount text box control**. On the **REPORT DESIGN TOOLS DESIGN tab**, in the **Grouping & Totals group**, click the **Totals** button, and then click **Sum** to insert a calculated control into the **Report Footer** section.

4 ▸ **Save** 🖫 the subreport, and then **Close** ⊠ *7B Orders Subreport*.

To view the results of the changes made to the subreport in the main report, you first must close the subreport.

5 ▸ Switch *7B MWB Suppliers Report* to **Report** view. Notice that the horizontal scroll bar no longer displays, and in the subreport controls, **Record 1** displays a total Amount of **$0.00** and **Record 2** displays a total Amount of **$90.23**. Scroll down to display **Record 5**, which displays a total Amount of **$535.33**.

Adding a sum to a field in the subreport causes the sum to display in the subreport control on the main form.

6 ▸ Switch to **Design** view. On the **REPORT DESIGN TOOLS DESIGN tab**, in the **Tools group**, click the **Subreport in New Window** 🖾 button. Click the **Report Footer section bar**, and then press F4 to display the **Property Sheet** for the **Report Footer** section. On the **Property Sheet Format tab**, click in the **Visible** property setting box, which displays **Yes**. Click the **arrow**, and then click **No**.

The data in the Report Footer section will not display when the report is displayed in any view other than Design view. You will be displaying the calculated field in the main form, so it is being hidden from view.

7 In the **Report Footer** section, click the **calculated control**. The **Property Sheet** displays *Selection type: Text Box*, and the **Selection type** box displays *AccessTotalsAmount*. Click the **Property Sheet Other tab**, and then click in the **Name** property setting box. Select **AccessTotalsAmount**, type **Total Amount** and then press [Enter]. Compare your screen with Figure 7.38.

The Selection type box displays Total Amount, which is the new name of the text box control that displays the sum of the amount field. Rename controls to easily remember the name, especially if the control name is used somewhere else in the form. You will be using this control name to display the total of the amount field in the main form.

FIGURE 7.38

8 **Close** ⊠ the **Property Sheet**, **Save** 🖫 the report, and then **Close** ⊠ *7B Orders Subreport*. Switch *7B MWB Suppliers Report* to **Report** view, and notice that the sum of the Amount field no longer displays in the subreport control.

9 Switch to **Design** view. On the **REPORT DESIGN TOOLS DESIGN tab**, in the **Controls group**, click the **Text Box** [abl] button. Move the mouse pointer down to the **Detail** section until the top of the plus (+) sign aligns with the **6-inch mark on the horizontal ruler** and with the **1-inch mark on the vertical ruler**, and then click. Compare your screen with Figure 7.39.

A text box control with an associated label control displays in the Detail section. The text box control displays Unbound because the control is not linked to a field.

FIGURE 7.39

10 In the **Detail** section, click the **label control** that is associated with the unbound text box control, and then press [F4] to display the **Property Sheet** for the **label control**. Click the **Property Sheet Format tab**, select the text in the **Caption** property setting box, and then type **Total Amt:** Select the text in the **Width** property setting box, type **.75** and then press [Enter] to increase the width of the label control.

The Caption property setting controls the text that is displayed in the label control associated with the unbound text box control.

11 ▸ In the **Detail** section, click the **unbound text box control**. If the control is hidden behind the **Property Sheet**, decrease the width of the **Property Sheet** by dragging the left edge of the **Property Sheet** to the right. Click the **Property Sheet Data tab**, and then in the **Control Source** property setting box, click the **Build** button ⌊···⌋.

> The Expression Builder dialog box displays. Although you can type the expression directly in the Control Source property setting box, the Expression Builder dialog box is similar to the Zoom dialog box, where you can see the entire typed expression. The Control Source property setting is used to link the text box control to a field.

12 ▸ In the **Expression Builder** dialog box, using your own first and last names and double-clicking the correct objects as they appear in the list, type **=IIf(IsError([Lastname Firstname 7B Orders Subreport].[Report]![Total Amount]),0,[Lastname Firstname 7B Orders Subreport].[Report]![Total Amount])** and then compare your screen with Figure 7.40.

> The expression starts with an equal (=) sign and is followed by the IsError function within the IIf function. The IIf function checks for the #Error message in the Total Amount field of 7B Orders Subreport. If #Error is found, 0 is displayed in the field; otherwise, the data in the Total Amount field is displayed. A period separates the report name from the object name, which is also enclosed in brackets. The object name, in this case [Report], is only necessary if the name of the report is the same as the underlying record source. The exclamation (!) mark is called the ***bang operator***. The bang operator tells Access that what follows it is an object that belongs to the object that precedes it in the expression. In this expression, Total Amount is an object in the 7B Orders Subreport report.

FIGURE 7.40

🔄 **ANOTHER WAY**   If the subreport contained data for each control on the main report, you could have typed a more simple expression of =[Lastname Firstname 7B Online Orders Subreport].[Report]![Total Amount]. The expression starts with an equals (=) sign and is followed by the name of the report enclosed in brackets. A period separates the report name from the object name—Report—which is also enclosed in brackets. The bang operator is used to identify Total Amount as an object in the 7B Orders Subreport report. If the subreport does not contain any data for any control on the main report, the control on the main report displays #Error when printed using the simplified expression.

13 ▸ In the **Expression Builder** dialog box, click **OK**, and then press ⌊↓⌋.

> The expression displays in the Control Source property setting box.

14 ▸ Click the **Property Sheet Format tab**. Click in the **Format** property setting box, click the displayed **arrow**, and then click **Currency**. **Close** ⌊×⌋ the **Property Sheet**.

> The data that was typed in the Control Source property setting box displays in the text box control.

15 With the **text box control selected**, point to the small gray box that displays in the upper left corner of the text box control until the pointer displays. Drag to the left until the left edge of the text box control aligns with the right edge of the label control that displays *Total Amt:*.

Dragging the small box that displays in the upper left corner of a control enables you to move only that control. If you point to any other part of the control before dragging, the control and its associated controls are moved.

16 Save 🖫 the report, and click **Yes** in the dialog box if necessary. Switch to **Report** view. Scroll down to display **Records 6 and 7**, and then compare your screen with Figure 7.41.

The sum of the Amount field in the subreport is displayed in the main report and is formatted as Currency.

FIGURE 7.41

ALERT!   **Does an Enter Parameter Value Message Box Display?**

If an Enter Parameter Value message box displays, you probably typed the name of the subreport or the name of the field incorrectly. If this occurs, repeat Steps 11 and 12, ensuring that you type the expression correctly.

17 If you are instructed to submit this result, view the report in **Print Preview**, and then create a paper or electronic printout.

18 **Close** the **Print Preview** window and the **report**, and then **Open** « the **Navigation Pane**. Rename the 7B MWB Suppliers Report to **Lastname Firstname 7B MWB Suppliers Report**

Objective 5   Create a Report Based on a Parameter Query

Video A7-5

Recall that a ***parameter query*** prompts you for criteria before running the query. Using a parameter query as the record source for a report enables the user to set the criteria for the report when the report is opened. Recall that when a report is opened, the underlying table or query in the report is read to ensure that the report displays the most current data. MWB Productions maintains a table to keep track of the website orders. A parameter query was created to display the orders between a range of dates.

Activity 7.13 │ Creating a Report Based on a Parameter Query

In this activity, you will view the design of the *7B Orders Parameter Query*, and then create a report based on the parameter query.

1 In the **Navigation Pane**, under **Tables**, double-click **7B Online Orders** to open the table in **Datasheet** view. Notice that the **Order Date** data ranges from 6/2/2017 to 9/22/2017.

When you run the parameter query, if you enter a range for which there is no data or if you enter the data incorrectly, the resulting fields will be empty.

2 Close ⊠ the table. In the **Navigation Pane**, under **Queries**, double-click **7B Orders - Parameter Query**. In the **Enter Parameter Value** message box, under **Enter first date**, type **6/1/17** and then click **OK**. In the second message box, under **Enter second date**, type **July 31, 2017** and then click **OK**.

Because the Order Date field has a data type of Date, you can enter the date in several formats. The query is run and displays orders between June 1, 2017, and July 31, 2017.

3 Close ⊠ the query, and then **Close** « the **Navigation Pane**. On the **CREATE tab**, in the **Reports group**, click the **Report Wizard** button.

Because the query was selected in the Navigation Pane, the *7B Orders - Parameter Query* displays in the Tables/Queries box.

4 In the **Report Wizard** dialog box, click the **All Fields** >> button to move all of the fields from the **Available Fields** box to the **Selected Fields** box, and then click **Next**.

5 In the second **Report Wizard** dialog box, click **Next**. In the third **Report Wizard** dialog box, **sort** the records by **Order Date** in **Ascending** order, and then click **Next** two times.

6 In the last **Report Wizard** dialog box, name the report **Lastname Firstname 7B Orders by Date Range** and then click **Finish**.

An Enter Parameter Value message box displays. Because the report is based on a parameter query, you must enter the parameter values.

7 For the first date, type **6/1/17** and click **OK**. For the second date, type **7/31/17** Click **OK**, and then compare your screen with Figure 7.42.

Six records are extracted from the underlying tables based on the parameter values entered. Five fields are included in the report, but all data may not be visible on this page. In that case, adjustments will need to be made to controls so all data is visible and the report prints on one page.

FIGURE 7.42

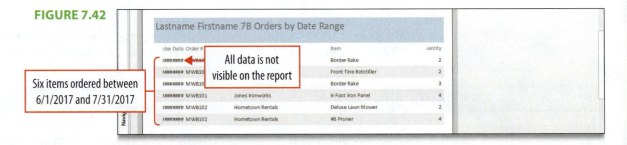

8 Switch to **Layout** view. Close the Field List, if necessary. Resize the text box controls and label controls for the **Item** and **Supplier Name** so they are just wide enough to display the longest item in each column. Resize the **Order Date** field to fully display the data, and then resize the **Quantity** field to fit the **label control**. Adjust the field placement so all fields display on the page.

9 Switch to **Design** view. In the **Page Footer** section, click to select the **Page Numbering** text box. Point to the small gray box that displays in the upper left corner of the text box control until the ⬚ pointer displays. Drag to the left until the right edge of the text box control aligns with the right edge of the **Quantity** controls. Resize the width of the report to **7.25 inches**. Save ⊟ the report.

Activity 7.14 | Printing the Parameters in the Report

The parameters used in the creation of the report can be printed as a part of the report by adding a text box control to a section. In this activity, you will add a text box control to the Report Header section to display the parameter values as a subtitle.

1 Point to the top of the **Page Header section bar** until the pointer displays. Drag downward to the top of the **Detail section bar** to increase the size of the **Report Header**.

2 On the **REPORT DESIGN TOOLS DESIGN tab**, in the **Controls group**, click the **Text Box** ab| button. In the **Report Header** section, align the top of the plus (+) sign of the pointer **one dot** from the left margin and **three dots** below the label control for the report title, and then click.

> Recall that adding a text box control to the design also adds an associated label control that can be used to describe the data in the text box control.

3 Click the **label control** that is associated with the newly added text box control, and then press Delete.

4 Click the unbound **text box control**, and then press F4 to display the Property Sheet for the control. Click the **Property Sheet Data tab**, click in the **Control Source** property setting box, and then click the **Build** button ⋯ . In the displayed **Expression Builder** dialog box, type **="Between** press Spacebar, and then continue typing **"&[Enter first date]&"** Press Spacebar, and then type **and** Press Spacebar again, and then continue typing **"&[Enter second date]** Compare your screen with Figure 7.43.

> Recall that an expression must begin with an equals sign (=). The word *Between* and a space will print. The & symbol concatenates the string with the next part of the expression. *Enter first date* is enclosed in square brackets because it is part of the criteria that is retrieved from the parameter query. You must type the criteria exactly as it displays in the criteria of the parameter query. The criteria will be concatenated with the space, the word *and*, and another space. This is concatenated with the second criteria.

FIGURE 7.43

String expression: Spaces should occur after *Between* and before and after *and*

Expression Builder dialog box

Control Source property

Criteria must be entered exactly as it displays in parameter query

5 In the **Expression Builder** dialog box, click **OK**, and then press ↓ to save the property setting.

ALERT! **Did a Message Box Display?**

If a message box displays stating that the expression you entered contains invalid syntax, click OK. Click the Control Source Build button, and then view Figure 7.43 to be sure that you typed the expression correctly. Common errors include not typing the equals sign, using parentheses instead of square brackets, leaving out the beginning or ending quotation marks, or leaving out one of the & symbols.

---

6 **Close** ✕ the **Property Sheet**. On the **REPORT DESIGN TOOLS FORMAT tab**, in the **Font group**, click the **Font Color button arrow** A▾. Under **Theme Colors**, on the sixth row, click the fourth color—**Dark Blue, Text 2, Darker 50%**.

7 With the text box control selected, in the **Font group**, click the **Font Size button arrow** 11 ▾, and from the displayed list, click **14**. Increase the width of the text box until the entire expression displays.

8 On the **REPORT DESIGN TOOLS ARRANGE tab**, in the **Sizing & Ordering group**, click the **Size/Space** button, and then click **To Fit**.

> The height of the text box control is increased to fit the size of the text, and the width of the text box control will adjust to fit the title that displays in Layout view, Report view, and Print Preview view.

9 **Save** 🖫 the report, and switch to **Report** view. For the first date, enter **6/1/17** and for the second date, enter **7/31/17**

> The report displays with a subtitle of *Between 6/1/17 and 7/31/17*. When the criteria is displayed in the report, be sure to enter the criteria in a consistent manner. For example, do not enter 6/1/17 for the first date and July 31, 2017, for the second date. If you do, the subtitle will display as *Between 6/1/17 and July 31, 2017*.

ALERT!   **Did Another Message Box Display?**

If an unexpected Enter Parameter Value message box displays when you try to print or preview a report, you may have misspelled one of the criteria or a field name in the expression. If this happens, click Cancel to return to Design view and correct the error. The parameter criteria in this report must match exactly to the parameter criteria used in the query.

---

10 Switch to **Print Preview** view. If you are instructed to submit this result, create a paper or electronic printout. **Close** the **Print Preview** window and the **report**, and then **Open** » the **Navigation Pane**.

Objective 6   Create an Alphabetic Index

Video A7-6

A report can display an *alphabetic index*, similar to the grouping of addresses in an address book. An alphabetic index groups items by a common first character. For example, all of your contacts can be sorted by last name in ascending order. All of the last names beginning with the letter *A* are grouped together under the letter *A*. All of the last names beginning with the letter *B* are grouped together under the letter *B*, and so on.

Activity 7.15 │ Creating an Alphabetic Index

In this activity, you will create an alphabetic index of the suppliers' names from the *7B MWB Suppliers* table, using the *7B MWB Supplier Names Query*.

1 In the **Navigation Pane**, under **Queries**, double-click **7B MWB Supplier Names Query**. Take a moment to review the data in the query, and then switch to **Design** view.

> The query displays the Supplier Name field in ascending order from the *7B MWB Suppliers* table.

2 **Close** ✕ the query, and then **Close** « the **Navigation Pane**.

3 On the **CREATE tab**, in the **Reports group**, click the **Report Wizard** button.

4 Because the query was selected in the **Navigation Pane**, in the **Report Wizard** dialog box, in the **Tables/Queries** box, **Query: 7B MWB Supplier Names Query** displays. If it does not display, click the **Tables/Queries arrow**, and then click **Query: 7B MWB Supplier Names Query**.

5 Under **Available Fields**, double-click **Supplier Name** to add the field name to the **Selected Fields** box, and then click **Next**.

Because the query sorts the Supplier Name in ascending order, the field will automatically be sorted in the same manner in the report.

6 Click **Next**. Under **Layout**, verify that the **Tabular** option button is selected. Under **Orientation**, verify that the **Portrait** option button is selected, and then click **Next**.

7 For the title of the report, type **Lastname Firstname 7B Supplier Alphabetic Index** and then click **Finish**. Compare your screen with Figure 7.44.

The report displays in Print Preview.

FIGURE 7.44

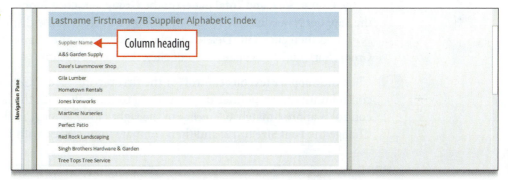

8 **Close** Print Preview. In **Design** view, click anywhere in an empty area of the design grid to deselect the controls, if necessary, and then click the **Supplier Name label control**. Be sure that the orange border only displays around the **Supplier Name label control**. Press Delete to remove the **Supplier Name label control** from the report.

9 **Save** the report, and then switch to **Layout** view. If necessary, expand the width of the **Supplier Name text box control** so that all of the data displays for every record.

10 On the **REPORT LAYOUT TOOLS DESIGN tab**, in the **Grouping & Totals group**, click the **Group & Sort** button. In the **Group, Sort, and Total pane**, click **Add a group**. From the displayed list, click **Supplier Name**.

The report must be grouped by Supplier Name to create an alphabetic index of the names.

11 In the **Group, Sort, and Total pane**, on the **Group bar**, click the **More arrow**. Click the **by entire value arrow**, and from the displayed list, click the **by first character** option button. Verify that the second option from the right displays with a header section. Click in an empty area of the report, and then compare your screen with Figure 7.45.

The first letter of the Supplier Name displays above the supplier names along with a label control that displays Supplier Name. You can select more than one character for the index.

FIGURE 7.45

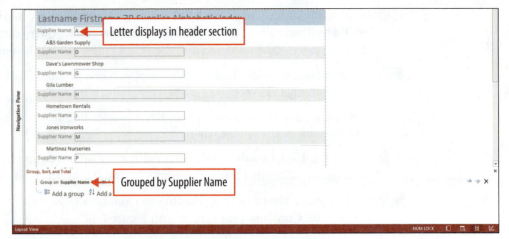

12 ▸ In the **Group, Sort, and Total pane**, on the **Group bar**, click **More**. To the right of **with title**, click the **Supplier Name** link. With *Supplier Name* selected, in the displayed **Zoom** dialog box, press Delete , and then click **OK**. Delete the placeholder from the **Supplier Name control**. Close ⊠ the **Group, Sort, and Total pane**—do *not* click the Delete button.

13 ▸ Click the **Supplier text box control** for the first record—*A&S Garden Supply*. Point to the control until the ↔ pointer displays. Drag to the right until the left edge of the text box control is approximately **0.5 inches** to the right of the letter *A* in the **Supplier Name header**. Change the **Font Size** to **12**, and then compare your screen with Figure 7.46.

FIGURE 7.46

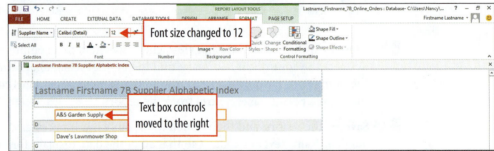

14 ▸ Click the **text box control** that displays the letter *A*, and change the **Font Size** to **16**. Change the **Font Color** to **Dark Blue, Text 2**, and then add **Bold** formatting to the text.

15 ▸ Save ⊟ the report, and then switch to **Report** view. Compare your screen with Figure 7.47.

FIGURE 7.47

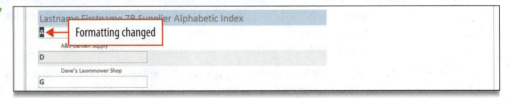

16 ▸ Switch to **Print Preview** view. If you are instructed to submit this result, create a paper or electronic printout. On the **PRINT PREVIEW tab**, in the **Close Preview group**, click the **Close Print Preview** button.

17 ▶ **Close** ☒ the report, and then **Open** » the **Navigation Pane**. **Close** the database, and **Exit** Access.

18 ▶ As directed by your instructor, submit your database and the paper or electronic printouts of the four reports that are the result of this project. Specifically, in this project, using your own name you created the following database and printouts or electronic printouts:

1. Lastname_Firstname_7B_Online Orders	Database file
2. Lastname Firstname 7B Orders Main Report	Report (printed or electronic printout)
3. Lastname Firstname 7B MWB Suppliers Report	Report (printed or electronic printout)
4. Lastname Firstname 7B Orders by Date Range	Report (printed or electronic printout)
5. Lastname Firstname 7B Supplier Alphabetic Index	Report (printed or electronic printout)

END | You have completed Project 7B

END OF CHAPTER

SUMMARY

Advanced forms can display data from one or more record sources. Split forms display data from one table in two different ways in the same form, Form view and Datasheet view.

Subforms display data from related tables on one form; they can be created using the Form Tool and the Form Wizard or by dragging a related table onto an existing form. Forms can be displayed on multiple pages by using the tab control.

Reports can be simple or complex; advanced reports use some of the same techniques as advanced forms. Subreports can be created using the SubReport Wizard and by dragging a related table onto a report.

A report can be created from a parameter query, and the criteria can be displayed in an unbound control in the report. A report can also use grouping and sorting features to display an alphabetic index.

GO! LEARN IT ONLINE

Review the concepts and key terms in this chapter by completing these online challenges, which you can find at **www.pearsonhighered.com/go**.

Matching and Multiple Choice:
Answer matching and multiple choice questions to test what you learned in this chapter. MyITLab®

Crossword Puzzle:
Spell out the words that match the numbered clues, and put them in the puzzle squares.

Flipboard:
Flip through the definitions of the key terms in this chapter and match them with the correct term.

END OF CHAPTER

REVIEW AND ASSESSMENT GUIDE FOR ACCESS CHAPTER 7

Your instructor may assign one or more of these projects to help you review the chapter and assess your mastery and understanding of the chapter.

	Review and Assessment Guide for Access Chapter 7		
Project	**Apply Skills from These Chapter Objectives**	**Project Type**	**Project Location**
7C	Objectives 1–3 from Project 7A	**7C Skills Review** A guided review of the skills from Project 7A.	On the following pages
7D	Objectives 4–6 from Project 7B	**7D Skills Review** A guided review of the skills from Project 7B.	On the following pages
7E	Objectives 1–3 from Project 7A	**7E Mastery (Grader Project)** A demonstration of your mastery of the skills in Project 7A with extensive decision making.	In MyITLab and on the following pages
7F	Objectives 4–6 from Project 7B	**7F Mastery (Grader Project)** A demonstration of your mastery of the skills in Project 7B with extensive decision making.	In MyITLab and on the following pages
7G	Objectives 1–6 from Projects 7A and 7B	**7G Mastery (Grader Project)** A demonstration of your mastery of the skills in Projects 7A and 7B with extensive decision making.	In MyITLab and on the following pages
7H	Combination of Objectives from Projects 7A and 7B	**7H GO! Fix It** A demonstration of your mastery of the skills in Projects 7A and 7B by creating a correct result from a document that contains errors you must find.	Online
7I	Combination of Objectives from Projects 7A and 7B	**7I GO! Make It** A demonstration of your mastery of the skills in Projects 7A and 7B by creating a result from a supplied picture.	Online
7J	Combination of Objectives from Projects 7A and 7B	**7J GO! Solve It** A demonstration of your mastery of the skills in Projects 7A and 7B, your decision-making skills, and your critical thinking skills. A task-specific rubric helps you self-assess your result.	Online
7K	Combination of Objectives from Projects 7A and 7B	**7K GO! Solve It** A demonstration of your mastery of the skills in Projects 7A and 7B, your decision-making skills, and your critical thinking skills. A task-specific rubric helps you self-assess your result.	On the following pages
7L	Combination of Objectives from Projects 7A and 7B	**7L GO! Think** A demonstration of your understanding of the chapter concepts applied in a manner that you would use outside of college. An analytic rubric helps you and your instructor grade the quality of your work by comparing it to the work an expert in the discipline would create.	On the following pages
7M	Combination of Objectives from Projects 7A and 7B	**7M GO! Think** A demonstration of your understanding of the chapter concepts applied in a manner that you would use outside of college. An analytic rubric helps you and your instructor grade the quality of your work by comparing it to the work an expert in the discipline would create.	Online
7N	Combination of Objectives from Projects 7A and 7B	**7N You and GO!** A demonstration of your understanding of the chapter concepts applied in a manner that you would use in a personal situation. An analytic rubric helps you and your instructor grade the quality of your work.	Online

GLOSSARY

Alphabetic index Grouping of items by a common first character.

Bang operator The exclamation (!) mark that tells Access that what follows it is an object that belongs to the object that precedes it in the expression.

Bound report A report that displays data from an underlying table, query, or SQL statement as specified in the report's Record Source property.

Conditional formatting A way to apply formatting to specific controls based on a comparison to a rule set.

Junction table A table that breaks down the many-to-many relationship into two one-to-many relationships.

Linked form A form related to the main form that is not stored within the main form.

Main form A form that contains a subform.

Main report A report that contains a subreport.

Many-to-many relationship A relationship between tables where one record in one table has many matching records in a second table, and a single record in the related table has many matching records in the first table.

mini toolbar A miniature, semitransparent toolbar that is used to work with objects on the screen.

Multi-page form A form that displays the data from the underlying table or query on more than one page.

Nested subform A subform that is embedded within another subform.

Parameter query A query that prompts an individual for criteria before running the query.

Split form An object that displays data in two views—Form view and Datasheet view—on a single form.

SQL statement An instruction using Structured Query Language.

Subform A form that is embedded within another form.

Subreport A report that is embedded within another report.

Syntax The set of rules by which words and symbols in an expression are combined.

Tab control A control that is used to display data on the main form on different tabs, similar to the way database objects, such as forms and tables, display on different tabs.

Unbound report A report that does not display data from an underlying table, query, or SQL statement and has an empty Record Source property setting.

CHAPTER REVIEW

Apply 7A skills from these Objectives:

1 Create a Split Form
2 Create a Form and a Subform
3 Create a Multi-Page Form

Skills Review | Project 7C Historical Gardens

Matthew Lee, coordinator for cultural and historical events of MWB Productions, wants the database forms to display related data. For example, he is interested in displaying the contacts for the historical gardens on one form. In this project, you will customize the company's forms to display data in two ways on the same form, to display data from multiple tables on one form, and to display data on multiple pages on a form. Your completed work will look similar to Figure 7.48.

PROJECT FILES

For Project 7C, you will need the following files:

a07C_Historical_Gardens
a07C_MWB_Logo
A new blank Word document

You will save your files as:

Lastname_Firstname_7C_Historical_Gardens
Lastname_Firstname_7C_Tab_Control_Form

PROJECT RESULTS

FIGURE 7.48

(Project 7C Historical Gardens continues on the next page)

CHAPTER REVIEW

1 Start Access. Open the **a07C_Historical_Gardens** file. Save the database in your **Access Chapter 7** folder as **Lastname_Firstname_7C_Historical_Gardens** If necessary, enable the content.

2 In the **Navigation Pane**, click **7C Contacts** to select the table. **Close** the **Navigation Pane**.

a. On the **CREATE tab**, in the **Forms group**, click the **More Forms** button, and then click **Split Form**. **Save** the split form as **Lastname Firstname 7C Contacts Split Form**

b. On the **FORM LAYOUT TOOLS DESIGN tab**, in the **Tools group**, click the **Property Sheet** button. Click the **Selection type arrow**, and then click **Form**.

c. Click the **Form Property Sheet Format tab**, if necessary. In the **property setting** box for **Split Form Printing**, click the **arrow**, and then click **Form Only**.

d. Switch to **Design** view. Click in the **Split Form Orientation** property setting box, and then click the **arrow**. Click **Datasheet on Top**, and then **Close** the **Property Sheet**.

e. Switch to **Layout** view. Point to the **splitter bar** until the pointer displays. Drag upward until the dark line displays between the fourth and fifth records.

f. On the **FORM LAYOUT TOOLS DESIGN tab**, in the **Header/Footer group**, click the **Logo** button. Navigate to the student data files, and then double-click **a07C_MWB_Logo**. Display the **Property Sheet**. Click in the **Size Mode** property box, click the arrow, and then click **Zoom**. Increase the width of the **logo control** to **1.5 inches**. **Close** the **Property Sheet**.

g. Click the **title's label control**. Click at the beginning of the title, and then type your **Lastname Firstname**

h. **Save** the form, and then switch to **Form** view. Press **PageDown** until **Record 4** displays. In the form section, change the **Phone Number** for *Chicago Botanical Garden* to **800-555-1136**

i. On the left side of the form, click the **Record Selector** bar, and then if you are instructed to submit this result, create a paper or electronic printout of only Record 4—the selected record. **Close** the form. **Open** the **Navigation Pane**.

3 Under **Tables**, click **7C Gardens**. On the **CREATE tab**, in the **Forms group**, click the **Form** button. **Close** the **Navigation Pane**.

a. Switch to **Design** view. In the **Detail** section, click on the **Layout Selector** to select the controls in the main form and subform. On the **FORM DESIGN TOOLS ARRANGE tab**, in the **Table group**, click the **Remove Layout** button. Click an empty area of the design grid to deselect the controls.

b. Switch to **Layout** view. In the main form, click the **Garden Name text box control**, if necessary. Press **Shift** and then click each of the text boxes in the main form. Point to the right edge of one of the text box controls until the pointer displays, and then drag to the left until there is **1 inch** of space between *Gardens* and the right edge of the text box control. Click the **subform control** to select it. Point to the right edge of the **subform control** until the pointer displays. Drag to the left until there is approximately **0.25 inches** of space after the **Subject control** in the subform.

c. Switch to **Design** view. Change the form title to **Lastname Firstname 7C Gardens and TV Shows Subform** Click to the right of **Gardens**. Hold down **Shift**, and then press **Enter**. **Save** the form as **Lastname Firstname 7C Gardens and TV Shows Subform**

d. Using the techniques you have practiced, insert **a07C_MWB_Logo** in the **Form Header** section, and change the **Picture Size Mode** property to **Zoom**.

e. Point to the middle right sizing handle of the **logo control** until the pointer displays. Drag to the right between *TV* and *Shows*.

f. Click in an empty area of the design grid, and then click the **title's label control**. Point to the right edge of the **title's label control** until the pointer displays. Drag to the left until the right edge of the label control aligns with the **6-inch mark on the horizontal ruler**. With the **title's label control** selected, on the **FORM DESIGN TOOLS FORMAT tab**, in the **Font group**, click the **Center** button.

g. Point to the right edge of the main form until the pointer displays. Drag to the left until the edge aligns with the **6.5-inch mark on the horizontal ruler**.

h. **Save** the form, and then switch to **Form** view. If you are instructed to submit this result, create a paper or electronic printout of only Record 1—the selected record. **Close** the form.

(Project 7C Historical Gardens continues on the next page)

CHAPTER REVIEW

4 ▶ **Open** the **Navigation Pane**. Under **Forms**, open **7C Gardens Main Form** in **Design** view.

a. On the **FORM DESIGN TOOLS DESIGN tab**, in the **Controls group**, verify that the **Use Control Wizards** button is active. In the form, point to the top of the **Form Footer section bar** until the pointer displays. Drag downward **1 inch**.

b. In the **Navigation Pane**, under **Tables**, drag **7C Contacts** onto **7C Gardens Main Form** at the **1.75-inch mark on the vertical ruler** and even with the left edge of the form.

c. In the **SubForm Wizard** dialog box, click **Define my own**. Under **Form/report** fields, in the **first list box**, click the **arrow**, and then click **Garden Name**. Under **Subform/subreport** fields, in the **first list box**, click the **arrow**, and then click **Garden Name**. Click **Next**. Under **What name would you like for your subform or subreport?**, type **Lastname Firstname 7C Garden Contact Subform** and then click **Finish**. **Close** the **Navigation Pane**.

d. **Save** the form. With the **subform** selected, on the **FORM LAYOUT TOOLS DESIGN tab**, in the **Tools group**, click **Property Sheet**. Verify that the Selection type is *Form*. Change the **Default View** property to **Single Form**. **Close** the **Property Sheet**.

e. In the subform, click the **Garden Name label control**, press Shift, click the **Garden Name text box control**, and then press Delete. Move the other controls up to close the empty space. Switch to **Layout** view.

f. Reduce the size of the **First Name**, **Last Name**, and **Phone Number** controls so there is approximately **0.5 inches** of blank space to the right of the data. Point to the bottom right corner of the **subform control** until the pointer displays. Drag to the left and up until the **right edge of the subform control** aligns with the **right edge of the text box controls** and the **bottom edge of the subform control** aligns with **bottom of the E-mail controls**.

g. Delete the **subform label control**, which displays *Lastname Firstname 7C Garden Contact Subform*.

h. Switch to **Design** view. Change the title of the form to **Lastname Firstname 7C Gardens and Contacts** and then place *7C Gardens and Contacts* on the second line. Adjust the width of the **title's label**

control so that the **right edge of the title's label control** aligns with the **right edge of the main form field's text box controls**.

i. **Save** the form. Switch to **Form** view. If you are instructed to submit this result, create a paper or electronic printout of only the first record. **Close** the form. **Open** the **Navigation Pane**. In the **Navigation Pane**, under **Forms**, Rename *7C Gardens Main Form* to **Lastname Firstname 7C Gardens and Contacts Form**

5 ▶ In the **Navigation Pane**, under **Forms**, open **7C Contacts TC Form** in **Design** view, and then **Close** the **Navigation Pane**.

a. Point to the top of the **Form Footer section bar**, and drag downward to the **3-inch mark on the vertical ruler**. On the **FORM DESIGN TOOLS DESIGN tab**, in the **Controls group**, click the **Tab Control** button. Move the pointer into the **Detail** section until the plus (+) sign of the pointer is aligned approximately with the **0.25-inch mark on the horizontal and vertical rulers**, and then click.

b. In the selected **tab control**, point to the **right middle sizing handle** until the pointer displays. Drag to the right until the right edge of the tab control aligns with the **6-inch mark on the horizontal ruler**.

c. On the **FORM DESIGN TOOLS DESIGN tab**, in the **Tools group**, click the **Add Existing Fields** button. In the **Field List**, click **Garden Name**. Hold down Shift, and then click **Last Name**. Point to a selected field, and then drag onto the first tab until the top of the arrow of the pointer aligns with the **1.5-inch mark on the horizontal ruler** and with the **0.75-inch mark on the vertical ruler**. **Close** the **Field List**.

d. Click anywhere in the report to deselect the controls. Click the **Garden Name text box control**, and point to the **right edge** of the control until the pointer displays. Drag to the right until the right edge aligns with the **5-inch mark on the horizontal ruler**.

e. Click to select the **Last Name label control**, press Shift, and click to select the **Last Name text box control**. Drag the controls to the right and upward until they align with the **First Name controls** and there is approximately **0.5 inches** of space between the two text box controls.

(Project 7C Historical Gardens continues on the next page)

f. In the **Detail** section, click the **second tab**, which has no controls. On the **FORM DESIGN TOOLS DESIGN tab**, in the **Tools group**, click the **Add Existing Fields** button. In the **Field List**, click **Phone Number**. Hold down `Shift`, and then click **E-mail**. Point to the selected fields, and then drag onto the second tab until the top of the pointer arrow aligns with the **1.5-inch mark on the horizontal ruler** and the **0.75-inch mark on the vertical ruler**. **Close** the **Field List**. **Save** the form.

g. Click the **first page tab**. Right-click the **first page**, and then click **Properties**. The **Property Sheet** displays *Selection type: Page*. Click in the **Caption** property setting box, type **Contact Name** and then press `Enter`.

h. Click the **second tab** to display its **Property Sheet**. Click in the **Caption** property setting box, type **Contact Information** and then press `Enter`. **Close** the **Property Sheet**.

i. In the form, click the **Contact Name** to display the first page of the form. Change the form's **title** to **Lastname Firstname 7C Contacts Tab Control Form** and then place *7C Contacts Tab Control Form* on the second line. Align the right edge of the title's label control with the right edge of the tab control, and then switch to **Form** view.

j. **Save** the form, and navigate to **Record 4**. Press `Alt` + `PrintScrn` to place a copy of the form into the Office Clipboard. In **Microsoft Office Word 2013,**

Open a New, Blank document. Type your **Firstname Lastname** and then press `Enter`. Type **Project 7C Step 5J** and then press `Enter`. On the **HOME tab**, in the **Clipboard group**, click the **Paste** button. Press `Ctrl` + `End` to move to the end of the Word document, and then press `Ctrl` + `Enter` to insert a page break. **Minimize** the Word window.

k. In the **Access** window, on the form, click the **Contact Information tab**. Press `Alt` + `PrintScrn`. On the taskbar, click the **Microsoft Word** button to display the Word document. **Paste** the screen into the Word document. On the **Quick Access Toolbar**, click the **Save** button, and save the file as **Lastname_ Firstname_7C_Tab_Control_Form** in your **Access Chapter 7** folder. If you are instructed to submit this result, create a paper or electronic printout of the document. **Close** the **Word** window.

6 If necessary, on the taskbar, click the **Access** button. In the **Access** window, **Close** the form, and then **Open** the **Navigation Pane**. Rename the *7C Contacts TC Form* as **Lastname Firstname 7C Tab Control Form**

7 **Close** the database, and then **Exit** Access.

8 As directed by your instructor, submit your database and the paper or electronic printouts of the three objects—two forms and one Word document—that are the result of this project. Specifically, in this project, using your own name you created the following database and printouts or electronic printouts:

1. Lastname_Firstname_7C_Historical_Gardens	Database file
2. Lastname Firstname 7C Contacts Split Form	Form (printed or electronic printout)
3. Lastname Firstname 7C Gardens and TV Shows Subform	Form (printed or electronic printout)
4. Lastname Firstname 7C Tab Control Form	Word document (printed or electronic document)

END | You have completed Project 7C

CHAPTER REVIEW

ACCESS

7

Skills Review Project 7D Featured Gardens

Apply 7B skills from these Objectives:

4 Create and Modify a Subreport

5 Create a Report Based on a Parameter Query

6 Create an Alphabetic Index

MWB Productions maintains a database of the historic gardens that are featured in the *Midwest Botanicals* television show. Creating advanced reports will help the president and officers of the production company view the information in the database in a different way. In this project, you will create advanced reports that display data from multiple tables and from a parameter query. You will also create an alphabetic index of historic gardens. Your completed reports will look similar to Figure 7.49.

PROJECT FILES

For Project 7D, you will need the following file:

a07D_Featured_Gardens

You will save your database as:

Lastname_Firstname_7D_Featured_Gardens

PROJECT RESULTS

FIGURE 7.49

(Project 7D Featured Gardens continues on the next page)

Project 7D: Featured Gardens | Access **503**

CHAPTER REVIEW

1 Start Access. Open the **a07D_Featured_Gardens** file. Save the database in your **Access Chapter 7** folder as **Lastname_Firstname_7D_Featured_Gardens** If necessary, enable the content.

2 Make a copy of the *7D Gardens Report*, name it **Lastname Firstname 7D Gardens Main Report** and then open in **Design** view. **Close** the **Navigation Pane**.

a. In the **Report Header** section, click the **title label control**. Add your **Lastname Firstname** before the title.

b. In the report, point to the top of the **Page Footer section bar**, and then drag it downward to the **1-inch mark on the vertical ruler**.

c. On the **REPORT DESIGN TOOLS DESIGN tab**, in the **Controls group**, verify the **Use Controls Wizard** button is active. In the **Controls group**, click the **Subform/Subreport** button. Point to the **Detail** section so the plus sign (+) aligns with the **0.25-inch mark on the horizontal ruler** and the **0.5-inch mark on the vertical ruler**, and then click.

d. In the dialog box, **Use existing Tables and Queries** should be selected, and then click **Next**. Select **Table: 7D TV Shows**. Under **Available Fields**, double-click **TV Show #**, **Original Air Date**, and **Subject**. Click **Next** two times. Name the report **Lastname Firstname 7D TV Shows Subreport** Click **Finish**.

e. Delete the **subreport label control**. Select the **label controls** in the **subreport Report Header**, and then, on the **REPORT DESIGN TOOLS FORMAT tab**, in the **Font group**, click the **Font Color button arrow**. Under **Theme Colors**, on the first row, click the first color—**White, Background 1**. In the subreport, right-click the **Report Header** and click the **Fill/Back Color arrow**. Under **Standard Colors**, on the sixth row, click the seventh color—**Green 5**. **Save** the report.

f. Switch to **Layout** view. In the subreport, click the **Original Air Date** text box control. On the **REPORT LAYOUT TOOLS FORMAT tab**, in the **Control Formatting group**, click the **Conditional Formatting** button. In the dialog box, click the **New Rule** button. Click the arrow to the right of the box that displays *between*, and select **less than**. Click inside the empty text box, and type **1/1/18**

g. Click the **Bold** button, and then click the **Font color button arrow**. Under **Standard Colors**, on the sixth row, click the sixth color—**Maroon 5**. Click **OK** two times.

h. Scroll down to the subreport for *Missouri Botanical Gardens*, and select the **TV Show # label** and **text box controls**. Resize them so they are just wide enough to display the data. Select the **Original Air Date label** and **text box controls**. Resize them so they are just wide enough to display the data. Select the **Subject label** and **text box controls**, and then drag to the left until there is approximately **0.25 inches** after *Original Air Date*. Move the controls to the left to close the blank space. Resize the **subreport control** so it is just wide enough to display the data. **Save** the changes to both reports.

i. Switch to **Design** view. Select the **subreport control**. On the **REPORT DESIGN TOOLS FORMAT tab**, in the **Control Formatting group**, click the **Shape Outline button**. Under **Theme Colors**, on the first row, click the eighth color—**Blue-Gray, Accent 4**. For the logo control in the Report Header, add a **Blue-Gray, Accent 4, 1 pt** border, and then **Save** the form.

j. Click any **subreport control**, and then on the **REPORT DESIGN TOOLS DESIGN tab**, in the **Tools group**, click the **Subreport in New Window** button. Resize the subreport to **5.75 inches wide**. In the **Detail** section, click the **TV Show # text box control**. On the **REPORT DESIGN TOOLS DESIGN tab**, in the **Grouping & Totals group**, click the **Totals** button, and then click **Count Records** to insert a calculated control.

k. Click the **Report Footer section bar**, and then press [F4]. On the **Property Sheet Format tab**, click in the **Visible** property setting box. Set it to **No**.

l. Click the **Count calculated control**, and then click the **Property Sheet Other tab**. In the **Name** property setting box, type **Count of Shows Close** the **Property Sheet**. **Save** and **Close** the subreport.

m. On the **REPORT DESIGN TOOLS DESIGN tab**, in the **Controls group**, click the **Text Box** button. Move the mouse pointer to the **Detail** section until it aligns with the **6.5-inch mark on the horizontal ruler** and the **1.5-inch mark on the vertical ruler**, and then click.

(Project 7D Featured Gardens continues on the next page)

n. Click the associated **label control**, and then press F4. Click the **Property Sheet Format tab**, and in the **Caption** property setting box, type **# of TV Shows:** In the **Width** property setting box, type **1** and then press Enter. Drag the **# of TV Shows** unbound control until it aligns with the right edge of the label control.

o. Click the **unbound text box control**. Click the **Property Sheet Data tab**, and then click in the **Control Source** property setting box. Click the **Build** button. In the dialog box, using your own first and last names and double-clicking objects from the list, type **=IIf(IsError([Lastname Firstname 7D TV Shows Subreport].[Report]![Count of Shows]),0,[Lastname Firstname 7D TV Shows Subreport].[Report]![Count of Shows])** In the **Expression Builder** dialog box, click **OK**. **Close** the **Property Sheet**. Resize the textbox control so the right edge aligns with the **7-inch mark on the horizontal ruler**. Resize the report to **7.25 inches wide**.

p. **Save** the report. If you are instructed to submit this result, view the report in **Print Preview**, and then create a paper or electronic printout of the first page. **Close** the **Print Preview** window and the **report**.

3 Open the **Navigation Pane**. Make a copy of **7D Gardens Report**, name it **Lastname Firstname 7D Featured Gardens Report** and then open in **Design** view.

a. In the **Report Header** section, click the **title label control**. Select the text, type **Lastname Firstname 7D Garden Contacts** and then press Enter.

b. Point to the top of the **Page Footer section bar**, and drag downward to the **1-inch mark on the vertical ruler**.

c. In the **Navigation Pane**, under **Tables**, click **7D Contacts**, and then drag the table onto the **Detail** section until the pointer aligns with the **0.5-inch mark on the horizontal and vertical rulers**. In the **SubReport Wizard** dialog box, verify that **Choose from a list** is selected and **Show 7D Contacts for each record in 7D Gardens using Garden Name** is selected, and then click **Next**. Name the subreport **Lastname Firstname 7D Contacts Subreport** and then click **Finish**.

d. If necessary, select the subreport, press F4, and then **Close** the **Navigation Pane**. Click the **Property Sheet**

Data tab, click in the **Link Master Fields** property setting box, and then click the **Build** button. In the **Subreport Field Linker** dialog box, click **OK**. On the **Property Sheet Format tab**, in the **Width** property setting box, type **8.5 Close** the **Property Sheet**.

e. Switch to **Layout** view. In the subreport, delete the controls for **Garden Name**. Adjust the widths and positions of the remaining controls to fit data without gaps of blank space between fields.

f. Switch to **Design** view, saving changes. Resize the **subreport control** to **6.25 inches wide**. Select the **subreport label control**, and drag to the right until it is approximately centered across the subreport control.

g. With the **label control** selected, click the **Font Color** button. Under **Theme Colors**, on the sixth row, click the fourth color—**Dark Purple, Text 2**, and then **Bold** the text.

h. In the subreport, in the **Report Header**, apply a **Background Color** of **Dark Purple, Text 2**. Select the **label controls** in the subreport **Report Header**, and change the **Font Color** to **White**.

i. Adjust the width of the report to **7 inches wide**. **Save** the report, click **Yes** in the dialog box, and then switch to **Report** view.

j. If you are instructed to submit this result, view the report in **Print Preview**, and then create a paper or electronic printout of the first page. **Close** the Print Preview window and the report.

4 On the **CREATE tab**, in the **Reports group**, click the **Report Wizard** button.

a. In the **Report Wizard** dialog box, **Select** the **Query: 7D TV Shows Parameter Query**. Move all of the fields to the **Selected Fields** box, and then click **Next** two times. Sort the records by **Original Air Date** in **Ascending** order, and then click **Next**. Under *Orientation*, click **Landscape**, and then click **Next**. Name the report **Lastname Firstname 7D 2017 TV Shows** and then click **Finish**. For the first date, type **1/1/17** and for the second date, type **12/31/17**

b. Switch to **Layout View**. For the first date, type **1/1/17** and for the second date, type **12/31/17** Resize and move all label and text box controls to fit the data within the page constraints. **Save** the report, and then switch to **Design** view.

(Project 7D Featured Gardens continues on the next page)

CHAPTER REVIEW

c. Point to the top of the **Page Header section bar**, and drag downward to the top of the **Detail section bar**.

d. On the **REPORT DESIGN TOOLS DESIGN tab**, in the **Controls group**, click the **Text Box** button. In the **Report Header** section, align the top of the plus (+) sign of the pointer with the **0.25-inch mark on the horizontal ruler** and the **0.5-inch mark on the vertical ruler**, and then click. Click the associated **label control**, and then press ⌫ Delete.

e. Click the **unbound text box control**, and then press ⌫ F4 . Click the **Property Sheet Data tab**, click in the **Control Source** property setting box, and then click the **Build** button. In the displayed **Expression Builder** dialog box, type **="Original Air Date Between "&[Enter first date]&" and "&[Enter second date]** making sure that you press ⌫ Spacebar after *Between* and before and after *and*. Click **OK**. **Close** the **Property Sheet**.

f. With the text box control selected, on the **REPORT DESIGN TOOLS FORMAT tab**, in the **Font group**, click the **Center** button. In the **Font group**, click the **Font Size button arrow**, and click **14**. Increase the size of the text box control until it is the same size and aligns with the right edge of the Report title.

g. **Save** the report, and switch to **Report** view. For the first date, enter **1/1/17** and for the second date, enter **12/31/17** Switch to **Print Preview** view. If you are instructed to submit this result, create a paper or electronic printout. **Close** the **Print Preview** window and the **report**, and then **Open** the **Navigation Pane**.

5 In the **Navigation Pane**, under **Queries**, click **7D Garden Contacts Query**, and then **Close** the **Navigation Pane**. On the **CREATE tab**, in the **Reports group**, click the **Report Wizard** button.

a. In the **Report Wizard** dialog box, **Query: 7D Garden Contacts Query** should display. Move all of the fields to the **Selected Fields** box, and then click **Next**. Click

the **Remove Field** button to remove the grouping. Click **Next** three times. For the title of the report, type **Lastname Firstname 7D Contacts Index** and then click **Finish**. **Close Print Preview**.

b. **Save** the report, and then switch to **Layout** view. Adjust the width of all controls so that all of the data displays for every record.

c. On the **DESIGN tab**, in the **Grouping & Totals group**, click the **Group & Sort** button. In the **Group, Sort, and Total pane**, click **Add a group**. From the displayed list, click **Last Name**. On the **Group bar**, click the **More arrow**. Click the **by entire value arrow**, and click the **by first character** option button. Click in an empty area of the report.

d. In the **Group, Sort, and Total pane**, on the **Group bar**, click **More**, and then to the right of **with title**, click the **Last Name** link. With *Last Name* selected, in the displayed **Zoom** dialog box, press ⌫ Delete, and then click **OK**. Delete the empty label control box placeholder. **Close** the **Group, Sort, and Total pane**.

e. Click the **text box control** that displays the letter *B*. On the **REPORT LAYOUT TOOLS FORMAT tab**, in the **Font group**, change the **Font Size** to **16**. Resize the control to approximately **1 inch**.

f. **Save** the report, and then switch to **Report** view. If you are instructed to submit this result, switch to **Print Preview** view, and then create a paper or electronic printout of the report. **Close** Print Preview.

g. **Close** the report, and then **Open** the **Navigation Pane**. **Close** the database, and **Exit** Access.

6 As directed by your instructor, submit your database and the paper or electronic printouts of the four reports that are the result of this project. Specifically, in this project, using your own name you created the following database and printouts or electronic printouts:

1. Lastname_Firstname_7D_Featured_Gardens	Database file
2. Lastname Firstname 7D Gardens Main Report	Report (printed or electronic printout)
3. Lastname Firstname 7D Featured Gardens Report	Report (printed or electronic printout)
4. Lastname Firstname 7D 2017 TV Shows	Report (printed or electronic printout)
5. Lastname Firstname 7D Contacts Index	Report (printed or electronic printout)

END | You have completed Project 7D

Apply 7A skills from these Objectives:

1 Create a Split Form
2 Create a Form and a Subform
3 Create a Multi-Page Form

MWB Productions maintains a database where customers can place telephone orders for the gardening supplies that are featured in the *Midwest Botanicals* television show. Ruthann Hansen, president of MWB Productions, wants the database forms to display related data. For example, she is interested in displaying the orders on one form. She also wants to display the CSR (customer service representative) information in a tab control form. In the following project, you will customize the company's forms to display data in two ways on the same form, to display data from multiple tables on one form, and to display data on multiple pages on a form. Your completed forms will look similar to Figure 7.50.

PROJECT FILES

For Project 7E, you will need the following files:

a07E_Phone_Orders
a07E_MWB_Logo
A new blank Word document

You will save your files as:

Lastname_Firstname_7E_Phone_Orders
Lastname_Firstname_7E_Tab_Control_Form

PROJECT RESULTS

FIGURE 7.50

(Project 7E Phone Orders continues on the next page)

1 Start Access. Locate and open the **a07E_Phone_Orders** file. Save the database in your **Access Chapter 7** folder as **Lastname_Firstname_7E_Phone_Orders** If necessary, enable the content.

2 In the **Navigation Pane**, click 7E MWB CSRs and then **Close** the **Navigation Pane**. Create a split form, and **Save** it as **Lastname Firstname 7E MWB CSRs Split Form**

3 Switch to **Design** view. In the **Property Sheet**, click the **Selection type arrow**. Click **Form** to display the **Form Property Sheet**. Click the **Split Form Printing** property setting box arrow, and then click **Form Only**. Click the **Split Form Orientation** property setting box arrow, and then click **Datasheet on Top**. **Close** the **Property Sheet**.

4 Switch to **Layout** view. Move the **Split Form Splitter Bar** between records 3 and 4. Select the **Photo controls** for *Andi Shell*. On the **FORM LAYOUT TOOLS ARRANGE tab**, click **Tabular** to remove the **Photo field** from the layout. Delete the **Photo label control**. Click the **Photo control**. In the **Property Sheet**, click the **Picture Alignment** property setting box arrow, and then click **Top Right**. **Close** the **Property Sheet**. Align the left edge of the **Photo control** with the left edge of the photograph. **Save** the form.

5 Add the **a07E_MWB_Logo** to the form, and change the **Picture Size Mode** property to **Zoom**. Increase the width of the logo control to **2 Close** the **Property Sheet**. Click the **title's label control**, and then type your **Lastname Firstname** at the beginning. Resize the **label control** to fit the title. **Save** the form.

6 Switch to **Form** view, and then navigate to **Record 3**. In the form section, change the **Last Name** from *Kay* to **Martin Save** the form. If you are instructed to submit this result, create a paper or electronic printout of only **Record 3**. **Close** the form. **Open** the **Navigation Pane**.

7 Click the **7E Phone Orders** table. Click the **CREATE tab**, and then click the **Form** button. **Close** the **Navigation Pane**. In the main form, click the **Supplier Name combo box control**. Resize the **text box control** so there is approximately **1 inch** of space between *Shop* and the right edge of the text box control.

8 Switch to **Design** view. Remove the **subform** from the stacked layout. Drag the right edge of the **subform** to the left until it aligns with the **3-inch mark on the horizontal ruler**. Move the subform under and to the center of the bottom of the main form. Drag the bottom edge upward until it aligns with the **3-inch mark on the vertical ruler**.

9 **Save** the form as **Lastname Firstname 7E Orders and Details** Add the **a07E_MWB_Logo** to the form, and change the **Picture Size Mode** property to **Zoom**. Drag the right bottom corner of the control downward to the top of the **Detail** section bar and to the right until it aligns with the **2-inch mark on the horizontal ruler**.

10 Select the **Title label control** box and resize the placeholder so the right edge aligns with the **6.25-inch mark on the horizontal ruler**. Edit the **title** to be **Lastname Firstname 7E Phone Orders and Details** with only your name on the first line. **Center** the title text.

11 Point to the right edge of the form. Drag to the left until the right edge of the form aligns with the **6.5-inch mark on the horizontal ruler.**

12 **Save** the form, and then switch to **Form** view. If you are instructed to submit this result, create a paper or electronic printout of only **Record 2**. **Close** the form. **Open** the **Navigation Pane**.

13 Open **7E MWB Suppliers TC Form** in **Design** view. Drag the **Form footer section bar** downward **2 inches**. Insert a tab control at the **0.5-inch mark on the horizontal ruler** and the **0.25-inch mark on the vertical ruler**. Increase the size of the tab control by dragging to the right until the right edge aligns with the **6-inch mark on the horizontal ruler**.

14 To the **first page** of the **tab control**, at the **1.5-inch mark on the horizontal ruler** and the **top edge of the tab sheet**, add the **Supplier #** and **Supplier Name** fields. Resize the **Supplier # text box control** so the right edge aligns at the **2-inch mark on the horizontal ruler**. Position the **Supplier Name** controls so the left edge of the **Supplier Name label control** is at the **2.25-inch mark on the horizontal ruler** and the top edge of the controls are aligned with the top edge of the **Supplier # text box control**. Resize the **Supplier Name text box control** so the right edge aligns at the **6-inch mark on the horizontal ruler**. On the first page of the tab control, change the **Caption** property to **Supplier**

(Project 7E Phone Orders continues on the next page)

15 To the **second page** of the **tab control**, at the **1.5-inch mark on the horizontal ruler** and the **top edge of the tab sheet**, add the following fields: **Address**, **City**, **State**, **Postal Code**, and **Phone**. Extend the widths of all text box controls to the **4-inch mark on the horizontal ruler**. Edit the **Caption** property to display **Directory Information**

16 Change the **title** of the form to **Lastname Firstname 7E Suppliers Tab Control Form** placing *Tab Control Form* on a second line. Align the right edge of the title's label control with the **5.5-inch mark on the horizontal ruler**. **Center** the text of the title. Resize the form to **6.5 inches** wide. Switch to **Form** view.

17 **Save** the form and navigate to **Record 7**. Using the Office Clipboard, **Copy** and **Paste** the first and second

tabs into a Word document. **Save** this document as **Lastname_Firstname_7E_Tab_Control_Form** If you are instructed to submit this result, create a paper or electronic printout of the **Word** document.

18 **Close** Word. In the **Access** window, **Close** the form, and then **Open** the **Navigation Pane**. **Close** the database, and then **Exit** Access.

19 As directed by your instructor, submit your database and the paper or electronic printouts of the three objects—two forms and one Word document—that are the result of this project. Specifically, in this project, using your own name you created the following database and printouts or electronic printouts:

1. Lastname_Firstname_7E_Phone Orders	Database file
2. Lastname Firstname 7E MWB CSRs Split Form	Form (printed or electronic printout)
3. Lastname Firstname 7E Phone Orders and Details	Form (printed or electronic printout)
4. Lastname Firstname 7E Tab Control Form	Word document (printed or electronic printout)

END | You have completed Project 7E

CONTENT-BASED ASSESSMENTS

Mastering Access   Project 7F Customer Service

MWB Productions maintains a customer service order phone line where viewers can order gardening supplies that are featured in the *Midwest Botanicals* television show. Creating advanced reports will help the president and officers of the production company study the information in the database in a different way. In the following project, you will create advanced reports that display data from multiple tables and from a parameter query. You will also create an alphabetic index of the last names of the customer service representatives. Your completed reports will look similar to Figure 7.51.

PROJECT FILES

For Project 7F, you will need the following files:

a07F_Customer_Service
a07F_MWB_Logo

You will save your database as:

Lastname_Firstname_7F_Customer_Service

PROJECT RESULTS

FIGURE 7.51

(Project 7F Customer Service continues on the next page)

CONTENT-BASED ASSESSMENTS

1 **Start** Access. Open the **a07F_Customer_Service** file. Save the database in your **Access Chapter 7** folder as **Lastname_Firstname_7F_Customer_Service** If necessary, enable the content.

2 Make a copy of the **7F CSR Report** and save it as **Lastname Firstname 7F CSR Orders** Open the report in **Design** view. **Close** the **Navigation Pane**.

3 Edit the **Title** of the report by changing *Lastname Firstname* to your first and last names. **Center** the text in the control.

4 Drag the **Page Footer section bar** down to the **1.5-inch mark on the vertical ruler**. Insert a **Subform/ Subreport** control at the **0.5-inch mark on the horizontal and vertical rulers**.

5 Using the **SubReport Wizard**, select **Use existing Tables and Queries**. From the **7F Orders** table, select the following fields in this order: **Order #**, **Order Date**, **Supplier Name**, and **Amount**. Show **7F Orders** for each record in **7F MWB CSRs** using **ID#**. Add your **Lastname Firstname** to the beginning of the subreport's default name.

6 Switch to **Layout** view. Delete the **subreport label control**. Scroll down to see the **subreport** for *Singh Brothers Hardware and Garden*. Resize the label and text box controls to just fit the data. Move the controls to close blank space between fields. Add a border of **Line Color Green 5** under **Standard Colors** and **2 pt Thickness** to the subreport. **Save** the report.

7 Switch to **Design** view. Select the **subreport**, and open it in its own window. Resize the **subreport control** to **5.0 inches wide**. Change the **Back Color report header** in the subreport to **Brown 5**. Select the label controls, and then change the **Font Color** to **White, Background 1**. **Save** and **Close** the subreport. Resize the **subreport control** until it is **5.25 inches wide**. If necessary, drag the **Page Footer section bar** back up to the **1.5-inch mark on the horizontal ruler**. Resize the report to **7.5 inches wide**.

8 Switch to **Layout** view. In any **subreport control**, click the **Amount text box control**. Display the **Conditional Formatting** dialog box, and create a **New Rule** to format the font for any **Amount** greater than **500** as **Green, Bold**. **Save** the report.

9 If you are instructed to submit this result, view the report in **Print Preview**, and then create a paper or electronic printout of only the first page of the report. **Close** the report, and then **Open** the **Navigation Pane**.

10 Click to select the **7F CSR Parameter Query**. Using the **Report Wizard**, add all **Available Fields** to the **Selected Fields** list. View the data by **7F Orders**. Group on the **ID#** field. **Sort Ascending** by **Order Date**. Use **Stepped** layout and **Portrait** orientation. Title the report **Lastname Firstname 7F Orders by CSR** Select **Modify the report's design**, and then click **Finish**. **Close** the **Navigation Pane**. **Save** the report.

11 Delete the **label** and **textbox controls** for the **ID** field. Resize the **Order Date** controls so the entire label is visible. Resize the **First Name** and **Last Name controls** to **1.25 inches** each. Move the fields to remove the blank space between them.

12 Delete the **report title control box**. To the **Report Header section**, add the **a07F_MWB_Logo**. Expand the width of the logo to the **2-inch mark on the horizontal ruler** and to the bottom of the **Report Header section**. Delete the **Title** placeholder. Add a **text box control** at the **2.25-inch mark on the horizontal ruler**. Delete the **text box label control**. Click the **unbound text box control**. Click the **Property Sheet Data tab**, and then click in the **Control Source** property setting box. Open the **Expression Builder** dialog box. Type the following concatenated string in the text control box: **="7F Orders Taken by "&[First Name]&" "&[Last Name]** Align and resize the title between the **2.25-** and **6.5-inch marks on the horizontal ruler**. **Center** the text in the control. Change the font size to **14**. Size the textbox **To Fit**.

13 In the **Page Footer section**, click in the **Now()** control box to the right of the equals sign. Type **"Report prepared by Firstname Lastname on "&** Widen the control so the right edge aligns with the **4.5-inch mark on the horizontal ruler**. Resize the **Page number control** so it displays between the **5.5-inch** and **7-inch mark on the horizontal ruler**. Resize the report to **7 inches wide**. **Save** the report.

14 Switch to **Report** view. In the **Enter Parameter Value** message box, under **Enter CSR #**, type **0559**

15 If you are instructed to submit this result, create a paper or electronic printout. **Close** the report, saving changes. **Open** the **Navigation Pane**.

(Project 7F Customer Service continues on the next page)

CONTENT-BASED ASSESSMENTS

16 Click **7F CSR Last Names Query**. Create a report using the **Report Wizard**. From the **Available Fields** list, add **Last Name** to the **Selected Fields** list. No sorting is required. Use **Tabular** layout and **Portrait** orientation. Title the report **Lastname Firstname 7F CSR Index Close Print Preview**.

17 Switch to **Layout** view. In the **Group, Sort, and Total** pane, click **Add a group**, and then click **Last Name**. On the **Group bar**, click the **More arrow**. Click the **by entire value arrow**, and click the **by first character** option button. Click in an empty area of the report. Click **do not keep group together on one page**, and from the displayed list, click **keep whole group together on one page**. Remove the **Lastname** title and placeholder. **Save** the report.

18 Click the **text box control** that displays the letter *A*, and change the **Font Size** to **16**. Click the **Font Color**

button arrow. Under **Theme Colors**, on the first line, click the sixth color—**Red, Accent 2**—and then apply **Bold** and **Italic**.

19 **Save** the report, and then switch to **Print Preview**. If you are instructed to submit this result, create a paper or electronic printout of the first page of the report.

20 **Close** the report, and then **Open** the **Navigation Pane**. **Close** the database, and then **Exit** Access.

21 As directed by your instructor, submit your database and the paper or electronic printouts of the three reports that are the result of this project. Specifically, in this project, using your own name you created the following database and printouts or electronic printouts:

1. Lastname_Firstname_7F_Customer Service	Database file
2. Lastname Firstname 7F CSR Orders	Report (printed or electronic printout)
3. Lastname Firstname 7F Orders by CSR	Report (printed or electronic printout)
4. Lastname Firstname 7F CSR Index	Report (printed or electronic printout)

END | You have completed Project 7F

CONTENT-BASED ASSESSMENTS

Mastering Access Project 7G Garden Tours

Apply 7A and 7B skills from these Objectives:

3 Create a Multi-Page Form

5 Create a Report Based on a Parameter Query

MWB Productions produces the television show *Midwest Botanicals*. The show's hosts present tours of public and private gardens that showcase the various styles. Matthew Lee maintains an updated database about the tours of the featured historic gardens. In this project, you will design a multi-page form for the gardens and tour information that will be used to update this part of the production. You will also create a report based on a parameter query using the name of the garden. Your completed work will look similar to Figure 7.52.

PROJECT FILES

For Project 7G, you will need the following files:

a07G_Garden_Tours

A new blank Word document

You will save your files as:

Lastname_Firstname_7G_Garden_Tours

Lastname_Firstname_7G_Garden_Tours_Tabs

PROJECT RESULTS

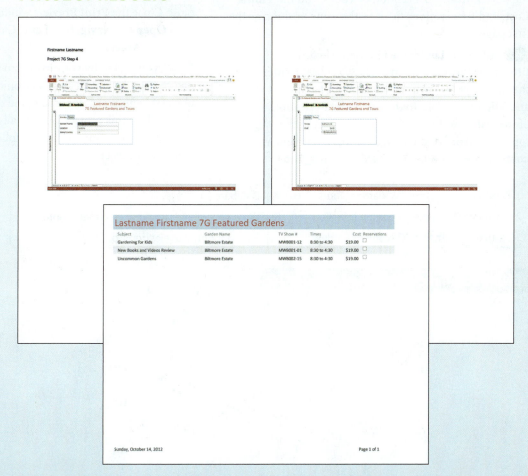

FIGURE 7.52

(Project 7G Garden Tours continues on the next page)

CONTENT-BASED ASSESSMENTS

1 Start Access. Open the **a07G_Garden_Tours** file. Save the database in your **Access Chapter 7** folder as **Lastname_Firstname_7G_Garden_Tours** If necessary, enable the content.

2 Open **7G Featured Gardens and Tours Form** in **Design** view, and then **Close** the **Navigation Pane**. Drag the top of the **Form footer section bar** down to the **3-inch mark on the vertical ruler**. In the **Detail section**, add a **tab control** at the **0.25-inch mark on the vertical and horizontal rulers**.

3 Extend the right edge of the **tab control** to the **5.5-inch mark on the horizontal ruler**. To the first page of the **tab control**, on the **Property Sheet**, add a caption of **Garden** From the Field List, add the **Garden Name**, **Location**, and **State/Country** field at the **1.5-inch mark on the horizontal ruler** and the **0.75-inch mark on the vertical ruler**. Extend the **text box controls** to the **4.5-inch mark on the horizontal ruler**. To the second page of the **tab control**, add a caption of **Tours** Add the **Times**, **Cost**, and **Reservations** fields to the same position as the first page.

4 Add your **Lastname Firstname** before the **title** of the form, and then press Shift + Enter. **Center** the title. **Save** the form. Use the Office Clipboard and Microsoft Word to display both tab controls of **Record 6**. Add your name and activity at the top of the Word document. Save this document as **Lastname_Firstname_7G_Garden_Tours_Tabs**

5 If you are instructed to submit this result, create a paper or electronic printout of the document. Close **Word**. Return to the **Access** window, **Close** the form, and then **Open** the **Navigation Pane**

6 Click the **7G Garden and Tours Query**. **Close** the **Navigation Pane**. Create a report using the **Report Wizard**. Use all of the fields. Do not add any grouping levels. **Sort** by **Subject** in **Ascending** order. Use **Tabular** layout and **Landscape** orientation. Title it **Lastname Firstname 7G Featured Gardens** Modify the report's design.

7 Select the **title control**. Change the **Font Color** to **Red, Accent 2** and the font size to **24**. Resize the control to fit the title. Resize the controls so the report width can be adjusted to **9.5 inches** wide.

8 Switch to **Layout** view. In the **Enter Parameter Value** message box, type **Biltmore Estate** Save the report.

9 If you are instructed to submit this result, create a paper or electronic printout.

10 **Close** the **Print Preview** window and the report, and then **Open** the **Navigation Pane**. **Close** the database, and then **Exit Access**.

11 As directed by your instructor, submit your database and the paper or electronic printouts of the two objects—one Word document and one report—that are the result of this project. Specifically, in this project, using your own name you created the following database and printouts or electronic printouts:

1. Lastname_Firstname_7G_Garden_Tours	Database file
2. Lastname Firstname 7G Garden Tours Tabs	Word document (printed or electronic printout)
3. Lastname Firstname 7G Featured Gardens	Report (printed or electronic printout)

END | You have completed Project 7G

CONTENT-BASED ASSESSMENTS

GO! Fix It	Project 7H Contests	Online
GO! Make It	Project 7I Advertising	Online
GO! Solve It	Project 7J Host Travel	Online
GO! Solve It	Project 7K Special Programming	

Apply a combination of the **7A** and **7B** skills.

PROJECT FILES

For Project 7K, you will need the following files:

a07K_Special_Programming
a07K_MWB_Logo
A new blank Word document

You will save your files as:

Lastname_Firstname_7K_Special_Programming
Lastname_Firstname_7K_TV_Shows_Form

Ruthann Hansen, president of MWB Productions, has scheduled special programming segments for the *Midwest Botanicals* television show. These segments will focus on holiday and seasonal topics.

Open the **a07K_Special_Programming** database and save it as **Lastname_Firstname_7K_Special_Programming** In this project, you will use the 7K TV Shows Form to create a multi-page form. To the first tab, add the TV Show # and the Original Air Date fields with a caption of **Show** To the second tab, add the Subject, Featured Garden, and Program fields with a caption of **Programming** Adjust all controls to display all data. In the title, replace *Lastname Firstname* with your first and last names. Save the form as **Lastname Firstname 7K TV Shows Form** Create a Microsoft Word document to show the contents of both tabs for Record 15. Save this document as **Lastname_Firstname_7K_TV_Shows_Form** If you are instructed to submit this result, create a paper or electronic printout of this document.

Open the 7K Special Programs report in Design view. Add the 7K Show Sponsors table as a subreport. Link the forms using the TV Show # field. Accept the default name for the subreport. Remove the TV Show # controls from the subreport and reduce the width to 3 inches. Delete the subreport label control. Add a logo and title to the report. Add your name in the Report Footer. Apply color in backgrounds, outlines, and fonts to create a well-formatted report on a portrait page. Save the report. If you are instructed to submit this result, create a paper or electronic printout of the first page of the report.

Create an alphabetic index on 7K Special Programs using the Program field sorted in Ascending order. Format the text box controls containing the letters. Arrange and adjust label and text box controls to display all data. Save as **Lastname Firstname 7K Special Programming Index** If you are instructed to submit this result, create a paper or electronic printout of the report.

(Project 7K Special Programming continues on the next page)

CHAPTER REVIEW

Performance Level

Performance Criteria		Exemplary	Proficient	Developing
	Create 7K TV Shows Form	Form created with the correct controls and formatted as directed.	Form created with no more than two missing elements.	Form created with more than two missing elements.
	Modify 7K Special Programs Report	Report created and formatted correctly.	Report created with no more than two missing elements.	Report created with more than two missing elements.
	Modify 7K Special Programming Index	Index modified to include the correct controls, grouping, sorting, and formatting.	Index modified with no more than two missing elements.	Index modified with more than two missing elements.

END | You have completed Project 7K

OUTCOMES-BASED ASSESSMENTS

RUBRIC

The following outcomes-based assessments are open-ended assessments. That is, there is no specific correct result; your result will depend on your approach to the information provided. Make Professional Quality your goal. Use the following scoring rubric to guide you in how to approach the problem and then to evaluate how well your approach solves the problem.

The *criteria*—Software Mastery, Content, Format and Layout, and Process—represent the knowledge and skills you have gained that you can apply to solving the problem. The *levels of performance*—Professional Quality, Approaching Professional Quality, or Needs Quality Improvements—help you and your instructor evaluate your result.

	Your completed project is of Professional Quality if you:	Your completed project is Approaching Professional Quality if you:	Your completed project Needs Quality Improvements if you:
1-Software Mastery	Choose and apply the most appropriate skills, tools, and features and identify efficient methods to solve the problem.	Choose and apply some appropriate skills, tools, and features, but not in the most efficient manner.	Choose inappropriate skills, tools, or features, or are inefficient in solving the problem.
2-Content	Construct a solution that is clear and well organized, contains content that is accurate, appropriate to the audience and purpose, and is complete. Provide a solution that contains no errors in spelling, grammar, or style.	Construct a solution in which some components are unclear, poorly organized, inconsistent, or incomplete. Misjudge the needs of the audience. Have some errors in spelling, grammar, or style, but the errors do not detract from comprehension.	Construct a solution that is unclear, incomplete, or poorly organized; contains some inaccurate or inappropriate content; and contains many errors in spelling, grammar, or style. Do not solve the problem.
3-Format & Layout	Format and arrange all elements to communicate information and ideas, clarify function, illustrate relationships, and indicate relative importance.	Apply appropriate format and layout features to some elements, but not others. Overuse features, causing minor distraction.	Apply format and layout that does not communicate information or ideas clearly. Do not use format and layout features to clarify function, illustrate relationships, or indicate relative importance. Use available features excessively, causing distraction.
4-Process	Use an organized approach that integrates planning, development, self-assessment, revision, and reflection.	Demonstrate an organized approach in some areas, but not others; or, use an insufficient process of organization throughout.	Do not use an organized approach to solve the problem.

OUTCOMES-BASED ASSESSMENTS

GO! Think	Project 7L Plants

PROJECT FILES

For Project 7L, you will need the following files:

a07L_Plants
a07L_MWB_Logo

You will save your database as:

Lastname_Firstname_7L_Plants

As a promotion for the *Midwest Botanicals* television show, Ruthann Hansen, president of MWB Productions, is always looking for ways to increase the attendance in the live studio audience. She has decided to offer a featured plant to the guests in the audience.

Open the **a07L_Plants** database and save it as **Lastname_Firstname_7L_Plants** In this project, you will create a split form based on the **7L Flower/Plant** table. In the form, adjust label and text box controls to display all data. Delete the Photo label control and arrange the label and text box controls so that the first column contains the ID#, Photo, Common Name, and Scientific Name fields. The photo should align with the left edge of the text boxes in the first column. The second column should display the other four fields. Add the **a07L_MWB_Logo** to the form header, change the size to Zoom, and resize the logo. Edit the form title to include your first and last names. Select the option to print the form only. Save the form as **Lastname Firstname 7L Flower/Plant Split Form** If you are instructed to submit this result, create a paper or electronic printout of the form of Record 3 only.

Open the **7L TV Shows Form** in Design view. Drag the **7L Historical Gardens** table to the design grid. Link Featured Garden to Garden Name. Drag the **7L Flower/Plant** table to the design grid to the right of the Historical Gardens subform. Link Featured Plant to ID#. Rename the form as **Lastname Firstname 7L Shows and Flowers/Plants Form** Open each of the subforms and change the Default View property to Single Form. Modify each of the subform label controls to be a descriptive title. Size the subforms to display all controls and eliminate any scroll bars. If you are instructed to submit this result, select Record 14 of the main form on a single landscape page.

END	You have completed Project 7L

GO! Think	Project 7M Seminars	Online

You and GO!	Project 7N Club Directory	Online

Creating Macros

GO! to Work
Video A8

PROJECT 8A

OUTCOMES
Create and modify macros.

PROJECT 8B

OUTCOMES
Build macro groups.

OBJECTIVES

1. Create a Standalone Macro with One Action
2. Add Multiple Actions to a Standalone Macro
3. Create an Embedded Macro
4. Print Macro Details

OBJECTIVES

5. Create a Macro Group
6. Associate a Macro with a Session
7. Create a Data Macro

In This Chapter

Macros provide a way to automate tasks that you may need to perform repeatedly. For example, you may create a report or query that you open and print on a weekly basis. You can create a macro that prints the query or report when the user clicks a command button. You may also use a macro to perform a set of actions every time a database is opened. Related macros can be created in a group. Macros can be run automatically, through the Navigation Pane, or by associating them with other actions like clicking a button on a form or report. Data macros are created to validate and ensure the accuracy of data in a table.

Providence and Warwick Hospital serves the metropolitan area of Providence, Rhode Island, and the surrounding cities that include Warwick, Rhode Island, and Fall River, Massachusetts. It is a world-class medical facility providing care to adults and children through the hospital as well as a number of social service and multidisciplinary facilities, such as the Asthma Center and Adult Metabolism Clinic. Scientists at the hospital conduct research and clinical trials of new drugs. The hospital's medical staff focuses on innovation and new technologies to provide quality patient care to patients at every stage of life.

PROJECT

8A

Employee Records

MyITLab®
Project 8A Training

PROJECT ACTIVITIES

In Activities 8.01 through 8.07, you will help Jordan Jones, human resources director for Providence and Warwick Hospital, customize the database to make it easier for his staff to use. You will create macros to automatically display a form and message box when an individual opens the database. The form will be ready for the staff to edit and update employment data for the hospital. Jones also wants you to add a button with an embedded macro to a form and embed a macro within a report. Finally, you will display and print a report that documents the details of the macros you created. When completed, your results will look similar to Figure 8.1.

PROJECT FILES

For Project 8A, you will need the following file: You will save your database as:

a08A_Employee_Records   Lastname_Firstname_8A_Employee_Records

PROJECT RESULTS

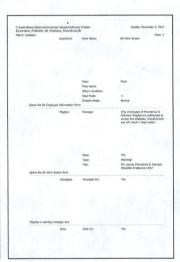

FIGURE 8.1 Project 8A Employee Records

Video A8-1

A *macro* is a series of actions grouped as a single command to accomplish a task or multiple tasks automatically. A *standalone macro* is an object displayed under Macros in the Navigation Pane. Some of the more commonly used actions are to open a report, find a record, or apply a filter to an object. An *action* is a self-contained instruction that can be combined with other actions to automate tasks.

Before creating a macro, you should list the actions you want to occur and in what order. You should determine if an argument applies to the action. An *argument* is a value that provides information to the action, such as the words to display in a message box. You should also determine if any conditions should be specified. A *condition* specifies that certain criteria must be met before the macro executes.

Activity 8.01 | Creating a Standalone Macro

In this activity, you will create a standalone macro that will display the *8A Employee Information Form* when the macro is run.

1 Start Access. Navigate to the location where the student data files for this textbook are saved. Locate and open the **a08A_Employee_Records** file. Display **Backstage** view, and click **Save As**, and then, under *File Types*, double-click **Save Database As**. In the **Save As** dialog box, navigate to the drive on which you will be saving your folders and projects for this chapter. Create a new folder named **Access Chapter 8** and save the database as **Lastname_Firstname_8A_ Employee_Records** in the folder. If necessary, add the Access Chapter 8 folder to the Trust Center.

> For this chapter, you must add the Access Chapter 8 folder to the Trust Center—you cannot just enable the content, because some of the macros will not execute properly if the database is not trusted.

2 In the **Navigation Pane**, under **Forms**, click **8A Employee Information Form** to select the form.

3 **Close** the **Navigation Pane**.

4 On the **CREATE tab**, in the **Macros & Code group**, click the **Macro** button, and then compare your screen with Figure 8.2.

> The *Macro Designer* displays, which allows you to build the list of actions to be carried out when the macro runs. The Add New Action bar displays in the Macro Designer window, and the Action Catalog task pane displays on the right side of the screen. The buttons on the MACRO TOOLS DESIGN tab are used to run, test, or modify a macro; to expand or collapse actions; and to display panes in the Macro Designer or to display more actions.

FIGURE 8.2

5 In the **Macro Designer,** in the **Add New Action bar,** click the displayed **arrow,** and then compare your screen with Figure 8.3.

Because the Show All Actions button is not active, a shorter list of macro actions displays. These macro actions can be used in a database that is not trusted. You can click the Show All Actions button to display a longer list of macro actions; however, if the database is not trusted and you select a macro action that requires the database to be trusted, the macro will not execute. Instead, a message box will display.

FIGURE 8.3

6 Scroll down the displayed list, and then click **OpenForm** to display the **OpenForm Action Block.** Compare your screen with Figure 8.4.

FIGURE 8.4

7 In the **Form Name** box, click the displayed **arrow,** and then click **8A Employee Information Form.**

This is a required argument.

8 In the **View** box, click the **arrow.** Notice that you can open the form in Form view, Design view, Print Preview, Datasheet view, PivotTable view, PivotChart view, or Layout view. Be sure that **Form** is selected.

The OpenForm action opens a form in Form view by default.

9 Point to the **Filter Name** box until the ScreenTip appears; read the description. Repeat the process in the **Where Condition** box and the **Data Mode** box. Be sure that these arguments are left blank.

> The Data Mode argument is used for forms that open in either Form view or Datasheet view. If left blank, Access opens the form in the data entry mode set in the form's Allow Edits, Allow Deletions, Allow Additions, and Data Entry property settings.

10 Point to the **Window Mode** box, and then read the description. Click the **arrow**, and notice the options for displaying the form. Be sure that the **Window Mode** setting is **Normal**.

11 In the **Action Catalog pane**, under **Program Flow**, double-click **Comment**. In the **Comment** text box that displays below the **OpenForm Action Block**, type **Displays the 8A Employee Information Form when the macro is run** Compare your screen with Figure 8.5.

> You should always enter a description of a macro so that you and others can determine easily the actions that will occur when the macro runs. A green arrow displays to the right of the Comments dialog box. Click it to move the comment above the action arguments.

FIGURE 8.5

> **BY TOUCH**   In the Action Catalog, tap Comment and drag below the OpenForm Action Block.

12 On the **DESIGN tab**, in the **Tools** group, click the **Run** button.

> A message displays stating that you must save the macro before you run it.

13 In the displayed message box, click **Yes** to save the macro. In the **Save As** dialog box, type **Lastname Firstname Open 8A Employee Information Form** and then click **OK**.

> The macro is saved and runs. When the macro runs, it displays the 8A Employee Information Form.

14 Close ☒ the **8A Employee Information Form**, and then **Close** ☒ the **Macro Designer**. **Open** ☒ the **Navigation Pane**, and then compare your screen with Figure 8.6.

> In the Navigation Pane, a new group—Macros—displays, and the newly created macro object displays under the group name.

FIGURE 8.6

15 In the **Navigation Pane**, under **Macros**, double-click **Open 8A Employee Information Form**.

Double-clicking a macro object causes the macro to run.

16 Close ⌧ the form.

Activity 8.02 | Opening a Form in Its Own Window

In this activity, you will modify the properties of a form to create a pop-up, modal window. A *pop-up window* displays (pops up), usually contains a menu of commands, and stays on the screen until the user selects one of the commands. A *modal window* is a child (secondary window) to a parent window—the original window that opened the modal window—that takes over control of the parent window. A user cannot press any controls or enter any information in the parent window until the modal window is closed. Both pop-up and modal windows are commonly used when the database designer wants to direct a user's focus to the information in the window.

1 In the **Navigation Pane**, under **Forms**, double-click **8A Intro Screen** to open the form in **Form** view.

Like most of the objects you have opened, the form displays with its own tab.

2 Switch to **Design** view. On the **FORM DESIGN TOOLS DESIGN tab**, in the **Tools group**, click the **Property Sheet** button. If the Property Sheet does not display *Selection type: Form*, click the **Selection type** arrow, and then click **Form**.

3 On the **Property Sheet**, click the **Other tab**. Click the **Pop Up property setting arrow**, and then click **Yes**. Click in the **Modal property setting box**, click the **arrow**, and then click **Yes**. Compare your screen with Figure 8.7.

The Pop Up property setting of Yes displays the object in its own window on top of all other opened objects. A setting of No displays the object as a tabbed object. Changing the Pop Up setting to Yes is most common for objects that you want to get the attention of the individual using the database. The Modal property setting is used to keep the focus on the opened form, because you cannot change the focus to another database object until the form is closed.

FIGURE 8.7

4 Close ⊠ the **Property Sheet**, and then **Close** ⊠ the form, saving changes when prompted. In the **Navigation Pane**, under **Macros**, double-click **Open 8A Employee Information Form**, and then under **Forms**, double-click **8A Intro Screen** to open both forms in **Form** view. Notice the text in the title bar of the pop-up window. In the **Navigation Pane**, under **Forms**, double-click **Departments Form**, and notice that the form does not open. Compare your screen with Figure 8.8.

8A Employee Information opens as a tabbed object, and *8A Intro Screen* opens in its own pop-up window. The pop-up window can be moved or closed. Until it is closed, the focus cannot be changed to another database object; that is why you cannot open the *8A Departments Form*. The *8A Intro Screen* form does not display Minimize or Maximize buttons, only a Close button, because the Modal property setting is Yes. A Modal property setting of No can display the Minimize and Maximize buttons.

FIGURE 8.8

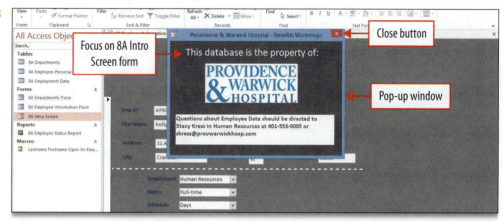

5 Close ⊠ the **8A Intro Screen** form, and then **Close** ⊠ the **8A Employee Information Form**. In the **Navigation Pane**, open the **8A Intro Screen** form in **Design** view.

6 On the **FORM DESIGN TOOLS DESIGN tab**, in the **Tools** group, click the **Property Sheet** button. Verify that the **Selection type** box displays **Form**. On the **Property Sheet**, click the **Format tab**, and then take a moment to review some of the property settings for this form while comparing your screen with Figure 8.9.

The text entered in the Caption property displays on the title bar of the form when in Form view. The Allow Form View property setting is Yes, while all of the other views are disabled.

The Border Style property setting is Dialog, which is a thick border that can include a title bar with a Close button. The form cannot be resized, maximized, or minimized with this border style. Because this is a custom form that does not display any records from an underlying table or query, the Record Selectors, Navigation Buttons, and Scroll Bars property settings have been set to No or Neither.

FIGURE 8.9

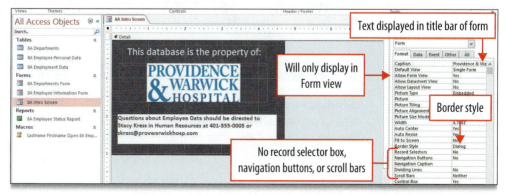

7 Close ⊠ the **Property Sheet**, **Close** ⊠ the form, and then **Close** « the **Navigation Pane**.

Activity 8.03 | Creating a Standalone Macro That Executes Automatically

In this activity, you will create another standalone macro that will open the 8A Intro Screen form when the database is opened.

1 On the **CREATE tab**, in the **Macros & Code group**, click the **Macro** button to display the **Macro Designer**.

2 In the **Macro Designer**, in the **Add New Action bar**, click the **arrow**, scroll down, and then click **OpenForm**. In the **OpenForm Action Block**, click the **Form Name arrow**, and then click **8A Intro Screen**.

3 If necessary, on the **MACRO TOOLS DESIGN tab**, in the **Show/Hide group**, click the **Action Catalog** button to display the **Action Catalog pane**. In the **Action Catalog pane**, point to **Comment**, and drag it below the OpenForm action. In the Comment box, type **Opens the 8A Intro Screen form** Compare your screen with Figure 8.10.

> In addition to double-clicking an action in the Action Catalog, an action can also be added by dragging it to place it in the correct position.

FIGURE 8.10

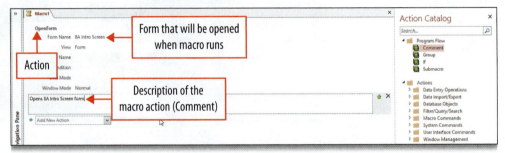

4 On the **Quick Access toolbar**, click the **Save** button. In the **Save As** dialog box, type **autoexec** and then click **OK**.

> When a macro is named *Autoexec*, Access automatically runs or executes the macro each time the database is opened. There can be only one macro in a database named *Autoexec*.

5 **Close** ☒ the **Macro Designer**, and then **Open** ☒ the **Navigation Pane**. Notice that in the **Navigation Pane**, under **Macros**, **autoexec** displays. Double-click **autoexec** to run the macro.

> The *8A Intro Screen* form displays in its own pop-up, modal window.

6 **Close** the form. Display **Backstage** view, and then click **Close**. In **Backstage** view, click **Open**. Under **Recent**, click **Lastname_Firstname_8A_Employee_Records**.

> The macro automatically executes or runs when the *8A_Employee_Records* database opens, and it displays the pop-up, modal *8A Intro Screen* form. Because this is a trusted macro action, the macro will execute even if the database has not been trusted or the content enabled.

🔄 **ANOTHER WAY**   The preferred method to open an object when the database is opened is the following. Display Backstage view, and then click Options. In the Access Options window, on the left side, click Current Database. Under Application Options, click the Display Form arrow, and then click the form that should be displayed when the database is opened.

Because you will add more actions to the standalone macro, it is appropriate to open the 8A Intro Screen form as an auto executable action.

---

7 **Close** ☒ the form.

Video A8-2

In the previous activities, you created macros that each contained only one action—opening a form. A macro can contain multiple actions that are executed in a specified order. For example, you can display a busy icon as the macro executes, which is especially useful for macros with multiple actions, to let the user know that Access is working on a process. This can be followed by an action that runs another standalone macro—for example, opening a form. And then you can select the title bar on the form, maximize the form, and then turn off the busy icon.

Activity 8.04 | Adding Multiple Actions to an Existing Standalone Macro

In this activity, you will modify the Autoexec macro and add more actions to the macro.

1 In the **Navigation Pane**, under **Macros**, right-click **autoexec**, and then click **Design View**. **Close** **«** the **Navigation Pane**.

2 In the **Action Catalog pane**, click in the **Search** box, and then type **dis** Under **System Commands**, double-click **DisplayHourglassPointer** to display the **DisplayHourglassPointer Action Block**. Notice that the default argument is *Yes*. Compare your screen with Figure 8.11.

When you search for an action using the Action Catalog pane, a description of the macro selected appears at the bottom of the pane. The Hourglass action changes the normal pointer to a busy icon to inform the user that some action is taking place. On a slower computer, the icon will keep the user from thinking that something is wrong with the database. If the computer is fast, the busy icon may not display. When the macro finishes running, the normal mouse pointer displays.

FIGURE 8.11

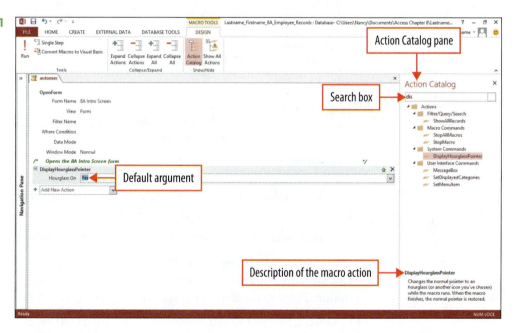

3 Click inside the **Add New Action bar**, and type **'Turns mouse pointer to a busy icon to show that the macro may take a few seconds to execute** and then press Enter.

Typing a single quote before the comment identifies the text that follows as a comment. The Comment block displays after you press Enter.

4 On the **MACRO TOOLS DESIGN tab**, in the **Show/Hide** group, click the **Show All Actions** button.

> Recall that the default list of macros displays only trusted macro actions. The next macro action that you will add to the macro is not a trusted macro action. For the macro to execute properly, you must add the location of the database to Trusted Locations or enable the content. Because this macro is used to open a pop-up, modal window, the database location must be trusted. The modal form will open automatically when the database is opened, and you cannot enable the content until the form is closed.

5 In the **Action Catalog pane**, click in the **Search** box, and then replace any existing text with **ech** Under **Macro Commands**, double-click **Echo**. In the **Echo Action Block**, in the **Echo On** box, click the **arrow**, and then click **No**. Click in the **Status Bar Text** box, and type **Macro is running** Click inside the **Add New Action bar** and type '**Hides the flickering screen as the macro actions execute** and then press Enter. Compare your screen with Figure 8.12.

> The Echo macro action hides or displays the results of the macro while it runs; however, it will not hide error messages or property sheets. Changing the Echo On argument to *No* hides the results. The Status Bar Text argument displays text on the status bar while the macro is running with Echo On set to No. The icon that displays in the Action Argument box indicates that the macro action is not safe.

FIGURE 8.12

6 In the **Action Catalog pane**, click in the **Search** box, and then replace any existing text with **run** Under **Macro Commands**, double-click **RunMacro**.

> The RunMacro action is used to run a macro from within another macro.

7 In the **RunMacro Action Arguments Block**, click the **Macro Name box arrow**, and then click **Open 8A Employee Information Form**. Point to the **Repeat Count** box, and then read the description. Point to the **Repeat Expression** box, and then read the description.

> The Repeat Count and Repeat Expression action arguments are used when the macro should be run more than one time. Left blank, the macro will run only one time.

8 Click inside the **Add New Action bar**, type '**Opens the 8A Employee Information Form** and then press Enter.

9 In the **Action Catalog pane**, click in the **Search** box, and then replace any existing text with **mes** Under **User Interface Commands**, double-click **MessageBox**.

> The MessageBox macro action is a trusted action that displays a message box that contains a warning or informational message. The MessageBox macro action can contain up to four arguments.

10 ► In the **Action Arguments** box, click in the **Message** box, and then type **Only employees of Providence & Warwick Hospital are authorized to access this database. Unauthorized use will result in legal action.**

11 ► Point to the **Beep** box, and read the description of the Beep argument. Verify that the Beep argument is **Yes**. Click the **Type arrow**, and then compare your screen with Figure 8.13.

There are five different message types listed. Each has a different icon that is displayed in the message box. None is the default message type because no icon displays in the message box.

FIGURE 8.13

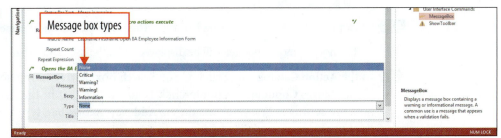

12 ► In the displayed list, click **Warning!** Point to the **Title** box, and read the description of the argument. Click in the **Title** box, and type **For Use by Providence & Warwick Hospital Employees Only!**

13 ► Click inside the **Add New Action bar**, type **'Displays a warning message box** and press Enter.

14 ► Scroll to the top of the **Designer** window. Click the **OpenForm** action to make it active. At the right edge of the title, click the green downward pointing arrow two times to move the action below the **DisplayHourglassPointer** action. (Be sure to click twice, not double-click.) Click the green downward pointing arrow in the **OpenForm** action box five more times or until it appears below the comment *Opens the 8A Employee Information Form.* Compare your screen with Figure 8.14.

FIGURE 8.14

 ANOTHER WAY

Alternatively, you can point to the right edge of the Action or Comment block and drag it to a new position. When you point to the top edge of an Action or Comment block to move it, the mouse pointer does not change in appearance. As you drag the box, an orange line will appear at positions where the box can be dropped.

15 ► Click the downward pointing green arrow to the right of the **OpenForm macro comment** until you move it below the **OpenForm macro action**. In the **Designer** window, scroll down until the **Add New Action bar** is displayed.

16 In the **Action Catalog pane**, click in the **Search** box, and then replace any existing text with **dis** Under **System Commands**, drag **DisplayHourglassPointer** above the **Add New Action bar**, and release the mouse button. In the **Action Arguments** box, click the **Hourglass On arrow**, and then click **No**.

Dragging an action into the Designer window gives the user more control over the placement of the action in the macro.

17 Click inside the **Add New Action bar**, type **'Restores the normal mouse pointer** and then press Enter.

The normal mouse pointer will be displayed to let the user know that the macro is finished executing.

18 In the **Action Catalog pane**, click in the **Search** box, and then replace any existing text with **ech** Under **Macro Commands**, double-click **Echo**. Notice that in the **Action Block**, in the **Echo On** box, the setting is **Yes**. Click inside the **Add New Action bar**, type **'Displays screen results** and then press Enter.

Screen actions will no longer be hidden from the individual using the database. Status Bar Text is not displayed because the Echo On argument is set to Yes.

NOTE   **Turning Off Macro Actions**

Access automatically restores Hourglass and Echo to the default settings after a macro has finished running to protect inexperienced macro programmers from causing the system to continue displaying the hourglass icon, which might lead the user to think that the database is operating incorrectly or is frozen. Even though Access restores these settings, it is good practice to always restore what you turn off. This will lead to better coding if you write Visual Basic code to execute commands.

---

19 On the **Quick Access Toolbar**, click the **Save** button. On the **MACRO TOOLS DESIGN tab**, in the **Tools group**, click the **Run** button. Point to the Intro Screen title bar, and then compare your screen with Figure 8.15.

Access does not always wait for one action to complete before going on to the next action. Notice that the *8A Employee Information Form* is not yet open; however, the *8A Intro Screen* is open with a message box displayed on top of it. A beep sounded when the message box displayed. The hourglass displays, and the status bar displays *Macro is running*.

FIGURE 8.15

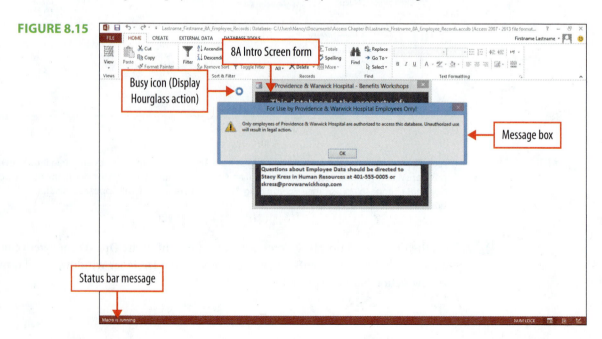

20 ▶ In the displayed message box, click **OK**. The **8A Employee Information Form** displays underneath the **8A Intro Screen** form. **Close** ⊠ the **8A Intro Screen** form. On the **tab row**, right-click any tab, and then click **Close All**.

21 ▶ Display **Backstage** view, and then click **Close**. Display **Backstage** view, and then click **Open** and then, under **Recent**, click **8A_Employee_Records**.

The Autoexec macro automatically executes or runs when the *8A_Employee_Records* database opens, and it displays the pop-up, modal *8A Screen* form with the message box on top of it.

22 ▶ In the displayed message box, click **OK**. **Close** ⊠ the **8A Intro Screen** form.

More Knowledge   **Debugging a Macro**

Debugging is using a logical process to find and reduce the number of errors in a program. To debug a macro, you can use *single stepping*, which executes one action at a time. Single stepping allows you to observe the results of each macro action to isolate an action that may be causing an error or producing unwanted results.

To single step through a macro, open the macro in Design view. On the MACRO TOOLS DESIGN tab, in the Tools group, click the Single Step button. In the Tools group, click the Run button. The Macro Single Step dialog box displays information about the macro, including the macro name, the condition, the action name, the arguments, and an error number. An error number of 0 indicates that no error has occurred. In this dialog box, you can carry out the macro action by clicking Step. You can stop the macro and close the dialog box by clicking Stop All Macros, or you can turn off single stepping and run the rest of the macro by clicking Continue.

When the macro has fully executed, be sure to turn off single stepping on the MACRO TOOLS DESIGN tab in the Tools group by clicking the Single Step button.

Objective 3   Create an Embedded Macro

Video A8-3

An *embedded macro* is a macro that is stored in the Session properties of forms, reports, or controls. Embedded macros are not displayed in the Navigation Pane under Macros. They are easier to manage because you do not have to keep track of the separate macro objects. Unlike standalone macros, when objects containing embedded macros are copied, imported, or exported, the macros are also copied, imported, or exported. Any standalone macro can be created as an embedded macro.

Activity 8.05   Creating an Embedded Macro on a Form

In this activity, you will create an embedded macro that will execute when the *Department Info* button is clicked on the *8A Employee Information Form*.

1 ▶ Switch the **8A Employee Information Form** to **Design** view. On the **FORM DESIGN TOOLS DESIGN tab**, in the **Controls group**, click the **Button** button ▭. In the **Details** section, align the plus sign (+) of the pointer at **4.5 inches on the horizontal ruler** and **2.5 inches on the vertical ruler**, and then click. Compare your screen with Figure 8.16.

The button displays at the set position, and the Command Button Wizard dialog box displays.

FIGURE 8.16

> **2** In the **Command Button Wizard** dialog box, click **Cancel**.

Recall that the Command Button Wizard can be used to associate a button with a preset action. Cancel the wizard to embed or assign a macro to the button. Because no name or picture has been associated with the button, it displays Command55. The number following the word Command may differ.

> **3** Right-click the button, and then click **Properties**. Verify that the **Property Sheet** displays *Selection type: Command Button* and the **Selection type** box displays *Command55*, identifying your command button. On the **Property Sheet Other tab**, in the **Name** property box, select the existing text and type **btnDeptInfo** and press [Enter].

The button name has been updated to *btnDeptInfo*. The button name will now display in the Selection type box for easy identification.

> **4** On the **Property Sheet Format tab**, in the **Caption** property box, select the existing text and type **Dept Info** and press [Enter]. Compare your screen with Figure 8.17.

The button label has been updated to *Dept Info*, reflecting the caption property. However, no actions have been associated with the button.

FIGURE 8.17

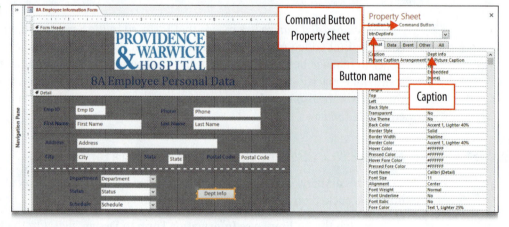

> **5** On the **Property Sheet**, click the **Event tab**. In the **On Click** property setting box, click the **Build** button ⋯ , and then compare your screen with Figure 8.18.

The Choose Builder dialog box displays for you to select the Macro Builder, the Expression Builder, or the Code Builder. You have previously used the Macro Builder and the Expression Builder. The *Code Builder* is used for programming in Microsoft Visual Basic.

FIGURE 8.18

> **6** In the **Choose Builder** dialog box, if necessary, click **Macro Builder**, and then click **OK** to display the Macro Designer.

> **7** In the **Macro Designer**, add the **OpenForm** action using one of the techniques you have learned. In the **OpenForm Action Block**, click the **Form Name arrow**, and then click **8A Departments Form**. Click in the **Where Condition** box, type **[Dept ID]=[Forms]![8A Employee Information Form]![Department]** selecting items as they appear in the list to reduce errors, and then compare your screen with Figure 8.19.

> The Where Condition property selects the records from the *8A Departments Form* for the Department displayed on the *8A Employee Information Form*.

FIGURE 8.19

> **8** In the **OpenForm Action Block**, click the **Data Mode arrow**, and then click **Read Only** to enable the user to only view the data in the *8A Departments Form*. Add the following comment: **Opens 8A Departments Form for department indicated on 8A Employee Information Form**

> **9** Close ⊠ the **Macro Designer**. In the displayed message box, click **Yes** to save the changes made to the macro and to update the **On Click** property. Compare your screen with Figure 8.20.

> In the Property Sheet, the On Click property displays *[Embedded Macro]*. To display the macro, click the Build button.

FIGURE 8.20

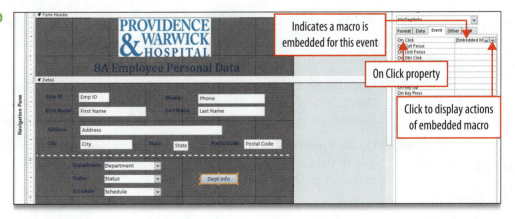

10 On the **Property Sheet**, click the **Format tab**. In the **Caption** box, click to the left of **Dept Info**, and then type **&** to create a shortcut key using the letter *D*. **Close** ✕ the **Property Sheet**, **Save** the form, and then switch the *8A Employee Information Form* to **Form** view.

The ampersand (&) causes the letter that follows it to be underlined on the button, which will enable the user to use a shortcut key combination to access the button instead of clicking on the button. The user presses Alt + the letter to activate the button. For this button, the shortcut is Alt + D.

11 On the **8A Employee Information Form**, click the **Dept Info** button. Alternatively, press Alt + D.

The *8A Departments Form* displays as a pop-up window and provides directory information about the Human Resources department, the Department listed on the *8A Employee Information Form*.

12 **Close** ✕ the *8A Departments Form*. In the **8A Employee Information Form**, in the record navigator, click the **Last record** button. In the **8A Employee Information Form**, click the **Dept Info** button, and then compare your screen with Figure 8.21.

The pop-up window displays directory information for the Facilities department, the same department displayed on the *8A Employee Information Form*, as indicated by the Filtered button to the right of the record navigator in the *8A Departments Form*.

FIGURE 8.21

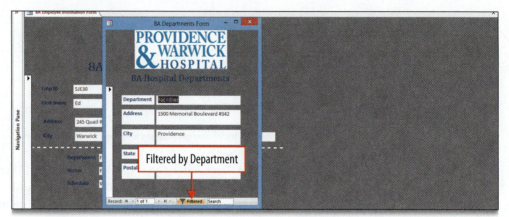

13 **Close** ✕ the *8A Departments Form*, and then **Close** ✕ the *8A Employee Information Form*, saving changes, if necessary. **Open** » the **Navigation Pane**. Notice that under **Macros**, the macro you created to display the *8A Departments Form* does not display—embedded macros do not display in the **Navigation Pane**.

Activity 8.06 | Creating an Embedded Macro on a Report

In this activity, you will create an embedded macro that will execute when the *Emp ID* text box is clicked on the *8A Employee Status Report*.

1 Open the **8A Employee Status Report** in **Design** view. **Close** « the **Navigation Pane**. In the **Detail** section, right-click the **Emp ID** text box, and then click **Properties**. Verify that the **Property Sheet** displays *Selection type: Text Box* and the **Selection type** box displays *Emp ID*.

2 On the **Property Sheet Event tab**, in the **On Click** property setting box, click the **Build** button ⋯. In the **Choose Builder** dialog box, verify that **Macro Builder** is selected, and then click **OK** to display the **Macro Designer**.

3 In the **Macro Designer**, add the **OpenForm** action using one of the techniques you have learned. In the **OpenForm Action Block**, click the **Form Name arrow**, and then click **8A Employee Information Form**. Click in the **Where Condition** box, type **[Emp ID]=[Reports]![8A Employee Status Report]![Emp ID]** selecting items as they appear in the list to reduce errors and then compare your screen with Figure 8.22.

> The Where Condition property selects the records from the *8A Employee Information Form* for the Employee selected on the *8A Employee Status Report*.

FIGURE 8.22

4 In the **OpenForm Action Block**, click the **Data Mode arrow**, and then click **Read Only**. Add the following comment: **Opens 8A Employee Information Form for the employee selected on 8A Employee Status Report**

5 Close ☒ the **Macro Designer**. In the displayed message box, click **Yes** to save the changes made to the macro and to update the **On Click** property. Close ☒ the **Property Sheet**. **Save** the report.

6 Switch to **Report** view. On the **8A Employee Status Report**, click the **Emp ID** text box for *BOM22* to run the macro.

> The *8A Employee Information Form* displays and provides information about Maria Bartello, the employee whose Emp ID was selected on the *8A Employee Status Report*.

7 Close ☒ the **8A Employee Information Form**. Close ☒ the **8A Employee Status Report**, saving changes if necessary. **Open** ☒ the **Navigation Pane**. Notice that under **Macros**, the macro you created to display the *8A Employee Information Form* does not display because embedded macros do not display in the **Navigation Pane**.

Objective 4 | Print Macro Details

Video A8-4

Use the ***Database Documenter*** to create a report that contains detailed information about the objects in a database, including macros, and to create a paper record.

Activity 8.07 | Printing Macro Details

In this activity, you will use the Database Documenter to print out the details of the macros that you have created in this project.

1 Close ☒ the **Navigation Pane**. On the **DATABASE TOOLS tab**, in the **Analyze group**, click the **Database Documenter** button. In the displayed **Documenter** dialog box, click the **Macros tab**, and then compare your screen with Figure 8.23.

> The Documenter dialog box displays tabs for each object type and a tab for the current database. Only standalone macros display on the Macros tab. Macros that are embedded with an object and will display as a property of the object.

FIGURE 8.23

2 In the **Documenter** dialog box, click the **Options** button, and then compare your screen with Figure 8.24.

The Print Macro Definition dialog box displays. Properties, actions, arguments, and permissions by user and group can be displayed in the printed report.

FIGURE 8.24

3 If necessary, click the **Permissions by User and Group** check box to clear it, and then click **OK**. In the **Documenter** dialog box, click **Select All**, and then click **OK**. Click in the middle of the document to zoom in, scroll up to display the top of the report, and then compare your screen with Figure 8.25.

The Object Definition opens in Print Preview, and displays the first page of information about the macro named *Autoexec*, including actions, arguments, conditions, and comments.

FIGURE 8.25

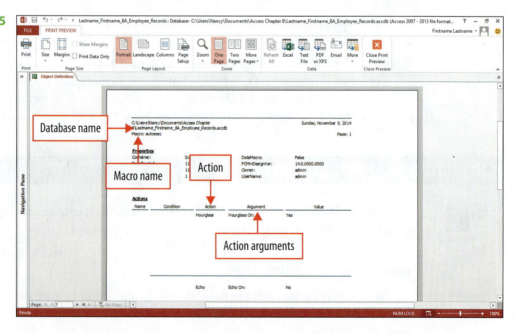

4 If you are instructed to submit this result, create a paper or electronic printout. Include the project, activity, and step number in the file name if you create an electronic printout. On the **PRINT PREVIEW tab**, in the **Close Preview group**, click the **Close Print Preview** button.

5 On the **DATABASE TOOLS tab**, in the **Analyze group**, click the **Database Documenter** button. In the **Documenter** dialog box, click the **Forms tab**. Click the **Options** button. In the **Print Form Definition** dialog box, if necessary, clear the check boxes for **Properties** and **Permissions by User and Group**, and then click **OK**.

6 In the **Documenter** dialog box, click the **8A Employee Information Form** check box.

This form has an embedded macro.

7 In the **Documenter** dialog box, click **OK**. In the **Object Definition** print preview, zoom in, and then scroll up to display the top of the first page, noticing that the report displays properties of the **8A Employee Information Form**. Click the **Next Page** button **three** times. Scroll down to display the bottom half of the page. Compare your screen with Figure 8.26.

The properties of the Dept Info button—Command Button: btnDeptInfo—display.

FIGURE 8.26

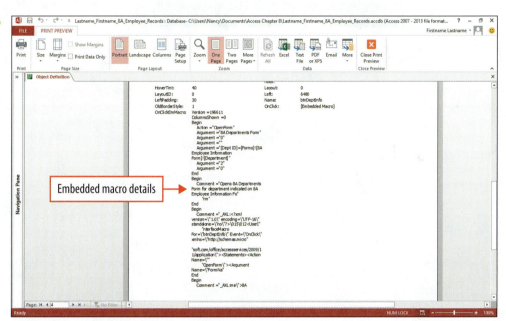

Embedded macro details

8 If you are instructed to submit this result, create a paper or electronic printout of page 4 only. Include the project, activity, and step number in the file name if you create an electronic printout. On the **PRINT PREVIEW tab**, in the **Close Preview group**, click the **Close Print Preview** button.

9 On the **DATABASE TOOLS tab**, in the **Analyze group**, click the **Database Documenter** button. In the **Documenter** dialog box, if necessary, click the **Reports tab**. Click the **Options** button. In the **Print Report Definition** dialog box, if necessary, clear the check boxes for **Properties** and **Permissions by User and Group**, and then click **OK**.

10 In the **Documenter** dialog box, click the **8A Employee Status Report** check box, and then click **OK**.

11 In the **Object Definition** print preview, zoom in, and click the **Next Page** button **four** times. Scroll down to display the bottom of the page.

The OnClick property displays the embedded macro.

12 If you are instructed to submit this result, create a paper or electronic printout of page 5 only. Include the project, activity, and step number in the file name if you create an electronic printout. On the **PRINT PREVIEW tab**, in the **Close Preview group**, click the **Close Print Preview** button.

13 Open » the **Navigation Pane. Close** ⊠ the database, and then **Exit** Access.

14 As directed by your instructor, submit your database and the paper or electronic printouts of the three Database Documenter reports that are the results of this project. Specifically, in this project, using your own name you created the following database and printouts or electronic printouts:

1. Lastname_Firstname_8A_Employee_Records	Database file
2. Lastname_Firstname_8A_Activity8.07_Step4	Database Documenter report (printed or electronic printout)
3. Lastname_Firstname_8A_Activity8.07_Step8	Database Documenter report (printed or electronic printout)
4. Lastname_Firstname_8A_Activity8.07_Step12	Database Documenter report (printed or electronic printout)

END | You have completed Project 8A

Employee Benefits

PROJECT ACTIVITIES

In Activities 8.08 through 8.12, you will help Margo Dalton, vice president of operations for Providence and Warwick Hospital, create a macro group. She also wants to add buttons on the form to automate some of the most common tasks, such as finding a training session. When completed, your results will look similar to Figure 8.27.

PROJECT FILES

For Project 8B, you will need the following file:

a08B_Employee_Benefits

You will save your database as:

Lastname_Firstname_8B_Employee_Benefits

PROJECT RESULTS

FIGURE 8.27 Project 8B Employee Benefits

Video A8-5

In the previous activities, you created a standalone macro with one action and another standalone macro with multiple actions. As you continue to create more macros, you may want to group related macros by creating a *macro group*. A macro group is a set of submacros grouped by a common name that displays as one macro object in the Navigation Pane. For example, you might want to create a macro group that opens several forms or reports in a database.

Activity 8.08 | Creating the First Macro in a Macro Group

In this activity, you will create the first macro in the macro group that will open the *8B Search Sessions Dialog Box* form.

1 ▶ Start Access. Navigate to the location where the student data files for this textbook are saved. Locate and open the **a08B_Employee_Benefits** file. **Save** the database in your **Access Chapter 8** folder as **Lastname_Firstname_8B_Employee_Benefits**

2 ▶ In the **Navigation Pane**, under **Forms**, double-click **8B Session Details**, and then double-click **8B Search Sessions Dialog Box** to open the forms in **Form** view. Point to the title bar of the **Search Sessions Dialog Box**, and then drag the pop-up form downward and to the right until, on the **8B Session Details** form, the Find Session button under the title displays. Compare your screen with Figure 8.28.

In this activity, you will create a macro group that executes and opens the *8B Search Sessions Dialog Box* form when a user clicks the Find Session button on the *8B Session Details* form.

FIGURE 8.28

3 ▶ Close ⊗ the **Search Sessions Dialog Box**, and then **Close** ⊗ the **8B Session Details** form. **Close** ⊗ the **Navigation Pane**.

4 ▶ On the **CREATE tab**, in the **Macros & Code group**, click the **Macro button**. On the **MACRO TOOLS DESIGN tab**, in the **Show/Hide group**, click the **Show All Actions** button.

Recall that the Show All Actions button displays trusted and untrusted macro actions.

5 ▶ In the **Action Catalog pane**, double-click **Group**. In the **Macro Designer**, in the **Group** box, type **8B Find Session Macro Group** to identify the group. Add the following comment: **Purpose: To enable the user to search for a specific session in the 8B Session Details form**

It is a good practice to start a macro group with a name and the purpose of the macro group.

6 ▶ In the **Action Catalog pane**, double-click **Submacro** and type **OpenSearchDialogBox**

In macro groups, submacro names are needed to distinguish the individual macros from one another. Within a macro group, the submacro name is entered before the macro actions in each submacro. The macro ends when *end submacro* is encountered. Macro names are limited to 64 characters. Because macros perform an action or actions, it is good practice to start the name of the macro with a verb—in this case, *Open*.

7 In the **Submacro**, using one of the techniques you have learned, add an **OpenForm** action. In the **OpenForm Action Block**, click the **Form Name arrow**, and then click **8B Search Sessions Dialog Box**. Click the **Data Mode arrow**, and then click **Edit**. Add the following comment: **Opens the 8B Search Sessions Dialog Box form** Compare your screen with Figure 8.29.

> Editing is enabled so that the user can enter a Session name in the combo box on the *8B Search Sessions Dialog Box* form. Because the form property has been set to open as a pop-up window, the Window Mode setting of Normal is appropriate.

FIGURE 8.29

8 **Save** the macro group as **Lastname Firstname 8B Find Session Macro Group**

9 On the **DATABASE TOOLS tab**, in the **Macro group**, click the **Run Macro** button, and then, in the **Macro Name** list, click the **arrow**, and then click **8B Find Session Macro Group. OpenSearchDialogBox**. Click **OK**, and then **Close** ☒ the form.

> Because the macro is associated with a Macro group, it must be run using the Run Macro button on the DATABASE TOOLS tab. Keep in mind that some macro actions are dependent upon other macro actions that have previously executed, and independently, a macro action may not execute properly if run out of order.

Activity 8.09 | Creating a Second Macro in a Macro Group

In this activity, you will create a second macro in the macro group that will check to see if a value is entered for the Session name in the *8B Search Sessions Dialog Box*, hide the *8B Search Sessions Dialog Box* form, change the focus to the *8B Session Details* form, select the title of the Session on the *8B Session Details* form, sort the records by the Session name, find the requested Session, close the *8B Search Sessions Dialog Box* form, and display a message to the user with a reminder to display all of the records.

1 In the **Macro Designer**, in the **Action Catalog pane**, double-click **Submacro** and type **SearchForSession** In the **Action Catalog pane**, double-click **If**.

> The If Action Argument block displays in the SearchForSession submacro to control the program flow. In some macros, an action should execute only if a condition is true. For example, if the user does not select a value in the combo box on the *8B Search Sessions Dialog Box* form, the macro should not execute.

2 In the **Submacro**, to the right of the **If** textbox, click the **Build** 🛠 button. In the **Expression Builder** dialog box, type **IsNull([Forms]![8B Search Sessions Dialog Box]![SessionName])** selecting items as they appear in the list to reduce errors. Compare your screen with Figure 8.30.

> The expression used for the condition checks the SessionName combo box in the *8B Search Sessions Dialog Box* form to determine if the combo box is blank—IsNull. Recall that the exclamation (!) mark is the bang operator that separates the object type from the object name.

FIGURE 8.30

3 In the **Expression Builder** dialog box, click **OK**. In the **If Arguments Block**, add the **CloseWindow** action using one of the techniques you have learned. In the **CloseWindow Action Block**, click the **Object Type arrow**, and then click **Form**. Click the **Object Name arrow**, and then click **8B Search Sessions Dialog Box**. Click the **Save arrow**, and then click **No**. Add the following comment: **If a session is not selected, then close the 8B Search Sessions Dialog Box form**

If Access finds that the Sessions combo box is blank, it will close the *8B Search Sessions Dialog Box* form without saving changes made to the form. Recall that the warning symbol in the row selector box indicates that this Macro Action is not trusted.

4 In the **If Arguments Block**, add the **StopMacro** action. Notice that there are no action arguments for the **StopMacro** action. Add the following comment: **Exits the macro**

If the Sessions combo box is blank, and the form closes, the macro stops executing.

5 In the **Macro Designer**, click the **Submacro:SearchForSession** textbox to activate the **Add New Action bar** below the **End If** label. Add the **SetValue** action. In the **SetValue Action Block**, to the right of the **Item** text box, click the **Build** button to open the **Expression Builder**. Compare your screen with Figure 8.31.

The SetValue macro action is an untrusted action used to set the value of a field, control, or property on a form, a form datasheet, or a report. The item is the name of the field, control, or property whose value you want to set. You must use the full syntax to refer to the item—do not just type the field, control, or property name. *Syntax* refers to the spelling, grammar, and sequence of characters of a programming language.

The operator buttons and list boxes in the Expression Builder can help you build the expression using correct syntax. As you select an object in the first list box, the second and third list boxes will populate. In the first list box, the plus sign (+) next to an object indicates that more items display under the object; click the plus sign (+) or double-click the object name to expand the list. The minus sign (−) indicates that the list under the object is fully expanded. Click the minus sign (−) or double-click the object name to collapse the list.

FIGURE 8.31

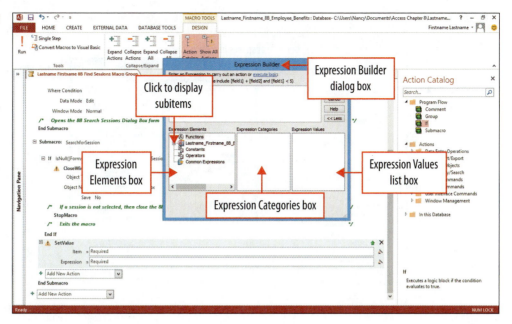

6 In the **Expression Builder** dialog box, in the **Expression Elements** list box, click the plus sign to the left of **Lastname_Firstname_8B_Employee_Benefits.accdb** to display the list of objects in the database—use the horizontal scroll bar to display the entire name of the database. Double-click **Forms** to expand the list, and double-click **All Forms**. Scroll down, and then click **8B Search Sessions Dialog Box**—use the horizontal scroll bar to display the entire name of the form.

The Expression Categories list box displays controls on the form. The Expression Values list box displays property settings and Sessions that can be associated with the form or the controls on the form. An *event* is any action that can be detected by a program or computer system, such as clicking a button or closing an object. Selecting an object in the Expression Categories list box causes the values or Sessions in the Expression Values list box to change, because different objects have different property settings or Sessions associated with them.

7 In the **Expression Categories** list box, verify that **<Form>** is selected. In the **Expression Values** list box, scroll down, double-click **Visible**, and then compare your screen with Figure 8.32.

The Expression Builder displays the correct syntax for the Visible property of the *8B Search Sessions Dialog Box*, which is a form. Instead of using the Expression Builder, you can type the expression in the Item box in the Action Block. An advantage of using the Expression Builder is that Access will insert square brackets and parentheses where they are required.

FIGURE 8.32

Square brackets required because of spaces in form name

Type of object

Property of object

Object name

8 In the **Expression Builder**, click **OK**. In the **SetValue Action Block**, click in the **Expression** box, and then type **False**

This macro action sets the Visible property setting of the *8B Search Sessions Dialog Box* form to False; in other words, it will hide the *8B Search Sessions Dialog Box* form.

9 Add the following comment: **Hides the 8B Search Sessions Dialog Box form** Compare your screen with Figure 8.33.

FIGURE 8.33

Property setting is changed

Sets Visible property to False—hides the form

SetValue is an untrusted action

10 In the **Submacro**, add the **SelectObject** action. In the **SelectObject Action Block**, click the **Object Type arrow**, and then click **Form**. Click the **Object Name arrow**, and then click **8B Session Details**. Verify that the **In Database Window** box displays **No**. Add the following comment: **Changes the focus to the 8B Session Details form**

The SelectObject action is used to put the focus on a specified database object so that an action can be applied to that object. Recall that the *8B Session Details* form is automatically opened when the database is opened. Therefore, the In Database Window setting should be set to No. If the form is not open, Access needs to open it from the Navigation Pane, and the In Database Window setting should be set to Yes.

So far, the macro group will open the *8B Search Sessions Dialog Box* form and then check to see if the Sessions field displays data. If not, the macro stops executing. If data is displayed in the Sessions field, the *8B Search Sessions Dialog Box* form will be hidden, and the focus will shift to the *8B Session Details* form.

11 In the **Submacro**, add the **GoToControl** action. In the **GoToControl Action Block**, in the **Control Name** box, type **Title** Add the following comment: **Places focus on Title field on 8B Session Details form** Compare your screen with Figure 8.34.

In the previous action, the focus was changed to the *8B Session Details* form. With this action, the focus is placed on a specific text box control named *Title* on that form.

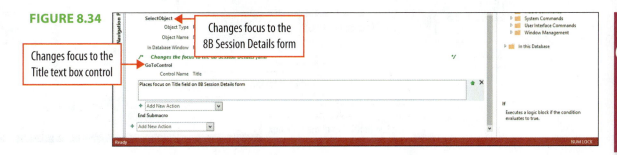

FIGURE 8.34

Changes focus to the 8B Session Details form

Changes focus to the Title text box control

12 ▶ In the **Submacro**, add the **RunMenuCommand** action. In the **RunMenuCommand Action Block**, click the **Command box arrow**, scroll down, and then click **SortAscending**. Add the following comment: **Sorts the session name (Title) in ascending order**

    The RunMenuCommand action is used to execute an Access command, such as Sort Ascending or Save a Record.

13 ▶ In the **Submacro**, add the **FindRecord** action. In the **FindWhat** box, type **=[Forms]![8B Search Sessions Dialog Box]![SessionName]** selecting items as they appear in the list to reduce errors. Verify that you have entered the expression correctly. Click the **Match box arrow**, and then click **Start of Field**. Point to each of the other Action Arguments boxes, reading the description of each argument and being sure not to change any of the settings. Add the following comment: **Finds the Title on the 8B Session Details form that matches the entry in the SessionName combo box on the 8B Search Sessions Dialog Box form** and then compare your screen with Figure 8.35.

    The FindRecord action locates the first or next record that meets the specified search criteria; in this case, the data in the SessionName field of the *8B Search Sessions Dialog Box* form must match the data in the Title field of the *8B Session Details* form. This macro action is similar to using the Find button on the HOME tab.

FIGURE 8.35

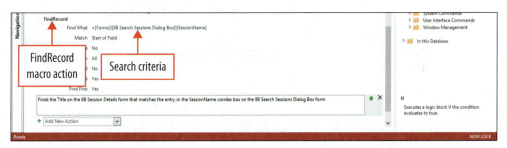

FindRecord macro action

Search criteria

14 ▶ In the **Submacro**, add the **CloseWindow** action. In the **CloseWindow Action Block**, click the **Object Type arrow**, and then click **Form**. Click the **Object Name arrow**, and then click **8B Search Sessions Dialog Box**. Verify that **Prompt** appears in the **Save** box. Add the following comment: **Closes 8B Search Sessions Dialog Box form**

    The Close action closes a specified object. If no object is specified in the Object Name box, the active object is closed.

15 ▶ In the **Submacro**, add the **MessageBox** action. In the **MessageBox Action Block**, click in the **Message** box, and then type **To display the records in their original sort order: On the HOME tab, in the Sort & Filter group, click the Remove Sort button.** Click the **Type box arrow**, and then click **Information**. Click in the **Title** box, and then type **Search for Session Name** Add the following comment: **Displays a message with instructions for clearing the sort** Compare your screen with Figure 8.36.

    Recall that if an individual filters or sorts records and closes the database, when the database is reopened, the filter or sort is still applied to the object.

FIGURE 8.36

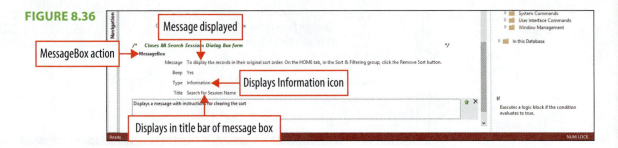

FIGURE 8.36

Message displayed

MessageBox action

Displays Information icon

Displays in title bar of message box

> **16** **Save** the macro group.

Activity 8.10 | Creating a Third Macro in a Macro Group

In this activity, you will create a third and final macro in the macro group that will close the *8B Session Name Search* form.

> **1** In the **Macro Designer**, in the **Action Catalog pane**, double-click **Submacro**, and type **CancelSearch** to name the macro. Add the **CloseWindow** action. In the **CloseWindow Action Block**, click the **Object Type arrow**, and then click **Form**. Click the **Object Name arrow**, and then click **8B Search Sessions Dialog Box**. Verify that **Prompt** appears in the **Save** box. Add the following comment: **Closes 8B Search Sessions Dialog Box form when search is cancelled**

> This macro will be used to close the *8B Search Sessions Dialog Box* form when the Cancel button on the form is clicked.

> **2** In the **Submacro**, add the **SelectObject** action. In the **SelectObject Action Block**, click the **Object Type arrow**, and then click **Form**. Click the **Object Name arrow**, and then click **8B Session Details**. Verify that the **In Database Window** box displays **No**. Add the following comment: **Changes the focus to 8B Session Details form** Compare your screen with Figure 8.37.

> After the *8B Search Sessions Dialog Box* form is closed, the focus is placed on the *8B Session Details* form.

FIGURE 8.37

Closes 8B Search Sessions Dialog Box form

Third macro in macro group

Changes focus to 8B Session Details form

> **3** **Save** the macro group. **Close** ☒ the **Macro Designer**, **Open** ☒ the **Navigation Pane**, and notice that under **Macros**, the macro group displays as one macro object.

> Double-clicking the macro does not cause this macro to execute because the macro has not been associated with the buttons on the *8B Session Details* form or the *8B Search Sessions Dialog Box* form.

Video A8-6

Recall that a session is any action that can be detected by a program or computer system, such as clicking a button or closing an object. For example, clicking the Find Session button on the 8B Session Details form causes a system session, upon which Access can execute a macro.

Activity 8.11 | Associating a Command Button with a Macro

In this activity, you will associate clicking the Find Session button on the *8B Session Details* form with a macro—the *8B Find Session Macro Group* macro. Clicking the Find Session button will cause the macro to execute.

1 In the **Navigation Pane**, under **Forms**, double-click **8B Session Details** to display the form in **Form** view. On the form, click the **Find Session** button, and notice that nothing happens because the button is not associated with any session.

2 Close « the **Navigation Pane**, and then switch the form to **Design** view. In the **Form Header section**, right-click the **Find Session** button, and then click **Properties**. Verify that the **Property Sheet** displays *Selection type: Command Button* and that the **Selection type** box displays *cmdFindSession*.

3 On the **Property Sheet**, click the **Event tab**, if necessary. Click the **On Click property setting arrow**. Notice that the complete names of some of the macros do not display. Point to the **left edge** of the **Property Sheet** until the pointer ↔ displays. Drag to the left to the **6.5-inch mark on the horizontal ruler** or until the complete names display. Click the **On Click property setting arrow**, and then compare your screen with Figure 8.38.

All of the macros that have been created display in the list.

FIGURE 8.38

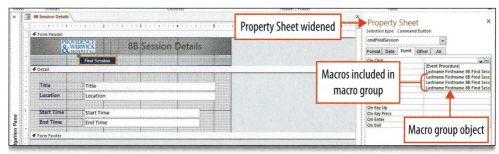

4 In the displayed list, click **8B Find Session Macro Group.OpenSearchDialogBox**.

When you click on the Find Session button in the *8B Session Details* form, the OpenSearchDialogBox macro in the *8B Find Session Macro Group* will execute.

5 On the **Property Sheet**, click the **Format tab**. In the **Caption** property setting box, click to the left of **Find Session**, and then type **&**

Recall that the ampersand (&) causes the letter that follows it to be underlined on the button, which will enable the user to use a shortcut key combination (Alt + the letter) to access the button instead of clicking on the button.

6 Close × the **Property Sheet**, **Save** the form, and then switch to **Form** view. Notice that on the **Find Session** button, the letter **F** is underscored, which indicates that pressing Alt + F is the same action as clicking on the button.

7 Click the **Find Session** button, and then compare your screen with Figure 8.39.

The Search Sessions dialog box displays, which is the *8B Search Sessions Dialog Box* form.

FIGURE 8.39

8 Close ⊠ the **Search Sessions** dialog box.

ALERT!   **Did the Find and Replace Dialog Box Display?**

If you use the shortcut key and the Find and Replace dialog box displays instead of the Search Sessions dialog box, you held down Ctrl instead of Alt.

9 Do not close the **8B Session Details** form. **Open** » the **Navigation Pane**. Under **Forms**, right-click **8B Search Sessions Dialog Box** and then click **Design View**. **Close** « the **Navigation Pane**.

10 Right-click the **OK** button, and then click **Properties**. On the **Property Sheet**, click the **Event tab**. Click the **On Click property setting arrow**, and then click **8B Find Session Macro Group. SearchForSession**. On the **Property Sheet**, click the **Format tab**. In the **Caption** box, click to the left of **OK**, and then type **& Close** the **Property Sheet**. **Save** the form, and then switch the form to **Form** view.

> When the OK button is clicked or the user presses Alt + O, the second macro in the *8B Find Session Macro Group* executes.

11 In the **Enter a Session Name combo box**, click the **arrow**, and then click **Eye Care Plan**. Click **OK**, and then compare your screen with Figure 8.40.

> The macro executes, the *8B Session Details* form displays the first record—Record 3—with a session name (Title) of Eye Care Plan, and a message box displays, telling you to click the Remove Sort button to display the records in the original sort order.

FIGURE 8.40

12 In the displayed message box, click **OK**. Press Alt + F to display the **Search Sessions** dialog box. In the **Search Sessions** dialog box, in the **Enter a Session Name combo box**, type **pr** and notice that Access displays Prescription Plan. Press Alt + O. In the displayed message box, click **OK**.

> Instead of selecting an item from the list, you can type the first few letters of the Session name. If Access finds the Session name in the list, it displays in the combo box. Record 7 is displayed.

13 On the **HOME tab**, in the **Sort & Filter** group, click the **Remove Sort** button.

---

14 Open ⟩⟩ the **Navigation Pane**. Under **Forms**, open the **8B Search Sessions Dialog Box** form in **Design** view, and then **Close** ⟪ the **Navigation Pane**.

15 Right-click the **Cancel** button, and then click **Properties**. On the **Property Sheet**, click the **Event tab**, click the **On Click property setting arrow**, and then click **8B Find Session Macro Group.CancelSearch**. Click the **Property Sheet Format tab**. In the **Caption** property setting box, click to the left of **Cancel**, type **&** and then **Close** ⨯ the **Property Sheet**. **Save** the form, and then switch the form to **Form** view.

> Clicking the Cancel button on the *8B Search Sessions Dialog Box* form causes the third macro in the macro group to execute.

16 In the **Search Sessions** dialog box, click the **Cancel** button. Alternatively, press ⎇Alt + C.

> The form closes, and the focus is placed on the 8B Session Details form.

17 **Close** the **8B Session Details** form.

18 On the **DATABASE TOOLS tab**, in the **Analyze group**, click the **Database Documenter** button.

> The Documenter dialog box displays tabs for each object type and a tab for the current database. Only standalone macros display on the Macros tab. Macros that are run are embedded with an object and will display as a property of the object.

19 In the **Documenter** dialog box, if necessary, click the **Macros tab**. Click the **Options** button. If necessary, click the **Permissions by User and Group** check box to clear it, and then click **OK**. In the **Documenter** dialog box, click the **Select All** button. Click **OK**.

20 Click in the middle of the document to zoom in to display the details of the **8B Find Session Macro Group** macro.

21 If you are instructed to submit this result, create a paper or electronic printout. Include the project, activity, and step number in the file name if you create an electronic printout. On the **PRINT PREVIEW tab**, in the **Close Preview group**, click the **Close Print Preview** button. Open ⟩⟩ the **Navigation Pane**.

Objective 7 | Create a Data Macro

Video A8-7

You have created macros using the Macro Designer and Macro Builder. Data macros are created and managed while you are viewing a table in Datasheet view. A ***data macro*** is a macro that is triggered by events, such as adding, updating, or deleting data within a table, form, or query. The macro is used to validate the accuracy of data in a table. It is also known as an event-driven macro.

Activity 8.12 | Creating an Event-Driven Macro

In this activity, you will create an event-driven macro to determine the status of each session based on the # Enrolled.

1 In the **Navigation Pane**, under **Tables**, double-click **8B Sessions** to display the table in **Datasheet** view. Review the data displayed in the table. **Close** « the **Navigation Pane**.

The # Enrolled field displays how many employees have signed up for the session, and the Capacity field displays the maximum capacity in that room. The Status field will be used to display whether the session is still open for enrollment.

2 On the **TABLE TOOLS TABLE tab**, in the **Before Events** group, click the **Before Change** button to display the **Macro Designer**.

3 In the **Macro Designer**, add the **If** action using one of the techniques you have learned. In the **If Action Block**, click in the **If** box, and type **[# Enrolled]>=[Capacity]** selecting items as they appear in the list to reduce errors.

The Conditional expression comparison is used to determine the action that will occur.

4 In the **If Arguments Block**, add the **SetField** action using one of the techniques you have learned. In the **SetField Action Block**, click in the **Name** box, and type **Status** Click in the **Value** box, and type **"Closed"** and then compare your screen with Figure 8.41.

The SetField action will update the *Status* field if the condition is true.

FIGURE 8.41

5 In the **If Arguments Block**, click the **Add Else** hyperlink on the right of the screen to add an additional condition to the If Arguments block. In the **Else Arguments Block**, add the **SetField** action using one of the techniques you have learned. In the **SetField Action Block**, click in the **Name** box, and type **Status** Click in the **Value** box, and type **"Open"**

The SetField action will update the *Status* field if the original Conditional expression is false.

6 **Close** × the **Macro Designer**. In the displayed message box, click **Yes** to save the changes made to the macro and to update the property. **Save** 🖫 the table.

7 In Record 7, click in the **# Enrolled** field, and type **30**. Press ↓ to move to the next record, and type **22** and click in the first **ID** field. Notice the updates to the **Status** field. Compare your screen with Figure 8.42.

FIGURE 8.42

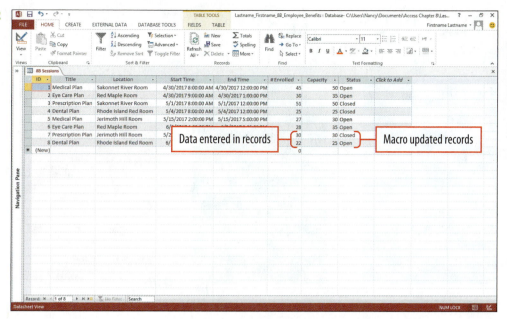

8 ▸ View the table in **Print Preview**. On the **PRINT PREVIEW tab**, in the **Page Layout group**, click the **Landscape** button. If you are instructed to submit this result, create a paper or electronic printout. On the **PRINT PREVIEW tab**, in the **Close Preview group**, click the **Close Print Preview** button.

9 ▸ **Close** ⊠ the database, and then **Exit** Access.

10 ▸ As directed by your instructor, submit your database and the paper or electronic printouts of the Planning and Managing Your Career two objects—one Database Documenter report and one table—that are the results of this project. Specifically, in this project, using your own name you created the following database and printouts or electronic printouts:

1. Lastname_Firstname_8B_Employee_Benefits	Database file
2. Lastname_Firstname_8B_Activity8.11_Step21	Database Documenter report (printed or electronic printout)
3. 8B Sessions	Table (printed or electronic printout)

END | You have completed Project 8B

END OF CHAPTER

SUMMARY

Macros are created to automate database tasks. A database must be trusted in order for all macro actions to be enabled. The Database Documenter is used to print details of objects, including macros.

Standalone macros can run from the Navigation Pane. An autoexec macro runs automatically when the database is opened. Macros can also be embedded within buttons; embedded macros do not display in the Navigation Pane.

A macro group is a set of submacros grouped together and displayed as a single macro in the Navigation Pane. Submacros can then be associated with a macro with the clicking of a button on a form or report.

Data macros are associated with a table and triggered by events, such as adding, updating, or deleting data in a table, form, or query. Data macros are used to validate the accuracy of data in a table.

GO! LEARN IT ONLINE

Review the concepts and key terms in this chapter by completing these online challenges, which you can find at **www.pearsonhighered.com/go**.

Matching and Multiple Choice:
Answer matching and multiple choice questions to test what you learned in this chapter. MyITLab®

Crossword Puzzle:
Spell out the words that match the numbered clues, and put them in the puzzle squares.

Flipboard:
Flip through the definitions of the key terms in this chapter and match them with the correct term.

END OF CHAPTER

REVIEW AND ASSESSMENT GUIDE FOR ACCESS CHAPTER 8

Your instructor may assign one or more of these projects to help you review the chapter and assess your mastery and understanding of the chapter.

	Review and Assessment Guide for Access Chapter 8		
Project	**Apply Skills from These Chapter Objectives**	**Project Type**	**Project Location**
8C	Objectives 1–4 from Project 8A	**8C Skills Review** A guided review of the skills from Project 8A.	On the following pages
8D	Objectives 5–7 from Project 8B	**8D Skills Review** A guided review of the skills from Project 8B.	On the following pages
8E	Objectives 1–4 from Project 8A	**8E Mastery (Grader Project)** A demonstration of your mastery of the skills in Project 8A with extensive decision making.	In MyITLab and on the following pages
8F	Objectives 5–7 from Project 8B	**8F Mastery (Grader Project)** A demonstration of your mastery of the skills in Project 8B with extensive decision making.	In MyITLab and on the following pages
8G	Objectives 1–7 from Projects 8A and 8B	**8G Mastery (Grader Project)** A demonstration of your mastery of the skills in Projects 8A and 8B with extensive decision making.	In MyITLab and on the following pages
8H	Combination of Objectives from Projects 8A and 8B	**8H GO! Fix It** A demonstration of your mastery of the skills in Projects 8A and 8B by creating a correct result from a document that contains errors you must find.	Online
8I	Combination of Objectives from Projects 8A and 8B	**8I GO! Make It** A demonstration of your mastery of the skills in Projects 8A and 8B by creating a result from a supplied picture.	Online
8J	Combination of Objectives from Projects 8A and 8B	**8J GO! Solve It** A demonstration of your mastery of the skills in Projects 8A and 8B, your decision-making skills, and your critical thinking skills. A task-specific rubric helps you self-assess your result.	Online
8K	Combination of Objectives from Projects 8A and 8B	**8K GO! Solve It** A demonstration of your mastery of the skills in Projects 8A and 8B, your decision-making skills, and your critical thinking skills. A task-specific rubric helps you self-assess your result.	On the following pages
8L	Combination of Objectives from Projects 8A and 8B	**8L GO! Think** A demonstration of your understanding of the chapter concepts applied in a manner that you would use outside of college. An analytic rubric helps you and your instructor grade the quality of your work by comparing it to the work an expert in the discipline would create.	On the following pages
8M	Combination of Objectives from Projects 8A and 8B	**8M GO! Think** A demonstration of your understanding of the chapter concepts applied in a manner that you would use outside of college. An analytic rubric helps you and your instructor grade the quality of your work by comparing it to the work an expert in the discipline would create.	Online
8N	Combination of Objectives from Projects 8A and 8B	**8N You and GO!** A demonstration of your understanding of the chapter concepts applied in a manner that you would use in a personal situation. An analytic rubric helps you and your instructor grade the quality of your work.	Online

GLOSSARY

GLOSSARY OF CHAPTER KEY TERMS

Action A self-contained instruction that can be combined with other actions to automate tasks.

Argument A value that provides information to the macro action, such as the words to display in a message box, or the control upon which to operate.

Code Builder A window used to type programming code in Microsoft Visual Basic.

Condition A statement that specifies that certain criteria must be met before the macro action executes.

Data macro A macro that is triggered by events, such as adding, updating, or deleting data within a table, form, or query. It is used to validate the accuracy of data in a table; also known as an event-driven macro.

Database Documenter An option used to create a report that contains detailed information about the objects in a database, including macros, and to create a paper record.

Debugging A logical process to find and reduce the number of errors in a program.

Embedded macro A macro that is stored in the Session properties of forms, reports, or controls.

Event Any action that can be detected by a program or computer system, such as clicking a button or closing an object.

Macro A series of actions grouped as a single command to accomplish a task or multiple tasks automatically.

Macro Designer Window that allows you to build the list of actions to be carried out when the macro runs.

Macro group A set of macros grouped by a common name that displays as one macro object on the Navigation Pane.

Modal window A child (secondary) window to a parent window—the original window that opened the modal window—that takes over control of the parent window.

Pop-up window A window that suddenly displays (pops up), usually contains a menu of commands, and stays on the screen only until the user selects one of the commands.

Single stepping Debugging a macro using a process that executes one action at a time.

Standalone macro A macro contained in a macro object that displays under Macros on the Navigation Pane.

Syntax The spelling, grammar, and sequence of characters of a programming language.

CHAPTER REVIEW

ACCESS

8

Margo Dalton, vice president of operations for Providence and Warwick Hospital, wants to customize her database of supervisory staff. In this project, you will create macros to automatically display a form and message box when the database is opened and embed macros within a form. Finally, you will display and print a report that documents the details of the macros you created. Your completed work will look similar to Figure 8.43.

PROJECT FILES

For Project 8C, you will need the following file:

a08C_Supervisory_Staff

You will save your database as:

Lastname_Firstname_8C_Supervisory_Staff

PROJECT RESULTS

FIGURE 8.43

(Project 8C Supervisory Staff continues on the next page)

CHAPTER REVIEW

1 Start Access. Locate and open the **a08C_Supervisory_Staff** file. Save the database in your **Access Chapter 8** folder as **Lastname_Firstname_8C_Supervisory_Staff** and then **Close** the Navigation Pane.

2 On the **CREATE tab**, in the **Macros & Code group**, click the **Macro button**.

a. In the **Macro Designer**, in the **Add New Action bar**, click the **arrow**, and then click **OpenReport**. In the **OpenReport Action Block**, in the **Report Name** box, click the **arrow**, and then click **8C Supervisory Staff**. In the **View** box, verify that **Report** is selected. The **Filter Name** and **Where Condition** boxes should be blank. In the **Window Mode** box, verify that the setting is **Normal**.

b. In the **Action Catalog pane**, double-click **Comment**, and type **Opens 8C Supervisory Staff report in Report view**

c. On the **MACRO TOOLS DESIGN tab**, in the **Tools group**, click the **Run** button. In the displayed message box, click **Yes** to save the macro. In the **Save As** dialog box, type **Lastname Firstname 8C Open Supervisory Staff report** and then click **OK**. **Close** the **8C Supervisory Staff** report, and then **Close** the Macro Designer.

3 **Open** the Navigation Pane. Under **Forms**, right-click **8C Intro Screen**, and then click **Design View**. On the **FORM DESIGN TOOLS DESIGN tab**, in the **Tools group**, click the **Property Sheet** button. On the **Property Sheet Other tab**, click the **Pop Up property setting arrow**, and then click **Yes**. Click in the **Modal** property setting box, click the **arrow**, and then click **Yes**. **Close** the **Property Sheet**, and then **Close** the form, saving changes when prompted. **Close** the Navigation Pane.

4 On the **CREATE tab**, in the **Macros & Code group**, click the **Macro button**.

a. In the **Macro Designer**, add the **OpenForm** action. In the **OpenForm Action Block**, click the **Form Name arrow**, and then click **8C Intro Screen**. Add the following comment: **Opens 8C Intro Screen form**

b. On the **Quick Access Toolbar**, click the **Save** button. In the **Save As** dialog box, type **autoexec** and then click **OK**. **Close** the Macro Designer, and then **Open**

the Navigation Pane. In the **Navigation Pane**, under click **autoexec** to run the macro. **Close** the form.

5 In, .txt file, the **Navigation Pane**, under **Macros**, right-click **Autoexec**, and then click **Design View**. **Close** the Navigation Pane.

a. Add the **DisplayHourglassPointer** action. Notice that the default argument is *Yes*. Add the following comment: **Turns mouse pointer into a Busy icon**

b. On the **MACRO TOOLS DESIGN tab**, in the **Show/Hide group**, click the **Show All Actions** button. In the **Macro Designer**, add the **Echo** action. In the **Echo Action Block**, click the **Echo On arrow**, and then click **No**. Click in the **Status Bar Text** box, and type **Macro is running** Add the following comment: **Hides the flickering screen as the macro runs**

c. Add the **RunMacro** action. In the **RunMacro Action Block**, click the **Macro Name arrow**, and then click **8C Open Supervisory Staff Report**. The **Repeat Count** box and the **Repeat Expression** box should be blank. Add the following comment: **Runs 8C Open Supervisory Staff Report macro**

d. Add the **MessageBox** action. In the **MessageBox Action Block**, click in the **Message** box, and then type **Only supervisors at Providence & Warwick Hospital are authorized to access this database.** In the **Beep** box, verify that the Beep argument is **Yes**. Click the **Type box arrow**, and then click **Warning!** Click in the **Title** box, and then type **For Use by Providence & Warwick Hospital Supervisors Only!** Add the following comment: **Displays a warning message box**

e. In the **Macro Designer**, add the **DisplayHourglassPointer** action. In the **DisplayHourglassPointer Action Block**, click the **Hourglass On arrow**, and then click **No**. Add the following comment: **Restores the mouse pointer**

f. Add the **Echo** action. Add the following comment: **Displays screen results**

g. Scroll to the top of the **Action Argument** box. Click the **OpenForm** action to make it active, and then move the action below the comment **Runs 8C Open Supervisory Staff Report**

h. Move the **OpenForm macro comment** below the **OpenForm action**.

(Project 8C Supervisory Staff continues on the next page)

CHAPTER REVIEW

i. **Save** the macro. On the **MACRO TOOLS DESIGN tab**, in the **Tools group**, click the **Run** button. In the displayed message box, click **OK**. **Close** the **8C Intro Screen** form. On the **tab row**, right-click any tab, and then click **Close All**. **Open** the **Navigation Pane**.

6 ▶ Open the **8C Supervisors Form** in **Design** view. **Close** the **Navigation Pane**. On the **FORM DESIGN TOOLS DESIGN tab**, in the **Controls group**, click the **Button** button. In the **Details** section, align the plus sign (+) of the pointer at **3 inches on the horizontal ruler** and **2 inches on the vertical ruler**, and then click.

a. In the **Command Button Wizard** dialog box, click **Cancel**.

b. Right-click the button, and then click **Properties**. Verify that the **Property Sheet** displays *Selection type: Command Button* and the **Selection type** box displays *Command0*, identifying your command button. On the **Property Sheet Other tab**, in the **Name** property box, select the existing text and type **btnEmpl**

c. On the **Property Sheet Format tab**, in the **Caption** property box, select the existing text and type **Employee List** and press Enter.

d. On the **Property Sheet Event tab**, in the **On Click** property setting box, click the **Build** button.

e. In the **Choose Builder** dialog box, click **Macro Builder**, if necessary, and then click **OK** to display the Macro Designer.

f. In the **Macro Designer**, add the **OpenForm** action using one of the techniques you have learned. In the **OpenForm Action Block**, click the **Form Name arrow**, and then click **8C Employees**. Click in the **Where Condition** box, and type **[Department]=[Forms]![8C Supervisors]![Department]** selecting items as they appear in the list to reduce errors.

g. In the **OpenForm Action Block**, click the **View arrow**, and then click **Datasheet**. Click the **Data Mode arrow**, and then click **Read Only**. Add the following comment: **Opens 8C Employees form for department indicated on 8C Supervisors form**

h. **Close** the **Macro Designer**. In the displayed message box, click **Yes** to save the changes made to the macro and to update the **On Click** property.

7 On the **Property Sheet**, click the **Format tab**. In the **Caption** box, click to the left of **Employee List**, and then type **&** to create a shortcut key using the letter *E*. **Close** the **Property Sheet**, **Save** the form, and then switch the *8C Supervisors form* to **Form** view.

a. On the **8C Supervisors** form, click the **Employee List** button. Alternatively, press Alt + E.

b. **Close** the *8C Employees* form, and then **Close** the *8C Supervisors* form, saving changes, if necessary. **Open** the **Navigation Pane**.

8 Open the **8C Departments** report in **Design** view. **Close** the **Navigation Pane**. In the **Detail** section, right-click the **Dept ID** text box, and then click **Properties**. Verify that the **Property Sheet** displays *Selection type: Text Box* and the **Selection type** box displays *Dept ID*.

a. On the **Property Sheet Event tab**, in the **On Click** property setting box, click the **Build** button. In the **Choose Builder** dialog box, verify that **Macro Builder** is selected, and then click **OK** to display the Macro Designer.

b. In the **Macro Designer**, add the **OpenForm** action using one of the techniques you have learned. In the **OpenForm Action Block**, click the **Form Name arrow**, and then click **8C Supervisors** form. Click in the **Where Condition** box, type **[Dept ID]=[Reports]![8C Departments]![Dept ID]** selecting items as they appear in the list to reduce errors.

c. In the **OpenForm Action Block**, click the **Data Mode arrow**, and then click **Read Only**. Add the following comment: **Opens 8C Supervisors form for the Dept ID selected on 8C Departments report**

d. **Close** the **Macro Designer**. In the displayed message box, click **Yes** to save the changes made to the macro and to update the **On Click** property. **Close** the **Property Sheet**. **Save** the report.

e. Switch to **Report** view. On the **8C Departments** report, click the **Dept ID** text box for *1233-D* to run the macro.

f. **Close** the **8C Supervisors** form. **Close** the **8C Departments** report, saving changes.

9 On the **DATABASE TOOLS tab**, in the **Analyze group**, click the **Database Documenter** button.

(Project 8C Supervisory Staff continues on the next page)

CHAPTER REVIEW

a. In the **Documenter** dialog box, click the **Macros tab**, and then click the **Options** button. If necessary, click the check box to deselect **Permissions by User and Group**, and then click **OK**. In the **Documenter** dialog box, click **Select All**.

b. In the **Documenter** dialog box, click the **Forms tab**, and then click the **Options** button. If necessary, click the check box to deselect **Properties** and **Permissions by User and Group**, and then click **OK**. In the **Documenter** dialog box, click the **8C Supervisors** form check box.

c. In the **Documenter** dialog box, click the **Reports tab**, and then click the **Options** button. If necessary, click the check box to deselect **Properties** and **Permissions by User and Group**, and then click **OK**. In the **Documenter** dialog box, click the **8C Departments** report check box, and then click **OK**.

d. If you are instructed to submit this result, create a paper or electronic printout of the pages that contain the two embedded macros and the autoexec macro. Include the project number, 8C, in the file name if you create an electronic printout. On the **Print Preview tab**, in the **Close Preview group**, click the **Close Print Preview** button.

10 **Open** the **Navigation Pane**. **Close** the database, and then **Exit** Access.

11 As directed by your instructor, submit your database and the paper or electronic printouts of the two Database Documenter reports that are the result of this project. Specifically, in this project, using your own name you created the following database and printouts or electronic printouts:

1. Lastname_Firstname_8C_Supervisory_Staff	Database file
2. Lastname_Firstname_8C_Database_Documenter_Embedded_ Macros	Database Documenter report (printed or electronic printout)
3. Lastname_Firstname_8C_Database_Documenter_Autoexec	Database Documenter report (printed or electronic printout)

END | You have completed Project 8C

CHAPTER REVIEW

Apply 8B skills from these Objectives:

5 Create a Macro Group

6 Associate a Macro with a Session

7 Create a Data Macro

Skills Review | Project 8D Hospital Departments

Margo Dalton, vice president of operations for Providence and Warwick Hospital, wants to customize her database of department information, including automating the process to add new departments. You will associate command buttons with a macro group's submacros, and create a data macro. Your completed work will look similar to Figure 8.44.

PROJECT FILES

For Project 8D, you will need the following file:

a08D_Hospital_Departments

You will save your database as:

Lastname_Firstname_8D_Hospital_Departments

PROJECT RESULTS

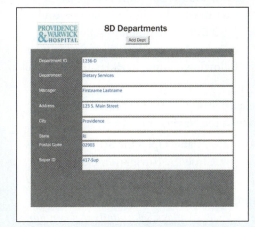

FIGURE 8.44

(Project 8D Hospital Departments continues on the next page)

CHAPTER REVIEW

1 Start Access. Locate and open the **a08D_Hospital_Departments** file. Save the database in your **Access Chapter 8** folder as **Lastname_Firstname_8D_Hospital Departments** and then **Close** the **Navigation Pane**.

2 On the **CREATE tab**, in the **Macros & Code group**, click the **Macro button**. On the **MACRO TOOLS DESIGN tab**, in the **Show/Hide group**, click the **Show All Actions** button.

a. In the **Action Catalog pane**, double-click **Group**. Click in the **Group** box, and type **Lastname Firstname 8D Add Dept Macro Group** Add the following comment: **Purpose: To enable a user to add a department using the 8D Departments form** On the **tab row**, right-click **Macro1**, click **Save**, and then type **Lastname Firstname 8D Add Dept Macro Group** Click **OK**.

b. In the **Action Catalog pane**, double-click **Submacro**, and type **GoToNewRecord** In the **Submacro**, add the **GoToRecord** action. In the **GoToRecord Action Block**, click the **Object Type arrow**, and then click **Form**. Click the **Object Name arrow**, and then click **8D Departments**. Verify that **New** appears in the **Record** box. Add the following comment: **Goes to new record in 8D Departments form**

c. In the submacro, add the **GoToControl** action. In the **GoToControl Action Block**, click in the **Control Name box**, and then type **Department ID** Add the following comment: **Changes focus from button to Department ID field**

d. In the submacro, add the **SetValue** action. In the **SetValue Action Block**, click in the **Item** box, and type **[Forms]![8D Departments]![cmdAddNew].[Visible]** Click in the Expression box, and type **No** Add the following comment: **Hides the Add Dept button**

e. In the submacro, add the **SetValue** action. In the **SetValue Action Block**, click in the **Item** box, and type **[Forms]![8D Departments]![cmdShowAll].[Visible]** Click in the **Expression** box and type **Yes** Add the following comment: **Displays the Show All button**

f. In the **Action Catalog pane**, double-click **Submacro**, and type **ShowAll** In the **ShowAll Submacro**, under **Add New Action**, click the arrow, and then click

ShowAllRecords. Add the following comment: **Shows all records and exits data entry**

g. In the submacro, add the **GoToControl** action. In the **GoToControl Action Block**, click in the **Control Name** box, and type **Department ID** Add the following comment: **Changes focus from button to Department ID field**

h. In the submacro, add the **SetValue** action. In the **SetValue Action Block**, to the right of the **Item** box, click the **Build** button. In the **Expression Builder**, select items or type **[Forms]![8D Departments]![cmdAddNew].[Visible]** and then click **OK**. Click in the **Expression** box, and type **Yes** Add the following comment: **Shows the Add Dept button**

i. In the submacro, add the **SetValue** action. In the **SetValue Action Block**, click in the **Item** box, and type **[Forms]![8D Departments]![cmdShowAll].[Visible]** Click in the **Expression** box, and then type **No** Add the following comment: **Hides the Show All button**

j. **Save** the macro group. **Close** the **Macro Designer**, and then **Open** the **Navigation Pane**.

3 In the **Navigation Pane**, **Open** the **8D Departments** form in **Design** view. **Close** the **Navigation Pane**.

a. In the **Form Header section**, right-click the **Add Dept** button, and then click **Properties**. Verify that the **Property Sheet** displays *Selection type: Command Button* and that the **Selection type** box displays *cmdAddNew*.

b. If necessary, point to the **left edge** of the **Property Sheet** until the pointer displays. Drag to the **7.25-inch mark on the horizontal ruler**.

c. On the **Property Sheet Event tab**, click the **On Click property setting arrow**. In the displayed list, click **Lastname Firstname 8D Add Dept Macro Group. GoToNewRecord**. On the **Property Sheet Format tab**, in the **Caption** property setting box, click to the left of **Add Dept**, and then type **&**

d. On the **Property Sheet**, in the **Selection type** box, click **cmdShowAll**. On the **Property Sheet Event tab**, click the **On Click property setting arrow**. In the displayed list, click **Lastname Firstname 8D Add Dept Macro Group.ShowAll**. On the **Property Sheet Format tab**, in the **Caption** property setting box,

(Project 8D Hospital Departments continues on the next page)

CHAPTER REVIEW

click to the left of **Show All**, and then type **& Close** the **Property Sheet**.

e. Switch to **Form** view. Click the **Add Dept** button. In the **Department ID** field type **1236-D** Press Tab, and type **Dietary Services** Enter your information for all of the remaining fields except Super ID. In the **Super ID** field, type **417-Sup**

f. If you are instructed to submit this result select and print the current record to create a paper printout, or create an electronic printout. **Close** the **8D Departments** form, saving changes.

4 On the **DATABASE TOOLS tab**, in the **Analyze** group, click the **Database Documenter** button.

a. In the **Documenter** dialog box, click the **Macros tab**, and then click the **Options** button. If necessary, click the check box to deselect **Permissions by User and Group**, and then click **OK**. In the **Documenter** dialog box, click **Select All**, and then click **OK**. If you are instructed to submit this result, create a paper or electronic printout. Include the project number, 8D, in the file name if you create an electronic printout. On the **Print Preview tab**, in the **Close Preview** group, click the **Close Print Preview** button.

5 Open the **8D Department Inspections** table in **Datasheet** view.

a. On the **TABLE TOOLS TABLE tab**, in the **Before Events** group, click the **Before Change** button to display the **Macro Designer**.

b. In the **Macro Designer**, add the **If** action using one of the techniques you have learned. In the **If Arguments Action Block**, click in the **If** conditional expression box, and type **[FD Inspection]=Yes and [Safety Inspection]=Yes and [HD Inspection]=Yes**

selecting items as they appear in the list to reduce errors.

c. In the **If Arguments Block**, add the **SetField** action using one of the techniques you have learned. In the **SetField Action Block**, click in the **Name** box, and type **Inspection Status** Click in the **Value** box, and type **"Inspections Complete"**

d. In the **If Arguments Block**, click the **Add Else** hyperlink to add an additional action to the If Arguments Block. In the **Else Arguments Block**, add the **SetField** action using one of the techniques you have learned. In the **SetField Action Block**, click in the **Name** box, and type **Inspection Status** Click in the **Value** box, and type **"Schedule Necessary Inspections"**

e. **Close** the **Macro Designer**. In the displayed message box, click **Yes** to save the changes made to the macro and to update the property. **Save** the table.

f. In the **HD Inspections** field, click in the following Dept IDs: **1212-D**, **1233-D**, **1265-D**, and **1459-D**. Notice the updates to the **Inventory Status** field.

g. View the table in **Print Preview**. If you are instructed to submit this result, create a paper or electronic printout in **Landscape** orientation. On the **PRINT PREVIEW tab**, in the **Close Preview group**, click the **Close Print Preview** button.

6 **Close** the database, and then **Exit** Access.

7 As directed by your instructor, submit your database and the paper or electronic printouts of the three objects— one form, one Database Documenter report, and one table—that are the result of this project. Specifically, in this project, using your own name you created the following database and printouts or electronic printouts:

1. Lastname_Firstname_8D_Hospital_Departments	Database file
2. 8D Departments	Form (printed or electronic printout)
3. Lastname_Firstname_8D_Database_Documenter	Database Documenter report (printed or electronic printout)
4. 8D Department Inspections	Table (printed or electronic printout)

END | You have completed Project 8D

CONTENT-BASED ASSESSMENTS

Mastering Access   Project 8E Gift Shop

Margo Dalton, vice president of operations for Providence and Warwick Hospital, wants to customize the gift shop database and automate common tasks. In this project, you will create a macro to automatically display a form and message box when the user opens the database. In addition, you will embed macros within a form and report. Your completed work will look similar to Figure 8.45.

Apply 8A skills from these Objectives:

1 Create a Standalone Macro with One Action

2 Add Multiple Actions to a Standalone Macro

3 Create an Embedded Macro

4 Print Macro Details

PROJECT FILES

For Project 8E, you will need the following file:

a08E_Gift_Shop

You will save your database as:

Lastname_Firstname_8E_Gift_Shop

PROJECT RESULTS

FIGURE 8.45

(Project 8E Gift Shop continues on the next page)

CONTENT-BASED ASSESSMENTS

1 Start Access. Locate and open the **a08E_Gift_Shop** file. Save the database in your **Access Chapter 8** folder as **Lastname_Firstname_8E_Gift_Shop** Close the **Navigation Pane**.

2 Create a macro to open the **8E Intro Screen** form with a comment: **Opens 8E Intro Screen form**. On the **DESIGN tab**, in the **Show/Hide group**, verify the **Show All Actions** button is active. **Save** the macro as **Autoexec**

3 Modify the **Autoexec** macro. Add the action **DisplayHourglassPointer** with the **Comment Displays the busy icon** Add the **Echo** action with the **Comment Hides the flickering screen as the macro runs** In the **Echo Action Block**, change the **Echo On** box to **No**. In the **Status Bar Text** box, type **Macro is running** Move the **OpenForm** action and comment below the **Echo** macro comment.

4 In the **Macro Designer**, at the bottom of the current list of actions, add a **MessageBox** action. Type a **Message** that displays **All gift shop inventory transfers must be recorded in the transfer log.** Add a **Beep**, and change the **Type** box to **Information**. Title the **Message** box **Inventory Transfers** Add a **Comment** that reads **Displays transfer procedure message**

5 In the **Macro Designer**, add an **Echo** action. In the **Echo Action Block**, verify the **Echo On** box is set to **Yes**. Add a **Comment** that says **Displays screen results**

6 In the **Macro Designer**, add a **DisplayHourglassPointer** action. In the **DisplayHourglassPointer Action Block**, change the **Hourglass On** box to **No**. Add a **Comment** that says **Restores the mouse pointer**

7 Close the Macro Designer, and **Save** the macro. **Open** the **Navigation Pane**.

8 Open the **8E Storage Locations** form in **Design** view. **Close** the **Navigation Pane**. In the **Details** section, add a **Button** control at **1.5 inches on the horizontal ruler** and **0.25 inches on the vertical ruler**. In the **Command Button Wizard** dialog box, click **Cancel**. Right-click the button, and then click **Properties**. On the **Property Sheet Other tab**, change the **Name** to **btnInv** On the **Property Sheet Format tab**, change the **Caption** to **Inventory List** On the **Property Sheet Event tab**, in the **On Click** property setting box, click the **Build** button. In the **Choose Builder** dialog box, verify that **Macro Builder** is selected, and then click **OK** to display the Macro Designer.

9 In the **Macro Designer**, add the **OpenForm** action to open the **8E Inventory List** form. In the **Where Condition** box, type **[Category]=[Forms]![8E Storage Locations]![Category]** For **View**, select **Datasheet**. For **Data Mode**, select **Read Only**. Add the comment: **Opens 8E Inventory List form for category indicated on 8E Storage Locations form** Close the **Macro Designer**, saving changes and updating the **On Click** property.

10 On the **Property Sheet Format tab**, in the **Caption** box, insert an **&** to the left of **Inventory List**. **Close** the **Property Sheet**, **Save** the form, and then switch **8E Storage Locations** to **Form** view. Click the **Inventory List** button. **Close** the **8E Inventory List** form. **Close** the **8E Storage Locations** form. **Open** the **Navigation Pane**.

11 Open the **8E Inventory Report** in **Design** view. **Close** the **Navigation Pane**. In the **Detail** section, display the **Property Sheet** for the **Category** text box. Verify that the **Property Sheet** displays *Selection type: Text Box* and the **Selection type** box displays *Category*. On the **Property Sheet Event tab**, in the **On Click** property setting box, click the **Build** button, and display the Macro Designer.

12 In the **Macro Designer**, add the **OpenForm** action to open the **8E Storage Locations** form. Add the **Where Condition [Category]=[Reports]![8E Inventory Report]![Category]** Change the **Data Mode** to **Read Only**. Add the comment: **Opens 8E Storage Locations form for the category selected on 8E Inventory Report** Close the **Macro Designer,** saving changes and updating the **On Click** property. **Close** the **Property Sheet**. **Save** the report.

13 Switch to **Report** view. On the **8E Inventory Report**, click the **Category** text box for *Food* to run the macro. **Close** the **8E Storage Locations** form. **Close** the **8E Inventory Report**, saving changes.

14 Open the **Database Documenter**. In the **Documenter** dialog box, click the **Macros tab**, and click **autoexec**. If necessary, in the **Options** dialog box, deselect **Permissions by User and Group**. In the **Documenter** dialog box, on the **Forms tab**, select the **8E Storage Locations** form. If necessary, in the **Options** dialog box, clear the **Properties** and **Permissions by User and Group** check boxes. In the **Documenter** dialog box, on the **Reports tab**, select the **8E Inventory Report** and then click **OK**. If you are instructed to submit this result, create a paper or electronic printout of the pages for the embedded (form and report) and autoexec macros.

(Project 8E Gift Shop continues on the next page)

Include the project number, 8E, in the file name if you create an electronic printout. **Close Print Preview**.

15 ▶ **Close** the database, and then **Exit** Access.

16 ▶ As directed by your instructor, submit your database and the paper or electronic printouts of the

two Database Documenter reports that are the result of this project. Specifically, in this project, using your own name you created the following database and printouts or electronic printouts:

1. Lastname_Firstname_8E_Gift_Shop	Database file
2. Lastname_Firstname_8E_Database_Documenter_Embedded	Database Documenter report (printed or electronic printout)
3. Lastname_Firstname_8E_Database_Documenter_Autoexec	Database Documenter report (printed or electronic printout)

END | You have completed Project 8E

Mastering Access | Project 8F Orthopedic Supplies

Margo Dalton, vice president of operations for Providence and Warwick Hospital, wants to customize the orthopedic supplies database using macros. In this project, you will create a macro group, associate command buttons with a macro, and create a data macro. Your completed work will look similar to Figure 8.46.

Apply 8B skills from these Objectives:

5 Create a Macro Group

6 Associate a Macro with a Session

7 Create a Data Macro

PROJECT FILES

For Project 8F, you will need the following file:

a08F_Orthopedic_Supplies

You will save your database as:

Lastname_Firstname_8F_Orthopedic_Supplies

PROJECT RESULTS

FIGURE 8.46

(Project 8F Orthopedic Supplies continues on the next page)

CONTENT-BASED ASSESSMENTS

1 Start Access. Locate and open the **a08F_ Orthopedic_Supplies** file. Save the database in your **Access Chapter 8** folder as **Lastname_Firstname_8F_ Orthopedic_Supplies** Close the **Navigation Pane**.

2 Create a **Macro Group** to print the reports. Name this macro group **Lastname Firstname 8F Report Group** with a comment: **Purpose: Allows user to select report printing options**

3 Create a **Submacro** named **Options** with the action **OpenForm** opening the **8F Report Options** form in Form view and Edit mode. Add the comment: **Opens 8F Report Options form**

4 Create a **Submacro** named **PrintReport** Add an **If** argument **1=[Forms]![8F Report Options]![Options]** and the **RunMacro** action for the **8F Report Group. ReportAlpha** macro. Add the comment: **Runs the macro for option 1** and then add the **StopMacro** action below the **RunMacro** action. In the submacro, below the first End If, add another **If** argument **2=[Forms]![8F Report Options]![Options]** and the **RunMacro** action for the **8F Report Group.ReportID** macro. Add the comment: **Runs the macro for option 2** and then add the **StopMacro** action.

5 Create a **Submacro** named **ReportAlpha** Add an action to **DisplayHourglassPointer**. Add the **RunMacro** for **8F Report Group.Cancel**, and add the comment: **Closes 8F Report Options form** Add the **OpenReport** action to open **8F Suppliers Alpha** report in Print Preview. Add the comment: **Opens report in print preview** Add the **SelectObject** action to select the **8F Suppliers Alpha** report, and add the comment: **Changes focus to 8F Suppliers Alpha report** Finally, add a macro action to turn off the hourglass with the comment: **Default mouse pointer displays**.

6 Create a **Submacro** named **ReportID** Add an action to **DisplayHourglassPointer** with the comment: **Displays busy icon while macro is running**. Add the **RunMacro** for **8F Report Group.Cancel**, and add the comment: **Closes 8F Report Options form** Next, add the **OpenReport** action to open **8F Suppliers by ID** report in **Print Preview**. Add the comment: **Opens report in print preview** Add the **SelectObject** action to select the **8F Suppliers by ID** report, and add the comment: **Changes focus to 8F Suppliers by ID report** Finally, add a macro action to

turn off the hourglass with the comment: **Default mouse pointer displays**.

7 Create a **Submacro** named **Cancel** Add the **CloseWindow** action to close the **8F Report Options** form; add the comment: **Closes 8F Report Options form**

8 **Close** the **Macro Designer**, saving the group as **Lastname Firstname 8F Report Group**

9 Open the **8F Report Options** form in **Design** view. Open the **Property Sheet** for the **Print Report** button. On the **Property Sheet Event tab**, click the **On Click property setting box arrow**, and click **8F Report Group. PrintReport**. On the **Property Sheet Format tab**, click in the **Caption** property setting and type **&** before *Print Report*. On the Design grid, click the **Cancel** button. On the **Event tab**, in the **On Click** property setting, select **8F Report Group.Cancel**. On the **Property Sheet Format tab**, click in the **Caption** property setting and type **&** before *Cancel*. **Close** the **Property Sheet** and **Save** the form.

10 Switch to **Form** view, saving changes. Test each report option and **Close Print Preview**. **Close** the **8F Suppliers** form.

11 Open the **Database Documenter**. In the displayed **Documenter** dialog box, on the **Macros tab**, click **Select All**. If necessary, in the **Options** dialog box, clear the **Permissions by User and Group** check box. In the **Documenter** dialog box, click **OK**. If you are instructed to submit this result, create a paper or electronic printout. Include the project number, 8F, in the file name if you create an electronic printout. **Close Print Preview**.

12 Open the **8F Supplies** table in **Datasheet** view. Add a data macro **Before Change**. Add the **If Arguments Block** with the condition **[# On Hand]<=36** Add the **SetField** action to set **Reorder Point** to **"Reorder Now"** In the **If Arguments Block**, add an **Else Arguments Block**, and then add the **SetField** action to set **Reorder Point** to **"Inventory OK"** Close the **Macro Designer**, saving changes. **Save** the table. In the record for **Supply ID** 519-Supp, update the **# on Hand** to **70** In the record for 525-Supp, update the **# on Hand** to **32** Click in the first field in the first record, and notice the updates to the **Reorder Point** field. View the table in **Print Preview**. If you are instructed to submit this result, create a paper or electronic printout in **Landscape** orientation. On the **PRINT PREVIEW tab**, in the **Close Preview group**, click the **Close Print Preview** button.

(Project 8F Orthopedic Supplies continues on the next page)

13   **Close** the database, and then **Exit** Access.

14   As directed by your instructor, submit your database and the paper or electronic printouts of the two objects—one Database Documenter report and one table—that are the result of this project. Specifically, in this project, using your own name you created the following database and printouts or electronic printouts:

1. Lastname_Firstname_8F_Orthopedic_Supplies	Database file
2. Lastname_Firstname_8F Database Documenter	Database Documenter report (printed or electronic printout)
3. 8F Supplies	Table (printed or electronic printout)

END | You have completed Project 8F

CONTENT-BASED ASSESSMENTS

Apply 8A and 8B skills from these Objectives:

1 Create a Standalone Macro

3 Create an Embedded Macro

4 Print Macro Details

7 Create a Data Macro

Maria Bartello, facilities director of the Providence and Warwick Hospital in Providence, Rhode Island, is analyzing proposed expansion projects. In this project, you will create macros to automate the process. Your completed work will look similar to Figure 8.47.

PROJECT FILES

For Project 8G, you will need the following file:

a08G_Hospital_Expansion

You will save your database as:

Lastname_Firstname_8G_Hospital_Expansion

PROJECT RESULTS

FIGURE 8.47

(Project 8G Hospital Expansion continues on the next page)

CONTENT-BASED ASSESSMENTS

1 Start Access. Locate and open the **a08G_Hospital_Expansion** file. Save the database in your **Access Chapter 8** folder as **Lastname_Firstname_8G_Hospital_Expansion**

2 **Open** the **8G Intro Screen** form in **Design** view. Change the **Pop Up** and **Modal** properties to **Yes**. **Save** and **Close** the form.

3 Create a macro to open the **8G Intro Screen** form with an appropriate comment. In the **Show/Hide group**, be sure the **Show All Actions** button is active. **Save** the macro as **autoexec**

4 Modify the **autoexec** macro. Add the action **OpenForm** to open the **8G Projects** form with an appropriate comment. Add the action **DisplayHourglassPointer** with the **Comment Displays the busy icon** Add the **Echo** action. In the **Echo Action Block**, change the **Echo On** box to **No**. Click in the **Status Bar Text** box, and then type **Macro is running** Add the **Comment Hides the flickering screen as the macro runs** Move the first **OpenForm** action and comment below the **Echo** macro comment. **Save** and **Close** the macro. **Close** the database, and then reopen it.

5 **Close** the **8G Intro Screen**. Switch the **8G Projects** form to **Design** view. In the **Form Header**, add a Button control at the **3-inch mark on the horizontal ruler** and **0.5-inch mark on the vertical ruler** with the caption **&Summary** Embed a macro to **Open** the **8G Projects** report in **Report** view. **Save** and **Close** the macro. **Save** the form. Switch to **Form** view, and test the macro. **Close** the report and the form.

6 Run the **Database Documenter**. Select the **Forms** tab, if necessary, and select **8G Projects**. Click the **Options**

button and under **Include for Form**, select the **Code** check box only, if necessary. Click the **Properties** button. Under **Print Categories**, be sure only **Other Properties** is selected. Click **OK** two times. Click the **Macros** tab, and click **Select All**. Click **OK**. If you are instructed to submit this result, create a paper or electronic printout of the report. Include the project number, 8G, in the file name if you create an electronic printout. **Close Print Preview**.

7 Open the **8G Projects** table in **Datasheet** view. Add a data macro **Before Change**. Add the **If Arguments Block** with the condition **[Total Bid Amount]<=[Budget Amount]** Add the **SetField** action to set **Bid Status** to **"Accepted"** In the **If Arguments Block**, add an **Else Arguments Block**, and then add the **SetField** action to set **Bid Status** to **"Rejected"** **Close** the **Macro Designer**, saving changes. **Save** the table. In Record 6, update the **Total Bid Amount** to **86941000** In Record 7 update the **Total Bid Amount** to **100036** Click in the first field in the first record, and notice the updates to the **Bid Status** field. View the table in **Print Preview**. If you are instructed to submit this result, create a paper or electronic printout in **Landscape** orientation. **Close Print Preview**.

8 **Open** the **Navigation Pane**. **Close** the database, and then **Exit** Access.

9 As directed by your instructor, submit your database and the paper or electronic printout of the two objects—one Database Documenter report and one table—that are the result of this project. Specifically, in this project, using your own name you created the following database and printouts or electronic printouts:

1. Lastname_Firstname_8G_Hospital_Expansion	Database file
2. 8G Database Documenter	Database Documenter report (printed or electronic printout)
3. 8G Projects	Table (printed or electronic printout)

END | You have completed Project 8G

CONTENT-BASED ASSESSMENTS

Apply a combination of the 8A and 8B skills.

GO! Fix It	Project 8H Medical Transcription	Online

GO! Make It	Project 8I Recruiting Events	Online

GO! Solve It	Project 8J Dictation Department	Online

GO! Solve It	Project 8K Stay Length	

PROJECT FILES

For Project 8K, you will need the following file:

a08K_Stay_Length

You will save your database as:

Lastname_Firstname_8K_Stay_Length

The vice president for operations at the Providence and Warwick Hospital, Margo Dalton, is preparing for the upcoming recruiting season. Open the **a08K_Stay_Length** database and save it as **Lastname_Firstname_8K_Stay_Length** Create an autoexec standalone macro to display the 8K Intro Screen form. On the **8K Facilities** form, embed a macro in the **Patients** button to display the **8K Patients** form for the facility selected in Datasheet view. In the **8K Facility** table, create a **Before Change** data macro to display **Outpatient** in the Facility type field if the Beds = 0; otherwise, it should display **Inpatient** Test the macro by entering **65** for the SMC facility and **0** for the WAC facility.

If you are instructed to submit this result, create a paper or electronic printout of the table in Landscape orientation. If you are instructed to submit the macro details, create a paper or electronic printout.

Performance Level

Performance Element	Exemplary: You consistently applied the relevant skills.	Proficient: You sometimes, but not always, applied the relevant skills.	Developing: You rarely or never applied the relevant skills.
Create autoexec macro	Autoexec created with the correct actions, arguments, and comments.	Autoexec created with no more than two missing actions, arguments, or comments.	Autoexec created with more than two missing actions, arguments, or comments.
Create embedded macro in Patients button on 8K Facilities form	Embedded macro created with the correct actions, arguments, and comments.	Embedded macro created with no more than two missing actions, arguments, or comments.	Embedded macro created with more than two missing actions, arguments, or comments.
Create Before Change data macro in 8K Facility table	Data macro created with the correct actions, arguments, and comments.	Data macro created with no more than two missing actions, arguments, or comments.	Data macro created with more than two missing actions, arguments, or comments.

END | You have completed Project 8K

OUTCOMES-BASED ASSESSMENTS

RUBRIC

The following outcomes-based assessments are open-ended assessments. That is, there is no specific correct result; your result will depend on your approach to the information provided. Make Professional Quality your goal. Use the following scoring rubric to guide you in how to approach the problem and then to evaluate how well your approach solves the problem.

The *criteria*—Software Mastery, Content, Format and Layout, and Process—represent the knowledge and skills you have gained that you can apply to solving the problem. The *levels of performance*—Professional Quality, Approaching Professional Quality, or Needs Quality Improvements—help you and your instructor evaluate your result.

	Your completed project is of Professional Quality if you:	Your completed project is Approaching Professional Quality if you:	Your completed project Needs Quality Improvements if you:
1-Software Mastery	Choose and apply the most appropriate skills, tools, and features and identify efficient methods to solve the problem.	Choose and apply some appropriate skills, tools, and features, but not in the most efficient manner.	Choose inappropriate skills, tools, or features, or are inefficient in solving the problem.
2-Content	Construct a solution that is clear and well organized, contains content that is accurate, appropriate to the audience and purpose, and is complete. Provide a solution that contains no errors in spelling, grammar, or style.	Construct a solution in which some components are unclear, poorly organized, inconsistent, or incomplete. Misjudge the needs of the audience. Have some errors in spelling, grammar, or style, but the errors do not detract from comprehension.	Construct a solution that is unclear, incomplete, or poorly organized; contains some inaccurate or inappropriate content; and contains many errors in spelling, grammar, or style. Do not solve the problem.
3-Format & Layout	Format and arrange all elements to communicate information and ideas, clarify function, illustrate relationships, and indicate relative importance.	Apply appropriate format and layout features to some elements, but not others. Overuse features, causing minor distraction.	Apply format and layout that does not communicate information or ideas clearly. Do not use format and layout features to clarify function, illustrate relationships, or indicate relative importance. Use available features excessively, causing distraction.
4-Process	Use an organized approach that integrates planning, development, self-assessment, revision, and reflection.	Demonstrate an organized approach in some areas, but not others; or, use an insufficient process of organization throughout.	Do not use an organized approach to solve the problem.

OUTCOMES-BASED ASSESSMENTS

GO! Think   Project 8L Patient Charges

PROJECT FILES

For Project 8L, you will need the following file:

a08L_Patient_Charges

You will save your database as:

Lastname_Firstname_8L_Patient_Charges

Paul Sandheinrich, CEO for Providence and Warwick Hospital, wants to study the patient charges accrued over the past few months at each of the facilities. Open the **a08L_Patient_Charges** database, close the Intro Screen, and save the database as **Lastname_Firstname_8L_Patient_Charges** Create a standalone macro to open the **8L Patient Charges** report in Report view for the user to enter a facility name and then close the **8L Display Charges** form. Save this macro as **Lastname Firstname 8L Charge Report** and associate the macro with the button on the **8L Display Charges** form. Using the form, generate the report for the P&W Rehab Center. Open the **8L Patient Charges** report in Design view and embed macros in both buttons in the Report Header. In the **Display Another Facility** button, embed a macro to close the current report without saving and open the **8L Display Charges** form to allow selection of a different facility. In the **Close Database** button, embed a macro to close the report without saving and close the database.

If you are instructed to submit this result, create a paper or electronic printout of the report and macro details.

END | You have completed Project 8L

GO! Think   Project 8M Clinical Trials   Online

You and GO!   Project 8N Club Directory   Online

Integrating Access with Other Applications

GO! to Work
Video A9

9
ACCESS 2013

Minerva Studio/Fotolia

In This Chapter

Using Access with other applications maximizes the efficiency of managing information. Data can be imported from another source or linked to data in an external source, such as a Word table, an Excel worksheet, or another Access database. Data can also be exported from an Access database into other applications and platforms. For example, Access data can be used to create individualized letters in Word or analyze data in Excel. In addition, tables, forms, queries, or reports can be exported using HTML or XML, a markup language similar to HTML, the markup language used to create webpages.

Liberty Motors has one of eastern Missouri's largest inventories of popular car brands, sport utility vehicles, hybrid cars, sports cars, and motorcycles. Liberty also offers extensive customization options for all types of vehicles through its accessories division. Its sales, service, and finance staff are all highly trained and knowledgeable about their products, and the company takes pride in its consistently high customer satisfaction ratings in both sales and service. Liberty Motors and its employees are active members of their local community, where they sponsor and participate in activities and events.

Liberty Motors

PROJECT
9A

PROJECT ACTIVITIES

In Activities 9.01 through 9.08, you will assist Phillip Garrett, president of Liberty Motors, and Jeanine Thomas, finance manager, in bringing data from Word, Excel, and other Access databases into a new Access database to create queries and reports. They need to import data from Microsoft Word and Excel as well as link information from another Access database. Your completed document will look similar to Figure 9.1.

Build from
Scratch

PROJECT FILES

For Project 9A, you will need the following files:

New blank Access database
a09A_Employees.docx
a09A_Used_Auto_Inventory.xlsx
a09A_Logo.jpg
a09A_Used_Auto_Chart.xlsx
a09A_SUVs_and_Motorcycles.accdb

You will save your files as:

Lastname_Firstname_9A_Liberty_Motors.accdb
Lastname_Firstname_9A_Employees_Table.txt

PROJECT RESULTS

FIGURE 9.1 Project 9A Liberty Motors

Video A9-1

When you create a database, you can type the records directly into a table. You can also *import* data from a variety of sources. Importing is the process used to bring in a copy of data from one source or application to another application. For example, you can import data from a Word table or Excel spreadsheet into an Access database.

Data can be imported in various ways. An imported table can overwrite an existing table or append data to an object with the same name in the existing database. Linked data can change the data in the database, and the change will be updated in the source document and vice versa; imported data will not be synchronized between the imported object and the source object.

Activity 9.01 | Preparing a Word Table for Importing

In this activity, you will create an empty database to store an imported Word table and then prepare the Word table for the import process.

1 Start Access. In the Access startup window, click **Blank desktop database**. In the **Blank desktop database** dialog box, to the right of the **File name** box, click the **Browse** button. In the **File New Database** dialog box, navigate to the location where you are saving your databases for this chapter, create a **New folder** named **Access Chapter 9** and then press Enter. In the **File name** box, using your own name, replace the existing text with **Lastname_Firstname_9A_Liberty_Motors** and then click **OK** or press Enter. In the **Blank desktop database** dialog box, click **Create**, and then **Close** × the displayed table.

You have created an empty database to store the table that you will import from Word.

2 **Close** the database, and then **Exit** Access.

3 Start Word, and then click **Open Other Documents**. Navigate to the location where the student data files for this textbook are saved. Locate and open the **a09A_Employees** file. Notice that employee data is saved in a table in this Word document.

4 Verify that the insertion point is in the table. On the **TABLE TOOLS LAYOUT tab**, in the **Data group**, click the **Convert to Text** button, and then compare your screen with Figure 9.2.

To import data from a Word table into an Access table, the data must be *converted* or changed to a *delimited file*—a file where each record displays on a separate line and the fields within the record are separated by a single character called a *delimiter*. A delimiter can be a paragraph mark, a tab, a comma, or another character.

FIGURE 9.2

5 In the displayed **Convert Table to Text** dialog box, verify that the **Tabs** option button is selected—this is the delimiter character you will use to separate the data into fields—and then click **OK**.

6 On the **HOME tab**, in the **Paragraph group**, click the **Show/Hide** button ¶ to display formatting marks if they are not already displayed. Click anywhere in the document to deselect the text, and then compare your screen with Figure 9.3.

> Clicking the Show/Hide button enables you to see the tabs between the fields and the paragraph marks at the end of each line. Word also flags some proper names as spelling errors because they are not listed in the Word dictionary.

FIGURE 9.3

7 Display **Backstage** view, click **Save As**, and then navigate to the **Access Chapter 9** folder. In the **Save As** dialog box, in the **File name** box, select the existing text, and then type **Lastname_Firstname_9A_Employees_Table** Click the **Save as type arrow**, and from the displayed list, scroll down, and then click **Plain Text**. In the **Save As** dialog box, click **Save**, and then compare your screen with Figure 9.4.

> A Word table must be converted to a delimited text file and then saved as either *Plain Text* or Rich Text. Data stored in Plain Text format contains no formatting, such as bold or italics. Plain Text stores the data using the *ASCII*—American Standard Code for Information Interchange—character set. The File Conversion dialog box displays for you to confirm the conversion to a text file.

FIGURE 9.4

8 In the displayed **File Conversion** dialog box, accept the default settings by clicking **OK**. **Close** ⊠ the document, and **Exit** ⊠ Word.

Activity 9.02 | Importing Data from a Word Table

In this activity, you will import the Word table data that is stored in a delimited text file into your 9A_Liberty_Motors database.

1 Start Access. On the left side of the opening screen, under **Recent**, click **9A_Liberty_Motors** to open the empty database. Enable the content or add the **Access Chapter 9** folder to the **Trust Center**. Notice that in the **Navigation Pane**, there are no tables in the database.

2 On the **EXTERNAL DATA tab**, in the **Import & Link group**, click the **Text File** button. In the displayed **Get External Data - Text File** dialog box, to the right of the **File name** box, click **Browse**. Navigate to your **Access Chapter 9** folder. In the **File Open** dialog box, double-click **9A_Employees_Table**, and then compare your screen with Figure 9.5.

The source file—the one being imported—is listed in the File name box. When importing, if a table with the same name as the imported table does not exist, Access creates the object. If a table with the same name exists in the database, Access may overwrite its contents with the imported data. If you modify data in the original text file, the data will not be updated in the Access database.

A *link* is a connection to data in another file. When linking, Access creates a table that maintains a link to the source data. You cannot change or delete data in a linked Access table; however, you can add new records.

FIGURE 9.5

---

3 In the **Get External Data - Text File** dialog box, verify that the **Import the source data into a new table in the current database** option button is selected, and then click **OK**. Compare your screen with Figure 9.6.

The Import Text Wizard dialog box displays, indicating that the data seems to be in a delimited format, using a comma or tab to separate each field.

FIGURE 9.6

4 In the **Import Text Wizard** dialog box, verify that the **Delimited** option button is selected, and then click **Next**.

In this Import Text Wizard dialog box, you select the delimiter that you used when you created the text file.

5 Click each **delimiter** option button, and notice how the text is affected in the preview window. When you are finished, verify that the **Tab** option button is selected. Click the **First Row Contains Field Names** check box to convert the field names to column headings instead of first record data. Click the **Text Qualifier arrow**, and notice that a single quotation mark and a double quotation mark display. If you are working with a file that includes text in quotation marks, you would indicate this by selecting either the single quotation mark or the double quotation mark. Verify that {**none**} is selected, and then compare your screen with Figure 9.7.

FIGURE 9.7

6 Click **Next**, and then compare your screen with Figure 9.8.

In this Import Text Wizard dialog box, under Field Options, you can change the field name, set the data type, index the field, or skip the importing of the field.

FIGURE 9.8

Field options for selected field

Select to not import the selected field

Scroll to display more records

Scroll to display more fields

NOTE — **Saving Data as a New Table or Appending Data**

If there is an existing table in the database, another Import Text Wizard dialog box displays before the one enabling you to change field options. This dialog box enables you to save the imported table as a new table or in an existing table. If you select the existing table, the data will be *appended*—added—to the end of the existing table.

---

7 ▸ Verify that the **Field Options** for the **Last Name** field are correct. Use the horizontal scroll bar to display the fields on the right. Click in the **Postal Code** field to select the field. Under **Field Options**, click the **Data Type arrow**, and then click **Short Text**.

Because Access determined that the Postal Code field contained all numbers, it assigned a data type of Long Integer. Recall that fields containing numbers that are not used in calculations should have a data type of Short Text.

8 ▸ Click **Next** to display primary key options, and then compare your screen with Figure 9.9.

FIGURE 9.9

Primary key options

Access adds ID field as primary key

9 ▸ Verify that the **Let Access add primary key** option button is selected, and then click **Next**. Import to the new table named **Lastname Firstname 9A Employees**

In this dialog box, you can accept the default name of the table or type a new name.

10 ▸ Click **Finish**. Because there are no errors in the imported file, the **Get External Data - Text File** dialog box displays, which enables you to save the import steps for future use.

When you import or export data in Access, you can save the settings you used so that you can repeat the process at any time without using the wizard. The name of the source file, the name of the destination database, primary key fields, field names, and all the other specifications you set are saved. Even though all of the specifications are saved, you can still change the name of the source file or destination file before running the import or export specification again. You cannot save the specifications for linking or exporting only a portion of a table.

ALERT!   **Did an Error Message Box Display After Clicking Finish?**

If a message box displays, there may be extra blank lines at the end of the text file, which cause blank records to be inserted into the database. If this occurs, click OK two times. Open the new table, delete any empty records, display the table in Design view, and then set the appropriate field as the primary key.

---

11 ▸ Select the **Save import steps** check box to display additional options. Click in the **Description** box, and then type **Imports a tab-delimited file that was a Word table** Notice that if you are using Outlook, you can create an Outlook Task to remind you when to repeat the import operation. Click **Save Import**, and notice that in the **Navigation Pane**, the **9A Employees** table displays.

Access creates and saves the import specification in the current database. You cannot move or copy the specification to another database.

12 ▸ On the **EXTERNAL DATA tab**, in the **Import & Link group**, click the **Saved Imports** button, and then compare your screen with Figure 9.10.

The Manage Data Tasks dialog box displays with two tabs—one for Saved Imports, and one for Saved Exports. Clicking the Run button performs the operation using the selected specification. You can schedule execution by clicking the Create Outlook Task button or delete a specification by clicking the Delete button. You can change the name or description of a specification, change the source file in an import operation, or change the destination file in an export operation by clicking the appropriate section in the specification.

FIGURE 9.10

13 ▸ In the **Manage Data Tasks** dialog box, click **Close**.

14 ▸ Double-click **9A Employees** to open the table in **Datasheet** view, and then **Close** ⟨«⟩ the **Navigation Pane**. Adjust the widths of all of the fields to display all of the data and the entire field name for each field.

All of the data from the Word table, which was converted to a delimited file, has been imported successfully into a table within the database, saving you from typing the data.

---

15 ▶ If you are instructed to submit this result, create a paper or electronic printout of the **first page** of the table in **Landscape** orientation, changing the margins, if necessary, to print all of the fields, and ensuring that the table name displays in the header. **Save** 🖬 the table, and then **Close** ✕ the table.

Objective 2 | Import Data from an Excel Workbook

Video A9-2

Jessie Pine, the auto sales manager, keeps an inventory of used cars, SUVs, and motorcycles in an Excel workbook. A *workbook* is an Excel file that contains one or more worksheets. A *worksheet* is the primary document used in Excel to save and work with data that is arranged in columns and rows. You can import the data from an Excel workbook into Access by copying the data from an open worksheet and pasting it into an Access datasheet, by importing a worksheet into a new or existing Access table, or by creating a link to a worksheet from an Access database. There is no way to save the workbook as an Access database within Excel; the individual worksheets within a workbook must be imported into an Access database.

Activity 9.03 | Importing Data from an Excel Worksheet

In this activity, you will import an Excel worksheet containing the used car inventory, creating a new table in your database.

1 ▶ If necessary, click the **EXTERNAL DATA tab**. In the **Import & Link group**, click the **Excel** button.

The Get External Data - Excel Spreadsheet dialog box displays, indicating that you can import the source data into a new table, append a copy of the records to an existing table, or link to the Excel worksheet.

2 ▶ In the **Get External Data - Excel Spreadsheet** dialog box, to the right of the **File name** box, click the **Browse** button. Navigate to the location where the student data files for this textbook are saved. Locate the **a09A_Used_Auto_Inventory** file, and then notice the icon to the left of the file name; it indicates the file is an Excel Worksheet file. **Open** the file.

3 ▶ In the **Get External Data - Excel Spreadsheet** dialog box, click **OK**, and then compare your screen with Figure 9.11.

The first Import Spreadsheet Wizard dialog box displays. A *spreadsheet* is another name for a worksheet. On this page you can select one worksheet—you can import only one worksheet at a time during an import operation. If you want to import several worksheets, save the import specification, and then change the source data. The first row displays column headings.

FIGURE 9.11

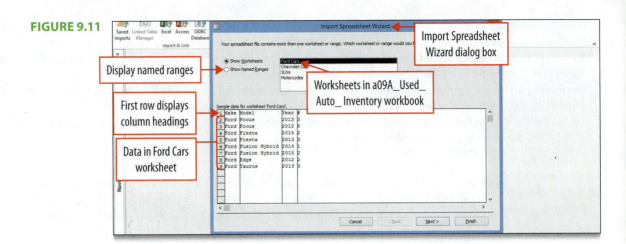

4 ▸ In the **Import Spreadsheet Wizard** dialog box, click the **Show Named Ranges** option button, and then in the box, click **Ford**.

This is the same data that displays in the *Ford Cars* worksheet, but without the column headings. If the Excel worksheet contains named ranges, you can select the Show Named Ranges option button. A *range* includes two or more selected cells on a worksheet that can be treated as a single unit. A *named range* is a range that has been given a name, making it easier to use the cells in calculations or modifications. A *cell* is the small box formed by the intersection of a column and a row.

5 ▸ Click the **Show Worksheets** option button, and verify that **Ford Cars** is selected. Click **Next** to display the second **Import Spreadsheet Wizard** dialog box. Notice that the wizard assumes that the first row contains column headings, and that Access uses the column headings as field names.

6 ▸ Click **Next** to display the third **Import Spreadsheet Wizard** dialog box.

Just as you did when importing a text file, you can change the field name, index the field, set the data type, or remove the field from the import operation.

7 ▸ Click **Next**. In the fourth **Import Spreadsheet Wizard** dialog box, verify that **Let Access add primary key** is selected, and then click **Next**.

8 ▸ In the final **Import Spreadsheet Wizard** dialog box, in the **Import to Table** box, type **Lastname Firstname 9A Cars** and then click **Finish**. Because you do not want to save the import steps, in the **Get External Data - Excel Spreadsheet** dialog box, click **Close**. Open ⌐»⌐ the **Navigation Pane**, and then notice that the table displays in the Navigation Pane.

9 ▸ In the **Navigation Pane**, double-click **9A Cars** to open the table in **Datasheet** view. **Close** ⌐«⌐ the **Navigation Pane**, and then compare your screen with Figure 9.12.

The data from the *Ford Cars* worksheet in the *a09A_Used_Auto_ Inventory* Excel workbook has been imported into this new table.

FIGURE 9.12

10 > **Close** ⊠ the table.

> **More Knowledge** | **Importing from a Workbook That Contains a Chart**
>
> If a workbook contains a chart on a separate worksheet, when you try to import any worksheet into Access, a message box displays stating that the wizard cannot access the information in the file and that you should check the file you want to import to see if it exists and if it is in the correct format. You should make a copy of the workbook, open the copied workbook, and then delete the worksheet containing the chart or move the chart to the sheet with the related data. Save the workbook, close it, and then import the data from any of the worksheets.

Activity 9.04 | Appending Data from Excel to an Access Table

In this activity, you will append data from an Excel worksheet to the 9A Cars table. To append data, the table must already be created.

1 > If necessary, click the **EXTERNAL DATA tab**. In the **Import & Link group**, click the **Excel** button. In the **Get External Data - Excel Spreadsheet** dialog box, click **Browse**. If necessary, navigate to the location where the student data files for this textbook are saved. Locate and **Open** the **a09A_Used_Auto_Inventory** file.

2 > Under **Specify how and where you want to store the data in the current database**, click **Append a copy of the records to the table**. Click the **table name box arrow** to display the names of the two tables that are saved in the database. Verify that **9A Cars** is selected, and then click **OK**.

3 > In the first **Import Spreadsheet Wizard** dialog box, click the **Chevrolet Cars** worksheet, and then click **Next**. In the second **Import Spreadsheet Wizard** dialog box, notice that Access has determined that the first row matches the field names contained in the existing table and that you cannot clear the check box. Click **Next**.

4 > In the **Import Spreadsheet Wizard** dialog box, click **Finish** to import the data into the **9A Cars** table in the current database.

5 > In the **Get External Data - Excel Spreadsheet** dialog box, click **Close**, and then **Open** » the **Navigation Pane**. Double-click **9A Cars** to display the table in **Datasheet** view. **Close** « the **Navigation Pane**, and then compare your screen with Figure 9.13.

> The data from the *Chevrolet Cars* worksheet in the *a09A_Used_Auto_Inventory* workbook is appended to the *9A Cars* table in your database.

FIGURE 9.13

6 > If you are instructed to submit this result, create a paper or electronic printout of the table. **Close** ⊠ the table.

Video A9-3

A *chart* is a graphic representation of data. Data presented in a chart is easier to understand than a table of numbers. *Column charts* display comparisons among related numbers, *pie charts* display the contributions of parts to a whole amount, and *line charts* display trends over time. Excel is the best tool for creating a chart because there are a wide variety of chart types and formatting options.

Activity 9.05 | Creating a Query and a Report

In this activity, you will create a query. Using the query, you will create a report that will be used in the next activity.

1 On the **CREATE tab**, in the **Queries group**, click the **Query Design** button. In the **Show Table** dialog box, double-click **9A Cars** to add the table to the Query Design workspace, and then **Close** ☒ the **Show Table** dialog box.

2 If necessary, expand the field list to display the entire table name. In the field list, click **Make**. Hold down (Shift), and then click # to select all four fields. Drag the selected fields down into the first column of the design grid, and then compare your screen with Figure 9.14.

FIGURE 9.14

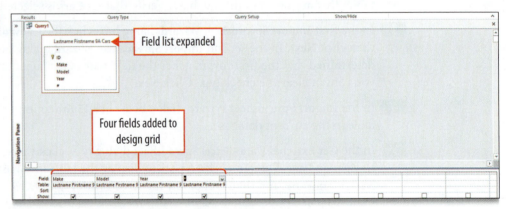

Field list expanded

Four fields added to design grid

BY TOUCH   To resize the file list, touch the file list with two or more fingers and then stretch your fingers apart to zoom out.

3 In the design grid, under **Make**, click in the **Criteria** box, type **Ford** and then press (Enter).

4 On the **QUERY TOOLS DESIGN tab**, in the **Results group**, click the **Run** button to display only the Ford cars.

5 Switch the query to **Design** view. In the design grid, under **Make**, on the **Show** row, clear the check box, and then **Run** the query.

   Recall that clearing the Show check box hides the field from the query. Because this query only displays Ford cars, hiding this field is appropriate.

6 Save 🖫 the query as **Lastname Firstname 9A Ford Cars Query** and then **Close** ☒ the query. **Open** » the **Navigation Pane**, and then notice that the query displays in the Navigation Pane.

7 In the **Navigation Pane**, under **Queries**, click **9A Ford Cars Query** to select the query, and then **Close** « the **Navigation Pane**.

8 On the **CREATE tab**, in the **Reports group**, click the **Report** button. Switch to **Design** view.

9 In the **Report Header** section, in the **title**, delete the space before **9A**, and then press (Shift) + (Enter). Double-click **Query** to select the word, and then type **Report** Press (Enter).

10 ▸ Click the image to the left of the title to select it. On the **REPORT DESIGN TOOLS DESIGN tab**, in the **Header/Footer group**, click the **Logo** button. If necessary, navigate to the location where the data files for this chapter are saved, and then double-click **a09A_Logo** to insert the logo. In the **Tools group**, click the **Property Sheet** button. Display the **Property Sheet Format tab**. Click in the **Size Mode** property box, and select **Zoom**. Resize the image so the right edge aligns with the **1-inch mark on the horizontal ruler**. **Close** ✕ the **Property Sheet**.

11 ▸ In the **Report Header** section, delete the **Date** and **Time text box controls**. In the **Page Footer** section, delete the **Page number text box control**. Resize the report to 6.5 inches wide. Compare your screen with Figure 9.15.

FIGURE 9.15

12 ▸ **Save** 🖫 the report as **Lastname Firstname 9A Ford Cars Report**

Activity 9.06 | Inserting an Excel Chart into a Report

In this activity, you will insert an Excel chart into 9A Ford Cars Report.

1 ▸ In the report, in **Design** view, point to the top of the **Report Footer section bar** until the pointer displays. Drag the section down to the **3-inch mark on the vertical ruler** to increase the size of the **Page Footer** section.

2 ▸ Start Excel. If necessary, maximize the Excel window. Display **Backstage** view, and then click **Open Other Workbooks**. Navigate to the location where the data files for this chapter are saved, and then double-click **a09A_Used_Auto_Chart** to open the workbook. Compare your screen with Figure 9.16.

The workbook opens with the *Cars* worksheet displaying. A pie chart has been saved in the worksheet and displays the number of cars for each model of Ford vehicles.

FIGURE 9.16

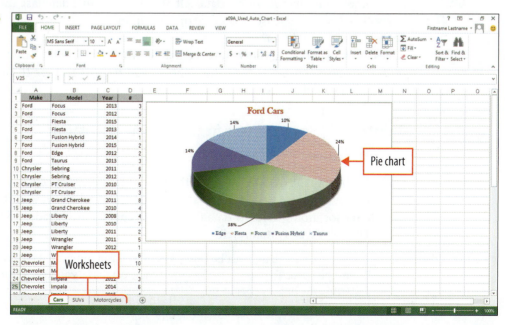

3 ▶ Click the outside edge of the **pie chart** to select the entire chart. On the **HOME tab**, in the **Clipboard group**, click the **Copy** 📋 button to place a copy of the pie chart in the Office Clipboard. **Close** ☒ Excel.

4 ▶ Click the **Access** button on the taskbar to activate the **9A Ford Cars Report** in the database. In the **9A Ford Cars Report**, right-click the **Page Footer section bar**, and then click **Paste**. Compare your screen with Figure 9.17.

The pie chart is pasted into the Page Footer section of the report.

FIGURE 9.17

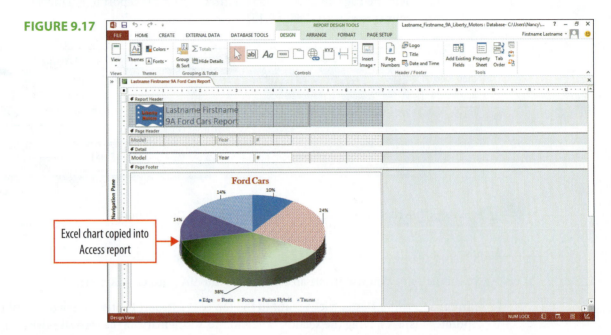

Excel chart copied into Access report

5 ▶ **Save** 💾 the report, and then switch to **Report** view. If you are instructed to submit this result, create a paper or electronic printout. **Close** ☒ the report.

Objective 4   Import from and Link to Another Access Database

Video A9-4

When you import data from another Access database, Access creates a copy of the source data without altering the source data. All of the objects in a database can be imported or copied to another Access database in a single operation. Import data from another Access database when you need to create similar tables or when you want to use the structure of the source database tables. Link to data in another Access database when the data is shared among multiple databases or if someone else needs to have the ability to add records and use the data, but not change the structure of the table.

Activity 9.07 | Importing Data from Another Access Database

In this activity, you will import the data contained in another Access database.

1 ▶ On the **EXTERNAL DATA tab**, in the **Import & Link group**, click the **Access** button. In the **Get External Data - Access Database** dialog box, click **Browse**. If necessary, navigate to the location where the data files for this chapter are saved, and then double-click **a09A_SUVs_and_Motorcycles**.

The source database must be closed before you can import data from it. The destination database must be open. To import the data into a new database, you must create a blank database before starting the import operation.

2 ▷ Verify that the **Import tables, queries, forms, reports, macros, and modules into the current database** option button is selected, and then click **OK**. In the **Import Objects** dialog box, click the **Tables tab**.

The Import Objects dialog box displays the two tables contained in the *a09A_SUVs_and_Motorcycles* database. To choose multiple types of objects, first select one object, click the relevant tab, and then click the desired object on that tab. To cancel a selected object, click the object again.

3 ▷ In the **Import Objects** dialog box, click **9A SUVs**, and then compare your screen with Figure 9.18.

FIGURE 9.18

4 ▷ In the **Import Objects** dialog box, click the **Queries tab**, and then click **9A Toyota SUVs Query**. Click the **Forms tab**, and then click **9A SUVs Form**. Click the **Reports tab**, click **9A Toyota SUVs Report**, and then click **OK**.

The Get External Data - Access Database dialog box displays, enabling you to save the import steps. If Access encounters any errors in the import operation, messages will display. To cancel the import operation during the importing process, press `Ctrl` + `Break`.

5 ▷ In the **Get External Data - Access Database** dialog box, click **Close**.

6 ▷ Open ⟩⟩ the **Navigation Pane**, resize the pane so all object names are visible, and then compare your screen with Figure 9.19.

A table, query, form, and report have been imported to the open database.

NOTE **Importing Queries, Forms, and Reports**

You can import table relationships, custom menus and toolbars, saved import/export specifications, and custom Navigation Pane groups. For tables, you can import the table definition and data or only the table definition. The *definition* is the structure of the database—the field names, data types, and field properties. You can import queries as queries or as tables. If you import a query as a query, you must also import the underlying table or tables used to create the query.

Importing a query, form, report, subform, or subreport does not automatically import the underlying record sources. If you create one of these objects using the data in two related tables, you must also import those two tables; otherwise, these objects will not open properly.

FIGURE 9.19

ALERT!   **Were All Four Objects Not Imported?**

If all four objects were not imported, you may not have clicked the object in the Import Objects dialog box. To correct this, run the import operation again, and select the missing object or objects. Do not select objects that were imported correctly. For example, if you correctly imported the *9A SUVs* table, and then you import it again, a second *9A SUVs* table will be imported and will be named *9A SUVs1*.

7 In the **Navigation Pane**, under **Reports**, right-click **9A Toyota SUVs Report**, and then click **Layout View**. Click the title one time to select it. Click to the left of **9A** to enter into editing mode, type your **Lastname Firstname** and then press Shift + Enter. Press Enter. On the **REPORT LAYOUT TOOLS FORMAT tab**, in the **Font group**, click the **Background Color arrow**, and then, under **Theme Colors**, in the second row, select the fifth color—**Blue, Accent 1, Lighter 80%**.

8 Switch to **Report** view. **Save** 🖫 the report. If you are instructed to submit this result, create a paper or electronic printout.

9 **Close** ✕ the report, and then **Close** « the **Navigation Pane**.

More **Knowledge**   **Recover Data from a Backup File**

If you are missing objects or they have become corrupt, import the clean objects from the most recent backup file.

Activity 9.08 | Linking to a Table in Another Access Database

In this activity, you will link to the data in the 9A Motorcycles table in the *a09A_SUVs_and_Motorcycles* database. You can link only to tables in another Access database; you cannot link to queries, forms, reports, macros, or modules.

1 On the **EXTERNAL DATA tab**, in the **Import & Link group**, click the **Access** button. In the **Get External Data - Access Database** dialog box, **Browse** to the location where the data files for this chapter are saved, and then double-click **a09A_SUVs_and_Motorcycles**.

2 In the **Get External Data - Access Database** dialog box, click the **Link to the data source by creating a linked table** option button, and then click **OK**.

Changes made to the data in Access will be propagated to the source data and vice versa. If the source database requires a password, that password is saved with the linked table. You cannot make changes to the structure of the table in the linked table.

3 In the **Link Tables** dialog box, on the **Tables tab**, click **9A Motorcycles**, and then click **OK**.

4 **Open** » the **Navigation Pane**, if necessary, and then compare your screen with Figure 9.20.

The 9A Motorcycles linked table displays in the Navigation Pane under Tables. The arrow that displays to the left of the icon indicates that this is a linked object.

FIGURE 9.20

Linked Access table

5 In the **Navigation Pane**, under **Tables**, right-click **9A Motorcycles**, and then click **Rename**. Click at the beginning of the line, type your **Lastname Firstname** press [Spacebar], and then press [Enter].

6 In the **Navigation Pane**, under **Tables**, double-click **9A Motorcycles** to display the table in **Datasheet** view. Adjust the widths of the columns as necessary.

7 If you are instructed to submit this result, create a paper or electronic printout. If you submit this database electronically, also submit **a09A_SUVs_and_Motorcycles.accdb** in order to view the linked objects properly. **Close** [×] the table, saving changes when prompted. **Close** the database, and then **Exit** [×] Access.

8 As directed by your instructor, submit your database, text file, and the paper or electronic printouts of the four objects—two tables and two reports—that are the result of this project. Specifically, in this project, using your own name you created the following database and printouts or electronic printouts:

1. Lastname_Firstname_9A_Liberty_Motors	Database file
2. Lastname_Firstname_9A_Employees_Table.txt	Text file
3. Lastname Firstname 9A Employees	Table (printed or electronic printout)
4. Lastname Firstname 9A Ford Cars Report	Report (printed or electronic printout)
5. Lastname Firstname 9A Toyota SUVs Report	Report (printed or electronic printout)
6. Lastname Firstname 9A Motorcycles	Table (printed or electronic printout)

END | You have completed Project 9A

Used Inventory

PROJECT ACTIVITIES

In Activities 9.09 through 9.15, you will help the sales staff at Liberty Motors use information from Access databases in other applications. In addition, you need to help the webmaster include data on the company's website. Access enables you to export data from an Access database into other applications, such as Word, Excel, or another Access database, and merge data from an Access database with a Word document. You can also export data to be used on a webpage. Your completed files will look similar to Figure 9.21.

PROJECT FILES

For Project 9B, you will need the following files:

a09B_Used_Inventory.accdb
a09B_Memo.docx

You will save your files as:

Lastname_Firstname_9B_Used_Inventory.accdb
Lastname_Firstname_9B_Jeeps_Exported.rtf
Lastname_Firstname_9B_Jeeps.docx
Lastname_Firstname_9B_Custom_Memo.docx
Lastname_Firstname_9B_Memo_Main.docx
Lastname_Firstname_9B_Used_Vehicles.xlsx
Lastname_Firstname_9B_Jeeps_in_Stock.html
Lastname_Firstname_9B_Jeeps_in_Stock.rtf
Lastname_Firstname_9B_XML_Jeeps_File.htm
Lastname_Firstname_9B_XML_Jeeps_File.xml
Lastname_Firstname_9B_XML_Jeeps_File.xsl

PROJECT RESULTS

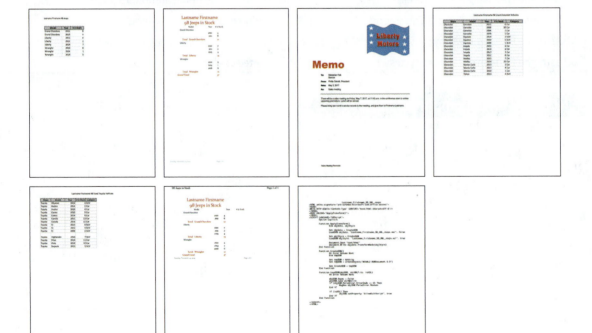

FIGURE 9.21 Project 9B Used Inventory

Video A9-5

You can *export* a table, query, form, or report to Word 2013. Exporting is the process used to send out a copy of data from one source or application to another application. You can then email the Word document rather than the entire database. Exporting to Word is also helpful if you have a table that you want to format more than you can in an Access table. When you export an Access object, the Export Wizard creates a copy of the object's data in a Microsoft Word Rich Text Format file; an extension of .rtf is used. Hidden fields are not exported with tables, queries, and forms; visible fields and records display as a table in the Word document. When you export a report, the Export Wizard copies the report data and the design layout, making the Word document resemble the report as closely as possible.

Activity 9.09 │ Exporting an Access Query to Word

In this activity, you will export a query to Word 2013. The database must be open in Access to perform the export operation because there is no Access import feature in Word.

1 ▶ Start Access. Navigate to the location where the student data files for this textbook are saved. Locate and open the **a09B_Used_Inventory** file. Save the database in your **Access Chapter 9** folder as **Lastname_Firstname_9B_Used_Inventory** Enable the content, or add the **Access Chapter 9** folder to the **Trust Center**.

2 ▶ In the **Navigation Pane**, **Rename** the two queries and one report by adding your **Lastname Firstname** to the beginning of the object names. Under **Queries**, double-click **9B Jeeps** to run and display the query results.

The query displays the model name, the year of the vehicle, and the number of Jeeps in stock.

3 ▶ Switch the query to **Design** view, expand the field lists so all data displays fully, and then compare your screen with Figure 9.22.

The underlying source of this query is the *9B Used Vehicles* query. In the design grid, in the last column, the criteria is *Jeep*, which extracts records with this criteria in the Make field. The field is hidden from the results because the data is redundant.

FIGURE 9.22

4 **Close** ⊠ the query, saving changes if necessary. In the **Navigation Pane**, under **Queries**, right-click **9B Jeeps**, point to **Export**, and then click **Word RTF File**. Alternatively, click the **EXTERNAL DATA tab**, and then in the **Export** group, click the **More** button, and then click **Word**. Compare your screen with Figure 9.23.

> The Export - RTF File dialog box displays, which enables you to select the destination for the data you want to export. Because the Export Wizard always exports formatted data, this option is selected and inactive. An option is available to display the Word document after the export operation is complete. The last selection—*Export only the selected records*—is inactive. If you want to export some of the records, before you begin the export operation, open the object and select the records.

FIGURE 9.23

5 In the **Export - RTF File** dialog box, click **Browse**. Navigate to the **Access Chapter 9** folder. In the **File name** box, select the existing file name, type **Lastname_Firstname_9B_Jeeps_Exported** and then click **Save**.

> **NOTE**   **Exporting Data into an Existing Word Document**
>
> When you export from Access to Word, the data is always exported into a new Word document. If you select an existing document, the Export Wizard overwrites the Word document with the new data. To insert the data into an existing Word document, export the data from Access into a new Word document, and then copy the data from the new Word document and paste it into the existing Word document. Alternatively, copy rows directly from an Access table, query, form, or report, and then paste them into the existing Word document.

6 In the **Export - RTF File** dialog box, under **Specify export options**, select the **Open the destination file after the export operation is complete** check box, and then click **OK**. Compare your screen with Figure 9.24.

> The query data is exported to a Word document. Because the Word document did not exist, a new document was created. The data is displayed as a table in Word with the field names as column headings. The hidden field—Make—does not display. In the title bar of the Word document, *[Compatibility Mode]* displays because this document has an .rtf extension instead of the standard .docx extension.

FIGURE 9.24

7 In Word, click the **INSERT tab**. In the **Header & Footer group**, click the **Header** button. In the **Built-in** gallery, click **Austin**. Click the **[Document title]** text, and then type **Lastname Firstname 9B Jeeps** to replace it. In the **Close group**, click the **Close Header and Footer** button.

8 On the **Quick Access Toolbar**, click the **Save** button, and then compare your screen with Figure 9.25.

> A message may display stating that a feature in the document is not supported by earlier versions of Word, meaning that a document with an .rtf extension cannot display the data in the same manner as Word. Although the summary is cryptic, in this case, an .rtf document cannot display content controls. If you click Continue, Word converts the header data to static text.

FIGURE 9.25

9 In the message box, click **Cancel**. Display **Backstage** view, click **Save As**, and double-click the **Access Chapter 9** folder. In the **Save As** dialog box, click in the **Save as type** box, and select **Word Document**. Change the file name to **Lastname_Firstname_9B_Jeeps** and then click **Save**.

> A message box may display stating that you are about to save your document to one of the new file formats and that changes may be made in the layout of the document.

10 In the displayed message box, click **OK**. If you are instructed to submit this result, create a paper or electronic printout.

11 Close ✕ Word. In the **Export - RTF File** dialog box, click **Close**.

Activity 9.10 | Exporting an Access Report to Word

In this activity, you will export the 9B Jeeps in Stock report to a Word document.

1 In the **Navigation Pane**, under **Reports**, double-click **9B Jeeps in Stock** to open the report. Switch to **Layout** view. Click the title—**9B Jeeps in Stock**—two times to enter into editing mode. Click to the left of **9B**, type **Lastname Firstname** using your own first and last names, and then press Shift + Enter. Press Enter, and then **Save** the report.

> The report displays Jeep models, the year, and the number of vehicles in stock for each year of the model. Each model is summed, and at the bottom of the report, the total number of Jeeps displays.

2 Close ✕ the report. In the **Navigation Pane**, under **Reports**, right-click **9B Jeeps in Stock**, point to **Export**, and then click **Word RTF File**. Verify that the **File name** box displays the correct path to your **Access Chapter 9** folder. In the **File name** box, select the existing file name, and type **Lastname_Firstname_9B_Jeeps_in_Stock** Under **Specify export options**, click the **Open the destination file after the export operation is complete** check box, and then click **OK**. Compare your screen with Figure 9.26.

> A message box displays, and then the document opens in Word. Although all of the data is exported, it is not aligned as nicely as it was in the Access report. You would probably want to do some further formatting in Word. All of the data is separated by tabs.

FIGURE 9.26

3 If you are instructed to submit this result, create a paper or electronic printout. **Close** ☒ Word. In the **Export - RTF File** dialog box, click **Close**.

Objective 6 Use Mail Merge to Integrate Access and Word

Video A9-6

Using Word's **_mail merge_** feature, letters or memos are created by combining, or **_merging_**, two documents—a **_main document_** and a **_data source_**. The main document contains the text of a letter or memo. The data source—an Access table or query—contains the names and addresses of the individuals to whom the letter, memo, or other document is being sent. Use the Mail Merge Wizard within Access to create a direct link between the table or query and the Word document.

Activity 9.11 | Merging an Access Table with a Word Document

In this activity, you will create individual memos to the employees of Liberty Motors to inform them of an upcoming staff meeting. You will create the memos by merging the individual names and position or department in the 9B Employees Table with a memo created in Microsoft Word.

1 In the **Navigation Pane**, click the **9B Employees** table to select the table. On the **EXTERNAL DATA tab**, in the **Export group**, click the **Word Merge** button.

The Microsoft Word Mail Merge Wizard starts. In this first dialog box, you can link the data in the table to an existing Word document or create a new Word document and then link the data in the table to the new document.

2 Verify that **Link your data to an existing Microsoft Word document** is selected, and then click **OK**. In the **Select Microsoft Word Document** dialog box, navigate to the location where the student data files for this textbook are saved. Locate and open the **a09B_Memo** file; click the **Microsoft Word** button on the taskbar to view the memo, and then compare your screen with Figure 9.27.

Microsoft Word opens with the memo on the left and the Mail Merge pane on the right.

FIGURE 9.27

3 ▶ On the **Microsoft Word** title bar, click the **Maximize** □ button. At the bottom of the **Mail Merge** pane, notice that the wizard is on **Step 3 of 6**.

Because you are using an existing Word document, the first two steps are already defined.

4 ▶ In the **Mail Merge** pane, under **Select recipients**, verify that the **Use an existing list** option button is selected. Under **Use an existing list**, click **Edit recipient list**, and then compare your screen with Figure 9.28.

The Mail Merge Recipients dialog box displays, enabling you to sort the list, filter the list, find duplicate entries, find a particular recipient or group of recipients, validate addresses, add recipients to the list, or remove recipients from the list.

FIGURE 9.28

5 ▶ In the **Mail Merge Recipients** dialog box, on the row for **Phillip Garrett**, clear the **check box** to the left of **Garrett** to remove this record from the list of recipients. Click the **Last Name arrow**, and then click **Sort Ascending**. Notice that the first record is empty. In this empty record, clear the **check box** to the left of where the last name would display, and then click **OK**.

Because the memo is from Phillip Garrett, a memo should not be addressed to him.

6 ▶ In the **Mail Merge** pane, under **Step 3 of 6**, click **Next: Write your letter**. Take a moment to read the information in the **Mail Merge** pane. If necessary, on the **HOME tab**, in the **Paragraph group**, click the **Show/Hide** button to display the paragraph marks. On the left side of the screen in the memo, click to the right of **To:** and to the left of the paragraph symbol, above the letter **P** in *Phillip*. In the **Mail Merge** pane, under **Write your letter**, click **More items**, and then compare your screen with Figure 9.29.

The Insert Merge Field dialog box displays, which enables you to select a field from the database to insert into the memo. The Match Fields button enables you to map the fields in the table to the mail merge fields that are built into Word. For example, this table contains a field named Position/ Department that could be mapped to the Word mail merge field entitled Job Title.

FIGURE 9.29

7 In the **Insert Merge Field** dialog box, under **Fields**, click **First Name**, and then click **Insert**. Alternatively, double-click the field. Click **Last Name**, and then click **Insert**. Click **Position/ Department**, and then click **Insert**. Click **Close**, and then compare your screen with Figure 9.30.

Word inserts each field name surrounded with the characters < and >. There are no spaces between the field names.

 ANOTHER WAY Instead of inserting all of the fields together, you can insert each field from the Mailings tab. In the Write & Insert Fields group, click the Insert Merge Field arrow button to view a list of available fields. Click the appropriate field desired as needed.

FIGURE 9.30

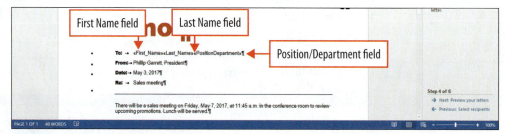

8 In the **memo**, click to the left of «**Last_Name**», and then press [Spacebar] to insert a space between the First_Name and Last_Name fields. Click to the left of «**PositionDepartment**», hold down [Shift], and then press [Enter] to move the field to the next line. Compare your screen with Figure 9.31.

Because the memo has built-in formatting, you must press [Shift] + [Enter] to insert a line break to align the Position/Department field directly under the First Name field. If you press [Enter] to insert a paragraph break, the Position/Department field will align at the left margin and a blank line will display above it.

FIGURE 9.31

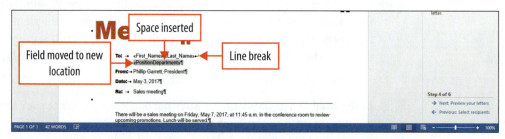

9 In the **Mail Merge** pane, under **Step 4 of 6**, click **Next: Preview your letters**. Notice that the first memo displays with a recipient name of **Adam Bristow**. In the **Mail Merge** pane, under **Preview your letters**, click the **Next record** ▶ button to display the memo for the next recipient. Continue clicking the **Next record** button until the letter addressed to *Sebastian Falk* (Recipient 11) displays.

10 In the **Mail Merge** pane, under **Step 5 of 6**, click **Next: Complete the merge**, and notice that in this step, you can either print the memos or edit the memos. In the **Mail Merge** pane, under **Merge**, click **Edit individual letters**.

By clicking *Edit individual letters*, you can customize one or more of the merged memos.

11 In the displayed **Merge to New Document** dialog box, click **Current record**, and then click **OK**.

The memo addressed to Sebastian Falk displays. At the end of the memo, a section break displays to demonstrate the end of the merged information for that record.

12 Press Ctrl + End to move to the end of the memo after the section break. Using your own first and last names, type **Please bring last month's service records to the meeting, and give it to Firstname Lastname.** and then compare your screen with Figure 9.32.

FIGURE 9.32

Custom message

13 On the **Quick Access toolbar**, click the **Save** button. In the **Save As** dialog box, navigate to your **Access Chapter 9** folder, and then **Save** the Word document as **Lastname_Firstname_9B_Custom_Memo** If you are instructed to submit this result, create a paper or electronic printout.

14 Close ✕ Word to exit the custom document. Notice that the memo to Sebastian Falk without the custom message displays in the Mail Merge Wizard.

15 From the **Backstage** view, click **Save As**. In your **Access Chapter 9** folder, **Save** the Word document as **Lastname_Firstname_9B_Memo_Main** and then **Close** ✕ Word. If the database is not displayed, on the status bar, click the **Microsoft Access** button to restore the Access window to the screen.

Objective 7 | Export Data to Excel

Video A9-7

You can copy data from an Access database into a worksheet by exporting a table, form, or query to an Excel workbook; however, you cannot export reports, macros, or modules to Excel. When you export a table or form that contains subdatasheets or subforms, only the main datasheet or main form is exported. You can export only one database object in a single export operation; however, you can merge the data in multiple worksheets in Excel after completing the individual export operations.

Export data to Excel if users share the data and some work with Access while others work with Excel. You can store the data in Access and then export it to Excel to analyze the data.

Activity 9.12 | Exporting Selected Records to Excel

In this activity, you will export selected records—Chevrolet vehicle data—from an Access query to an Excel workbook.

1 In the **Navigation Pane**, under **Queries**, double-click **9B Used Vehicles** to run the query and to display the results. **Close** « the **Navigation Pane**.

2 Click the arrow to the right of **Make** in the title row of the query results. Click the **Select All** check box to remove the check mark displaying all makes. Click the check box next to **Chevrolet** to filter the table to display only that make of vehicle. Click **OK**. Select the filtered records, and then compare your screen with Figure 9.33.

FIGURE 9.33

3 On the **EXTERNAL DATA tab**, in the **Export group**, click **Excel**.

4 In the displayed **Export - Excel Spreadsheet** dialog box, in the **File name** box, verify that the path to your **Access Chapter 9** folder is correct. In the **File name** box, select the existing file name, and type **Lastname_Firstname_9B_Used_Vehicles** Notice that in the **File format** box, the file will be saved as an Excel Workbook with an extension of .xlsx, which is the extension used for Excel 2013.

5 In the **Export - Excel Spreadsheet** dialog box, under **Specify export options**, click the **Export data with formatting and layout** check box. Click the **Open the destination file after the export operation is complete** check box, and then click the **Export only the selected records** check box.

Because you selected records in the query, the *Export only the selected records* option is active.

6 In the **Export - Excel Spreadsheet** dialog box, click **OK**, and then compare your screen with Figure 9.34.

Excel opens and displays the exported data in a worksheet within the workbook. The worksheet name is the same as the query from which the data was exported. The workbook name displays in the Excel window title bar.

FIGURE 9.34

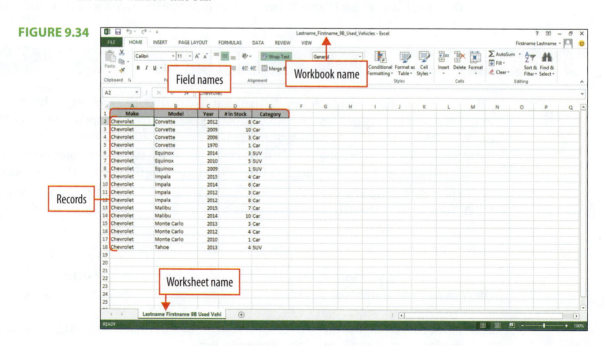

7 At the bottom of the worksheet, right-click the **Worksheet tab**, and then click **Rename**. Type **9B Chevrolet** and then press Enter. **Save** 💾 the workbook, and then **Minimize** ▬ the Excel workbook.

8 If necessary, click the **Microsoft Access** button on the taskbar to restore the Access window and display the query.

Activity 9.13 | Copying Selected Records to an Existing Excel Workbook

In this activity, you will export selected records—Toyota vehicle data—from an Access query to an Excel workbook by copying and pasting the records.

1 In the datasheet, using the techniques you practiced in the previous activity, filter the table and select all of the records displaying a **Make** of **Toyota**.

2 On the **HOME tab**, in the **Clipboard group**, click the **Copy** button. Alternatively, right-click in a blank area of the datasheet, and then click **Copy**; or press Ctrl + C.

3 On the taskbar, click the **Microsoft Excel** button to make the Excel window active.

4 At the bottom of the worksheet, to the right of the **9B Chevrolet tab**, click the **New Sheet** ⊕ button. Compare your screen with Figure 9.35.

> A blank worksheet is inserted to the right of the *Chevrolet* worksheet. A dark border displays around cell A1.

FIGURE 9.35

5 With cell **A1** selected, on the **HOME tab**, in the **Clipboard group**, click the **Paste** button. Alternatively, press Ctrl + V.

> The selected records are pasted into the *9B_Used_Vehicles* workbook on a separate worksheet.

N O T E	**Exporting Data into an Existing Workbook**
	If you use the Export Wizard to export selected records into an existing workbook, the original data in the Excel workbook is overwritten.

---

6 Point to the column border between **B** and **C** until the pointer displays. Drag to the right until all of the data in cell **B12**—*Highlander*—displays on one line.

7 Using the techniques you practiced in the previous activity, **Rename** the worksheet as **9B Toyota** and then compare your screen with Figure 9.36.

There are now two worksheets in the *9B_Used_Vehicles* workbook— *9B Chevrolet* and *9B Toyota*. The *9B Toyota* worksheet is active.

FIGURE 9.36

8 Save the workbook. On the **INSERT tab**, in the **Text group**, click the **Header & Footer** button. In the **header** box, type **Lastname Firstname 9B Used Toyota Vehicles** Click anywhere in the worksheet to move the insertion point out of the header box.

9 At the bottom of the workbook, click the **9B Chevrolet tab**. Insert a **Header** of **Lastname Firstname 9B Used Chevrolet Vehicles** and then click anywhere in the worksheet to move the insertion point out of the header box.

10 Save the workbook. Unless you are required to submit your files electronically, display **Backstage** view, and then click **Print**. Under **Settings**, click the **Print Active Sheets arrow**, and then click **Print Entire Workbook**. If you are directed to submit an electronic printout of this workbook, display **Backstage** view, and then click **Export**. Double-click **Create PDF/XPS Document**. In the **Publish a PDF or XPS** dialog box, click the **Options** button, and then select **Entire workbook**. Click **OK**, and then click **Publish**.

Both worksheets print with the header information at the top of the page.

11 Close Excel. In the Access window, **Close** the **9B Used Vehicles** query without saving, and then **Open** the **Navigation Pane**.

More Knowledge | **Exporting Data to Another Access Database**

You can copy data from one Access database into another Access database. Copying and pasting is easiest, but exporting offers you more options. You can export all of the database objects into another database. However, to export selected records, you must copy and paste the records.

Exporting an object to another database is similar to importing the object from the first database, although you cannot export multiple objects in a single operation. If you want to export multiple objects, it is easier to open the destination database and perform an import operation. You cannot export table relationships, import and export specifications, custom menu bars, custom toolbars, or a query as a table.

Video A9-8

If you need to display an Access object on a webpage, you can export the object to an *HTML* format, *HyperText Markup Language*—the language used to display webpages. Webpages are text files that contain text and codes—known as *tags*—that the web browser interprets as the page is loaded. A tag begins with the < character and ends with the > character; for example, to apply bold formatting to the word Access, you would add a beginning and an ending tag to the word— <b>Access</b>. The <b> tag identifies where the bold formatting begins. The </b> tag identifies where the bold formatting ends.

XML, *Extensible Markup Language*, is the standard language for describing and delivering data on the web. Similar to HTML, XML uses tags to organize and present data. Unlike HTML, which uses standard tags, XML enables you to create your own set of tags. With an XML document, the data can be displayed on a webpage, included in a Word document, analyzed in Excel, imported into a different database, or imported into many other programs that recognize XML files.

Activity 9.14 | Exporting a Report to an HTML File

In this activity, you will export the 9B Jeeps in Stock report to an HTML file.

1 In the **Navigation Pane**, under **Reports**, right-click **9B Jeeps in Stock**, point to **Export**, and then click **HTML Document**.

2 In the displayed **Export - HTML Document** dialog box, in the **File name** box, verify that the file will be saved in the **Access Chapter 9** folder. In the **File name** box, select the existing file name, and type **Lastname_Firstname_9B_Jeeps_in_Stock.html** Under **Specify export options**, select the **Open the destination file after the export operation is complete** check box, and then click **OK**.

3 In the displayed **HTML Output Options** dialog box, click **OK**, and then compare your screen with Figure 9.37.

The document displays in Microsoft Internet Explorer or in your default web browser.

FIGURE 9.37

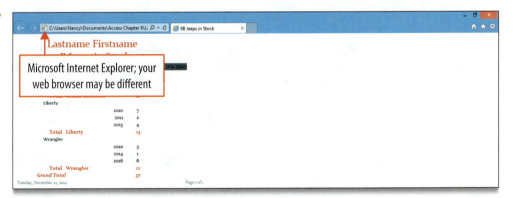

4 If you are instructed to submit this result, create a paper or electronic printout of the webpage.

5 **Close** [**×**] the web browser window. In the **Export - HTML Document** dialog box, click the **Close** button.

Activity 9.15 | Exporting a Report to an XML File

In this activity, you will export the 9B Jeeps in Stock report to an XML file.

1 In the **Navigation Pane**, under **Reports**, right-click **9B Jeeps in Stock**, point to **Export**, and then click **XML File**.

2 In the displayed **Export - XML File** dialog box, in the **File name** box, verify that the file will be saved in the **Access Chapter 9** folder. Select the file name, and then type **Lastname_ Firstname_9B_XML_Jeeps.xml** Click **OK**, and then compare your screen with Figure 9.38.

The Export XML dialog box displays. When you export data to XML, multiple files can be created. An **XML schema** is a document with an .xsd extension that defines the elements, entities, and content allowed in the document. It defines the tag names and defines the order, relationships, and data type you use with each tag. The schema is essential to ensure that all of the table relationships and data types are preserved when the data is imported into another database. An XML file cannot be viewed directly in a web browser. **XML presentation files** can be created so that the data can be viewed in a web browser.

FIGURE 9.38

3 In the **Export XML** dialog box, verify that the **Data (XML)** check box is selected, and then click the **Presentation of your data (XSL)** check box. Click **OK**. In the **Export - XML File** dialog box, click **Close**.

Because XML files are typically imported into other applications, there is no option to view the file after the export operation.

4 On the taskbar, click the **File Explorer** button. Navigate to the location where the **Access Chapter 9** folder is saved, and open the folder. Compare your screen with Figure 9.39.

In Details view, the name, size, and type of each file is displayed, in addition to the date and time the file was modified. Your dates and times will differ. The Type column shows two HTML documents— *9B_Jeeps_in_Stock* and *9B_XML_Jeeps*. *9B_Jeeps_in_Stock* is the HTML file that you created when you exported to an HTML file. *9B_XML_Jeeps* is an HTML presentation file that was created when you selected the *Presentation of your data (XSL)* check box while exporting to an XML file.

There is also an *XSL Stylesheet* file named *9B_XML_Jeeps*. This is the second presentation file that is used to create the HTML file. Finally, there is an XML document that stores the data that was exported.

FIGURE 9.39

5 Locate the **9B_XML_Jeeps** file that displays a **Type** of **HTML Document**. Right-click the file name, and then click **Open with**. From the shortcut menu, click **Notepad**. The procedure may differ depending upon your web browser. Compare your screen with Figure 9.40.

> The HTML code displays in a Notepad window. *Notepad* is a simple text editor that comes with the Windows operating system. This is the actual document that was exported. The web browser interprets the HTML tags and displays the text as a readable document. If you know HTML coding, you can format this document so that the column headings are more readable.

FIGURE 9.40

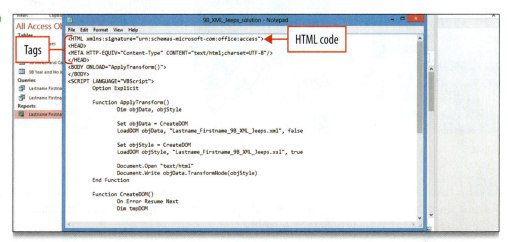

6 If you are instructed to submit this result, create a paper or electronic printout of the source code. **Close** ☒ the Notepad window.

7 **Close** ☒ the Access Chapter 9 window. **Close** the database, and then **Exit** Access.

More Knowledge   **Exporting Data to Alternate Formats**

If you have data in your Access database that you would like to export to other applications, explore the options on the EXTERNAL DATA tab, in the Export group.

- Objects can be shared by others as a PDF document or by emailing them in a format that the recipient can view and use. These export options do not require the recipient to have Access or any other database software.
- In the Export group, click the More button for additional export formats. A SharePoint List, as you recall, is a list of documents maintained on a server running Microsoft Office SharePoint Server. You also can export data to other database applications, such as ODBC databases. Recall that ODBC stands for Open Database Connectivity, a standard that enables databases using SQL statements to interface with one another.

---

8 As directed by your instructor, submit your database and the paper or electronic printouts of the seven objects that were the result of this project—two RTF documents, two Word documents, one Excel workbook, and two HTML documents. Specifically, in this project, using your own name you created the following database and printouts or electronic printouts:

1. Lastname_Firstname_9B_Used_Inventory	Database file
2. Lastname_Firstname_9B_Jeeps_Exported	RTF document (printed or electronic printout)
3. Lastname_Firstname_9B_Jeeps	Word document (printed or electronic printout)
4. Lastname_Firstname_9B_Jeeps_in_Stock	RTF document (printed or electronic printout)
5. Lastname_Firstname_9B_Custom_Memo	Word document (printed or electronic printout)
6. Lastname_Firstname_9B_Used_Vehicles	Excel workbook (printed or electronic printout)
7. Lastname_Firstname_9B_Jeeps_in_Stock	HTML document (printed or electronic printout)
8. Lastname_Firstname_9B_XML_Jeeps	Source code document (printed or electronic printout), XML and XLS files

END | You have completed Project 9B

END OF CHAPTER

SUMMARY

Importing is the process of copying data from another application. For example, a Word table can be converted to a text file for import, or data can come from an Excel worksheet or another database.

Linking is the process of connecting to data in another application. If a table exists in another database, it can be linked to share the table in the original database.

Exporting is the process of copying data to another application to use its features. For example, an Access query can be exported to perform a mail merge or selected records can be exported to Excel.

Access objects can be exported to HTML and XML files, formats used for viewing webpages. From File Explorer, files are opened using a web browser; however, the formatting differs from the Access report.

GO! LEARN IT ONLINE

Review the concepts and key terms in this chapter by completing these online challenges, which you can find at **www.pearsonhighered.com/go.**

Matching and Multiple Choice:
Answer matching and multiple choice questions to test what you learned in this chapter. MyITLab®

Crossword Puzzle:
Spell out the words that match the numbered clues, and put them in the puzzle squares.

Flipboard:
Flip through the definitions of the key terms in this chapter and match them with the correct term.

END OF CHAPTER

REVIEW AND ASSESSMENT GUIDE FOR ACCESS CHAPTER 9

Your instructor may assign one or more of these projects to help you review the chapter and assess your mastery and understanding of the chapter.

	Review and Assessment Guide for Access Chapter 9		
Project	**Apply Skills from These Chapter Objectives**	**Project Type**	**Project Location**
9C	Objectives 1–4 from Project 9A	**9C Skills Review** A guided review of the skills from Project 9A.	On the following pages
9D	Objectives 5–8 from Project 9B	**9D Skills Review** A guided review of the skills from Project 9B.	On the following pages
9E	Objectives 1–4 from Project 9A	**9E Mastery (Grader Project)** A demonstration of your mastery of the skills in Project 9A with extensive decision making.	In MyITLab and on the following pages
9F	Objectives 5–8 from Project 9B	**9F Mastery (Grader Project)** A demonstration of your mastery of the skills in Project 9B with extensive decision making.	In MyITLab and on the following pages
9G	Objectives 1–8 from Projects 9A and 9B	**9G Mastery (Grader Project)** A demonstration of your mastery of the skills in Projects 9A and 9B with extensive decision making.	In MyITLab and on the following pages
9H	Combination of Objectives from Projects 9A and 9B	**9H GO! Fix It** A demonstration of your mastery of the skills in Projects 9A and 9B by creating a correct result from a document that contains errors you must find.	Online
9I	Combination of Objectives from Projects 9A and 9B	**9I GO! Make It** A demonstration of your mastery of the skills in Projects 9A and 9B by creating a result from a supplied picture.	Online
9J	Combination of Objectives from Projects 9A and 9B	**9J GO! Solve It** A demonstration of your mastery of the skills in Projects 9A and 9B, your decision-making skills, and your critical thinking skills. A task-specific rubric helps you self-assess your result.	Online
9K	Combination of Objectives from Projects 9A and 9B	**9K GO! Solve It** A demonstration of your mastery of the skills in Projects 9A and 9B, your decision-making skills, and your critical thinking skills. A task-specific rubric helps you self-assess your result.	On the following pages
9L	Combination of Objectives from Projects 9A and 9B	**9L GO! Think** A demonstration of your understanding of the chapter concepts applied in a manner that you would use outside of college. An analytic rubric helps you and your instructor grade the quality of your work by comparing it to the work an expert in the discipline would create.	On the following pages
9M	Combination of Objectives from Projects 9A and 9B	**9M GO! Think** A demonstration of your understanding of the chapter concepts applied in a manner that you would use outside of college. An analytic rubric helps you and your instructor grade the quality of your work by comparing it to the work an expert in the discipline would create.	Online
9N	Combination of Objectives from Projects 9A and 9B	**9N You and GO!** A demonstration of your understanding of the chapter concepts applied in a manner that you would use in a personal situation. An analytic rubric helps you and your instructor grade the quality of your work.	Online

GLOSSARY

GLOSSARY OF CHAPTER KEY TERMS

Appended When data is added to the end of an existing table.

ASCII An acronym for American Standard Code for Information Interchange, a character set.

Cell The small box formed by the intersection of a column and a row in a worksheet.

Chart A graphic representation of data.

Column chart A chart used to display comparisons among related numbers.

Converted Changed.

Data source An Access table or query that contains the names and addresses of the individuals to whom the letter, memo, or other document is being sent in a mail merge.

Definition The structure of the database—the field names, data types, and field properties.

Delimited file A file in which each record displays on a separate line, and the fields within the record are separated by a single character.

Delimiter A single character; can be a paragraph mark, a tab, a comma, or another character.

Export The process used to send out a copy of data from one source or application to another application.

Extensible Markup Language The standard language for defining and storing data on the web.

HTML An acronym for HyperText Markup Language.

HyperText Markup Language The language used to display webpages.

Import The process used to bring in a copy of data from one source or application to another application.

Line chart A chart used to display trends over time.

Link A connection to data in another file.

Mail merge Letters or memos that are created by combining two documents.

Main document The document that contains the text of a letter or memo for a mail merge.

Merging Combining two documents to create one.

Named range A range that has been given a name, making it easier to use the cells in calculations or modifications.

Notepad A simple text editor that comes with the Windows operating systems.

ODBC An acronym for Open Database Connectivity.

Open Database Connectivity A standard that enables databases using SQL statements to interface with one another.

Pie chart A chart used to display the contributions of parts to a whole amount.

Plain Text A document format that contains no formatting, such as bold or italics.

Range An area that includes two or more selected cells on a worksheet that can be treated as a single unit.

SharePoint List A list of documents maintained on a server running Microsoft Office SharePoint Server.

SharePoint Server A server that enables you to share documents with others in your organization.

Spreadsheet Another name for a worksheet.

Tags Codes that the web browser interprets as the page is loaded; they begin with the < character and end with the > character.

Workbook An Excel file that contains one or more worksheets.

Worksheet The primary document used in Excel to save and work with data that is arranged in columns and rows.

XML An acronym for Extensible Markup Language.

XML presentation files Files that can be created so that the data can be viewed in a web browser.

XML schema A document with an *.xsd* extension that defines the elements, entities, and content allowed in the document.

CHAPTER REVIEW

Apply **9A** skills from these Objectives:

1 Import Data from a Word Table

2 Import Data from an Excel Workbook

3 Insert an Excel Chart into a Report

4 Import from and Link to Another Access Database

Skills Review | Project 9C Cars and Motorcycles

Liberty Motors maintains many of its records in Word, Excel, and Access files. Phillip Garrett, president, and Jeanine Thomas, finance manager, want to bring the data from these files into an Access database to create queries and reports. In this project, you will import data from Word, Excel, and another Access database and create a link to data in another application. Your completed files will look similar to Figure 9.41.

PROJECT FILES

Build from Scratch

For Project 9C, you will need the following files:

New blank Access database
a09C_Used_Cars_Inventory.accdb
a09C_Motorcycles.accdb
a09C_Logo.jpg
a09C_Domestic_Chart.xlsx
a09C_Customers.docx
a09C_Sports_Car_Sales.xlsx

You will save your files as:

Lastname_Firstname_9C_Cars_ and_Motorcycles.accdb
Lastname_Firstname_9C_ Customers_Table.txt

PROJECT RESULTS

FIGURE 9.41

(Project 9C Cars and Motorcycles continues on the next page)

CHAPTER REVIEW

1   Start Access. In the Access startup window, click **Blank desktop database**. In the **Blank desktop database** dialog box, to the right of the **File name** box, click the **Browse** button. In the **File New Database** dialog box, navigate to your **Access Chapter 9** folder. In the **File New Database** dialog box, click in the **File name** box, type **Lastname_Firstname_9C_Cars_and_Motorcycles** and then press [Enter]. In the **Blank desktop database** dialog box, click **Create**. **Close** the displayed table.

2   Start Word. Click **Open Other Documents**. Click **Computer**, click **Browse**, and then navigate to the location where the student data files for this textbook are saved. Locate and open the **a09C_Customers** file.

   a.   Verify that the insertion point is in the table. On the **TABLE TOOLS LAYOUT tab**, in the **Data group**, click the **Convert to Text** button. In the dialog box, verify that the **Tabs** option button is selected, and then click **OK**. Click anywhere to deselect the text.

   b.   Display **Backstage** view, double-click **Save As**, and then navigate to the **Access Chapter 9** folder. Save the file as **Lastname_Firstname_9C_Customers_Table** Click the **Save as type arrow**, and from the displayed list click **Plain Text**. Click **Save**, and then click **OK**. **Close** Word.

3   **Return** to Access. On the **EXTERNAL DATA tab**, in the **Import & Link group**, click the **Text File** button. In the dialog box, to the right of the **File name** box, click **Browse**. Locate **9C_Customers_Table**, and double-click.

   a.   Verify that the **Import the source data into a new table in the current database** option button is selected, and then click **OK**. In the **Import Text Wizard** dialog box, verify that the **Delimited** option button is selected. Click **Next**. Verify that the **Tab** option button is selected, and then click the **First Row Contains Field Names** check box. In the **Text Qualifier** box, verify that {**none**} is selected, and click **Next**.

   b.   Click in the **Postal Code** field to select the field. Under **Field Options**, click the **Data Type arrow**, and then click **Short Text**. Click **Next**. Verify that the **Let Access add primary key** option button is selected, and then click **Next**. Change the name to **Lastname Firstname 9C Customers** Click **Finish**.

   c.   Click the **Save import steps** check box. Click in the **Description** box, and then type **Imports a tab-delimited text file that was a Word table** Click **Save Import**. On the **EXTERNAL DATA tab**, in

the **Import & Link group**, click the **Saved Imports** button, and confirm that your import file is there. **Close** the dialog box.

4   In the **Navigation Pane**, double-click **9C Customers** to open it, and then **Close** the **Navigation Pane**.

   a.   In **record 25**, add yourself as a customer. Adjust the widths of all of the fields to display all of the data and the entire field name for each field.

   b.   If you are instructed to submit this result, create a paper or electronic printout of the table in **Landscape** orientation, changing margins, if necessary, to print all of the fields. **Save**, and then **Close** the table.

5   On the **EXTERNAL DATA tab**, in the **Import & Link group**, click the **Excel** button. In the dialog box, click the **Browse** button. Locate and open the **a09C_Sports_Car_Sales** file. Verify **Import the source data into a new table in the current database** is selected, and then click **OK**.

   a.   In the **Import Spreadsheet Wizard** dialog box, verify that **Show Worksheets** is selected and **In Stock** is highlighted. Click **Next**.

   b.   Verify that the **First Row Contains Column Headings** check box is selected. Click **Next** two times.

   c.   Select **Choose my own primary key**. If necessary, click the **field name box arrow**, click **Vehicle#**, and then click **Next**. In the **Import to Table** box, type **Lastname Firstname 9C Sports Cars** and then click **Finish**. In the **Get External Data - Excel Spreadsheet** dialog box, click **Close**.

6   On the **EXTERNAL DATA tab**, in the **Import & Link group**, click the **Excel** button. Locate and **Open** the **a09C_Sports_Car_Sales** file.

   a.   Click **Append a copy of the records to the table**. If necessary, click the **table name box arrow** and select **9C Sports Cars**. Click **OK**. In the **Import Spreadsheet Wizard** dialog box, be certain that **Show Worksheets** is selected. Click **Special Order**, and then click **Next** two times. Click **Finish**.

   b.   In the **Get External Data - Excel Spreadsheet** dialog box, click **Close**, and then **Open** the **Navigation Pane**. Double-click **9C Sports Cars** to open the table. If you are instructed to submit this result, create a paper or electronic printout of the table. **Close** the table, and then **Close** the **Navigation Pane**.

(Project 9C Cars and Motorcycles continues on the next page)

CHAPTER REVIEW

7 On the **CREATE tab**, in the **Queries group**, click the **Query Design** button. In the **Show Table** dialog box, double-click **9C Sports Cars**, and then click **Close**. In the field list, click **Vehicle#**. Hold down Shift, and then click **Color**. Drag the fields down into the first column of the design grid. In the design grid, under **Domestic**, click in the **Criteria** box, type **Y** and then on the **Show** row, clear the check box. On the **QUERY TOOLS DESIGN tab**, in the **Results group**, click the **Run** button. **Save** the query as **Lastname Firstname 9C Domestic** and then **Close** the query.

8 **Open** the **Navigation Pane**. Under **Queries**, click **9C Domestic** to select the query, and then **Close** the **Navigation Pane**. On the **CREATE tab**, in the **Reports group**, click the **Report** button.

a. Switch to **Design** view. Click the image to the left of the title. On the **REPORT DESIGN TOOLS DESIGN tab**, in the **Header/Footer group**, click the **Logo** button. Locate **a09C_Logo**, and then double-click. In the **Tools group**, click the **Property Sheet** button. On the **Property Sheet Format tab**, change the **Size Mode** property to **Zoom**. **Close** the **Property Sheet**. In the **Report Header** section, delete the **Date** and **Time text box controls**. In the **Page Footer** section, delete the **Page number text box control**. In the **Report Footer** section, delete the **Count calculated control** and **line**, and then drag the bottom of the **Report Footer** section to the bottom of the section bar.

b. **Save** the report as **Lastname Firstname 9C Domestic Report** Point to the top of the **Report Footer section bar** until the pointer displays. Drag the section down to the **3-inch mark on the vertical ruler**.

c. Start Excel. If necessary, maximize the Excel window. Click **Open Other Workbooks**. Locate and open **a09C_Domestic_Chart**. Click the outside edge of the **column chart** to select the entire chart. Right-click the chart, and then click **Copy**. **Close** the workbook without saving, and then **Exit** Excel. In the **9C Domestic Report**, right-click the **Page Footer section bar**, and then click **Paste**. Remove any blank space in the **Report Footer** section. **Save** the report, and then switch to **Report** view. If you are instructed to submit this result, create a paper or electronic printout. **Close** the report.

9 On the **EXTERNAL DATA tab**, in the **Import & Link group**, click the **Access** button. In the **Get External Data - Access Database** dialog box, click **Browse**. Locate and then double-click **a09C_Used_Cars_Inventory**. Verify that the **Import tables, queries, forms, reports, macros, and modules into the current database** option button is selected, and then click **OK**.

a. In the **Import Objects** dialog box, click the **Tables tab**, and then click **9C Used Vehicles**. Click the **Queries tab**, and then click **9C Corvettes**. Click the **Reports tab**, click **9C Corvettes in Stock**, and then click **OK**.

b. In the dialog box, click **Close**. **Open** the **Navigation Pane**.

10 In the **Navigation Pane**, under **Reports**, right-click **9C Corvettes in Stock**, and then click **Layout View**. Click the title *9C Corvettes* one time to select the title. Click to the left of *9C*, type **Lastname Firstname** using your name, and then press Shift + Enter. Press Enter, and **Save** the report. If you are instructed to submit this result, create a paper or electronic printout of the report. **Close** the report.

11 On the **EXTERNAL DATA tab**, in the **Import & Link group**, click the **Access** button. In the **Get External Data - Access Database** dialog box, **Browse** to locate and then double-click **a09C_Motorcycles**. Click the **Link to the data source by creating a linked table** option button, and then click **OK**.

a. In the **Link Tables** dialog box, click **9C Motorcycles**, and then click **OK**.

b. In the **Navigation Pane**, under **Tables**, right-click **9C Motorcycles**, and then click **Rename**. Click to the left of **9C**, type **Lastname Firstname** using your name, and then press Spacebar. Press Enter.

c. Double-click **9C Motorcycles** to display the table. Adjust the widths of all of the columns. Unless you are required to submit your database electronically, **Print** the table. If you submit this database electronically, also submit **a09C_Motorcycles** to view the linked objects properly. **Close** the table, saving changes when prompted.

12 **Close** the database, and then **Exit** Access.

(Project 9C Cars and Motorcycles continues on the next page)

CHAPTER REVIEW

13 As directed by your instructor, submit your database, .txt file, and the paper or electronic printouts of the five objects that are the result of this project—three tables and two reports. Specifically, in this project, using your own name you created the following database, .txt file, and printouts or electronic printouts:

1. Lastname_Firstname_9C_Cars_and_Motorcycles	Database file
2. Lastname_Firstname_9C_Customers_Table	.txt file
3. Lastname Firstname 9C Customers	Table (printed or electronic printout)
4. Lastname Firstname 9C Sports Cars	Table (printed or electronic printout)
5. Lastname Firstname 9C Domestic Report	Report (printed or electronic printout)
6. Lastname Firstname 9C Corvettes in Stock	Report (printed or electronic printout)
7. Lastname Firstname 9C Motorcycles	Table (printed or electronic printout)

END | You have completed Project 9C

CHAPTER REVIEW

Apply 9B skills from these Objectives:

5 Export Data to Word

6 Use Mail Merge to Integrate Access and Word

7 Export Data to Excel

8 Export Data to an HTML File and an XML File

The employees at Liberty Motors would like to be able to analyze their sports car inventory data in other applications in addition to Access. Access enables you to export data from an Access database into applications like Word and Excel, including merging Access data with a Word document. You can also export data to be displayed on a webpage. In this project, you will export data to several types of applications. Your completed files will look similar to Figure 9.42.

PROJECT FILES

For Project 9D, you will need the following files:

a09D_Sport_Vehicles.accdb
a09D_SC_Letter.docx

You will save your files as:

Lastname_Firstname_9D_Sport_Vehicles.accdb
Lastname_Firstname_9D_Imports_Query.rtf
Lastname_Firstname_9D_Letter.docx
Lastname_Firstname_9D_Letter_Main.docx
Lastname_Firstname_9D_Imports.docx
Lastname_Firstname_9D_Imports_RTF.rtf
Lastname_Firstname_9D_15-16_Models.xlsx
Lastname_Firstname_9D_Corvettes_HTML
Lastname_Firstname_9D_Corvettes_XML.htm
Lastname_Firstname_9D_Corvettes_XML.xml
Lastname_Firstname_9D_Corvettes_XML.xsl

PROJECT RESULTS

FIGURE 9.42

(Project 9D Sport Vehicles continues on the next page)

CHAPTER REVIEW

1 Start Access. Navigate to the location where the student data files for this textbook are saved. Locate and open the **a09D_Sport_Vehicles** file. Save the database in the **Access 2013 Database** format in your **Access Chapter 9** folder as **Lastname_Firstname_9D_Sport_Vehicles** Enable the content or add the **Access Chapter 9** folder to the **Trust Center.**

2 In the **Navigation Pane**, under **Queries**, right-click **9D Imports**, point to **Export**, and then click **Word RTF File**. In the **Export - RTF File** dialog box, click **Browse.** Navigate to the **Access Chapter 9** folder. In the **File name** box, select the existing file name, type **Lastname_Firstname_9D_Imports_Query** and then click **Save**. In the **Export - RTF File** dialog box, under **Specify export options**, select the **Open the destination file after the export operation is complete** check box, and then click **OK**.

   a. On the **INSERT tab,** in the **Header & Footer group**, click the **Header** button. In the **Built-In** gallery, click **Banded.**Click the [DOCUMENT TITLE] text, and then type **Lastname Firstname 9D Imported Sports Cars** In the **Close group**, click the **Close Header and Footer** button.

   b. Display **Backstage** view, click **Save As**, and navigate to the **Access Chapter 9** folder. Change the file name to **Lastname_Firstname_9D_Imports** Verify that the **Save as type** box displays **Word Document**, which means the file will be given a .docx extension. In the **Save As** dialog box, click **Save**. In the displayed message box, click **OK**. If you are instructed to submit this result, create a paper or electronic printout. **Close** Word. In the **Export - RTF File** dialog box, click **Close**.

3 Click the **9D Customers** table to select it. On the **EXTERNAL DATA tab**, in the **Export group**, click the **Word Merge** button. Verify that **Link your data to an existing Microsoft Word document** is selected, and then click **OK**. In the **Select Microsoft Word Document** dialog box, locate and **Open** the **a09D_SC_Letter** file. Click the **Microsoft Word** button on the taskbar, and **Maximize** the Word window.

   a. In the **Mail Merge** task pane, under **Select recipients**, verify that **Use an existing list** is selected. Under **Step 3 of 6**, click **Next: Write your letter**. Click to the right of **Dear**, and then press Spacebar. In the **Mail Merge** pane, under **Write your letter**, click **More items.**

In the **Insert Merge Field** dialog box under **Fields**, double-click **First Name**. Double-click **Last Name**, and then click **Close**. In the letter, click to the left of «**Last_Name**», and then press Spacebar. Type a **colon** after the «**Last Name**» field.

   b. In the **Mail Merge** task pane, click **Next: Preview your letters**; the first letter displays with a recipient name of **Thomas Walker**. In the **Mail Merge** pane, under **Make changes**, click the **Exclude this recipient** button.

   c. In the **Mail Merge** pane, click **Next: Complete the merge**. In the **Mail Merge** pane, under **Merge**, click **Edit individual letters**. In the displayed **Merge to New Document** dialog box, click **From** and type **24** Under **To**, also type **24** Click **OK**. In the letter, click at the end of the paragraph that begins *Liberty Motors*, and then press Enter two times. Type **You will look great in that red Corvette!**

   d. On the **Quick Access toolbar**, click the **Save** button. In the **Save As** dialog box, **Save** the Word document as **Lastname_Firstname_9D_Letter** If you are instructed to submit this result, create a paper or electronic printout of the **current page**.

   e. **Save** the main document as **Lastname_Firstname_9D_Letter_Main Close** Word. If necessary, on the status bar, click the **Microsoft Access** button to restore the Access window to the screen.

4 In the **Navigation Pane**, under **Reports**, double-click **9D Imports** to open the report. Switch to **Layout** view. Click the title—**9D Imports**—two times to enter into editing mode. Click to the left of **9D**, type **Lastname Firstname** using your own first and last names, and then press Shift + Enter. Press Enter, and then **Save** the report.

   a. **Close** the report. In the **Navigation Pane**, under **Reports**, right-click **9D Imports**, point to **Export**, and then click **Word RTF File**. Verify that the **File name** box displays the correct path to your **Access Chapter 9** folder. Rename the file **Lastname_Firstname_9D_Imports_RTF** Under **Specify export options**, select the **Open the destination file after the export operation is complete** check box, and then click **OK**.

   b. If you are instructed to submit this result, create a paper or electronic printout. **Close** the Word window. In the **Export - RTF File** dialog box, click **Close**.

(Project 9D Sport Vehicles continues on the next page)

CHAPTER REVIEW

Skills Review   Project 9D Sport Vehicles (continued)

5 ▶ In the **Navigation Pane**, under **Queries**, double-click **9D 14-16 Models** to open the query in **Datasheet** view. **Close** the **Navigation Pane**. In the title row of the query results, click the arrow to the right of **Year**. Click the **Select All** check box and then click **2015** to filter the data to view only 2015 models. Click **OK**. Select all of the records displayed in the filtered query. Click the **EXTERNAL DATA tab**, and in the **Export group**, click **Excel**.

a. In the **Export - Excel Spreadsheet** dialog box, in the **File name** box, verify that the path to your **Access Chapter 9** folder is correct. In the **File name** box, select the existing file name, and type **Lastname_Firstname_9D_15-16_Models** Notice that in the **File format** box, the file will be saved as an Excel Workbook (*.xlsx). Under **Specify export options**, click all three check boxes. Click **OK**.

b. At the bottom of the worksheet, right-click the **Worksheet tab**, and then click **Rename**. Type **9D 2015** and then press Enter. **Save** the workbook, and then **Minimize** Excel.

c. If necessary, on the taskbar, click the **Microsoft Access** button to restore the Access window. Filter the query to display only the 2016 models. Select all of the displayed records. On the **HOME tab**, in the **Clipboard group**, click the **Copy** button. On the taskbar, click the **Microsoft Excel** button to make the Excel window active. At the bottom of the worksheet, to the right of the **9D 2015**, click the **New sheet button**.

d. With cell **A1** selected, on the **HOME tab**, in the **Clipboard group**, click the **Paste** button. Point to the column border between **B** and **C** until the pointer displays. Drag to the right until all of the data in cell **B1**—*Customer ID*—displays. Using the techniques you have practiced, **Rename** the worksheet as **9D 2016 Save** the workbook.

e. On the **INSERT tab**, in the **Text group**, click the **Header & Footer** button. In the header box, type **Lastname Firstname 2016 Models** Click anywhere in the worksheet to move the insertion point out of the **header** box.

f. At the bottom of the workbook, click the **9D 2015 tab**. Insert a **Header** of **Lastname Firstname 9D 2015 Models** and then click anywhere in the worksheet to move the insertion point out of the **header** box.

g. **Save** the workbook. Unless you are required to submit your files electronically, print the **Entire workbook**, and then click **OK**. **Close** Excel.

h. In the Access window, in the title row, click the arrow to the right of **Year**. Click the **Select All** check box to remove the filter, and click **OK**. **Close** the **9D 14-16 Models** query without saving, and then **Open** the **Navigation Pane**.

6 ▶ In the **Navigation Pane**, under **Reports**, right-click **9D Corvettes in Stock**, and open the report in **Design** view. Add your **Lastname Firstname** to the beginning of the report title, and press Shift + Enter to move **9D Corvettes** to the second line of the title. **Save** and **Close** the report. Right-click **9D Corvettes in Stock**, point to **Export**, and then click **HTML Document**.

a. In the **Export - HTML Document** dialog box, in the **File name** box, verify that the file will be saved in the **Access Chapter 9** folder. In the **File name** box, select the existing file name, and type **Lastname_Firstname_9D_Corvettes_HTML** Under **Specify export options**, select the **Open the destination file after the export operation is complete** check box, and then click **OK**. In the **HTML Output Options** dialog box, click **OK**.

b. If you are instructed to submit this result, create a paper or electronic printout of the webpage. **Close** the web browser window. In the **Export - HTML Document** dialog box, click the **Close** button.

7 ▶ In the **Navigation Pane**, under **Reports**, right-click **9D Corvettes in Stock**, point to **Export**, and then click **XML File**. In the **Export - XML File** dialog box, in the **File name** box, verify that the file will be saved in the **Access Chapter 9** folder. Select only the file name, and then type **Lastname_Firstname_9D_Corvettes_XML** Click **OK**. In the **Export XML** dialog box, verify that the **Data (XML)** check box is selected, and then click the **Presentation of your data (XSL)** check box. Click **OK**. In the **Export - XML File** dialog box, click **Close**.

(Project 9D Sport Vehicles continues on the next page)

CHAPTER REVIEW

8 Display the **File Explorer**. Navigate to the location where the **Access Chapter 9** folder is saved, and open the folder. If necessary, click the **View tab**, and, in the Layout group, click **Details**. **Maximize** the window.

a. Locate the **9D_Corvettes_XML** file that displays a **Type** of **HTML Document**. Right-click the file name, click **Open with**, and then click **Notepad**.

b. If you are instructed to submit this result, create a paper or electronic printout of the code. **Close** the Notepad window, and then **Close** the Access Chapter 9 window.

9 **Close** the database, and then **Exit** Access.

10 As directed by your instructor, submit your database, supporting files, and the paper or electronic printouts of the seven objects that are the result of this project—three Word documents, one RTF document, one Excel workbook, one HTML file, and one source code file. Specifically, in this project, using your own name you created the following database and printouts or electronic printouts:

1. Lastname_Firstname_9D_Sports_Vehicles	Database file
2. Lastname_Firstname_9D_Letter_Main.docx	Word document (printed or electronic printout)
3. Lastname_Firstname_9D_Imports	Word document (printed or electronic printout)
4. Lastname_Firstname_9D_Letter	Word document (printed or electronic printout)
5. Lastname_Firstname_9D_Imports_RTF	RTF document (printed or electronic printout)
6. Lastname_Firstname_9D_15-16_Models	Excel workbook (printed or electronic printout)
7. Lastname_Firstname_9D_Corvettes_HTML	HTML file (printed or electronic printout)
8. Lastname_Firstname_9D_Corvettes_XML	Source code file (printed or electronic printout) and XML and XSL supporting files

END | You have completed Project 9D

CONTENT-BASED ASSESSMENTS

Liberty Motors offers extensive customization options for all types of vehicles through its accessories division. In this project, you will import a Word table as a plain text file. You will import data from an Excel worksheet and create a report with an imported Excel chart. Your completed work will look similar to Figure 9.43.

Apply 9A skills from these Objectives:

1 Import Data from a Word Table

2 Import Data from an Excel Workbook

3 Insert an Excel Chart into a Report

4 Import from and Link to Another Access Database

Build from Scratch

PROJECT FILES

For Project 9E, you will need the following files:

New blank Access database
a09E_Custom_Features.docx
a09E_Package_Sales.xlsx
a09E_Employees.accdb
a09E_Logo.jpg

You will save your files as:

Lastname_Firstname_9E_Customized_Cars.accdb
Lastname_Firstname_9E_Custom_Features.txt

PROJECT RESULTS

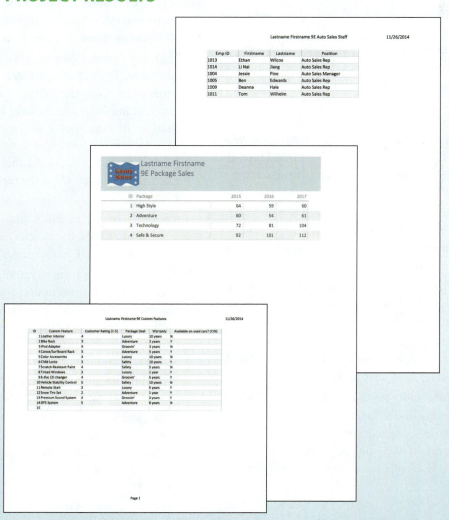

FIGURE 9.43

(Project 9E Customized Cars continues on the next page)

1 Start Access. In your **Access Chapter 9** folder, create a new blank database called **Lastname_Firstname_9E_ Customized_Cars Close** the displayed table.

2 Start Word. Locate and open the **a09E_Custom_ Features** document. On the **TABLE TOOLS LAYOUT tab**, in the **Data group**, click the **Convert to Text** button. Separate the text with **Tabs**.

3 **Save** the file as **Plain Text** using the name **Lastname_Firstname_9E_Custom_Features** In the displayed **File Conversion** dialog box, accept the default settings, and then **Exit** Word.

4 Return to the Access **9E Customized_Cars** empty database. Import the **9E_Custom_Features** text file. Verify that the **Import the source data into a new table in the current database** option button is selected, and then click **OK**.

5 In the **Import Text Wizard** dialog box, verify that the **Delimited** option button is selected, and click **Next**. Verify that the **Tab** option button is selected. Select the **First Row Contains Field Names** check box. In the **Text Qualifier** box, verify that {**none**} is selected, and then click **Next**.

6 Change the **Data Type** in the **Customer Rating (1-5)** field to **Short Text**. Click **Next**. Verify that the **Let Access add primary key** option button is selected, and then click **Next**. Edit the table name by replacing the underscores with spaces. Click **Finish**.

7 Select the **Save import steps** check box to display additional options. Click in the **Description** box, type **Imports a tab-delimited text file that was a Word table** and then click **Save Import**.

8 Open the **9E Custom Features** table in **Datasheet** view, and adjust the widths of all of the fields to display all of the data and the entire field name for each field.

9 If you are instructed to submit this result, create a paper or electronic printout of the table in **Landscape** orientation. **Save**, and then **Close** the table.

10 Import the **a09E_Package_Sales** workbook file. Verify **Import the source data into a new table in the current database** is selected, and then click **OK**. In the **Import Spreadsheet Wizard** dialog box, verify that **Show Worksheets** is selected and **Packages** is highlighted. Click

Next. Select the **First Row Contains Column Headings** check box. Click **Next** two times. Verify **Let Access add primary key** is selected, and then click **Next**. Name the table **Lastname Firstname 9E Package Sales** and then click **Finish**. In the **Get External Data - Excel Spreadsheet** dialog box, click **Close**.

11 Select the **9E Package Sales** table and create a new **Report**. Switch to **Design** view. Select the image placeholder to the left of the title and replace with the **a09E_Logo** with a **Size Mode** property of **Zoom**. Resize the logo to approximately **1 inch** tall by **1 inch** wide. In the **Report Header** section, delete the **Date** and **Time text box controls**. Move **9E Package Sales** to the second line of the title. In the **Page Footer** section, delete the **Page number text box control**. In the **Report Footer** section, delete the **Count calculated control** and the **line**. Increase the size of the **Page Footer** section to the **2.75-inch mark** on the horizontal ruler. **Save** the report as **Lastname Firstname 9E Package Sales**

12 Start Excel. **Open** the **a09E_Package_Sales** workbook. In the **Package Totals** worksheet, select the entire chart. **Copy** the chart to the **Office Clipboard**. **Exit** Excel. In the Access **9E Package Sales** report, **Paste** the chart in the **Page Footer**. Resize the report to **7 inches wide**. **Save** the report, and then switch to **Report** view. If you are instructed to submit this result, create a paper or electronic printout. **Close** the report.

13 Import data from the **a09E_Employees** database. Click the **Link to the data source by creating a linked table** option button, and then click **OK**. In the **Link Tables** dialog box, click **9E Employees**, and then click **OK**.

14 Import data from the **a09E_Employees** database. Verify that the **Import tables, queries, forms, reports, macros, and modules into the current database** option button is selected, and then click **OK**. In the **Import Objects** dialog box, click the **Queries** tab, click **9E Auto Sales Staff**, and then click **OK**. Click **Close**. Rename **9E Auto Sales Staff** by adding your **Lastname Firstname** to the beginning of the query name.

15 Double-click **9E Auto Sales Staff**. If you are instructed to submit this result, create a paper or electronic printout. **Close** the query, and then **Exit** Access.

(Project 9E Customized Cars continues on the next page)

CONTENT-BASED ASSESSMENTS

16 ▶ As directed by your instructor, submit your databases and the paper or electronic printouts of the three objects that are the result of this project—one table, one report, and one query. Specifically, in this project, using your own name you created the following databases and printouts or electronic printouts:

1. Lastname_Firstname_9E_Customized_Cars	Database file
2. a09E_Employees	Database file (for linking purposes only)
3. Lastname Firstname 9E Custom Features	Table (printed or electronic printout)
4. Lastname Firstname 9E Package Sales	Report (printed or electronic printout)
5. Lastname Firstname 9E Auto Sales Staff	Query (printed or electronic printout)

END | You have completed Project 9E

CONTENT-BASED ASSESSMENTS

Apply 9B skills from these Objectives:

5 Export Data to Word

6 Use Mail Merge to Integrate Access and Word

7 Export Data to Excel

8 Export Data to an HTML File and an XML File

The accessories staff would like to be able to analyze data related to luxury features and package sales using Word and Excel. They would also like to be able to display data on the web. Access enables you to export data from an Access database into these applications and onto a webpage. In this project, you will export data to several types of applications, including merging Access data with a flyer created in Word. Your completed files will look similar to Figure 9.44.

PROJECT FILES

For Project 9F, you will need the following files:

a09F_Custom_Packages.accdb
a09F_Flyer.docx

You will save your files as:

Lastname_Firstname_9F_Custom_Packages.accdb
Lastname_Firstname_9F_Accessory_Staff.docx
Lastname_Firstname_9F_Flyers.docx
Lastname_Firstname_9F_Flyer_Main.docx
Lastname_Firstname_9F_Safety_Features.xlsx
Lastname_Firstname_9F_Package_Sales.html
Lastname_Firstname_9F_XML_Package_Features.xml
Lastname_Firstname_9F_XML_Package_Features.htm
Lastname_Firstname_9F_XML_Package_Features.xsl

PROJECT RESULTS

FIGURE 9.44

(Project 9F Custom Packages continues on the next page)

CONTENT-BASED ASSESSMENTS

1 Start Access. Locate and open the **a09F_Custom_Packages** file. **Save** the database in the **Access 2013 Database** format in your **Access Chapter 9** folder as **Lastname_Firstname_9F_Custom_Packages**

2 In the **Navigation Pane**, under **Queries**, right-click **9F Accessory Staff**, point to **Export**, and then click **Word RTF File**. Navigate to the **Access Chapter 9** folder, and name the file **Lastname_Firstname_9F_Accessory_Staff**

3 Under **Specify export options**, select the **Open the destination file after the export operation is complete** check box, and then click **OK**. On the Word ribbon, click the **INSERT tab**. In the **Header & Footer group**, click the **Header** button. In the **Built-In** gallery, click **Blank**, and then in the **Type text box**, type **Lastname Firstname 9F Accessory Staff** Close the Header. Using the default file name, Save the document as a **Word Document** in the **Access Chapter 9** folder. If necessary, in the displayed message box, click **OK**. If you are instructed to submit this result, create a paper or electronic printout. **Close** the Word window. In the **Export - RTF File** dialog box, click **Close**.

4 Export the **9F Custom Features** table using the **Word Merge** button. Verify that **Link your data to an existing Microsoft Word document** is selected, and then click **OK**. Locate and open the **a09F_Flyer** file. Click the **Microsoft Word** button on the task bar, and maximize the Word window.

5 In the Word **Mail Merge** task pane, under **Select recipients**, verify that **Use an existing list** is selected, and then click **Next: Write your letter**. One at a time, click to the right of **Package Deal**, **Custom Feature**, and **Warranty**, inserting the appropriate field names. At the bottom of the flyer, replace **Firstname Lastname** with your first and last names. Preview and then complete the merge. Click **Edit Individual Letters**, and then merge records **3–4** only. **Save** your document in the **Access Chapter 9** folder as **Lastname_Firstname_9F_Flyers** Unless you are required to submit your files electronically, **Print** the document.

6 **Close** Word to exit the merged document. **Save** the document as **Lastname_Firstname_9F_Flyer_Main** and **Close** Word. Restore the Access window to the screen.

7 In the **9F Custom Features** table, **Filter** the results to display only the *Safe & Secure Package Deal* records; select the records. On the **EXTERNAL DATA tab**, in the **Export group**, click **Excel**.

8 **Save** the file in your **Access Chapter 9** folder as **Lastname_Firstname_9F_Safety_Features** Under **Specify export options**, select all three check boxes, and then click **OK**. Rename the worksheet **9F Safe & Secure** Insert a **Header**, and type **Safe & Secure Package Sales Rep: Firstname Lastname** Save the workbook. If you are instructed to submit this result, create a paper or electronic printout. **Close** the **Excel workbook** and **Excel**. In the Access window, **Close** the **9F Custom Features** table, but do not save the changes.

9 In the **Navigation Pane**, under **Reports**, open the **9F Package Sales** report in **Design** view. Add your **Lastname Firstname** to the beginning of the title. **Save** and **Close** the report. Right-click the **9F Package Sales** report, point to **Export**, and then click **HTML Document**. Navigate to the **Access Chapter 9** folder, and name the file **Lastname_Firstname_9F_Package_Sales.html** Under **Specify export options**, click the **Open the destination file after the export operation is complete** check box, and then click **OK**. In the **HTML Output Options** dialog box, click **OK**. Click **OK** if you are prompted about the section width.

10 If you are instructed to submit this result, create a paper or electronic printout of the webpage. **Close** the web browser window. In the **Export - HTML Document** dialog box, click the **Close** button.

11 In the **Navigation Pane**, under **Reports**, open the **9F Package Features** report in **Design** view. Replace **Lastname Firstname** with your first and last names. **Save** and **Close** the report. Right-click **9F Package Features**, point to **Export**, and then click **XML File**. **Save** the file in the **Access Chapter 9** folder as **Lastname_Firstname_9F_XML_Package_Features.xml** and then click **OK**. In the **Export XML** dialog box, verify that the **Data (XML)** check box is selected, and then click the **Presentation of your data (XSL)** check box. Click **OK**. In the **Export - XML File** dialog box, click **Close**.

12 Locate the **9F_XML_Package_Features** file that displays a **Type** of **HTML Document** and display the source code in **Notepad**. If you are instructed to submit this result, create a paper or electronic printout of the document. **Close** the document window, and then **Close** the Access Chapter 9 window.

(Project 9F Custom Packages continues on the next page)

CONTENT-BASED ASSESSMENTS

13 ▶ **Exit** Access.

14 ▶ As directed by your instructor, submit your database and the paper or electronic printouts of the six objects that are the result of this project—three Word documents, one Excel workbook, one HTML file, and one source code file. Specifically, in this project, using your own name you created the following database and printouts or electronic printouts:

1. Lastname_Firstname_9F_Custom_Packages	Database file
2. Lastname_Firstname_9F_Accessory_Staff	Word document (printed or electronic printout)
3. Lastname_Firstname_9F_Flyers	Word document (printed or electronic printout)
4. Lastname_Firstname_9F_Flyer_Main.docx	Word document (printed or electronic printout)
5. Lastname_Firstname_9F_Safety_Features	Excel workbook (printed or electronic printout)
6. Lastname_Firstname_9F_Package_Sales	HTML file (printed or electronic printout)
7. Lastname_Firstname_9F_XML_Package_Features	Source code file (printed or electronic printout), and XML and XSL supporting documents

END | You have completed Project 9F

CONTENT-BASED ASSESSMENTS

Mastering Access | Project 9G Monthly Promotions

Gregory Burton, accessories sales manager, and Jessie Pine, auto sales manager, at Liberty Motors have teamed up to offer special monthly promotions to encourage customers to revisit the showroom. In this project, you will import an Excel worksheet that contains the customer list and a Word table that contains the promotion details. You will use mail merge to inform the customers about the promotions. You will export a form created from the promotions table to an HTML file so it can be viewed as a webpage. Your completed files will look similar to Figure 9.45.

Apply 9A and 9B skills from these Objectives:

1 Import Data from a Word Table

2 Import Data from an Excel Workbook

6 Use Mail Merge to Integrate Access and Word

8 Export Data to an HTML File and an XML File

PROJECT FILES

For Project 9G, you will need the following files:

New blank Access database
a09G_Promotions_Letter.docx
a09G_Customers.xlsx
a09G_Monthly_Promotions.txt
a09G_Logo.jpg

You will save your files as:

Lastname_Firstname_9G_Monthly_Promotions. accdb
Lastname_Firstname_9G_Promotions_Letter.docx
Lastname_Firstname_9G_Letter_Main.docx
Lastname_Firstname_9G_Monthly_Promotions_ HTML.html

Build from Scratch

PROJECT RESULTS

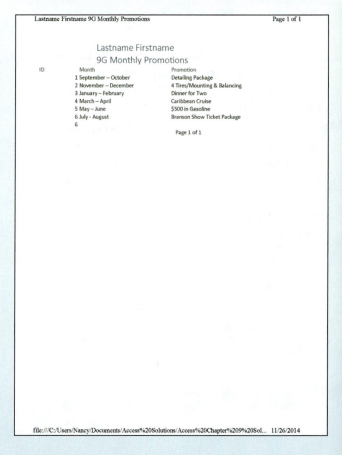

FIGURE 9.45

(Project 9G Monthly Promotions continues on the next page)

CONTENT-BASED ASSESSMENTS

1 Start Access. **Create** a new blank database and **Save** it in the **Access Chapter 9** folder as **Lastname_Firstname_9G_Monthly_Promotions Close** the table.

2 Import **External Data** from the **a09G_Customers** Excel file into a new table in the **9G_Monthly_Promotions** database. The **first row contains column headings**. Change the data type for the **Postal Code** field to **Short Text**. **Let Access add primary key**. Import to table **Lastname Firstname 9G Customers**

3 Open the **9G Customers** table, and **AutoFit** all columns. **Save** and **Close** the table. Merge it with the existing Microsoft Word document **a09G_Promotions_Letter**. The recipients will be selected from the existing list in the **9G Customers** table. Verify the **Show/Hide** button is active. Place your insertion point at the beginning of the fifth blank line after the current date. Add the **Address Block**, and click **OK**. Insert the **First Name** and **Last Name** fields between the space and the colon in the salutation line. Place a space between these fields.

4 In the closing of the letter, replace **Firstname Lastname** with your first and last names. **Save** the document in your **Access Chapter 9** folder as **Lastname_Firstname_9G_Letter_Main**

5 **Preview your letters** and **Complete the merge** for only the eighth record. **Save** the Word document in your **Access Chapter 9** folder as **Lastname_Firstname_9G_Promotions_Letter** Unless you are required to submit your files electronically, **Print** the letter. **Close** the Word window, and then **Exit** Word, saving changes if necessary. **Close** the **9G Customers** table.

6 **Import External Data** from the text file **a09G_Monthly_Promotions**. Import the source data into a new table in the current database. Use the **tab delimiter**. The **first row contains field names**. The data types are correct. **Let Access add primary key**. Import this text to **Lastname Firstname 9G Monthly Promotions** Do not save the import steps.

7 From the **9G Monthly Promotions** table, **Create** a report. In the **Title** of the report, move **9G Monthly Promotions** to a second line. Add the **a09G_Logo** to the report header. With the **Size Mode** property set to **Zoom**, resize the **logo control** until it reaches the **1.5-inch mark on the horizontal ruler**. Delete the **Date** and **Time** controls. Resize the report to **6.5 inches** wide. **Save** the report as **Lastname Firstname 9G Monthly Promotions** and then **Close** the report.

8 Export the **9G Monthly Promotions** report as an **HTML Document**. **Save** the document in your **Access Chapter 9** folder as **Lastname_Firstname_9G_Monthly_Promotions_HTML** Open the destination file after the export operation is complete. In the **HTML Output Options** dialog box, click **OK**.

9 If you are instructed to submit this result, create a paper or electronic printout of the webpage. **Close** the web browser window. In the **Export - HTML Document** dialog box, click the **Close** button.

10 **Exit** Access.

11 As directed by your instructor, submit your database and the paper or electronic printouts of the three objects that are the result of this project—two Word documents and one HTML file. Specifically, in this project, using your own name you created the following database and printouts or electronic printouts:

1. Lastname_Firstname_9G_Monthly_Promotions	Database file
2. Lastname_Firstname_9G_Letter_Main	Word document
3. Lastname_Firstname_9G_Promotions_Letter	Word document (printed or electronic printout)
4. Lastname_Firstname_9G_Monthly_Promotions_HTML	HTML file (printed or electronic printout)

END | You have completed Project 9G

CONTENT-BASED ASSESSMENTS

Apply a combination of the 9A and 9B skills

GO! Fix It	Project 9H Customer Service	Online

GO! Make It	Project 9I Sponsored Events	Online

GO! Solve It	Project 9J Sales Data	Online

GO! Solve It	Project 9K Advertisements	

PROJECT FILES

For Project 9K, you will need the following files:

a09K_Advertisements.accdb
a09K_Ad_Staff.txt

You will save your files as:

Lastname_Firstname_9K_Advertisements.accdb
Lastname_Firstname_9K_Ads_Workbook.xlsx

Jessie Pine, auto sales manager of Liberty Motors, explores many different venues to advertise the business. Most of the data for the advertisements is kept in a database. Some of the employees would like to see the data arranged in a worksheet to create a what-if analysis. Open the **a09K_Advertisements** database, and then save it as **Lastname_Firstname_9K_Advertisements** Import the **a09K_Ad_Staff.txt** file as a table, using the first row as field names, assigning a Short Text data type to the Postal Code field, and letting Access assign the primary key. Save the table as **Lastname Firstname 9K Ad Staff** and then AutoFit all columns in the table. Export the **9K Advertisements** table to an Excel workbook with formatting and layout. Save the workbook as **Lastname_Firstname_9K_Ads_Workbook** Rename the sheet tab **9K Data** If necessary, AutoFit the columns. Copy all of the data from the **9K Cost Analysis** query to a second sheet in the same workbook. Rename this sheet **9K Analysis** Type **Lastname Firstname 9K Advertisements** as a header for each of the sheets. Unless you are required to submit your files electronically, print both worksheets in landscape orientation.

Performance Level

Performance Criteria		Exemplary	Proficient	Developing
	Import the a09K_Ad_Staff.txt file as a table	Table created with correct fields and settings as directed.	Table created with no more than two missing fields or settings.	Table created with more than two missing fields or settings.
	Export the 9K Advertisements table to Excel	Worksheet created with correct fields and settings as directed.	Worksheet created with no more than two missing fields or settings.	Worksheet created with more than two missing fields or settings.
	Export the 9K Cost Analysis query to Excel	Worksheet created with correct fields and settings as directed.	Worksheet created with no more than two missing fields or settings.	Worksheet created with more than two missing fields or settings.

END | You have completed Project 9K

OUTCOMES-BASED ASSESSMENTS

RUBRIC

The following outcomes-based assessments are open-ended assessments. That is, there is no specific correct result; your result will depend on your approach to the information provided. Make Professional Quality your goal. Use the following scoring rubric to guide you in how to approach the problem and then to evaluate how well your approach solves the problem.

The *criteria*—Software Mastery, Content, Format and Layout, and Process—represent the knowledge and skills you have gained that you can apply to solving the problem. The *levels of performance*—Professional Quality, Approaching Professional Quality, or Needs Quality Improvements—help you and your instructor evaluate your result.

	Your completed project is of Professional Quality if you:	Your completed project is Approaching Professional Quality if you:	Your completed project Needs Quality Improvements if you:
1-Software Mastery	Choose and apply the most appropriate skills, tools, and features and identify efficient methods to solve the problem.	Choose and apply some appropriate skills, tools, and features, but not in the most efficient manner.	Choose inappropriate skills, tools, or features, or are inefficient in solving the problem.
2-Content	Construct a solution that is clear and well organized, contains content that is accurate, appropriate to the audience and purpose, and is complete. Provide a solution that contains no errors in spelling, grammar, or style.	Construct a solution in which some components are unclear, poorly organized, inconsistent, or incomplete. Misjudge the needs of the audience. Have some errors in spelling, grammar, or style, but the errors do not detract from comprehension.	Construct a solution that is unclear, incomplete, or poorly organized; contains some inaccurate or inappropriate content; and contains many errors in spelling, grammar, or style. Do not solve the problem.
3-Format & Layout	Format and arrange all elements to communicate information and ideas, clarify function, illustrate relationships, and indicate relative importance.	Apply appropriate format and layout features to some elements, but not others. Overuse features, causing minor distraction.	Apply format and layout that does not communicate information or ideas clearly. Do not use format and layout features to clarify function, illustrate relationships, or indicate relative importance. Use available features excessively, causing distraction.
4-Process	Use an organized approach that integrates planning, development, self-assessment, revision, and reflection.	Demonstrate an organized approach in some areas, but not others; or, use an insufficient process of organization throughout.	Do not use an organized approach to solve the problem.

OUTCOMES-BASED ASSESSMENTS

Apply a combination of the 9A and 9B skills

GO! Think   Project 9L Employee Recognition

PROJECT FILES

For Project 9L, you will need the following files:

a09L_Employee_Recognition.accdb
a09L_Birthday_List.docx
a09L_Birthday_Card.docx

You will save your files as:

Lastname_Firstname_9L_Employee_Recognition.accdb
Lastname_Firstname_9L_Birthday_List.txt
Lastname_Firstname_9L_Card.docx
Lastname_Firstname_9L_Card_Main.docx
Lastname_Firstname_9L_HTML_List.html

You have been asked to help with an employee recognition project at Liberty Motors. You will import the data from a Word table into a database table and then merge this table with cards created in Word. The birthday list will be uploaded to the company intranet, so it will need to be exported to HTML.

Open **a09L_Employee_Recognition** and save it as **Lastname_Firstname_9L_Employee_ Recognition** Open **a09L_Birthday_List**, and then convert the table to text. Save as a text file named **Lastname_Firstname_9L_Birthday_List** and then import it into your database as a table named **Lastname Firstname 9L Birthday List** using the first row as field names and no primary key. AutoFit all columns, and add your name and birthday to the table. Merge it with **a09L_Birthday_Card** so the person's full name appears on the line after Happy Birthday and their favorite cake appears before the word "Cake." Adjust the spacing as necessary. Merge your card only (Record 13), and save it as **Lastname_Firstname_9L_Card** Save the main document as **Lastname_Firstname_9L_Card_Main** If you are instructed to submit this result, create a paper or electronic printout of your birthday card.

Export the **9L Birthday List** table to HTML. Save the file as **Lastname_Firstname_9L_ HTML_List.html** Unless you are required to submit your files electronically, print the webpage.

END | You have completed Project 9L

OUTCOMES-BASED ASSESSMENTS

Build from
Scratch

GO! Think	Project 9M Service Records	Online

| You and GO! | Project 9N Club Directory | Online |

Administering Databases and Writing SQL Statements

GO! to Work
Video A10

PROJECT	OUTCOMES
10A	Manage Access files.

OBJECTIVES

1. Create a Navigation Form
2. Use Microsoft Access Analysis Tools
3. Modify Access Views and Behaviors
4. Use the Database Splitter
5. Encrypt and Decrypt Databases
6. Create a Locked Database (ACCDE File)

PROJECT	OUTCOMES
10B	Write SQL statements.

OBJECTIVES

7. Modify a Query in SQL View
8. Create a Query in SQL View
9. Create a Union Query Using SQL
10. Create Calculated Fields and SQL Aggregate Functions

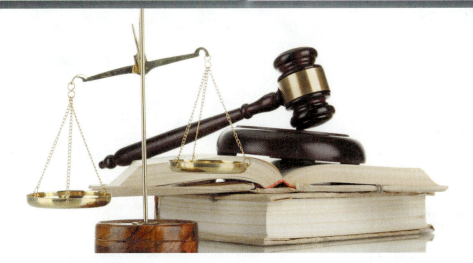

Africa Studio/Fotolia

In This Chapter

Throughout the life of a database, tables are added; design changes are made to queries, forms, and reports; and data is constantly updated and added. Understanding how to maintain a database is critical to the success of the individuals who rely on its data. Analysis tools enable users to identify potential problems and then fix them. Access also provides a set of security settings including password protection and a means to ensure the security of a database that you plan on sharing. Finally, Access provides a view for creating and modifying the SQL, or Structured Query Language, that makes all of its queries work.

Attorneys at **Loren-Renner Law Partners** counsel clients on a wide variety of issues including contracts, licensing, intellectual property, taxation, and the unique needs of the sports and entertainment industries. Entertainment clients include production companies, publishers, talent agencies, actors, writers, artists—anyone doing business in the entertainment industry. Sports clients include colleges and universities, professional sports teams, athletes, and venue operators. Increasingly, amateur and community sports coaches and organizations with concerns about liability are seeking the firm's specialized counsel.

PROJECT ACTIVITIES

Loren-Renner Law Partners uses Access databases to organize various operations. The firm uses one database to maintain its recruitment efforts and one that contains lawyer data, corporate client data, and corporate case data. In Activities 10.01 through 10.12, you will administer and secure the data by creating a navigation form, applying several file management tools, splitting a database, encrypting a database, and locking the database. You will also generate printouts that will look similar to those in Figure 10.1.

PROJECT FILES

For Project 10A, you will need the following files:

a10A_Recruitment
a10A_Icon
a10A_Lawyers

You will save your files as:

Lastname_Firstname_10A_Recruitment
Lastname_Firstname_10A_Screens
Lastname_Firstname_10A_Lawyers
Lastname_Firstname_10A_Lawyers_be
Lastname_Firstname_10A_ACCDE

PROJECT RESULTS

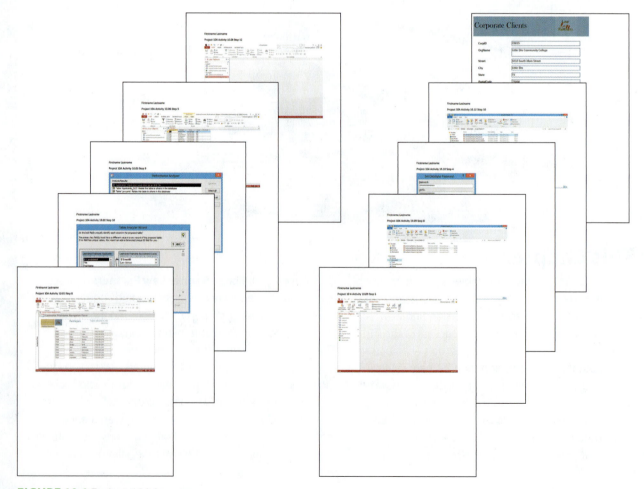

FIGURE 10.1 Project 10A Lawyers

Video A10-1

A *navigation form* is a form that displays navigational controls that enable you to display forms and reports in your database. Navigation forms are useful when your database is web-based because browsers do not display Access's Navigation Pane. Navigation forms do not have to display controls for all of your database objects; you can design a navigation form for a specific purpose, such as managing recruitment events.

Activity 10.01 | Creating a Navigation Form Using the Navigation Form Tool

You can create a navigation form in Design or Layout view by using the Blank Form tool or by using the Navigation Form tool. In this activity, you will create a navigation form to enable web access to one form and two reports in your Recruitment database.

1 ▶ Start Access. Navigate to the location where the student data files for this textbook are saved. Locate and open the **a010A_Recruitment** file. Display **Backstage** view, click **Save As**, and then, under *File Types*, double-click **Save Database As**. In the **Save As** dialog box, navigate to the drive on which you will be saving your folders and projects for this chapter. Create a new folder named **Access Chapter 10** and **Save** the database as **Lastname_Firstname_10A_Recruitment** in the folder. Enable the content or add the **Access Chapter 10** folder to the **Trust Center**.

2 ▶ On the **CREATE tab**, in the **Forms group**, click the **Navigation** button, and notice the six design layouts you can select for your navigation form. Compare your screen with Figure 10.2.

    Each layout provides tabs in different locations that you can use to switch to a database object.

FIGURE 10.2

3 ▶ In the list, click **Vertical Tabs, Left**. If the Field List displays, close it. Compare your screen with Figure 10.3.

FIGURE 10.3

4 In the **Navigation Pane**, under **Forms**, point to **Lawyer Information**. Hold down the left mouse button, drag up and to the right to [**Add New**], and then release the mouse button.

The Lawyer Information form is added to the navigation form as the first tab in the form.

🔄 **BY TOUCH**   Touch the Lawyer Information form, and drag it up and to the right. Drop it on [Add New].

5 Using the technique you just practiced, add the **Lawyer Directory** and the **Paralegal Directory** reports as the second and third tabs in the navigation form.

If you add an object as a tab in the navigation form by mistake, right-click the tab, and then click Delete.

6 At the top of the form, click the **Navigation Form** title to select it, and then click to the left of the N in *Navigation*. Type your Lastname Firstname press Spacebar, and then press Enter. Compare your screen with Figure 10.4.

FIGURE 10.4

7 Save 🖫 the navigation form as **Lastname Firstname Navigation Form Close** « the **Navigation Pane**. Switch to **Form** view.

8 Press Alt + PrintScrn. Create a new, blank Word document. In the **Word** document, type your first and last names, press Enter, and then type **Project 10A Activity 10.01 Step 8** Press Enter, and then **Paste** the screenshot. Save 🖫 the document in your **Access Chapter 10** folder with the name **Lastname_Firstname_10A_Screens** Leave the Word document open.

9 Return to **Access**. **Close** ✕ the navigation form, and **Open** » the **Navigation Pane**.

Objective 2   Use Microsoft Access Analysis Tools

Video A10-2

Microsoft Access contains several analysis tools that provide useful information to the database administrator. One tool scans tables for redundant data and then provides a mechanism to split them into smaller, related tables. Another tool analyzes all database objects and lists possible design flaws that decrease performance. Another analysis tool creates a highly detailed report listing the attributes for the entire database. These analysis tools are used to improve database performance and increase data reliability.

Activity 10.02 | Using the Table Analyzer

Employees at Loren-Renner Law Partners notice that when they enter invoices into the database, they spend a significant amount of time typing the same recruitment information into multiple records. In this activity, you will use the Table Analyzer to see if the table needs to be split. The *Table Analyzer* searches for repeated data in a table and then splits the table into two or more related tables to avoid data redundancy.

1 Open the **Applicants** table in **Datasheet** view. Click the **EventID column arrow**, and then click **Sort A to Z**. Scroll through the table, observe the duplicate entries in the **EventID**, **Law School**, and **Event Date** columns, and then **Close** ⊠ the table, saving changes. **Close** « the **Navigation Pane**.

The data in the Applicants table repeats information numerous times within the table, making it redundant.

2 On the **DATABASE TOOLS tab**, in the **Analyze group**, click the **Analyze Table** button. If the wizard displays a screen called **The Table Analyzer: Looking at the Problem**, review the information, and click the **Next** button two times. Verify that the **Applicants** table is selected, and then compare your screen with Figure 10.5.

If the *Show introductory pages?* check box is selected, two extra screens will display the next time the Table Analyzer is started. These two screens explain the normalization process.

FIGURE 10.5

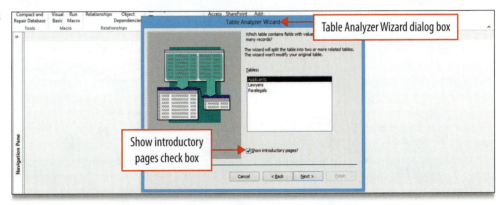

3 Click the **Next** button. In the displayed wizard dialog box, read the directions. Verify that the **Yes, let the wizard decide** option button is selected, and then click **Next**.

4 In the displayed wizard dialog box, read the directions. In the **Table1** field list, scroll down to display *Lookup to Table2*, and then compare your screen with Figure 10.6.

The wizard suggests placing the event data into a related table currently named Table2. It suggests using EventID as its primary key. In the proposal for Table1, a lookup field will be inserted to relate the two tables.

FIGURE 10.6

5 Double-click the **Table1** title bar. In the displayed dialog box, type **Lastname Firstname Applicants** and then click **OK**. If necessary, widen the field list until the entire table name is displayed.

6 Double-click the **Table2** title bar. In the displayed dialog box, type **Lastname Firstname Recruitment Events** and then click **OK**. If necessary, widen the field list until the entire table name is displayed.

7 Click the **Next** button, and then read the directions displayed in the wizard dialog box. In the **Applicants** table, click **Candidate#**, and then click the **Set Unique Identifier** 🔑 button.

8 Press Alt + PrintScrn. In the **Word** document, press Enter, and then press Ctrl + Enter to insert a page break. Type your first and last names, press Enter, and then type **Project 10A Activity 10.02 Step 10** Press Enter, **Paste** the screenshot, and then click **Save** 💾. Leave the Word document open.

9 Switch to the **Access** window. Click **Next**, and then read the directions displayed in the wizard dialog box. Verify that the **Yes, create the query** option button is selected, and then click **Finish**.

10 **Close** ✖ the displayed **Access Help** window, and **Close** ✖ the query. **Open** » the **Navigation Pane**, and then compare your screen with Figure 10.7.

The two tables have been created and the original table has been renamed Applicants_OLD. A query named Applicants is created so that the reports and forms that relied on the old Applicants table will still work.

FIGURE 10.7

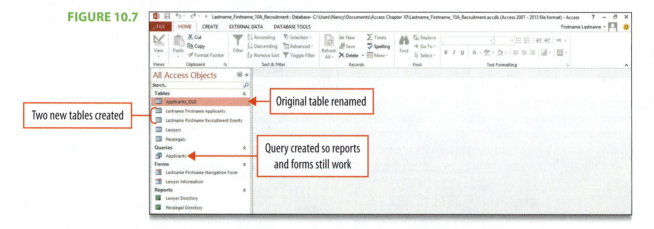

11 **Close** « the **Navigation Pane**.

NOTE | **Preventing Accidental Deletion of Records During the Conversion Process**

Access creates the relationship between the Applicants and Recruitment Events tables with the Enforce Referential Integrity and Cascade Update Related Records options selected. The Cascade Delete Related Records is not selected so that you cannot accidentally delete any records.

Activity 10.03 | Using the Performance Analyzer

Poor database design impairs performance, especially when the database is used to store large amounts of data. Loren-Renner Law Partners needs to analyze its database to increase its performance. In this activity, you will use the *Performance Analyzer* to identify and fix problems with the database. The Performance Analyzer is a wizard that analyzes database objects and then offers suggestions for improving them.

1 ▶ On the **CREATE tab**, in the **Queries group**, click the **Query Design** button. Add the **Paralegals** table and the **Lawyers** table, and then **Close** ☒ the **Show Table** dialog box. If necessary, expand the field lists until all fields and table names display.

2 ▶ From the **Paralegals** table, add the **Paralegal** and **Phone** fields to the design grid. From the **Lawyers** table, add the **FName** and **LName** fields.

3 ▶ From the **Paralegals** table, drag **Lawyer** and drop it over **LawyerID** in the **Lawyers** table. Compare your screen with Figure 10.8.

An *indeterminate relationship* between the two tables is established using Lawyer as the common field. An indeterminate relationship is one that does not enforce referential integrity. The relationship applies to this query only and is not defined for the entire database.

FIGURE 10.8

4 ▶ In the **Results group**, click the **Run** button. Click **Save** 🖫, type **Lastname Firstname Paralegal Assignments** and then click **OK**. **Close** ☒ the query.

5 ▶ On the **DATABASE TOOLS tab**, in the **Analyze group**, click the **Analyze Performance** button.

6 ▶ In the displayed **Performance Analyzer** dialog box, click the **All Object Types tab**. Click the **Select All** button, and then click **OK**. Compare your screen with Figure 10.9.

The Performance Analyzer provides three levels of suggestions: Recommendations, Suggestions, and Ideas. For this database, the Performance Analyzer has no recommendations, one suggestion, and several ideas.

FIGURE 10.9

7 ▶ Under **Analysis Results**, click the suggestion **Table 'Paralegals': Relate to table 'Lawyers'**. Click the **Optimize** button.

A one-to-many relationship between the two tables is defined, and the Performance Analyzer displays a check mark next to the item.

8 ▸ Click the first item labeled with the **Idea** icon. Notice that the **Optimize** button is unavailable.

Access fixes only those problems identified as a recommendation or suggestion.

9 ▸ Press Alt + PrintScrn. In the **Word** document, press Enter, and then press Ctrl + Enter to insert a page break. Type your first and last names, press Enter, and then type **Project 10A Activity 10.03 Step 9** Press Enter, **Paste** the screenshot, and then click **Save** 💾. Leave the document open.

10 ▸ Return to **Access**. Read through the remaining ideas, and then click the **Close** ❌ button.

Activity 10.04 | Viewing Object Dependencies

The Object Dependencies pane shows the dependencies between database objects. A **dependency** is an object that requires, or is dependent on, another database object. For example, several forms, reports, and queries may rely on a single table. Deleting that table would "break" those dependent objects. In this activity, you will use the Object Dependencies pane to determine whether any objects depend on the Applicants_OLD table. If not, you will delete the table.

1 ▸ Open ≫ the **Navigation Pane**. Click the **Lawyers** table to make it active. On the **DATABASE TOOLS tab**, in the **Relationships group**, click the **Object Dependencies** button. If a message displays, click **OK**. On the right side of the Access window, notice that the **Object Dependencies** pane displays.

2 ▸ If a message box displays, click **OK**. Widen the pane so all object names are visible. If necessary, click the *Objects that depend on me* option button. Compare your screen with Figure 10.10.

The Paralegals table, Paralegal Assignments query, Lawyer Information form, and Lawyer Directory report all depend on the Lawyers table.

FIGURE 10.10

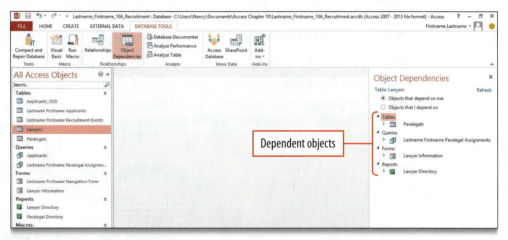

3 ▸ In the **Navigation Pane**, click the **Applicants_OLD** table, and then in the **Object Dependencies** pane, click **Refresh**. If a message displays, click **OK**. Notice that no database objects depend on the **Applicants_OLD** table.

4 ▸ Close ❌ the **Object Dependencies** pane. Click the the **Applicants_OLD** table, and then press Delete. In the message box, click **Yes**.

More Knowledge | **Deleting Database Objects**

If there were objects dependent on the table that you deleted, they would no longer operate correctly. Any dependent objects will also need to be deleted or redesigned. Forms, reports, queries, and macros can all be deleted using the same technique.

---

5 On the **DATABASE TOOLS tab**, in the **Analyze group**, click the **Analyze Performance** button. In the displayed **Performance Analyzer** dialog box, click the **All Object Types** tab, click the **Select All** button, and then click **OK**.

With the deletion of the old Applicants table, only two ideas are given by the Performance Analyzer.

6 In the **Performance Analyzer** dialog box, click the **Close** ☒ button. **Close** « the **Navigation Pane**.

Objective 3   Modify Access Views and Behaviors

Video A10-3

Access has many options that affect database views and behaviors. These options are changed using the Access Options dialog box. For example, there are options to alter colors and borders, options for how text is formatted, and settings that alter how windows display. The Access Options dialog box is also used to add and remove commands from the Quick Access Toolbar. You can create a custom interface by changing the options for the Navigation Pane. Hundreds of option settings are available to the database designer.

Activity 10.05 │ Modifying Access Options

Loren-Renner Law Partners would like its database to have a unique look and feel. In this activity, you will use the Access Options dialog box to customize the appearance of all databases opened on this computer.

1 Display **Backstage** view, and click **Options**. If necessary, click **General**. Compare your screen with Figure 10.11.

The left pane displays several option groups that, when clicked, display their settings in the larger pane. The settings for the General option group currently display.

FIGURE 10.11

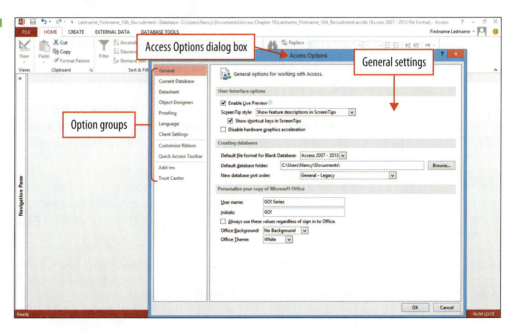

2 Under **Personalize your copy of Microsoft Office**, in the **User name** box, type your first and last names. In the **Initials** box, type your first, middle, and last initials.

3 Under **Personalize your copy of Microsoft Office**, in the **Office Background** box, click the **Office Background box arrow**, and then click **Circuit**.

An ***Office background*** is a small graphic in the top right corner of the Access application window used to personalize Office 2013.

4 Click **OK**, and then observe the changes to the top of the database window.

These changes will affect every database opened on this computer as well as documents in the other Office 2013 applications.

5 Display **Backstage** view, and then click **Options**. In the left pane, click **Datasheet**.

6 Under **Gridlines and cell effects**, clear the **Horizontal** check box.

7 Under **Default font**, click the **Size arrow**, and then click **9**.

8 In the left pane, click **Object Designers**. Under **Table design view**, in the **Default text field size**, replace the existing value with **50**

The default field size for new text fields will be 50 instead of 255.

9 Click **OK**. **Open** » the **Navigation Pane**. Open the **Paralegals** table in **Datasheet** view, and compare your screen with Figure 10.12.

The horizontal gridlines no longer display between the records. The font size is smaller for the entire table, allowing the columns to be smaller and still display all of the data.

FIGURE 10.12

10 **Close** × the **Paralegals** table. **Close** « the **Navigation Pane**.

Activity 10.06 | Customizing the Quick Access Toolbar

Any Access command, including those not available on the Ribbon, can be added to the Quick Access Toolbar. Loren-Renner Law Partners would like to add its commonly used commands to the Quick Access Toolbar. In this activity, you will use two different methods to customize the Quick Access Toolbar.

1 Display **Backstage** view, and then click **Options**. In the left pane, click **Quick Access Toolbar**. Alternatively, on the **Quick Access Toolbar**, click the **Customize Quick Access Toolbar arrow** ▾, and then click **More Commands**. Compare your screen with Figure 10.13.

Under *Choose commands from*, the commands from the Popular Commands group display. Under *Customize Quick Access Toolbar*, the commands on the current Quick Access Toolbar are listed. The *Customize Quick Access Toolbar* menu provides two options—the Quick Access Toolbar can be modified for all databases or just the current database.

FIGURE 10.13

Customizes all databases or current database only

Current commands on Quick Access Toolbar—yours may differ

2 In the list below **Popular Commands**, click **Close Database,** and then click the **Add** button.

Loren-Renner Law Partners would like this button added for all databases opened on this computer.

3 In the upper-right corner, click the **Customize Quick Access Toolbar arrow**, and then click the path to the currently open database. In the list below **Popular Commands**, scroll down. Click **Quick Print**, and then click the **Add** button.

The firm would like this change for the currently opened database only.

4 Click **OK**, and then compare your screen with Figure 10.14.

The Close Database and Quick Print icons have been added to the Quick Access Toolbar. Icons added to just one database are placed to the right of the other icons.

FIGURE 10.14

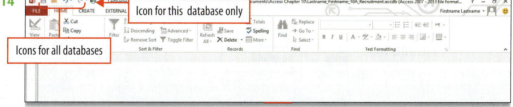

Icon for this database only

Icons for all databases

5 Open ⟩⟩ the **Navigation Pane**. Open the **Paralegals** table in **Datasheet** view. Press Alt + PrintScrn . In the **Word** document, press Enter , and then press Ctrl + Enter to insert a page break. Type your first and last names, press Enter , and then type **Project 10A Activity 10.06 Step 5** Press Enter , **Paste** the screenshot, and then click **Save** 🔒. Leave the Word document open.

6 In **Access, Close** ✕ the **Paralegals** table.

Activity 10.07 | Setting Current Database Options

The Current Database group provides several useful options you can change. These options enable the database designer to create the look and feel of a custom application. Loren-Renner Law Partners would like its database to have a unique look and feel, and the company does not want end users to make design changes. In this activity, you will create a custom application title and application icon for the database, and then disable Layout view.

1 Display **Backstage** view, click **Options**, and then in the left pane, click **Current Database**.

2 Under **Application Options**, in the **Application Title** box, type **L-R Law Partners**

> The *application title* is the text that displays in the Access title bar when that database is open. If the Application Title box is left blank, the file path, name, file, and application name display instead.

3 To the right of **Application Icon** box, click the **Browse** button. In the displayed **Icon Browser** dialog box, change the file type to **Bitmaps (*.bmp)**.

4 In the **Icon Browser** dialog box, navigate to where the student files for this project are stored. Locate and click **a10A_Icon**, and then click **OK**. Click the check box next to *Use as Form and Report Icon.*

5 To the right of the **Display Form** box, click the down-pointing arrow, and then click **Navigation Form** to display this form when the database is opened.

> Because the Navigation Pane does not display in web-based databases, the navigation form should be set to display as the default form when the database is opened.

6 Under **Application Options**, select the **Compact on Close** check box.

> With this option selected, the database will be compacted and repaired each time it is closed. *Compact & Repair* is a process in which an Access file is rewritten to store the objects and data more efficiently.

7 Clear the **Enable Layout View** check box to remove the checkmark.

> With the checkmark removed, Layout view is disabled.

8 Click **OK**, read the displayed message, and then click **OK** again.

9 From **Backstage** view, click **Close**, and then display **Backstage** view. Under *Recent*, click **Lastname_Firstname_10A_Recruitment**.

10 **Close** ☒ the **Navigation Form**. **Open** the **Lawyer Directory** report in **Report** view, and then compare your screen with Figure 10.15.

> The application title displays in the title bar. The application icon displays in the report's tab and in the upper left corner of the screen. If the database file or icon image file is renamed or moved to another location, the icon will no longer display.

FIGURE 10.15

11 **Close** ☒ the report.

Activity 10.08 | Set Navigation Options

The database designer can choose to customize the Navigation Pane to create a custom interface for the end user. Loren-Renner Law Partners would like its users to see objects in specialized groups in the Navigation Pane. In this activity, you will customize the Navigation Pane by adding a custom category and two groups. You will then add the form and report to their respective groups.

1 ▶ Display **Backstage** view, click **Options**, and then in the left pane, if necessary, click **Current Database**.

2 ▶ Under **Navigation**, click the **Navigation Options** button, and then compare your screen with Figure 10.16.

The existing categories for the Navigation Pane display on the left and the groups for each existing category display on the right. Categories and Groups are edited using the buttons below the two columns.

FIGURE 10.16

3 ▶ Click the **Add Item** button, type **L-R Law Partners** and then press Enter.

L-R Law Partners displays as a category. A ***Navigation Pane category*** is a top-level listing that displays when the Navigation Pane arrow is clicked.

4 ▶ With the **L-R Law Partners** category selected, click the **Add Group** button. Type **Lawyers** and then press Enter.

Lawyers displays as group. A ***Navigation Pane group*** is a second-level listing that displays when a Navigation Pane category is selected.

5 ▶ Click the **Add Group** button. Type **Paralegals** and then press Enter. Click **OK** three times to close the dialog boxes.

6 ▶ From **Backstage** view, **Close** the database. Display **Backstage** view. Under *Recent*, click **Lastname_Firstname_10A_Recruitment. Close** ⊠ the **Navigation Form**.

7 ▶ Click the **Navigation Pane arrow** ⊙, and then click **L-R Law Partners**. In the **Navigation Pane**, under **Unassigned Objects**, drag the **Lawyers** table and drop it over the **Lawyers** group. Drag the **Lawyer Information** form and drop it over the **Lawyers** group. Drag the **Lawyer Directory** report and drop it over the **Lawyers** group.

8 ▶ Drag the **Paralegals** table and drop it over the **Paralegals** group. Drag the **Paralegal Directory** report and drop it over the **Paralegals** group. Compare your screen with Figure 10.17.

The objects display as shortcuts within their respective Navigation Pane groups, and they are no longer listed under Unassigned Objects.

FIGURE 10.17

9 Display **Backstage** view, click **Options**, and then under **Navigation**, click the **Navigation Options** button. In the **Categories** column, click **L-R Law Partners**. In the **Groups** column, clear the **Unassigned Objects** check box, and then click **OK** two times to close the dialog boxes. Click **OK** to close the message box.

> The two objects that you assigned earlier display in the Navigation Pane. You will need to close and reopen the database for the options to take effect.

10 Display **Backstage** view, and then click **Close**. From **Backstage** view, click **Open Other Files**. Under *Open*, double-click **Computer**, navigate to your **Access Chapter 10** folder, and then double-click **Lastname_Firstname_10A_Recruitment**.

11 Right-click the **Lawyers** table, and in the displayed shortcut menu, click **Rename Shortcut**. Add your **Lastname Firstname** at the beginning of the object name. Use this same technique to add your last and first names to the other objects displayed in the **Navigation Pane**.

12 Press [Alt] + [PrintScrn]. In the **Word** document, press [Enter], and then press [Ctrl] + [Enter] to insert a page break. Type your first and last names, press [Enter], and then type **Project 10A Activity 10.08 Step 12** Press [Enter], **Paste** the screenshot, and then click **Save** [💾]. Leave the Word document open.

13 Return to **Access**. On the **Quick Access Toolbar**, right-click the **Close Database button**, and then click **Remove from Quick Access Toolbar**. Use this same technique to remove the **Quick Print** button from the **Quick Access Toolbar**.

14 Display **Backstage** view, click **Options**, and then click **General**. Click the **Office Background arrow**, and then click **No Background**.

15 Click **Datasheet**. Click the **Default Font size button arrow**, and then click **11**. Under **Default gridlines showing**, select the **Horizontal** check box.

16 Click **Object Designers**, and then set the **Default text field size** back to **255**

17 Click **OK** to close the **Access Options** dialog box and then click **OK** to close the message box. Close the **10A_Recruitment** database.

Objective 4 Use the Database Splitter

Video A10-4

Business databases are often divided into two parts—a back end and a front end. The **back end** consists of the database tables and their data. The back end is typically placed on a server and is not directly seen by the end user. In Access, the **front end** comprises the database forms, queries, reports, and macros. The end users open the front end to work with the data stored in the back-end tables. Dividing the database enables the database administrator to maintain a single source of data while designing multiple front ends to meet the needs of various departments in the company.

Activity 10.09 | Splitting a Database

A **split database** is an Access database that is split into two files—one containing the back end, and one containing the front end. Several departments at Loren-Renner Law Partners need their own forms, reports, and queries. Instead of trying to coordinate separate databases, the company would like to place all of the database tables on a network server. Each department will then have its own custom front end that links to the tables in the back-end file. In this activity, you will use the Split Database tool to create two separate files—one for the back end, and one for the front end.

1 Navigate to the location where the student data files for this textbook are saved and open the **10A_Lawyers** database. Save the database in your **Access Chapter 10** folder, as **Lastname_Firstname_10A_Lawyers** If necessary, enable the content.

2 On the **DATABASE TOOLS tab**, in the **Move Data group**, click **Access Database**. Compare your screen with Figure 10.18.

FIGURE 10.18

3 In the displayed **Database Splitter** dialog box, read the message, and then click the **Split Database** button. Compare your screen with Figure 10.19.

FIGURE 10.19

4 In the **Create Back-end Database** dialog box, if necessary, navigate to your **Access Chapter 10** folder. Notice the suggested file name, and then click the **Split** button. Read the displayed message, click **OK**, and then compare your screen with Figure 10.20.

In the Navigation Pane, the tables display the linked table icon and the other objects display as before. Recall that a linked table is a table that resides in a separate database file.

FIGURE 10.20

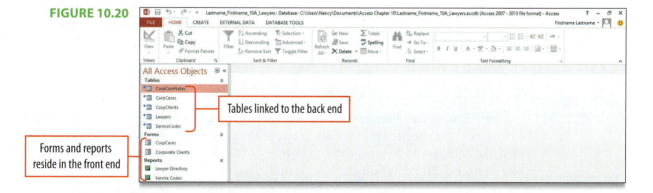

5 Press [Alt] + [PrintScrn]. In the **Word** document, press [Enter], and then press [Ctrl] + [Enter] to insert a page break. Type your first and last names, press [Enter], and then type **Project 10A Activity 10.09 Step 5** Press [Enter], **Paste** the screenshot, and then click **Save** 🖫. Leave the Word document open.

6 On the taskbar, click the **File Explorer** button. Navigate to the location where the **Access Chapter 10** folder is saved, and open the folder. Double-click **Lastname_Firstname_10A_Lawyers_be**, and Enable Content if necessary. Compare your screen with Figure 10.21.

> The five linked tables reside in this back-end database file. Typically, the file containing the back end would reside on a network server that all departments can access. Notice that none of the front-end objects in the Lawyers database were copied to this back-end file.

FIGURE 10.21

More **Knowledge** | **Moving the Back End to a Microsoft SQL Server**

Instead of moving the back end into a separate Access database file, it can be placed on a Microsoft SQL Server. *Microsoft SQL Server* is a database application designed for high-end business uses. If a database contains thousands of records, or if it will be accessed by multiple users at the same time, moving the back-end files to a Microsoft SQL Server will dramatically improve performance.

---

7 **Close** the database, and **Exit** this instance of Access to return to the **File Explorer** window.

8 Press [Alt] + [PrintScrn]. In the **Word** document, press [Enter], and then press [Ctrl] + [Enter] to insert a page break. Type your first and last names, press [Enter], and then type **Project 10A Activity 10.09 Step 8** Press [Enter], Paste the screenshot, and then click **Save**. Leave the Word document open.

9 Return to **Access**. Close the database.

Objective 5   Encrypt and Decrypt Databases

Video A10-5

The data stored in any company's database is one of that company's most valuable assets. If proprietary knowledge is made public, the company could lose its competitive advantage. Further, personal information stored in the database needs to be protected from unauthorized access. For these reasons, the data needs to be hidden until the correct password is entered. Only authorized users should know what that password is.

Activity 10.10 | Encrypting a Database with a Password

Loren-Renner Law Partners has a moral and legal responsibility to keep the data it collects hidden from unauthorized individuals. If one of the company computers or laptops is ever lost or stolen, the data should be unreadable to anyone outside of the company. In this activity, you will make an Access 2013 database unreadable until a password is entered.

1 Start Access. Click **Open Other Files**. Under **Open**, double-click **Computer**. In the **Open** dialog box, open the **Access Chapter 10** folder, and then click **Lastname_Firstname_10A_Lawyers** one time. In the lower right corner of the **Open** dialog box, click the **Open button arrow**, and compare your screen with Figure 10.22.

> Three additional open modes display. *Open Read-Only* opens the database so that all objects can be opened and viewed, but data and design changes cannot be made. *Open Exclusive* opens the database so that changes can be made, but no one else may open the database at the same time. *Open Exclusive Read-Only* opens the database in both Exclusive and Read-Only modes.

FIGURE 10.22

2 Click **Open Exclusive**.

The database must be opened in exclusive mode before it can be encrypted. To *encrypt* means to hide data by making the file unreadable until the correct password is entered.

3 Display the **Backstage** view, and under *Info*, click the **Encrypt with Password** button. Compare your screen with Figure 10.23.

FIGURE 10.23

4 In the **Set Password** dialog box, in the **Password** box, type **GO!Access2013** Access passwords are case sensitive, so be sure to capitalize exactly as shown. In the **Verify** box, type **GO!Access2013** and then press [Alt] + [PrintScrn]. In the **Word** document, type your first and last names, and then press [Enter]. Type **Project 10A Activity 10.10 Step 4** press [Enter], and then **Paste** the screenshot. **Save** 💾 the file. Leave the Word document open.

> *Strong passwords* are created so they will be hard to guess and the database is secure. They use a combination of upper- and lowercase letters, special characters, numbers, and spaces in a character string. A *weak password* is a password that is easy to guess. Weak passwords may lead to costly losses of valuable data.

5 In **Access**, in the **Set Database Password** dialog box, click **OK**. If a message box displays, click **OK**. From **Backstage** view, click **Close**.

6 Display **Backstage** view to reopen the database. In the displayed **Password Required** dialog box, type **GO!Access2013** and then click **OK**. Alternatively, type the password, and then press [Enter]. **Close** the database.

> With encrypted Access 2013 files, individuals must enter a password to access the database. There is no way to retrieve a forgotten password to be able to open an encrypted database. Be sure to store passwords in a safe place away from the data they protect, in case it is ever necessary.

Activity 10.11 | Decrypting a Database with a Password

Loren-Renner Law Partners periodically resets the passwords used for its database to make them more secure. In this activity, you will remove a password currently used to open the Lawyers database so it will be ready to reset later. When you no longer want a password required to open a database, you must *decrypt* the file or unset the password.

1 Using the technique you practiced in the previous exercise, open the **10A Lawyers** database using the **Open Exclusive** option. In the **Password Required** dialog box, type **GO!Access2013** and click **OK**.

2 Display the **Backstage** view, and under *Info*, click the **Decrypt Database** button to display the **Unset Password** dialog box. Compare your screen with Figure 10.24.

To prohibit any user from removing the password encryption applied to a database, the password must be entered to discontinue the password requirement for opening the current database.

FIGURE 10.24

Enter password to remove encryption

Unset Database Password dialog box

3 Type **GO!Access2013** and then click **OK**. Alternatively, type the password, and then press Enter. From **Backstage** view, click **Close**.

4 Display **Backstage** view, and open the **10A Lawyers** database.

Notice the database opens without asking you to provide a password.

Objective 6 | Create a Locked Database (ACCDE File)

Video A10-6

A business may want to secure the design of certain objects in the database when providing a working copy of the database for staff. An *ACCDE file* is an Access 2013 file format that prevents users from creating forms and reports and making design changes to forms, reports, and macros while performing other regular database tasks. Because design changes might be necessary in the future, a copy of the original database should be stored in a secure place.

Activity 10.12 | Creating a Secure ACCDE File

Loren-Renner Law Partners wants to provide a locked-down version of its database so users cannot make any design changes. In this activity, you will create and test an ACCDE file.

1 If necessary, open the **10A_Lawyers** database.

2 Display **Backstage** view, and click **Save As**. In the right column under **Advanced**, double-click **Make ACCDE**. Compare your screen with Figure 10.25.

FIGURE 10.25

> **3** Verify that the path for your **Access Chapter 10** folder displays. In the **File name** box, change the file name to **Lastname_Firstname_10A_ACCDE** and then click **Save** 🖫.

> **4** **Exit** Access. Switch to the **File Explorer** window, and then compare your screen with Figure 10.26.

The Type description for the ACCDE file is Microsoft Access ACCDE Database. A padlock is added to the icon to indicate the file's "locked-down" status.

FIGURE 10.26

> **5** In the **File Explorer** window, double-click **Lastname_Firstname_10A_ACCDE**. If the Microsoft Office Access Security Notice displays, click **Open**.

> **6** Click the **CREATE tab**, and then compare your screen with Figure 10.27.

The forms and reports creation tools are dimmed, indicating that new forms and reports cannot be created.

FIGURE 10.27

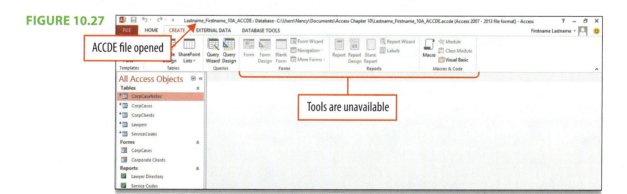

> **7** In the **Navigation Pane**, under **Reports**, right-click **Lawyer Directory**, and notice that the **Design View** command is dimmed. Design changes cannot be made in an ACCDE file.

8 Double-click the **Corporate Clients** form to open it in **Form** view. Add a new record using the following information. Replace **Firstname Lastname** with your first and last names. **Close** ☒ the form.

CorpID	C0025
OrgName	Little Elm Community College
Street	1010 South Main Street
City	Little Elm
State	TX
PostalCode	75068
Phone	(214) 555-5011
Representative	Firstname Lastname

The form can be used for normal database tasks as long as no Design view features are used.

9 If you are instructed to submit this result, create a paper or electronic printout of the current form only. **Close** the database, and then **Exit** Access.

10 In **File Explorer**, with the **Access Chapter 10** folder contents active, press Alt + PrintScrn. In the **Word** document, press Ctrl + End to go to the end of the document. Press Ctrl + Enter to go to a new page, and then type your first and last names and press Enter. Type **Project 10A Activity 10.12 Step 10** press Enter, and then **Paste** the screenshot. **Save** 💾 the file. If you are instructed to submit this result, create a paper or electronic printout of the Word document. **Close** Word, and **Close** the File Explorer window.

11 As directed by your instructor, submit your databases and the paper or electronic printouts of the two objects—one Word document and one form—that are the result of this project. Specifically, in this project, using your own name you created the following databases and printouts or electronic printouts:

1. Lastname_Firstname_10A_Recruitment	Database file
2. Lastname_Firstname_10A_Lawyers	Database file
3. Lastname_Firstname_10A_Screens	Word document (printed or electronic printout)
4. Corporate Clients	Form (printed or electronic printout)
5. Lastname_Firstname_10A_Lawyers_be	Back-end database file
6. Lastname_Firstname_10A_ACCDE	Locked database file

END | You have completed Project 10A

Overdue Accounts

PROJECT ACTIVITIES

Loren-Renner Law Partners stores billing information in two unrelated tables. It needs queries that combine the data from both tables so the firm can call those clients that need to pay their bill. The only way to combine these two queries is to work in SQL view. The partners have given you several tables from their database, each with a small sample of data. Once the queries are working properly, they can be applied to the full data set. In Activities 10.13 through 10.18, you will write queries in SQL view. Using this view, you will be able to create queries that cannot be created in Design view. Your completed queries and report will look similar to the printouts shown in Figure 10.28.

PROJECT FILES

For Project 10B, you will need the following database:

a10B_Accounts_Due

You will save your database as:

Lastname_Firstname_10B_Accounts_Due

PROJECT RESULTS

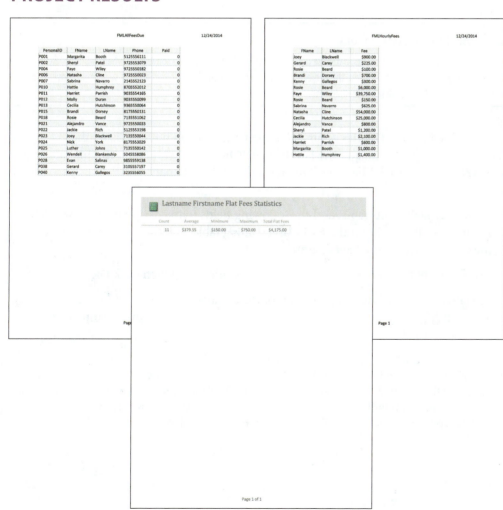

FIGURE 10.28 Project 10B Overdue Accounts

Video A10-7

All Access queries use SQL. *SQL*, or *Structured Query Language*, is a language used by many database programs to view, update, and query data in relational databases. In Access, queries can be created in Design view and then modified in SQL view. Starting in Design view saves time and is a good way to become familiar with writing SQL.

Activity 10.13 | Modifying a Query in SQL View

Loren-Renner Law Partners needs a query that lists each client who was charged a flat fee and has not yet paid that fee. In this activity, you will create that query in Design view and then modify it in SQL view.

1 ▶ Start Access. Navigate to the location where the student data files for this textbook are saved. Locate and then open the **a10B_Accounts_Due** database. Display **Backstage** view, click **Save As**, and then, under *File Types*, double-click **Save Database As**. In the **Save As** dialog box, navigate to your **Access Chapter 10** folder, and then **Save** the file as **Lastname_Firstname_10B_ Accounts_Due** in the folder. Enable the content if necessary.

2 ▶ Rename each table by adding **FML** to the beginning of each object name. Be sure to replace *FML* with your own initials, and do not use any spaces in the table names. **Close** ⟪ the **Navigation Pane**.

> **NOTE**   **Table and Field Naming Conventions**
>
> You will be creating queries by writing SQL. To simplify the SQL statements, database designers usually choose a naming convention where table and field names are abbreviated terms and do not contain any spaces. For this reason, this project follows what is known as the Upper Camel Case naming convention, and you will add your initials to the table names instead of your first and last names.

3 ▶ On the **CREATE tab**, in the **Queries group**, click the **Query Design** button. Using the techniques you have practiced, add the **FMLPersonalClients** and **FMLFlatFeeBilling** tables to the query design workspace. **Close** the **Show Table** dialog box. Expand the field lists to display all data.

4 ▶ From the **FMLPersonalClients** table, add the following fields to the design grid: **PersonalID**, **FName**, **LName**, and **Phone**. From the **FMLFlatFeeBilling** table, add the **Paid** field to the design grid. In the **Criteria** box for the **Paid** column, type **No**

5 ▶ Click **Save** 🖬, type **FMLFlatFeesDue** using your own initials, and then click **OK**.

6 ▶ Locate the status bar in the lower right corner of the database window, and then click the **SQL View** button 🔲. Click any blank area in the SQL workspace, and then compare your screen with Figure 10.29.

> When you work in Query Design view, Access builds the equivalent SQL statement. An *SQL statement* is an expression that defines the SQL commands that should be performed when the query is run. SQL statements typically contain several SQL clauses that begin with keywords. *Keywords* are commands built into the SQL programming language. Keywords are typically written using uppercase letters. In SQL view, statements are edited in the design grid.

FIGURE 10.29

SQL statement

Design grid

SQL View button

7 ▶ In the SQL statement, click to the left of the keyword *FROM*, and then press Enter.

This SQL statement starts with a SELECT clause. A **SELECT clause** lists which fields the query should display. The second clause in this SQL statement is a FROM clause. A **FROM clause** lists which tables hold the fields used in the SELECT clause.

8 ▶ Click to the left of the keyword *INNER*, and then press Enter two times.

A **JOIN clause** defines the join type for a query. Recall that an inner join displays only those records that have a corresponding record in both of the related tables. A **WHERE clause** defines the criteria that should be applied when a query is run.

9 ▶ Click to the left of the keyword *WHERE*, and then press Enter. In the **WHERE** clause, remove all six parentheses.

These parentheses would be needed only if a more complex WHERE clause were written. Often, the SQL generated while in Design view will not be as efficient as the SQL written by a database designer in SQL view.

10 ▶ Click **Save** 🖫. On the **QUERY TOOLS DESIGN tab**, in the **Results group**, click the **Run** button. Click the **LName column arrow**, and then click **Sort A to Z**. Compare your screen with Figure 10.30.

Brandi Dorsey and Faye Wiley are each listed two times. This type of duplication may lead to duplicate phone calls being made to the client.

FIGURE 10.30

Duplicate listings

11 In the status bar, click the **SQL View** button [SQL]. Click to the right of the keyword SELECT, press [Spacebar] and then type **DISTINCT**

>   The *DISTINCT* keyword removes duplicates from query results. It always follows the SELECT keyword, and is added only in SQL view.

12 **Run** the query and notice that duplicate records no longer display. **Save** [icon], and then **Close** [×] the query.

Objective 8   Create a Query in SQL View

Video A10-8

Many database designers find it easier to design their queries in SQL view. The typical SQL query uses the same three-step sequence. Understanding this sequence removes much of the complexity of the typical SQL statement. Working in SQL view enables the designer to write more efficient SQL, and also provides more control than Design view. Many types of queries can be created only when working in SQL view.

Activity 10.14   Creating an SQL Statement

Loren-Renner Law Partners needs a query that lists each client who was charged an hourly rate and has not yet paid the fee. Due to the nature of this query, you will need to work in SQL view to write a query not available in Design view. In this activity, you will create that query in SQL view.

1 On the **CREATE tab**, in the **Queries group**, click the **Query Design** button. **Close** the displayed **Show Table** dialog box, and then in the status bar, click the **SQL View** button [SQL].

>   Because you started with a select query, the SELECT keyword displays followed by a semicolon. Semicolons are used to mark the end of SQL statements.

2 Click before the semicolon, press [Spacebar] and then type the following, substituting FML with your own initials: **FMLPersonalClients.PersonalID, FMLPersonalClients.FName, FMLPersonalClients.LName, FMLPersonalClients.Phone, FMLHourlyBilling.Paid** Compare your screen with Figure 10.31.

>   In a SELECT clause, both the table name and field name are included and are separated by a period. Multiple fields must be separated by commas.

FIGURE 10.31

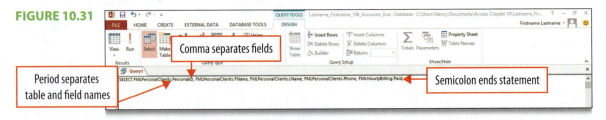

Period separates table and field names

Comma separates fields

Semicolon ends statement

3 Press [Enter], and then type the following FROM clause, substituting your own initials: **FROM FMLPersonalClients, FMLHourlyBilling**

>   All tables used in the SELECT clause must be listed in the FROM clause and are separated by commas.

4 Press [Enter], and then type the following WHERE clause, substituting your own initials: **WHERE FMLHourlyBilling.Paid=No**

>   Recall that in the WHERE statement, the criteria for the query is defined.

5 Be sure that the semicolon is at the end of the query. Click **Save** 🖫, and then, substituting your own initials, type **FMLHourlyFeesDue** Click **OK**.

6 Click the **Run** button, and then compare your screen with Figure 10.32. If you receive a message that the query has errors or the **Enter Parameter Value** dialog box displays, go back and check your typing very carefully.

> The result of this query is a cross join query. Recall that in a cross join query, every possible combination of records between two related tables will be returned. If no join type is defined or if there is a mistake in the WHERE clause, SQL returns a cross join query. When tables contain a large number of records, cross join queries will take a very long time to run. In this query, the join type needs to be defined.

FIGURE 10.32

7 **Save** 🖫 your query, and then return to **SQL** view.

Activity 10.15 | Specifying the Join Type in SQL

The Hourly Billing Due query currently returns a cross join. Once a join type is specified in the query, it will display one record per customer. In this activity, you will add an SQL clause so that the two tables used in the query use an inner join.

1 In **SQL** view, in the **FROM** clause, click between *FMLPersonalClients* and the comma, and then press Enter.

2 Press Delete to remove the comma.

3 Type the following JOIN clause, **INNER JOIN**

> The INNER JOIN keyword instructs the query to use an inner join between two tables.

4 Click to the right of *FMLHourlyBilling*, press Spacebar, and type the following ON clause:
ON FMLPersonalClients.PersonalID = FMLHourlyBilling.PersonalID

> The **ON** keyword is used to specify which field is common to two tables. The combination of the INNER JOIN and ON keywords creates a relationship between the two tables. In this query the PersonalID field is used to join the tables.

5 **Save** 🖫, and then **Run** the query. Sort the **LName** column in alphabetical order, and then compare your screen with Figure 10.33.

> The tables are joined correctly, but customers with more than one outstanding bill are listed two or more times.

FIGURE 10.33

Duplicate values

6 ▶ Return to **SQL** view. After the **SELECT** keyword, press [Spacebar], and then type **DISTINCT**

7 ▶ **Run** the query. Check that no customer is listed more than once. **Save** 🖫, and then **Close** ✕ the query.

Objective 9 | Create a Union Query Using SQL

Video A10-9

Using SQL, the results of two or more queries can be displayed in one query. A ***union query*** combines the results of two or more similar select queries. The combined queries must have the same number of columns and the same data types in each corresponding column. Union queries are created only in SQL view.

Activity 10.16 | Creating a Union Query in SQL View

Recall that Loren-Renner Law Partners needs a list of all personal clients with amounts owed. In earlier projects, you built two separate queries, one for flat fees and the other for hourly fees. In this activity, you will use SQL to combine the results of both queries into a single query.

1 ▶ On the **CREATE tab**, in the **Queries group**, click the **Query Design** button. **Close** the displayed **Show Table** dialog box.

2 ▶ In the **Query Type group**, click the **Union** button. Notice that the query switches to **SQL** view.

3 ▶ **Open** ⏵ the **Navigation Pane**. Open the **FMLFlatFeesDue** query, and then in the status bar, click the **SQL View** button 🔲. With the entire SQL statement selected, right-click anywhere in the design grid, and then click **Copy**.

4 ▶ **Close** the **FMLFlatFeesDue** query. In the union query, right-click anywhere in the design grid, and then click **Paste**.

5 ▶ At the end of the SQL statement, delete the semicolon, and then press [Enter] **two** times.

6 ▶ Type **UNION** and then press [Enter] **two** times. Compare your screen with Figure 10.34.

The ***UNION*** keyword is used to combine one or more queries in a union query.

FIGURE 10.34

UNION keyword

7 Open the **FMLHourlyFeesDue** query, and then in the status bar, click the **SQL View** button. With the entire SQL statement selected, right-click anywhere in the design grid, and then click **Copy**.

8 **Close** the **FMLHourlyFeesDue** query. In the union query that you are building, right-click next to the insertion point, and then click **Paste**.

9 Click **Save**, type **FMLAllFeesDue** using your own initials, and then click **OK**.

10 In the **Navigation Pane**, notice the union query icon to the left of the query's name. In the **Results group**, click the **View button arrow**, and notice that Design view is not available for this query.

11 **Run** the query, and then compare your results with Figure 10.35.

FIGURE 10.35

12 If you are instructed to submit this result, create a paper or electronic printout of the query. Click **Save**, and then **Close** the query. **Close** the **Navigation Pane**.

Objective 10 Create Calculated Fields and SQL Aggregate Functions

Video A10-10

SQL is a powerful language that does far more than create select queries. SQL provides commands to create calculated fields and summarize data using aggregate functions. Recall that an aggregate function performs a calculation on a column of data and returns a single value. When creating calculated fields, many developers prefer to work in SQL view because long expressions can be viewed without having to use the Zoom feature.

Activity 10.17 │ Creating Calculated Fields in SQL

Loren-Renner Law Partners needs a list of total amounts due for the clients who were billed at an hourly rate. In this activity, you will write an SQL statement with a field that calculates fees by multiplying the number of hours by the hourly rate.

1 On the **CREATE tab**, in the **Queries group**, click the **Query Design** button.

2 Use the displayed **Show Table** dialog box to add the **FMLPersonalClients** and **FMLHourlyBilling** tables, and then **Close** the **Show Table** dialog box. Expand the field lists so all field names are displayed

3 From the **FMLPersonalClients** table, add the **FName** field, and then add the **LName** field.

4 In the status bar, click the **SQL View** button.

Starting this query in Design view saves you from having to type the SELECT, FROM, and INNER JOIN clauses.

5 To the right of the entire SELECT clause, type a comma, press [Spacebar], and then type the following using your own initials: **FMLHourlyBilling.Hours * FMLHourlyBilling.Rate AS Fee**

A calculated field with the caption *Fee* will display the product of the Hours and Rate fields for each record. The *AS* keyword creates captions for fields.

6 At the end of the SQL statement, click to the left of the semicolon, press [Enter], and then type the following WHERE clause using your own initials: **WHERE FMLHourlyBilling.Paid = No**

7 Click **Save** 💾, type **FMLHourlyFees** using your own initials, and then click **OK**.

8 **Run** the query, and then compare your screen with Figure 10.36.

FIGURE 10.36

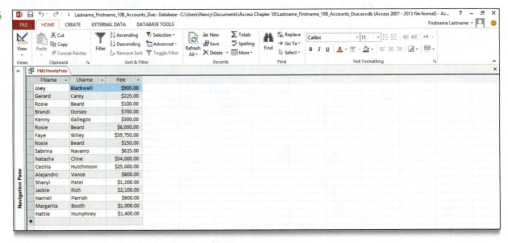

9 If you are instructed to submit this result, create a paper or electronic printout of the query. **Close** ✕ the query.

Activity 10.18 | Writing SQL Aggregate Functions

Loren-Renner Law Partners needs a report showing summary statistics for the amounts due from clients paying flat fees. In this activity, you will use SQL aggregate functions to calculate summary statistics and then create a report based on the query.

1 On the **CREATE tab**, in the **Queries group**, click the **Query Design** button. **Close** ✕ the displayed **Show Table** dialog box. In the status bar, click the **SQL View** button 🟥.

2 In the design grid, delete the semicolon, press [Spacebar], and then, substituting *FML* with your own initials, type the following: **Count(FMLFlatFeeBilling.Fee) AS Count**

Count is an SQL aggregate function.

3 Press [Enter], and then type the following FROM clause: **FROM FMLFlatFeeBilling**

4 Press [Enter], and then type the following WHERE clause: **WHERE FMLFlatFeeBilling.Paid = No;**

5 Click **Save** 💾, type **FMLFlatFeesStats** using your own initials, and then click **OK**.

6 Click the **Run** button, and then compare your screen with Figure 10.37.

The number of records in the query displays in a column that has *Count* as its caption.

FIGURE 10.37

7 Return to **SQL** view. Click to the right of the entire **SELECT** clause, and then type a comma. Press [Enter], and then type the following using your own initials: **Avg(FMLFlatFeeBilling.Fee) AS Average,** and then press [Enter].

8 Continue adding to the SELECT clause as by typing **Min(FMLFlatFeeBilling.Fee) AS Minimum,** and then press [Enter]. Type **Max(FMLFlatFeeBilling.Fee) AS Maximum,** and press [Enter]. Type **Sum(FMLFlatFeeBilling.Fee) AS [Total Flat Fees]**

Because Total Flat Fees contains spaces, it must be enclosed in square brackets. In Access SQL statements, any table name or field name that has spaces must be enclosed in square brackets. If there are no spaces, then the square brackets are optional. After [Total Flat Fees], no comma is needed because it is the end of the SELECT clause.

9 Compare your screen with Figure 10.38. **Save** 🖫 and then **Run** the query.

FIGURE 10.38

10 **Close** the query. **Open** » the **Navigation Pane**, and then click to select the **FMLFlatFeesStats** query. On the **CREATE tab**, in the **Reports group**, click the **Report** button.

11 Click anywhere in the **Total Flat Fees** column to select the column. On the **REPORT LAYOUT TOOLS DESIGN** tab, in the **Grouping & Totals group**, click the **Totals** button, and then click **Sum** to remove the second displayed total for that column. Click the **Total** line, and press [Delete].

12 Delete the **Date** and **Time** boxes in the **Report Header**. Change the report's title to **Lastname Firstname Flat Fees Statistics** If necessary, resize the text box so the title fits in one line. If you are instructed to submit this result, create a paper or electronic printout.

13 Click **Save** 🖫, and then accept the **Report Name** by clicking **OK**.

14 **Close** ☒ the report, and then **Close** the database and **Exit** Access.

15 As directed by your instructor, submit your database and the paper or electronic printouts of the three objects—two queries and a report—that are the result of this project. Specifically, in this project, using your own name you created the following database and printouts or electronic printouts:

1. Lastname_Firstname_10B_Accounts_Due	Database file
2. FMLAllFeesDue	Query (printed or electronic printout)
3. FMLHourlyFees	Query (printed or electronic printout)
4. Lastname Firstname Flat Fees Statistics	Report (printed or electronic printout)

END | You have completed Project 10B

END OF CHAPTER

SUMMARY

A navigation form is a form that displays navigational controls to display forms and reports in your database; it is useful for a web-based database where the Navigation Pane is not displayed.

Analysis tools improve performance. The Table Analyzer and Performance Analyzer analyze objects and offer improvement ideas. Viewing object dependencies protects the database before deleting objects.

Access Options customize database views, including the Navigation Pane. Using a locked-down ACCDE file format, a split database with the back end stored on a server, or a password provides security.

SQL provides more control and flexibility than Design view when designing queries, and more options. SQL was used to join two queries in a union query, create calculated fields, and create statistics.

GO! LEARN IT ONLINE

Review the concepts and key terms in this chapter by completing these online challenges, which you can find at **www.pearsonhighered.com/go.**

Matching and Multiple Choice:
Answer matching and multiple choice questions to test what you learned in this chapter. **MyITLab®**

Crossword Puzzle:
Spell out the words that match the numbered clues, and put them in the puzzle squares.

Flipboard:
Flip through the definitions of the key terms in this chapter and match them with the correct term.

Your instructor may assign one or more of these projects to help you review the chapter and assess your mastery and understanding of the chapter.

	Review and Assessment Guide for Access Chapter 10		
Project	**Apply Skills from These Chapter Objectives**	**Project Type**	**Project Location**
10C	Objectives 1–6 from Project 10A	**10C Skills Review** A guided review of the skills from Project 10A.	On the following pages
10D	Objectives 7–10 from Project 10B	**10D Skills Review** A guided review of the skills from Project 10B.	On the following pages
10E	Objectives 1–6 from Project 10A	**10E Mastery (Grader Project)** A demonstration of your mastery of the skills in Project 10A with extensive decision making.	In MyITLab and on the following pages
10F	Objectives 7–10 from Project 10B	**10F Mastery (Grader Project)** A demonstration of your mastery of the skills in Project 10B with extensive decision making.	In MyITLab and on the following pages
10G	Objectives 4, 5, 7–10 from Projects 10A and 10B	**10G Mastery (Grader Project)** A demonstration of your mastery of the skills in Projects 10A and 10B with extensive decision making.	In MyITLab and on the following pages
10H	Combination of Objectives from Projects 10A and 10B	**10H GO! Fix It** A demonstration of your mastery of the skills in Projects 10A and 10B by creating a correct result from a document that contains errors you must find.	Online
10I	Combination of Objectives from Projects 10A and 10B	**10I GO! Make It** A demonstration of your mastery of the skills in Projects 10A and 10B by creating a result from a supplied picture.	Online
10J	Combination of Objectives from Projects 10A and 10B	**10J GO! Solve It** A demonstration of your mastery of the skills in Projects 10A and 10B, your decision-making skills, and your critical thinking skills. A task-specific rubric helps you self-assess your result.	Online
10K	Combination of Objectives from Projects 10A and 10B	**10K GO! Solve It** A demonstration of your mastery of the skills in Projects 10A and 10B, your decision-making skills, and your critical thinking skills. A task-specific rubric helps you self-assess your result.	On the following pages
10L	Combination of Objectives from Projects 10A and 10B	**10L GO! Think** A demonstration of your understanding of the Chapter concepts applied in a manner that you would apply outside of college. An analytic rubric helps you and your instructor grade the quality of your work by comparing it to the work an expert in the discipline would create.	On the following pages
10M	Combination of Objectives from Projects 10A and 10B	**10M GO! Think** A demonstration of your understanding of the Chapter concepts applied in a manner that you would apply outside of college. An analytic rubric helps you and your instructor grade the quality of your work by comparing it to the work an expert in the discipline would create.	Online
10N	Combination of Objectives from Projects 10A and 10B	**10N You and GO!** A demonstration of your understanding of the Chapter concepts applied in a manner that you would apply in a personal situation. An analytic rubric helps you and your instructor grade the quality of your work.	Online

GLOSSARY

GLOSSARY OF CHAPTER KEY TERMS

ACCDE file An Access file format that prevents individuals from making design changes to forms, reports, and macros.

Application title The text that displays in the Access title bar when that database is open.

AS An SQL keyword that creates captions for fields.

Back end A file that consists of the database tables and their data. The back end is typically placed on a server and is not directly seen by the end user.

Compact & Repair A process where an Access file is rewritten to store the objects and data in more efficiently.

Decrypt An action that removes a file's encryption or unsets a password.

Dependency An object that requires, or is dependent on, another database object.

DISTINCT An SQL keyword that removes duplicates from query results.

Encrypt A process to hide data by making the file unreadable until the correct password is entered.

FROM clause An SQL statement that lists which tables hold the fields used in the SELECT clause.

Front end A file that includes the database forms, queries, reports, and macros. The end users open the front end to work with the data stored in the back-end tables.

Indeterminate relationship a relationship that does not enforce referential integrity.

JOIN clause An SQL statement that defines the join type for a query.

Keywords Commands built into the SQL programming language

Microsoft SQL Server A database application designed for high-end business uses.

Navigation form A form that displays navigational controls that enable you to display forms and reports in your database.

Navigation Pane category A top-level listing that displays when the Navigation Pane arrow is clicked.

Navigation Pane group A second-level listing that display when a Navigation Pane category is selected.

Office background A small graphic in the top right corner of the Access application window used to personalize Office 2013.

ON An SQL keyword that is used to specify which field is common to two tables.

Open Exclusive An option that opens the database so that changes can be made, but no one else may open the database at the same time.

Open Exclusive Read-Only An option that opens the database in both Exclusive and Read-Only modes.

Open Read-Only An option that opens the database so that all objects can be opened and viewed, but data and design changes cannot be made.

Performance Analyzer A wizard that analyzes database objects, and then offers suggestions for improving them.

SELECT clause An SQL statement that lists which fields the query should display.

Split database An Access database that is split into two files—one containing the back end, and one containing the front end.

SQL (Structured Query Language) A language used by many database programs to view, update, and query data in relational databases.

SQL statement An expression that defines the SQL commands that should be performed when the query is run.

Strong password A password that is very difficult to guess.

Table Analyzer A wizard that searches for repeated data in a table, and then splits the table into two or more related tables.

UNION An SQL keyword that is used to combine one or more queries in a union query.

Union query A query type that combines the results of two or more similar select queries.

Weak password A password that is easy to guess.

WHERE clause An SQL statement that defines the criteria that should be applied when a query is run.

CHAPTER REVIEW

Apply **10A** skills from these Objectives:

1 Create a Navigation Form
2 Use Microsoft Access Analysis Tools
3 Modify Access Views and Behaviors
4 Use the Database Splitter
5 Encrypt and Decrypt Databases
6 Create a Locked Database (ACCDE file)

Skills Review | Project 10C Paralegals

Loren-Renner Law Partners wants to secure the database tables used by its paralegals. You will encrypt the database using a secure password, create a locked ACCDE file, and split the database to allow Human Resources to design separate front-end databases to be used by various departments. Your completed documents will look like those shown in Figure 10.39.

PROJECT FILES

For Project 10C, you will need the following files:

a10C_Paralegals
a10C_Icon

You will save your files as:

Lastname_Firstname_10C_Paralegals
Lastname_Firstname_10C_Screens
Lastname_Firstname_10C_Paralegals_ACCDE
Lastname_Firstname_10C_Paralegals_be

PROJECT RESULTS

FIGURE 10.39

(Project 10C Paralegals continues on the next page)

CHAPTER REVIEW

1 Start Access. Locate and then open the **a10C_ Paralegals** file. Save the database in your **Access Chapter 10** folder as **Lastname_Firstname_10C_Paralegals** If necessary, add the Chapter 10 folder to the Trust Center or Enable Content.

2 On the **CREATE tab**, in the **Forms group**, click the **Navigation** button, and then click **Horizontal Tabs**. If the Field List displays, close it.

3 In the **Navigation Pane**, under **Forms**, point to **PersonalServiceCodesForm**, hold down the left mouse button, drag up and to the right to [**Add New**], and then release the mouse button. Using the technique you practiced, add the **PersonalClientsForm** and the **PersonalClientsList** report as the second and third tabs in the navigation form.

a. At the top of the form, edit the title to read **Lastname Firstname 10C Paralegals Navigation Form**

b. **Save** the navigation form as **Lastname Firstname Paralegals Navigation Form Close** the **Navigation Pane**. Switch to **Form** view.

c. Press [Alt] + [PrintScrn]. Create a new, blank Word document. In the **Word** document, type your first and last names, press [Enter], and then type **Project 10C Step 3** Press [Enter], and then **Paste** the screenshot. **Save** the document in your **Access Chapter 10** folder with the name **Lastname_Firstname_10C_Screens** Leave the Word document open.

d. Return to **Access**, and **Close** the **Paralegals Navigation Form**.

4 On the **DATABASE TOOLS tab**, in the **Analyze group**, click the **Analyze Table** button. If the introductory page displays, click **Next** two times.

a. Under **Tables**, verify that **Cases** is selected, and then click **Next**. Verify that **Yes, let the wizard decide** is selected, and then click **Next**.

b. Double-click the **Table1** title bar, type **Lastname Firstname Cases** and then click **OK**. Double-click the **Table2** title bar, type **Lastname Firstname Paralegals** and then click **OK**.

c. Click **Next**. In the **Cases** table, click **PCaseID**, and then click the **Set Unique Identifier** button.

d. Click **Next**, and then click **Finish**. **Close** the **Access Help** window, and then **Close** the **Cases** query. **Open** the **Navigation Pane**.

5 Select the **Cases_OLD** table. On the **DATABASE TOOLS tab**, in the **Relationships group**, click the **Object Dependencies** button. In the displayed message box, click **OK**.

a. In the **Object Dependencies** pane, check that no database objects depend on the **Cases_OLD** table. Press [Alt] + [PrintScrn], and then **Close** the **Object Dependencies** pane.

b. In the **Word** document. Type your first and last names, press [Enter], and then type **Project 10C Step 5** Press [Enter], and then **Paste** the screenshot. Leave the document open.

c. In **Access**, delete the **Cases_OLD** table. **Close** [«] the **Navigation Pane**.

6 On the **CREATE tab**, in the **Queries group**, click the **Query Design** button. Add the **Cases** and **PersonalServiceCodes** tables, and then **Close** the dialog box. Expand the field lists so all fields and table names display.

a. From the **Cases** table, add the **PCaseID**, **Description**, and **Closed?** fields, and then from the **PersonalServiceCodes** table, add the **Service** field.

b. Click **Save** , type **Lastname Firstname Case Information** and then click **OK**. **Run** and then **Close** the query.

7 On the **DATABASE TOOLS tab**, in the **Analyze group**, click the **Analyze Performance** button. Click the **All Object Types tab**, click the **Select All** button, and then click **OK**.

a. Under **Analysis Results**, click the suggestion with the green question mark. Click the **Optimize** button.

b. Press [Alt] + [PrintScrn], and then **Close** the **Performance Analyzer** dialog box. In the **Word** document, press [Enter], and then press [Ctrl] + [Enter] to insert a page break. Type your first and last names, press [Enter], and then type **Project 10C Step 7** Press [Enter], **Paste** the screenshot, and then click **Save**. Leave the document open.

c. Return to **Access**. From **Backstage** view, click **Options**.

8 Click **Current Database**, and then in the **Application Title** box, type **L-R Law Partners: Paralegals**

a. In the **Application Icon** box, browse to select **a10C_ Icon**, a bitmap file located within the student files.

(Project 10C Paralegals continues on the next page)

b. Clear the **Display Status Bar** check box.

c. In the **Display Form** box, click the **arrow** and then click the **Paralegals Navigation Form**.

9 Under **Navigation**, click the **Navigation Options** button.

a. Click the **Add Item** button, type **Paralegals** and then press Enter.

b. Click the **Add Group** button, type **Clients** and then press Enter.

c. Click the **Add Group** button, type **Cases** and then press Enter. Click **OK** two times to close the dialog boxes.

d. Read the displayed message, and then click **OK**.

e. From **Backstage** view, click **Close**, and then display **Backstage** view to reopen the database. **Close** the navigation form and **Open** the **Navigation Pane**.

10 Click the **Navigation Pane arrow**, and then click **Paralegals**.

a. Drag the **PersonalClients** table and drop it into the **Clients** group. Drag the **PersonalClientsForm** and drop it into the **Clients** group. Drag the **PersonalClientsList** report and drop it into the **Clients** group.

b. Drag the **Cases** table and drop it into the **Cases** group. Drag the **PersonalServiceCodes** table and drop it into the **Cases** group. Drag the **PersonalServiceCodesForm** and drop it into the **Cases** group. Drag the **Case Information** query and drop it onto the **Cases** group.

11 From **Backstage** view, click **Options**. If necessary, click **Current Database**, and then under **Navigation**, click the **Navigation Options** button.

a. In the **Categories** column, click **Paralegals**. In the **Groups** column, clear the **Unassigned Objects** check box, and then click **OK** three times. Close and reopen the database.

12 From **Backstage** view, click **Options**, and then click **Quick Access Toolbar**.

a. In the list of **Popular Commands**, scroll down, click **New**, and then click the **Add** button.

b. Click the **Customize Quick Access Toolbar arrow**, and then click the path for the current database. In the list below **Popular Commands**, click **Open**, and

then click the **Add** button. Click **OK** twice to close the dialog and message boxes. Close and reopen the database. **Close** the **Paralegals Navigation Form**.

13 On the **DATABASE TOOLS tab**, in the **Move Data group**, click the **Access Database** button.

a. In the **Database Splitter** dialog box, click the **Split Database** button.

b. In the **Create Back-end Database** dialog box, verify your **Access Chapter 10** folder is open.

c. Click the **Split** button, accepting the default name for the back-end file, and then click **OK**. Click **OK** to close the message box.

d. Press Alt + PrintScrn. In the **Word** document, press Enter, and then press Ctrl + Enter to insert a page break. Type your first and last names, press Enter, and then type **Project 10C Step 13** Press Enter, **Paste** the screen-shot, and then click **Save**.

14 In **Access**, on the **Quick Access Toolbar**, click the down-pointing arrow. Click **New** to remove the icon from the Quick Access **Toolbar**.

a. Open the **PersonalServiceCodesForm**, and enter the following record:

ServiceCode	Service	Type
PS010	**Insurance Disputes**	**Personal Service/ Agent**

b. If you are instructed to submit this result, print the current form only. **Close** the form.

15 Display the **Backstage** view, and then click **Close Database**.

a. From the **Backstage** view, click **Open**. Under *Open*, double-click **Computer**. Navigate to your **Access Chapter 10** folder, and then click **Lastname_ Firstname_10C_Paralegals** one time.

b. In the lower right corner of the **Open** dialog box, click the **Open button arrow**, and then click **Open Exclusive**.

16 Display the **Backstage** view, and click the **Encrypt with Password** button.

a. In the **Set Database Password** dialog box, in the **Password** box, type **GO!Access10C** In the **Verify** box, type **GO!Access10C** and then click **OK**. If a message box displays, click **OK** to close it.

(Project 10C Paralegals continues on the next page)

CHAPTER REVIEW

b. Display the **Backstage** view. **Close** and then reopen the **10C Paralegals** database. In the displayed **Password Required** dialog box, type **GO!Access10C** and then click **OK**. Alternatively, type the password, and then press Enter.

17 Display the **Backstage** view, click **Save As**, and then, under **Advanced**, double-click the **Make ACCDE** button.

a. In the **Save As** dialog box, verify that your **Access Chapter 10** folder is open. Save the locked database as **Lastname_Firstname_10C_Paralegals_ACCDE**

18 **Open** File Explorer, and then open your **Access Chapter 10** folder.

a. If necessary, maximize the **File Explorer** window and switch to **Details** view. Verify that all the files created in this project display and that the columns are wide enough to display all of the Name and Type descriptions.

b. Press Alt + PrintScrn, and then **Close** File Explorer.

c. In the **Word** document, press Enter, and then press Ctrl + Enter to insert a page break. Type your first and last names, press Enter, and then type **Project 10C Step 18** Press Enter, and **Paste** the screenshot.

d. Click **Save**. If you are instructed to submit this result, create a paper or electronic printout of the Word document. **Close** Word.

19 **Exit** Access. As directed by your instructor, submit your databases and the paper or electronic printouts of the two objects—one form and one Word document—that are the result of this project. Specifically, in this project, using your own name you created the following databases and printouts or electronic printouts:

1. Lastname_Firstname_10C_Paralegals	Database file
2. PersonalServiceCodesForm	Form (printed or electronic printout)
3. Lastname_Firstname_10C_Screens	Word document (printed or electronic printout)
4. Lastname_Firstname_10C_Paralegals_be	Back-end database file
5. Lastname_Firstname_10C_Paralegals_ACCDE	Locked database file

END | You have completed Project 10C

CHAPTER REVIEW

Skills Review | Project 10D Top Accounts

Loren-Renner Law Partners wants a report that lists its top corporate accounts. To build the report, you will create two queries using SQL view. You will join the two queries into a single query. You will then create a query that summarizes the data in the union query and build the report from this query. Your completed report will look similar to the report shown in Figure 10.40.

PROJECT FILES

For Project 10D, you will need the following file:

a10D_Corporate_Accounts

You will save your database as:

Lastname_Firstname_10D_Corporate_Accounts

PROJECT RESULTS

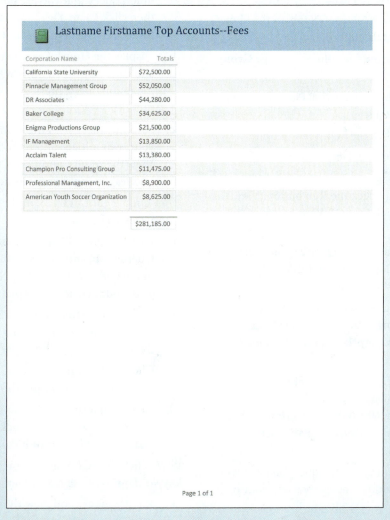

Lastname Firstname Top Accounts--Fees

Corporation Name	Totals
California State University	$72,500.00
Pinnacle Management Group	$52,050.00
DR Associates	$44,280.00
Baker College	$34,625.00
Enigma Productions Group	$21,500.00
IF Management	$13,850.00
Acclaim Talent	$13,380.00
Champion Pro Consulting Group	$11,475.00
Professional Management, Inc.	$8,900.00
American Youth Soccer Organization	$8,625.00
	$281,185.00

Page 1 of 1

FIGURE 10.40

(Project 10D Top Accounts continues on the next page)

CHAPTER REVIEW

1 Start Access. Locate and open the **a10D_Corporate_Accounts** file. **Save** the database in your **Access Chapter 10** folder as **Lastname_Firstname_10D_Corporate_Accounts** Enable content, if necessary.

a. **Rename** the database tables by adding **FML** to the beginning of each table name using your own initials.

2 On the **CREATE tab**, in the **Queries group**, click the **Query Design** button.

a. In the displayed **Show Table** dialog box, add the **CorpAccounts** and **FlatFees** tables to the query. Resize field lists so all fields are visible.

b. From the **CorpAccounts** table, add the **CorpName** field to the design grid. From the **FlatFees** table, add the **Fee** field to the design grid.

3 On the **QUERY TOOLS DESIGN tab**, in the **Show/Hide group**, click the **Totals** button.

a. In the **Total** row for the **Fee** column, change **Group By** to **Sum**.

b. **Save** the query with the name **FMLFlatFeesQuery** using your own initials.

4 In the status bar, click the **SQL View** button.

a. After the *AS* keyword, replace the text *SumofFee* with **Totals**

b. In the **Results group**, click the **Run** button. View the results, and then click the **SQL View** button. Click **Save**.

5 On the **CREATE tab**, in the **Queries group**, click the **Query Design** button. **Close** the **Show Table** dialog box, and then click the **SQL View** button.

a. Replace the existing text with the following SELECT clause using your own initials: **SELECT FMLCorpAccounts.CorpName, Rate * Hours AS Totals**

b. On a new line, enter the following FROM clause using your own initials: **FROM FMLCorpAccounts INNER JOIN FMLHourlyFees ON FMLCorpAccounts.CorpID = FMLHourlyFees. CorpID;**

c. Click the **Run** button to test the query so far. **Save** the query as **FMLHourlyFeesQuery** using your own initials.

6 Click the **SQL View** button. In the SELECT clause, replace the text *Rate * Hours* with **Sum(Rate * Hours)**

a. At the end of the SQL statement, delete the semicolon, press Enter, and then type the following clause: **GROUP BY FMLCorpAccounts.CorpName**

b. Click the **Run** button, view the results, and then click **Save**.

7 On the **CREATE tab**, in the **Queries group**, click the **Query Design** button. **Close** the **Show Table** dialog box, and then in the **Query Type group**, click the **Union** button.

a. Display the **FlatFeesQuery** query in **SQL** view. Select the entire SQL statement, right-click, and then from the displayed shortcut menu, click **Copy**. Display the union query that you are building, right-click, and then click **Paste**. Delete the semicolon, press Enter **two** times, and then type **UNION**

b. Display the **HourlyFeesQuery** query in **SQL** view, and then **Copy** the entire SQL statement. Display the union query, press Enter **two** times, and then press Ctrl + V.

c. **Save** the query with the name **FMLFeesUnion** using your own initials, and then click the **Run** button. View the results, and then **Close** all three open queries, saving changes as needed.

8 On the **CREATE tab**, in the **Queries group**, click the **Query Design** button.

a. In the displayed **Show Table** dialog box, click the **Queries tab**, and then add the **FMLFeesUnion** query to the query. Add the **CorpName** field to the design grid, and then add the **Totals** field.

b. In the **Show/Hide group**, click the **Totals** button. In the **Total** row for the **Totals** column, change **Group By** to **Sum**.

c. Click in the **Sort** row for the **Totals** column. Click the displayed arrow, and then click **Descending**.

d. **Save** the query with the name **FMLTopFeeAccounts** using you own initials. Click the **Run** button and view the results. **AutoFit** columns as necessary.

9 Click the **SQL View** button. After the SELECT keyword, press Spacebar, and then type: **TOP 10**

a. **Run** the query and view the results.

b. Click **Save**, and then **Close** the query.

(Project 10D Top Accounts continues on the next page)

CHAPTER REVIEW

10 ▶ On the **Navigation Pane**, click to select the **TopFeeAccounts** query. On the **CREATE tab**, in the **Reports group**, click the **Report** button.

a. In the **Report Header**, delete the date and time text box controls.

b. Change the report **Title** text box to **Lastname Firstname Top Accounts—Fees** Make adjustments so the title fits on one line. Change the **CorpName** label to **Corporation Name**

c. At the top of the **Totals** column, change the **SumofTotals** label to **Totals** At the bottom of the **Totals** column, click the text box that calculates the

grand total, and then apply the **Currency** format. Resize the control so the total is visible.

d. **Save** the report with the name suggested by Access.

11 ▶ If you are instructed to submit this result, create a paper or electronic printout of the report. **Close** the report.

12 ▶ **Exit** Access. As directed by your instructor, submit your database and the paper or electronic printout of the report that is the result of this project. Specifically, in this project, using your own name you created the following database and printout or electronic printout:

| 1. Lastname_Firstname_10D_Corporate_Accounts | Database file |
| 2. FMLTopFeeAccounts | Report (printed or electronic printout) |

END | You have completed Project 10D

CONTENT-BASED ASSESSMENTS

Mastering Access Project 10E Accountants

Loren-Renner Law Partners wants to secure the databases used by its accounting and marketing departments. You will also create a new workgroup information file for the database used by the marketing department. Your results will look similar to that shown in Figure 10.41.

Apply 10A skills from these Objectives:

1 Create a Navigation Form

2 Use Microsoft Access Analysis Tools

3 Modify Access Views and Behaviors

4 Use the Database Splitter

5 Encrypt and Decrypt Databases

6 Create a Locked Database (ACCDE file)

PROJECT FILES

For Project 10E, you will need the following files:

a10E_Accountants
a10E_Icon

You will save your files as:

Lastname_Firstname_10E_Accountants
Lastname_Firstname_10E_Screens
Lastname_Firstname_10E_Accountants_be
Lastname_Firstname_10E_ACCDE

PROJECT RESULTS

FIGURE 10.41

(Project 10E Accountants continues on the next page)

1 Start Access. Locate and open the **a10E_Accountants** file. **Save** the database in the **Access Chapter 10** folder as **Lastname_Firstname_10E_Accountants** If necessary, enable content.

2 Create a navigation form, **Vertical Tabs, Right**. If the Field List displays, close it. Add the **Cases Form**, **Clients Form**, and **Client Directory** to the navigation form. Edit the title to read **Lastname Firstname Navigation Form** **Save** the navigation form as **Lastname Firstname Navigation Form**

3 **Close** the **Navigation Pane**. Switch to **Form** view. Press [Alt] + [PrintScrn]. **Close** the **Navigation Form**. Create a new, blank Word document. In the **Word** document, type your first and last names, press [Enter], and then type **Project 10E Step 3** Press [Enter], and then **Paste** the screenshot. **Save** the document in your **Access Chapter 10** folder with the name **Lastname_Firstname_10E_Screens** Leave the Word document open.

4 Use the **Table Analyzer Wizard** to analyze the **Billing** table. Have the wizard decide how to split the table, and then rename the suggested tables as follows:

Suggested Table	New Name
Table1	**Lastname Firstname Billing**
Table2	**Lastname Firstname Accountants**

5 In the **Billing** table, set **InvoiceID** as the **unique identifier**. Choose the option to create the query, and then **Finish** the wizard. **Close** the **Help** window, and **Close** the query.

6 Display all database objects that depend on the **Billing_OLD** table. Press [Alt] + [PrintScrn], and then **Close** the **Object Dependencies** pane. In the **Word** document, press [Enter], and then press [Ctrl] + [Enter] to insert a page break. Type your first and last names, press [Enter], and then type **Project 10E Step 6** Press [Enter], and then **Paste** the screenshot. **Save** the document.

7 Delete the **Billing_OLD** table. Rename the **Clients** table as **Lastname Firstname Clients** Rename the **Cases** table to **Lastname Firstname Cases**

8 Start a new query in **Query Design** view, and then add the **Clients** and **Cases** tables to the query. Resize the field lists so all fields and table names are visible. From the **Clients** table, add the **OrgName** field. From the **Cases** table, add the **CaseID** and **Closed?** fields. Create an indeterminate relationship between the **ClientID** field in the **Clients** table and the **Client** field in the **Cases** table, if necessary. **Save** the query as **Lastname Firstname Client-Cases** Run and then **Close** the query.

9 Run the **Performance Analyzer** wizard for **All Object Types**. Optimize the item with the **Suggestion** icon. Press [Alt] + [PrintScrn], and then **Close** the dialog box. In the **Word** document, press [Enter], and then press [Ctrl] + [Enter] to insert a page break. Type your first and last names, press [Enter], and then type **Project 10E Step 9** Press [Enter], **Paste** the screenshot, and then click **Save**.

10 From **Backstage** view, display the **Access Options** dialog box. Under **Current Database**, change the **Application Title** to **Loren-Renner Law Partners Accounting Department** For the **Application Icon**, assign **a10E_Icon**. Display the **Navigation Form**, and disable **Layout** view.

11 Edit the following **Navigation Pane** options: add a new item named **Accounting Dept** and then add a new group named **Clients** and one named **Accounting** In the **Navigation Pane**, display the **Accounting Dept** category. Drag the **Cases** and **Clients** tables into the **Clients** category. Drag the **Client-Cases** query into the **Clients** category. Drag the **Cases Form** and **Clients Form** into the **Clients** category. Drag the **Client Directory** report into the **Clients** category. Drag the **Accountants**, **Billing**, and **Services** tables into the **Accounting** category. Using the **Navigation** options, do not display **Unassigned Items** in the **Navigation Pane** when the **Accounting Dept** category is selected.

12 For the current database only, add the following commands to the **Quick Access Toolbar: Import Access database**, **Import Excel spreadsheet**, and **Open**.

13 **Close** all open dialog boxes and database objects. Press [Alt] + [PrintScrn]. In the **Word** document, press [Enter], and then insert a page break. Type your first and last names, press [Enter], and then type **Project 10E Step 13** Press [Enter], **Paste** the screenshot, and then click **Save**. If you are instructed to submit this result, create a paper or electronic printout of the screenshots document.

14 Split the database into a back-end and front-end file. **Save** the back-end file in your **Access Chapter 10** folder with the name suggested by Access. **Close** the database.

(Project 10E Accountants continues on the next page)

CONTENT-BASED ASSESSMENTS

15 Open **10E_Accountants_be**. Press [Alt] + [PrintScrn], and then **Close** the database. In the **Word** document, press [Enter], and then insert a page break. Type your first and last names, press [Enter], and then type **Project 10E Step 15** Press [Enter], and then **Paste** the screenshot. **Save** the document.

16 Open **10E_Accountants** using the **Open Exclusive** command. Encrypt the database using the password **GO!Office2013** Click **OK**, and then **Close** the database.

17 Open **10E_Accountants** using the password. Create a secure ACCDE version of the database file. Save the ACCDE file in your **Access Chapter 10** folder as **Lastname_Firstname_10E_ACCDE**

18 **Close** the database, and **Exit** Access.

19 Open **File Explorer**, and then open your **Access Chapter 10** folder. If necessary, maximize the **File** **Explorer** window and switch to **Details** view. Verify that all the files created in this project display and that the columns are wide enough to display all of the Name and Type descriptions. Press [Alt] + [PrintScrn], and then **Close** File Explorer.

20 In the **Word** document, press [Enter], and then press [Ctrl] + [Enter] to insert a page break. Type your first and last names, press [Enter], and then type **Project 10E Step 20** Press [Enter], **Paste** the screenshot, and then click **Save**. If you are instructed to submit this result, create a paper or electronic printout of the Word document.

21 As directed by your instructor, submit your databases and the paper or electronic printout of the Word document that is the result of this project. Specifically, in this project, using your own name you created the following databases and printout or electronic printout:

1. Lastname_Firstname_10E_Accountants	Database file
2. Lastname_Firstname_10E_Screens	Word document (printed or electronic printout)
3. Lastname_Firstname_10E_Accountants_be	Back-end database file
4. Lastname_Firstname_10E_ACCDE	Locked database file

END | You have completed Project 10E

CONTENT-BASED ASSESSMENTS

Mastering Access Project 10F Legal Services

Loren-Renner Law Partners wants a report that describes the various services that it provides to corporations and organizations. To build the report, you will create two queries using SQL view. You will join the two queries into a single query. You will then create a query that summarizes the data in the union query and build the report from this query. Your completed report will look similar to the report shown in Figure 10.42.

MyITLab®
grader

Apply 10B skills from these Objectives:

7 Modify a Query in SQL View

8 Create a Query in SQL View

9 Create a Union Query Using SQL

10 Create Calculated Fields and SQL Aggregate Functions

PROJECT FILES

For Project 10F, you will need the following file:

a10F_Legal_Services

You will save your database as:

Lastname_Firstname_10F_Legal_Services

PROJECT RESULTS

Lastname Firstname Services	Friday, December 26, 2014 1:51:14 PM
Service	**Average**
Arbitration	$664.29
Contracts	$743.68
Copyright	$1,906.25
Licensing	$886.11
Litigation	$19,212.50
NCAA Compliance	$2,400.00
Risk Management	$3,934.43
Taxation	$1,754.17
Trademark	$1,028.57

Page 1 of 1

FIGURE 10.42

(Project 10F Legal Services continues on the next page)

CONTENT-BASED ASSESSMENTS

1 Start Access. Locate and open the **a10F_Legal_Services** file. **Save** the database in the **Access Chapter 10** folder as **Lastname_Firstname_10F_Legal_Services** Enable content, if necessary. At the beginning of each table name, add **FML** using your own initials and no space.

2 Start a new query in **Design** view. Add the **Services** and **FlatFees** tables to the query. If necessary, expand the fields lists to display all field names. From the **Services** table, add the **Service** field to the design grid. From the **FlatFees** table, add the **Fee** field.

3 In the **Show/Hide group**, click the **Totals** button. In the **Total** row for the **Fee** column, change **Group By** to **Avg**.

4 In **SQL** view, adapt the SELECT statement so that the calculated field's caption will display as **Average** Run the query and view the results. **Save** the query as **FMLFlatServices** using your own initials.

5 Start a new query in **Design** view, and then switch to **SQL** view. Add a SELECT statement that displays the *Service* field from the **Services** table.

6 Add a calculated field to the SELECT statement that multiplies the **Rate** and **Hours** fields.

7 Add a **FROM** clause that joins the **Services** table to the **HourlyFees** table with an inner join that uses the **ServiceCode** fields from each table. If needed, use the FROM clause in the query created earlier in this project as your reference.

8 For the calculated field, add an SQL aggregate function that calculates the average (AVG) of the **Rate** field multiplied by the **Hours** field .Write the SQL needed so that the calculated field's caption displays as **Average** Add a GROUP BY clause that groups the query by each

Service. If needed, use the query created earlier in this project as your reference.

9 Run the query and view the results. **Save** the query as **FMLHourlyServices** using your own initials.

10 Create a new **Union** query. **Copy** and **Paste** the SQL from the two queries created earlier and join them using the UNION keyword. **Run** the query, view the results, and then **Save** the query as **FMLServicesUnion** using your own initials.

11 Create a new query in **Design** view. In the displayed **Show Table** dialog box, click the **Queries tab**, add the **ServicesUnion** query, and then **Close** the dialog box. Add the **Service** field to the design grid, and then add the **Average** field.

12 In the **Show/Hide group**, click the **Totals** button. In the **Total** row for the **Average** column, change **Group By** to **Avg**. **Save** the query with the name **FMLServicesQuery** using your own initials. Click the **Run** button, view the results, and then **Close** all open queries.

13 Create a **Report** using the **ServicesQuery** query.

14 Change the **Title** text box to **Lastname Firstname Services** Change the **AvgofAverage** label to **Average** At the bottom of the **Average** column, delete the text box and line controls.

15 Save the report using the name suggested by Access. If you are instructed to submit this result, create a paper or electronic printout. **Close** the report, and then **Exit** Access.

16 As directed by your instructor, submit your database and the paper or electronic printout of the report that is the result of this project. Specifically, in this project, using your own name you created the following database and printout or electronic printout:

1. Lastname_Firstname_10B_Accounts_Due	Database file
2. FMLServices	Report (printed or electronic printout)

END | You have completed Project 10F

CONTENT-BASED ASSESSMENTS

Mastering Access   Project 10G Bonuses

Apply 10A and 10B skills from these Objectives:

4 Use the Database Splitter

5 Encrypt and Decrypt Databases

7 Modify a Query in SQL View

8 Create a Query in SQL View

9 Create a Union Query Using SQL

10 Create Calculated Fields and SQL Aggregate Functions

The two lead partners, Alex Loren and David Renner, need to secure the front end of the database with a password before creating a confidential query that lists the lawyers who have generated the most business. You will create two queries using SQL view, join them in a union query, and then build another query summarizing the union query. Your completed report will look similar to Figure 10.43.

PROJECT FILES

For Project 10G, you will need the following database:

a10G_Bonuses

You will save your files as:

Lastname_Firstname_10G_Bonuses
Lastname_Firstname_10G_be

PROJECT RESULTS

FIGURE 10.43

(Project 10G Bonuses continues on the next page)

CONTENT-BASED ASSESSMENTS

1 Start Access. Locate and then open the **a10G_ Bonuses** database. **Save** the database in your **Access Chapter 10** folder as **Lastname_Firstname_10G_Bonuses** At the beginning of each table name, add **FML** using your own initials and no space.

2 **Split** the database using the name Access suggests for the back end and **Save** it in your **Access Chapter 10** folder.

3 **Close** the database. **Open** it again in **Exclusive mode**, and then encrypt it using the password **10GBonusGO!** If a message box displays, click **OK**.

4 Start a new query in **Design** view. Add the **Lawyers** and **FlatFees** tables to the query, expanding the field lists as necessary. From the **Lawyers** table, add the **FName** and **LName** fields to the design grid. From the **FlatFees** table, add the **Fee** field.

5 In the **Show/Hide group**, click the **Totals** button. In the **Total** row for the **Fee** column, change **Group By** to **Sum**.

6 In **SQL** view, change the caption for the calculated field to **Total Run** the query and view the results. **Save** the query as **FMLFlatFeesQuery** using your own initials.

7 Start a new query in **Design** view, and then switch to **SQL** view. Using the earlier query as your guide, write a SELECT statement that displays the **FName** and **LName** fields from the **Lawyers** table.

8 Add a calculated field to the SELECT clause that multiplies the **Rate** and **Hours** fields from the **HourlyFees** table. Write the SQL needed so that the calculated field's caption displays as **Total**

9 For the calculated field, add an SQL aggregate function that calculates the sum of the **Rate** field multiplied by the **Hours** field.

10 Add a FROM clause that joins the **Lawyers** table to the **HourlyFees** table with an inner join that uses the **LawyerID** fields from each table.

11 **Copy** the GROUP BY clause from **FlatFeesQuery** and **Paste** it into the current query. **Run** the query and view the results. **Save** the query as **FMLHourlyFeesQuery** using your own initials.

12 Create a new **Union** query. **Copy** and **Paste** the **SQL** statements from the two queries created earlier and join them using the **UNION** keyword. **Run** the query, view the results, and then **Save** the query as **FMLUnion** using your own initials. **Close** all open queries.

13 Create a new query in **Design** view, add the **Union** query, and then add the **FName**, **LName**, and **Total** fields to the design grid. Add the **Total row** to the design grid, and then in the **Total row** for the **Total** column, change **Group By** to **Sum**.

14 In the **Total** column, change the **Sort** row value to **Descending**. Display the **Property Sheet**, and then, on the **General** tab, change the format to **Currency**.

15 In **SQL** view, after SELECT, add the **TOP 4** keyword. **Save** the query as **FMLTopLawyers** using your own initials. **Run** the query, and then **Close** the query.

16 Create a report based on the **FMLTopLawyers** query to display all fields. Change the report title to read **Lastname Firstname Top Four Lawyers** on one line. Change the **SumofTotal** label to read **Total** Remove the **Count** total and line control from under the **FName** field. In the **Report Header**, delete the date and time controls. If you are instructed to submit this result, create a paper or electronic printout. **Save** the report as **Lastname Firstname Top Lawyers Report Close** the report and **Exit** Access.

17 As directed by your instructor, submit your databases and the paper or electronic printout of the report that is the result of this project. Specifically, in this project, using your own name you created the following databases and printout or electronic printout:

1. Lastname_Firstname_10G_Bonuses	Database file
2. Lastname_Firstname_Bonuses_be	Back-end database
3. Lastname Firstname Top Lawyers Report	Report (printed or electronic printout)

END | You have completed Project 10G

CONTENT-BASED ASSESSMENTS

GO! Fix It	Project 10H Annual Dinner	Online

Apply a combination of the 10A and 10B skills.

GO! Make It	Project 10I Professional Seminars	Online

GO! Solve It	Project 10J Law Library	Online

GO! Solve It	Project 10K Contracts	

PROJECT FILES

For Project 10K, you will need the following database:

a10K_Contracts

You will save your files as:

Lastname_Firstname_10K_Contracts
Lastname_Firstname_10K_Screen

Loren-Renner Law Partners needs a list of each client that has asked for assistance with contracts. To start, open **a10K_Contracts**, and save it as **Lastname_Firstname_10K_Contracts** At the beginning of each table name, add **FML** using your own initials.

Create a Navigation Form using a Horizontal tab style. Add the form and both reports to the Navigation Form. Edit the title to read **Lastname Firstname Navigation** Save the form using the same name. Close the Navigation Pane, switch to Form view, and capture the screen. Paste it into a Word document and save it as **Lastname_Firstname_10K_Screen** If you are instructed to submit this result, create a paper or electronic printout of the Word document.

Using SQL, create a query that lists personal clients who have cases listed in the **Cases** table. List only the clients where the *ServiceCode* is equal to SC08. Include the *Name*, *Street*, *City*, *State*, and *PostalCode* fields. Add the necessary SQL command so that clients are not listed more than one time in the query's results. Save the query as **FMLPersonalQuery** using your own initials.

Using SQL, create a query that lists corporate clients who have cases listed in the **Cases** table. List only the clients where the *ServiceCode* is equal to **SC08**. Include the *CompanyName*, *Street*, *City*, *State*, and *PostalCode* fields. Add the necessary SQL command so that clients are not listed more than one time in the query's results. Save the query as **FMLCorporateQuery** using your own initials.

Create a union query that combines the two queries. Save the query as **FMLAllClients** using your own initials. If you are instructed to submit this result, create a paper or electronic printout of the query.

Submit the database as directed by your instructor.

(Project 10K Contracts continues on the next page)

CONTENT-BASED ASSESSMENTS

Performance Level

	Exemplary	Proficient	Developing
Create Contracts Navigation Form	Form created with correct tabs and title.	Form created with no more than two missing elements.	Form created with more than two missing elements.
Create PersonalQuery using SQL	Query created with correct syntax and format.	Query created with no more than two missing elements.	Query created with more than two missing elements.
Create CorporateQuery using SQL	Query created with correct syntax and format.	Query created with no more than two missing elements.	Query created with more than two missing elements.
Create AllClients union query using SQL	Query created with correct syntax and format.	Query created with no more than two missing elements.	Query created with more than two missing elements.

Performance Criteria (left side label)

END | You have completed Project 10K

RUBRIC

The following outcomes-based assessments are open-ended assessments. That is, there is no specific correct result; your result will depend on your approach to the information provided. Make Professional Quality your goal. Use the following scoring rubric to guide you in how to approach the problem and then to evaluate how well your approach solves the problem.

The *criteria*—Software Mastery, Content, Format and Layout, and Process—represent the knowledge and skills you have gained that you can apply to solving the problem. The *levels of performance*—Professional Quality, Approaching Professional Quality, or Needs Quality Improvements—help you and your instructor evaluate your result.

	Your completed project is of Professional Quality if you:	Your completed project is Approaching Professional Quality if you:	Your completed project Needs Quality Improvements if you:
1-Software Mastery	Choose and apply the most appropriate skills, tools, and features and identify efficient methods to solve the problem.	Choose and apply some appropriate skills, tools, and features, but not in the most efficient manner.	Choose inappropriate skills, tools, or features, or are inefficient in solving the problem.
2-Content	Construct a solution that is clear and well organized, contains content that is accurate, appropriate to the audience and purpose, and is complete. Provide a solution that contains no errors in spelling, grammar, or style.	Construct a solution in which some components are unclear, poorly organized, inconsistent, or incomplete. Misjudge the needs of the audience. Have some errors in spelling, grammar, or style, but the errors do not detract from comprehension.	Construct a solution that is unclear, incomplete, or poorly organized; contains some inaccurate or inappropriate content; and contains many errors in spelling, grammar, or style. Do not solve the problem.
3-Format & Layout	Format and arrange all elements to communicate information and ideas, clarify function, illustrate relationships, and indicate relative importance.	Apply appropriate format and layout features to some elements, but not others. Overuse features, causing minor distraction.	Apply format and layout that does not communicate information or ideas clearly. Do not use format and layout features to clarify function, illustrate relationships, or indicate relative importance. Use available features excessively, causing distraction.
4-Process	Use an organized approach that integrates planning, development, self-assessment, revision, and reflection.	Demonstrate an organized approach in some areas, but not others; or, use an insufficient process of organization throughout.	Do not use an organized approach to solve the problem.

OUTCOMES-BASED ASSESSMENTS

PROJECT FILES

For Project 10L, you will need the following files:

a10L_Case_History
a10L_Icon

You will save your files as:

Lastname_Firstname_10L_Case_History
Lastname_Firstname_10L_ACCDE
Lastname_Firstname_10L_Screen

Loren-Renner Law Partners needs to secure the database containing a list of past cases. Open **a10L_Case_History** and save it as **Lastname_Firstname_10L_Case_History** Create an ACCDE file named **Lastname_Firstname_10L_ACCDE** At the beginning of each table name, add **FML** using your own initials. Customize the Access Options so the Application Title **L-R Case History** displays along with the **a10L_Icon**. Add the Open and Close Database icons to the Quick Access Toolbar for this database only. Capture the screen and paste it into a Word document named **Lastname_Firstname_10L_Screen** If you are instructed to submit this result, create a paper or electronic printout of the Word document.

Using SQL, create a query that lists corporate clients who have past cases listed in the *Cases* table. List only the client name and how many cases they have had. Group the data by *CompanyName*, and then display the count as **PastCases** Save the query as **FMLHistory** using your own initials. If you are instructed to submit this result, create a paper or electronic printout of the query.

Submit the project as directed by your instructor.

END | You have completed Project 10L

Glossary

ACCDE file An Access file format that prevents individuals from making design changes to forms, reports, and macros.

Action A self-contained instruction that can be combined with other actions to automate tasks.

Action query A query that creates a new table or changes data in an existing table.

Address bar (Internet Explorer) The area at the top of the Internet Explorer window that displays, and where you can type, a URL—Uniform Resource Locator—which is an address that uniquely identifies a location on the Internet.

Address bar (Windows) The bar at the top of a folder window with which you can navigate to a different folder or library, or go back to a previous one.

Aggregate functions Calculations such as Min, Max, Avg, and Sum that are performed on a group of records.

Alignment The placement of text or objects relative to the left and right margins.

Alignment guides Green lines that display when you move an object to assist in alignment.

Alphabetic index Grouping of items by a common first character.

AND condition A compound criteria used to display records that match all parts of the specified criteria.

App The term that commonly refers to computer programs that run from the device software on a smartphone or a tablet computer—for example, iOS, Android, or Windows Phone—or computer programs that run from the browser software on a desktop PC or laptop PC—for example Internet Explorer, Safari, Firefox, or Chrome.

App for Office A webpage that works within one of the Office applications, such as Excel, and that you download from the Office Store.

Append To add on to the end of an object; for example, to add records to the end of an existing table.

Append query An action query that adds new records to an existing table by adding data from another Access database or from a table in the same database.

Appended When data is added to the end of an existing table.

Application title The text that displays in the Access title bar when that database is open.

Apps for Office 2013 and SharePoint 2013 A collection of downloadable apps that enables you to create and view information within your familiar Office programs.

Argument A value that provides information to the macro action, such as the words to display in a message box, or the control upon which to operate.

Arithmetic operators Mathematical symbols used in building expressions.

AS An SQL keyword that creates captions for fields.

Ascending order A sorting order that arranges text alphabetically (A to Z) and numbers from the lowest number to the highest number.

ASCII An acronym for American Standard Code for Information Interchange, a character set.

AutoNumber data type A data type that describes a unique sequential or random number assigned by Access as each record is entered and that is useful for data that has no distinct field that can be considered unique.

Back end A file that consists of the database tables and their data. The back end is typically placed on a server and is not directly seen by the end user.

Back up A feature that creates a copy of the original database to protect against lost data.

Backstage tabs The area along the left side of Backstage view with tabs to display screens with related groups of commands.

Backstage view A centralized space for file management tasks; for example, opening, saving, printing, publishing, or sharing a file. A navigation pane displays along the left side with tabs that group file-related tasks together.

Bang operator The exclamation (!) mark that tells Access that what follows it is an object that belongs to the object that precedes it in the expression.

Best Fit An Access command that adjusts the width of a column to accommodate the column's longest entry.

Between ... And operator A comparison operator that looks for values within a range.

Blank desktop database A database that has no data and has no database tools—you must create the data and tools as you need them; the database is stored on your computer or other storage device.

Bound A term used to describe objects and controls that are based on data that is stored in tables.

Bound control A control that retrieves its data from an underlying table or query; a text box control is an example of a bound control.

Bound report A report that displays data from an underlying table, query, or SQL statement as specified in the report's Record Source property.

Button control A control that enables individuals to add a command button to a form or report that will perform an action when the button is clicked.

Calculated control A control that contains an expression, often a formula or function, that most often summarizes a field that contains numerical data.

Calculated field A field that stores the value of a mathematical operation.

Caption A property setting that displays a name for a field in a table, query, form, or report other than that listed as the field name.

Cascade Delete Related Records A cascade option that enables you to delete a record in a table on the *one* side of the relationship and also delete all of the related records in related tables.

Cascade options Relationship options that enable you to update records in related tables when referential integrity is enforced.

Cascade Update Related Fields A cascade option that enables you to change the data in the primary key field in the table on the *one* side of the relationship and update that change to any fields storing that same data in related tables.

Cell The small box formed by the intersection of a column and a row in a worksheet.

Center alignment The alignment of text or objects that is centered horizontally between the left and right margins.

Chart A graphic representation of data.

Click The action of pressing and releasing the left button on a mouse pointing device one time.

Clip art Downloadable predefined graphics available online from Office.com and other sites.

Clipboard A temporary storage area that holds text or graphics that you select and then cut or copy.

Cloud computing Refers to applications and services that are accessed over the Internet, rather than to applications that are installed on your local computer.

Cloud storage Online storage of data so that you can access your data from different places and devices.

Code Builder A window used to type programming code in Microsoft Visual Basic.

Collaborate To work with others as a team in an intellectual endeavor to complete a shared task or to achieve a shared goal.

Column chart A chart used to display comparisons among related numbers.

Combo box A control that enables individuals to select from a list or to type a value.

Commands An instruction to a computer program that causes an action to be carried out.

Common dialog boxes The set of dialog boxes that includes Open, Save, and Save As, which are provided by the Windows programming interface, and which display and operate in all of the Office programs in the same manner.

Common field A field in two or more tables that stores the same data.

Compact & Repair A process where an Access file is rewritten to store the objects and data in more efficiently.

Comparison operators Symbols that are used to evaluate data in the field to determine if it is the same (=), greater than (>), less than (<), or in between a range of values as specified by the criteria.

Compound criteria Multiple conditions in a query or filter.

Compressed file A file that has been reduced in size and thus takes up less storage space and can be transferred to other computers quickly.

Compressed folder A folder that has been reduced in size and thus takes up less storage space and can be transferred to other computers quickly; also called a *zipped* folder.

Concatenation Linking or joining strings.

Condition A statement that specifies that certain criteria must be met before the macro action executes.

Conditional formatting A way to apply formatting to specific controls based on a comparison to a rule set.

Context menus Menus that display commands and options relevant to the selected text or object; also called *shortcut menus*.

Context-sensitive commands Commands that display on a shortcut menu that relate to the object or text that you right-clicked.

Contextual tabs Tabs that are added to the ribbon automatically when a specific object, such as a picture, is selected, and that contain commands relevant to the selected object.

Control An object on a form or report that displays data or text, performs actions, and lets you view and work with information.

Control layout The grouped arrangement of controls on a form or report; for example, the Stacked layout.

ControlTip Displays descriptive text when the mouse pointer is paused over the control.

Converted Changed.

Copy A command that duplicates a selection and places it on the Clipboard.

Criteria Conditions in a query that identify the specific records you are looking for.

Cross join A join that displays when each row from one table is combined with each row in a related table, usually created unintentionally when you do not create a join line between related tables.

Crosstab query A query that uses an aggregate function for data that is grouped by two types of information and displays the data in a compact, spreadsheet-like format. A crosstab query always has at least one row heading, one column heading, and one summary field.

Currency data type An Access data type that describes monetary values and numeric data that can be used in mathematical calculations involving values with one to four decimal places.

Custom web app A database that you can publish and share with others over the Internet.

Cut A command that removes a selection and places it on the Clipboard.

Data Facts about people, events, things, or ideas.

Data entry The action of entering the data into a record in a database table or form.

Data macro A macro that is triggered by events, such as adding, updating, or deleting data within a table, form, or query. It is used to validate the accuracy of data in a table; also known as an event-driven macro.

Data source The table or tables from which a form, query, or report retrieves its data.

Data type The characteristic that defines the kind of data that can be stored in a field, such as numbers, text, or dates.

Data validation Rules that help prevent invalid data entries and ensure data is entered consistently.

Database An organized collection of facts about people, events, things, or ideas related to a specific topic or purpose.

Database Documenter An option used to create a report that contains detailed information about the objects in a database, including macros, and to create a paper record.

Database management system (DBMS) Database software that controls how related collections of data are stored, organized, retrieved, and secured; also known as a *DBMS*.

Database template A preformatted database that contains prebuilt tables, queries, forms, and reports that perform a specific task, such as tracking events.

Datasheet view The Access view that displays data organized in columns and rows similar to an Excel worksheet.

Date control A control on a form or report that inserts the current date each time the form or report is opened.

DBMS An acronym for *database management system*.

Debugging A logical process to find and reduce the number of errors in a program.

Decrypt An action that removes a file's encryption or unsets a password.

Default The term that refers to the current selection or setting that is automatically used by a computer program unless you specify otherwise.

Default value A value displayed for new records.

Definition The structure of the database—the field names, data types, and field properties.

Delete query An action query that removes records from an existing table in the same database.

Delimited file A file in which each record displays on a separate line, and the fields within the record are separated by a single character.

Delimiter A single character; can be a paragraph mark, a tab, a comma, or another character.

Dependency An object that requires, or is dependent on, another database object.

Descending order A sorting order that arranges text in reverse alphabetical order (Z to A) and numbers from the highest number to the lowest number.

Deselect The action of canceling the selection of an object or block of text by clicking outside of the selection.

Design grid The lower area of the query window that displays the design of the query.

Design view The Access view that displays the detailed structure of a query, form, or report; for forms and reports, may be the view in which some tasks must be performed, and only the controls, and not the data, display.

Desktop In Windows, the screen that simulates your work area.

Desktop app The term that commonly refers to a computer program that is installed on your computer and requires a computer operating system like Microsoft Windows or Apple OS to run.

Destination table The table to which you import or append data.

Detail section The section of a form or report that displays the records from the underlying table or query.

Dialog box A small window that contains options for completing a task.

Dialog Box Launcher A small icon that displays to the right of some group names on the ribbon, and which opens a related dialog box or pane providing additional options and commands related to that group.

DISTINCT An SQL keyword that removes duplicates from query results.

Document properties Details about a file that describe or identify it, including the title, author name, subject, and keywords that identify the document's topic or contents; also known as *metadata*.

Drag The action of holding down the left mouse button while moving your mouse.

Dynamic An attribute applied to data in a database that changes.

Edit The process of making changes to text or graphics in an Office file.

Ellipsis A set of three dots indicating incompleteness; an ellipsis following a command name indicates that a dialog box will display if you click the command.

Embedded macro A macro that is stored in the Session properties of forms, reports, or controls.

Encrypt A process to hide data by making the file unreadable until the correct password is entered.

Enhanced ScreenTip A ScreenTip that displays more descriptive text than a normal ScreenTip.

Event Any action that can be detected by a program or computer system, such as clicking a button or closing an object.

Export The process of copying data from one file into another file, such as an Access table into an Excel spreadsheet.

Expression A combination of functions, field values, constants, and operators that produces a result.

Expression Builder A feature used to create formulas (expressions) in calculated fields, query criteria, form and report properties, and table validation rules.

Extensible Markup Language The standard language for defining and storing data on the web.

Extract To decompress, or pull out, files from a compressed form.

Field A single piece of information that is stored in every record; represented by a column in a database table.

Field list A list of field names in a table.

Field properties Characteristics of a field that control how the field displays and how data can be entered in the field.

File A collection of information stored on a computer under a single name, for example, a Word document or a PowerPoint presentation.

File Explorer The program that displays the files and folders on your computer, and which is at work anytime you are viewing the contents of files and folders in a window.

Fill The inside color of an object.

Filter by Form An Access command that filters the records in a form based on one or more fields, or based on more than one value in the field.

Filter by Selection An Access command that displays only the records that contain the value in the selected field and hides the records that do not contain the value.

Filtering The process of displaying only a portion of the total records (a subset) based on matching specific values to provide a quick answer to a question.

Find Duplicates Query A query used to locate duplicate records in a table.

Find Unmatched Query A query used to locate unmatched records so they can be deleted from the table.

First principle of good database design A principle of good database design stating that data is organized in tables so that there is no redundant data.

Flagged A highlighted word that Spell Check does not recognize from the Office dictionary.

Flat database A simple database file that is not related or linked to any other collection of data.

Focus An object that is selected and currently being acted upon.

Folder A container in which you store files.

Folder window In Windows, a window that displays the contents of the current folder, library, or device, and contains helpful parts so that you can navigate the Windows file structure.

Font A set of characters with the same design and shape.

Font styles Formatting emphasis such as bold, italic, and underline.

Footer A reserved area for text or graphics that displays at the bottom of each page in a document.

Foreign key The field that is included in the related table so the field can be joined with the primary key in another table for the purpose of creating a relationship.

Form A database object that you can use to enter new records into a table, or to edit, delete, and display existing records in a table.

Form Footer Information at the bottom of the screen in Form view or Layout view that is printed after the last detail section on the last page of a printout.

Form Header Information such as a form's title that displays at the top of the screen in Form view or Layout view and is printed at the top of the first page when records are printed as forms.

Form selector The box in the upper left corner of a form in Design view where the rulers meet; used to select the entire form.

Form tool An Access tool that creates a form with a single mouse click, which includes all of the fields from the underlying data source (table or query).

Form view The Access view in which you can view, modify, delete, or add records in a table; but you cannot change the layout or design of the form.

Form Wizard An Access tool that walks you step by step through the creation of a form and that gives you more flexibility in the design, layout, and number of fields in a form.

Formatting The process of establishing the overall appearance of text, graphics, and pages in an Office file—for example, in a Word document.

Formatting marks Characters that display on the screen, but do not print, indicating where the Enter key, the Spacebar, and the Tab key were pressed; also called *nonprinting characters*.

Free/Busy information In the Outlook calendar, one of four indicators—Busy, Free, Tentative, or Out of Office—associated with your availability for a specific date and time.

FROM clause An SQL statement that lists which tables hold the fields used in the SELECT clause.

Front end A file that includes the database forms, queries, reports, and macros. The end users open the front end to work with the data stored in the back-end tables.

Gallery An Office feature that displays a list of potential results instead of just the command name.

Gradient fill A fill effect in which one color fades into another.

Group Footer Information printed at the end of each group of records; used to display summary information for the group.

Group Header Information printed at the beginning of each new group of records; for example, the group name.

Group, Sort, and Total pane A pane that displays at the bottom of the screen in which you can control how information is sorted and grouped in a report; provides the most flexibility for adding or modifying groups, sort orders, or totals options on a report.

Groups On the Office ribbon, the sets of related commands that you might need for a specific type of task.

Header A reserved area for text or graphics that displays at the top of each page in a document.

HTML An acronym for HyperText Markup Language.

HyperText Markup Language The language used to display webpages.

Image control A control that enables individuals to insert an image into any section of a form or report.

Import The process of copying data from another file, such as a Word table or an Excel workbook, into a separate file, such as an Access database.

Indeterminate relationship A relationship that does not enforce referential integrity.

Index A special list created in Access to speed up searches and sorting.

Info tab The tab in Backstage view that displays information about the current file.

Information Data that is organized in a useful manner.

Inner join A join that allows only the records where the common field exists in both related tables to be displayed in query results.

Innermost sort field When sorting on multiple fields in Datasheet view, the field that is used for the second level of sorting.

Input mask A field property that determines how the data displays and is stored.

Insertion point A blinking vertical line that indicates where text or graphics will be inserted.

Instance Each simultaneously running Access session.

Is Not Null A criteria that searches for fields that are not empty.

Is Null A criteria that searches for fields that are empty.

Join A relationship that helps a query return only the records from each table you want to see, based on how those tables are related to other tables in the query.

JOIN clause An SQL statement that defines the join type for a query.

Join line In the Relationships window, the line joining two tables that visually indicates the common fields and the type of relationship.

Junction table A table that breaks down the many-to-many relationship into two one-to-many relationships.

Keyboard shortcut A combination of two or more keyboard keys, used to perform a task that would otherwise require a mouse.

KeyTip The letter that displays on a command in the ribbon and that indicates the key you can press to activate the command when keyboard control of the ribbon is activated.

Keywords Commands built into the SQL programming language. Also, custom file properties in the form of words that you associate with a document to give an indication of the document's content; used to help find and organize files. Also called *tags*.

Label control A control on a form or report that contains descriptive information, usually a field name or title.

Landscape orientation A page orientation in which the paper is wider than it is tall.

Layout Options A button that displays when an object is selected and that has commands to choose how the object interacts with surrounding text.

Layout selector A small symbol that displays in the upper left corner of a selected control layout in a form or report that is displayed in Layout view or Design view; used to move or format an entire group of controls.

Layout view The Access view in which you can make changes to a form or report while the object is running—the data from the underlying data source displays.

Left outer join A join used when you want to display all of the records on the *one* side of a one-to-many relationship, whether or not there are matching records in the table on the *many* side of the relationship.

Line chart A chart used to display trends over time.

Line control A control that enables an individual to insert a line into a form or report.

Link A connection to data in another file.

Linked form A form related to the main form that is not stored within the main form.

List box A box containing a list of choices for a lookup field.

Live Preview A technology that shows the result of applying an editing or formatting change as you point to possible results—*before* you actually apply it.

Location Any disk drive, folder, or other place in which you can store files and folders.

Logical operators Operators that are used to evaluate data to determine if a condition is met (true) or not met (false). With two criteria, AND requires that both conditions be met and OR requires that either condition be met for a record to display in the query results.

Lookup field A way to restrict data entered in a field.

Macro A series of actions grouped as a single command to accomplish a task or multiple tasks automatically.

Macro Designer Window that allows you to build the list of actions to be carried out when the macro runs.

Macro group A set of macros grouped by a common name that displays as one macro object on the Navigation Pane.

Mail merge Letters or memos that are created by combining two documents.

Main document The document that contains the text of a letter or memo for a mail merge.

Main form A form that contains a subform.

Main report A report that contains a subreport.

Make table query An action query that creates a new table by extracting data from one or more tables.

Many-to-many relationship A relationship between tables where one record in one table has many matching records in a second table, and a single record in the related table has many matching records in the first table.

Merging Combining two documents to create one.

Message Bar The area directly below the ribbon that displays information such as security alerts when there is potentially unsafe, active content in an Office document that you open.

Metadata Details about a file that describe or identify it, including the title, author name, subject, and keywords that identify the document's topic or contents; also known as *document properties*.

Microsoft SQL Server A database application designed for high-end business uses.

Mini toolbar A small toolbar containing frequently used formatting commands that displays as a result of selecting text or objects.

Modal window A child (secondary) window to a parent window—the original window that opened the modal window—that takes over control of the parent window.

MRU Acronym for *most recently used*, which refers to the state of some commands that retain the characteristic most recently applied; for example, the Font Color button retains the most recently used color until a new color is chosen.

Multi-page form A form that displays the data from the underlying table or query on more than one page.

Multiple-items form A form that enables you to display or enter multiple records in a table.

Multivalued field A field that holds multiple values.

Named range A range that has been given a name, making it easier to use the cells in calculations or modifications.

Navigate The process of exploring within the organizing structure of Windows.

Navigation area An area at the bottom of the Access window that indicates the number of records in the table and contains controls in the form of arrows that you click to navigate among the records.

Navigation form A form that displays navigational controls that enable you to display forms and reports in your database.

Navigation Pane An area of the Access window that displays and organizes the names of the objects in a database; from here, you open objects for use.

Navigation Pane category A top-level listing that displays when the Navigation Pane arrow is clicked.

Navigation Pane group A second-level listing that display when a Navigation Pane category is selected.

Nested subform A subform that is embedded within another subform.

Nonprinting characters Characters that display on the screen, but do not print, indicating where the Enter key, the Spacebar, and the Tab key were pressed; also called *formatting marks*.

Normalization The process of applying design rules and principles to ensure that your database performs as expected.

Notepad A simple text editor that comes with the Windows operating systems.

Notification bar An area at the bottom of an Internet Explorer window that displays information about pending downloads, security issues, add-ons, and other issues related to the operation of your computer.

Number data type An Access data type that describes numbers that might be used in calculations.

Object tab In the object window, a tab that identifies the object and which enables you to make the open object active.

Object window An area of the Access window that displays open objects, such as tables, queries, forms, or reports; by default, each object displays on its own tab.

Objects The basic parts of a database that you create to store your data and to work with your data; for example, tables, queries, forms, and reports.

ODBC An acronym for Open Database Connectivity.

Office 365 Administrator In Office 365, the person who creates and manages the account, adds new users, sets up the services your organization wants to use, sets permission levels, and manages the SharePoint team sites.

Office background A small graphic in the top right corner of the Access application window used to personalize Office 2013.

Office Web Apps The free online companions to Microsoft Word, Excel, PowerPoint, Access, and OneNote.

ON An SQL keyword that is used to specify which field is common to two tables.

One-to-many relationship A relationship between two tables where one record in the first table corresponds to many records in the second table—the most common type of relationship in Access.

Open Database Connectivity A standard that enables databases using SQL statements to interface with one another.

Open dialog box A dialog box from which you can navigate to, and then open on your screen, an existing file that was created in that same program.

Open Exclusive An option that opens the database so that changes can be made, but no one else may open the database at the same time.

Open Exclusive Read-Only An option that opens the database in both Exclusive and Read-Only modes.

Open Read-Only An option that opens the database so that all objects can be opened and viewed, but data and design changes cannot be made.

Option button In a dialog box, a round button that enables you to make one choice among two or more options.

Options dialog box A dialog box within each Office application where you can select program settings and other options and preferences.

OR condition A compound criteria used to display records that match at least one of the specified criteria.

Outer join A join that is typically used to display records from both tables, regardless of whether there are matching records.

Outermost sort field When sorting on multiple fields in Datasheet view, the field that is used for the first level of sorting.

Page Footer Information printed at the bottom of every page in a report; most often includes the page number.

Page Header Information printed at the top of every page in a report.

Page number control A control on a form or report that inserts the page numbers when displayed in Print Preview or when printed.

Pane A separate area of a window.

Paragraph symbol The symbol ¶ that represents the end of a paragraph.

Parameter A value that can be changed.

Parameter query A query that prompts an individual for criteria before running the query.

Paste The action of placing text or objects that have been copied or cut from one location to another location.

Paste Options gallery A gallery of buttons that provides a Live Preview of all the Paste options available in the current context.

Path A sequence of folders that leads to a specific file or folder.

PDF The acronym for Portable Document Format, which is a file format that creates an image that preserves the look of your file; this is a popular format for sending documents electronically because the document will display on most computers.

Performance Analyzer A wizard that analyzes database objects, and then offers suggestions for improving them.

Picture Alignment property A property that determines where the background picture for a form displays on the form.

Picture Size Mode property A property that determines the proportion of a picture in a form.

Pie chart A chart used to display the contributions of parts to a whole amount.

Plain Text A document format that contains no formatting, such as bold or italics.

Point The action of moving your mouse pointer over something on your screen. Also, a measurement that is 1/72 of an inch.

Pointer Any symbol that displays on your screen in response to moving your mouse.

Populate The action of filling a database table with records.

Pop-up window A window that suddenly displays (pops up), usually contains a menu of commands, and stays on the screen only until the user selects one of the commands.

Portable Document Format A file format that creates an image that preserves the look of your file, but that cannot be easily changed; a popular format for sending documents electronically, because the document will display on most computers.

Portrait orientation A page orientation in which the paper is taller than it is wide.

Primary key The field in a table that uniquely identifies a record; for example, a Student ID number at a college.

Print Preview A view of a document as it will appear when you print it.

Progress bar In a dialog box or taskbar button, a bar that indicates visually the progress of a task such as a download or file transfer.

Propagate To disseminate or apply changes to an object.

Properties The characteristics that determine the appearance, structure, and behavior of an object.

Property Sheet A list of characteristics—properties—for fields or controls on a form or report in which you can make precise changes to each property associated with the field or control.

Property Update Options button An option button that displays when you make changes to the design of a table; it enables individuals to update the Property Sheet for a field in all objects that use a table as the record source.

Protected View A security feature in Office 2013 that protects your computer from malicious files by opening them in a restricted environment until you enable them; you might encounter this feature if you open a file from an email or download files from the Internet.

pt The abbreviation for *point*; for example, when referring to a font size.

Query A database object that retrieves specific data from one or more database objects—either tables or other queries—and then, in a single datasheet, displays only the data you specify.

Quick Access Toolbar In an Office program window, the small row of buttons in the upper left corner of the screen from which you can perform frequently used commands.

Range An area that includes two or more selected cells on a worksheet that can be treated as a single unit.

Read-Only A property assigned to a file that prevents the file from being modified or deleted; it indicates that you cannot save any changes to the displayed document unless you first save it with a new name.

Record All of the categories of data pertaining to one person, place, event, thing, or idea; represented by a row in a database table.

Record selector bar The vertical bar at the left edge of a record when it is displayed in a form that is used to select an entire record.

Record selector box The small box at the left of a record in Datasheet view that, when clicked, selects the entire record.

Record source The tables or queries that provide the underlying data for a form or report.

Record Source property A property that enables you to specify the source of the data for a form or a report. The property setting can be a table name, a query name, or an SQL statement.

Redundant In a database, information that is duplicated in a manner that indicates poor database design.

Referential integrity A set of rules that Access uses to ensure that the data between related tables is valid.

Relational database A sophisticated type of database that has multiple collections of data within the file that are related to one another.

Relationship An association that you establish between two tables based on common fields.

Report A database object that summarizes the fields and records from a query or table in an easy-to-read format suitable for printing.

Report Footer Information printed at the bottom of the last page of a report.

Report Header Information printed on the first page of a report; used for logos, titles, and dates.

Report tool An Access tool that creates a report with one mouse click and displays all of the fields and records from the record source that you select.

Report Wizard An Access tool that walks you step by step through the creation of a report and that gives you more flexibility in the design, layout, and number of fields in a report.

Required A field property that ensures a field cannot be left empty.

Ribbon A user interface in both Office 2013 and File Explorer that groups the commands for performing related tasks on tabs across the upper portion of the program window.

Rich Text Format (RTF) A standard file format that contains text and some formatting such as underline, bold, italic, font sizes, and colors; RTF documents can be opened in many word processing programs and text editors.

Right outer join A join used when you want to display all of the records on the *many* side of a one-to-many relationship, whether or not there are matching records in the table on the *one* side of the relationship.

Right-click The action of clicking the right mouse button one time.

Run The process in which Access searches the records in the table(s) included in the query design, finds the records that match the specified criteria, and then displays the records in a datasheet; only the fields that have been included in the query design display.

Sans serif font A font design with no lines or extensions on the ends of characters.

ScreenTip A small box that that displays useful information when you perform various mouse actions such as pointing to screen elements or dragging.

Scroll bar A vertical or horizontal bar in a window or a pane to assist in bringing an area into view, and which contains a scroll box and scroll arrows.

Scroll box The box in the vertical and horizontal scroll bars that can be dragged to reposition the contents of a window or pane on the screen.

Second principle of good database design A principle stating that appropriate database techniques are used to ensure the accuracy and consistency of data as it is entered into the table.

Section bar In Design view, a gray bar in a form or report that identifies and separates one section from another; used to select the section and to change the size of the section.

Secure environment A system that uses controlled servers to ensure the security and privacy of email, to control the storage and use of information and to protect against the loss of confidential data.

SELECT clause An SQL statement that lists which fields the query should display.

Select query A type of Access query that retrieves (selects) data from one or more tables or queries, displaying the selected data in a datasheet; also known as a *simple select query*.

Selecting Highlighting, by dragging with your mouse, areas of text or data or graphics, so that the selection can be edited, formatted, copied, or moved.

Serif font A font design that includes small line extensions on the ends of the letters to guide the eye in reading from left to right.

Server A computer that provides services on a network such as an email server or a file server.

SharePoint Collaboration software with which people in an organization can set up team sites to share information, manage documents, and publish reports for others to see.

SharePoint List A list of documents maintained on a server running Microsoft Office SharePoint Server.

SharePoint Server A server that enables you to share documents with others in your organization.

Short Text data type An Access data type that describes text, a combination of text and numbers, or numbers that are not used in calculations, such as a Postal Code.

Shortcut menu A menu that displays commands and options relevant to the selected text or object; also called a *context menu*.

Simple select query Another name for a select query.

Single stepping Debugging a macro using a process that executes one action at a time.

Single-record form A form that enables you to display or enter one record at a time in a table.

Sizing handles Small squares that indicate a picture or object is selected.

SkyDrive Microsoft's free cloud storage for anyone with a free Microsoft account.

Sorting The process of arranging data in a specific order based on the value in a field.

Source file When importing a file, refers to the file being imported.

Source table The table from which records are being extracted or copied.

Split button A button divided into two parts and in which clicking the main part of the button performs a command and clicking the arrow opens a menu with choices.

Split database An Access database that is split into two files—one containing the back end, and one containing the front end.

Split form An object that displays data in two views—Form view and Datasheet view—on a single form.

Spreadsheet Another name for a worksheet.

SQL (Structured Query Language) A language used by many database programs to view, update, and query data in relational databases.

SQL statement An expression that defines the SQL commands that should be performed when the query is run.

Stacked layout A control layout format that is similar to a paper form, with label controls placed to the left of each text box control; the controls are grouped together for easy editing.

Standalone macro A macro contained in a macro object that displays under Macros on the Navigation Pane.

Start search The search feature in Windows 8 in which, from the Start screen, you can begin to type and by default, Windows 8 searches for apps; you can adjust the search to search for files or settings.

Static data Data that does not change.

Status bar The area along the lower edge of an Office program window that displays file information on the left and buttons to control how the window looks on the right.

Status Bar Text property A form property that enables individuals to enter text that will display in the status bar for a selected control.

String A series of characters.

Strong password A password that is very difficult to guess.

Structure In Access, the underlying design of a table, including field names, data types, descriptions, and field properties.

Style A group of formatting commands, such as font, font size, font color, paragraph alignment, and line spacing that can be applied to a paragraph with one command.

Subdatasheet A format for displaying related records when you click next to a record in a table on the *one* side of the relationship.

Subfolder A folder within a folder.

Subform A form that is embedded within another form.

Subreport A report that is embedded within another report.

Subset A portion of the total records available.

Synchronization The process of updating computer files that are in two or more locations according to specific rules—also called *syncing*.

Syncing The process of updating computer files that are in two or more locations according to specific rules—also called *synchronization*.

Syntax The set of rules by which words and symbols in an expression are combined.

System tables Tables used to keep track of multiple entries in an attachment field that you cannot view or work with.

Tab control A control that is used to display data on the main form on different tabs, similar to the way database objects, such as forms and tables, display on different tabs.

Tab order The order in which the insertion point moves from one field to another in a form when you press the Tab key.

Table A format for information that organizes and presents text and data in columns and rows; the foundation of a database.

Table Analyzer A wizard that searches for repeated data in a table, and then splits the table into two or more related tables.

Table area The upper area of the query window that displays field lists for the tables that are used in a query.

Tables and Related Views An arrangement in the Navigation Pane that groups objects by the table to which they are related.

Tabs (ribbon) On the Office ribbon, the name of each activity area.

Tags Custom file properties in the form of words that you associate with a document to give an indication of the document's content; used to help find and organize files; also called *keywords*. Also, codes that the web browser interprets as the page is loaded; they begin with the < character and end with the > character.

Taskbar The area along the lower edge of the desktop that displays buttons representing programs.

Template A preformatted document that you can use as a starting point and then change to suit your needs.

Text box control A bound control on a form or report that displays the data from the underlying table or query.

Text string A sequence of characters.

Theme A predesigned set of colors, fonts, lines, and fill effects that look good together and that can be applied to all of the objects in the database or to individual objects in the database.

Title bar The bar at the top edge of the program window that indicates the name of the current file and the program name.

Toggle button A button that can be turned on by clicking it once, and then turned off by clicking it again.

Toolbar In a folder window, a row of buttons with which you can perform common tasks, such as changing the view of your files and folders or burning files to a CD.

Totals query A query that calculates subtotals across groups of records.

Triple-click The action of clicking the left mouse button three times in rapid succession.

Truncated Refers to data that is cut off or shortened because the field or column is not wide enough to display all of the data or the field size is too small to contain all of the data.

Trust Center An area of Access where you can view the security and privacy settings for your Access installation.

Trusted Documents A security feature in Office that remembers which files you have already enabled; you might encounter this feature if you open a file from an email or download files from the Internet.

Trusted source A person or organization that you know will not send you databases with malicious content.

Unbound control A control that does not have a source of data, such as the title in a form or report.

Unbound report A report that does not display data from an underlying table, query, or SQL statement and has an empty Record Source property setting.

Unequal join A join used to combine rows from two data sources based on field values that are not equal; can be created only in SQL view.

Uniform Resource Locator An address that uniquely identifies a location on the Internet.

UNION An SQL keyword that is used to combine one or more queries in a union query.

Union query A query type that combines the results of two or more similar select queries.

Unmatched records Records in one table that have no matching records in a related table.

Update query An action query used to add, change, or delete data in fields of one or more existing records.

URL The acronym for Uniform Resource Locator, which is an address that uniquely identifies a location on the Internet.

USB flash drive A small data storage device that plugs into a computer USB port.

Validation rule An expression that precisely defines the range of data that will be accepted in a field.

Validation text The error message that displays when an individual enters a value prohibited by the validation rule.

Weak password A password that is easy to guess.

WHERE clause An SQL statement that defines the criteria that should be applied when a query is run.

Wildcard character In a query, a character that serves as a placeholder for one or more unknown characters in criteria; an asterisk (*) represents one or more unknown characters, and a question mark (?) represents a single unknown character.

Window A rectangular area on a computer screen in which programs and content appear, and which can be moved, resized, minimized, or closed.

Wizard A feature in Microsoft Office that walks you step by step through a process.

Workbook An Excel file that contains one or more worksheets.

Worksheet The primary document used in Excel to save and work with data that is arranged in columns and rows.

XML An acronym for Extensible Markup Language.

XML Paper Specification A Microsoft file format that creates an image of your document and that opens in the XPS viewer.

XML presentation files Files that can be created so that the data can be viewed in a web browser.

XML schema A document with an *.xsd* extension that defines the elements, entities, and content allowed in the document.

XPS The acronym for XML Paper Specification—a Microsoft file format that creates an image of your document and that opens in the XPS viewer.

Zero-length string An entry created by typing two quotation marks with no spaces between them ("") to indicate that no value exists for a required text or memo field.

Zipped folder A folder that has been reduced in size and thus takes up less storage space and can be transferred to other computers quickly; also called a *compressed* folder.

Zoom The action of increasing or decreasing the size of the viewing area on the screen.

Index

Layout view (Access), 77
  formatting/deleting controls, 239
  modifying controls, 240–241
  modifying forms, 220–225
    applying themes, 221
    control layout, 222–223
    formatting controls, 224–225
    grouping controls, 220–221
  modifying reports, 233–235
left outer join, 375, 380
less than (<), 156
  convert to lowercase (input mask
    character), 306
  less than, in expressions, 312
less than or equal to (<=), 312
Like operator, 312
Limit to List property setting, 302–303,
  314–315
line charts, 584, 606
linked forms, 469, 498
linking
  importing versus, 577
  table to another database, 588–589
links
  definition, 62, 577, 606
  hyperlinks
    data type, 298
    in reports, 425
list box, 301, 320
Live Preview, definition, 12
locations, definition, 13
logical operators, definition, 158
logo controls, 404, 406–407, 426
Long Text, 298, 300
lookup fields
  Allow Multiple Values check box, 303
  creating, 301–303
  definition, 301, 320
  Limit to List property setting, 302–303,
    314–315
Lookup Wizard, 298, 301–303
lowercase conversion, input mask
  character, 306

M

Macro Designer
  definition, 521, 554
  using, 521–522
macro group
  creating
    first macro, 540–541
    second macro, 541–546
    third macro, 546
  definition, 540, 554
MACRO TOOLS DESIGN tab, 521, 526,
  528, 530–531, 540
macros
  actions
    arguments, 521, 554
    definition, 521, 554
    Echo macro action, 528, 531

FindRecord action, 545
    MessageBox macro action, 528
    multiple, standalone macro, 527–531
    OpenForm macro action, 529
    turning off, 530
  command button with, 547–549
  conditions, 521, 554
  debugging, 531, 554
  definition, 521, 554
  embedded
    definition, 531, 554
    on form, 531–534
    on report, 534–535
  event-driven (data macros)
    creating, 549–551
    definition, 549, 554
  macro group
    first macro, 540–541
    second macro, 541–546
    third macro, 546
  printing details, 535–538
  with session, 547–549
  single stepping, 531, 554
  standalone
    automatic execution, 526
    creating, 521–524
    definition, 554
    multiple actions in, 527–531
Mail Merge feature, 594–597, 606
main document, 594, 606
main form
  creating, 465–470
  definition, 465, 498
  modifying, 470–473
  switching main form and subforms, 469
main report
  definition, 481, 498
  subreport total on, 486–489
Make Table dialog box, 362–363
make table queries
  aggregate functions in, 362
  definition, 361, 380
  expressions in, 362
  select queries
    converting to make table query, 362–363
    creating, 361–362
managing tables, 279–287
many-to-many relationships, 134,
  465–466, 468, 481, 498
margins, alignment guides, 28
MAX function, queries, 166–168, 347
Maximize button, 7
menus
  context, definition, 9
  shortcut, definition, 9
merging
  Access table with document, 594–597
  definition, 594, 606
message, in status bar, 412–413
Message Bar, definition, 128
MessageBox macro action, 528
metadata, definition, 14

Microsoft accounts
  creating, 42–43
  signing in to, 24
Microsoft Clip Art collection, 26
Microsoft Office, signing in to
  accounts, 24
Microsoft Office 365
  Outlook Calendar, 176
  Outlook Meeting tool, 98
Microsoft Office Help, Excel, 40–41
Microsoft Office Trusted Location dialog
  box, 280–281
Microsoft SQL Server. See SQL Server
Microsoft Visual Basic, 530, 532, 554
MIN function, queries, 166–168, 347
mini toolbar, definition, 9, 460, 498
Minimize button, 7
misspelled words, checking spelling,
  9–10
modal window, 524, 526, 528, 554
modifying. See also formatting
  borders of controls, 411–412
  controls, 240–241
  data types, 59
  forms
    Design view, 225–227
    Layout view, 220–225
  joins, 373–377
  main form, 470–473
  options, Access Options dialog box,
    635–636
  query design, 141–142
  records, 289–290
  reports, 78–80
    design, 238–243
    Layout view, 233–235
    Report Wizard, 420–421
  sections of reports, 423–424
  subforms, 470–473
  subreports, 483–484
  table column widths, 69–70
  table structure, 281–282
  tables, 287–293
More Commands dialog box, 25
moving
  controls, forms, 222–223
  fields, 290–292
MRU (most recently used), 33
multi-page forms, 476–479, 498
multiple actions, in standalone macro,
  527–531
multiple fields
  aggregate functions in, 348
  for row headings, in crosstab query, 351
  sorting records in tables, 137–138
multiple primary key fields, 466
multiple tables, in field list, 422
multiple-items forms, 86–88
  building tables by entering records in,
    86–88
  definition, 86
multiplication operator (*), 342